STATE OF THE NATION
South Africa 2005-2006

Edited by Sakhela Buhlungu, John Daniel,
Roger Southall & Jessica Lutchman

First published in South Africa by HSRC Press
Private Bag X9182, Cape Town, 8000, South Africa
www.hsrcpress.ac.za

Published in the rest of the world by Michigan State University Press
East Lansing, Michigan, 48823, United States of America
www.msupress.msu.edu

© 2006 Human Sciences Research Council

First published 2006

All rights reserved. No part of this book may be reprinted or reproduced or utilised in any form or by any electronic, mechanical, or other means, including photocopying and recording, or in any information storage or retrieval system, without permission in writing from the publishers.

Copy editing by Vaun Cornell
Typeset by Jenny Wheeldon
Cover by Farm
Cover photograph by Elsabe Gelderblom
Print management by comPress
Printed in the Republic of South Africa by Creda Communications

Distributed in South Africa by Blue Weaver Marketing and Distribution
PO Box 30370, Tokai, Cape Town, 7966, South Africa
Tel: +27 +21 701-4477
Fax: +27 +21 701-7302
email: orders@blueweaver.co.za

Distributed in the rest of the world by Michigan State University Press
Suite 25, Manly Miles Building, 1405 South Harrison Road
East Lansing, MI 48823, United States of America
Tel: +1 517 355-9543 ext 101
Fax: +1 517 432-2611
www.msupress.msu.edu

In South Africa
ISBN 0-7969-2115-6
In the rest of the world
ISBN 0-87013-778-6

Contents

List of tables   vi

List of figures   ix

Foreword   xi
   Mark Orkin

Acronyms   xiii

Introduction: can South Africa be a developmental state?   xvii
   Roger Southall

Part I: Politics

   Introduction   3

1   Putting numbers to the scorecard: presidential targets and the state of delivery   11
   David Hemson and Michael O'Donovan

2   Towards a Constitution-based definition of poverty in post-apartheid South Africa   46
   Wiseman Magasela

3   Delivery and disarray: the multiple meanings of land restitution   67
   Cherryl Walker

4   Assessing the constitutional protection of human rights in South Africa during the first decade of democracy   93
   Karthy Govender

5   More than a law-making production line? Parliament and its oversight role   123
   Judith February

6   The state of the national gender machinery: structural problems and personalised politics   143
   Amanda Gouws

Part II: Economy

Introduction 169

7 Black empowerment and present limits to a more democratic capitalism in South Africa 175
Roger Southall

8 The state of labour market deracialisation 202
Percy Moleke

9 The state of the informal economy 223
Richard Devey, Caroline Skinner and Imraan Valodia

10 Work restructuring and the future of labour in South Africa 248
Sakhela Buhlungu and Eddie Webster

11 The state of research and experimental development: moving to a higher gear 270
Michael Kahn and William Blankley

Part III: Society

Introduction 299

12 The state of South Africa's cities 303
Bill Freund

13 Guns and the social crisis 333
Jacklyn Cock

14 The Chinese communities in South Africa 350
Janet Wilhelm

15 Winning the Cup but losing the plot? The troubled state of South African soccer 369
Merryman Kunene

16 The state of mathematics and science education: schools are not equal 392
Vijay Reddy

Part IV: South Africa in the world
>   Introduction   419

17   South Africa's evolving foreign trade strategy: coherence or confusion?   427
     Jesmond Blumenfeld

18   South Africa's relations with the People's Republic of China: mutual opportunities or hidden threats?   457
     Sanusha Naidu

19   South Africa in Africa: scrambling for energy   484
     John Daniel and Jessica Lutchman

Contributors   510

Index   512

List of tables

Table 1.1   Scorecard on the RDP   19
Table 1.2   Anticipated housing delivery and backlog   24
Table 1.3   Percentage of households with access to public electricity supply   29
Table 1.4   Household electrification   30
Table 1.5   Incidence of malaria reported   34
Table 1.6   Actual and targeted staffing levels of SAPS   35

Table 2.1   Comparison of selected poverty lines for South Africa, 1993   54

Table 3.1   Restitution budget, 1997/98–2005/06 (R'000s)   71
Table 3.2   National progress on settling claims, April 1995–March 2005   72
Table 3.3   Provincial breakdown for lodged claims   76
Table 3.4   Provincial breakdown of settled claims as of February 2005   77
Table 3.5   National settled claims by locality and settlement type, February 2005   78
Table 3.6   Claims requiring settlement, by regional office of the Commission, February 2005   78
Table 3.7   Categories and scale of land dispossession, 1960–1983   83

Table 7.1   Share ownership on the JSE by percentage of market capitalisation   182
Table 7.2   *Financial Mail's* top 20 businesspeople in South Africa, 2003   192
Table 7.3   Selected BEE deals, 2004   193

Table 8.1   Distribution of workers within sectors, by percentage, race and skills level   206
Table 8.2   Distribution of workers in occupational groups, percentage by race, 2001–03   208
Table 8.3   Racial distribution of managers by age groups, 2004   210
Table 8.4   Distribution of workers, percentage by race and gender within skill levels, 2002–04   210

LIST OF TABLES

Table 8.5　Highest level of education among those aged 20 and older, percentage by race, 2001　216
Table 8.6　Degrees, diplomas, and certificates awarded by public universities, percentage by race and field of study, 2002　217
Table 8.7　Proportion of workers trained in relation to total employees by race group and occupational category　219

Table 9.1　Formal and informal employment – definitional differences　229
Table 9.2　Informal employment as a proportion of non-agricultural employment　229
Table 9.3　Labour market status of workers in South Africa, 1997–2003　231
Table 9.4　Formal employment, informal employment and domestic work, percentage by sex and race　234
Table 9.5　Labour market status of workers, February 2002 to March 2004　239
Table 9.6　Labour market status of informal economy workers, February 2002 to March 2004　239
Table 9.7　Shifts between informal work and other labour market status　240

Table 10.1　Security of job tenure of Cosatu members, 2004　254
Table 10.2　Occupational category of Cosatu members surveyed, as defined by the company　255
Table 10.3　Age profile of Cosatu members, 1994, 1998 and 2004　256
Table 10.4　Highest formal educational levels of Cosatu members　256
Table 10.5　Gender composition of Cosatu membership, 1994, 1998 and 2004　257
Table 10.6　Year in which Cosatu member joined the union　258

Table 11.1　South Africa's percentage share of world exports in technology, 1992 and 2002　273
Table 11.2　Manufactured exports revenue ranked by South African Rands, 1992 and 2002　274
Table 11.3　R&D expenditure by sector, 2003/04　279

Table 11.4   Patents of South African origin granted at the United States Patent and Trademark Office, 1993–2003   280
Table 11.5   Researcher full-time equivalents, 1992 and 2004   282
Table 11.6   Mathematics higher-grade candidates and passes (thousands), 1997–2003   283
Table 11.7   R&D expenditure by socio-economic objective, 2001/02   288
Table 11.8   R&D expenditure by biotechnology-related research field 108, 2002 and 2004 (R millions)   289
Table 11.9   Patents registered under the PCT, 1999–2004   291

Table 16.1   Participation and performance in mathematics in 1990, percentage by racial groups   393
Table 16.2   Public schools in Gauteng offering mathematics in 2003, categorised by ex-racial Departments of Education and poverty rankings   402
Table 16.3   Trend of mathematics participation in public schools in Gauteng   404
Table 16.4   Higher-grade mathematics participation in Gauteng (no. and % of entrants)   404
Table 16.5   Trends of schools in Gauteng offering only standard-grade mathematics (no. and %)   405
Table 16.6   Trends of higher-grade mathematics performance in Gauteng schools, by ex-racial department   406
Table 16.7   Trend in correlation of school quality in Gauteng for ex-DET and ex-HoA schools   409
Table 16.8   Established and emergent schools in Gauteng   409

Table 19.1   South African exports, imports and trade balance by region, 2004 (R millions)   488

List of figures

Figure 1.1   The line of delivery in basic water   26
Figure 1.2   The sanitation backlog, 1996–2016   28

Figure 6.1   Structure and components of the national gender machinery   148

Figure 8.1   Distribution of skill profiles within racial groups as at March 2004   212

Figure 9.1   Labour force by type of work in South Africa, 1997–2003   231
Figure 9.2   Workers in informal enterprises by sector, March 2004   232
Figure 9.3   Incomes in informal enterprises, March 2004   233

Figure 11.1   GERD:GDP, 1983–2003   278
Figure 11.2   Expenditure on R&D by major research fields, 2003 and 2004   279
Figure 11.3   Demographics of researchers (headcounts) in the NSI, 2001/02   284

Figure 16.1   TIMSS 2003 mean mathematics scores of schools categorised by ex-racial departments   399
Figure 16.2   TIMSS 2003 mean mathematics scores by provinces   400
Figure 16.3   Mathematics school quality in Gauteng public schools in 2003, by ex-racial department and independent schools   407
Figure 16.4   Change in school quality in Gauteng over time (1999, 2003), for ex-DET and ex-HoA schools   408

Figure 18.1   South Africa's bilateral trade statistics with China   469
Figure 18.2   China–South Africa bilateral trade   469
Figure 18.3   Commodity imports from China to South Africa   470

Figure 19.1   South African exports by region, 2003 and 2004   488
Figure 19.2   South African imports by region, 2003 and 2004   489
Figure 19.3   South Africa's trade balance by region, 2003 and 2004   489
Figure 19.4   South African business activity in Africa by sector,
              2000–03   490
Figure 19.5   Organogram of the Central Energy Fund   496
Figure 19.6   South Africa's involvement in the African oil and natural gas
              markets, by company   504

Foreword

This is the third edition of *State of the Nation*, now an annual collection of original essays upon the politics, economy, society and international relations of contemporary South Africa. Like the previous two editions, the present volume draws together a wide and exciting set of analyses, written by contributors from universities, civil society organisations and the media as well as from the Human Sciences Research Council (HSRC). We are confident that it will receive as favourable a reception as the previous editions.

We are gratified at how quickly *State of the Nation* has become established as part of the annual South African scholarly calendar. Coverage in the media, international as well as South African, has been extensive; individual essays have been cited as authoritative; controversies have been stirred; both previous volumes have been prescribed as university texts; they have found their way into South African embassies across the world and foreign embassies in South Africa; and perhaps most importantly, many ordinary South Africans have purchased the books simply to find out more about the complex and fascinating country we live in.

The considerable success of the series rests in part upon its sure foundations: the precedent of the *South African Review* series of the 1980s; the now well-established practice of the President in delivering annual 'State of the Nation' speeches which, as well as indicating new directions in government strategy, have recently established targets and invited accountability; the rigour applied by the editors; and their brief to suitably qualified contributors that they subject developments to thoughtful and evidence-based scrutiny 'without fear or favour'.

However, the success is also a product of the care taken by the HSRC Press. Under Director Garry Rosenberg, assisted by Karen Bruns and Mary Ralphs, and by the Publications Review Committee chaired by John Daniel, the Press has rapidly emerged as one of the leading academic publishers in South Africa. As a non-profit publisher, mandated to disseminate the work of HSRC researchers and other social scientists in the public interest, it has played a vital role in enabling *State of the Nation* to become a flagship project of the HSRC.

We are grateful for the energy and thoroughness which the Press has brought to *State of the Nation*, as indeed to the impressive list of its other titles.

It would be impossible to undertake such an ambitious annual publishing project as *State of the Nation* without external financial support to complement the parliamentary funds that we allocate to it. We are deeply grateful to Atlantic Philanthropies, the Ford Foundation and the Charles Mott Foundation, who have all been generous and delightful partners with whom to work. We are equally grateful to the Konrad Adenauer Foundation, which has organised and funded 'launch workshops' around the country, sessions that serve to inform the media about the book and provoke vigorous debate about its contents. Without the backing of these supporters, *State of the Nation* would have been unable to achieve the success that it has enjoyed.

Finally, I would like to congratulate the editors, John Daniel, Jessica Lutchman, and Roger Southall, who this year have been joined in their task by Sakhela Buhlungu of the Department of Sociology of the University of the Witwatersrand. Theirs has been a huge effort, although *State of the Nation* has evidently become more a labour of love than a burden of the workplace.

As this third edition was being prepared for printing I was concluding my five-year term as President and Chief Executive Officer of the HSRC. I am delighted to commend this enormously worthwhile project to my successor, Dr Olive Shisana, and to wish *State of the Nation* the very best of fortune in the years ahead. Long may it continue, as our first edition put it, to 'celebrate and irritate'!

Dr Mark Orkin

President and Chief Executive Officer
HSRC
August 2000–July 2005

Acronyms

AGM	annual general meeting
AGOA	US African Growth and Opportunity Act
ANC	African National Congress
ART	anti-retroviral treatment
AU	African Union
BEE	black economic empowerment
BERD	business and not-for-profits R&D
BIG	basic income grant
BLNS	Botswana, Lesotho, Namibia and Swaziland
BNC	Bi-National Commission
C2005	Curriculum 2005
CAF	Confederation of African Football
CBD	central business district
CCP	Chinese Communist Party
CEF	Central Energy Fund
CEO	Chief Executive Officer
CGE	Commission on Gender Equality
Cofesa	Confederation of Employers of Southern Africa
COGSI	Cape Oil and Gas Supply Initiative
Comesa	Common Market for Eastern and Southern Africa
Cosatu	Congress of South African Trade Unions
CSG	child support grant
CSIR	Council for Scientific and Industrial Research
DA	Democratic Alliance
DLA	Department of Land Affairs
DME	Department of Minerals and Energy
DoE	Department of Education
DoSD	Department of Social Development
DRC	Democratic Republic of Congo
DTI	Department of Trade and Industry
DWAF	Department of Water Affairs and Forestry
EC	European Commission
EFTA	European Free Trade Association

EU	European Union
Fasa	Football Association of South Africa
FDI	foreign direct investment
FET	further education and training
Fifa	Federation of International Football Associations
FRD	Foundation for Research Development
FTA	free trade area
FTE	full-time equivalent
FTP	fixed tariff preference
GATT	General Agreement on Tariffs and Trade
GDP	gross domestic product
GEAR	Growth, Employment and Redistribution strategy
Geda	Gauteng Economic Development Agency
GEIS	General Export Incentive Scheme
GERD	gross expenditure on R&D
GES	Global Economic Strategy
GFSA	Gun Free South Africa
GHS	general household survey
GNU	Government of National Unity
HERD	higher education R&D
HSL	household subsistence level
HSRC	Human Sciences Research Council
ICLS	International Conference for Labour Statistics
ICT	information communication technology
IDP	integrated development plan
IFP	Inkatha Freedom Party
ILO	International Labour Organisation
IMF	International Monetary Fund
Instraw	International Research and Training Institute for the Advancement of Women (United Nations)
ISD	Institutions Supporting Democracy
ISS	Institute for Security Studies
JMC	Joint Monitoring Committee on the Improvement of the Quality of Life and the Status of Women
JRC	Joint Rules Committee

JSE	Johannesburg Securities Exchange
LFS	labour force survey
LSBC	local business services centre
MK	Umkhonto we Sizwe
MLL	minimum living level
MP	Member of Parliament
MRC	Medical Research Council
NA	National Assembly
Nafcoc	National African Federated Chamber of Commerce
NCAC	National Conventional Arms Control Bill
NCACC	National Conventional Arms Control Committee
NCOP	National Council of Provinces
Nedlac	National Economic Development and Labour Council
Nepad	New Partnership for Africa's Development
NGF	National Gender Forum
NFL	National Football League
NGM	national gender machinery
NGO	non-governmental organisation
NNP	New National Party
NPSL	National Professional Soccer League
NSDS	National Skills Development Strategy
NSI	national system of innovation
NSL	National Soccer League
OEM	original equipment manufacture
OHS	October household survey
OPEC	Organisation of the Petroleum Exporting Countries
OSW	Office of the Status of Women
PAC	Pan Africanist Congress
PBMR	pebble-bed modular nuclear reactor
PDL	poverty datum line
PLAAS	Programme for Land and Agrarian Settlement
PRC	People's Republic of China
PSL	Premier Soccer League
QR	quantitative restrictions
R&D	research and experimental development
RDP	Reconstruction and Development Programme

SAA	South African Airways
SACP	South African Communist Party
SACU	Southern African Customs Union
SADC	Southern African Development Community
SADCC	Southern African Development Coordination Conference
Safa	South African Football Association
SAHRC	South African Human Rights Commission
SALGA	South African Local Government Association
Sanco	South African National Civics Organisation
SANDF	South African National Defence Force
SAPS	South African Police Service
SARS	South African Revenue Service
SAWID	South African Women in Dialogue
Scopa	Select Committee on Public Accounts
SETA	Sector Education and Training Authority
SMME	small, medium and micro-enterprise
SOE	state-owned enterprise
SPP	Surplus People Project
Stats SA	Statistics South Africa
SWOP	Sociology of Work Unit
SYSTEM	Students and Youth in Science, Technology and Mathematics
TAC	Treatment Action Campaign
TDCA	Trade, Development and Co-operation Agreement (EU-South Africa)
TIMSS	Trends in International Mathematics and Science Study
UDHR	Universal Declaration of Human Rights
UN	United Nations
UNDP	United Nations Development Programme
Ussasa	United Schools Sports Association of South Africa
VIP	ventilated improved privy
WHO	World Health Organization
WNC	Women's National Coalition
WTO	World Trade Organization

Introduction: can South Africa be a developmental state?

Roger Southall

In the introduction to *State of the Nation: South Africa 2004–2005*, the editors noted that 'the African National Congress (ANC) is in the throes of shifting from the Growth, Employment and Redistribution (GEAR) strategy to a more interventionist, developmental state' (Daniel, Southall & Lutchman 2005: xxxi). Since then, this change has become sufficiently explicit for it to have initiated the beginnings of a serious debate about the changing nature and role of the state as the second Mbeki presidency unfolds.

The editors argued that this shift in orientation – which articulated a comprehensive agenda for transformation put forward by Thabo Mbeki at the beginning of his final term as President – flowed less from the ANC's past or present engagements with socialism, than from its seeking to apply lessons learnt from the idea of an Asian-style (capitalist) 'developmental state' (Daniel et al. 2005: xxviii). However, it was suggested that if the ANC were to transform South Africa into a developmental state, it would have to meet three particular challenges: first, the state would have to confront major deficiencies in its capacity, notably those resulting from the skewed human resource patterns inherited from its racialised past; second, whereas the developmental patterns of the classic Asian developmental states were structured by propitious post-Second World War conditions which facilitated their growth, contemporary South Africa operates in a highly globalised production system in which the capacity of (especially less powerful) individual states to steer their own economic fortunes has been massively eroded; and third, whereas the governments of developmental states were enabled to trade high rates of growth for low levels of democracy, the relatively high levels of popular mobilisation and low levels of social coherence which South Africa has inherited from the struggle against apartheid would require that the ANC seeks to combine development and democracy.

Our interpretation of this change was shared by others. Itumeleng Mahabane, writing in the *Financial Mail* (25.02.05), for instance, observed of President Mbeki's latest 'State of the Nation' address that it 'continued a shift to a transformative and developmental state, aimed at entrenching the principle of shared growth by making all our people part of the economy'. His analysis followed that of the *Financial Mail* (01.10.04) which saw the move as following from the government's reaction to its *Ten year review* (PCAS 2003). This had stated that although much had been achieved, the pressures of poverty and inequality would soon become overwhelming if the 'first economy', linked to the global economy, continued on a present trajectory which saw those who were located in a 'second economy' excluded from the benefits of growth by lack of employment, education, skills, capital and opportunity. The conclusion had been that the state should become more active in correcting the market's failures, a stance which Neva Makgetla (2005) has confirmed subsequently became a subject of increasing debate within the Tripartite Alliance (which links the ANC to the Congress of South African Trade Unions [Cosatu] and the South African Communist Party [SACP] to the ANC). However, such deliberations are themselves mere reflections of the growing boldness with which the government and the ANC have latterly come to openly espouse the 'developmental state'.

Government strategy: 'turning the ship of state around'?[1]

In his 'State of the Nation' speech for 2005, delivered on 11 February, President Mbeki provided an assessment of the government's success in achieving the goals which it had outlined following its victory in the 2004 general election, that is, 'to achieve higher rates of economic growth and development, improve the quality of life of all our people, and consolidate our social cohesion'. Noting that while South Africa has been underperforming compared to its 'emerging-market' peer group, he insisted that the country has positioned itself upon a sustainable higher growth path. Unemployment remains far too high, but employment has gradually begun to improve. Furthermore, the government is making marked progress towards its various targets. Ninety per cent of those deemed eligible are now receiving social grants; over ten million people have gained access to potable water; and over two million housing subsidies have been allocated to the poor since 1994. Likewise, whereas 4.1 million out of 11.2 million households lived on an income of R9 600 or less per year in 2001, by

2004 this figure had decreased to 3.6 million households. The President also claimed that of the 307 'concrete actions' promised in his previous speech, 51 per cent with specific time frames had been achieved, 21 per cent had been undertaken with 'slight delays', and 28 per cent had not been carried out. If, as O'Donovan and Hemson suggest in this volume, the President was putting a favourable gloss upon performance, he was nonetheless highlighting the government's determined efforts to streamline delivery.

President Mbeki declared that the broad objectives of the coming year were 'to increase investment, lower the cost of doing business, improve economic inclusion and provide the skills required by the economy'. Central to this were the continuing plans for public investment, notably with regard to transport logistics, electricity and water resources, while additionally steps had been taken to improve the management of administered prices through the use of independent regulation and more rigorous monitoring. Bold steps were being taken to liberalise the telecommunications industry; sectoral black economic empowerment (BEE) charters were being refined; a new National Skills Development Strategy for 2005–2010 had been approved; government would extend exemptions for small business with regard to taxes, levies and central bargaining and other labour arrangements; new measures were being considered to improve foreign capital inflows; and development strategies were being developed with regard to a range of different industrial sectors. Critically, also, plans were afoot for a thorough review of the functioning of the governmental system with a view to upgrading public service skills and competencies (Mbeki 2005a).

Further elaboration of the government's plans was provided by Alec Erwin, Minister of Public Enterprises. After undertaking major surgery upon the state-owned enterprises (SOEs), the latter were now ready to 'undertake a major investment and efficiency programme'. SOEs were to become 'drivers of growth and development': with a turnover of R83.7 billion in 2004 (larger than the combined turnover of BHP Billiton, Anglogold and Telkom), they combine assets of R175.5 billion, and employ 136 000 people, constituting some 1.2 per cent of formal sector employment of 11 million (*ANC Today* 5[15], 15–21.04.05). Their past performance had been anything but satisfactory. Transnet, the transport and logistical holding state company, had recorded a reduction in value of its net assets in 2003/04 of R8.7 billion; one of its operations, South African Airways (SAA) had lost R15 billion over two years;

Denel (defence) had similarly posted poor results; and while Eskom was financially sound, important policy issues had to be resolved. Confirming major restructuring plans for each, Erwin reiterated the government's commitment to retaining the state's 'core assets' and transforming the key parastatals into companies that would operate efficiently and which would work closely with the private sector where this was appropriate *(Business Report* 17.04.05).

In commenting on the 2005 Budget, the *Financial Mail* (18.02.05) argued that the ANC had now moved closer to the old Afrikaner establishment with which it shares statist views favouring a strong central government that actively leads economic growth. Although movement was slow, 'like turning a massive oil tanker around', government was clearly involved in 'a basic shift in approach and strategy'. Yet was this necessarily in the direction of a developmental state?

That it was definitely intended to be was soon confirmed by Mbeki when he addressed the National Assembly on 25 May (Mbeki 2005b). On this occasion, he reflected upon the decline of the 'Washington Consensus', the ideas which had set the stage for the reduction of the role of the state in the 'development thinking' of global bodies such as the International Monetary Fund and the World Bank since the 1980s. Noting a new acceptance that development 'requires an effective state, one that plays a catalytic, facilitating role', he reiterated earlier statements he had made in 1999 that a minimalist state would be incapable of addressing the backlog of poverty in South Africa. He therefore went on to assert the need for a 'strong state'. To this end, he noted that Cabinet had charged the Forum of South African Directors-General to appraise both the 'capacity of our democratic state' and the challenges of 'social cohesion' (both factors which we identified as key issues confronting any attempt to promote a developmental state in our editorial last year, and which are taken up in different contexts this year in the chapters by both Cock and Kunene). National government having already announced that it would take measures to assume greater decision-making powers over the provinces and local government and to unify the public service across all three levels of government *(Mail & Guardian* 18–24.02.05; *Financial Mail* 11.03.05), Mbeki further insisted that 'as a developmental state', it was vital for government to ensure that all three spheres of governance 'have the necessary professional, managerial and skilled personnel to enable the state machinery to discharge its developmental responsibilities'.

Complementary to the President's latest oration was the release by the ANC of a discussion document which addressed 'Development and underdevelopment'. Proclaiming the government's success on the macroeconomic front, the document nonetheless noted that great challenges remain, notably those of high unemployment, low growth, low savings, low investments, continued mass poverty and deep inequalities based on class, race, gender and region. Addressing these would demand an approach involving focused state-led interventions to ensure the integration of South Africa's 'two economies', poverty alleviation, job creation and sustained growth. During the last half of the twentieth century, it continued, there had been three major successful efforts to overcome the problems of underdevelopment and poverty, and each of these had rested upon the ability of government to act as a developmental state. These efforts were, respectively, the Marshall Plan (whereby US loans had stimulated Western European post-war construction); the East Asian Growth and Development Plan (whereby US aid and capital flows to interventionist governments had created prosperous and stable anti-communist states); and more recently, the European Integration Programme (whereby the European Union is structuring market forces to promote growth and overcome regional inequalities). Observing key aspects of all these programmes from which South Africa needed to draw appropriate lessons, the paper argued that whilst the Washington Consensus has few supporters left in high quarters today, it has not been replaced by any serious attempt seeking to replicate the examples of successful development cited earlier. Consequently (the document implies rather than states), it is up to the government to make its own decisive interventions to overcome the inherited duality of the post-apartheid economy, with key strategies being: first, to raise the level of investment by lowering the cost of capital; and second, to reform the labour market so that more labour is absorbed (notably by amending the applicability of minimum wage and current labour regulations to small businesses). Nonetheless, for all that the paper suggests that South Africa should learn from all three successful post-war development experiences, it leaves little doubt that its principal inspiration is that of the East Asian developmental model (ANC 2005: 26).

It would seem, in sum, that the ANC and the government's latest thinking asserts the necessity of a developmental state that is 'strong' in the sense of having the intellectual resources to plan, monitor and stimulate high growth (notably through revitalised SOEs), 'strong' in the sense of having legislative and administrative capacity to share and direct policy, and 'strong' in the sense of being able to mobilise and deploy capital into sectors where private industry will not venture. Yet how are such ideas being received, and what are the prospects of their realisation?

The nascent debate about the developmental state in South Africa

Three broad (overlapping) positions concerning the developmental state have appeared, put forward, firstly, by economic liberals; secondly, by 'Jacobins'; and thirdly, by advocates or admirers of the developmental state. They have been expressed as follows.

The economic liberals

This perspective, which is promoted by vigorous advocates of the private sector, combines both doubts about the wisdom of the nature of state intervention into the market with fears that attempted implementation of a developmental state will hobble enterprise and growth.

The essence of this position was expressed by an important editorial in *Business Day* on 8 March 2005, concerning what it termed the government's new ideology of 'developmentalism'. The 'developmental state', it proclaimed, citing Thandika Mkandawire ('a senior United Nations economist'), was one that saw itself as having a mission to achieve high rates of accumulation and industrialisation and derived its legitimacy from its ability to do so. The elites of such a state subscribe to this mission, whilst importantly, the state itself has the capacity to implement policies and is sufficiently autonomous from 'myopic private interests' to be able to make long-term strategy. 'Recognise any of this?' *Business Day* asked, and went on to observe that:

> It was when President Thabo Mbeki turned to developmentalism that privatization was dropped as a policy, pressure for empowerment was stepped up as a way of ensuring the loyalty of the new elite Mkandawire says is so critical to developmental success, and that a 300-plus point action plan became the Holy Grail for his second and final term.

However, a key peril was one of state incapacity:

> The problems may just be too big for a democracy. The model developmental states are East Asian – autocratic if not dictatorial. Here, chaos rules in too many places and the danger is that when the Developmentalist-in-Chief leaves office, the economic model might go with him, a fine idea poorly executed and leaving a vacuum for more popular ideologies to fill. By that time business and capital may have been so tied up in red tape, empowerment codes, broad-based consortiums, public–private partnerships, training levies and endless promises of a dynamic new infrastructure that it will no longer be able to argue the case for a viable alternative. *(Business Day* 08.03.05)

Lawrence Schlemmer has proffered a related analysis *(ThisDay* 18.08.04). Joseph Schumpeter had predicted some 60 years ago that the need to tame long-term business cycles would lead to growing intervention, bureaucratised corporations and the ascendancy of state socialism. However, his predictions have been defeated by the persistence of innovation, new wealth creation, rising mass prosperity in the developed world and the increasing sophistication of short-term economic management. However, South Africa looks set to provide an unwelcome, belated vindication of his fears. Whereas the developmental states of the Far East ('although over-idealised') have shown that a government can work with business in non-directive partnerships to target market opportunities and facilitate investment and technology, South Africa seems set upon another path. Certainly, since 1996, fiscal control has been tightened, firm targets for lowering inflation have been adhered to and growth was to be boosted by the privatisation of state assets. However, growth and investment did not follow because the macroeconomic formula was not backed by deregulation of the microeconomy and labour markets. Private fixed investment lagged, labour absorption fell, and mass poverty and inequality deepened. As a result, ANC popularity slumped in the opinion polls, and protests by Cosatu and the SACP signalled mass discontent, with the result that the government swung left in anticipation of the 2004 general election. Subsequently, privatisation has stalled, the state has reasserted its economic role, corporations are increasingly subject to a maze of legislation about BEE, and all spheres of life are progressively being subjected to regulation. In short, the ANC's version of the developmental state will fail to bring sustained investment, technological innovation and growth and will condemn South Africa to 'mediocrity in perpetuity'.

Others share Schlemmer's fears that the economy is over-regulated. It is important to acknowledge that to describe them as advocates of an unrestricted 'free market' may parody their position. For instance, Tony Leon, leader of the Democratic Alliance (DA), repudiates criticisms of his party which suggest that it does not accept the need for government intervention strategies which both address the social needs of the poor and provide for their economic empowerment. He nonetheless argues vigorously that if South Africa's private sector is to be enabled to maximise growth, then there needs to be a radical reduction of state control over the market, notably concerning its attempt to legislate 'race representivity' (Leon, *Financial Mail* 11.03.05).[2] Similar positions are put forward by those who argue that urgently needed, faster job creation would be fostered by a shift away from labour market regulation towards greater labour flexibility, although some also balance this with fears that big business is in bed with government and that the capital (especially the financial) market also needs to be deregulated (Abedian, *Financial Mail* 01.10.04; Bernstein, *Business Day* 17.09.04). In a word, the economic liberals fear an ideological 'developmentalism' that is at best misguided, at worst designed to promote the narrow interests of the ANC elite.

The Jacobins

Mahabane has adopted the name 'The New Jacobins' for his provocative column in the *Financial Mail* where he analyses the strategies of the government with particular regard to the economy. In so doing, he is suggesting that, in echo of the most radical wing of the bourgeois revolutionaries in France after 1789, the ANC ruling elite are intent upon using the state to promote a social transformation which, while not socialist, nonetheless has the potential – in Hobsbawm's phrase – to go 'too far for bourgeois comfort' (Hobsbawm 2000: 63).[3] For instance, it might be proposed that whilst welcoming state economic strategies which emphasise fiscal discipline and market competitiveness, large-scale capital remains nervous about transformative policies such as BEE which threaten to impinge upon their profitability and mode of operation. Yet according to Mahabane, transformation should not stop at BEE, but should extend to the very nature of our thinking on economic development policy: 'Liberals often say SA cannot afford empowerment. What we cannot afford is liberalism' *(Sunday Times* 17.04.05). What South Africa needs, as with China, is a broad industrial policy to underpin demand and create more sustainable economic acceleration – 'In SA, the state ineluctably has to intervene in the economy'.

Yet Mahabane has severe doubts as to whether the ANC elite has the capacity to make its own revolution *(Financial Mail* 25.02.05). A development state requires an intellectual, cultural and philosophical shift that South Africa has not yet made, nor appears ready to make. In such a state, the state bureaucracy is composed of the nation's brightest and best, following administrative careers which are not subject to the whims of political fortune. A technocratic and meritocratic civil service would be fired not only by the ambition of achieving economic growth, but also of promoting national interests as defined by the administrative elite. In contrast, South Africa remains obsessed by politics, correcting the racialised past:

> Our obsession with politics suggests that we are victims of our own minds. Our pathos is not of empowered people who have the means to shape a better future. Our mentality is of people who must continue to fight to assert themselves…We are in fact a political state. Transformation must be about development, not politics; race cannot be the sole consideration. (Mahabane, *Sunday Times* 17.04.05)

A similar view is put forward by Moeletsi Mbeki (*The Star* 08.04.05) who – whilst likewise favouring emulation of the developmental states of East Asia – suggests that existing government policies are likely to distort the development of the black capitalist class which is necessary for South Africa's advance. South Korea's transformation into an industrial power was directed by the state but implemented by the private sector. The government used its control of the commercial banks to borrow from abroad and then channelled those funds to companies investing in approved exporting industries. Attempts to attract foreign investment were eschewed in favour of educating the Korean population, and while industrialisation was initially (between 1962 and 1987) driven by an authoritarian regime, the latter nonetheless promoted measures that minimised social inequality. Furthermore, incentives were provided to the private sector at the same time as measures were taken to augment the state's entrepreneurial activity. By focusing upon promoting Korean entrepreneurs, the government assisted South Korean companies to acquire the capacity and skills to become major players in the world economy. In contrast, South African

BEE policies are creating a class of rent-seeking entrepreneurs who are living off existing industries, and in this they suggest that the country is following the regressive example of the rest of post-colonial Africa. Yet this need not be so.

Whereas development in the advanced economies is driven by the private sector, in Africa the latter is made up principally of peasants and subsidiaries of multinational companies who lack full freedom to operate because they are dominated locally by political elites. On the one hand, these elites use their control of the state to extract surplus which peasants would otherwise have invested; on the other, productive companies – which are largely owned by multinationals or non-Africans – are subject to a wide range of impositions, from official and unofficial taxes to customs dues, backhanders and often artificially high electricity and service charges. The result is that manufacturing in Africa is stunted. Yet South Africa is different, for while the political elite has much the same characteristics as elsewhere on the continent, its room for manoeuvre is hemmed in by three factors. These are: first, the fact that it does not have a peasantry to exploit; second, that there is a dynamic and constitutionally-protected private sector largely owned by (mainly white) South African citizens; and third, that to defeat apartheid it was forced into an alliance with a highly organised black working class. As both the private sector and the working class have a strong interest in growth, the opportunity and capacity of the political elite to extract surplus and indulge in unproductive consumption is therefore severely constrained. Against this, BEE – which is encouraged by elements of the super-rich who are seeking government favours – indicates that the political elite is actively seeking to siphon savings from the private sector, even if the latter has considerable muscle to resist dispossession. For this pattern to be broken and for growth to be maximised, the private sector needs to be unleashed and strengthened, and BEE should be refigured to promote genuine entrepreneurship. In the countryside, communal tenure must be abolished in favour of freehold to allow peasants to become the real owners of their land; they must be allowed to sell their products directly to the market without the intervention of the state; and financial institutions that are independent of the political elite should provide for the financial needs of peasants and small business.

> What socio-economic system would these changes bring about? Certainly not socialism! These changes would, for the first time, bring into being in Africa a capitalist market economy that answers to the needs of African producers. (M Mbeki, *Financial Mail* 13.08.04)

In summary, the Jacobins espouse what is at heart a radical nationalist position which views African economic liberation as involving a radical transformation of ownership and control in favour of black capitalists and producers. Only a genuinely South African capitalism – rather than one externally directed by monopolistic multinationals – can set the country upon a development path of benefit to all its people. South Africa, in short, requires a genuinely 'patriotic' bourgeoisie. Simultaneously, the Jacobin position incorporates the paradox (or is it a dialectic?) that a strong state is needed to set this patriotic bourgeoisie free!

The developmentalists

According to Jeremy Cronin, Deputy General Secretary of the SACP and an ANC Member of Parliament, 'there is now a growing intra-ANC alliance consensus on the need for a strong, developmental state' (*ThisDay* 16.08.04). However, there would seem to be rather little consensus as to what this consensus is about! On the one hand, flowing out of the ANC's theory of the national democratic revolution, there is strong overlap with the Jacobin position concerning the need for the state to promote a class of black capitalists. On the other hand, there is simultaneously much more caution with regard to the developmental benefits of a 'deracialised' free market, and correspondingly more concern to both control the new black capitalist class and render the political economy responsive to mass social needs and interests. Yet the difficulty is that first, the term 'developmental state' means different things to different people, and second, as Makgetla (2005) observes, it is 'used without much investigation of its intellectual origins or significance in international development theory'.

For all that key government actors may have turned to the idea of the developmental state in the wake of the market's failure to promote adequate growth and create enough desperately needed jobs, its present popularity may well be that it can serve as an ideological glue to hold the Alliance together. Indeed, its emergence in 2004 – an election year when the ANC leadership successfully calmed prior highly vocal disagreements between itself and Cosatu and the SACP concerning economic strategy – was probably no accident. Yet this is not to suggest that its appearance did not have deeper origins.

The Jacobin perspective emphasises that the developmental state idea has strong anti-colonial origins – Japan's determination to escape Western domination, South Korea's own drive to escape the thrall of both pre-Second World War Japanese colonialism and post-war US imperialism, and so on. It is therefore scarcely surprising that the rapid growth achieved by the developmental states should be hailed by Third World nationalist elites, and that prestige may be gained by 'looking east' and associating with such states and their strategies. It is perhaps no less surprising that, for all that the successful East Asian states were simultaneously capitalist states, influential thinkers within the Tripartite Alliance should be looking to contemporary China as, if not a developmental state itself, then at least a country which is learning from their experiences.

Describing how the SACP has sought to 're-imagine socialism' following the collapse of the Berlin Wall, Cronin identifies the Chinese Communist Party as not so much embracing the market as engaging the capitalist-dominated world as 'a risky but unavoidable way' of defending and advancing socialist gains. 'There are technologies and there are markets controlled by capitalism, but which, in the pursuit of their own profits, might also be harnessed to a different project' (*ThisDay* 16.08.04). Hence, faced with a decline of their exports to their crisis-ridden Asian neighbours in the late 1990s, the Chinese increased wages in their vast public sector by some 25 per cent to create a compensatory demand. Socialism, in short, is not a self-contained system, and it is more useful to think of it as 'the struggle, in the midst of capitalism, for the hegemony of a political economy of social needs over the dominance of private profits'.

Cronin observes that such an argument takes us straight back to different conceptions of the national democratic revolution. In the old tradition of viewing history as a succession of stages, some within the Alliance appear to think that because contemporary South Africa is not socialist, it has to be capitalist. It is only after it has been deracialised and normalised (and some revolutionary capitalists have got extremely rich), that a move to socialism can be contemplated. On the other hand, the democratic state can be seen as a terrain contested by capitalist and popular forces in which, given the failure of capitalism to address the needs of the poor, the latter are struggling to achieve an alternative social economy. From this perspective, the present consensus around the developmental state contains both those who see a strong state as necessary to get the balance right between public interests and the capitalist market, and those for whom a strong public sector combines with embedded traditions in the liberation movement of participatory democracy to become part of a far more ambitious transformational agenda.

Makgetla has joined Cronin in looking to China for lessons (*Business Day* 22.04.05). This is in response to a flurry of interest about that country's economic model, resulting not only from admiration of its recent high levels of growth,[4] but also from concern about the rapid expansion of South Africa's trade imbalance with China (in part due to the import of cheap Chinese clothing imports, which has had a highly deleterious impact upon the local textile industry). While the economic liberals propose that recent Chinese experience highlights the need for maximising competitiveness through labour flexibility, achieving high rates of savings and attracting foreign investment (Leon, *The Star* 21.04.05), Makgetla looks rather to the Chinese government role in promoting relative income equality, subsidising necessities to compensate for low monetary wages, undervaluing the currency (to boost exports) and controlling many basic inputs such as finance to restrain production costs. Yet Makgetla's position is not that China is a developmental state for she recognises that that term describes the ability of a state to mobilise a nation for rapid development within the capitalist system. While China might fit the description of a development state as she sees the term being generally used in South Africa – that is, to mean little more than a 'state that drives development, in contrast to a free market approach' – she argues the value of using the concept of a development state as it has been elaborated in the international development literature if appropriate lessons are going to be drawn from East Asia.

Citing Chalmers Johnson and other prominent authors, Makgetla defines developmental states as having engaged in a revolutionary project which, unlike Leninism, viewed the market as a better instrument for achieving their objectives of rapid modernisation than central planning. From this perspective, the developmental state classically had two principal characteristics. First, 'in class terms, the development state was closely allied to business but able to maintain the autonomy needed to drive development of new industries', maintaining mass support through a combination of nationalist propaganda and improvements in living standards for workers and small businesspeople, while associating these with rapidly increasing employment and paternalistic labour relations in larger companies. Second, in policy terms, 'the state intervened vigorously to develop new industries, using a combination of massive amounts of subsidized credit, strong tariff protection, substantial training and infrastructure development'. However, such actions could not take place in a vacuum, and the success of Japan, South Korea and Taiwan 'resulted as much from peculiar international and national circumstances as from good policies'. After 1945, the US and Western Europe saw these three countries as a bulwark against communism, and hence provided substantial foreign aid, preferential access for exports and indirect support through US spending throughout the East Asian region. Meanwhile, capital in all three countries was disorganised after the second World War, hence less able to resist radical land reform or exert pressure to retain resource-based production, existing industries and traditional forms of inequality and subordination. In short, while offering a critique of both free market models of development as well as of the distorted patterns of (under)development pursued by numerous Third World countries, the developmental state idea offers experiential support for the view that states in the South must intervene extensively (but appropriately) in business decisions if they are to achieve rapid growth. Yet it does not offer 'general truths that must be slavishly adopted', only ideas 'about possible causes of failure and solutions'.

Pursuing the debate

All three broad perspectives seek to promote South Africa's rapid development as well as sharing a number of overlapping concerns – about unemployment, inequality, social coherence and so on. Yet they also address different remedies for South Africa's travails.

Challenges to South Africa as a developmental state

Let us now examine the way in which the different approaches can throw light on challenges facing South Africa if it is to aspire to becoming a developmental state, namely, the issues of historical specificity, state capacity, and the purported democracy/development trade-off.

THE DEVELOPMENT STATE: CAN HISTORY BE REPEATED?

Marx once famously said that history repeats itself, firstly as tragedy, secondly as farce. His aphorism speaks to the folly of mechanical attempts to reproduce past experiences out of time and place, and in the present context, raises the issue of historical specificity: were the conditions which allowed or promoted the developmental state in Japan, South Korea and Taiwan peculiar to their post-war situation and, if so, what does this imply?

It has recently been proposed by Doner, Ritchie and Slater (2005: 327–362) that the political origins of developmental states are located in conditions of 'systemic vulnerability', or the simultaneous interplay of three separate constraints: (i) broad coalitional commitments, (ii) scarce resource endowments, and (iii) severe security threats. Their argument is that 'the interactive condition of systemic vulnerability is both a necessary and sufficient condition for developmental states', and that unless political leaders are confronted by all three of these constraints simultaneously, they will find less challenging ways of staying in power than constructing a developmental state. 'Systemic vulnerability' thus makes the reconciliation of coalitional, geopolitical and fiscal constraints a matter of ruling elites' political survival.

To elaborate:
- Politicians need to build a broad coalition when revenues are desperately needed for national defence, and when there is little revenue to go round. Only by expanding the national pie through sustained growth, yet without pursuing cheap labour policies, can such an inclusive coalition be sustained. Systemic vulnerability therefore presses elites to abandon low-wage-based export growth for a higher-skill, quality-based export trajectory. Elites thus have to make 'side payments' (in this case higher wages) without draining the national treasury or raising exporters' costs.
- Strong states arise in response to security threats, in part by appealing to nationalism and patriotism. But external threats do not in themselves develop institutional capacity. The key factor is whether threatened states are forced to turn inwards to meet the financial challenges of defence or war.
- A state's ease of access to revenue influences institutional development, with an abundance of resources potentially encouraging the creation of distributive rather than extractive state institutions. Yet countries of similar resource endowments develop different institutional capacities. Some elites merely satisfice in revenue collection, that is, they only collect the minimum amount of revenue needed to survive politically. But the

demands of maintaining broad coalitions and meeting external security threats force developmental states to maximise revenue. The need to reconcile these competing pressures likewise compels elites to develop collaborative public–private linkages, redistribute assets such as land, identify areas for investment, improve the competitiveness of firms and upgrade skills. 'Easy' development strategies are not viable.

Doner et al. conclude that whereas Taiwan, South Korea and, they believe, Singapore responded to the combination of all three challenges by forming developmental states, other fast-growing, yet less successful, 'intermediate' states in South East Asia (Malaysia, Indonesia, Philippines and Thailand) did not, and display lower bureaucratic coherence and less effective public–private linkages.

The parsimonious nature of this approach suggests that few other countries are likely to become developmental states. Similarly Wade (1999: 345–350) proposes that whereas the successful East Asian countries were enabled to 'govern their markets' because of the favourable historical and industrial conditions in which their policies were implemented, subsequently developing countries faced immensely more hostile environments: they confronted a new protectionism limiting their exports to Western markets, a fall in the demand for unskilled labour and raw materials per unit of industrial production attendant upon dramatic changes in technology, a more volatile global financial market and so on. Theorists also argue that the globalisation which has taken place since the 1980s has taken its own toll on the mercantilist basis of the developmental states, eroding their political and economic autonomy and rendering them more market oriented (Kim 1999). Following Wade (1999: 348, 381), it may be assumed, therefore, that adoption of policies by governments to impart an East Asian directional thrust will have a smaller effect than they had in East Asia. Yet this does not detract from the wisdom of developing countries studying the East Asian experience to see how government and capitalism have been arranged in states where growth has been a top national priority for decades.

This approach urges a mixture of the scepticism of the economic liberals and the caution of the developmentalists towards the applicability of the developmental state idea to South Africa. At one level, the liberals fear that, however well-intentioned, growing state regulation of the market is likely to misfire, and will lack the sophistication of the East Asian examples. Rather than promoting development, state intervention is more likely to stifle it, a belief which, it must be said, also follows from the ahistoric nature of much neoclassical economic thinking which commends the minimal state as a prerequisite for growth. At another level, the liberals share the concerns of the Jacobins that state controls over the economy imposed by the ANC may not only be unproductive, but may work to drain surplus into the pockets of an avaricious emergent black bourgeoisie for private consumption.

Yet it is undoubtedly the developmentalists, represented in this context by Makgetla, who have most to say about this issue. For a start, she warns against the ahistoric embrace of a generic 'developmental statism' as merely the ideological obverse of free-marketry. Compared to the East Asian states, the South African economy has pursued an entirely different and far more unfavourable historical trajectory. Whereas the former faced national capital groups that saw industrial growth as their main road to profit, South African capital was shaped by mining, and financial institutions, parastatals and even agriculture were geared to ensuring that it succeeded. While Afrikaner nationalists enjoyed some success in getting mining interests to support manufacturing from the 1920s, manufacturing remained oriented to providing consumer goods for higher income groups and was based heavily on imported inputs and capital equipment. The mines and financial institutions remained largely foreign owned until the 1980s, and when the economy was reopened at the end of apartheid, they rapidly reintegrated into global markets. While this background does not imply that the South African state is powerless, it does suggest that it is likely to face far greater resistance to industrial restructuring than was found in the successful Asian economies. Nonetheless, just as dos and don'ts can be learnt from contemporary China, so the developmental state idea can be used to inform state policy for maximising employment-creating growth, building export industries on the back of an expanding domestic market, ensuring real increases in living standards for workers (for example by subsidising the cost of transport and holding down the value of the rand), and ensuring that BEE strategies are broad-based.

South Africa is clearly not subject to the 'systemic vulnerability' which Doner et al. view as both the necessary and sufficient conditions for the creation of a developmental state, but this does not mean that appropriate lessons cannot be learnt from East Asian (and other) examples. However, implementation of any policies is dependent upon state capacity, about which there remain many doubts.

STATE CAPACITY

The key thrusts of the three competing perspectives towards state capacity are as follows. First, in arguing that state intervention into the economy is always fraught with perils, the economic liberals stress that in South Africa this is compounded by the added danger of policy-driven attempts to achieve demographic representivity. These accentuate the widely acknowledged skills deficiencies of the state and undermine the values of the democratic Constitution. Second, while favouring meritocracy, the Jacobins espouse a radical capitalist agenda which, by implication, demands a strong Africanist state capable of simultaneously controlling, directing and mediating conflicts between national capital (inclusive of the new black bourgeoisie), multinational capital and the organised working class. Third, the developmentalists, in urging the necessity of the developmental state achieving 'transformation' and growth simultaneously, seek to will it into existence and hence seek to implement policies designed to achieve desired ends (delivery, growth and so forth). Such a view, whilst recognising the state as 'a site of struggle', assumes the capacity of the state to reconcile conflicting interests and to pursue its goals democratically. All three perspectives provide considerable insight, yet equally they are all partial (and partisan), and need to be complemented by a more systematic approach towards the highly complex issue of the state.

Gerhard Maré (2004) argued in the first *State of the Nation* that any assessment of the post-apartheid state needed to be made in terms of four broad issues: What social inequalities had it inherited and how was it attempting to address this legacy? What were the sources of political legitimacy, and to what extent did these provide for a durable relationship between citizens and state? To what extent were state structures able to meet the needs of the country's new inclusiveness, and how effective were they as a delivery mechanism? Finally, who was gaining what, and on what basis were they fighting for what? He concluded that, with all its multiple contradictions, the new state had resolved the tensions between reform and repression that characterised the apartheid state through the incorporation of all South Africans under equal citizenship rights. However, the transition also demanded measures that maintained South Africa's mode of incorporation into global capitalism. The key questions which followed, therefore, were: Should South Africa be placed within the long line of African transitions that utilised the state for enrichment of a bureaucracy and rapid class formation into a dependent bourgeoisie? Or is the South African state better understood as a complex set of class, gender and race contestations, occurring under conditions, internally and globally, vastly different from those that applied during the wave of decolonisation?

Maré only addressed the issue of state 'capacity' obliquely. In contrast, this has formed a central concern of theorists of the developmental state, who in broad terms have divided between an approach which argues that the key to successful economic performance rests with 'strong' states imbued with a high level of autonomy, and those who contend that state power derives from the extent to which states are 'embedded' in society. A recent attempt to bridge the gap between these positions is offered by Cummings and Norgaard (2004), who propose that state capacity can be best understood by examining it along four closely interrelated dimensions: ideational, political, technical and implementational.

- *Ideational state capacity* refers to the degree to which the state is legitimated and embedded in state institutions. If the ideas of the elite are to become influential, and if state institutions comprise groups of individuals in power, then the elite's ideas need to have the endorsement of those individuals. The more that functions and policies are perceived to be addressing collective problems, the better ideas fit officials' sense of their role and identity, and the more the ideas are regarded as legitimate by the public, the stronger the state's ideational capacity.
- *Political state capacity* refers to what makes for an effective structure of governance, both horizontally (how individuals and departments work together internally with government) and vertically (how individuals and departments relate to the domestic and international community).
- *Technical state capacity* refers to the intellectual and organisational resources owned by a state, such as internal or external expertise, that may be brought to bear on the policy-making process so as to design coherent, viable and politically feasible policies.
- *Implementational state capacity* refers to the ability of the state to carry out decisions that have been taken, dependent upon such factors as material resources or the blocking of implementation by particularist groups.

This multidimensional approach provides one potential framework for encapsulating the concerns of our three perspectives and taking forward our thinking about the capacity of the South African state. Space is too short to argue this comprehensively, but the following considerations may be suggestive:

- Maré's assessment that the post-apartheid state has provided an inclusive basis for its political legitimacy is widespread, as are upbeat assessments about consequential outcomes. South Africa, notes a leading business spokesman, has achieved a 'virtuous circle' of high growth, democratic governance and social development (Parsons, *Business Day* 05.10.04). Whereas the apartheid ideology was fundamentally and purposefully divisive, the constitutional foundation of the post-apartheid state upon democratic values of individual freedoms, racial and gender equality, and state accountability is acclaimed by all major political actors, even if (as the contributions in this volume by February, Gouws and Govender indicate) their realisation is imperfect. Nonetheless, South Africa's *ideational state capacity* may be said to be severely limited by at least two ideological fractures. The first concerns the mode of the government's attempt to address the history of racial inequality, with liberals contesting the official drive for promoting 'representivity' by favouring black appointments and promotions in both state and societal institutions as 're-racialising' South Africa, and being joined by the Jacobins in arguing that presently constructed BEE policies compromise efficiency and encourage entitlement over achievement. (This, however, is not to say that Jacobins' perspectives are wholly consistent, for their espousal of a meritocratic civil service is curiously quiet about the implication that at this stage of South Africa's history this could well slow extension of African/black/majority control over the machinery of state.) The second fracture revolves around economic strategy and the resultant nature of South Africa's post-apartheid capitalism. As already suggested, the state's own promotion of the idea of the development state may at one level be an attempt to forge a 'broad coalition' concerning this issue amongst the ruling party's multiple constituencies, whilst simultaneously drawing closer to national (especially Afrikaner?) capital. Yet the extent to which the state's robustly conservative fiscal policies have contributed to entrenching social inequalities, not least through shifting the balance of employment towards the informal market (see Valodia et al., Buhlungu & Webster, and Moleke in this volume) and by raising questions about whether South Africa's present capitalist path can be socially redistributive (see Southall in this volume), has excited much controversy, especially among developmentalists within the Tripartite Alliance.

- As reiterated in the 2005 'State of the Nation' speech, the government recognises the state's limited *political capacity* as indicated notably by provincial and local government failures to implement policies. Its proposed remedy is the restructuring of the public service to give greater powers of control to the centre, while simultaneously using its fiscal muscle to reward efficiency and punish the reverse. Its most notable critics in this regard are economic liberals, who fear that not only are financial and administrative breakdowns propelling a creeping centralisation which is leading to reduced accountability at provincial and local government levels, but that government's ambitions shoot far beyond its resources, notably of competent senior managers (Schlemmer, *Business Day* 04.03.05). In contrast, Jacobins praise the government's aspirations towards the developmental state, but concur that the state has too limited a capacity to make strategic interventions, citing in particular its alleged lack of a coherent industrial policy (Mahabane, *Financial Mail* 13.08.04), a theme which is taken up with regard to South Africa's evolving trade strategy by Blumenfeld in this volume.

- Nothing has been more influential in promoting the new popularity of the developmental state than the government's new emphasis upon restructuring the SOEs and making them 'drivers of growth'. Their performance has been so problematic (with exceptions, notably Eskom) that criticism of the policy shift has been muted. Hence, although the government has been widely censured for its alleged mismanagement of the privatisation of the telecommunications industry, the urgent necessity of the state shaking up the railways to lower freight costs is barely disputed (for example, Lunsche, *Financial Mail* 29.10.04). Related positions concerning *technical state capacity* are expressed across the ideological spectrum. For instance, Jacobin criticisms of the limitations of existing industrial policy have been endorsed by other commentators who argue that government should do more to shift South Africa from a capital-intensive growth pattern to a more integrated policy that increases the economy's international competitiveness by, *inter alia*, increasing local demand, curbing exchange rate volatility, and developing a rational national public transport policy. As Kahn and Reddy do in this volume, they also stress the need for the

co-ordination of educational, technological, skills and industrial policy (Machaka, Mohammed, Phele & Roberts, *Mail & Guardian* 15–21.10.04).
- President Mbeki's espousal of firm targets for the delivery of services in 2004 was part and parcel of the government's adoption of new performance strategies to render the post-apartheid public service more efficient, as has been a concerted attempt to make monitoring and evaluation of policy implementation central to official practice. While such initiatives designed to improve *implementational state capacity* are widely welcomed in principle, failure to realise targets often invites criticisms that inefficiencies follow from the government's ideological impulse to control from above, and reveals its inability to 'loosen the shackles of state regulation and adopt policies that stimulate private initiative' (Honey, *Financial Mail* 22.04.05).

It is scarcely surprising that debate is more vigorous around ideational and political rather than technical and implementational state capacities. Yet what is equally notable is how all three perspectives remain remarkably reluctant to confront the issue of a democracy/development trade-off.

SHADOW DEBATING A DEMOCRACY/DEVELOPMENT TRADE-OFF

There is no subject more out of bounds in South Africa's contemporary political discourse than any suggestion that development may require constraints upon democracy. Democratic rights for the majority in South Africa have been so hard won that any hint that they have costs is distinctly unwelcome. The ANC clings to its identity as the liberation movement which freed South Africa from the shackles of apartheid, the DA identifies itself as the embodiment of individual rights, and the New National Party found the burden of ridding itself of its apartheid past so great that it recently collapsed itself, unlamented, into the new ruling party. Everyone favours 'freedom' and academic commentators concur with the new global orthodoxy that the struggle for political and socio-economic rights democratises development whilst also developing democracy (Graham 2005). Yet as the *Business Day* editorial (08.03.05) pointed out, developmental states have been autocratic if not actually authoritarian, and whilst scholars such as Doner et al. concede that developmental states may have become democratic, 'side payments' compromising various freedoms were often necessary to get them to that destination. It is scarcely surprising, therefore, that this problematic aspect of the developmental state has been downplayed by its promoters. This needs surprisingly little elaboration.

For the developmentalists, the debate about the developmental state has been largely restricted to one of economic strategy. Yet ironically this ignores the foundations of the developmental state as it was originally analysed by such academics as Chalmers Johnson. He argued that in contrast to early industrialising, *market-rational* states such as the US, where the state's economic role was *regulatory*, late industrialising developmental states were *plan-rational*, that is, they assumed as their dominant feature the setting of substantive social and economic goals. Most relevantly: first, the plan-rational system depends upon the existence of widely agreed upon overarching goals for the society, such as high-speed growth; second, in a plan-rational state the government will prioritise industrial policy, that is, promote an industrial structure that enhances the nation's international competitiveness; third, in a plan-rational system decision-making is centred in an elite bureaucracy, whereas in a *market-rational* system it is located in a parliamentary assembly. In the plan-rational system, therefore, change will be characterised by internal bureaucratic disputes, factional infighting and conflict among ministries, whereas, in a market-rational state it will be fought over via strenuous parliamentary contests over legislation and by election battles. In short, in the developmental state, economic interests are explicitly subordinated to political objectives.

Liberal critics of the ANC argue precisely that its intention is to extend its political control over all aspects of the state and the economy. In contrast, the ANC responds that all suggestions that it is misusing its political dominance to inhibit opposition and accountability are derogatory of its own historical role as the harbinger of democracy, and often racist (Southall 2005). It also recognises that in an era when the maintenance of liberal-democratic institutions is much vaunted as a foundation of political stability and an attraction to foreign investment, any moves by government to centralise control and narrow political space have to be justified in avowedly market-rational rather than plan-rational terminology. In any case, for all that the government may wish to promote commandism in the interests of efficiency, it remains uncomfortably aware of its limited capacity to impose order upon unruly protests about delivery failures without aping the strategies of its oppressive forbears. The dilemma remains, therefore, of how to combine plan-rationality with liberal democracy, yet on the whole developmentalists choose to ignore it.

The Jacobins' position is in many ways the most interesting, because it is rarely made explicit. Yet there is undoubtedly a hint of revolutionary authoritarianism. As expressed by the DA's Ryan Coetzee (*ThisDay* 29.07.04), who characterises the entire ANC leadership as Jacobin, the Jacobin conception of democracy has its roots in Rousseau's conception of the 'general will'. From this perspective, the ANC is said to see itself as the organic representative of the majority, and from there conflates 'the people' with the 'party' and the 'state'. Whereas liberal democrats seek to balance the desires of the majority against the rights of individuals, Jacobins believe that individuals must submit their desires to the general will.

This interpretation is certainly reflected in Moeletsi Mbeki's analysis of how South Africa is to escape the fate of African underdevelopment: as well as undertaking to constrain unproductive private accumulation by the new black elite, the ruling party must undertake a radical restructuring of the capitalist relations in both town and countryside to free the market and liberate all citizens to become entrepreneurs. Only a 'strong' state will be capable of doing this, and hence by implication the further suggestion is that if reactionary elements of capital get in the way, they will have to be pushed aside or even appropriated. If the one face of the Jacobins is that of Margaret Thatcher, the other is that of Robert Mugabe!

In their rejection of the developmental state, the economic liberals espouse an uncomplicated relationship between democracy and development. Individual political and economic freedoms, overseen by a market-regulatory state, maximise economic opportunity and hence entrepreneurship and growth. Yet theirs is a different problem, for they fail to confront the despotism inherent in their gospel of labour market flexibility. As Webster and von Holdt (2005) elaborate, corporate restructuring and the reorganisation of work are pointing to an emergent crisis of social reproduction in post-apartheid South Africa: in the formal economy, the dominant trend is towards managerial authoritarianism, resulting in worker dissatisfaction, alienation, resistance and inefficiency; within the non-core of informal work, workers are subject to job insecurity, low wages and alienation, with more and more workers being pushed over the edge into poverty; in the third zone of the economy, one of unemployment and informal subsistence, households are placed under devastating pressures of impoverishment and hunger. While economic liberals imply that only an intensification of present market trends, notably by weakening the trade unions, can lead to long-term growth and wealth, Webster and von Holdt propose the alternative of the state assuming a developmental role, one which in part it will be propelled into undertaking by a 'counter-movement' of trade unions and social movements – realities of political economy which economic liberals too readily forget.

Concluding thoughts

The burden of this discussion is that while the aspiration for South Africa to become a developmental state is understandable and in many ways admirable, it must nonetheless be regarded with caution. Most certainly we need to go well beyond the employment of the term as a 'feel-good' label if the concept of the developmental state is to retain any heuristic value. A number of conclusions follow.

First, there are clear indications that the experience of the developmental states cannot be replicated as a matter of will. It may well be that in their analysis of the 'systemic vulnerability' of the East Asian states Doner et al. adopt a too severe definition of the developmental state, for other writers such as Evans (1995), whose distinction between predatory, developmental and intermediate states was discussed previously (Daniel, Southall & Lutchman 2005), adopt a broader perspective which would allow the application of the term to a wider array of high-growth developing economies. Nonetheless, the point is well taken both that the nature of South Africa's internal political economy (a now largely black-controlled state, still mainly white-owned industry, a black working class, an impoverished black informal sector and a propertyless black rural population heavily dependent upon transfers from urban areas for their subsistence), as well as the nature of its location into the global political economy (continuing heavy reliance upon the export of minerals), is so very different from what faced ruling elites in post-war Japan, Taiwan and South Korea that no easy analogies can be drawn. It is also clear that while the recent shift in government strategy to restructuring the SOEs does represent a major initiative which has been overwhelmingly favoured by private capital, a strengthened public sector does not itself add up to the 'plan-rationality' which saw developmental states politically establishing economic goals, devising a far-reaching industrial policy and directing the investment behaviour of their largest corporations. Finally, it needs to be noted that, as presently conducted, the debate about South Africa as a developmental state is overwhelmingly addressed to its internal strategies and arrangements, and it is strangely silent about how it does or should relate to the global and African continental economies. However, as is eloquently explored in the chapters by Blumenfeld, Naidu, and Daniel and Lutchman in this volume, this is hugely problematic: links between industrial and trade policies are weak, China's relations to South Africa are dictated by considerations of *realpolitik* more than benevolence, and South Africa's proactive search for energy self-sufficiency is encouraging behaviour that is leading it into collaborative relations with some of the most unaccountable, corrupt and abusive regimes in Africa.

Despite these problems, a second conclusion is that important lessons (negative as well as positive) can be learnt from the developmental states. As stressed notably by the developmentalists, these mainly concern matters of economic strategy, notably about how to boost internal demand, deploy state resources to promote domestic industrial capacity, and combine employment growth with redistribution. From this perspective, the developmental states provide important models from which broad orientations as well as particular policies can be pragmatically borrowed and implemented, just as relevant lessons may be drawn from contemporary China, whose developmental path has been so different from its East Asian capitalist neighbours. However, in this regard, the warnings of both the economic liberals and the Jacobins should not be easily discounted. While they differ fundamentally about the wisdom and necessity of state intervention into the economy, they converge around the issue of the seriously limited capacity of the South African state as it is today and raise important questions about the simultaneous short-term pursuit of 'demographic representivity' and 'efficiency', objectives which they view as being in tension. Beyond this, furthermore, their concerns overlap with those of the developmentalists about how 'state capacity' can be both analysed and improved, a dimension to which recent thinking about the developmental state could well add considerable value if pursued systematically.

A final contribution of the notion of the developmental state is that it may compel new thinking in South Africa around the issue of how democracy can be combined with development. What 'broad coalitions' are necessary or desirable for growth to be achieved? What bargains have to be struck between which groups in society, and what 'side payments' have to be made if stability and development are to be combined? If strategic intervention by the state is necessary to bring about a shift in an employment and wealth-creating direction, does it have costs which are either inherent or an outcome of particular policies? Our three schools of thought tend to provide different answers, but it is in their clash of ideas that innovative and productive solutions may emerge.

Afterword

As with our previous volumes, this edition of *State of the Nation* takes its cue from the President's own annual assessments of the country's condition and surrounding ideas of where it is going. If this editorial has highlighted the emergent debate around the developmental state, the issues which that is raising come through strongly in all the chapters that follow, although equally all our authors range widely across their topics and extend their analysis beyond the confines of contemporary discussion as it has been presented here. Taken together, however, they allow this collection to pose the pressing question: if democratic South Africa is to achieve its objectives of growth and equity, will it need to become 'a developmental state of a special type'?

Notes

1 Editorial headline, *Financial Mail* 18.02.05.
2 'What is the state of our nation? The answer: the nation is strong; the state is the problem' (Leon, *Financial Mail* 11.03.05).
3 'After 1794 it would be clear to moderates that the Jacobin regime had driven the Revolution too far for bourgeois comfort and prospects, just as it would be clear to revolutionaries that "the sun of 1793", if it were to rise again, would have to shine on a non-bourgeois society. Again, the Jacobins could afford radicalism because in their time no class existed which could provide a coherent social alternative to theirs. Such a class only arose in the course of the industrial revolution, with the 'proletariat' or, more precisely, with the ideologies and movements based on it'. (Hobsbawm 2000: 62–63)
4 Officials from the Presidency were said to be hugely impressed by the Chinese government-led growth model after a visit to China in early 2005 (*Mail & Guardian* 11.02.05).

References

ANC (African National Congress) (2005) Development and underdevelopment. Discussion document for the National General Council, 29.06–03.07.05.

Cummings S & Norgaard O (2004) Conceptualising state capacity: Comparing Kazakhstan and Kyrgyzstan, *Political Studies* 52: 685–708.

Daniel J, Southall R & Lutchman J (eds.) (2005) *State of the Nation: South Africa 2004–2005*. Cape Town: HSRC Press.

Doner R, Ritchie K & Slater D (2005) Systemic vulnerability and the origins of developmental states: Northeast and Southeast Asian in comparative perspective, *International Organization* 59(2): 327–362.

Evans P (1995) *Embedded autonomy: States and industrial transformations*. Princeton: Princeton University Press.

Graham P (2005) Socio-economic rights: Cornerstone or capstone of democracy? In P Jones & K Stokker (eds.) *Democratising development: The politics of socio-economic rights in South Africa*. Norway: Martinus Nijhoff.

Hobsbawm E (2000, first published 1962) *The age of revolution: Europe 1789–1848*. London: Phoenix Press.

Johnson C (1999) The developmental state: Odyssey of a concept. In M Woo-Cumings (ed.) *The developmental state*. Ithaca and London: Cornell University Press.

Kim YT (1999). Neoliberalism and the decline of the developmental state, *Journal of Contemporary Asia* 29(4): 441–461.

Makgetla N (2005) A developmental state for South Africa? Discussion paper for Cosatu's 2005 Central Committee.

Maré G (2004) The state of the state: Contestation and race re-assertion in a neo-liberal terrain. In J Daniel, A Habib & R Southall (eds.) *State of the Nation 2003–04*. Cape Town: HSRC Press.

Mbeki T (2005a) Address of the President of South Africa, Thabo Mbeki, to the second joint sitting of the third democratic Parliament. Cape Town, 11.02.05.

Mbeki T (2005b) Speech of the President of the Republic of South Africa, Thabo Mbeki, on the occasion of the Budget Vote of the Presidency, National Assembly, Cape Town, 25 May.

PCAS (Presidency Policy Co-ordination and Advisory Services, South Africa) (2003) *Towards a ten year review: Synthesis report on implementation of government programmes*. Pretoria: Government Communications and Information Systems.

Southall R (2005) The 'dominant party debate' in South Africa, *Afrika Spectrum* 39(1): 61–82.

Wade R (1999) *Governing the market: Economic theory and the role of government in East Asian industrialization*. Princeton: Princeton University Press.

Webster E & von Holdt K (eds.) (2005) *Beyond the apartheid workplace: Studies in transition*. Scottsville, South Africa: University of Kwazulu-Natal Press.

Part I: Politics

Politics: introduction

Jessica Lutchman

The politics section in this volume moves away from the party-political focus of the first two *State of the Nation* volumes to concentrate on some of the political issues and institutions which have dominated the political landscape of the last 12 months. We open with the issue which more than any other concerns the Mbeki government, namely, improving the quality of life of those located in what it terms 'the second economy' and examine how well or otherwise the ambitious service-delivery targets identified in the President's May 2004 'State of the Nation' address are being reached. Our second article follows on from this by looking critically at the conceptualisation of the notion of poverty in the post-apartheid era. We then turn to one of the more contentious of current issues, that of land restitution as a means of redressing the inequities of the past. This flows into an examination of the promotion of human rights post-1994 and, in particular, how the Constitutional Court is interpreting the Constitutional Bill of Rights. We then look at the national Parliament and how it is exercising its watchdog role over the executive and the public purse. Finally, we examine how women's interests are being served by the network of institutions and bodies that make up what is known as the national gender machinery (NGM).

David Hemson and Michael O'Donovan assess how close government has come to accomplishing the delivery targets defined in the May 2004 speech. They suggest that such a public enunciation of its goals signals not only an official commitment by government to new forms of public accountability and open government, but demonstrates a 'rational model' of government. They echo a theme developed by Roger Southall in the introduction to this volume when they suggest that there seems to be a new 'form of presidential rule' emerging as 'the Presidency itself takes on the responsibility of setting targets and ensuring that they are carried out' – a function more usually undertaken by national departments and local government structures. This, they argue, as does Southall, is characteristic of the interventionist and centralising characteristics of the 'development-state' model.

With regard to the targets set out by the President in 2004, the authors make the point that few of these were new; instead, what was presented was largely a new packaging of old promises. The authors point out that assessing the delivery of these 'old promises' has not been easy for a number of reasons. One has been the problem of acquiring relevant data against which to verify the effectiveness and efficiency of government in service delivery. In part, they argue, this is due to the fact that the necessary data are not always provided by national departments and when provided, they are not always reliable or easily checked. They also point to a difficulty caused by what could be termed fancy methodological footwork, particularly in regard to the more ambitious or difficult of the goals or ones in which the government is clearly falling short. In these circumstances, the authors note that the attainment of targets tends to be measured in terms of inputs (how much is to be, or is being, spent) rather than results (reduction in backlogs, improved health and well-being).

Nonetheless, utilising the available data, the authors conclude that although some significant progress has been made in the areas of public housing, water, electricity, sanitation, social security, health and education, the progress has been insufficient to offset the sizeable backlogs in most of these areas. The two exceptions, they note, are the provision of electricity and social security services such as the child-support grant and pensions. There, quotas have been exceeded. They conclude that there is a continuing need for academics and civil society to develop and keep ongoing scorecards of government's performance and/or underperformance in this huge task it has set itself. The Human Sciences Research Council will certainly continue to be part of that process and future editions of this volume will report their findings.

One of the youngest contributors to this volume, Oxford doctoral student Wiseman Magasela, takes a fresh look at an old issue, that of poverty in South Africa. He argues that researching poverty in South Africa is still 'in its formative stages when considering developments and advances at the international level'. He suggests that this is an opportune time to question the 'conceptualisation and measurement' of poverty, the more so because South Africa does not have a reliable or recent 'official definition of poverty or a poverty line' and, more often than not, most poverty-related studies in South Africa have 'relied uncritically on income and absolute definitions and measures of poverty'. The first official review of poverty after 1994,

'Key indicators of poverty in South Africa', undertaken by the World Bank, was based on 'income poverty' alone and failed to take into account socio-economic perspectives. He also suggests that South Africa's most widely used poverty surveys – the household subsistence and minimum living level – were both constructed during the apartheid era and remain unchanged.

This, he argues, is problematic as the post-apartheid period in South Africa is fundamentally different from that which preceded it. Therefore, to conceptualise poverty solely on the basis of quantitative analysis (narrow income measures) is unwise as the results produced tend to be distorted. The author concludes that a strongly qualitative perspective (for example, socio-economic rights enshrined in the Constitution) should be adopted in future poverty research in South Africa. Poverty is multidimensional in nature; it is not merely about 'income-related measures' but also about 'access to infrastructure' and 'a quality of life' to which every South African is entitled. If the South African government is to create effective anti-poverty policies, Magasela concludes, a better conceptualisation of poverty in the post-apartheid period is required.

In her article, Cherryl Walker (KwaZulu-Natal's Land Claims Commissioner between 1994 and 1999) takes stock of the land restitution process and assesses the extent to which the programme has contributed to the goals of redress and redistributive justice. Despite the rhetorical importance government assigns to land reform and redress, Walker argues that since 1994 the budget for land restitution and the restitution process itself have fallen far short of what is required. She suggests that in actuality restitution has not been a top government priority and has ranked below that of other African National Congress development goals. However, an increased budget in 2005/06 and a reference to restitution in the 2005 'State of the Nation' address signal the state's determination to wind up the process by the new deadline of March 2008.

In evaluating the implementation of the restitution process, Walker suggests that the programme of land restitution has suffered from what she calls 'misplaced agrarianisation'. What this refers to is the fact that, in her view, land restitution is firstly conceptualised as primarily a rural phenomenon, while the urban dimension is often underestimated; secondly, she argues that the success of restitution is primarily assessed in terms of land-based development rather than financial compensation; and finally, she sees this reflected in a developmental moralism which insists that claimants should choose land restoration instead of financial compensation. Most land activists see taking money as a 'betrayal of restitution principles'.

Walker concludes by arguing that, despite the positive ambitions of land restitution in the early 1990s, 'achievements have been modest' thus far and the programme has fallen short in terms of 'historical reach, developmental impact and overall contribution to land reform'. To date, 'the goals of social justice, redress and rebuilding communities have turned out to be more elusive than previously imagined' and she suggests that a 'reassessment of the criteria by which the programme is judged' needs to be developed.

Karthy Govender, a legal academic and member of the national South African Human Rights Commission, tracks the progress made in the past decade in regard to the acceptance and implementation of the fundamental rights and freedoms enshrined in South Africa's Constitution. He concentrates on the Bill of Rights, crafted to safeguard not only first generation (civil and political) rights, but also second (economic, social and cultural) and third (collective or societal rights, such as the right to a clean environment) generation rights. As Govender explains, the vision behind the Bill of Rights was not only that of constraining the exercise of state power, but also an egalitarian vision requiring the state to take positive measures to promote a better life for all. This extensive protection of rights, at least in theory, has led to South Africa's Constitution being once memorably described as a 'Rolls Royce' among constitutions. The problem remains the translation of theory into practice, in a country facing massive challenges with limited resources. Many of the constitutional rights, Govender shows, have been tested at the level of the Constitutional Court as individuals have sought a better quality of life by challenging state conduct and lower-court interpretations of various statutes. Govender reviews and assesses Constitutional Court judgements relating to equality and dignity, democracy, and socio-economic rights, including the rights to health and shelter.

On the whole, Govender argues, the Constitutional Court has done well in upholding the constitutional rights protected by the Constitution, whilst at the same time not second-guessing the actions of the executive to an unacceptable degree. The judges' determinations on government policies have at times, perhaps inevitably, been the source of tension between the executive and judiciary, as in the Constitutional Court ruling on the Treatment Action Campaign's case in which the Court concluded that the policy of the state to restrict the supply of Nevirapine to the limited test or pilot sites and not to extend it to all state hospitals was a violation of section 27 (the right to access healthcare services) of the Constitution and the state was thus ordered to supply the drug to all public hospitals. He predicts, however, that in the decade ahead this tension could rise. After an era characterised by law-making, the years immediately ahead will largely be ones of implementation and it is at this stage that vested rights and interests 'are most likely to be adversely affected'. He cites dispensing doctors and pharmacists as groups which have been affected by the re-regulation of democratic South Africa. There will be others. Simultaneously, Govender foresees that there are likely to be further challenges in the years ahead, made by or on behalf of the marginalised, for speedier and more decisive delivery, and this will strain the resources of the state. In the conflicts that await, it will be the courts – and the Constitutional Court in particular – which will be called upon to determine whether the state is living up to its constitutional obligations. The litmus test of our maturing democracy will, in this view, 'be the response of the executive to unfavoured decisions. Any response which has the effect of devaluing the institution of the courts…will…subvert much of the gains made in the first decade of democracy'. Watch this space.

In contrast to Govender's generally positive assessment of the work of the Constitutional Court, which he feels 'has crafted a solid foundation upon which the future development of constitutional law and human rights law can be based', Judith February's portrait of the legislative end of South Africa's democratic framework in the same period is unflattering. 'As an institution', she argues, Parliament 'has played its role patchily, unevenly, and sometimes hesitantly', especially when it has been at loggerheads with the executive. This less than flattering view she particularly applies to the legislature's constitutionally assigned oversight role. The result, she shows, is a generally negative public perception of Parliament, citing some recent survey data to support her view.

February constructs her argument around three case studies, from which in only one instance does Parliament emerge with any credit. That was the Protection of Constitutional Democracy against Terrorism Bill, in regard to which the relevant portfolio committee and special interest groups joined together effectively to force the executive to backtrack and rewrite key clauses before it was enacted. This was a rare instance where Parliament displayed the will to face off with the executive. This did not happen in the other two cases, the National Conventional Arms Control Act and the Strategic Defence Procurement Package (or so-called 'arms deal'). Here, she argues, Parliament displayed both ineptitude and a craven lack of political independence, succumbing meekly to the crippling of the legislature's most important oversight body, the Select Committee on Public Accounts. Of course, given recent developments relating to former Deputy President Zuma and the arms deal, and calls from the opposition for the investigation to be reopened, the Select Committee on Public Accounts (and Parliament in general) has an ideal opportunity to redeem itself. However, given the almost casual response of the Portfolio Committee on Minerals and Energy to the 'Oilgate' revelations, it seems no lessons have been drawn from the whole saga.

February also looks at two other parliamentary functions designed to promote oversight and finds that both fail to deliver the goods. The one is in respect of public participation in the committee process of the legislature through lobbying and other forms of input and representation. Where it has occurred to good effect, February suggests it has been by entities favouring the 'wealthy or better-resourced special interest groups representing the worlds of big business and finance'. But the lack of input from more marginal and less-resourced non-governmental organisations is not the only problem; another relates to the committees themselves, which lack expertise and are often badly run. Frequently, too little notice is given to the public to make representations and then not enough time is given over to hearing and interrogating submissions. The other mechanism is the twice-weekly question-time sessions, where Members of Parliament (MPs) can probe and challenge the actions of government departments through probing and information-gathering questions. This too, she suggests, has been largely ineffective for a range of reasons: most importantly, MPs do not ask enough of the right questions, answers are often delayed for months or even years, and in any case, when they come, are often inadequate, all of which means that the media tends to ignore them. This tendency has been dubbed 'question dodging' and February suggests it is becoming more and more frequent.

In her chapter, Amanda Gouws assesses the work of a network of gender institutions – some linked to Parliament – collectively referred to as the

NGM. Crafted in the wake of the 1994 democratic election, the NGM carried the 'hope and expectation' that it would 'influence policy-making from a gender perspective and put women's interests on the political agenda'. Gouws concentrates on three structures within the machinery, namely, the Office of the Status of Women located within the Presidency, Parliament's Joint Monitoring Committee on the Improvement of the Quality of Life and the Status of Women, and the Commission on Gender Equality, one of the so-called 'Chapter 9 (constitutionally-required) institutions'. Gouws's argument is that despite the state having created an enabling environment for gender equality, the NGM cannot be said to fall into a category of bodies with 'high influence and high access'. Even so, it has not been devoid of achievement, for it has made a number of successful inputs in regard to pending legislation; it has facilitated access of gender groups to the legislature's committee processes; and, in general, she suggests it has contributed to a greater degree of gender consciousness in South Africa.

Nonetheless, Gouws suggests that these advances could have been greater had it not been for problems of institutional design and what she calls 'personal politics'. The overlapping of mandates between structures, the lack of co-ordination between and within structures, the lack of communication with the wider public, the inability of a strong women's movement to hold the NGM accountable, overwhelming workloads and the lack of strategic leadership have all worked to blunt the success of South Africa's post-apartheid gender machinery.

With the exception of Govender, it would seem from this introduction that each of the contributors to this section is negative – or at least somewhat disappointed – at government's post-1994 performance in the areas of land, gender, delivery and so on. While this would not be a wholly unfounded view, it would not be a fair depiction either of their thinking. Each article is set against a backdrop in which the enormity of the challenge is acknowledged – as is the fact that South Africa has made huge strides forward since it embarked upon democratic politics in 1994. The essential point each of these studies is making, however, is that much still remains to be done if the aspirations of the Constitution are to be realised.

1 Putting numbers to the scorecard: presidential targets and the state of delivery

David Hemson and Michael O'Donovan

In his 'State of the Nation' address in 2004, President Mbeki outlined the achievements of the past ten years and the challenges to be met.[1] He spelt out several dozen long-term objectives to guide his administration, on the basis of clear targets, promises of open government, and a concern for efficient public administration. This initiative won general approval (Habib 2004): here was a president determined to set out concrete objectives in the language of commitment and statecraft.

Mbeki's address offers an insightful yardstick for gauging how much has changed since 1994. But it also raises questions of a review along a range of policy prescriptions that have become part of the broad objectives of South African government and society over the past decade. This chapter assesses shifts in policy instruments ranging from the classical declarations of the Freedom Charter, to the broad programmatic Reconstruction and Development Programme (RDP), to White Papers and sectoral policies readily crystallised in statutes and to current presidential pronouncements and strategies. These commitments will be reviewed against shifts in priorities: the changing, raising, lowering or even dropping of targets and benchmarks over time, and problems of verifying claims and commitments will be examined. Finally, a broad appraisal will be made of the achievements of delivery over the past ten years.

New objectives, new promises

This review comes at a time when the African National Congress (ANC) is planning celebrations of the fiftieth anniversary of the Freedom Charter and has stated that, 'We must base our vision, programmes and actions on that historic manifesto of the people of South Africa, the Freedom Charter' (ANC 2005). The Freedom Charter set out in broad brushstrokes the hopes of the oppressed and impoverished: 'The people shall share in the country's wealth; There shall be work and security; The doors of learning and culture shall be opened; There shall be houses, security and comfort!' Within these bold statements, the objectives for the ANC were defined as restoring the national wealth of the country to the people, transferring ownership of key sectors to the people 'as a whole', recognising the right to work and 'full unemployment benefits', free education for all children, decent housing for all, an end to hunger, a preventive health scheme and free medical care and hospitalisation, and the abolition of slums (ANC 1955).

Aspects of the visionary declarations of the Freedom Charter were, with significant modifications, carried over into the celebrated RDP, which put forward definite targets and set standards by which these could be measured. That programme of ten years ago has been adjusted over time and modified by sectoral White Papers and budgetary shifts. Many of its champions have moved to the business sector and its responsibilities to line departments. This organisational reshuffle was associated with a shift in economic policy from a relatively expansionist policy aiming at redistribution to the successor Growth, Employment and Redistribution strategy (GEAR), which prioritised financial stability. GEAR has been criticised for producing negative consequences for poor people and for compromising the outcome of social programmes, particularly in relation to sustained access to basic services (Habib 2004: 2). Although some of the conservatism of budgetary policy has now ebbed, in the crucial years of delivery there were impacts on the budgets for key social objectives. Undoubtedly, also, the emphasis on efficiency and effectiveness is derived from the struggle to do more with the limited resources available.

This review will focus on a dozen or so of the 80-odd objectives cited in the address which are directly related to the delivery of services to the poor. These read, in the direct language of the address (Mbeki 2004), as follows:

Household services
1. 'To intensify the housing programme…in the next three years we will spend R14.2 billion to help our people to have access to basic shelter.'
2. 'Within the next five years all households will have access to clean running water.'

3. 'During the current year more than 300 000 households will be provided with basic sanitation.'
4. 'Within the next eight years ensure that each household has access to electricity.'

Social security
5. 'Ensure social grants reach all 7.7 million beneficiaries…within two years add about 3.2 million children who will be eligible for child-support grant.'

Health
6. 'Reduce malaria cases by ten per cent each year.'
7. 'Implementation of our Comprehensive Plan on HIV and AIDS: 113 health facilities will be fully operational by March 2005 and 53 000 people will be on treatment at that time.'

Education
8. 'By the end of this financial year we shall ensure that there is no learner or student learning under a tree, mud school or any dangerous conditions that expose learners or teachers to the elements.'
9. 'By the end of the current financial year we expect all schools to have access to clean water and sanitation.'

Security
10. 'By 2006 there will be 152 000 officers on active duty in the South African Police Services (SAPS).'
11. 'In the current year establish at least two community courts in each province.'
12. 'In the next three months we will set up special joint teams to target and focus on serious crime with an immediate objective of apprehending the top 200 criminals in the country.'

This review will set out a scorecard for these specific objectives and explore how these commitments are being monitored. Is there effective parliamentary and public oversight, with readily available reliable statistics, which can put these goals to the test?

Presidential rule and ministerial delivery

The spelling out of goals with definite targets has been welcomed as a form of more open government with a heightened emphasis on delivery. At one level the turn to explicit objectives reflects on executive ability as the Presidency itself takes on the responsibility for setting targets and ensuring they are carried out. The emphasis in management is shifting from ministerial government to the Presidency itself, particularly as local government increasingly has the responsibility of ensuring the constitutional guarantees (in housing, water and energy) to its citizens.

Presidentialism, the location of power within the executive, is being fleshed out in both political direction and a growing staff, and combined with the drive for business efficiency in government.[2] Although there are notions of equity in policy (notably concerning poverty alleviation), the focus is on effectiveness, ensuring the task is done, and efficiency, working to ensure resources are not wasted. In many ways the turn in objectives takes the form of the model of new public administration first presented by Osborne and Gaebler (1983) and extolled as a new way of 'reinventing government' to get efficiency and effectiveness around the notion of value for public money in a period of neoliberalism.

Changed administrative mechanisms are regarded internationally as providing the most striking trends in government over the past period. They are made up of the following elements:
- A focus on management, performance appraisal and efficiency rather than policy;
- The disaggregation of public bureaucracies into agencies which deal with each other on a user pay basis;
- Cost cutting;
- A style of management which emphasises, *inter alia*, output targets, limited term contracts, monetary incentives and freedom to manage (Hood, quoted in Chandler 1996).

It is also widely regarded as involving a transition from a 'bureaucratic model' to public administration organised around the 'goal-oriented fulfilment of public tasks' (Bauer 2004). Increasingly, strategies provide for further advancement of public mandates, although these may be broken up through deregulation and rebuilt around new funding structures. All of this involves the application of management principles to public institutions to allow forms of regulation and control.

Most importantly for this discussion are the strategies and tools which provide for increased decentralisation. This is achieved not by replicating bureaucracies at different levels but through increasing responsibility of executives at all levels by focusing on results or *outputs* and the necessary effects or *outcomes*, controlled through performance reports, cost accounting, competition, and finally through impact analysis or *evaluation* (Bauer 2004). Overall there is not a loss of control by national government as goals are set from the centre, new controlling strategies are put in place to control from a distance, and there is continuous benchmarking. The emphasis is on improving services to 'customers' rather than 'citizens' with the greatest public efficiency for the least cost.

The change in management appears to offer an authoritative control over the affairs of public servants; checking on the administration, providing overall direction, and exercising overall supervision. The commitments of the 'State of the Nation' speech place the President in the role of giving direction, guidance and leadership on all the issues of the time. This style is reinforced by the *izimbizo* held shortly before the 2004 election in which ordinary people voiced their frustration with water, housing and other basic services. This seemed to be a level of democracy in action, with citizens able to place their demands directly to government and getting some immediate response. In the election campaign, delivery was presented as the key to political advance and the targets announced in the 2004 'State of the Nation' speech were a way of driving ministers to meet public expectations.

What is also emerging is a new form of presidential direction. The government's plan of action is now to be co-ordinated by the Cabinet office, which is to triple its income from R6.9 million in 2004/05 to R21.8 million in 2005/06, while the Presidency itself is being allocated R240 million, an increase of R100 million (some 70 per cent) on the previous year (*Mail & Guardian* 25.02–03.03.05). In funding and in personnel the Presidency is gaining ascendancy within the state, and filling the Union Building, which once housed the entire national government. There is undoubtedly increased capacity in the presidential purview of ministerial and local government policies, implementation and impact and this is often welcomed.

The Presidency has been characterised also by adaptation of public management, in particular the setting of public targets and the channelling of funds through new agencies and mechanisms. The projection of targets of delivery has a purpose of disciplining ministers to keep their eyes on the overall political aspects of delivery and ensuring that government is seen to have its focus on social goals. The emphasis is on managing resources efficiently to ensure that there is an easing of the social burden of the poor while clearing the way for capital accumulation.

Working on this basis, the President finds it possible to reflect on weaknesses in government. In the 'State of the Nation' address of 2005, the President identified the following problem areas in delivery:
- Weaknesses in the governance system which mean that plans to build school infrastructure 'are unfolding at a much slower pace than envisaged';
- The misapplication of the policies of free basic electricity which 'are accruing mainly to those who are relatively well-off';
- Slow transfers of the Municipal Infrastructure Grant to municipalities reflecting a 'lack of all-round capacity particularly in technical areas with regard to water, sanitation and public works projects'. (Mbeki 2005)

There are three points to be made in relation to presidential oversight. The first is that the turn towards public statement of goals and objectives of government is in line with the precepts of new public management and a formally rational model of government. The second is that the key aspects of assessment, 'customer' empowerment and targets are being ordered carefully to achieve political effect. Finally, the trend in policy towards decentralisation is also, and contradictorily, reinforcing the power of the political centre.

Managing backlogs and information

There are a number of problems in making an objective assessment of progress on goals, two of which warrant particular attention here. The first is the basis on which backlogs are measured and the second is the availability and reliability of data to estimate progress to achieving targets and ending backlogs.

The problem with all estimates of backlogs in any service, is that politicians and planners often operate with a view of a static population. At the inception of the community water programme of the Department of Water Affairs and Forestry (DWAF) in 1994, for instance, it was mentioned that there were 12 million people without water and 21 million without sanitation (DWAF 2003). The celebration of delivery of water to ten million people after ten years creates the impression that government is rapidly ending the backlog. Departmentally approved statistics, however, show that the problem remains. A recent review of the entire water sector concluded that five million people had no access to safe water and a further 6.5 million did not have access to 'defined basic service levels' and that 18.1 million did not have adequate sanitation (DWAF 2003: iii). In other words, about 11.5 million people still lacked a basic access service to safe water in 2003. This is just short of the figure in 1994; the *proportion* of total population is, of course, much smaller.

These figures are not symptoms of statistical tricks or oddities; and there is little perception generally of the effects that changes in population have on backlogs. Since services are generally to *households* rather than individuals or 'population', it is at this level that the growth in demand for services is faced. While population growth has been increasing at a rate of approximately 2.25 per cent per annum (although it is now reported to be easing), the rate of increase in households has been increasing at a level of five per cent. Significantly, the rapid increase in households is concentrated among the majority of poor most dependent on public services: of the increase in households from 1996–2001, 93 per cent were among African people. This is associated with sharp decline in the average size of families among Africans over the same period from 4.8 to 3.9.[3] These population shifts, including migration into growth areas such as Gauteng, warp a linear conception of delivery, one which starts with a conception of a definite population, registers delivery and, over a few years, measures the reduced backlog. With low levels of delivery, the backlogs may be growing even as delivery increases. Such are the dimensions of the problem that backlogs among the dispossessed tend to grow faster than delivery in many sectors. Unfortunately the assessment of the targets and benchmarks set out by government often does not take these considerations into account.

A rational model of public administration is also undermined by the growing tendency for government to evince an attitude of scepticism, doubt, or rejection of statistical trends which do not reflect progress in the past decade. Defensive attitudes and scepticism are particularly marked, not only in relation to HIV/AIDS but also to other aspects of government policy and evaluation. Statistics South Africa (Stats SA) is formally independent, yet reports to the Minister of Finance. Nonetheless, the government tends to disregard or ridicule statistical conclusions from this body which show different trends from those anticipated by public policy. There are trends which government holds as inherently invalid or impossible, for instance, that poor black people are poorer (in terms of income poverty) than they were in 1994 or that unemployment has increased dramatically over the past ten years. Hence, in a recent interview, Minister of Finance Trevor Manuel stated that there would be a 'revolution' if the unemployment rate was 40 per cent, and thus the figure could not be true (*Business Report* 28.02.05). This rejection of unemployment statistics has been repeated by the President who wrote recently that millions walking the streets in search of work are not visible (*Sunday Times* 22.05.05). In short, the current mood in government is to strongly criticise studies which show growing or continued impoverishment or backlogs, even if these make reasoned use of official statistics. Hence, the United Nations Development Programme (UNDP) national *Human Development Report* (2004), which relied on such a method, was construed as out of sympathy with the attempt to achieve transformation in South Africa, and as making 'little acknowledgement of progress' (GCIS 2004).

The doubts about statistics expressed by ministers make it difficult to assess social progress against basic indicators. But they can also have something of a positive or democratic side if they lead to reasoned discussion. It is therefore encouraging that the scepticism about statistics is increasingly also expressed by professionals and local government in relation to official delivery figures. These doubts appear to be derived from different perspectives. Nationally there is pressure to show achievements, but often locally, municipal officials are not unhappy to disclose a poor record of delivery as, ironically, a larger backlog would attract increased funding.[4] Even senior officials express reservations (normally privately) about the internal statistical records of departments and state that authoritative statistics require independent surveys. Scepticism arises even with reports from authoritative scientific bodies in relation to such issues as the quality of water discharge as they are seen to work on a contractual basis with government bodies and do not release their studies for public scrutiny. There is greater public concern, too, that statistics should be 'believable' and authoritative in the sense of being independently verified. These points are made by civil society from one perspective, insisting statistics should be publicly available, and also by defensive civil servants from another.

Assessing progress through the RDP

When compared to the ambitious aspirations of the RDP, South Africa's second decade is marked by a far more modest set of objectives and by the lowering of the improved standards which were to be applied.[5] Indeed, the goals set out to be achieved and exceeded in the past decade in areas such as housing, land, water, and sanitation are repeated to be achieved in the present. In 1994 the RDP programme envisaged, *inter alia*, universal access to water and sanitation facilities as well as the elimination of hunger and malnutrition, all to be achieved on the basis of people's participation in development and within the coming decade – 1994 to 2004.

Table 1.1 offers a brief synopsis of the major objectives of the RDP programme and the backlog in 2002.

Table 1.1 *Scorecard on the RDP*

Sector	Short-term RDP objective	Medium-term RDP objective	Situation in 2002
Housing		At least one million houses within five years (1994–99)	Long-term RDP objective: Shelter for all by 2003. The one-millionth house was delivered in 2003. The number of households living in shacks doubled between 1994 and 2002 to reach 1.8 million.
Water	20–30 litres per person per day within 200m of residence	50–60 litres per person per day within 200m	Households with access to piped water within 200m increased by 2m after 1994. Prevalence of the service at this level, however, remained unchanged at 73% in 2001. In that year approx. 2.9 million households were still unserviced.*

Sector	Short-term RDP objective	Medium-term RDP objective	Situation in 2002
Telecommunication	Universal access to 'affordable' telecommunications for schools and clinics within two years	Provide universal affordable access for all as rapidly as possible	Between 1994 and 2002 the prevalence of fixed line telephone facilities dropped from 31% to 24%. In 2002, 9 million households were unserviced.**
Sanitation facilities	Adequate facilities should be provided to at least 75% of rural households	Provide adequate sanitation facilities to all within five years (1994–99)	Between 1994 and 2002 an additional 1.3 million households obtained ventilated improved privy toilet facilities or better. However, this was insufficient to change coverage at the basic level which has declined from 67% to 62%. In 2002, 4.6 million households were unserved with basic sanitation.
Refuse removal	All homes serviced		Between 1994 and 2002 the rate of refuse removal improved by 2% to reach 55% of households. In 2002, 5.2 million households were still not serviced.
Electricity		By 2000, 2.5 million homes connected; Universal access for schools and clinics	Over 4 million households electrified by 2000. In 2002, 2.8 million households were still unserviced.
Nutrition	Eliminate malnutrition and fear of hunger within three years		In 2002, 31% percent of households with children reported being unable to feed them at some stage in the last year. In 1994 the figure was 41%.

Source: Estimates of backlogs are own calculations derived from Stats SA's LFS 2002[6]

Notes:
* The figure for water services establishes delivery as piped water to the dwelling, yard, or within 200m of a communal tap and uses the 1994 October Household Survey (OHS) as the benchmark compared to a similar question in the Labour Force Survey (LFS) of March 2001 (the most recent source), which provides a calculation of the 200m standard in a question which asks whether households can access piped water within three minutes.
** During this period there was a dramatic uptake in the use of cellular phones. However, as the objective was described in terms of 'affordable' services this component has not been factored in. In addition, landline connections provide the basic infrastructure for easing the digital gap between urban and rural areas.

A scan of Table 1.1 shows that while progress was generally made on all fronts (with the notable and important exception of telecommunications), and in one instance there was advance greater than the promise (electricity), few of the *objectives* were met. A number of targets were not met in the time period and others were quietly dropped. The one million houses which were to be achieved in five years eventually took just under ten years to build, the backlog in water and sanitation was far from met and the increase to 50 litres per person per day in 1999 was not mentioned, while refuse removal only increased marginally. On the other hand, there has been a significant decline in the number of householders reporting that they were unable to feed their children.

Despite progress, a thorough review of the targeting, planning, and funding of delivery was not made after the RDP office was closed. Nor was there an open review and assessment by Parliament of the precise targets, budgetary allocations, and institutional capacity, which would have shown the basis on which progress was achieved or delivery held up. The assignment of the RDP's objectives to line departments prior to their apportionment to local government appears to have left an assessment of its crucial social objectives to internal mechanisms rather than to an open debate involving all levels of government and civil society. Instead, a quiet conclusion seems to have been drawn that targets should be modest, that open review was not suitable, and that specific mechanisms (such as the RDP office) were not necessary. Instead of a thorough appraisal, broad statements of progress were made rather than a careful appraisal in cost-benefit analysis, parliamentary examination, or democratic review at the local level.

Undoubtedly, however, lessons were also drawn within government about the intractability of interdepartmental co-ordination, and one of the innovations of this period was the grouping of government departments into economic, social, governance, security and international 'clusters' in order to achieve better integration of delivery.

Does the RDP live on?

The objectives set out in the 'State of the Nation' speech in 2004 in a sense replaced the established RDP social objectives with a series of commitments which go well beyond service delivery to the poor to involve, among other issues, international relations, economic policy and security issues. This marks, in part, the inevitable expansion of government objectives with South Africa's advent as a power within the continent, but also indicates the displacement of old priorities by the new. Social delivery is marked by an attitude which could be summarised as follows: 'The RDP is dead, long live the RDP!' The slogan could be interpreted as follows: the RDP lives on in popular imagination, and its promises cannot be jettisoned and, indeed, should have been achieved with its expiration after a decade. However, its goals are now part of a much larger schema.

Yet to what extent, in practice, have the various delivery pledges made in the 'State of the Nation' addresses carried forward the original objectives of the RDP? Do these objectives live on (though without the original timelines) and/or are they being re-interpreted and repackaged? An answer to these questions is offered by the review of the six most substantive sectors (housing, water and sanitation, electricity, social security, education, and security).

Housing

Objective 1: Intensification of the housing programme
One of the most important considerations in service delivery is that basic services like potable water, refuse removal and electricity are provided to households. They are best analysed at that level but, unfortunately, many assessments are made in terms of population covered.

Currently the South African population is increasing at less than 2.5 per cent each year.[7] However, recent censuses and large-scale household surveys reveal that the total number of households in the country is increasing at approximately twice this rate.[8] In particular the number of African households increased by 32 per cent from 6 533 977 to 8 625 030 over the period, an increase of over two million households.

As households 'unbundle' into smaller (more nuclear?) units they create demand for services and housing over and above that created by population growth and immigration. The extent of household unbundling has therefore somewhat unexpectedly exacerbated service demands (particularly for housing subsidies) placed on the state.

Household services are directly influenced by housing developments (which largely reflect the situation of households) and thus by the state's housing subsidy scheme. Between 1994 and 2003 approximately one million houses were completed under the subsidy scheme and this had a strong bearing on service levels in general.⁹ These 'RDP' houses are typically serviced with on-site running water, sanitation and sewerage services as well as electricity. The housing subsidy scheme thus adds a substantial fillip to the prevalence of these ancillary services which are usually built in as construction proceeds. Of course, the level of these ancillary services is further supplemented by direct provision to existing (unserviced) housing stock.

The earliest estimates of housing and household services backlogs were given by Stats SA's 1994 October Household Survey (OHS). Since earlier censuses had systematically excluded the four formally independent homelands (Transkei, Bophuthatswana, Venda and Ciskei), this survey offered the first reliable estimate of service backlogs for the country as a whole. The general trends portrayed by the 1994 OHS were subsequently confirmed by the 1996 census. By comparing changes in housing profiles between 1996 and the most recent census of 2001, it is possible to see the impact of the new regime's tenure on service provision.

A comparison of these two censuses shows an increase in the number of people living in all major housing types. By 2001 the number of households living in shacks had increased to 26 per cent more than the 1996 figure. The number of households living in formal dwellings had increased more dramatically to 7.7 million, which is 32 per cent more than the 1996 figure. By contrast there was only a marginal increase in the number of households living in traditional dwellings.

Housing backlogs – the number of households located in 'informal' or similarly inadequate housing and also those households which are living in single rooms who qualify for a housing subsidy – are thus important in understanding how and where service backlogs are being rolled back. The backlogs strongly express the impact of the growth in the number of households.

The 'unbundling' of households greatly exacerbated the housing challenge facing the state. For example, the initial RDP target of one million houses would have been sufficient to eliminate the shacks that were then in place. However, the growth in households has been such that, despite state initiatives, the total number of households living in shacks continued to increase after 1996. Perversely, as the *rate* of delivery was half of that anticipated (the RDP set out a target of one million over five years, a target which was slightly exceeded only after ten years), the challenge facing the state in housing all citizens is now larger than it was in 1994.

In his 'State of the Nation' address in 2004, the President committed the government to spending R14.2 billion over the next three years to 'help our people to have access to basic shelter'. The promise has been supplemented by an additional R3.2 billion to make a new commitment of R17.4 billion (Social Sector Cluster, June 2005).

Table 1.2 *Anticipated housing delivery and backlog*

	Actual		Projected	
	1996	2001	2004	2008
House, flat, semi-detached, etc.	5 834 819	7 680 421	9 059 874	11 289 299
Traditional dwelling	1 644 386	1 654 787	1 661 659	1 670 322
Slum or other	1 580 364	1 870 498	2 066 911	2 363 764
Total households	9 059 569	11 205 706	12 788 444	15 323 384

Source: Census of 1996 and 2001 with figures for 2004 and 2008 based on a forward extrapolation on the basis of inter-censual trends

From Table 1.2 the 1996 and 2001 census housing data are brought into three basic sectors: formal housing, traditional dwellings, and slum dwellings. However, it must be borne in mind that government subsidies are not the sole source of housing. Between 1994 and 2003 it appears that less than half of all new housing stock could, to some extent, be attributed to the subsidy scheme and the remaining formal housing units were furnished by commercial developers or by households themselves.

From the changes between the censuses, the anticipated future figures are then extrapolated forward on the basis of an exponential trendline. On this basis it is anticipated that formal housing will increase to 11.3 million units, the number of traditional dwellings will remain stagnant, and slum housing will increase from 1.8 million in 2001 to 2.4 million in 2008.

At current subsidy levels the R17.4 billion would result in a total of 621 400 subsidies and, thus, anticipated additional houses. On this basis the state seemingly intends to provide an average of 207 142 dwellings each year for the next three years. This is well below what is required to eliminate the current backlog, which was estimated to include 2.1 million households in 2004. From the figures presented, the backlog could be in the order of 1.8 million in 2008/09 (that is, an anticipated 2.4 million in slums less 621 400 houses delivered). The forward extrapolation does take into account that there has been delivery which has diminished slum dwellings and that this will continue into the future. Nonetheless, if the recent trends are maintained, the numbers living in slums – a crucial target for elimination set by the Minister of Housing in a 'war on shacks'[10] – will not be reduced although the *proportion* of the population living in slums will.

Moreover, if the number of households continues to increase at the current rate (and there are indications that population growth is abating) then the increase in the number of households will rise to 630 000 each year. In terms of income criteria, almost 80 per cent of all households qualify for a housing subsidy,[11] although many are already housed. This indicates that housing allocations are woefully insufficient to meet the projected demand, and at current expenditure levels, less than a third of 'new' households will be catered for.

Government is anticipating that through negotiations, the financial sector will become committed to providing R42 billion for low-cost housing for households with incomes between R1 500 – R7 000 (Sisulu 2005). The history of housing loans to poor communities, which was full with promise in the early post-liberation period, has, however, become marked with conflict and it is uncertain whether the very large sums will be released for construction of new houses.

Although housing strategy is publicly expressed less in terms of the elimination of inadequate housing than in the upgrading of all informal settlements, it does appear that without massive growth in employment opportunities or a marked increase in state subsidies, shacks will continue to be a feature of the South African landscape for some time.

Water for all

Objective 2: Within the next five years all households will have access to clean running water
Clean drinking water for all has been a key objective of the RDP and remains so today. As mentioned earlier, despite considerable effort the backlog has

been declining unevenly over the past decade and there are fresh challenges in this sector as a number of studies have shown that there are difficulties in sustaining delivery in remote poor communities.[12] The transfer of water projects to local authorities is advancing but it is very far from being complete. When this is achieved there should be more dedicated funding for operations and maintenance.

Figure 1.1 *The line of delivery in basic water*

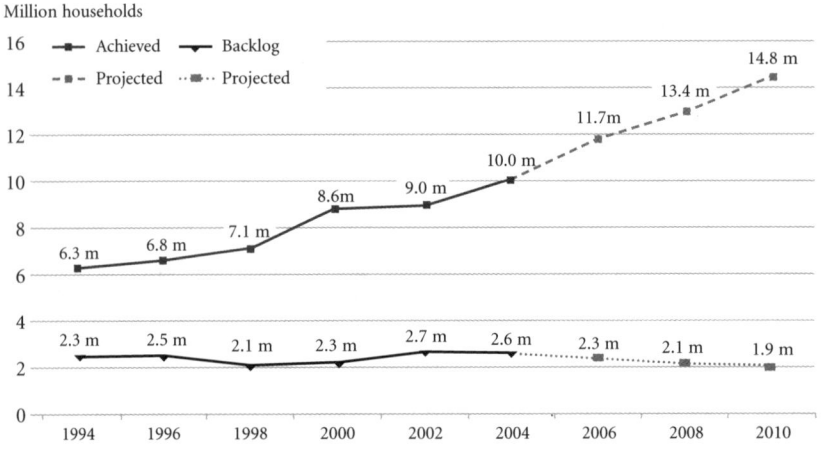

Source: Stats SA Surveys 1995 to 2003 with forward extrapolation beyond 2003 based on trend with the number of households modelled on 1996 and 2001 Census data

Figure 1.1 shows the statistics of delivery at the level of basic service (piped water within 200 metres of the household) or better. The largest part of delivery is connection to the dwelling or yard, the latter having shown the greatest expansion over the entire period and communal taps (though preferred in policy) considerably less. Somewhat surprisingly, given the high level of publicity given to water delivery, forward projections show that the backlog in water services is persistent, tending to decline slowly as a proportion of all households while delivery rises.[13] The rising line of delivery largely reflects additional houses built in urban areas as well as a smaller proportion in rural areas.

The backlog has increased slightly from 2.4 million to 2.7 million between 1994 and 2002, a marginal trend in a persistent backlog which is acknowledged in DWAF's 2003 *Strategic framework*. The difficulty has been that the increasing number of households, rising on annually from 388 606 in 1997 to a projected 616 812 in 2008, is tending to erode progress in reducing the backlog even as delivery is accelerated. On the basis of the extrapolation of trends forward, there is a slow decline in the numbers of the backlog.[14] However, unless there is increased spending and an improved delivery system, it appears that the target of water for all by 2008 will not be met, as on the current basis, there will be a projected 2.1 million households unserved.

This seems a surprising conclusion as water delivery is generally regarded as an exemplary sector. The apparent contradiction is explained by comparison to electricity: compared to the 600 000 to 700 000 household connections to the electricity grid a year, the highest claimed level of delivery in DWAF records is 400 000 households (1.5 million people) gaining access to clean water in a year.

In these conditions, with a relatively static proportion of the Budget going to water services (some 0.7 per cent), not only will the target of water for all by 2008 not be reached but considerable effort and considerable additional resources will be needed to reduce the numbers in the backlog.

Toilets for all

Objective 3: During the current year more than 300 000 households will be provided with basic sanitation

It is possibly significant that the promise of sanitation for all by 2010, along with commitments to bring sanitation to schools and clinics, to implement health and hygiene education and to eliminate bucket toilets by 2006, contained in the *Strategic framework* on the water sector, are not mentioned in the 2004 'State of the Nation' address. Instead of precise targets there is a commitment to step up delivery of basic sanitation to 300 000, a figure which implies a concentration on ventilated improved privies (VIPs), although it could also include other toilets. On the basis of projections of delivery of VIPs, it is likely that the 300 000 toilets will be achieved in 2006, although current information on delivery is unfortunately not available. The question, however, is what acceleration of sanitation delivery will happen in rural communities and slums?

Figure 1.2 *The sanitation backlog, 1996–2016*

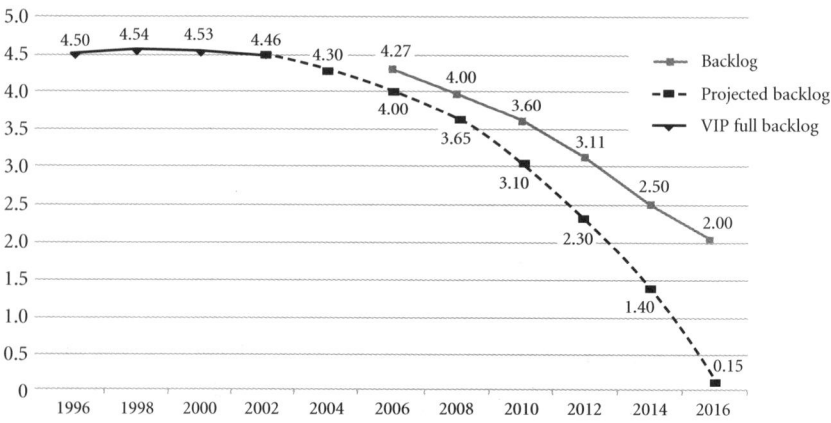

Source: Data based on Stats SA Survey 1998–2003 and extrapolated forward with number of households modelled on 1996 and 2001 Census data

Figure 1.2 shows changes within the backlog in sanitation at the VIP level or better. The curve represents the statistics derived from official surveys up to 2003 and thereafter on projections based on a model of household growth and level of delivery. In 2004 there were 4.5 million households without basic sanitation and, despite an acceleration of delivery, there has not been a significant decline in the backlog as yet. The decline in the forward projection of the backlog represents the results of recent accelerated delivery rather than accomplished fact.

On the current basis of expenditure, by 2010 – the target date to provide sanitation for all – there will still be some 3.7 million households without basic sanitation. From Figure 1.2 it appears that the commitment to provide sanitation for all by 2010 is, even on these most generous estimates, illusory. The second curve (VIP full backlog) indicates the additional task which arises from the fact that VIPs fill over five to eight years and need either to be replenished or emptied, and represents a sum of the backlog plus the additional task of either emptying pits or replacing them.[15] In rural conditions it is highly unlikely that pits can be emptied because of additional costs and accessibility. These full VIPs then become an additional burden on further delivery and the forward curve advances well beyond 2015.

Household electrification

Objective 4: Ensure that each household has access to electricity within the next eight years

Despite the considerable growth in the number of households requiring services, notable progress has nevertheless been made in several arenas. One particularly successful field has been the provision of electricity. In 1994 only 55 per cent of all households had access to mains electricity; by 2003 this had increased to 78 per cent.[16] The most marked improvements in the provision of electricity are evident in informal and traditional dwellings. In both these cases, more than a third of all dwellings were electrified after 1994. The improvement in electrification among formal households is less marked, but nevertheless impressive. By 2003 another 19 per cent of formal dwellings were electrified despite the rapid rise in the number of such dwellings.

Table 1.3 *Percentage of households with access to public electricity supply*

	1994	2003	Improvement
Formal dwellings	69	88	19
Traditional dwellings	6	41	35
Informal dwellings	20	54	34
Overall prevalence	55	78	23

Sources: Stats SA 1994, OHS: Lighting, access to electricity; 2003b

To achieve this improvement, an average of 562 000 households were electrified each year between 1994 and 2003. Table 1.4 compares electrification rates for two distinct periods after 1994. It shows that the tempo at which households were electrified increased from approximately 218 000 per annum (in the period 1994 to 1996) to 664 000 per annum (in the period 1997 to 2003). Should the current pace of electrification be maintained, some 3.3 million households could be electrified in the five years to which Mbeki refers.

Table 1.4 *Household electrification*

	1994	1996	2003
Total households	8 800 000	9 050 572	12 546 104
Total households electrified	4 797 720	5 233 372	9 811 308
Backlog	4 002 280	3 817 200	2 630 376
Prevalence of electricity	55%	57%	78%
Annual increment over preceding period		218 000	664 000

Sources: Stats SA 1994, OHS: Lighting, access to electricity; Census 1996, GHS 2003
Note: There is, unfortunately a considerable discrepancy between Stats SA figures and those of the National Electricity Regulator.

Unfortunately, significant as this figure is, it may be insufficient to offset the current backlog of 2.9 million households and the annual growth of the additional households each year. For the promise of electricity to all by 2012 to be met an extraordinary investment in electrification is called for precisely as Eskom, the main agent for the past success, is restructured.

Social security

Objective 5: Ensure social grants reach all 7.7 million beneficiaries…within two years add about 3.2 million children who will be eligible for child support grant
One of the most successful redistributive measures taken by the state has been the expansion of state grants and, in particular, the increased use of the child support grant (CSG). Not only has the value of grants increased in recent years, but eligibility for disability, child support and other grants has also widened. CSGs in particular have been made more accessible as the eligibility criteria widened. Between 2000 and 2004 there was a more than ten-fold increase in the total number of people who received this modest grant (R170 per month per child).

The main reason for the dramatic expansion in the uptake of CSGs has been a widening of the age of eligibility and better means of access. In early 2003, to qualify for the benefit the intended beneficiary had to be under nine years of age, the household had to meet a means criterion and satisfy the documentation requirements. By August 2003, the age criterion had widened to include children aged nine and ten. The age criterion will now be expanded until all children (that meet the income and documentation criteria) under the age of 14 will qualify for the benefit.

Because the age criterion is expanding more rapidly than the rate at which children age, no children are currently being removed as beneficiaries because of their age. However, theoretically, children may be removed as a result of their no longer meeting the means test. In 2004 the Children's Institute reported that only 0.57 per cent of applications for the CSG were rejected on the basis of the household's income (Leatt 2004), indicating that this is hardly ever used as a reason for refusing or lapsing a grant.[17]

Although the value of the grant has kept up with inflation, the means criterion has remained static in nominal terms. Inflation has thus expanded the eligibility criteria as it reduces the real value set by the means test. This widens the eligibility criteria in a way similar to tax 'bracket creep', which rises as incomes rise over time. The expansion in the number of beneficiaries is thus derived from:
- Improved documentation/registration of babies and their caregivers;
- Expansion of the age eligibility criterion; and
- Lower real value set by the means test.

However, a reduction in the number of beneficiaries is indicated by the age profile. There are typically fewer 0–4 year olds than there are 5–9 year olds. There are also typically fewer 5–9 year olds than 10–14 year olds (Stats SA 2003: 28). The reduction in the size of the relevant age cohort will inevitably be offset by the expansion brought about by the income 'bracket creep'. Precisely how the relevant dynamics interact is unknown as they depend on demographic trends and on economic performance. However, if the most recent trends are maintained the objective set by the President is likely to be met.

As this number of social grant beneficiaries has objectively already been attained, Mbeki was, in effect, giving a confirmation that service levels would not be undermined. Of particular importance has been the expansion of the uptake in CSGs. The number of beneficiaries of social grants is set to increase as eligibility criteria are widened and the target is likely to be achieved.

Education

Objective 6: No learning under a tree or in a mud school
In a briefing it was reported that in 2003 there were 494 cases of schools without any classrooms, which is defined as a school 'under trees'.[18] According to the Department of Education the number of these schools in September 2004 was 552. In April 2005 the Department established a task team to find ways of speeding up the provision of classrooms. In February 2005 a comprehensive audit was carried out which found there were 179 such schools concentrated mostly in KwaZulu-Natal and Limpopo. The evidence is of a sudden decline of 373 schools 'under trees' between 2004/05. The Minister of Education, Naledi Pandor, reported that, by June 2005, the task team was to report 'concrete plans to end the practice of teaching children outdoors'.[19]

The incidence of 'teaching under trees' is probably less a reflection of the absence of classrooms than it is of the quality of the buildings (poor ventilation) and of overcrowding, both of which lead teachers to teach outside. In a number of rural schools, there is great overcrowding; in a recent visit to a primary school near Bizana it was found there were 175 learners in Grade 1 in a single damp classroom built by parents and not less than 65 learners in each of the other classrooms.[20] The school was without sanitation as toilet structures had been blown down in a tornado and there was no water supplied. No plans had been made to redress the problems.

According to the Minister, open exposure and overcrowding and a lack of basic facilities would cost R50 billion to solve. It appears that there is some progress, and provincial educational departments are required to report on school infrastructure on a monthly basis.[21]

Objective 7: By the end of the current financial year we expect all schools to have access to clean water and sanitation
Schools should be the centres of health and hygiene education to improve the health, understanding and living standards of the rising generation. Teachers, officials, and public-health engineers should all be united to educate and provide services to schools, particularly in rural areas to counter the high levels of water-related diseases among children.

Schools, particularly in rural communities, are characterised by *inadequate* water and sanitation, but unfortunately it has not been possible to access the latest data at this level. There are, however, statistics relating to access. The figures of schools without *any* water supply alone are daunting: of a total of 27 458 schools, in July 2002 there were 7 817 entirely without water and this was reduced to 3 860 by June 2005. Of those without sanitation there were 3 420 in April 2004 and this was reduced to 3 220 in June 2005. Progress, it appears, is made most readily in access to water as, over the three years, 3 957 gained water while only 200 received sanitation.[22] At this rate it appears unlikely that the remaining 4 000 or so schools could receive both water and sanitation in a year. According to the updated Social Cluster report, 52 schools are in the planning phase to be provided with water and sanitation by March 2006,[23] the date all schools are to be upgraded.

The Minister has expressed concern that all provinces should provide statistics and in a media briefing on 28 May 2004, she reported that the matter 'will be attended to as a matter of urgency', and that some R200 million is required to eliminate the problem of sanitation in schools alone. An interdepartmental task team has been established and funding is being sought from donors as well as from the Treasury. Significantly, the President has identified delays in school infrastructure development as a problem (Mbeki 2005). It appears that this target will not be met by April 2006.

Health

Objective 8: Reduce malaria cases by ten per cent each year
In 1996 the government, persuaded by environmental interests, stopped using DDT to control malaria-carrying mosquitoes. This move was followed by a dramatic escalation in the number of malaria cases (and deaths). In the face of an impending health crisis, the moratorium was scrapped and the use of DDT was again adopted, although not in general application. The Medical Research Council has developed Geographic Information System monitoring of malaria cases, followed by a strategy of deploying teams with DDT to targeted homesteads and villages. The impact of the new policy on the number of malaria cases was dramatic. Between 2000 and 2001 the number of malaria cases reported dropped by 59 per cent. Between 2001 and 2002 it dropped by another 41 per cent.

Table 1.5 *Incidence of malaria reported*

Year	No. of cases reported	Difference previous year	Percentage change over previous year
2000	64 622		
2001	26 506	38 116	59
2002	15 619	10 887	41
2003	13 459	2 160	14
2004	13 399	60	0

Source: Department of Health http://www.doh.gov.za/issues/malaria/statistics.html, accessed 16.08.05

In this context, the promise of a sustained reduction in the number of cases of ten per cent each year appears feasible. In 2002–03, the number of cases reported dropped by 'only' 14 per cent and in the period 2003–04 it dropped negligibly. The downward trend is slowing and it is uncertain that the annual ten per cent can be re-established after 2004, although successful management held the numbers downward in the first half of 2005. Unfortunately these positive developments are threatened by the onset of global warming which is anticipated to increase the spread of malaria southwards.

Objective 9: Implementation of our Comprehensive Plan on HIV and AIDS. 113 health facilities will be fully operational by March 2002 and 53 000 people will be on treatment at that time

Despite the relative modesty of these objectives, there are reasons to doubt whether they had been attained before the end of the 2004/05 financial year. At the end of 2004, despite 129 state health facilities providing therapy, only half the targeted number of people living with HIV/AIDS were receiving anti-retroviral treatment (ART).[24] It is not clear how many of the 129 facilities were 'fully operational'. Unfortunately, the matter has been clouded by the Health Minister. At a briefing in 2005 it was stated that there were 50 009 patients on ART at 143 health facilities where comprehensive HIV/AIDS services were being provided (Social Sector Cluster briefing, June 2005). However, Minister Tshabalala-Msimang questioned these figures, saying she had not been informed of how the numbers were reached. Rather than confirming an achievement, she reported that she would try to establish how many people were on the government's anti-retroviral programme, how many had fallen out and 'how many had died as a result of the side effects' (*SAPA* 05.05.05).

This statement undermined the credibility both of the objective and the departmental figures (as the Minister added she was not concerned with figures but with 'quality') and, unfortunately, there has been no report on what she has established.

Security

Objective 10: Ensure that 152 000 officers are on active duty in the SAPS by 2006
This promise by Mbeki was a reaffirmation of the Enlistment Programme established by the South African Police Service (SAPS) in 2001. That programme sought to reverse the drop in the number of SAPS personnel prompted, *inter alia*, by an earlier moratorium on recruitment. The Enlistment Programme set staffing-level targets for 2003 and subsequent years. According to the plan, by March 2006 SAPS should have 152 560 officers on active duty. There is some difference whether civilians are included in the definition of 'officers on active duty'. The definition has a significant impact on whether the objective is being reached; the figures of 'staff including civilians' reach the target in 2005 but those of 'staff excluding civilians' do not. (Significantly, the SAPS website on police/population ratios refers to figures of police officers and excludes civilians.)[25] Although the March 2003 target was met that year, it was followed by another pronounced drop in staffing levels. By 2004 the combination of escalating targets and lower staffing levels resulted in staffing levels of officers being only 75 per cent of what was envisaged (see Table 1.6) and an additional 8 000 members and 3 000 support staff were subsequently recruited. Although the situation improved in the second half of 2004, the current rate of recruitment (10 640 per year) is insufficient to ensure that the promise of 'officers on active duty' for 2006 will be met.

Table 1.6 *Actual and targeted staffing levels of SAPS*

Date	Staff (excl. civilians)	Staff (civilian & officers)	Target
2002	119 560	123 000	No target
2003	*	132 310	131 560
2004	106 364	134 857	140 560
2005	115 056	148 454	147 560
2006	*	*	152 560
2007	*	*	156 760

Source: SAPS 2002 and data for staff (civilian and officers) from the Presidency 2004 and 2005
Note: * Indicates lack of data

Objective 11: In the current year establish at least two community courts in each province

In his address to Parliament in February 2005, Mbeki stated that (only) three community courts had been established: 'We have also launched three community courts and started eight pilots in six provinces.'[26] It is reported that four community courts have now been set up in Cape Town.

Objective 12: In the next three months we will set up special joint teams to target and focus on serious crime with an immediate objective of apprehending the top 200 criminals in the country

Although special joint task teams focused on serious crimes have been established, the effectiveness of these teams is unknown. Although the immediate task of these teams was to apprehend 'the top 200 criminals in the country', progress is being monitored by the Justice, Crime Prevention and Security Cluster. Although defining the 'top' criminals is a grey area, it is stated by the Presidency that the top 200 criminals 'for 2004' had been apprehended.[27] These are impressive statistics, but the question is whether top criminals and others are not only being apprehended but also convicted.

Conclusion

This chapter has sought to assess how close government has come to meeting its goals put forth in the 2004 'State of the Nation' addresses. This is in line with the official commitment to new forms of public accountability and open government. Yet effective review depends closely on the availability of data for providing an independent audit of public commitment to the poor and the performance of departments.

Departments are subject to review by Parliament and the annual 'State of the Nation' addresses also now offer something of a scorecard. Meanwhile, the government website[28] proclaims that the public disclosure of statistics has democratic objectives:

> This will allow the public to continue to follow progress in implementation of the government's programme. By facilitating transparent governance it will contribute to the conditions enabling all of society to work together to build a South Africa that truly belongs to all.

These are laudable aims, but greater reliance has still had to be placed on national surveys rather than departmental statistics, largely because these are not often readily available or verifiable. Yet well-developed departmental statistics are essential to assessment against specific targets and they therefore clearly need to be improved, and the means of their assembly be made publicly available.

More difficult to understand is the appearance and disappearance of specific targets in government pronouncements. Many key targets are set out but others are not. While it is difficult to imagine all targets being reported on in each 'State of the Nation' speech, some key commitments are not repeated, not even by line-department ministers. It is significant to note in what sectors promises are *not* made. Although jobs are widely regarded as the top priority of the nation (even more so than health), there are no specific commitments to job creation. Similarly, an RDP target such as housing for all by 2003 has disappeared without comment and has not been replaced by another target date. A 2004 election promise to create one million jobs over the next five years through expanded public works programmes has dropped from view.

The status of targets is often difficult to establish. A key commitment to sanitation for all by 2010 is made in the *Strategic framework on water services*, yet is not repeated in the 'State of the Nation' address or in the Social Cluster's priorities, but reappears in a recent Government Communication and Information System pamphlet. On the other hand, an objective which does not appear in the 'State of the Nation' address or in those of the social or economic cluster gains considerable additional expenditure of R6 billion to 'complete the land restitution programme' (Manuel 2005). It is not clear where the real priorities lie without intensive scrutiny of Treasury expenditure plans.

There is also evidence of disjunctures between the public-policy process and budgeting. A number of promises seem to stand alone without the funding to support them. White Papers set out broad objectives (of which the RDP was the most comprehensive) and targets always have the explicit endorsement of Cabinet before presentation. These targets, however, do not appear to be comprehensively absorbed into the government's programme of action or Budget.

A similar situation is found in relation to South Africa's realisation of the United Nations' Millennium Development Goals. Although these have been officially endorsed, the attitude of government is generally condescending. For instance, it is officially maintained that these goals will be reached or over-fulfilled, yet they are not often related to government's programme of action and do not appear incorporated in the objectives of the social cluster which sets the goals for basic services serving the poor. Since the Millennium Development Goals concentrate on outcomes, it is not clear whether many can be reached in relation to the goal of reducing infant and under-five mortality by two-thirds or by halving the proportion of people living in extreme poverty and hunger between 1990 and 2015.

The key indicators of life expectancy – infant and child mortality – are central to achieving the Millennium Development Goals. A recent statement by the Minister of Health states that some progress is recorded in reducing both the infant mortality rate and child mortality. There has been a welcome decline in infant mortality from 45 to 43/1 000 live births over five years, 1998 to 2003 (Tshabalala-Msimang 2005), but this masks the enormous change which still has to come in the next ten years to reduce infant mortality by more than half to 18/1 000 in 2015.[29] The other key indicator in the Millennium Development Goals is that of halving the proportion of the population living in extreme poverty and experiencing hunger by 2015. There has been preliminary work undertaken by departments together with the UNDP (UNDP 2003), but government objectives do not refer to progress in outcomes along these lines.

The executive has seemingly learnt from past experience and has steered away from enumerating outcomes. Targets consequently tend to be measured in terms of inputs rather than results. With a few exceptions, the emphasis is on departmental objectives rather than on final outcomes in human development. For example, rather than speaking of the extent to which the overall housing backlog will be reduced, the President refers to the amount to be spent on tackling the issue. Similarly, he speaks not of a reduction in crime rates but focuses on the inputs – the staffing levels of the SAPS, number of courts, and so on. While he promises that all households will have access to clean water and electricity, Mbeki is silent as to the extent to which this access will be translated into consumption via, for example, free basic allocations. Progress towards reducing poverty as a result of all these and other interventions is critical, yet curiously it is not mentioned as a measurable target towards 2015.

Clearly there is a complex process of new packing of old promises; housing, water and sanitation live on in the commitments of the social cluster of the government's programme of action, although timelines on basic services taken over from the RDP are either dropped or extended forwards. The executive can be seen to be capitalising on its service-delivery strengths and relying heavily on continued performance by the more efficient national institutions. Inputs and strategies are highlighted, and when there is a reference to outcomes, there has to be good reason for confidence around achieving the outcome. Hence, while government can proclaim its success in achieving targets such as 'placing two million children on social grants', there is silence on the more difficult issues of nutrition, refuse removal, sanitation and telecommunications that were cornerstones of the RDP. Several of the earlier objectives appear to have fallen by the wayside and are no longer mentioned, like increasing access to affordable communications, even though that goal remains vital to closing the digital gap between rich and poor and modernising the economy.

While progress in many sectors is being made, in others (water, sanitation, school infrastructure) the targets set out in 2004 are unlikely to be met. The cost of meeting fundamental social objectives is substantial and is not acknowledged in budgetary reviews. Clearly, many of the social goals will not be met unless there is substantial change in budgetary allocations in infrastructure delivery. Who will take responsibility for goals not being achieved? Unfortunately, as public statements are made of progress in terms of 'distance to target', there is the danger that old targets will slip off the record and be replaced by departmental inputs rather than achieved outcomes.

Objectives and their associated targets, while presented as part of the rational ordering of public management, are also essentially political in nature. The achievements of service delivery in a society of huge inequalities are intensely contested, and in this political context it is likely that government will play its stronger cards.

Nowhere is this clearer than in the management of the assessment of goals. Public accountability exercised by democratic control is central to notions of equity and effectiveness and cannot be replaced by the mechanisms of public management. In the recent period, there have been rising levels of community mobilisation to secure service delivery. The emphasis of new public administration is on models of efficiency rather than of building equity into all governmental processes. Greater efficiency can only be achieved with greater public accountability at every level of government: through rigorous parliamentary review, through democratic local government, and with the energetic involvement of civil society.

Notes

1   This chapter has benefited from extensive comment from Goolam Aboobaker from the Presidency who responded to the paper in a key discussion at the July 2005 Human Sciences Research Council (HSRC) Winter Conference. He felt that the view that there was centralisation of power in the Presidency was exaggerated. Criticism was also directed at some statistical trends which showed uneven progress towards targets; and mention was made particularly of South African Police Services (SAPS) staff figures and conditions in schools. These and other points have been taken into consideration and where there are contrasting figures, the sources are given for each.

2   It is argued by representatives of the Presidency that much of the additional financial support is not for personnel and that not all positions have been filled. The tendency towards centralisation is not peculiar to South Africa; a recent study of British politics identified prime ministerialism, greater power to the prime minister, as an important trend over time (Hennessy 2000).

3   Figures derived from the ten per cent samples of the 1996 and 2001 Censuses.

4   A high-ranking municipal official from the Eastern Cape recently rejected statistics derived from the 2001 Census and presented by one of the authors for being 'wrong, completely wrong' as they showed some progress in delivery. He felt that municipal statistics would show a much lower level of delivery.

5   In water delivery, for instance, the RDP set out that the quantity of water available should rise from 25 to 50 litres per person per day by 1999.

6   The figure for shacks in 1994 is of 757 000 free-standing and backyard shacks (from the 1994 OHS).

7   There is evidence that population growth is now declining substantially (see Stats SA, 2005b) and that the population growth halved between 2004/05 to 0.92 per cent. It is not clear yet what effect this is having on the trends identified in household growth.

PRESIDENTIAL TARGETS AND THE STATE OF DELIVERY

8   While a consistent reduction in household size is evident the magnitude of the decline is more problematic. There is some indication that domestic workers and migrant workers living in institutions were not treated in precisely the same way in 1996 and 2001.

9   The exact level of housing delivery has been complicated by language which refers to subsidies, 'housing starts', 'top structures', and so on, rather than completed houses. The figure of one million houses has been provided by the DWAF in private correspondence. Public sources for actual completed houses are difficult to source; the General Household Survey (GHS) of 2002 had 600 000 households responding that they had received a housing subsidy which is about half the number claimed to be 'built or under construction' by the Department of Housing. In 2002/03 the National Home Builders' Registration Council, which is required to register all housing, registered 43 000 RDP houses out of the 203 588 stated to be 'built or under construction' by the Department in that year.

10 The Minister of Housing, Lindiwe Sisulu, 'declared war on informal settlements' in a speech to the National Council of Provinces in Cape Town on 11 June 2004, and in a subsequent speech to the Public Policy Forum meeting of Cities Alliance on 1 November 2004 stated: 'Therefore by 2014 we would expect to be able to say that we have contributed towards the Millennium Development Goal in significantly improving the lives of over 2.2 million households which implies that we will have reached some nine million people.' On another occasion in 2004 she said, 'The ten-year target of clearing informal settlements is realistic' (available at http://www.dailytenders.co.za/General/News/Article/Article.asp?ID=1199).

11 This estimate is based on estimates of household earnings in 2001.

12 See, for instance, a review of the sustainability of rural water projects in KwaZulu-Natal conducted in 2003 which concluded that more than half the projects were not operating within the RDP standards. Of the 23 projects sampled, ten were found to be sustainable or functioning at RDP standards (43.4%), eight were working but problematic (34.9%), and the remaining five (21.7%) were not working (Hemson 2004).

13 The greatest controversy in delivery relates to those receiving piped water beyond 200 metres as the relevant question is no longer put in surveys after the LFS, February 2001. Equally, the proportion of households beyond 200 metres varies considerably in surveys. Unfortunately departmental statistics do not assist as they reflect access to 'safe' water, not necessarily piped water. The statistics since 2001 (that is, 2002 and 2004) of access to communal taps within 200 metres have been established by adjusting the number of households by a factor established in previous surveys.

14 The persistent backlog is partially explained by social surveys registering those actually receiving services, not those communities where infrastructure has been installed. The

numbers 'unserved' also include households where schemes have decayed and failed and who now draw water from other sources.

15　The figures are calculated on the basis of replenishment over ten years, a generous estimation of the lifespan of a typical latrine.

16　Figure derived from the 2003 Stats SA's general household survey.

17　This test is expressed in terms of the joint income of a child's caregiver and that person's spouse. In urban areas this income must not exceed R9 600 per annum and in rural areas it must not exceed R13 200.

18　Parliamentary media briefing by the Minister of Education, Naledi Pandor, 28.05.04. Available at http://www.info.gov.za/speeches/2004/04052809451002.htm.

19　See http://www.news24.com/News24/AnanziArticle/0,,2-7-1442_1691789,00.html.

20　Fieldnotes on a visit to Tsawana Junior School, KwaJali, 24.02.05.

21　Information provided by the Presidency.

22　Statistics compiled from those made available to one of the authors undertaking an assessment of water services for DWAF in 2004 and from the June 2005 Provincial Education Monthly Infrastructure report submitted to the Department of Education.

23　Social Cluster, updated 28.06.05, available at http://www.info.gov.za/aboutgovt/poa/report/social.htm.

24　Available at http://www.tac.org.za/Documents/ARVRollout/arvstats.htm.

25　See http://www.saps.gov.za/_dynamicModules/internetsite/buildingBlocks/basePage4/BP444.asp.

26　Available at http://www.anc.org.za/ancdocs/history/mbeki/2005/tm0211.html.

27　The latest Justice, Crime Prevention & Security Cluster on 29 June 2005 does not mention the matter. See http://www.nia.org.za/SPEECHES/speech/jcps_cluster_media_briefing%2029%20June.htm.

28　http://www.gov.za

29　Advanced industrial countries have achieved the rate of four or five deaths per 1 000 live births. For details of a preliminary assessment of all Millennium Development Goal indicators see UNDP 2003.

References

ANC (African National Congress) (1955) The Freedom Charter. Adopted at the Congress of the People, Kliptown, 26.06.55.

ANC (1994) *A basic guide to the Reconstruction and Development Programme.* Available at http://www.anc.org.za/ancdocs/policy/short.htm.

ANC (2005) Statement of the National Executive Committee of the African National Congress on the occasion of Year 93 of the ANC, Umtata, 08.01.05.

Bauer H (2004) Public management in Austrian government: Contribution to exploratory meeting. Available at http://www.pogar.org/publications/finances/oecd/bauer-pma.pdf.

Bradshaw D, Bourne D & Nannan N (2003) What are the leading causes of death among South African children? *MRC Policy Brief* No. 3, December 2003.

Chandler J (1996) New public management: Does it exist? The new public management and local governance. Proceedings of Political Studies Association. Available at http://www.psa.ac.uk/cps/1996.htm.

Department of Health (2003) *14th National malaria update 2003.* Pretoria: Department of Health. Available at http://www.doh.gov.za/issues/malaria/updates/2003/dec03.pdf.

DWAF (Department of Water Affairs and Forestry, South Africa) (2003) *Strategic framework for water services: Water is life, sanitation is dignity.* Pretoria: DWAF.

GCIS (Government Communications and Information System) (2004) Background notes on government's response to the 'South Africa Human Development Report' published by the UNDP 05.05.04. Available at http://www.info.gov.za/speeches/2004/04050609151001.htm.

Habib A (2004) The politics of economic policy-making: Substantive uncertainty, political leverage, and human development, *Transformation* 56: 90–103.

Hemson D (2004) Beating the backlog: Meeting targets and providing free basic services. Unpublished position paper for the National Treasury, January 2004.

Hennessy P (2000) *The Prime Minister: the Office and its holder since 1945.* Allen Kane: London.

Hood C (1991) A public management for all seasons? *Public Administration* 69: 3–19.

Leatt A (2004) Granting assistance: *An analysis of the Child Support Grant and its extension to seven and eight year olds.* Children's Institute Working Paper. Cape Town: University of Cape Town.

Leatt A & Solange R (2004) Social security implementation – granting assistance to the poor. Paper on behalf of the Children's Institute presented at Naledi Conference on Improving the impact of poverty eradication programmes in South Africa, September 2004.

Manuel T (2005) Budget Speech 2005 by Minister of Finance Trevor A Manuel, Cape Town, 25.02.05.

Mbeki T (2004) Address of the President of South Africa, Thabo Mbeki, to the first joint sitting of the third democratic Parliament. Cape Town, 21.05.04.

Mbeki T (2005) The Presidency response of the President of South Africa to the Debate of the State of the Nation Address, National Assembly. Cape Town, 17.02.05.

McLeod N (2005) Poverty reduction through better regulation. Information challenges: Dealing with information asymmetries. Presentation to Conference on Poverty Reduction through Better Regulation, 21–23.02.05, Rosebank, Johannesburg.

Osborne D & Gaebler T (1983) *Reinventing government: How the entrepreneurial spirit is transforming the public sector*. Reading: Addison-Wasley.

RSA (Republic of South Africa) (2005) *Government's programme of action: Social cluster*. Pretoria: Government Communication Information System.

SAPS (South African Police Service) (2002) *Annual Report of the SA Police Service 2001/2002. Annual report of the National Commissioner of the South African Police Service 2001–2002*. Pretoria: SAPS.

Sisulu, LN (2005) Minister of Housing at the Financial Sector Transformation Conference by the Financial Sector Campaign Coalition, Indaba Hotel, Fourways, Johannesburg, 26.07.05. Available at http://www.housing.gov.za/Content/media_desk/speeches/2005/26%20July%202005.ht.

Social Sector Cluster (2005) Media briefing by the Ministers of Health and Social Development on the Programme of Action of the Social Sector Cluster, Pretoria, 28.06.05.

Stats SA (Statistics South Africa) (1994) *October household survey 1994*. South African Data Archive (SADA 0061). Pretoria: Stats SA.

Stats SA (1998) *The people of South Africa: Population Census 1996, Census in brief*. Pretoria: Stats SA.

Stats SA (2002) *Labour force survey*. P0210. Pretoria: Stats SA.

Stats SA (2003a) *Census 2001*: Census in brief. Pretoria: Stats SA.

Stats SA (2003b) *General household survey*. P0318. Pretoria: Stats SA.

Stats SA (2004) *General household survey July 2003*. P0318. Pretoria: Stats SA.

Stats SA (2005a) *Non-financial census of municipalities for the year ended 30 June 2003*. P9115. Pretoria: Stats SA.

Stats SA (2005b) *Mid-year population estimates*. P0302. Pretoria: Stats SA.

Tshabalala-Msimang M (2005) 2005. Budget Speech by Minister of Health, 08.04.05. Available at http://www.pmg.org.za/briefings/050408health.htm.

UNDP (United Nations Development Programme) (2003) Millennium development indicators for South Africa. Available at http://www.sarpn.org.za/documents/d0000514/index.php.

UNDP (2004) *The challenge of sustainable development in South Africa: Unlocking people's creativity. South Africa Human Development Report, 2003*. Pretoria: UNDP.

Walsh K (1995) *Public service and market mechanisms*. London: MacMillan.

2 Towards a Constitution-based definition of poverty in post-apartheid South Africa

Wiseman Magasela

In the manifesto which it addressed to the voters in the 2004 general election, the African National Congress (ANC) dedicated itself to halving poverty in South Africa by 2014. Subsequently, having been returned to power by a sweeping victory, President Thabo Mbeki reiterated his government's commitment to:

> Mov[ing] our country forward decisively towards the eradication of poverty and underdevelopment...and achiev[ing] further and visible advances with regard to the improvement of the quality of life of all our people, affecting many critical areas of social existence. (Mbeki 2004)

Nobody doubts the nobility of this ambition. Nonetheless, it is fair to ask what the President and the ANC mean by the term 'poverty' in their various articulations. Furthermore, when we explore research, writings and statements on poverty in South Africa, what is the emerging understanding of poverty in the post-apartheid South African context and, importantly, on what assumptions is it based? And if we can find agreement about what poverty is, can we assess the present extent of poverty some 11 years after South Africa enshrined the ideals of improving *the quality of life of all citizens* and establishing a society based on *democratic values, social justice* and *fundamental human rights* in its Constitution?

The issue of agreeing how we separate those who are 'poor' from those who are 'not poor' is clearly a vexing one, yet it is not one which is peculiar to South Africa, for the definition and measurement of poverty shapes and influences choices which all (benign) governments have to make. As MacGregor observes, 'the academic debate about poverty has been largely about definitions' (1981: 62), while May, reviewing 24 studies of poverty in

11 developing countries, speaks of an 'elusive consensus' (2001: 23) when it comes to definitions, measurement and analysis of poverty. Not surprisingly, therefore, Everatt concludes that in South Africa 'poverty has many meanings within government and the progressive movement broadly, as it does among academics and commentators' (2003: 77).

This lack of consensus on the meaning of poverty and how to define and measure poverty has considerable political implications, for at the present time the government is having to face claims that there has been an increase in poverty since 1994. Many such assertions have been based on quantitative analysis of data derived from the 1995 and 2000 income and expenditure surveys and the 1996 and 2001 population censuses. The report *Earning and spending in South Africa: Selected findings and comparisons from the income and expenditure surveys of October 1995 and October 2000* (Stats SA 2002) is widely taken to have provided evidence of increases in poverty between 1995 and 2000. Other researchers have corroborated the findings of this report. Terreblanche has argued that 'the quality of life of the majority of South Africans deteriorated during the first eight years of the post-apartheid period'(2002: 18). Meth and Dias (2004) came to the conclusion that, while 'for many of them [the poor] the intensity of poverty has decreased because of the provision of a social wage' (2004: 83), overall poverty nonetheless increased over the three years from 1999 to 2001. Simkins, analysing the 1995 and 2000 income and expenditure survey, made the observation that 'on all the poverty measures, poverty increased between 1995 and 2000 against a constant real poverty line per person' (2004: 6). Recently, too, Hoogeveen and Özler have concluded that 'the depth and severity of poverty [has] increased' (2005: 22) in South Africa.

Are these claims, which fly in the face of the government's aspirations and efforts, valid? The answer, of course, is that it depends on what is meant by poverty. Commonly, research 'proving' increases in poverty in South Africa uses income poverty lines. Hence Terreblanche (2002), for instance, focuses on income, poverty rising within race inequalities, the marginal increase in gross domestic product (GDP) per capita and levels of unemployment. This he does whilst acknowledging an increase in social spending by government (welfare, health, education and housing) in the period 1995/96 to 2002/03.

The politics of poverty definition

This chapter explores what has become common and conventional practice in research on poverty in South Africa, that is, how it is conceptualised, defined and measured. This task requires recognition, first, that poverty is a 'contested political concept' (Alcock 1993: 3), and second, that there is an inextricable link and relationship between how poverty is conceptualised, definitions of poverty, explanations for it and policies designed to address it (Townsend 2000).

Poverty as a contested political concept

In South Africa there is continuing debate as to the extent and increasing levels of poverty between the government and other important actors. Central to the conflicting views is not only the meaning and definition of poverty, but also the question of who defines it. This is a crucial point, particularly in a country with a long history of racial discrimination that led to poverty being concentrated in only some groups in society.

Alcock observes:

> Most people of course claim that their understanding of poverty is the correct one, based on logical argument or scientific research. But as our exploration of the problem of understanding poverty will reveal, there is no one correct, scientific, agreed definition because poverty is inevitably a political concept, and thus inherently a contested one...therefore the first thing to understand is that poverty is not a simple phenomenon which we can learn to define by adopting the correct approach. It is a series of contested definitions and complex arguments which overlap and at times contradict each other. (1993: 3–4)

Yet apart from contending that the conceptualisation of poverty is highly contested, Alcock further insists that 'poverty is not just a state of affairs, it is an *unacceptable* state of affairs – it implicitly contains the question, what are we going to do about it?' (1993: 3). In a contemporary South Africa, where many arguments (based almost entirely on quantitative analysis of income poverty) have been put forward that poverty has increased rather than decreased since the democratic government came to power, it is inevitable therefore that the debate about poverty has become a contentious one.

Concepts, definitions, explanations and policies

The other relevant issue is the interrelatedness and interconnectedness of concepts, definitions, explanations and policies (Townsend 2000), for as Ravallion (1992) observes, 'measurement and policy' issues are often inseparable. Bradshaw (2000) makes the related point that in poverty research, the measure determines the result. It follows, therefore, that the definitions and measurements of poverty that are adopted have far-reaching implications for the success or failure of anti-poverty policies. Yet in today's South Africa, definitions of poverty abound, and much the same can be said of the anti-poverty policies that emanate from government departments.

Why definitions of poverty matter

When a society chooses a definition of poverty, and denotes specific characteristics with which to identify the poor, it thereby makes an explicit expression of its fundamental values. The state of being in poverty is directly related to a lack of an acceptable quality of life. As being poor is an unacceptable and undesirable state, defining poverty is a statement that has its basis in the dominant political, economic and social ideology in a society. This ideology is central in informing how poverty is understood and how, when research on poverty is undertaken, poverty is conceptualised. Furthermore, definitions of poverty inform those in power how to source and allocate resources directed at its eradication, while different definitions of poverty require different policy responses.

Against this background, the poverty issue in post-apartheid South Africa is reviewed as follows. First, an overview of key aspects of the economy, which are relevant to any discussion of poverty, is presented. Second, consideration is given to how poverty has been conceptualised, and how this has informed the predominating practice in poverty estimation. This is coupled with an exploration of studies of poverty conducted by and statements made by the government. Third, the approach to poverty that informs government policies is discussed. And fourth, the argument will be made that the democratic Constitution, and the values it enshrines, provides a compelling basis for a reconceptualisation of poverty in post-apartheid South Africa.

The economy: the labour market, wages, unemployment and poverty

Research undertaken in different parts of the world has conclusively demonstrated a strong relationship between poverty and employment. In South Africa the same has been shown to be true. The first post-apartheid study of poverty concluded that, among other aspects, 'poverty has a strong employment dimension' (Ministry in the Office of the President: Reconstruction and Development Programme 1995). The Presidency's *Towards a ten-year review* reached the same conclusion, as the 'persistence of poverty' is seen to be 'arising largely from unemployment and the apartheid legacy' (PCAS 2003: 31). Meanwhile, the country also has the problem of the 'working poor', that is, those who have jobs but remain in poverty. Poswell states that in South Africa 'high levels of poverty result from low real wages and high unemployment' (2002: 14). Similarly, Bhorat, Leibbrandt, Maziya, van der Berg and Woolard, using what they call an 'absolute' standard of R650 per month per household, found that:

> at least a quarter of all employed workers earn less than R650 per month…[and] the majority of working poor are Africans [82%] and coloured [15%]. They are mostly men, but women [particularly African women] tend to be overrepresented among them. (2001: 216)

Since 1994, the South African economy has seen positive, albeit modest, growth compared to the apartheid era. When the Growth, Employment and Redistribution (GEAR) strategy was adopted as the macroeconomic strategy for South Africa, it envisaged attaining a six per cent rate of growth and the creation of 400 000 jobs per year (Department of Finance 1996). These targets have proved to be too ambitious. Consequently, what compounds and worsens the state of poverty in South Africa is the failure of the economy to create and provide enough secure and quality jobs with decent wages for all job seekers. High levels of unemployment, low wages for a significant number of workers, and growing casualisation in some sectors have come to characterise the country's economy and labour market. Hence Poswell (2002), reiterating the point made by Bhorat et al. (2001), shows that in 1995, 30 per cent of employed Africans earned less than R1 001 per month and this figure grew to 49 per cent in 1999. Unemployment in South Africa remains high and the 'labour force is less successful is gaining employment at present, and is not yet equipped to find jobs in the future' (PCAS 2003: 89–90).

Definitions of poverty in post-apartheid South Africa

The household subsistence level (HSL) calculated by the Institute for Planning Research at the University of Port Elizabeth, and the minimum living level (MLL) calculated by the Bureau of Market Research at the University of South Africa, are two commonly used and uniquely South African poverty lines. Both the HSL and the MLL are what are called absolute income measures of poverty, which as literature shows, are minimalist definitions of poverty based on subsistence. Both the HSL and MLL and their derivatives are based on the poverty datum line (PDL). Budlender (1985) wrote a convincing critique of these measures. There is also the approach of creating what is called a 'relative' measure of poverty which selects cut-off points of 40 per cent and 20 per cent to identify 'poor' and 'ultra-poor' households in the country ranked by adult equivalent income. A further poverty line used is the US $1 per day. There are other difficulties too. In Britain, for instance, the use of subsistence poverty lines led to the belief that poverty had been eliminated under the post-war welfare state, but as Abel-Smith and Townsend (1965) demonstrated, there remained many people who still lived lives of hardship and deprivation and who were excluded from society's institutions and processes. Deprivation indices pioneered by Townsend (1979), in *Poverty in the United Kingdom: A survey of household resources and standards of living,* showed this clearly. A shift from absolute to relative conceptualisation, definition and measurement of poverty occurred. Poverty measurement moved from a preoccupation with physical efficiency to the understanding of the poor as social citizens with social, economic and political roles, responsibilities and needs.

South Africa today does not have an official definition of poverty. However, there are important statements and official government documents that contain specific definitions of poverty and which provide estimates of the extent of poverty. To explore the terrain of poverty definition in post-apartheid South Africa, it is necessary to start with the ANC's position in the period immediately prior to the 1994 elections, and trace subsequent developments after it moved into power.

ANC initiatives prior to the 1994 elections

Three documents adopted by the ANC outlined its approach to poverty during the period when it considered itself a government in waiting. The first was *Ready to Govern* (ANC 1992), which laid down plans on key social and economic policies with the institution of democracy, fighting poverty and combating inequality as the main targets for policy intervention. The Second Carnegie Enquiry into Poverty in South Africa, on which *Uprooting poverty: The South African challenge* (Wilson & Mamphela 1989) was based, had painted the bleak picture under which millions of South Africans lived, and the ANC was suitably apprised that tackling deep and extensive poverty was going to be the main challenge facing a post-apartheid democratic government. Consequently, out of concern to know in greater depth about the conditions under which South Africans lived, the ANC commissioned the *Project for Statistics on Living Standards and Development*, which was undertaken by the World Bank and South African researchers during the nine months leading up to the country's first democratic elections. This became an important milestone in poverty studies in post-1994 South Africa and 'is generally considered the benchmark for comprehensive poverty-related data in the country' (Roberts 2000: 3).

The third document was the *Reconstruction and Development Programme: A Policy Framework* (ANC 1994), which was presented as 'an integrated, coherent socio-economic policy framework' in which the ANC and its partners spelt out their approach to poverty in five key programmes: 'Meeting basic needs', 'Developing our human resources', 'Building the economy', 'Democratising the state and society', and 'Implementing the RDP'. In the Reconstruction and Development Programme (RDP), poverty is described as 'the single greatest burden of South Africa's people' (Point 2.1.1) and reference is made to the fact that 'there are at least 17 million people surviving below the minimum living level in South Africa' (Point 2.1.1). However, as noted by Everatt subsequently, the RDP had many critical weaknesses, one of which was 'the failure to settle on a clear definition of poverty' (2003: 82), even if in retrospect it is fair to observe that a political party which was still outside government could hardly have been expected to have arrived at a clear definition of poverty.

These articulations on poverty, significantly added to through other poverty studies and official state documents, marked the beginning of how poverty came to be understood in the post-apartheid period. The most important of developments in understanding poverty in democratic South Africa was the 1996 adoption of the country's Constitution with a Bill of Rights which specifies social and economic rights.

Further developments

The lack of comprehensive, reliable and up-to-date information on poverty in South Africa was a task that the democratic government sought urgently to address (May 1998; Mpambani 1994; Stats SA 2000). A particular responsibility was assumed by Statistics South Africa (Stats SA), which conducted the first post-1994 census in 1996, followed by another in 2001. Subsequently, two income and expenditure surveys were conducted in 1995 and 2001, and another was due in 2005. Furthermore, October household surveys (OHSs) were conducted after 1994 and later replaced by the general household survey (GHS). Overall, the collection of periodic information and statistics by the official statistics agency constitutes a major attempt to build a clear picture of primarily socio-economic conditions in the country, and has formed a major basis for the quantitative analysis of poverty.

The first official review of poverty in South Africa after 1994 was titled *Key indicators of poverty in South Africa*. This study, conducted by the World Bank, and published by the Ministry in the Office of the President: Reconstruction and Development (1995), was a quantitative analysis of the Project for Statistics on Living Standards and Development. Poverty definitions and measurement are clearly spelt out. Five different types of poverty lines are used to estimate poverty levels in South Africa. This is shown in Table 2.1.

The definitions of poverty and estimates of the numbers of poor people in South Africa used in *Key indicators of poverty in South Africa* (Ministry in the Office of the President: 1995) were subsequently used by other researchers and also appeared in official state documents. Except for different statistical manipulations providing poverty estimates, there is little variation in the conceptualisation and analysis of poverty which has departed from *Key indicators of poverty in South Africa*. Even so, for all its use of different poverty lines, the report was criticised in some quarters for focusing exclusively on income poverty: 'The arbitrary manner in which the income-poverty line was chosen', opined Hercules (1998: 19), 'raises the critical questions of who defines income-poverty?'

Table 2.1 *Comparison of selected poverty lines for South Africa, 1993*

Types of poverty lines	Amount/ month cut-off (R)	Population living below the poverty line (%)
1. Population cut-offs at the:		
40th percentile of households raked by adult equivalence	301.1	52.8
20th percentile of households raked by adult equivalence	177.6	28.8
2. Minimum per capita caloric intake (at 2 000 Kcal per day)	143.2	39.3
3. Minimum per capita adult-equivalent caloric intake (at 2 500 Kcal per day)	185.5	42.3
4. Minimum and supplemental living levels per capita set by the Bureau of Market Research, University of South Africa	220.1	567.0
Supplemental living level (SLL)	164.2	447.0
Minimum living level (MLL)		
5. Per adult equivalent household subsistence level (HSL) set by the Institute for Planning Research, University of Port Elizabeth	251.1	36.2

Source: Ministry in the Office of the President: Reconstruction and Development Programme (1995: 8)

The report *Poverty and inequality in South Africa* (May 1998) was a further significant addition to the understanding of poverty in post-apartheid South Africa and has been hailed by government (DoSD 2000) and researchers. May examined the poverty issue in a far more comprehensive manner. Pertinent issues in the understanding, definition and measurement of poverty are raised. The report starts by alluding to poverty definition as a contested enterprise and elaborates on conceptual issues for measurement. Holistic measures of poverty and deprivation, which capture the multidimensional nature of poverty (such as United Nations Development Programme's (UNDP) Human Development Index and the Capability Poverty Measure, created to overcome pitfalls of narrow income definitions) are discussed and analysed. Subjective measurement of poverty, poverty lines and the World Bank's definition of poverty all form important parts of the final report. When it came to defining, measuring and estimating poverty, the study relied on and adopted the practice used in *Key indicators of poverty in South Africa.*

There have been other contributions that have been influential in the formulation of policy concerning poverty in a variety of government departments. However, the most common feature of these reports and documents has been their inconsistency in their choice of poverty definition and measurement, reflecting the 'fact that "poverty" has many meanings within government' (Everatt 2003: 77). In 1995, for instance, the Presidency assembled a commission to investigate labour market policy in South Africa. The resulting report, *Restructuring the South African labour market* (DoL 1996), based its understanding of poverty and poverty levels on *Key indicators of poverty in South Africa*. In contrast, the *Report of the Lund Committee on child and family support* (DoSD 1996) based its understanding, definition and levels of poverty on the MLL. This latter approach was similarly adopted by the *Draft White Paper on population policy* (DoSD 1997a), which viewed the eradication of poverty as one of its guiding principles. In 2000, the Department of Social Development (DoSD) issued the *National report on social development 1995–2000* (DoSD 2000), which, after highlighting socio-economic rights enshrined in the 1996 Constitution, based its understanding of poverty on the assumptions, definitions and estimates of poverty made in *Key indicators of poverty in South Africa* and *Poverty and inequality in South Africa* (May 1998). In the same year *The state of South Africa's population report* (DoSD 2000), from the DoSD's National Population Unit, introduced its own perspective by adopting the so-called international poverty line of US$1 per day. A significantly different approach was adopted in *Measuring poverty in South Africa*, which sought to understand poverty:

> in common with the United Nations development reports, in a broader perspective than merely the extent of low income or low expenditure in the country. It is seen here as the denial of opportunities and choices most basic to human development to lead a long, healthy, creative life and to enjoy a decent standard of living, freedom, dignity, self-esteem and respect from others. (Stats SA 2000: 54)

The Committee of Inquiry into a Comprehensive System of Social Security for South Africa (DoSD 2002) projected its arguments from a completely different platform to the studies mentioned earlier. The Committee used the constitutional framework as the basis for understanding poverty and state intervention through social security measures. The issue of socio-economic rights is raised and the need to use these as the basis in constructing policies and measures in the fight against social exclusion, social deprivation and poverty is the central argument.

Academics continue to play a pivotal role in the understanding of poverty. As heads of committees and commissions and as participants in state-sponsored poverty research and studies, they are an important source of information and views which continue to shape the debates over definition and measurement. Importantly, the outcome is a growing body of research showing levels of poverty and trends over time, for example Whiteford & Posel (1995), Woolard & Leibbrandt (1999), Budlender (1999), May, Carter, Haddad & Maluccio (1999), Roberts (2000), Bhorat et al. (2001), Meth & Dias (2004), Roberts (2005), and Hoogeveen & Özler (2005). A reading of these publications shows that the issue of how poverty is understood and conceptualised in post-apartheid South Africa is not problematised, if considered at all. The second observation is that these studies rely on and use money metric definitions and measures of poverty. Some researchers even go to the extent of providing figures of the poverty gap, an amount, if properly targeted at the poor, which will remove the poor from poverty and in so doing eradicate poverty.

Building citizenship and tackling multidimensional poverty

A pertinent question that we have to ask is how the government sees and responds to the poverty issue in South Africa, bearing in mind the definitions of poverty discussed earlier. Nearly all government departments have policies and programmes formulated on the basis that such policies and programmes contribute to the improvement of the quality of life and tackle poverty. In fact what we see in the unfolding post-1994 social policy terrain is that whilst researchers measured poverty, official statements have continued to state the government's vision for South African society. The *White Paper on reconstruction and development* (RSA 1994) states the aim of economic policy as to:

> alleviate the poverty, low wages and extreme inequalities in wages and wealth generated by the apartheid system to meet basic needs, and thus ensure that every South African has a decent living standard and economic security.

Putting aside government failures and successes in its policies and programmes, the eradication of poverty is claimed to be the core objective and the primary focus of state departments. Anti-poverty programmes from the DoSD, public works programmes, the setting of minimum wage levels in non-unionised economic sectors, the provision of free healthcare for children from birth to the age of seven, the provision of free school meals in poverty-stricken areas, the limited but partially effective social security system, land restitution, and the provision of housing, water and sanitation are all policies designed to tackle poverty through direct state intervention. Poverty in these many initiatives is seen, not just as a lack of income, but as a multidimensional phenomenon and as an intersectoral, cross-cutting issue requiring measures that run across ministries and departments. For instance, the Department of Housing (2003) has proclaimed 'restoring and furthering human dignity and citizenship' as one of the key principles guiding housing policy and strategy, with access to housing being viewed as 'part of the state's response towards poverty reduction and improving the quality of life of all South Africans' (DoH 2004: 6). The Department of Water Affairs and Forestry (DWAF) views its policies in the same light. The Department's 'free basic water' policy provides poor households with 6 000 litres of water per household per month and this is seen as 'a level sufficient to promote healthy living' (DWAF 2001). Whilst these examples demonstrate the two departments' understanding of the objectives of their policies, criticisms of the level, content and quality of the provisions have been registered. Valid criticisms have been made against DWAF as to the adequacy of 6 000 litres of water per household per month to 'promote healthy living'. Similarly, against the Department of Housing it has been pointed out that many of the completed housing units have problems of size (they are small), inferior design, poor thermal performance and low resistance to damp (UNDP 2003).

The duty of the state to intervene and provide basic services, some of them for free, arises from the notion and status of citizenship enjoyed, for the first time since 1994, equally by all South Africans. State intervention, through the many programmes aimed at tackling multidimensional poverty, is aimed at ensuring that all South Africans 'participate fully in all spheres of social, economic and political life' (DoSD 1997b).

The Constitution and the conceptualisation of poverty

The South African Constitution encapsulates foundational values, aspirations and ideals for South African society. For the millions who live in poverty, it offers a clear expression of a set of material rights that must be enjoyed by all South Africans and must be respected, protected, promoted and fulfilled by the state in all its laws, policies and programmes. In so doing, the Constitution represents an acknowledgement of the social, political and economic consequences of South Africa's brutal history for the majority of citizens, and identifies challenges facing South African society as it tries to make a complete break with its past and create a just society.

The Constitution must be viewed in a political, socio-historical context. First and foremost, it represents a watershed in the struggle against white domination and the denial of rights to blacks. At different times, the aspirations of those who were oppressed, discriminated against, exploited and impoverished were crystallised in various documents. In 1943, at an annual conference of the ANC, *Africans' claims in South Africa* was adopted. Under a Bill of Rights (adapted from the Atlantic Charter of Rights), the same conference demanded that: 'We, the African people in the Union of South Africa, urgently demand the granting of full citizenship rights such as are enjoyed by all Europeans in South Africa' (ANC 1943).

In 1955, the Freedom Charter, expressing again the aspirations for an inclusive South African society, was adopted. The ANC's later documents, *Ready to Govern* (ANC 1992) and *Reconstruction and development programme: A policy framework* (ANC 1994), South Africa's Interim Constitution and the Constitution of the Republic of South Africa (1996) represent and embody the aspirations that informed the struggle for liberation. As such, they provide a compelling foundation for our understanding of the poverty issue in post-apartheid South Africa.

A 'citizenship with rights' is the definitive notion of post-apartheid democratic South Africa. The notion of citizenship enshrined in the country's Constitution is the key distinguishing difference between apartheid and democratic South Africa. The Bill of Rights articulates a 'citizenship' with civil, political, social and economic rights. There is a real and inextricable link between socio-economic rights and quality of life, and between socio-economic rights and poverty. Furthermore, South Africa has signed or ratified and adopted international declarations, conventions and covenants entrenching the importance of social and economic rights and the fight against poverty. Cognisant of the fact that poverty has been defined, measured and estimated in post-1994 South Africa, what we must investigate is whether there is any evidence of attempts to link socio-economic rights in the Bill of Rights and poverty in post-apartheid South Africa.

The first point of call must be to look at how the custodians of the Constitution, the Constitutional Court, understand and interpret social and economic rights and the poverty issue. Second, are there writers and researchers in South Africa who see this link? Thirdly, what about civil society formations and the relationship between the Constitution and poverty?

The vision of the South African Constitution, and specifically its aspirations and ideals on social justice and the improvement of the quality of life of all South Africans, has been confirmed on more than one occasion by Justices of the Constitutional Court. For instance, a National Judges' Symposium[1] held on 16 July 2003 stated that:

> The vision of our Constitution is to establish an open democracy committed to social justice and the recognition of human rights. It seeks to improve the quality of life of all citizens and free the potential of each person.

At the same symposium, Justice Pius Langa made the point that:

> No institution of government could fail to notice the high levels of poverty and deprivation of material necessities affecting large numbers of the South African population. It is clear that this constitutional objective…[improving the quality of life of all citizens]…will not be achieved until this state of dire need is eradicated…The socio-economic rights in the Constitution quite clearly reflect a commitment to social upliftment. (Langa 2003: 672)

The views of the Justices of the Constitutional Court in the judgement in *Soobramoney v Minister of Health, KZN, and others 1998*, without going into the merits of the case, are similarly reflective of the link between poverty and socio-economic rights. In this case, the Justices clarified the relevance of the Bill of Rights, socio-economic rights and their relationship with the poverty issue in South Africa. This passage captures the essence of the views of the Court:

> We live in a society in which there are great disparities in wealth. Millions of people are living in deplorable conditions and in great poverty. There is a high level of unemployment, inadequate social security, and many do not have access to clean water or to adequate health services. These conditions already existed when the Constitution was adopted and a commitment to address them, and to transform our society into one in which there will be human dignity, freedom and equality, lies at the heart of our new constitutional order. For as long as these conditions continue to exist that aspiration will have a hollow ring.[2]

Although the Constitution does not provide a precise definition of poverty, it offers through phrases such as 'democratic values', 'social justice', 'fundamental human rights', 'improve the quality of life of all citizens', and 'human dignity', together with the Bill of Rights and socio-economic rights, a compelling foundation for the understanding and conceptualisation of poverty from which definitions of poverty can be constructed. Understandably, it is inevitable that such definitions will at times be subject to contestations, power relations and social struggles.

When we consider writers and researchers on poverty in South Africa, the relationship between socio-economic rights and poverty has been established and investigated. The Community Law Centre at the University of the Western Cape, through projects such as the Socio-Economic Rights Project, leads in this regard. However, this work happens without exploring the link between socio-economic rights and the definitions, measurement and estimation of poverty used by researchers in this area in South Africa. As Liebenberg remarks:

> If the socio-economic rights in the Constitution are to amount to more than paper promises, they must serve as useful tools in enabling people to gain access to the basic social services and resources needed to live a life consistent with human dignity]… and]…socio-economic rights were included as justiciable rights in the Bill of Rights primarily to assist the poor to protect and advance their fundamental socio-economic needs and interests. These rights should therefore be interpreted in a way that promotes this purpose. (2002: 159–161)

De Vos similarly stresses the necessity for poverty studies to consider the 'transformative nature of the Constitution' and the fact that it 'does not only facilitate and necessitate the *political* transformation...but also aims to facilitate the country's *social and economic* transformation' (2001: 263).

Meanwhile, civil society campaigns, using Constitution-based rights, have been launched to address the plight of the poor. The Basic Income Grant Coalition bases its campaign around the fact that the Constitution recognises the right of everyone to social security. The Anti-Privatisation Forum, in its fight for free water provision, takes as its point of departure the constitutional principle that South Africans have a right to sufficient water. The Alliance for Children's Entitlement to Social Security takes the right of every child to basic nutrition, health, shelter, healthcare services and social services contained in the Bill of Rights to ground its campaign for the improvement of the quality of life of South Africa's children. Other such examples abound.

Civil society efforts to employ the Constitution to further the struggle against poverty are complemented by the role and function of the South African Human Rights Commission (SAHRC). This is a 'Chapter 9 institution' which, according to the Constitution,

> every year must require relevant organs of state to provide the Commission with information on the measures that they have taken towards the realisation of the rights in the Bill of Rights concerning housing, healthcare, food, water, social security, education and the environment.

In this monitoring role, the SAHRC had, by 2004, issued five reports on economic and social rights detailing how government departments had performed in the promotion and fulfilment of these rights in pursuit of improving the quality of life of South Africans.

What we have in South Africa is a Constitution articulating specific values, aspirations and ideals and expressing social and economic rights to be enjoyed by all South Africans. We have government departments with 'policies and programmes meeting constitutional obligations' (PCAS 2003).

Conclusion

Research on the poverty issue in post-apartheid South Africa is still in its formative stages. Issues of the contested nature of poverty, its conceptualisation, definition and measurement and the interrelatedness of concepts, definitions and policies are critical if a better understanding of poverty is to be developed. In contrast, the study of poverty in the post-apartheid period has remained too reliant upon income and absolute definitions and measures, and overall has failed to capture the multidimensional nature of poverty. The argument, here, therefore, is that the way forward for poverty research in South Africa is for it to capture the spirit and vision of the Constitution.

The Constitution provides a compelling and forceful basis for understanding poverty. We must ask, therefore, whether the income and absolute definitions of poverty used in poverty research reflect what South Africans, and not just experts, view as capturing the quality of life, which every citizen must, by right, enjoy. Research needs to be guided by the question: how do definitions of poverty correspond to the values, visions and socio-economic rights outlined in the Constitution?

The fact that government departments construct their policies for combating multidimensional poverty using the Constitution as their foundation, requires that research on poverty is based on similar lines. Indicators of multiple deprivations, which capture the multidimensional nature of poverty far better than absolute and minimalist income-based poverty lines, and are closely aligned with constitutional imperatives, must be explored in South Africa.

Notes

1   National Judges' Symposium (2003) Statement. Available at http://www.doj.gov.za/2004dojsite/m_statements/2003/2003%2007%2018%20statement_judges%20symposium.pdf.

2   *Soobramoney v Minister of Health, KZN, and others* 1998 (1) SA 765 (CC).

References

Abel-Smith B & Townsend P (1965) *The poor and the poorest: A new analysis of the Ministry of Labour's family expenditure surveys of 1953–54 and 1960*. London: Bell.

Alcock P (1993) *Understanding poverty*. London: Macmillan.

ANC (African National Congress) (1943) *Africans' claims in South Africa*. Annual conference of the African National Congress, Bloemfontein, 16.12.43. Available at http://www.anc.org.za/ancdocs/history/claims.html.

ANC (1992) *Ready to govern: ANC policy guidelines for a democratic South Africa* adopted at the National Conference 28–31.05.92. Available at http://www.anc.org.za/ancdocs/history/readyto.html.

ANC (1994) *Reconstruction and development programme: A policy framework*. Johannesburg: Umanyano Publications.

Bhorat H, Leibbrandt M, Maziya M, van der Berg S & Woolard I (2001) *Fighting poverty: Labour markets and inequality in South Africa*. Cape Town: UCT Press.

Bradshaw J (2000) The measurement of absolute poverty. Paper for the FISS Conference, Sigtuna, Sweden, 17–20.06.00.

Budlender D (1985) *A critique of poverty datum lines*. Saldru working paper, No. 63, Cape Town: Southern Africa Labour and Development Research Unit, University of Cape Town.

Budlender D (1999) Patterns of poverty in South Africa, *Development Southern Africa* 16(2): 197–219.

Chaskalson A (2003) Address at the opening of the Judges' Conference, *South African Law Journal* 120(4): 657–663.

Congress of the People (1955) Freedom Charter, adopted in Kliptown, 26 June 1955. Available at http://www.anc.org.za/ancdocs/history/charter.html.

Department of Finance (South Africa) (1996) *Growth, employment and redistribution: A macroeconomic strategy*. Pretoria: Department of Finance.

Department of Social Services and Poverty Alleviation (Provincial Government of the Western Cape) (2000) *The state of South Africa's population report 2000*. Cape Town: Department of Social Services and Poverty Alleviation.

De Vos P (2001) Grootboom, the right of access to housing and substantive equality as contextual fairness, *South African Journal on Human Rights* 17(2): 258–276.

DoH (Department of Housing, South Africa) (2003) *A social housing policy for South Africa. Towards an enabling environment for social housing development*. Pretoria: DoH.

DoH (2004) *Annual report 2003/04*. Pretoria: DoH.

DoL (Department of Labour, South Africa) (1996) *Restructuring the South African labour market: Report of the Presidential Commission to investigate labour market policy*. Pretoria: DoL.

DoSD (Department of Social Development, South Africa) (1996) *Report of the Lund Committee on child and family support*. Pretoria: DoSD.

DoSD (1997a) *Draft White Paper on population policy*. Pretoria: DoSD.

DoSD (1997b) *White Paper for Social Welfare*. Pretoria: DoSD.

DoSD (2000) *National report on social development 1995–2000*. Pretoria: DoSD.

DoSD (2002) *Transforming the present: Protecting the future. Report of the Committee of Inquiry into a comprehensive system of social security for South Africa*. Pretoria: DoSD.

DWAF (Department of Water Affairs and Forestry, South Africa) (2001) *Free basic water implementation strategy document*. Pretoria: DWAF.

Everatt D (2003) The politics of poverty. In D Everatt & V Maphai (eds.) The real state of the nation: South Africa after 1990, *Development Update Special Edition* 4: 75–100.

Hercules A (1998) *A profile of poverty in sub-Saharan Africa: Some critical issues*. Johannesburg: The Development Resources Centre.

Hoogeveen JG & Özler B (2005) *Not separate, not equal: Poverty and inequality in post-apartheid South Africa*. William Davidson Institute Working Paper No. 739.

Langa P (2003) The vision of the Constitution, *South African Law Journal* 120(4): 670–679.

Liebenberg (2002) South Africa's evolving jurisprudence on socio-economic rights: An effective tool in challenging poverty? *Law, Democracy and Development* 6(2): 159–191.

MacGregor S (1981) *The politics of poverty*. London: Longman.

May J (ed.) (1998) *Poverty and inequality in South Africa*. Report prepared for the Office of the Executive Deputy President and the Inter-Ministerial Committee for Poverty and Inequality, 13.05.98. Pretoria: DoSD.

May J (2001) An elusive consensus: Definitions, measurement and analysis of poverty. In A Grinspun (ed.) *Choices for the poor: Lessons from national poverty strategies*. New York: United Nations Development Programme.

May J, Carter MR, Haddad L & Maluccio J (1999) *KwaZulu-Natal income dynamics study (KIDS) 1993–1998: A longitudinal household data set for South African policy analysis*. CSDS Working Paper No. 21, School of Development Studies, University of Natal.

Mbeki T (2004) Address of the President of South Africa, Thabo Mbeki, to the second joint sitting of the third democratic Parliament, Cape Town, 06.02.04.

Meth C & Dias R (2004) Increases in poverty in South Africa: 1999–2002, *Development Southern Africa* 21(1): 59–85.

Ministry in the Office of the President: Reconstruction and Development Programme (1995) *Key indicators of poverty in South Africa*.

Mpambani SA (1994) Poverty profile of the Transkei region. In *Project for Statistics on Living Standards and Development*. Cape Town: SALDRU, University of Cape Town.

PCAS (2003) *Towards a ten-year review synthesis report on implementation of government programmes: Discussion document*. Pretoria: GCIS.

Poswell L (2002) *The post-apartheid South African labour market: A status report*. Cape Town: Development Policy Research Unit, University of Cape Town.

Ravallion M (1992) *Poverty comparisons: A guide to concepts and methods*. Living Standards Measurement Study Working Paper No. 88. Washington DC: World Bank.

Roberts B (2000) *Chronic and transitory poverty in post-apartheid South Africa: Evidence from KwaZulu-Natal*. CSDS Working Paper No. 28, School of Development Studies, University of Natal.

Roberts B (2005) Empty stomachs, empty pockets: Poverty and inequality in post-apartheid South Africa. In J Daniel, R Southall & J Lutchman (eds.) *State of the Nation South Africa 2004–2005*. Cape Town: HSRC Press.

RSA (Republic of South Africa) (1994) *White Paper on reconstruction and development*. Pretoria: Ministry in the Office of the President, Reconstruction and Development.

Saldru (Southern African Labour and Development Research Unit) (1993) *Project for Statistics on Living Standards and Development*. Cape Town: Saldru, University of Cape Town (UCT).

Simkins C (2004) *What happened to the distribution of income in South Africa between 1995 and 2001?* Available at http://www.sarpn.org.za/documents/d0001062/P1175-simkins_Nov2004.pdf.

Stats SA (Statistics South Africa) (2000) *Measuring poverty in South Africa*. Pretoria: Stats SA.

Stats SA (2002) *Earning and spending in South Africa: Selected findings and comparisons from the income and expenditure surveys of October 1995 and October 2000*. Pretoria: Stats SA.

Terreblanche S (2002) *A history of inequality in South Africa 1652–2002*. Pietermaritzburg: University of Natal Press.

Townsend P (1979) *Poverty in the United Kingdom: A survey of household resources and standards of living*. London: Penguin.

Townsend P (2000) Post-1945 poverty research and things to come. In J Bradshaw & R Sainsbury (eds.) (2000) *Researching poverty.* Ashgate: Aldershot.

UNDP (United Nations Development Programme) (2003) *South Africa: Human development report.* Available at http://hdr.undp.org/reports/global/2003.

Whiteford A & Posel D (1995) *A profile of poverty: Inequality and human development in South Africa.* Pretoria: Human Sciences Research Council.

Wilson F & Mamphela R (1989) *Uprooting poverty: The South African challenge, report for the Second Carnegie Inquiry into Poverty and Development in Southern Africa.* New York: WW Norton & Company.

Woolard I & Leibbrandt M (1999) *Measuring poverty in South Africa.* DPRU Working Paper No. 33, Development Policy Research Unit, University of Cape Town.

3 Delivery and disarray: the multiple meanings of land restitution

Cherryl Walker

Time to take stock

2005 marks the tenth anniversary of the establishment of the Commission on Restitution of Land Rights,[1] the institution tasked with the primary responsibility for settling land claims in terms of the Restitution of Land Rights Act of 1994. This is also the year that President Mbeki identified in his 'State of the Nation' address of 2002 as the final year for the programme: a crunch year, by the end of which all outstanding land claims were to be settled and this unwieldy programme of constitutionally mandated redress closed.

As several analysts anticipated, the advice on which President Mbeki based his 2002 projections has proved unreliable. Despite the Chief Land Claims Commissioner's reaffirmation of the target as recently as January 2005 (*The Mercury* 18.01.05), in February 2005 Land Affairs Minister Thoko Didiza quietly acknowledged that 'it will take an additional two years to redress the injustices of land seized under apartheid'.[2] The Commission is now working to a new deadline of 31 March 2008 (Commission 2005). Nevertheless, the rate at which land claims are being processed has certainly speeded up emphatically in recent years, while the considerable boost to the restitution allocation in the 2005/06 national Budget confirms that the Mbeki government is determined to wrap up the programme as quickly as possible. By early 2005, approaching 75 per cent of the nearly 80 000 land claims lodged with the Commission were reported as settled (calculated from DLA 2005). As a result, and in contrast to its beleaguered status in earlier years when claim settlements were few and far between, restitution enjoys something of the status of flagship for the state in its larger land reform programme (encompassing land redistribution and tenure reform as well).[3]

As the volume of settled claims has grown and the deadline of 2005 drawn nearer, so the media has begun to show a more critical, if selective, interest in restitution. At the same time, the body of independent research on land claims is growing. This means not only that more is known about the programme now than before, but also that more probing questions are being asked about its achievements – and, with greater public scrutiny, the disjunctures and tensions embedded in the ideal of restitution are becoming more apparent. One example is the unhappiness voiced publicly in February 2005 by the South African National Parks Authority about the threat posed to its conservation mandate by 37 unresolved and hitherto unpublicised claims on the Kruger National Park. 'National Parks cannot be turned into "The Lost City"...which is what communities see when they think of making money through land claims,' the *Mail & Guardian* (18–24.02.05) quoted a Parks spokesperson as saying. Another example is the investigation into the Khomani San restitution settlement of 1999 that the South African Human Rights Commission (SAHRC) undertook in late 2004 – a settlement that President Mbeki hailed at the time as signalling 'the rebirth of a people' (Commission 1999: 5), but the SAHRC described five years later as severely dysfunctional. According to Jody Kollapen, SAHRC Chairperson, 'What we found...was a community beset with many problems...their farms are in disarray' (*The Sunday Independent* 06.03.05).

2005 is, thus, an appropriate juncture at which to take stock of the restitution programme and tease out from the jumble of inconsistent reports on national delivery and local disarray an assessment of its achievements so far – the provisional nature of such an exercise necessitated by the incomplete status of the programme, the obstinately multidimensional character of the claims that it has unleashed, and significant gaps in the information. What is known about the state of land restitution in terms of its geographical distribution and historical reach? What has its contribution to redress and reconstruction in post-apartheid South Africa been? What might we learn from this hugely ambitious yet persistently marginal attempt by the state to compensate in the present the victims of land dispossession and forced removals in the past? How successful has it been – what, indeed, are the criteria by which success should be judged?

These are the large questions informing this review of the state of restitution in 2005. The discussion is organised into three sections. The first section provides an overview of the national numbers and discusses certain problems with an uncritical reliance on these figures as indicators of performance. The second section aims to ground the analysis in a more disaggregated account of the distribution of claims and the different types of settlement that have been reached. It highlights the significant but neglected urban dimensions of restitution and initiates a discussion on the fit between the current programme and the history of land dispossession that it is intended to address. In conclusion I point to the multiple meanings of land restitution and caution against what I term a 'misplaced agrarianisation' as the only lens through which to view its achievements. Restitution is not only about rural land reform and should not be judged simply by its contribution to this important national endeavour.

Given the limitations of space, the discussion is necessarily broad and important issues are neglected, including the extent of popular mobilisation around land, the range of responses from current landowners, and the worrying suggestions of corruption that have surfaced around land settlements in Mpumalanga.[4] The difficulties of community reconstruction once land has been restored to successful claimants are acknowledged but not discussed in any depth – this is a particularly important area, not simply for further research but, more urgently, for a serious and considered response by the state. The swirling debate on the merits and demerits of market-based land reform and the property clause in the Constitution is also dealt with only tangentially, although I raise a number of issues that are pertinent to it.

How much do the national numbers count?

Budgeting for restitution

The Restitution of Land Rights Act was the first piece of transformative legislation to be passed – amidst a standing ovation – by South Africa's newly democratic Parliament, in November 1994. At the launch of the Land Claims Commission a few months later, the African National Congress (ANC) Minister of Land Affairs, Derek Hanekom, declared triumphantly in a press release that restitution would put South Africa 'on the real road to reconciliation and reconstruction'. Redressing the massive land dispossessions suffered by black South Africans under white minority rule and protecting established (white) property rights were fiercely contested issues during the constitutional negotiations, leading to a compromise that tried, judiciously, to provide for both. In terms of this, people who had been dispossessed of land rights after the passage of the Natives Land Act in 1913, as a result of racially discriminatory laws and practices by the former state, could lodge claims against the new state for restitution. Restitution could take the form of restoration of the original land, provision of alternative land or other state benefits, or payment of financial compensation.[5] The public was given until 31 December 1998 to submit claims to the Commission for investigation, verification and settlement.

During the constitutional negotiations, activists, ideologues and pragmatists argued passionately the merits of various symbolically laden years – 1948, 1913, 1652 – as the most appropriate cut-off point for the history of land dispossession that the restitution programme should cover; this issue continues to simmer in political debate today. The special political and symbolic significance that land restitution has always carried in national debate has not, however, been matched by its ranking in terms of hard government priorities since 1994. As indicated by Table 3.1, the budget for land reform has always been tiny, while land restitution received no mention at all in President Mbeki's 2004 'State of the Nation' address, in which he outlined an extraordinarily detailed list of objectives and delivery targets for the ANC's third term of government (Mbeki 2004).

In 2005, however, the symbolic and the programmatic importance of land restitution appear to be moving closer together, as the state moves to wind up the programme. In this year's 'State of the Nation' address, President Mbeki invoked the fiftieth anniversary of the forced removal of Sophiatown in his opening remarks (Mbeki 2005a) and drew heavily on the 'covenant' represented by the constitutional agreement on restitution in defending his government's record on transformation in the parliamentary debate that followed (Mbeki 2005b: 5–6). At the same time, moving beyond rhetoric, Finance Minister Trevor Manuel approved a major injection of funds into the programme, with restitution garnering the bulk of the land reform budget.

Since 2001 the average annual increase in the restitution budget has been in the order of 54 per cent (National Treasury 2005). Although the total allocation of R9.9 billion for the period April 2005 to March 2008 falls well short of the R13 billion that Minister Didiza has said is required (*ThisDay*

20.10.04), it still represents a substantial investment in the process. Table 3.1 illustrates the minor place accorded the Department of Land Affairs (DLA) and its programmes in the national accounts since 1994, as well as the striking upward trend in the restitution allocation in recent years and its positive effects on the DLA budget.

Table 3.1 *Restitution budget, 1997/98–2005/06 (R'000s)*

Financial year	Restitution allocation (R'000's)	Share of DLA budget (%)	DLA budget as share of national Budget (%)
1997/98	64 147	9.3	0.20
1998/99	46 838*	5.9	0.35
1999/00	164 090	21.8	0.30
2000/01	265 138	29.6	0.36
2001/02	290 981	29.8	0.35
2002/03	394 265	36.6	0.36
2003/04	839 116	52.1	0.41
2004/05	1 156 144	56.9	0.55
2005/06	2 705 678	69.7	0.92

Sources: Walker 2001; National Treasury 2004, 2005
Note: * Actual expenditure, not allocation

Quantifying claim settlements

As the budget has increased and the Commission strained to meet its politically driven deadline, so the throughput of claims has gathered momentum. The official figures for settled claims have doubled in the past three years, rising from 29 887 at the end of January 2002 (Commission 2002) to 57 908 in March 2005 (Commission 2005); this figure likely excludes the approximately 2 500 claims found to be invalid by the end of 2002 (Commission n.d. [2003]).[6] This leaves a formidable but reassuringly bounded quantum of claims still to be processed – 17 866 in March 2005, of which 10 063 were reported as urban (which the Commission hoped to settle within 2005), and 7 803 rural (Commission 2005). The national statistics for the restitution programme in March 2005 are summarised in Table 3.2.

Table 3.2 *National progress on settling claims, April 1995–March 2005*

Settlement milestones	Amounts
Claim forms lodged with the Commission, April 1995 to cut-off date of 31.12.98	63 455
Adjusted number after several rounds of audit adjustments as of March 2005	79 696
Total number of claims settled in the first five years of the Commission	3 916
Total number of claims settled in the second five years of the Commission	53 992
Total number of settled claims as of March 2005	57 908
Total number of claims found not to be valid as of December 2002	2 544
Total number of claims still to be settled as of March 2005*	17 866
Total number of households benefiting from settled claims as of March 2005	170 485
Total hectares of land transferred through settled claims as of March 2005	854 444ha
Total value of financial compensation paid to claimants as of March 2005	R2.4 billion
Total value of restitution awards (land & financial compensation) as of March 2005	R4.7 billion

Sources: Commission 2001; Commission n.d. (2003); Commission 2005; DLA 2005
Note: * Subtracting the total number of settled, outstanding and invalid claims from the total number of lodged claims as reported by the Commission and DLA leaves a balance of 1 381 claims not accounted for.

Qualifying settlement claims

In her foreword to the Commission's Annual Report in 2004, Minister Didiza noted that 'we should all be delighted that 48 825 land claims have been settled during our lifetime, with more than 810 292 hectares of land transferred to more than 122 292 households' (Commission 2004: 3). But what do such aggregate numbers mean? How much do they count in terms of numbers and relevance for understanding the programme?

Although the Commission has undoubtedly made impressive progress in processing claims in recent years, the aggregate numbers should not be overly privileged in the analysis. Until now the national debate on restitution has concentrated on these apparently tangible measurements of performance (or non-performance). However, this information opens only a small window on the meaning of land restitution in post-apartheid South Africa. On their own the national statistics measure neither redress nor development and cannot be taken at face value as an accurate indicator of what is happening on the ground.

Even if completely reliable (which they are not), such figures say very little about the extent to which restitution is addressing the more subjective aspects of loss and redress and nothing about settlement quality. They also do not throw light on the relationship between restitution and broader developmental goals.

The concerns expressed primarily by civil society about the reliability of the data are real. As anyone who has tried to research the status of claims can attest, the overviews presented in annual reports and the Commission website do not mesh satisfactorily with the information in regional files or held by past and present officials, nor with reality on the ground. The reasons include weak information management systems and inadequate monitoring and evaluation capacity in both the Commission and the DLA. In part the poor quality of the data can be explained by the very pressure on these institutions to deliver macro-level results that demonstrate that claims are being settled at scale and land is being restored to 'the people' – not enough resources are devoted to rigorous data collection and management, while official performance is valued more in terms of quantity than quality. The combination of weak information systems and relatively high staff turnover means that both institutional and project memory is thin.

Recently the Programme for Land and Agrarian Settlement (PLAAS) at the University of the Western Cape, which has tracked the numbers over the years, pointed out that between February and September 2004 there was a 'dramatic downward revision' of the numbers of hectares reported as transferred through restitution in Mpumalanga province (from 240 042 to 97 938 hectares) – yet the total area transferred through restitution in this period remained exactly the same, at 810 292 hectares, that is, the downward movement of the Mpumalanga figures was offset by a serendipitously equivalent upward movement of the figures for five other provinces (PLAAS 2004: 4). It has been suggested that rather than risk revising figures that are already in the public domain, the Commission preferred to wait till further land-based settlements would justify new, higher and, it is to be hoped, more accurate national tallies (as were presented by the Commission to Parliament in March 2005).

A different order of problem lies with the way in which the data are collated and interpreted. Initially, considerable confusion existed around the definitions of 'claim' and 'claimant', with the numbers fluctuating depending on one's unit of analysis – the individual claim form (which could contain more than one claim), the claim as defined in law, the actual or projected number of households and/or of individuals standing to benefit from the claim, or the individual or group constituting the claimant (see Hall 2003.) Now a similar slipperiness applies to the definition of 'settlement', with comparable consequences in terms of uncertain accounting and premature conclusions. At what point is a claim settled and what does this mean in terms of the claim's status and national progress towards meeting the constitutional commitment to land restitution?

Many claims reported as settled in the national statistics are far from being resolved in the sense of land transferred or financial compensation paid or even, in some cases, negotiations finalised. For instance, in 2002 the Commission listed Knysna in a report to the World Summit on Sustainable Development on claims settled with land (Commission n.d. [2002]). The entry on Knysna reports that former victims of the Group Areas Act in this coastal town lodged a community claim in 1997 and 'after extensive negotiations an agreement was reached for the restoration of land rights to those claimants who opted for it and for other claimants...financial compensation' (Commission n.d. [2002]: 71). The settlement date is given as 25 February 2001, the day scheduled for a ceremonial cheque handover. However, this date did not represent the conclusion of the process. The initial negotiations had resulted in 1 079 claimants choosing financial compensation and 30 claimants settling for alternative land, but at the handover ceremony a third group of people complained to the Minister of Land Affairs that they had not known about the claim and, unusually, were allowed to join the process (Bohlin 2004). This resulted in the payout being delayed as well as the amount finally paid to claimants being reduced, as the original award was not recalculated but divided among the expanded group. Furthermore, by early 2005, four years after the claim was described as settled, the negotiations to acquire land owned by the Knysna municipality for the small group who had chosen land were in limbo. There were reportedly no state funds to purchase the land, its value had escalated wildly since 2001, and the municipality was reluctant to sell, arguing that this would unfairly benefit one small group.[7]

The national figures for beneficiaries and hectares can also not be read as proxy indicators of restitution's contribution to agrarian reform. The benefits of restored land cannot be assumed to devolve equally to all households, even less to all individual members of households who may be enumerated as beneficiaries of land-based settlements. The gender dimensions of restitution settlements are particularly hard to track, as the data are rarely disaggregated in gendered terms.[8] The extent to which land that has been restored is actually being used can also only be established on a case-by-case basis in the field. For instance at Cremin, a former 'black spot' near Ladysmith, KwaZulu-Natal (which I have described elsewhere as a relatively successful claim [Walker 2004]), a total of 85 claimants had title to their land restored in 1997/98, but by early 2004 only 17 had re-established a residential presence on the farm, of whom an even smaller number were attempting to work the land in a sustained manner (without government support). Another example of the gap between the overview numbers and practice on the ground is the claim by 101 former labour tenants to a portion of the Baynesfield Estate outside Pietermaritzburg. The settlement proposal approved by the Minister of Land Affairs in January 2000 involved the transfer of 265 hectares of Estate land to the 24 claimant households who wanted land, and financial compensation for the 77 households who preferred money (Tong 2002). By late 2004 no households were living on the Estate – yet DLA documents list this as a 2000 land-based settlement that has benefited 101 (not just 24) households (DLA n.d. [2003]).

The numbers also do not address the widespread concerns about the quality of the development plans drawn up for communities whose land is being restored, as well as the inadequacy of what is rather opaquely referred to as 'post-settlement support' for claimants once their land has been transferred and Commission officials have moved on. Drawing on an evaluation of six land-based restitution settlements in Limpopo, Tomkova notes:

> The widespread inexperience in land-use and agricultural production among restitution beneficiaries has significantly threatened the sustainability of restitution projects. Degeneration and depreciation of formerly productive land and commercially viable farms has been a disappointing trend...Inadequate infrastructure and access to services, decreasing outputs, stagnating production levels and indebtedness are commonly observed. (2004: 2)

All this is not to suggest that the national numbers have no analytical utility. However, they have to be treated cautiously as at best approximations of a much more fragmented reality. They also need to be disaggregated to more meaningful dimensions and regularly cross-checked against field-based information. As the following section indicates, that process has barely begun.

Grounding the numbers

The provincial dimensions of restitution

Table 3.3 gives a provincial breakdown of lodged claims in terms of their urban or rural classification in March 2001, the last date for which this level of detail has been obtained.[9] National figures reported for 2005 show that the proportion of urban to rural claims has been revised upwards, to 77 per cent of the total since then.[10]

Table 3.3 *Provincial breakdown for lodged claims*

	Total claims		Urban		Rural	
	No.	%	No.	%	No.	%
Eastern Cape	7 392	11	6 588	89	804	11
Free State	2 769	4	2 668	96	101	4
Gauteng	11 898	17	9 863	83	2 035	17
KwaZulu-Natal	14 807	22	11 997	81	2 810	19
Limpopo	5 607	8	1 494	27	4 113	73
Mpumalanga	6 436	9	1 226	19	5 210	81
North West	3 945	6	2 473	63	1 472	37
Northern Cape	3 200	5	1 200	38	2 000	62
Western Cape	11 938	18	11 343	95	595	5
Total as of March 2001*	67 992 [68 878]	100	48 852	72	19 140	28
National audit adjustment	4 983					
Total as of March 2003	72 975		69		31	
Claim adjustment 2003/05	6 721		No data		No data	
Total as of March 2005**	79 696	100	61 455	77	14 319	18

Sources: Commission 2001; Commission n.d. (2003); Commission 2005
Notes: * The Commission's 2001 figures show a discrepancy of 886 between its summary national total and its detailed rural/urban numbers, which total 67 992.
** The urban and rural totals are calculated from adding together settled and outstanding claims; this leaves a balance of 3 922 (5 per cent) unallocated claims when subtracted from the national total.

Table 3.4 summarises data presented by the Commission to Parliament in March 2005 on settled claims as of February 2005.

Table 3.4 *Provincial breakdown of settled claims as of February 2005*

Province	Claims settled (land & financial settlements)		Beneficiary households		Hectares transferred (land settlements)	
	No.	%	No.	%	No.	%
Eastern Cape	15 995	28	41 882	25	52 655	6
Free State	1 674	3	3 442	2	45 748	5
Gauteng	11 945	21	12 948	8	3 555	0.4
KwaZulu-Natal	10 593	18	28 358	17	209 560	25
Limpopo	1 350	2	23 145	14	134 604	16
Mpumalanga	1 572	3	27 778	16	99 662	12
North West	2 505	4	13 948	8	71 925	8
Northern Cape	1 953	3	5 722	3	233 634	27
Western Cape	10 321	18	13 262	8	3 101	0.4
Total	57 908	100	170 485	100	854 444	100

Source: Commission 2005

A comparison of Tables 3.3 and 3.4 shows that the number of claims reported as settled in the Eastern Cape by February 2005 is twice the number of claims reported as lodged in that province in 2001. This can be explained, at least in part, by the upward adjustment of numbers as a result of the various internal claim audits within the Commission, but the discrepancy illustrates the difficulty of working with the national statistics – it is not possible, for instance, to calculate the number of claims settled in each province by 2005 as a percentage of the number of claims reported as lodged in 2001, because the data sets are not consistent. What Table 3.4 does show is that the Eastern Cape currently has the largest number of settled claims, followed by Gauteng, KwaZulu-Natal and the Western Cape. The sequence for households that have benefited from the programme is, however, somewhat different. Eastern Cape still leads, by a considerable margin, followed by KwaZulu-Natal, but the next largest cohorts of beneficiaries are found in Mpumalanga and Limpopo, which is indicative of the community nature of the many rural claims in those provinces.

Because of data deficiencies, it is difficult to disaggregate settled claims in terms of their urban/rural distribution and settlement category (land or financial compensation) in provinces.[11] Table 3.5 sets out the national figures as of February 2005, while Table 3.6 shows Commission figures for rural and urban claims still requiring settlement.

Table 3.5 *National settled claims by locality and settlement type, February 2005*

	Land	Claim settlements Financial compensation	Other remedy	Total
Urban	15 035	33 880	2 477	51 392
Rural	3 217	3 283	16	6 516
Total	18 252	37 163	2 493	57 908
		Settlements as percentage of total claims		
Urban	26%	59%	4%	89%
Rural	6%	6%	0%	13%
Total	32%	65%	4%	100%

Source: Commission 2005 (appendix)

Table 3.6 *Claims requiring settlement, by regional office of the Commission, February 2005*

	Total claims		Urban		Rural	
	No.	%	No.	%	No.	%
Eastern Cape	3 834	21	2 869	29	965	12
Free State & Northern Cape	2 073	12	1 536	15	537	7
Gauteng & North West	723	4	71	0.7	652	8
KwaZulu-Natal	5 443	30	3 311	33	2 132	27
Limpopo	1 337	7	56	0.5	1 281	16
Mpumalanga	1 400	8	215	2	1 185	15
Western Cape	3 056	17	2 005	20	1 051	14
Total as of February 2005	17 866	100	10 063	100	7 803	100

Source: Commission 2005

As already noted, conclusions based on this high-level data must be treated with caution (more rural claims have still to be settled in the Eastern Cape in 2005 than were reported as lodged in 2001) and, given ongoing claim settlements, regularly reviewed against the updated numbers. Nevertheless, several points emerge about the profile of the restitution programme thus far.

The first point, although perhaps obvious, is worth making in view of the national expectations of restitution, and that is that the character of the restitution programme is not uniform across all nine provinces and a full evaluation requires engaging with the different provincial profiles. As could also be expected, claims in Gauteng and Western Cape have been predominantly urban (mainly the product of the Group Areas Act). Less expected, however, is the strongly urban character of claims in the more significantly rural Eastern Cape, Free State and KwaZulu-Natal. In recent years claim numbers in the Eastern Cape have been substantially boosted by adjustments to the numbers to reflect large clusters of claims in East London (East Bank and West Bank), as well as Port Elizabeth (notably the Port Elizabeth Land and Community Restoration Association[12] group claim) and Uitenhage (Kaba-Langa). In KwaZulu-Natal over 5 000 claims were lodged in the Cato Manor suburb of Durban alone. The two provinces with the largest number of rural claims are Mpumalanga and Limpopo. In 2004 the Chief Land Claims Commissioner indicated the magnitude of the settlement challenges here when he reported that up to 50 per cent of Northern Limpopo and Eastern Mpumalanga were under claim.[13] In April 2005 Glen Thomas, then Acting Director General for the DLA, further suggested that the DLA was worried about the potential impact of these rural claims on the agricultural economy, given that 'agriculture is the backbone of the economy in KwaZulu-Natal, Mpumalanga and Limpopo' (DLA 2005: slide 11).

The second point is that thus far most claim settlements, both rural and urban, have involved financial compensation, not land. Even more noteworthy, as of February 2005 more urban than rural claims had been settled with land, while slightly more rural settlements had been settled with financial compensation than with land – a striking inversion of common assumptions. This does not, of course, mean that the bulk of the land transferred to black ownership through the restitution programme has been urban. Given the nature of urban development and population densities, the amount of land involved in urban settlements is generally small; as more rural settlements come through, the rural proportion of land transfers will increase still further. Nor does it mean that the majority of households that have benefited from land restoration are urban, although the number of urban beneficiaries is not insignificant. Table 3.5 does, however, underscore the urban dimensions of restitution and the significance of financial compensation, issues which are returned to later.

Thirdly, thus far the contribution of restitution to broader land redistribution goals has been very limited. At 854 444 hectares (including urban land), its contribution is about one-quarter of the national figure of 3.5 million hectares transferred to black ownership through land reform by March 2005 (DLA 2005), although, as the remaining rural claims get settled, this could begin to shift. To date land restoration has been most extensive in the arid Northern Cape, a province that accounts for only five per cent of all lodged claims but, as of February 2005, held 27 per cent of all land transferred through restitution. The limited extent of land restoration before 2005 becomes even more evident when the Northern Cape statistics are unpacked to reveal that fully two-thirds of all land restored in that province – and almost one-fifth nationally – was accounted for by just three land-based settlements involving a few hundred households. All three of these claims have troubled social and economic histories: they are Riemvasmaak, involving 166 households and 74 562 hectares along the Orange River, and the interlocking Mier and Khomani San claims around the Kalahari Gemsbok Park, involving a couple of hundred households and a combined total of some 80 000 hectares of land adjoining the Park.[14]

Acknowledging the urban

Given South Africa's history of rural dispossession as well as extremely high levels of rural poverty, joblessness, and land-based conflict, rural claims certainly warrant prioritisation as part of a broader agrarian reform programme. However, the preceding figures demonstrate the significant urban dimensions of restitution, which mean that the programme cannot be analysed in terms of agrarian reform alone. Although making good use of the urban numbers in terms of aggregate throughput, the state tends to gloss the fact that so many settlements are urban and to conflate – inaccurately – urban claims with financial compensation. Some officials appear suspicious, even hostile, about the class and ethnic identity of urban claimants (about relative wealth and the presumed preponderance of 'Indian' or 'coloured' claimants over 'African'), feeding perceptions about a hierarchy of victimhood in which rural claimants warrant more state resources than urban.[15] In the academic literature, urban restitution is most commonly analysed in the niche areas of heritage and identity studies, which operate somewhat apart from – parallel to – research on policy development and the political economy of land and housing reform. To the extent that urban claims are discussed in the land and housing literature, it is usually not as a significant component of restitution that is deserving of analysis in its own right, but as a somewhat awkward addendum to a programme that is conceptualised as essentially about rural land reform.

In fact, although most urban claims have been settled by means of financial compensation, there have been some important attempts to meld urban restitution to community restoration projects and to low- and middle-income housing development. District Six in Cape Town is probably the most prominent and best-studied example, but other interesting projects deserving of further analysis include the Port Elizabeth Land and Community Restoration Association-led redevelopment initiative around central Port Elizabeth, the East Bank and West Bank settlements already mentioned in East London, and the Kipi and Burlington housing projects in Pinetown, Durban. Urban restitution is also interesting for the perspectives it affords on the restitution programme as a whole. Urban claims have highlighted most sharply the policy difficulties and dilemmas embedded in the programme's commitment to land restoration as the premier form of restitution. A detailed examination of the different ways in which urban claims have been accommodated since 1994 would also be revealing of the different political and social dynamics at work in urban reconstruction in the major urban centres.

The rural bias in the restitution programme is a product not only of current developmental imperatives but also of history and politics. That the population relocation policies of the apartheid state cut deeply through urban as well as rural communities and landscapes is well established, and a number of urban land struggles have acquired an iconographic status in the history of resistance to apartheid – District Six, Sophiatown (evidenced by President Mbeki's invocation in his 2005 'State of the Nation' address), and Umkhumbane in Cato Manor. However, those who worked most actively to secure land restitution as a constitutional commitment in the early 1990s were driven primarily by their experience in and knowledge of rural land dispossessions in the 1970s and 1980s (Walker forthcoming). Furthermore, at an early stage in the development of restitution policy, urban-sector specialists identified urban claims as a threat to, not an opportunity for, the reintegration of the apartheid city that forced removals had torn apart. These tensions were particularly acute in local authorities where prime vacant land was subject to claim, notably Cato Manor in Durban and District Six in Cape Town, and an early signal that the practice of land restitution was not always compatible with other public mandates, such as the provision of low-income housing, or with planners' blueprints.

At one stage consideration was given to excluding urban claims from the restitution process altogether, but this was rejected on equity grounds (see Walker forthcoming.) However, as a result of lobbying by certain alarmed urban planners, the restitution legislation allowed local authorities to apply to the Land Claims Court to exclude land restoration as a settlement option in localities where this was deemed not in the public interest. After 1994 both the Durban and Cape Town Metropolitan Councils tried to use this provision to subordinate land claims to their redevelopment plans for the strategically located sites of Cato Manor and District Six. The bruising legal and political battles that ensued tied up considerable Commission resources in its first term, with different outcomes in each site – in Cato Manor land claims were effectively sidelined from the redevelopment of the area for low-income housing, while in District Six a more formally claimant-centred process of urban renewal is still unfolding uncertainly (see, for example, Boyce 2003; Beyers 2004).

The historical dimensions of dispossession

In assessing the achievements of the restitution programme, one has to consider not only its geographical but also its historical reach – to what extent has it succeeded in reaching those who were eligible to claim in terms of the constitutional mandate hammered out in 1993? The answer requires extensive research and the following discussion must be considered provisional and exploratory.

No ready estimates exist for the scale of state-sanctioned land dispossessions between 1913 and 1948, but major forces at work in this period included the extension of white individual or corporate title over various tracts of black communal land that were not protected as 'native reserves', as well as the proclamation of conservation areas, including the Kalahari Gemsbok Park. Areas strongly impacted in this way include parts of Limpopo, Mpumalanga, the Northern Cape and northern KwaZulu-Natal.

The removals of the apartheid era are much better documented. The Surplus People Project (SPP) estimated that between 1960 and the early 1980s, when population relocation was at its most intense, some 3.5 million people (not households) were moved in seven major categories, while a further 1.9 million people were under threat of removal in 1983. (The SPP figures did not include the very large numbers moved in terms of 'betterment' planning in the reserves.[16]) The SPP estimates are summarised in Table 3.7. The totals and relative ranking for each category are merely indicative of the scale of dispossession under apartheid nationally, as removals began before 1960 and continued in varying degrees of intensity through the 1980s. The total number of people affected by 'black-spot' removals under apartheid was probably in the region of 700 000 (Walker 2003).

How well do the number and categories of post-1994 land claims correspond with this history?

Table 3.7 *Categories and scale of land dispossession, 1960–1983*

Category	People moved	%
Farmworkers and dwellers on white-owned farms	1 129 000	32
Landowners and tenants affected by the Group Areas Act	860 000	24
Residents of deproclaimed black townships situated in 'white' areas	730 000	21
Landowners and tenants on black- and church-owned 'black spots'	475 000	13
Residents of deproclaimed reserves affected by bantustan consolidation	139 000	4
Residents of cleared informal settlements	112 000	3
People moved for development, including forestry and strategic reasons	103 500	3
Total 1960–1983	3 548 500	100

Source: SPP 1983: 6

Clearly, the total number of households that have reportedly benefited from restitution to date (over 170 000 in early 2005) falls far short of the total number of households dispossessed of land rights for racially discriminatory purposes after 1913 – Table 3.7 suggests that upwards of 600 000 households were affected during the heyday of apartheid alone.[17] What is not certain at this stage is the impact of unsettled claims on this finding, in particular the nearly 8 000 rural claims. They are likely to boost the total number of beneficiary households substantially, but until the dimensions of each claim are known, the extent of this is unknown.

However, simply comparing the total numbers of restitution beneficiaries and dispossession victims is unsatisfactory, as the aggregate numbers do not compare actual dispossessions with actual settlements and may conceal major variations among the different categories of dispossession. Again, given the paucity of information on unsettled rural claims, it is premature to make confident projections about the eventual profile of rural restitution. What is probable is that former 'black-spot' communities will be disproportionately represented compared to former farm dwellers. Many black freehold communities were prominent in resisting relocation and campaigning for the restitution process (see Walker forthcoming). In addition, former black landowners and their descendants tend to be better educated and resourced than most rural dwellers, hence more likely to have known about and accessed the restitution programme in the mid-1990s.[18]

With regard to the historical reach of urban restitution, it is possible to be more categorical and conclude that this definitely falls far short of what was potentially possible. Most urban claims are individual claims stemming from the apartheid era and the application of the Group Areas Act and urban relocation policies. According to SPP, between 1960 and 1983 approximately 1 590 000 people were affected by these categories of dispossession. Assuming an average of six people per household, this translates into some 260 000 households – or, potentially, some 260 000 claims. However, as Tables 3.5 and 3.6 indicate, urban claims (settled and unsettled) amount to less than one-quarter (61 455) of this figure.

What requires further investigation is why so many potential claims were not lodged before the 1998 cut-off date. Critics have charged the Commission with not doing enough to make people aware of their rights and the cut-off date for lodging claims, although it did mount an extensive public awareness campaign in the latter part of 1998, which certainly led to a strong surge in lodged claims. For victims of forced removals who did know about the programme but still held back, anecdotal evidence suggests a variety of explanations, ranging from alienation and deep scepticism that the state would deliver, to reluctance to reopen old wounds, to political or moral discomfort with making such claims on the new, post-apartheid government.

Evaluating financial compensation

As Table 3.5 makes clear, the restitution programme has leaned heavily towards the payment of financial compensation. Since the late 1990s there has been a lively debate within the Commission about what has come to be called, disparagingly, 'cheque-book restitution' – even as the Commission has relied on cash settlements to move the national tallies along. For most land activists cash settlements compromise the very essence of restitution as land reform. Thus Nkuzi, a prominent land-sector non-governmental organisation (NGO) in Limpopo, responded to President Mbeki's invocation of the Sophiatown removals in his 'State of the Nation' address in February 2005 in the following terms:

> The President did not mention that those removed from Sophiatown, hundreds of whom lodged land claims, have not had their land returned. While the validity of their claims was undeniable the government decided that 'restoration of the land was not feasible…and alternative land within the same magisterial district was not available'…and therefore they offered only financial compensation to the claimants…If the removal of Sophiatown sent a message in the strongest terms that 'South Africa did not belong to all who live in it' and was a 'triumph for white supremacy', what does the failure to return those removed signify? What is the unequivocal message sent by the government of today when those dispossessed receive no land and the settlement of Triomf remains in place? (Nkuzi 2005: 9)

The issues at stake are, however, rather more complex than the standard criticisms of cash compensation suggest. Undoubtedly the unaccustomed windfall of relatively large sums of money (R17 500 and upwards)[19] can be quickly dissipated in poor households, without producing lasting benefit or a sense of closure around the injustices of the past. Undoubtedly, too, the option of money rather than land does not constitute the first choice for many claimants. In Cato Manor, for instance, several hundred former landowners objected to the court application by the Metropolitan Council to rule out land restoration. Most were driven by strong feelings about the injustices of the Group Areas Act and vivid memories of the community that they had lost.[20] However, as the difficult negotiations to acknowledge land claims in the redevelopment of Cato Manor wore on, many claimants resigned themselves, some in great bitterness, to financial compensation as the most pragmatic resolution – the Cato Manor being redeveloped on the hills where the market gardens and landmarks of their youth once stood was not the Cato Manor that they recalled.

However, as the urban planners who lobbied against the automatic presumption of land restoration argued, in many cases restoring land may not be feasible or desirable from a broader developmental perspective – land use, land values, zoning priorities and regional economies have not stood still in the intervening years. Clearly, as the Cato Manor case demonstrates, the decisions around what is feasible involve political, not simply technical, policy choices. The point is, however, that at times land restitution is not the only public interest at issue. Similar conundrums are coming to the fore in the rural context as well, around claims on conservation areas and, more controversially, on some highly productive, capital-intensive agricultural enterprises.

Furthermore, financial compensation does not always represent a coerced or inferior option for claimants (although they may complain about the amount of money received). In the rural Nazareth claim in KwaZulu-Natal, claimants divided over the choice between land restoration and financial compensation in interestingly gendered ways. Here a minority of claimants, mainly men, insisted on getting land while the majority, mainly older women, regarded money as more developmentally appropriate at their stage of life. They did not wish to relocate to undeveloped land again, but wanted to invest their restitution awards in their houses in the better-serviced closer settlement where they had been living for the past 20 years (Walker 2000). Bohlin's (2004) analysis of two very different Western Cape communities where financial compensation was paid (Riebeeck Kasteel and Knysna) describes the complex and context-specific dynamics shaping the different responses of individual claimants to their awards – as signifiers of both loss and gain, recognition and marginalisation, closure and further contestation.

The dominant discourse on restitution is heavily developmental. However, the motives for lodging a claim are not necessarily primarily economic. Furthermore, while the importance of land for livelihoods is a major argument driving the wider land reform programme, the linkages between land rights and individual or household well-being are neither inherent nor automatic.

The multiple meanings of restitution

Since 1995 the restitution programme has travelled an erratic path, alternatively lauded for its contribution to redress and redistributive justice, condemned for the limitations of its reach and berated or praised for its record of delivery. The discussion in this chapter suggests that major disjunctures lie at the heart of the programme – between its symbolic significance and its developmental reach as well as between the need to invest time and resources in developing robust, case-specific settlements and the political imperative to show delivery at scale. The particular symbolic significance of land restitution in national political debate – as marker of dispossession in the past and redistribution in the present – has not been matched by its consistently low ranking in terms of the ANC's developmental priorities. Restitution in practice, as opposed to restitution as an ideal, has found itself competing for budgets, attention, even legitimacy on occasion, in relation to other public goals.

What is clear is that compared to the ambitions vested in restitution in the early 1990s, its achievements have thus far been modest indeed. Historical reach, developmental impact, contribution to land reform – in all these areas the programme has fallen far short of what was hoped. The goals of social justice, redress and rebuilding communities have turned out to be more elusive than previously imagined. However, I am also arguing that more work is needed to deepen our understanding of what restitution has achieved, and that 2005 is an opportune time to reassess the criteria by which the programme is being judged.

Part of the challenge lies in the extraordinarily dense tangle of issues that restitution encompasses, dealing as it does not only with rural and urban histories of dispossession and reconstruction, but also with the intersection of the symbolic and the material, of rights and development, of the local as well as the national. In order to analyse restitution as a complex whole, one has to appreciate that it operates very differently at different levels. The measures of success that circulate in national political debate are not always congruent with those operating at the regional or sectoral level, where more hard-nosed questions about land-use impacts are likely to be asked by non-claimants, and not only those opposed in principle to restitution. At the level of individual claims, the assessment of success or failure, the meanings of redress and of reconstruction, are even more diverse and context-specific. There is no single 'community' or claimant response, no single moment of restitution either – hence no single, unilinear assessment of success or failure can be made. All the evidence points to multiple responses, depending on the location of the respondents in terms of age, gender, geographic location, class, social history, economic options and levels of social integration.

Misplaced agrarianisation?

In the last, heavy days of apartheid Colin Murray proposed that apartheid-era population relocation policies constituted a form of 'displaced urbanisation' – a term used to describe 'the concentration of black South Africans…in huge rural slums which are politically in the Bantustans and economically on the peripheries of the established metropolitan labour markets' (1988: 111). What I want to propose in conclusion is that, in large part in reaction to this grim history, the restitution programme has suffered from a kind of 'misplaced agrarianisation' in its original conceptualisation, and now in its evaluation. This article has highlighted a number of areas where this operates – the underestimation of the urban dimensions of restitution, the emphasis on measuring the success of restitution principally in terms of land-based development, and also what might be described as a sort of developmental moralism which insists that claimants ought to choose land restoration and that anything else is a betrayal of restitution principles.

The disintegration of the Khomani San settlement is an extreme illustration of the inadequacy of land restoration as a panacea for the far larger problems of historical marginalisation and social and economic dispossession, and the restitution programme cannot be expected to address these on its own.

Notes

1 Commission on Restitution of Land Rights is the formal name for this body but it is commonly called the Land Claims Commission. This, or the abbreviated 'Commission', is the term I use.
2 South African Press Association, report on media briefing by Minister of Agricultural and Land Affairs, 17.02.05, Sabinet online, Cape Town.
3 South Africa's post-1994 land reform programme comprises three main sub-programmes: land restitution for those who were dispossessed of land rights as a result of racially-discriminatory laws and practices after 1913; land redistribution for the landless and land-hungry who do not qualify for restitution; and tenure reform for those whose tenure is insecure, primarily workers and their families living on white-owned farms and residents on communal land in the former bantustans. The state has set itself a target of transferring 30 per cent of white-owned commercial farmland into black ownership by 2015 through land redistribution and restitution. As of March 2005 only 4.3 per cent of the total had been transferred nationally (DLA 2005). This total obscures significant regional variation; it also includes non-agricultural land from the urban component of restitution and former state land. The Land Claims Commission currently operates as a semi-autonomous branch within the Department of Land Affairs (DLA). Land redistribution and tenure reform are not discussed here, although a full assessment of land reform requires an integrated analysis of all three sub-programmes.
4 The Regional Land Claims Commissioner for Mpumalanga was suspended in late 2004 pending an investigation into these allegations. See Agriculture and Land Affairs Portfolio Committee 2005.
5 The Natives Land Act of 1913 scheduled seven per cent of the country as 'native reserves' and provided for the 'release' of additional land for these areas. The 1936 the Native Land and Trust Act set the total area for the reserves at approximately 13 per cent of South Africa.
6 The validation campaign involved the Commission screening all claim forms lodged with it to weed out duplicates and non-claims, establish information gaps and clarify the number of valid claims in the system.
7 Bohlin 2004, pers. comm.
8 My thanks to Ruth Hall for confirming this point.
9 The distinction between urban and rural is not always easy to draw. The initial classification is made in regional offices, generally in terms of the locality of the dispossessed land.

10 All percentages are rounded to the nearest whole number, and should be treated as illustrative of approximate proportions; thus some totals equal 101 per cent.

11 Hall (2003) provides a detailed assessment of rural, land-based settlements.

12 The Port Elizabeth Land and Community Restoration Association is a claimant organisation which organised individual claimants effectively from the early 1990s to work for the restoration and redevelopment of vacant land from which they had been removed under the Group Areas Act.

13 'Blacks claiming 20% of farms,' 07.01.04. Available at http://www.news24.com/ News24/South_Africa/News. Accessed 08.01.04.

14 Claimants also received access to 50 000ha in the Park, which remained a conservation area (Commission 1999; Tong 2002).

15 I have witnessed this in the negotiations around the restitution framework for Cato Manor, Durban.

16 The 'betterment' issue is complex and not addressed here. There were questions whether these removals qualified under the Restitution of Land Rights Act, and initially the Commission discouraged such claims. The Chatha claim in the Eastern Cape was a prominent exception; its successful settlement led to unsuccessful calls for the claim period to be reopened to accommodate further 'betterment' claims.

17 This number is merely illustrative, calculated by dividing 3.5 million people by six (assuming an average of six people per household). Once descendants of those dispossessed in the apartheid era are factored into the equation, the number of beneficiary households per claim would multiply still further.

18 Between 1960 and 1983 a total of 247 black-owned farms, encompassing some 150 000ha, were removed as 'black spots' (Walker 2003); these communities comprised both landowners and tenants.

19 The amount awarded to individual claimants has varied hugely, depending on the value of the original land right and the quality of legal or other representation. Developing consistent policy on the valuation of historical land rights was a major challenge for the Commission. Since 2000 there has been a move towards a 'Standard settlement offer' to individual claimants within groups sharing similar histories of dispossession, as a way of expediting the process.

20 This section draws on my personal observations of the process. I was Regional Land Claims Commissioner for KwaZulu-Natal from 1994 to 1999.

References

Agriculture and Land Affairs Portfolio Committee (South Africa) (2005) Irregularities in land restitution in Mpumalanga: Briefing by Minister. Unpublished report, 10.03.05, Parliament, Cape Town.

Beyers C (2004) State capacity and land restitution's 'rights-communities': The District Six case. Paper presented at Conference on Ten Years of Democracy in Southern Africa, Queen's University, Kingston, 2–5.05.04.

Bohlin A (2004) A price on the past: Cash as compensation in South African land restitution, *Canadian Journal of African Studies* 38(3).

Boyce B (2003) Linking land restitution and urban development: lessons for restructuring the apartheid city from the Kipi land claim, Durban Metropolitan Area. Unpublished Masters thesis, Development Studies, University of Natal, Durban.

Commission (Commission on Restitution of Land Rights, South Africa) (1999) *Annual report April '98 – March '99*. Pretoria: Commission on Restitution of Land Rights.

Commission (2001) *Annual report April 2000 – March 2001*. Pretoria: Commission on Restitution of Land Rights.

Commission (n.d. [2002]) *Restitution and sustainable development. A catalogue of settled restitution claims*. Pretoria: Commission on Restitution of Land Rights.

Commission (2002) *Restitution statistics*. Available at http://www.land.pwv.gov.za/restitution/updated. Accessed 20.05.02.

Commission (n.d. [2003]) *Report on the validation campaign to the Minister of Agriculture and Land Affairs and the Land Restitution trustees and Belgian Embassy*. Pretoria: Commission on Restitution of Land Rights.

Commission (n.d. [2004]) Cumulative statistics on settled restitution claims, 1995 – 31 March 2004. Unpublished document. Pretoria: Commission on Restitution of Land Rights.

Commission (2004) *Annual report 2003 – 2004*. Pretoria: Commission on Restitution of Land Rights.

Commission (2005) National implementation plan. Restitution high drive 2008. Presentation to the Portfolio Committee on Agriculture and Land Affairs, 18.03.05. Pretoria: Commission on Restitution of Land Rights.

DLA (Department of Land Affairs, South Africa) (n.d. [2003]) List of land restitution claims settled with the developmental component nationally. Unpublished memorandum. Pretoria: DLA.

DLA (2005) Presentation to the Select Committee on the 2005 Strategic Plan by Mr Glen Thomas, Acting Director General, 04.04.05. Pretoria: DLA.

Hall R (2003) *Rural restitution*. Evaluating Land and Agrarian Reform in South Africa series, No. 2, PLAAS, University of the Western Cape.

Mbeki T (2004) Address of the President of South Africa, Thabo Mbeki, to the first joint sitting of the third democratic Parliament. Cape Town, 21.05.04.

Mbeki T (2005a) Address of the President of South Africa, Thabo Mbeki, to the second joint sitting of the third democratic Parliament. Cape Town, 11.02.05.

Mbeki T (2005b) Response of the President of South Africa, Thabo Mbeki, to the debate of the State of the Nation Address, National Assembly, Cape Town: 17 February 2005.

Murray C (1988) Displaced urbanisation. In J Lonsdale (ed.) *South Africa in question*. London: James Currey.

National Treasury (South Africa) (2004) *2004 Estimates of national expenditure*. Pretoria: National Treasury.

National Treasury (2005) *2005 Estimates of national expenditure*. Pretoria: National Treasury.

Nkuzi Development Agency (2005) President skips land. In *Nkuzi Times* 25.02.05.

PLAAS (Programme for Land and Agrarian Settlement) (2004) *Umhlaba wethu*. Bellville, Cape Town: PLAAS.

SPP (Surplus People Project) (1983) *Forced removals in South Africa*. The SPP Reports, Vol. 1. Cape Town: SPP.

Tomkova J (2004) Post-settlement challenges of land reform in South Africa. Paper presented at Conference on Ten Years of Democracy in Southern Africa, Queen's University, Kingston, 2–5.05.04.

Tong M (2002) Lest we forget. The restitution digest on administrative decisions. Unpublished manuscript.

Walker C (2000) Relocating restitution, *Transformation* 44: 1–16.

Walker C (2001) Evolving government policies on land reform, 1999–2001. Unpublished report. Johannesburg: Centre for Development Enterprise.

Walker C (2003) Report on 'black spot' removals for the Legal Resources Centre, Pretoria. Unpublished report. Pretoria: Legal Resources Centre.

Walker C (2004) 'We are consoled' – Reconstructing Cremin, *South African Historical Journal*, 51: 199–223.

Walker C (forthcoming, 2005) The limits to land reform, *Journal of Southern African Studies*, 31(4).

4 Assessing the constitutional protection of human rights in South Africa during the first decade of democracy

Karthy Govender

Introduction: an assessment of universally-recognised fundamental rights and freedoms

Albie Sachs, writing extrajudicially, pithily captured the foundational principle upon which the South African Bill of Rights is premised, when he stated, 'We do not want bread without freedom, nor do we want freedom without bread; we want bread and we want freedom' (Sachs 2000: 1389).

After the atrocities and excesses of Second World War, it became apparent that public international law must, in addition to regulating the relationships between sovereign states, also protect, promote and monitor the observance of human rights within states. The Universal Declaration of Human Rights (UDHR) was an aspirational document that sought to lay down minimum norms of morality and decency that each sovereign state should respect in its relationship with persons within its territory. Not only did it protect fundamental civil and political rights such as the right to vote and participate in the democratic process, the freedom of speech, and the right to be treated equally, it also sought, by insisting that people are entitled to living conditions consistent with human dignity, to entrench respect for social and economic rights.

There is no unanimity on the specific sets of rights that would constitute universally accepted fundamental rights, freedoms and civil liberties. However, over the years a core content has developed, largely as a consequence of multilateral treaties. Most of these instruments have been interpreted and developed over a period of time. We have had access to this knowledge, both at the time of drafting our Constitution and when interpreting its provisions in relation to specific situations.

The two principal covenants in this regard are the International Covenant on Civil and Political Rights[1] and the International Covenant on Economic, Social and Cultural Rights.[2] Member states who are signatories are required to submit reports to the Human Rights Committee on measures that they have adopted to give effect to the rights recognised in the covenants.

Most liberal democracies regard the protection of civil and political rights as foundational to a constitutional democracy. These rights include the right to life; the right not to be subject to torture, cruel, inhuman or degrading treatment or punishment; the right not to be held in slavery; the right to liberty and the security of the person; the right when lawfully deprived of liberty to be treated with dignity; the right to be treated equally before courts and tribunals; the right not to be found guilty of a criminal offence regarding acts or omissions which did not constitute criminal conduct at the time of commission or omission; the right to privacy; the right to freedom of thought, conscience and religion; the right to express oneself and hold opinions; the right to assemble peacefully; the right to associate with others; the right to marry and found a family; the right of the child to protection without discrimination; and the right to be treated equally and not to be subject to any discrimination. These are sometimes referred to as first generation rights.

Socio-economic rights or second generation rights were, for some time, the subject of debate and disagreement as to whether they were justiciable and enforceable, given the direct budgetary implications of their enforcement. The covenant on economic, social and cultural rights recognises the right to work; the right to just and favourable conditions at work; the right to form and join trade unions; the right to social security; the right of everyone to adequate standards of living including the right to be free from hunger; the right to enjoy the highest attainable standard of physical and mental health; the right to free primary education and access to higher education; and the right to participate in the cultural life of the society.

In addition, special instruments have been enacted to give greater focus to certain rights in the main covenants – the Convention on the Elimination of All Forms of Racial Discrimination, the Convention on the Elimination of All Forms of Discrimination against Women, the Convention Relating to the Status of Refugees, the Convention on Torture and Other Cruel, Inhuman or Degrading Treatment or Punishment, and the Convention on the Rights of the Child are examples.

The first two generations of human rights focused primarily on the individual. A set of rights is afforded to the individual to ensure that he or she is able to engage in the democratic process, develop and grow, be reasonably content and live a life free from want. A subsequent set of rights, which inure to a collection of individuals or to society as a whole, has developed and is sometimes referred to as third generation rights – an example of this would be the right to a clean and healthy environment. This is a right that will benefit the entire society and is asserted as a collective right.

Ideological and economic differences resulted in serious chasms between the developed world and the developing world in their prioritisation and championing of the different categories of rights (Henkin 1995). The developing world charged that the developed world, by exclusively supporting civil and political rights, was impeding the necessary growth in social and economic development of its people. The developed world accused the developing world of using the need to realise social and economic rights as a pretext for failing to respect and comply with the civil and political rights of its people, and thus preventing their effective participation in governance. However, over time, this chasm narrowed and there is now a general acceptance that there is no hierarchy of rights, no set of rights enjoying greater priority over others, and that there is no inherent conflict between the different sets or generations of rights (Henkin 1995). Most democratic states have acceded to both covenants and most regional instruments recognise the necessity of ensuring the progressive realisation of socio-economic rights so that people enjoy standards of living that are consonant with human dignity and the need to respect basic civil and political rights.

This is not to say that there is unanimity as to the set of rights that should be included in every constitution. Established democracies differ as to whether capital punishment should be prohibited or permitted, whether a women ought to have the relatively unfettered right to terminate her pregnancy during the early periods of gestation, and on other issues. But as indicated earlier there are significant areas of consensus.[3]

In the decades following the signing of the UDHR, South Africa legally embraced apartheid and racism which were fundamentally at odds with the values of the declaration. This system was based on excluding black persons from the political process, denying them effective civil and political rights, suppressing dissent, and distributing and spending state resources in a racially discriminatory manner to optimally promote the interests and rights of white people whilst limiting and retarding the development of black people. South Africa, during this period, was thus one of the most conspicuous and consistent violators of these developing norms of human rights. In addition, dissent and opposition to apartheid were met with repression and persecution. Bannings of individuals and organisations, detention without trial, the suppression of opposition voices, and later extrajudicial killings and violence were used in a vain attempt to shore up apartheid and emasculate resistance to it. The apartheid policy, itself a violation of human dignity, was supported by measures and means that directly violated basic and fundamental human rights.

Drafting the final Constitution and commitment to the protection of universally-accepted fundamental rights and freedoms

The predicted race-based cataclysmic conflict was avoided when the National Party and its allies negotiated the Interim Constitution in 1993 with the liberation movements and their allies. In effect this Constitution was a peace treaty, which allowed for a cession of hostilities and a transfer of power to a democratically elected government.

It was agreed that the unelected negotiating parties would draft the Interim Constitution, which would come into effect in April 1994 with the advent of the new democratic government. This Constitution would remain in place for two years while the democratically elected legislature, acting as a Constitutional Assembly, would draft the final Constitution. A vital aspect of the settlement was that the new Constitution had to be consistent with a set of constitutional principles agreed to by the negotiators and listed in schedule 4 of the Interim Constitution. The newly created Constitutional Court was given the task of determining whether the Constitution drafted by the democratically elected legislature was consistent with constitutional principles. Thus a group of judges was given the awesome responsibility of determining whether a constitution drafted by the democratically elected representatives of the people of South Africa was consistent with a set of pre-existing principles. The Constitutional Assembly was thus not given an open-ended discretion to adopt the constitutional dispensation of its choice.

At the time the Constitution was drafted, the lessons of history were that a supreme constitution which gives adequate power to democratically elected leaders, while simultaneously structuring and confining the exercise of that power in order to prevent abuses, is the most viable that we have been able to come up with. It is extremely unlikely that, given the background in reaction to which the drafters were drafting, a totalitarian system, theocratic order, or a system based on parliamentary sovereignty would have been the preferred option in developing and sustaining a viable constitutional democracy.

Most of the basic structures that form the basis of our constitutional order, such as regular elections, multiparty democracy, open and transparent government, a supreme Constitution, an independent judiciary, separation of powers, commitment to the principle of equality and the protection and entrenchment of human rights, would have been included by the Constitutional Assembly irrespective of the imperative to comply with the constitutional principles. However, there would have been keen debate about the nature and extent of powers to the provinces, the need to accommodate traditional leaders and other specific issues.

Constitutional Principle II[4] insisted upon an expansive and justiciable Bill of Rights in the new Constitution by providing:

> Everyone shall enjoy all universally accepted fundamental rights, freedoms and civil liberties, which shall be provided for and protected by entrenched and justiciable provisions in the Constitution…

A pariah state, which regularly and constantly acted in contradiction to basic international human rights norms, was required to transform into a constitutional democracy where everyone enjoyed the protection of all fundamental rights, freedoms and civil liberties. The purpose of this paper is to assess the distance travelled by the country on this journey.

The main visions within the Bill of Rights

The South African Bill of Rights, based on international covenants, regional instruments and principles of customary international law, is an amalgam of the three generations of rights described earlier. There are two discernible visions in the document.

There is the constraining vision, which demarcates the boundaries of the rights into which neither the state nor (in appropriate instances) private persons may stray. Most of these rights can be described as civil and political rights and include the right to be treated equally; the right to human dignity; the right to life; the right to freedom and security; the right not to be subject to slavery, servitude and forced labour; the right to privacy; the freedom of religion; the freedom of expression and assembly; the freedom of association; the right to vote and participate in the political process; the rights of citizenship; the freedom of movement; the freedom of trade; the rights to fair labour practice; the right to property; the right to just administrative action; and the rights of accused, detained and arrested persons.

While these rights constrain state action, they often require the state to proactively create and safeguard the environment in which these rights can optimally be enforced. The responsibility of the state may vary from passing legislation to setting up administrative structures. For instance, the right to vote requires legislation, an impartial and independent electoral commission, an environment that is conducive to free and fair voting, and a fair and efficient voting and vote counting process. These rights often require more than passive non-interference on the part of the state.

The egalitarian vision requires the state to take reasonable legislative and other measures within available resources to improve the quality of life of all persons, and free the potential of all. The South African Bill of Rights protects a number of socio-economic rights such as the right of access to housing; the right to have access to healthcare, food, water and social security; various rights of the child; the right to basic education and the right to further education, which is to be made progressively available by the state.

In addition, a number of rights that are enjoyed in consort with others are also protected. The right to an environment that is not harmful to one's health or well-being is protected and so is the right to use one's language and to participate in and belong to cultural, religious and linguistic communities.

The reach and application of the Bill of Rights

The mandate given to the constitutional drafters was to entrench all universally accepted fundamental rights, freedoms and civil liberties, and to draft a bill of rights that was relevant to South Africa. The result was an expansive and ambitious Bill of Rights of wide application. However, operational provisions and limitations upon rights can impact significantly on the scope and ambit of substantive rights.

The legislature, executive, judiciary and all organs of state are explicitly bound by all the provisions of the Bill of Rights (section 8 [1]). Organs of state include all departments of state, and any other functionary, exercising a public power or performing a public function in terms of legislation (section 239). In *De Lille v Speaker of the National Assembly*, the courts held that all the actions of the national legislature are subject to the Constitution. Parliament was not allowed to claim supreme power subject to limitations on that power imposed by the Constitution. The founding premise is that the Constitution is supreme and law or conduct of Parliament that is inconsistent with the Constitution is invalid to the extent of the inconsistency. In setting aside the suspension of Ms De Lille by Parliament, the courts held that the process in terms of which the complaint against Ms De Lille was heard was procedurally unfair and that her freedom of expression as a parliamentarian was unjustifiably infringed. Parliament has to comply with all the provisions of the Bill of Rights when disciplining its members. Its constitutional responsibility was not restricted to passing laws that were consistent with the Constitution.

The Bill of Rights binds the executive even in its interaction with foreigners. In *Mohamed v President of RSA*,[5] officials of the state had arranged the removal of the applicant from South Africa to stand trial in the US for serious offences committed against US and Kenyan citizens in Kenya. South Africa failed to obtain an assurance from the US government that it would not impose the death penalty on Mohamed if he was convicted. The death penalty is a competent sentence in New York and not constitutionally permitted in South Africa. The Constitutional Court held that by extraditing Mohamed without receiving such an assurance the state had acted unconstitutionally. It reasoned that the state was bound to act in accordance with the Bill of Rights which provided that Mohamed had a right not to be put to death by the state. Extraditing him to a country where the death penalty was a competent verdict, without any undertaking that it would not be imposed, meant that Mohamed's rights were disregarded.

In addition, certain provisions of the Bill of Rights may, depending on the nature of the right and the nature of the duty required by the right, impose obligations on private and juristic persons.

Certain rights, such as the right not to be subject to unfair discrimination on the categories listed, are made explicitly horizontal and capable of being enforced by one individual against another private or juristic person. Thus, in addition to redefining the basis upon which the state and public institutions may interact with the individual, this Bill of Rights allows for the norms which regulate private relationships to be reappraised to bring them into line with the values and morality entrenched in Chapter 2.

The African customary rule of primogeniture, which only allowed the eldest male heir to inherit the deceased's estate, was held unconstitutional as it amounted to unfair discrimination against women.[6] Under the rule of primogeniture, in the case of *Bhe v Magistrate, Khayelitsha and Others* the deceased's father would have inherited the estate in preference to the daughters of the deceased. The Constitutional Court set aside the rule and as an interim measure declared that the provisions of the Intestate Succession Act would also be applicable to persons in the position of the applicants. The applicants were thus able to rely on the Bill of Rights to change legal principles that discriminated against them, alter the legal relationship between them, their deceased father and the surviving male heir, and as a consequence were able to retain the family home.

By extending the application and reach of the Bill of Rights to relationships beyond that between the state and the individual, the Constitution seeks to radiate the values of the Bill of Rights into private and semi-private relationships such as that which occurred in the Bhe case. One of the larger objects of the Bill of Rights is to create an open and democratic society based on human dignity, freedom and equality. In order to attain this broader objective, courts are required, when interpreting any law or when developing the common law or customary law, to promote the spirit, purport and objects of the Bill of Rights (section 39 [2]). If we are to attain the vision that we have set ourselves, then the Bill of Rights has to reach into the relationship between the state and individuals, and in some instances, between individuals themselves. The decisions changing the common law and customary law complement and supplement the process of ensuring that state action is consistent with the Constitution.

Limiting rights

Rights in a bill of rights cannot be used to unacceptably infringe the rights of others or to unreasonably and unjustifiably impede the state in its legitimate governance functions. If the exercise of rights impedes and retards legitimate state action, then a bill of rights can become a charter for the abuse of rights. In order to prevent this, most modern bills of rights contain limitation clauses that allow for rights to be limited in appropriate circumstances.

The South African Bill of Rights has a general limitation clause which is applicable to all rights. A limitations clause has to carefully define the conditions under which the state may limit rights. If the limitation clause is drafted too widely then the state may limit rights unjustifiably, and thus adversely affect the integrity of the bill of rights. If it is drafted too narrowly, then the state may not be able to act and limit rights when the interests of society require it to do so. The correct balance needs to be struck.

Any person seeking to set aside law or conduct on the basis that it infringes a right, must establish that the measure being impugned is inconsistent with the Constitution. This involves a two-stage process. Firstly, an assessment has to be made as to whether any of the rights have been infringed and, if so, secondly, whether that infringement is reasonable and justifiable in an open and democratic society. Inconsistency is established if a right is infringed and it is not reasonable and justifiable. The party asserting the infringement has the onus of proving the first stage and the party seeking to uphold the law or conduct has to prove the justification.[7]

In *S v Makwanyane*,[8] the Constitutional Court interpreting the limitations clause in the Interim Constitution required any limitation of right to be proportionate and achieve an appropriate balance between different interests. The Court held that in the balancing process, regard must be had to the nature of the right and its importance to an open and democratic society and to the purpose for which the right is limited and its importance to an open and democratic society. Consideration must be taken of the extent of the limitation, its effectiveness and whether the societal objectives could reasonably be achieved through other means that are less damaging of the right. In effect, the Court assesses the importance of the right against the purpose of the limitation and assesses whether the means chosen to achieve the objective is proportionate and reasonable.

The drafters of the final Constitution closely followed the suggestions made in *S v Makwanyane* when drawing up the limitations clause now contained in section 36 of the Constitution. Under section 36, limitations can only be justified if they are in terms of a law of general application and are reasonable and justifiable. If the limitation is not authorised by a law, then the limitations clause cannot be relied upon. In *August v Electoral Commission*,[9] the Independent Electoral Commission did not register prisoners, thus effectively disenfranchising them. As electoral legislation did not sanction this, the Commission was not allowed to rely on the limitations clause to justify their infringement of the right of prisoners to vote and was ordered to make appropriate arrangements for prisoners to vote. However, the substantive enquiry is whether the limitation is reasonable and justifiable.

In *Christian Education South Africa v Minister of Education*,[10] a collective of private schools challenged section 10 of the South African Schools Act which prohibited corporal punishment in all schools, including private or independent schools. The applicants argued that the prohibition violated a number of rights, including their right to freedom of religion as the Bible sanctioned, and in some instances advocated, moderate corporal chastisement. The court 'assumed without deciding' that the law violated the freedom of religion, but held it was reasonable and justifiable. The prohibition of corporal punishment was part of a national plan to transform and bring the education system into line with the Constitution. Further, there was a general obligation on the state to reduce the levels of violence and protect minors. The prohibition of corporal punishment symbolises the commitment of the state to protecting the dignity as well as the physical and emotional integrity of learners. While the freedom of religion is of central importance, the actual impact on the right was limited. Schools were not allowed to administer corporal punishment, but beyond that they were allowed to administer and run the schools in accordance with their religious beliefs and in accordance with the Constitution – making an exception for these schools would derogate substantially from the principle being protected. In the circumstances, the Court held that it was reasonable and justifiable to limit the freedom of religion to the extent that occurred in this case.

An infringement of fundamental rights is a serious matter in a constitutional democracy and warrants the state supplying a reasonable justification in support of its law or conduct. In deciding whether the explanation is constitutionally permissible, the importance of the right and the extent of the limitation are of crucial importance. However, not all rights weigh as heavily and not all limitations are egregious infringements. The proportionality approach requires the state to convince a court that it has acted reasonably. This somewhat flexible approach means that due regard is paid to fundamental rights without the developing state being hamstrung unjustifiably in the process of governance.

An assessment of the interpretation of certain substantive rights

Equality and dignity

As much as apartheid was about inequality, the Final Constitution is about the attainment of substantive equality. One of the founding values is the attainment of equality (section 1) and running through the fabric of the Bill of Rights is a commitment to an open and democratic society based on human dignity, equality and freedom. The first substantive right in the Bill of Rights is the right to be treated equally. The Court has developed an equality jurisprudence that is relevant to South Africa, incrementally and cautiously.

Section 9 (1) affirms the right of everyone to be equal before the law and to the equal protection and benefit of the law. However, it is the right not to be subject to unfair discrimination on the basis of listed and analogous grounds that has become the centrepiece of the developing law regarding equality (section 9 [3]). By defining equality to include the full and equal enjoyment of rights, substantive as opposed to formal equality is protected and affirmative measures endorsed as a means of achieving substantive equality. The right not to be subject to unfair discrimination is horizontally applicable and the Promotion of Equality and Prohibition of Unfair Discrimination Act of 2000 gives legislative effect to this right. Finally, in order to reduce the demanding burden of proof that has plagued applicants in other equality jurisdictions, there is a constitutional presumption that discrimination on one of the listed grounds is presumed to be unfair unless the contrary is established.

Differentiation is objectionable if burdens are imposed or benefits granted on the basis of categorisations that adversely impact on the dignity of the complainant. Thus the jurisprudence on equality had distinguished between categorisations that impact on dignity and those that do not. Categorisations that do not impact on dignity, such as differentiations between geographical areas, are not the central concern of section 9. The decision to have exacting planning and development laws in area A and less onerous planning laws in area B does not impact on dignity and is therefore not the main concern of section 9.

In respect of categorisations that do not impact on dignity, the courts have interpreted section 9 (1) to mean that state differentiation is permissible if the categorisation is rationally related to a legitimate state objective.[11] Section 9 (1) does not require the state to satisfy the more exacting requirement that its categorisation is reasonable. Choosing between different categories of beneficiaries and imposing burdens on some and not on others is integral to the process of governance. Provided that these differentiations do not adversely impact upon dignity and amount to discrimination, our courts are content to subject them to the non-exacting rationality review and afford a significant measure of latitude to government. These categorisations can be assessed under other provisions of the Bill of Rights, but any challenge under section 9 (1) would only succeed if the applicant is able to demonstrate irrational action on the part of the state.

Differentiation that amounts to discrimination is treated very differently by the courts. Section 9 (3) lists 17 grounds on which unfair discrimination is prohibited.[12] This list is not a closed one. The courts have held that differentiation on any one of the listed grounds amounts to discrimination.[13] In terms of section 9 (5) of the Constitution, discrimination on one of the listed grounds is presumed to be unfair unless the contrary is established. Proof of differentiation on a listed ground is converted relatively easily to a presumption of unfair discrimination. The listed grounds are deemed to have been used in the past to marginalise and oppress people and hence have the potential to adversely impact on their dignity.[14] If these grounds are the basis of classifications, then discrimination is deemed to have occurred and the presumption of unfairness is triggered. The onus will then be on the party differentiating on a listed ground to prove that the differentiation is fair and to provide an explanation for its decision. This process will allow an evaluation to be made on the merits of the case.

In addition to the listed grounds, differentiation on analogous grounds may also be constitutionally illegitimate. Analogous grounds referred to immutable characteristics that have the potential to impact adversely on human dignity. Grounds such as citizenship[15] and HIV status[16] have been held to be analogous grounds. In terms of section 9 (3), the applicant has to establish that the classification is on analogous grounds and then has the onus of proving that the discrimination is unfair. The presumption of unfairness does not operate in respect of analogous grounds.

The Constitution prohibits unfair discrimination. In determining whether the discrimination is unfair, regard must be had to the impact it has on the complainant.[17] Specifically, an assessment has to be made of whether the complainant belonged to a category of persons that were victims of past patterns of discrimination, whether the measure impairs the dignity of the complainant, and whether the measure is designed to achieve a laudable and important societal objective. In *Pretoria City Council v Walker*,[18] the Court had to consider whether the policy of differential tariffs was constitutional. The residents of the predominantly white part of Pretoria were charged a consumption-based tariff while residents of the African townships were charged a flat rate per household. The flat rate was significantly lower than the consumption-based tariffs. White residents argued that they were being unfairly discriminated against on the basis of race. While this was indirect discrimination on the basis of race, the Court concluded that the discrimination was not unfair. The Council had the constitutional mandate of equalising facilities and services to all within its region. The facilities in the townships were vastly inferior to those of white Pretoria. The homes in the townships, unlike those in 'white Pretoria', did not have individual meters to measure the consumption of water and electricity. The white residents, although a political minority, were not the victims of past patterns of discrimination. In the circumstances, it was not unfair to adopt the differential tariff scheme as an interim measure until meters were installed in the homes in the townships. Charging everyone the flat rate would decimate the coffers of the Council and make the realisation of its constitutional goals of improving the quality of life of all people impossible. The Court held that cross-subsidisation was permissible in a democracy and occurs in various aspects of our society.[19] Further, the Court held that the purpose of section 9 is to end the unfair discrimination. The issue is whether from an objective perspective, the discrimination is unfair. It need not be established that the person discriminating has the intention to discriminate.[20]

The equality jurisprudence has been developed in a manner that is directly relevant in the South African context. Non-discriminatory differentiation, such as economic measures, is subject to the non-exacting rationality review under the equality clause. The Court has made clear that the focus of the right to equality is to assess the fairness of differentiations that impact on dignity. It has chartered a course that requires justification by those differentiating on a listed ground as opposed to insisting that the applicants prove all the requirements of unfair discrimination, including intention.

The development of the right to equality has allowed marginalised and vulnerable communities the opportunity to develop and assert their rights. This is particularly so in the case of the gay and lesbian community. In 1994, there were criminal norms that made it an offence for consenting male adults to engage in sexual intercourse in private. In 2004, the Supreme Court of Appeals capped an incredible legal journey by finding that the common law definition of marriage, being restricted to a union of one man to one woman, was inconsistent with the Constitution. The journey started when the Court set aside laws criminalising consensual sexual conduct between males in private[21] and continued when it recognised the rights of gays and lesbians to adopt children, to bring their partners into the country,[22] to be entitled to the same employment benefits as spouses,[23] and finally to marry.[24]

In *Van Heerden v Minister of Finance*, the Court reaffirmed the constitutional commitment to the attainment of substantive equality. Affirmative action measures are constitutionally endorsed and are directed at achieving substantive equality. Affirmative action is thus not positive discrimination and neither is it reverse discrimination. It is a legitimate method of addressing pervasive and entrenched patterns of systemic discrimination. The US position of subjecting affirmative action measures to a demanding level of scrutiny is not directly applicable to South African law. An affirmative action measure, which falls within section 9 (2) of the Constitution, cannot simultaneously be unfair discrimination in terms of section 9 (3). A measure will fall within the ambit of section 9 (2) if it is aimed at advancing previously disadvantaged communities, designed to achieve the objective and promotes substantive equality. A measure that is reasonably likely to achieve its objective will be deemed to be adequately designed to achieve the objective. This flexible standard will allow the Court to make situation-specific assessments and have particular regard to whether the dignity of the complainant has been affected.

Dignity plays a decisive and crucial role in the right to equality. In declaring the sodomy laws unconstitutional, the Court concluded that as the law strikes at one of the ways in which gays give expression to their sexual orientation, it is a severe limitation of the gay man's rights to privacy, dignity and freedom.[25] A similar concern for dignity premised the decision in *Fourie v Minister of Home Affairs* recognising gay and lesbian marriages. Just as the laws criminalising gay sexual activity had a broader anti-gay radiating effect in our society, the changes in the law brought about by the Constitutional Court decision are having a similar radiating effect – this time positive from the perspective of respecting people. Changes in the law often led to adjustments in societal mores. An Afrikaner school[26] in the Durban area invited a priest to address the learners. A pupil who had a gay aunt was offended by the priest, who railed against gays and lesbians, and a complaint was lodged with the South African Human Rights Commission (SAHRC). During the mediation, the Commission pointed out that gays and lesbians have the constitutional right to adopt children and hence a public school must anticipate the possibility that children from gay parent unions may be attending their school. Thus an attack on gays would be perceived to be a direct attack on the parents of these learners. Once this was accepted, it became patent that the best interests of the child would require the school not to ally itself with anti-gay rhetoric. The school accepted this and offered the necessary apologies and the principal undertook to appraise his teachers of the implications and impact of developments in this area of the law. Societal interactions in a school in Pinetown have had to be reappraised in the light of the decisions of the Constitutional Court on gay rights.

The right to human dignity, in addition to being central to the right to equality, is also protected as a substantive right.[27] The Court has held that the right to dignity protects the rights of persons to marry freely and nurture a family.[28] Thus legislation that prohibits the establishment of such a relationship is inconsistent with the right to dignity. The right to marry and raise a family was read into the general right to dignity.

Democracy and human rights

Our Constitution seeks to entrench three types of democracy, namely, representative, participatory and direct democracy (de Waal, Currie & Erasmus

2001). In a constitutional democracy, power is given to legitimately elected rulers, subject to checks and balances. Universal adult suffrage, a national common voters' roll, regular elections and a multiparty system of democratic government (section 1 [d]) are founding provisions of the Constitution. The basis of representative democracy is section 19, which protects the political rights of citizens. These rights enable persons to form and participate in the activities of political parties, to vote in free, fair and regular elections, and to stand for and hold public office if elected. The management of national, provincial and municipal elections is entrusted by the Constitution to the Electoral Commission (section 190).

The national and provincial legislatures are elected through a party list proportional representation system. Voters thus vote for the political party of their choice and there is a direct relationship between the votes cast and the political power garnered. Elections are well organised and the representation of the political parties in Parliament genuinely reflects the popular support in the country. In order to maintain the integrity of this system, an anti-defection clause was included in the Constitution. This provided that a person loses membership of a legislature if that person ceases to be a member of the party that nominated him or her to the legislature.[29] This provision vested considerable powers in the hands of party bosses and arguably inhibited the ability of legislators to act contrary to the party wishes irrespective of their own views. However, it maintained a measure of stability in the early years of democracy.

A new party called the Democratic Alliance (DA), which comprised, amongst others, the Democratic Party and the New National Party (NNP), contested the October 2000 municipal elections. In November 2001, the NNP withdrew from the Alliance. The effect of this was that its local government representatives could not leave the DA and move with their party leaders without losing their seats, even though they were, in substance, voted in as NNP members. It was legitimate to cure this and allow the elected members of the NNP to leave the Alliance and retain their seats at local government level. The national Parliament passed four pieces of legislation, including two incidental constitutional amendments, to provide for a relaxation of the anti-defection clause in respect of the local, provincial and national spheres. The cumulative effect of these laws was to allow for a 15-day window period during the second and fourth year after an election to allow legislators to change parties and still retain their seats.

Defections during this period were subject to the requirement that at least ten per cent of the party defect simultaneously. However, in addition the legislation introduced a once-off 15-day period immediately after the commencement of the legislation during which legislators could change party allegiances without losing their seats. These defections were not subject to having to obtain a minimum of ten per cent of the party to defect. It thus allowed defection at the discretion of the individual legislator.

Laws permitting defectors to retain their seats in the legislature undoubtedly operate in favour of the ruling and larger parties. In South Africa, these laws almost precipitated a constitutional crisis when their full impact dawned on smaller parties. The most serious consequence would have been to deprive the Inkatha Freedom Party of its status as the dominant party in KwaZulu-Natal because some of its members, having been elected on its party list, defected to the African National Congress (ANC). The United Democratic Movement and others challenged the laws in the Constitutional Court.[30]

Allowing defections meant that political power would no longer correspond with the will of the electorate. It was argued that the relaxation of the anti-defection clause undermined one of the core structures of the Constitution. The Court held that it could not be argued that a proportional representation electoral system with an anti-defection clause was so fundamental that any change to it was implicitly prohibited. It further held that a multiparty democracy envisaged a political order in which it was permissible for different political groupings to organise and promote their views through public debate. The Court held that while a proportional representation system with an anti-defection clause was consistent with democracy, it could not be argued that a proportional representation system without an anti-defection clause was inconsistent with democracy.

According to the Court, a proportional representation system with an anti-defection clause is not an essential component of a multiparty democracy and hence the conclusion that the laws allowing for defections did not infringe the founding values in section 1, including the commitment to a multiparty system of government. The Court also concluded that it did not amount to a violation of the right to vote. The Court held that the right to vote was directed to elections, to voting, and to participation in political activities. However, between elections voters were deemed not to have control over the conduct of elected representatives. The only recourse that they had was to withhold their votes from candidates who had disappointed them in the next elections. In the circumstances, most of the substantive arguments of the applicants were rejected.

The changes to the anti-defection constitutional provisions were interpreted by some as evidence of the dominant party using its overwhelming majority to defeat the will of the electorate and wrest power in KwaZulu-Natal. Fortunately, from a perspective of maintaining a stable constitutional democracy, this did not transpire. In terms of the Constitution, Parliament was permitted to amend the constitutional anti-defection clause in so far as it applied to the national and provincial legislatures by passing ordinary legislation within a reasonable period after the promulgation of the Constitution. The Court held that Parliament had not passed the laws within a reasonable period of time, as the laws permitting defection were passed more than five years after the Constitution came into effect. Subsequently, the laws allowing partial defections at national and provincial level were not valid and legislators were not able to rely on them. Thus those who had defected on the basis of these laws were not able to retain their seats. To achieve their objective, Parliament would have to pass substantive constitutional amendments.

A subsequent substantive constitutional change that permitted defections was made prospective and had no material impact on the party controlling the KwaZulu-Natal provincial legislature. Very little was actually gained by these changes, yet considerable damage could have been done to the constitutional order. The fact that partial defections are constitutionally permissible does not mean, in the South African context, they are constitutionally desirable. Defections strip smaller parties of their political representatives and strengthen the dominant party beyond its electoral support. Electoral processes in a developing democracy must strive to achieve the greatest correlation possible between electoral support and political power and must eschew mechanisms than distort the will of the people. The dominant political party in South Africa has largely restricted itself to technical amendments to the Constitution and has resisted using its majority to attain far-reaching changes. The changes effected to the Constitution enabling floor-crossing are a lamentable exception and can have a corrosive effect on the constitutional order.

Directly related to political rights such as the freedom of expression is the right to assemble, demonstrate, picket and petition and the freedom of association. Section 16 protects the freedom of expression, which includes conduct intended to convey a message. The right to freedom of expression does not extend to propaganda for war, incitement of imminent violence or the advocacy of hatred based on race, ethnicity, gender or religion, and that which constitutes incitement to cause harm. Expression that is not protected in terms of section 16 (2) can be regulated and restricted by the state without having to satisfy the requirements of the limitation clause. Our courts have recognised the importance of the freedom of expression to a constitutional democracy and the close relationship between it and other rights.[31] While recognising its indispensability to a democracy, we have not adopted the American approach of regarding the freedom of expression as a pre-eminent right. The courts have emphasised that the foundational values of our Bill of Rights are respect for human dignity, equality, and freedom. The freedom of expression does not automatically trump other rights, but is worthy of the same protection as other core values.[32]

The right to assemble unarmed (section 17) is essential to the concept of direct democracy as it facilitates the conveyance of a message much more effectively than if individuals conveyed the same message. The right to assemble is regulated by the Regulations of Gatherings Act 205 of 1993, which requires the organisers of a gathering of more than 15 people in public to comply with certain notice and consultation provisions of the Act. Non-compliance may result in a prohibition of the gathering. These regulations are justified on the basis that they do not impact on the content of the message, but rather on the mode of expression. The requirement on the mode of expression is then balanced against the serious inconvenience caused to other persons using public facilities by uncontrolled demonstrations. The regulation of assemblies does not appear to be out of step with other democracies.

Participatory democracy enables persons to participate in decisions which impact on them. There is a direct constitutional obligation on the national and provincial legislatures to 'make rules and orders concerning its business, with due regard to representative and participatory democracy, accountability, transparency and public involvement'.[33] This enables public participation directly in the legislative process. In addition, and to promote transparency and accountability, persons have a right to lawful, reasonable and procedurally fair administrative action (section 33). The Promotion of Administrative Justice Act of 2000 provides further content to this. It provides that fair procedures have to be adopted in order to minimise erroneous decisions, that adequate reasons must be supplied for administrative actions that adversely affect rights, and that the administration must act lawfully and reasonably. This enables the courts to assess whether the decision made by the administration is a decision that a reasonable authority can make. Thus administrators have to engage with those affected by their decisions, justify their decisions when rights are adversely affected and convince a court that they have acted reasonably. These provisions have the effect of shining a spotlight into the bowels of the administration. The present legal provisions are profoundly different from the administrative law that prevailed prior to the last ten years, which was characterised by lack of accountability, no requirement to give reasons and restricted grounds of judicial review.

Improving the quality of life and freeing the potential of people

The Constitution seeks, unlike many other constitutions, to protect socio-economic rights. Some socio-economic rights are as directly enforceable as fundamental first generation rights, such as the freedom of expression. These include the right to basic education, including adult basic education (section 29 [1]), and the right not to be refused emergency medical treatment (section 27 [3]). The justiciability of other socio-economic rights varies. Everyone has the right to have access to adequate housing (section 26 [1]), to healthcare services, sufficient food and water and social security (section 27 [1]). In order to bolster the access rights and prevent them from simply being a wish list, a positive obligation is imposed on the state to take reasonable legislative and other measures, within its available resources, to achieve the progressive realisation of these rights.[34] In the Madisonian tradition of checks and balances, the SAHRC, an institution set up by the Constitution to support democracy,[35] is empowered, as one of its functions, to require the relevant organs of state 'to supply it with information on the measures that they have taken towards the realisation of rights in the Bill of Rights, concerning housing, healthcare, food, water, social security, education and the environment' (section 184 [3]).

However, the possibility that aspects or parts of socio-economic rights are directly enforceable in courts, has presented the South African courts with the unique challenge of ensuring that government acts in accordance with its constitutional mandate while simultaneously respecting the divide between the role of the judiciary and that of the elected representatives.

Mr Thiagaraj Soobramoney suffered from chronic renal failure and, after exhausting his private funds, sought renal dialysis from a public hospital. The policy of the hospital was to provide dialysis to people who were suitable candidates for a kidney transplant and whose kidneys could be resuscitated. Soobramoney fell outside the guidelines and was denied treatment. His argument before the Court was simple and poignant.[36] Had he been rich he would have been able to afford the dialysis and thus lived, but as he had no funds, this society was allowing him to die. He argued that the policy and the decision violated his right to life (section 11) and his right not to be denied emergency medical treatment.

Notwithstanding the inevitability of the conclusion reached by the Court, it was nonetheless tragic. It was common cause that the KwaZulu-Natal Department of Health had inadequate funds to effectively provide basic healthcare. If the court granted the order, all persons in the position of Soobramoney would have been prioritised and this would effectively have reordered the spending and planning priorities of the Department. The cost of affording Soobramoney dialysis would have been at the expense of others who depended on the public health system. The Court declined to grant Soobramoney's order, finding that the right to life was not applicable as there was a more specific right dealing with the issue. Section 27 (3) was restricted to receiving medical treatment as a consequence of a sudden catastrophe such as an accident or assault. It did not extend to ongoing treatment.

The concern with this judgement was not with the conclusion, but with the significant degree of deference accorded to the state in determining budgetary priorities. The Court held:

> A court will be slow to interfere with rational decisions taken in good faith by the political organs and medical authorities whose responsibility it is to deal with such matters.[37]

This non-exacting level of scrutiny raised fears that socio-economic rights, the enforcement of which has direct budgetary implications, would be reduced to a wish list as it would be extremely difficult to prove that government had acted irrationally and in bad faith.

These fears proved to be ill-founded as the Constitutional Court unequivocally held in the Grootboom case[38] that socio-economic rights are justiciable.[39] Mrs Grootboom was rendered homeless as a result of being evicted from the informal home which she had erected on private land and where she was living, together with others in her position, in deplorable conditions. She sought an order based on section 26 of the Constitution directing the government to provide them with adequate basic shelter until they obtained permanent housing. The government demonstrated that it had in place a comprehensive plan for formal housing over a period of time and argued that it was progressively realising the right of access to housing. The Court started from the premise that socio-economic rights are justiciable. The issue was how to enforce them in a given case.[40] The United Nations (UN) Committee on Economic, Social and Cultural Rights imposes an obligation on state parties to ensure the satisfaction of, at the very least, minimum essential levels of each of the rights.[41] These minimum levels must progressively increase.

The Constitutional Court held that the state's positive obligation is to take reasonable legislative and other measures to achieve the progressive realisation of the right within available resources. The ultimate standard is whether government is acting reasonably. The minimum core content may be taken into account in determining whether the state is acting reasonably. The requirement of reasonableness requires justification on the part of the state. The Court held that legislative measures by themselves are unlikely to ensure compliance. The state is required to achieve an intended result and legislative programmes must be reasonably implemented. Whether the state is acting reasonably is determined on a case-by-case basis and is context sensitive. While the state had in place legislative and implementation measures designed to provide people with formal housing, it had no direct poverty alleviation measures for those in dire need and who were waiting on lists to be allocated formal houses. Thus the very poor were not provided with temporary relief, such as waterproof shelter, portable water and basic sanitation and refuse services, while they waited for formal housing. This, according to the Constitutional Court, was not reasonable and in violation of section 26 of the Constitution.[42]

In its order, the Court endorsed, as a starting point, a poverty alleviation programme adopted by the Cape Metro Council called 'Accelerated Managed Land Settlement Programme'. This programme required the rapid release of land for families in crisis and the progressive provision of basic services. It was unreasonable, according to the Court, for the state to fail to provide shelter, basic sanitation and water to people living in intolerable conditions. The SAHRC was requested to monitor and report on the provision of these services.

The difference between the Soobramoney and Grootboom cases was that in the former case the applicants were seeking the full right to medical care, while in the latter, the applicants were seeking the minimum content of the right. Acknowledging that the minimum core content is relevant to the determination of whether governmental action is reasonable or not allows for the incremental realisation of the right while simultaneously recognising that some part of the right is immediately enforceable. It may be that the minimum core content, once determined, will be discounted against resource constraints and other legitimate state priorities in determining what is reasonable.

The third Constitutional Court judgement to consider the enforcement of socio-economic rights was *Minister of Health and Others v Treatment Action Campaign and others*.[43] In this case the Court considered the constitutionality of government policy not to supply Nevirapine to HIV-positive pregnant women in all state hospitals. The Treatment Action Campaign (TAC) and a host of non-governmental organisations argued that the failure to roll out the drug at all state hospitals and thus prevent mother to child transmission, amounted to a violation of section 27 (1) of the Constitution, which guaranteed the right of access to healthcare services. The government provided Nevirapine only at state facilities that were designated as pilot or test sites and not at all state hospitals. The applicants sought an order from the Court directing the government to implement a comprehensive programme of providing Nevirapine to all HIV-positive mothers attending state hospitals who, from a medical perspective, were deemed suitable to receive the drug.

Both the Medicines Control Council of South Africa and the World Health Organization (WHO) sanctioned the drug as being suitable to prevent mother to child transmission. The drug was used in the private sector to prevent mother to child transmission. The Constitutional Court held that the real enquiry in assessing whether the state has complied with its obligations to realise socio-economic rights is whether the state has acted reasonably. The Court held that the minimum core content of the right was not directly enforceable against the state.[44] The minimum core of the right, available resources and other factors must be taken into account when making this assessment.

The Constitutional Court held that from the evidence available to it, it was clear that Nevirapine was effective in preventing mother to child transmission during pregnancy and at birth. Further, it stated that the evidence demonstrated that the drug was reasonably efficacious, even in instances where the mother breastfed the child. The Court held that it was possible that both mother and child may become resistant to anti-retrovirals in future. However, this concern was speculative and was clearly outweighed by the benefits that accrue after the administration of the drug. The Court dismissed the concerns about toxicity as being hypothetical and found that there was no evidence that the drug was harmful. Both the (WHO) and the Medicine Health Council had approved the drug and the government was using the drug at its test sites.

The cost of providing the drug was not an issue in this case and was clearly within the capacity of the state. An important point in the deliberations of the Court was that the drug had the potential benefit of saving the life of the child. In terms of section 28 of the Constitution, a child has the right to basic nutrition, shelter, basic healthcare services and social services. The state is obliged, if the parents are unable to do so, to provide the necessary assistance to enable the child to enjoy these basic rights.

The Court finally concluded that the policy of the state to restrict the supply of Nevirapine to the limited test or pilot sites and not to extend it to all state hospitals was a violation of section 27 of the Constitution and the state was ordered to roll out the drug to all public hospitals. The state argued that under the doctrine of separation of powers, policy formulation was the responsibility of the executive and that the Court could not make an order which has the effect of requiring the executive to pursue a particular policy. The Court rejected this argument and held that where a breach of a right had occurred, it was obliged to provide effective relief.[45] The nature of the right and the nature of the infringement would determine appropriate relief, which may require the exercise of supervisory jurisdiction. To this end, detailed directions were given by the Court to ensure that Nevirapine was made available for the purpose of reducing the risk of mother to child transmission of HIV at public hospitals.

A striking feature of the judgement was the speedy manner in which the Court was able to dismiss the justifications submitted by the state in support of its policies. The state's arguments, when subject to legal scrutiny, fell short of what was required to demonstrate reasonableness. The short shrift manner in which the Court disposed of its arguments bears testimony to this fact. In many respects, the case was legally a very easy case – the cost of the drug was not an issue and neither was its efficacy in stopping mother to child transmission during pregnancy or birth. The failure to administer the drug could result in the transmission of the virus from mother to child. Using the drug gave the child reasonable hope of being HIV negative. In this scenario, the decision not to make it available in public hospitals had to be supported by strong justification. This, the state failed to do.

In this instance, civil society was able to change government policy regarding the supply of Nevirapine by analysing its justifications and convincing a court that these were not reasonable. The case of Mr Soobramoney was very different – an order in his favour would have impacted tremendously on the health budget and favoured those who were terminally ill at the expense of other vulnerable members of our society. Delicate and sensitive choices had to be made and it is best that the elected representatives make these choices. In the TAC case, there was no such dilemma or agonising choice to be made.

The ultimate conclusion that government acted unreasonably in dealing with an aspect of the AIDS pandemic is a stinging rebuke. These cases require government to justify its policy choices that impact on socio-economic rights to the benchmark mark of reasonableness. Government is not able to avoid this responsibility by reliance on the doctrine of separation of powers[46] or by reference to the margin of appreciation afforded to the elected representatives in determining budgetary issues. A constitutional democracy should require nothing less than this 'culture of justification' (Mureinik 1994: 31).

The SAHRC, after consulting with various role-players, developed a set of protocols to assist it in its reporting functions. The protocols require detailed information from organs of state on measures that have been taken to realise socio-economic rights for the period under review (SAHRC 2001). The responses received form the basis of the report to Parliament as required by the Constitution. In the segment dealing with health in the fifth socio-economic rights report, the SAHRC stated:

> There still remain huge gaps between policy and effective implementation in many areas of quality care service delivery, disparities along racial lines, urban and rural divides, between provinces and amongst 'race groups'. In short the road to equity seems long and arduous. (SAHRC 2004: 79)

So despite progressive laws, significant budgetary allocation for social spending, judicial enforcement of socio-economic rights and oversight by the SAHRC, the social deficit and inequality that we inherited is proving difficult to overcome and eradicate.

Further, Human Rights Watch have identified the rights of detained and accused persons, the excessive use of force by police, the lack of respect for the rights of foreign persons, violence against women, and the slow realisation of socio-economic rights (especially in the rural areas) as major human rights concerns in South Africa (Human Rights Watch 2005).

Conclusion

Over the next decade, the implementation of government policy is likely to be challenged on two fronts. After a decade of frenetic law-making, government is in the implementation phase. It is now concerned with implementing plans drawn up to restructure this society. It is at this stage that vested rights and interests are mostly likely to be adversely affected. As in the case of the dispensing doctors and the pharmacists, it is likely that those who are adversely affected by the re-regulation of this society are likely to challenge government action on the basis that a right in the Bill of Rights has been infringed. The right (section 33) to administrative action that is lawful, procedurally fair and reasonable will, no doubt, be frequently used to test the reasonableness of governmental implementation programmes.

Given the extent to which the ANC dominates the political process, many of these battles will be fought in the courts. Judges may be called upon to make policy determinations and this may result in tensions between the executive and judiciary. Given the constitutional role of the courts in enforcing a supreme Constitution, such tensions may be inevitable. The litmus test will be the response of the executive to unfavoured judicial decisions. Any response which has the effect of devaluing the institution of the courts in a constitutional democracy, will ultimately subvert many of the gains made in the first decade of democracy.

Simultaneously, there are likely to be more challenges from the marginalised in society, demanding speedier and more decisive action from government aimed at ameliorating their conditions, freeing their potential and allowing them to participate in the activities of this society. They will rely on the constitutional obligation to progressively realise the right to gain access to land, the right of access to adequate housing and the right of access to healthcare, food, water and social security.

The pulling and pushing of government in opposite directions will present the Court with the dilemma of choosing between alternative courses of action, both of which adversely affect rights. Thus, over the next few years, the Court will, of necessity, engage in a more complicated balancing of rights. Such a balancing was explicitly recognised by the Court in *Port Elizabeth Municipality v Various Occupiers*.[47] The Court, in interpreting the right to property, observed that while the Constitution recognised the right to own, use and occupy property, it also identified and protected the rights of the dispossessed to land. The rights of the dispossessed to land were not delineated in unqualified terms, but presupposed the adoption of measures by the state to open up access to land. The right to property sometimes clashed with the steps taken to eradicate the homelessness of the dispossessed. The Court held that the judicial function in those circumstances was not to establish a hierarchy of rights, but rather to balance out and reconcile the competing rights and interests in a just manner.

The drafters of the South African Bill of Rights were true to their mandate. The Bill of Rights is an expansive document incorporating all universally accepted fundamental rights and freedoms. In interpreting and applying the rights, the Court speedily established the minimum norms with which there had to be compliance and then incrementally and cautiously allowed the outer parameters of the rights to develop on a case-by-case basis. The Constitutional Court, in the first decade of its existence, has crafted a solid foundation upon which the future development of constitutional and human rights law can be based. By the persuasiveness of its reasoning, it has reinforced the importance of the institution of the courts and the vital role that it plays in a constitutional democracy. The development, nurturing and growth of the courts is a significant contribution to the African renaissance on a continent where the judiciary is often not accorded a status appropriate to the constitutional role required of it.

Notes

1 This covenant was adopted and opened for signing and ratification by the General Assembly of the United Nations in terms of resolution 2200 (XXI) of 16 December 1996. The covenant came into force on 23 May 1976.
2 This covenant was adopted and opened for signing and ratification by the General Assembly of the UN in terms of resolution 2200 (XXI) of 16 December 1966 and came into force on 3 January 1976.
3 *De Lille v Speaker of the National Assembly* 1998 (3) SA 430 (C); *Speaker of the National Assembly v De Lille* 1999 (4) SAA 863 (SCA).
4 Constitutional Principle II was one of a set of principles contained in schedule 4 of the Interim Constitution. The constitutional settlement provided that the final Constitution had to be consistent with all the constitutional principles contained in schedule 4 of the Interim Constitution.
5 *Mohamed v President of RSA* 2001 (3) SA 893 (CC).
6 *Bhe v Magistrate, Khayelitsha and Others* 2005 (1) BCLR 1(CC).
7 *Ferreira v Levin* NO 1996 (1) SA 984 (CC) para. 44.
8 *S v Makwanyane* 1995 (3) SA 391 (CC) at 104.
9 *August v Electoral Commission* 1999 (3) SA 1 (CC).
10 *Christian Education South Africa v Minister of Education* 2000 (4) SA 757 (CC).
11 *Prinsloo v van der Linde* 1997 (3) SA 1012 (CC).
12 The listed grounds are race, gender, sex, pregnancy, marital status, ethnic or social origin, colour, sexual orientation, age, disability, religion, conscience, belief, culture, language and birth.
13 *Harksen v Lane* NO 1998 (1) SA 300 (CC) para. 53.
14 *Harksen* para. 49 (see note 13).
15 *Larbi-Odam v MEC for Education* (North-West Province) 1998 (1) SA 745 (CC).

16 *Hoffman v South African Airways* 2000 (11) BCLR 1235 (CC).
17 *President of the Republic of South Africa v Hugo* 1997 (4) SA 1 (CC). *Harksen* para. 52 (see note 13).
18 *Pretoria City Council v Walker* 1998 (2) SA 363 (CC).
19 *Pretoria City Council* para. 62 (see note 18).
20 *Pretoria City Council* para. 43 (see note 18).
21 *National Coalition for Gay and Lesbians Equality v Minister of Justice* 1999 (1) SA 6.
22 *National Coalition for Gay and Lesbians Equality v Minister of Home Affairs* 2000 (2) SA1(CC).
23 *Satchel v President of the Republic of South Africa* 2002 (9) BCLR 986 (CC).
24 *Fourie v Minister of Home Affairs* 2005 (3) BCLR 241 (CC).
25 *National Coalition* para. 36 (see note 21).
26 This illustration is taken from the files of the South African Human Rights Commission office in Durban.
27 Section 10 provides that everyone has inherent dignity and the right to have their dignity protected.
28 *Dawood v Minister of Home Affairs* 2000 (3) SA 936 (CC).
29 Item 6(3) of schedule 6 of the Constitution.
30 *UDM v President of the Republic of South Africa* 2003(1) SA 495 (CC).
31 *South African National Defence Force Union v Minister of Defence* 1999 (4) SA 469 (CC) para. 8.
32 *S v Mamabolo* 2001 (3) SA 409 at 429.
33 Section 57 (1)(b), section 70 (1)(b) and section 116 (1)(b) of the Constitution.
34 This obligation is imposed on the state in section 25 (5) (the obligation to enable citizens to gain access to land), section 26 (2) (the obligation to realise the right of access to adequate housing) and in section 27 (2) (the obligation to realise the right of access to healthcare, food, water and social security).
35 Section 184 of the Constitution.
36 *Soobramoney v Minister of Health, KwaZulu-Natal* 1998 (1) SA 765(CC).
37 *Soobramoney* para. 29 (see note 36).
38 *Government of the Republic of South Africa and Others v Grootboom* 2000 (11) BCLR 1169 (CC).

39 Section 26 (right to housing), section 27 (the right to healthcare, food, water and social security), section 28 (the rights of the child) and section 29 (the right to education).

40 *Grootboom* para. 20 (see note 38).

41 *Grootboom* para. 29 (see note 38).

42 *Grootboom* para. 52 (see note 38).

43 *Minister of Health and Others v Treatment Action Campaign and others* 2002 (10) BCLR 1033 (CC).

44 Professor John Dugard (2004) has criticised this and has argued that the Court should have interpreted sections 26 and 27 as imposing minimum core obligations on the state which would entitle individuals to a basic level of services.

45 *Minister of Health and Others v Treatment Action Campaign and others* para. 106 (see note 43).

46 Professor Pieterse (2004) argues on the basis of this judgement that socio-economic rights are as justiciable as civil and political rights and that our model of separation of powers is radically different from that advocated by Locke and Montesque.

47 *Port Elizabeth Municipality v Various Occupiers* 2004 (12) BCLR 1268 (CC).

References

De Waal J, Currie L & Erasmus G (2001) *The Bill of Rights handbook*. Fourth edition. Cape Town: Juta.

Dugard J (2004) Twenty years of human rights scholarship and ten years of democracy, *South African Journal of Human Rights* 20(3): 345–354.

Henkin L (1995) *International law: Politics and value*. London: Martinus Nijhoff.

Human Rights Watch (2005) *World Report* 2005. Available at http://hrw.org/wr2k5.

Mureinik E (1994) A bridge to where? Introducing the Interim Bill of Rights, *South African Human Rights Journal* 10: 31–48.

Pieterse M (2004) Coming to terms with judicial enforcement of socio-economic rights, *South African Journal of Human Rights* 20(3): 383–417.

Sachs A (2000) Social and economic rights: Can they be justiciable? *Southern Methodist University Law Review* 1381(53): 1389.

SAHRC (South African Human Rights Commission) (2001) *Third economic and social rights report series 1999/2000*. Johannesburg: SAHRC.

SAHRC (2004) *Fifth economic and social rights report series 2002/2003*. Pretoria: SAHRC.

5 More than a law-making production line? Parliament and its oversight role

Judith February

> The purpose of Parliament is to improve the quality of government. An effective Parliament should be the basis for effective government. Parliament is the most important link between the public and the executive – it should keep government in touch with public feeling and alert to issues about which the public feels strongly.
>
> *Jacobs, Calland & Power 2001: 69*
>
> I'm not sure if Parliament has a sense of its strategic role and purpose in deepening democracy and in relation to the socio-economic challenges in the country.
>
> *Jeremy Cronin, Idasa round table 2004*

'Travelgate', 'Oilgate' and the public perception of Parliament

In his May 2004 'State of the Nation' address, President Mbeki (2004) unveiled his government's programme of action for improved service delivery and challenged Parliament to hold his government to account for the proper implementation of the ambitious programme. The President thus threw down the gauntlet to Parliament to exercise oversight over the executive by holding it to account for promises made. In so doing, he was invoking Parliament's constitutional mandate to keep executive power in check. This article examines Parliament's record in performing that oversight function and argues that it is a role that it has thus far declined to carve out for itself adequately or successfully.[1]

The last few years have been difficult ones for Parliament. It has often struggled to define and interpret its oversight role and has had to deal with a number of high-profile breaches of its own code of ethics. The arms deal particularly tested Parliament's mettle for holding the executive to account and it emerged from it with the reputation of its most powerful oversight watchdog, the Select Committee on Public Accounts (Scopa), badly tarnished.

In May 2005, Parliament released a strategic plan entitled *Mapping the Future 2004–2008* (South African Parliament 2005). Central to this plan is the notion of a 'people's Parliament' which is responsive and open to engagement and interaction with citizens and which will have as a priority the function of 'scrutinising and overseeing executive action'. Parliament, the plan suggests, intends to map a new course. It was unveiled at a time when the image of Parliament was at a low ebb, not least of which due to the continuing 'Travelgate' scandal. Early in 2005, 26 Members of Parliament (MPs) and former MPs were arrested and charged with defrauding Parliament through the abuse of travel vouchers. Earlier in the year five of those arrested had pleaded guilty and been convicted as part of a plea-bargaining agreement. They received sentences ranging from fines of from R40 000 (or one year's direct imprisonment) to R80 000 or three years' imprisonment. In June 2005, the other 21 MPs arrested appeared in court in connection with the scandal. The trial was adjourned to give the lawyers acting on behalf of the accused time to engage in plea-bargaining. While plea-bargaining is a widely used device and has the advantage often of speeding up the judicial process, it can also be seen as a form of impunity and as a means of getting the rich and powerful off the hook, particularly where it is employed in the case of public office-holders. What it does is reinforce public cynicism and a view that double standards apply in the case of the rich and the political elite.

While Parliament had itself initiated the travel fraud investigation, since the arrest of the MPs it has done little to assure the public that it attaches much importance to the fact of fraudulent conduct on the part of some of its members. None of those arrested – bar one Democratic Alliance (DA) MP – had been suspended from Parliament and neither had any of those convicted. However, this may still occur as African National Congress (ANC) Secretary General, Kgalema Motlanthe, announced in a statement on 30 May 2005 that those MPs found guilty of abusing travel vouchers would lose their seats. The statement added, however, that the ANC was waiting for all MPs to be tried before commencing internal disciplinary procedures. Laudable though that may be, the legal process is a slow one and it does not explain why individual

MPs are not required to step down as a matter of principle as and when they are found guilty. In the meantime, they continue to draw salaries from the public purse and enjoy the same perks as their more honest and honourable colleagues. Nor is it clear whether a successful plea bargain amounts to being found guilty. Press reports in June 2005 (*Business Day* 10.06.05) spoke of backbench discontent at the fact that only backbenchers had been charged and that none of the so-called 'party bigwigs' – in the form of four Cabinet ministers, two deputy ministers, two provincial premiers and some of Parliament's senior office bearers – had been charged. All of these had appeared, along with the backbenchers and others, on a list – published in 2003 – of those said to be under investigation by the National Prosecuting Authority. The *Business Day* report spoke of a view among the backbenchers that they had been set up 'to carry the can…while letting the party bigwigs off the hook'. None of this has done anything positive for the image of the national Parliament.

In May 2005 Parliament came under pressure again. This followed calls by the opposition DA and others for an investigation into fresh allegations in the so-called 'Oilgate' scandal. This story was uncovered by the *Mail & Guardian* (20–27.05.05) newspaper and involves allegations relating to financial dealings between the parastatal energy company, PetroSA, Imvume (a black economic empowerment grouping) and a Swiss firm, Glencore. It is alleged that in December 2003, PetroSA advanced $15 million to Imvume in order for Imvume to source oil condensate on its behalf. Instead, according to the *Mail & Guardian*, Imvume paid R11 million of this advance to the ANC in a bid to boost its cash stock ahead of the 2004 elections. It is further alleged that in January 2004, Glencore sought payment for its supply of condensate but it was not forthcoming. Instead, PetroSA paid the amount to Glencore. In other words, PetroSA paid for the same shipment of oil condensate twice.

Opposition parties in Parliament called for either a commission of enquiry into this matter – since the allegations are that public funds were used in effect to fund parts of the ANC's 2004 election campaign – or that Parliament itself investigate the matter. Initially the chair of the relevant oversight body, the Mineral and Energy Committee, declined the request before agreeing to look into the matter, but only three months down the line. In a related development, the Auditor-General raised several queries relating to the audit of PetroSA. These should be taken up by the body charged with scrutinising the expenditure of public funds, Scopa, but at the time of writing it had given no indication it would do so, or at least not as a matter of urgency. As in the case of 'Travelgate', Parliament looks set to fall short again of performing its required watchdog function.

There are other indications that Parliament is failing in regard to the issue of public trust. The most recent Afrobarometer[2] data is instructive. Its survey of 16 African countries found a lowering level of trust in elected representatives, and in this regard, South Africa was no different from other African countries. When asked whether they approved of the performance of their MP, only nine per cent of South Africans surveyed 'strongly approved', while 31.7 per cent 'disapproved' and 35.8 per cent 'approved'. Equally interesting were the responses of citizens when asked whether they had 'trust' in the National Assembly (NA). Of the South Africans surveyed, 20.1 per cent said 'not at all', 43 per cent responded 'a little bit', 24.5 per cent and 6.7 per cent indicated that they had 'a lot' or 'a very great deal' of trust in the NA, while 5.7 per cent said they 'don't know'. What the responses to these questions illustrate clearly is that much work needs to be done to persuade citizens that elected representatives do act in their best interests and that Parliament is worthy of their trust.

The oversight framework

Parliament's oversight role derives from the Constitution. Section 55 stipulates that the legislature's role is to pass, initiate or prepare legislation (except money bills), ensure executive accountability and exercise oversight over organs of state.

Specific oversight mechanisms are laid out in Parliamentary Rules, which state that the NA must provide for mechanisms to:
- Ensure that all executive organs of state in the national sphere of government are accountable to it; and
- Maintain oversight of national executive authority, including the implementation of legislation.

Section 92 (2) goes on to state that 'Members of the Cabinet are accountable collectively and individually to Parliament for the exercise of their powers and the performance of their functions.'

The national Parliament has two houses – the NA and the National Council of Provinces (NCOP). The NA has 400 seats and the NCOP 90. The two houses have distinct functions. In addition to oversight, the role of the NA is to initiate (except for money bills) and pass legislation. The NCOP's role does not expressly include oversight; while it has powers to pass and initiate legislation, its primary function is to ensure that provincial interests are taken into account in the national sphere of government. The composition of the NCOP is determined by provincial elections with its 90 members being made up of a delegation of ten members from each province. Each NCOP delegation has six permanent members and four special members (Calland 1999: 9). The NCOP is often perceived as the 'Cinderella' chamber because it has failed to stamp its authority on the law-making and oversight role and has been hidden by the long shadow of the NA. However, it does provide the entry point for provinces into the national policy-making process and is the connection between provincial and national government. In an important way it also compensates, at least in theory, for the limited powers provinces have individually (Murray & Nijzink 2002: 42).

In addition to the national Parliament, there are nine provincial legislatures with limited law-making functions but important oversight functions in relation to the performance of government at the provincial level. There are also a number of institutions set up to protect and promote constitutional democracy in terms of Chapter 9 of the Constitution. These include the Public Protector, the South African Human Rights Commission (SAHRC), the Commission for Gender Equality, the Auditor-General, the Electoral Commission and the Commission for the Promotion and Protection of the Rights of Cultural, Religious and Linguistic Communities. These so-called 'Chapter 9 institutions' are independent and accountable directly to Parliament and are crucial to the realisation of rights and to the creating of a culture of accountability.

The powers and functions of Parliament's committees

The architecture of Parliament has changed dramatically since 1994. It has been technologically modernised and linked electronically to the world of the twenty-first century. The old apartheid Parliament had no email connectivity, only one fax machine per floor, a library with limited holdings and virtually no support or research staff complement. It also had a very weak committee system that did not play any significant role in law-making or oversight. The post-1994 Parliament has an efficient operational infrastructure with good library facilities, large numbers of researchers and other administrative support staff. In less than a decade, Parliament, according to Calland, changed from 'a part-time, cynical rubber-stamp to a full-time, vibrant place of work' (1999: 1). When the democratic Parliament took office in 1994, it overhauled not only the rules governing the work of Parliament's committees but also opened them up to the public and the media. Overnight, committees moved from being a shadow of the executive to becoming the engine room of Parliament (Calland 1999) and the key instrument in Parliament's attempt properly to fulfil its oversight mandate.

The rules of Parliament grant the NA and NCOP committees extensive powers. These include powers to:
- Summon individuals to give evidence on oath or produce documents;
- Ask any person or institution to report to them;
- Receive petitions, representations or submissions from any interested person, group or institution. (Calland 1999: 31)

They are also empowered to monitor, investigate, enquire into, and make recommendations relating to any aspect of the legislative programme, Budget, rationalisation, restructuring and so on. In practice, committees differ in their effectiveness as overseers of executive action. In large part, this is often a function of the effectiveness of the relevant committee chair. These posts are much sought after by MPs, not just for their potential influence but for the additional remuneration which attends the post.

Currently there are 25 parliamentary portfolio committees. Political party representation on the committees is proportional to the number of seats held by each party in Parliament. The parliamentary committee system attempts to mirror the executive structure by having a committee for each government department. There are also a number of joint committees comprising members from both houses. These include the Joint Standing Committees on Defence, on Intelligence and on the Budget, the Joint Committee on the Improvement of Quality of Life and Status of Women and a Constitutional Review Committee. Parliament also has the power to convene ad hoc committees whenever there is a need for an investigation into a specific issue. The Joint Standing Committee on Intelligence and the Joint Standing Committee on Defence are statutory committees. This means that they are either established by the Constitution or by an Act of Parliament, as well as in terms of the rules of Parliament.

While the structure, powers and duties of Parliament are spelt out unambiguously and ambitiously in the Constitution, there remains a gap between the constitutional aspirations for Parliament and how Parliament and its committee structures have fulfilled its mandate. My argument in this paper is that Parliament as an institution has played its role patchily, unevenly, and sometimes hesitantly. This latter has particularly been the case where the legislature has found itself having to square up to the executive, and it has sometimes capitulated, particularly in the area of oversight. I will illustrate this conclusion by reference to three key case studies:

- The enactment of the so-called anti-terrorism legislation and the National Conventional Arms Control Act. These are cases which show the ways in which different committees have tussled with the executive during the law-making process. The outcomes of both these law-making processes will be analysed for what they tell us about the role of Parliament as law-maker and overseer of the executive.
- The government's multi-billion rand Strategic Defence Procurement Package (or the 'arms deal' as it is commonly known). The arms deal has been something of a litmus test for democratic accountability in South Africa for it has tested every institution, most notably Parliament, which was designed to promote and protect constitutional democracy. The case study will look at both the way in which Parliament dealt with allegations of corruption related to the deal and also the impact it had – and continues to have – on Parliament. In particular, it will explore the oversight role that Scopa exercised at the time of the investigation.

National Conventional Arms Control Act

During the apartheid era, South Africa was much criticised for its conduct in the arms arena, particularly for the many arms sales it made to countries with poor or worse human rights records. When the ANC came to power it pledged to clean up this trade and to apply ethical and human rights criteria to the dealings of its arms industry. To this end, a National Conventional Arms

Control Committee (NCACC) was established under the chairpersonship of Minister Kader Asmal. A former professor of international human rights law and prominent exile critic of South Africa's apartheid arms trade, Asmal was seen as the ideal choice to 'clean up' the local arms trade and to bring accountability to its dealings. The *White Paper on defence* released in the late 1990s went so far as to pledge that the 'principle of openness and transparency relating to the arms trade shall apply' (DoF 1999 chapter 8, para. 12), with the qualification that this transparency could be curtailed due to national security interests.

Little of this has materialised and while it is true that South Africa no longer sells arms to all and sundry, it still sometimes does deals with countries with dubious human rights credentials. Nor has the NCACC been either transparent or accountable in its operations. According to Thandi Modise, one-time Chairperson of the Portfolio Committee on Defence, 'for the first five years since the existence of the NCACC there has been a problem of the parliamentary committee being shut out of the NCACC processes' (Skosana 2002: 11).

In 1999, a draft National Conventional Arms Control Bill (NCAC) was introduced into the legislature in an attempt to legally direct the trade in arms. The Bill was drafted without any input from the portfolio committee that, according to Modise, saw it for the first time when it was tabled before it in July 2000. The Bill soon ran into trouble and was withdrawn, first in 2000 and then again in 2001, because it was argued that the Bill deviated in several respects from the provisions of the Constitution as endorsed in the *White Paper on defence* and consequently compromised the principles of transparency, responsibility and restraint. After various amendments, several important aspects of the Bill were improved to the satisfaction of both the Defence Committee and the NCACC.

However, one principal area of contention remained between the Committee and the executive. It involved the issue of parliamentary participation in the review of applications for the sale of arms (clause 23[1] of the Bill). It contained confidentiality provisions in terms of which information on weaponry exported by South Africa, as well as on their final destinations, would be confidential or reported under conditions of secrecy to the national legislature. The Committee criticised the provision as diverting from stated government policy. The clause was also perceived as being inconsistent with the *White paper on defence* cited earlier. The Chairperson of the NCACC, Minister Asmal, rejected the amendments proposed by the Portfolio Committee on the grounds that premature disclosure could have negative effects on the arms industry. The Bill was therefore withdrawn by the relevant minister and redrafted.

The redrafted Bill broadened the dispute between the executive and Parliament regarding the destination of arms sales, the transparency of such sales and the role of the legislature in the process. In December 2002, the NCAC Bill, albeit an amended version, was enacted despite the concerns of Parliament and civil society organisations with regard to issues of transparency. The clause entrenching prospective oversight had been removed. Parliament lost the battle in its stand-off with the executive despite the best intentions of, particularly, the Chair of the Defence Committee, Thandi Modise. Modise, a committed, strong-willed MP, had gone as far as possible in incorporating the comments from civil society organisations as well as expert drafting input from Laurie Nathan as a special advisor to the Committee. In the end, however, this was insufficient. Furthermore, after the 2004 elections Modise was 'redeployed' by the ANC to the Northern Province legislature as its Speaker. Many interpreted this as a punitive act by the ANC as a direct consequence of her stand-off with the executive. The fact that another independent woman MP, Speaker Frene Ginwala, was at the same time summarily removed from her post as Speaker of the NA reinforced the message of what befalls those who do not fully tow the party line. The fact that both were women was also not lost on observers.

The NCAC Act is an example of a tussle between the executive and the legislature about the content of legislation, where the legislature failed to stand its ground and hold the executive accountable for its actions and policies.

The Protection of Constitutional Democracy against Terrorism Act

In contrast to the case of the NCAC Act in which executive pressure prevailed over the concerns of the national legislature, the Protection of Constitutional Democracy against Terrorism Act of 2004 represents a case where determination on the part of Parliament to carry out its oversight function and represent the interests of the electorate in the face of executive pressure prevailed.

A draft anti-terrorism Bill was tabled for discussion in Parliament on 26 November 2002 and was the subject of public hearings at the Portfolio Committee on Safety and Security. The Bill was widely criticised as unconstitutional for its far-reaching provisions with regard to detention, bail and the extensive search-and-seizure powers granted to the police. The proposed draft Bill initially defined an act of terrorism as 'an unlawful act committed in or outside the Republic' while a 'terrorist organisation' was defined as 'an organisation declared as such by the Minister of Safety and Security and which is likely to intimidate the public or a segment of the public, or is likely to carry out a convention offence'.

Various interest groups argued that the Bill's broad definition of a 'terrorist' and 'terrorist organisation' could extend to legitimate protest activity and consequently argued for a more precise definition that would reduce the chances of arbitrary state action against individuals or organisations. In addition, the Bill raised concern due to the wide powers given to the Minister of Safety and Security, the National Directorate of Public Prosecutions, as well as the general law enforcement agencies. Non-governmental organisations (NGOs) that made submissions on the Bill raised concerns that its far-ranging provisions posed a threat to personal freedom, freedom of expression and freedom of the media.

Perhaps most significantly, the leading trade union organisation, the Congress of South African Trade Unions (Cosatu) opposed the Bill on the grounds that its definition of terrorism could lead to the outlawing of legitimate strike activities. The Bill was then redrafted in the form of the Protection of Constitutional Democracy against Terrorist and Other Related Activities Bill. When the redrafted version was referred to the NCOP in February 2004, the government announced that, under the threat of a nationwide strike by Cosatu, it was delaying a vote on the legislation until after the April 2004 elections.

After consultation with the government, the legislature revived the Bill on 22 June 2004. Thereafter, Parliament formally amended and adopted the Protection of Constitutional Democracy against Terrorist and Related Activities Bill. The Bill, signed into law on 12 November 2004, incorporated most of the concerns made by the unions and civil society organisations. While not everyone was pleased with the final product, the legislature had made a concerted effort to accommodate concerns. It must also be noted that Cosatu in particular had lobbied effectively and boldly in respect of this legislation. The lesson this suggests is that with sufficient will by those outside Parliament, solid gains can be made. It does, however, take a willingness by the legislature (and indeed the executive) to engage constructively and negotiate on the detail of legislation.

The arms deal and the hobbling of Scopa

The third case study is of an issue that has dogged the current Parliament more than any other in the 11 years of its existence. More than that it has impacted upon almost every one of the institutions set up to protect South Africa's hard-won constitutional democracy. These include the Public Protector, the National Prosecuting Authority, the Auditor-General's office and the judiciary. It also seriously damaged the effectiveness of one of Parliament's most important – if not the most crucial – standing committees, namely Scopa. In the space of two years, the arms deal turned one of Parliament's most effective, authoritative and non-partisan bodies into a feeble and partisan rubber stamp. It has not yet recovered its former stature and the consequence has been serious damage to Parliament's watchdog function. The arms deal provides an interesting perspective on what can become of oversight bodies when they encounter realpolitik head-on.

The background details are as follows. Between 1995 and 1996, the Ministry of Defence conducted a Strategic Defence Review of the capacity and requirements of the South African National Defence Force (SANDF). The purpose was, among other things, to identify key areas in which the SANDF required large capital expenditure. In April 1998, Parliament approved the Review and in September of that year the Cabinet provided details of the new arms and equipment it would purchase at a cost of R29.9 billion over 12 years. A year or so later, in December 1999, the executive entered into five major arms transactions involving submarines, corvettes, light-utility helicopters, lead-in fighter trainers, advanced light fighter aircraft and four maritime helicopters, the purchase of which was eventually deferred.

As part of his ordinary function and duty under the Constitution, the Auditor-General investigated certain aspects of the arms transactions and produced a report in September 2000 entitled *Special review of the selection processes of strategic defence packages for the acquisition of armaments at the Department of Defence* (Auditor-General's Office 2000). That report formed the subject of a further investigation by Parliament, through Scopa. In October 2000, Scopa produced its own report on the arms transactions. The two reports identified areas of concern and recommended that further investigations be conducted. There was no suggestion in those two reports of any corruption involved in the deal; they instead sought to highlight important areas in which they had questions and concerns.

Scopa's October 2000 report, for example, raised concerns about the procedural regularity of the arms transactions. Scopa has a very specific and significant role in the parliamentary oversight process. Its core function is to satisfy the legislature that money has been spent in accordance with decisions in the Budget. In other words, that the taxpayer is getting 'value for money'. Unlike other parliamentary committees, Scopa does not pass laws or policies as part of the ruling party's electoral mandate. To the contrary, its mandate is to perform a non-partisan oversight role to ensure the effective management of fiscal resources. As part of that function, the tradition has been that a member of the opposition should chair Scopa, because of its exceptional role. This, like many of the arcane traditions that have filtered through to the South African Parliament, is a widely observed Commonwealth parliamentary tradition. Its chairperson at the time of the arms deal investigation was an Inkatha Freedom Party (IFP) MP, Gavin Woods.

Prior to the arms deal, Scopa enjoyed a reputation as one of the best-run, most efficient committees in parliament. A body inherited from the apartheid era, the post-1994 Scopa took oversight of public expenditure seriously. This was possibly for the first time in its long existence. After 1994, MPs from all parties worked together in a non-partisan way, establishing a system of working groups that, assisted by the technical support of the parliamentary office of the Auditor-General, enabled the committee to cover effectively the broad sweep of its responsibilities.

The arms deal literally tore Scopa apart. The minutiae of what happened cannot be detailed here – suffice to say that a series of heavy-handed interventions from the ANC Whip's office, and on one occasion by Deputy President Zuma, gradually snuffed out the flame of non-partisanship and independence. The first blow was struck in 2001 when the cerebral Andrew Feinstein was removed as the head of the ANC study group within Scopa and replaced by a hitherto little-noticed fellow ANC MP, Vincent Smith.

He turned out to be an effective handmaiden of the ANC Whips. With the political storm over the arms deal growing ever more heated, Smith's task became that of the filibusterer, successfully employing stalling tactics to frustrate Woods's investigative efforts. Woods held onto his position as chair, albeit precariously, until the ANC majority on Scopa, led largely by Smith, pushed a report through to Parliament on its investigation, which, according to Calland and February (2001), was less than satisfactory and left several questions unanswered. He then resigned and was replaced by a National Party member.

Scopa is little heard from these days. Even the reports of a scandal involving the use of public funds by a state-owned corporation in the form of PetroSA appears not to have sparked any activity on the part of what was once, albeit briefly, a fiercely independent oversight grouping.

Public participation

Parliament as the articulator of the will of the people is at the heart of both representative and participatory governance. The Constitution[3] envisages not only formal democracy where citizens elect their representatives, but also an ongoing interaction between citizens and their elected representatives. For all the advantages of the proportional representation system, it does not allow for citizens to have much direct contact with their elected representatives. This has created a situation where the citizenry feels removed from those who are in power, and particularly in poor communities. An informal constituency system is in place in terms of which MPs are assigned a constituency and are expected, particularly during recesses, to visit their constituencies and listen to the concerns of citizens. The system has worked unevenly, often dependent on the diligence of the MP involved. In addition, constituency offices are often under-resourced and there is no clear way for MPs to channel their constituencies' concerns within the parliamentary system.

The South African Constitution provides an opportunity for citizens to be involved in the law-making process and institutional mechanisms exist for public participation in the legislature. Section 59 (1) states that the 'National Assembly must facilitate public involvement in the legislative and other processes of the Assembly and conduct its business in an open manner'.

The question is, how has this space for public input into the parliamentary process been used and by whom? Some NGOs and groups like the European Union have conducted fairly extensive public-education and public-outreach programmes to encourage citizen participation in the national and provincial legislatures, and to some good effect. However, the fact is that the issue of public participation in policy-making is one of those easier-said-than-done cases. A study by Albertyn (in Graham & Coetzee 2002) found that of the approximately 100 000 non-profit organisations in South Africa, mostly community-based, very few have engaged in formal participatory processes such as making submissions to Parliament. Those that have have tended to be the wealthy or better-resourced special interest groups or lobbies representing the worlds of big business and finance. There have been exceptions, however, like Cosatu, which maintains a permanent parliamentary office, and the Treatment Action Campaign. Conspicuous by their absence have been the poor and the marginalised as a consequence of four rather obvious factors – time, communication, transport and education (Fakir 2004).

In addition, the committees of Parliament do not themselves always make it easy for the public to make use of their fora. Implementation of the rules of participation has been uneven and often not conducive for effective public intervention. Committees often give outside bodies too little notice for them to prepare effective or detailed submissions and also often set aside too little time for full and proper hearings and debate. The ways in which committees deal with the submissions and how these are integrated into the committee's activities on a Bill also differ. As Habib and Herzenberg point out, there are no 'uniform rules applying to the weight attached to or the treatment of submissions' (2004: 174). There does not appear to be a systematic process in place whereby submissions are systematically reviewed, and valid or reasonable recommendations extracted and brought before the committee for its consideration.

Parliament does not have a central database on which all the submissions made since 1994 could have been captured. There is therefore no formal record of who has been accessing Parliament and making submissions. However, it is widely understood by those working in and around Parliament that the vast majority of groups participating in terms of making submissions and attending public hearings of committees are, as was noted earlier, limited to better-resourced NGOs and private-sector business interests. These groups are well placed to interact with the complex legislative language in Bills, can afford to travel to Parliament, and have the capacity to conduct research. A notable exception to this is the exceptionally effective Cosatu parliamentary office, which has managed through its deep understanding of politics and parliamentary procedure to carve a role for itself through making both oral and written submissions. Through its research and strategic positioning it has managed to extract certain gains within Parliament, particularly during the deliberations on the so-called anti-terrorism Bill.

Question time

Parliamentary question time is another of the institution's mechanisms of accountability, which, along with the committee system, offers the opportunity of holding the executive to account. In theory, question time provides ordinary members with the opportunity to seek specific, and perhaps embarrassing, information from the President, Deputy President and Cabinet Ministers on matters of importance.

Between 1994 and 2000, question time incorporated three mechanisms: interpellations, questions for oral response and questions for written reply. During this period questions for oral reply in the NA were placed on the question paper in the order in which they were received. It was felt by the ANC that this system was abused by certain parties as between 1994 and 1998 the New National Party, the Democratic Party and the IFP put a combined total of 5 105 questions to ministers as compared to the ANC's 588. Lia Nijzink attributes the infrequency of ANC questioning to the fact that the ANC appeared to regard Parliament as predominantly a venue for reviewing legislation and that many MPs were inexperienced in parliamentary procedure (Nijzink 2001). In 2000, question time was increased from 30 minutes to two hours per week, interpellations were abolished and a rotational system of question allocation, as determined by the numerical strength of the party in the House, introduced.

It cannot be said that question time as an oversight instrument has been a success. The media either show little interest in the weekly sessions or very little that is newsworthy emerges from them. I suspect both explanations apply. Nor does it seem that the Cabinet takes the obligation to answer questions fully very seriously. A frequent problem is what is termed 'question-dodging'. There have been many such cases but the worst is that of the

Minister of Foreign Affairs, Dr Nkosasana Zuma, who has failed to answer a single simple question for two years. In February 2002, she was asked by the DA to explain the circumstances surrounding the resignation of a previous Director-General of the Department, details of any financial arrangements relating to his resignation and steps taken to fill the vacancy. The query remained unanswered for two years until 2004 when the Minister replied in writing to the DA with the following: '(1), (2), (3) We now have a Director-General.'

There are currently no mechanisms for ensuring Cabinet members answer questions in a particular way but this response, whether intended or not, was tantamount to contempt of both the process and Parliament. It has been rare in the last 11 years that a question in the NA has opened up a national debate or even a degree of controversy. One exception was President Mbeki's response to an opposition question by the DA's Ryan Coetzee on HIV/AIDS in 2004 which sparked widespread debate and in some way again served to highlight weaknesses in government policy on the HIV/AIDS pandemic.

The 'Corder Report' of 1999

At the beginning of 1999, Parliament commissioned Professor Hugh Corder, Saras Jagwanth and Fred Soltau of the University of Cape Town's Law Faculty to identify the areas in which Parliament was required to exercise oversight, assess the existing mechanisms and procedures designed to hold the executive to account and to make recommendations to improve the efficiency and effectiveness of such mechanisms. The research report (the so-called 'Corder Report'), which was tabled in July of the same year, proposed, among other things, that Parliament introduce legislation to establish standard oversight practices and ensure the independence of the institutions supporting democracy (ISDs) (Chapter 9 of the Constitution).

In response to this report, the Joint Rules Committee (JRC) established an ad hoc Joint Sub-Committee on Oversight and Accountability, chaired by MP Fatima Chohan-Kota, in order to consider the Corder Report's recommendations and inform the JRC of its findings. The Joint Sub-Committee engaged in a series of meetings and interviewed key role-players before presenting the JRC with its final report in September 2002. Among the proposals included in the report were the recommendations that Parliament, through the JRC, compile a document 'landscaping' the constitutional provisions dealing with the interrelated themes of oversight, accountability and transparency; initiate a process aimed at drafting guidelines for portfolio and select committees to allow, *inter alia*, for joint planning of oversight work; enact legislation to allow it to formally participate in the Budget; investigate the resources available to committees and engage further with relevant stakeholders in terms of the legislature's relationship with the ISDs (Joint Sub-Committee on Oversight and Accountability Report 2002).

One of the most significant comments made by the Joint Sub-Committee concerned the role of the national legislature in the Budget. It noted that the Budget process was a 'fundamentally crucial moment in the lifespan of government, which brought the full scope of Parliament's oversight role to bear on government priorities' (Joint Sub-Committee on Oversight and Accountability 2002: 9). In this regard, the Joint Sub-Committee observed that the legislature did not effectively participate in the process and consequently recommended that Parliament enact legislation in accordance with section 72 (2) of the Constitution.

In August 2004, the JRC of the third Parliament agreed that a task team on oversight and accountability be formed to follow up on the deliberations and recommendations of the Joint Sub-Committee. It was agreed that the focus areas of the task team should include the operating procedures and practices of parliamentary committees, the role of Parliament in the Budget process, and the relationship between Parliament and the ISDs. To date the task team has held preliminary discussions concerning the implementation of its mandate.

Two comments are pertinent to the Corder Report process. One is the fact that Parliament convened the exercise in the first place was a recognition of the fact that the oversight process was in some ways not operating to maximal effect and that it could, at the least, be improved. The second is that the dilatory nature of Parliament's response to the report's recommendations speaks volumes about Parliament's reluctance to actually do something to make the system more effective. It would seem that the political will is lacking.

Conclusion

At the beginning of the life of the third democratic South African Parliament in 2004, the ANC's Chief Whip proclaimed that the focus of the third democratic Parliament would be on strengthening committees and their oversight over implementation of legislation and policy. So far it would seem that there is little to suggest that this was anything more than rhetoric or 'hot air' as some might call it. The question is whether the substance or the 'stuff' of our democracy measures up to the constitutional aspirations of representative and participatory democracy. Parliament faces some serious challenges in establishing a culture of oversight, in communicating its role to the nation, and in affirming its relevance against the backdrop of ever-increasing levels and instances of inequality, such as the tawdry 'Travelgate' investigation. The way in which Parliament deals with these challenges will have a huge influence on the nature and character of our politics in the years ahead. Judging by Parliament's performance to date, the signs are not propitious. Reconciling tensions between the executive and the legislature will always be difficult, particularly where government is headed by a powerful chief executive who appears to dominate a party with an overwhelming majority in the legislature. In these circumstances, the robustness of the legislature will ultimately be a question of political will. So far it would seem that that will is lacking.

In looking back on the performance of South Africa's democratic Parliament over 11 years, it is hard to resist those cliched adages so beloved of schoolteachers in their end-of-term reports, namely, 'must try harder' and 'could do better'.

Notes

1   My thanks to Perran Hahndiek, a researcher in the Political Information and Monitoring Service of the Institute for Democracy in South Africa (Idasa), who provided invaluable assistance in the background research to this paper. Thanks also to Richard Calland for reading the final draft and for his helpful comments.

2   Afrobarometer is a joint project of Idasa, CDD-Ghana and Michigan State University. It is an independent, non-partisan research project that measures the social, economic and political atmosphere in Africa. It conducts a comparative series of national public attitude surveys on democracy, markets and civil society in 16 countries in Africa (www.afrobarometer.org).

3 Section 1 of the Constitution details the founding values, which include, *inter alia*, 'human dignity, accountability, responsiveness and openness...'.

References

Auditor-General's Office (2000) *Special review of the selection processes of strategic defence packages for the acquisition of armaments at the Department of Defence*. Pretoria: Government Printers.

Calland R (1999) *The first five years: A review of South Africa's democratic Parliament.* Cape Town: Institute for Democracy in South Africa (Idasa).

Calland R & February J (2001) *Democracy and the arms deal: An interim review.* Cape Town: Idasa.

Corder H, Jagwanth S & Soltau F (1999) *Report on oversight and accountability*. Cape Town: University of Cape Town.

DoF (Department of Defence, South Africa) (1999) *White Paper on defence*. Pretoria: DoF.

Fakir E (2004) Building a strong civil society. In M Strom & H Boyte (eds.) *Lessons from the field*. Cape Town: Idasa.

Graham P & Coetzee A (2002) *In the balance: Debating the state of democracy in South Africa*. Cape Town: Idasa.

Habib A & Herzenberg C (2004) Popular control over decision-makers. In P Graham & R Calland (eds.) *Democracy in the time of Mbeki*. Cape Town: Idasa.

Idasa (Institute for Democracy in South Africa) (2004) Lessons from the field: A decade of democracy, a series of round tables held at Idasa in Cape Town from June to August 2004.

Jacobs S, Calland R & Power G (2001) *Real politics: The wicked issues*. Cape Town: Idasa.

Mbeki T (2004) Address of the President of South Africa, Thabo Mbeki, at the joint sitting of the third democratic Parliament, Cape Town, 21.05.04.

Murray C & Nijzink L (2002) *Building representative democracy*. Cape Town: European Union Parliamentary Support Programme.

Nijzink L (2001) Opposition in the new South African Parliament. Paper presented at the Konrad Adenauer Foundation Conference on Opposition Politics, Grahamstown.

Skosana X (2002) *The dynamics of post-1994 arms export control policy*. Institute for Security Studies: Pretoria.

South African Parliament (2003) *Ad hoc sub-committee on oversight and accountability: Report*. Cape Town: Government Printers.

South African Parliament (2005) *Mapping the future: The strategic plan of Parliament 2004–2008*. Cape Town: Government Printers.

The state of the national gender machinery: structural problems and personalised politics

Amanda Gouws

Introduction

The institutionalisation of state mechanisms to enhance gender equality in South Africa was part of the negotiated settlement that led to a democratic South Africa. The acceptance of the need to establish a national gender machinery followed a long and hard struggle by South African women to put gender on the political agenda – gender had been made subordinate to the struggle for racial equality for many decades. It was also the culmination of the 'Women's Charter process' when women, with the help of the Women's National Coalition (WNC) (a broad-ranging women's movement consisting of hundreds of women's organisations across party lines), drew up the Charter for Effective Equality and handed it to President Mandela in 1994.

The WNC embodied women's claims for representation and voice in the new democracy. This engagement with the state in South Africa reflected a change in the women's movement away from intense suspicion of government towards greater acceptance and a view of the state that was permeable to women's interests (Hassim 2003). Apart from greater representivity through an increasing number of women being elected to state structures,[1] the national gender machinery (NGM) was set up to serve as the structural nodes through which gender equality would be effected.

The NGM consists of structures that have been created within the state and civil society and reflects the success of feminist activists, academics and grassroots women in negotiating a space for women within the state (also known as 'state feminism'). Considered to be one of the most integrated and advanced sets of structures worldwide, the NGM (see Figure 6.1 on p. 146) encompasses:

- The Office of the Status of Women (OSW) and provincial offices of the Status of Women;
- The Joint Monitoring Committee on the Improvement of the Quality of Life and the Status of Women (JMC);
- The Women's Caucus in Parliament;
- The Women's Empowerment Unit;
- Gender focal points (such as gender desks in each national civil service department which are tasked with gender mainstreaming and monitoring legislation) on national and provincial level; and
- The autonomous Commission on Gender Equality (CGE).

While the institutionalisation of all the structures took time and encountered some difficulties, when the machinery was up and running on a national and provincial level, a great deal of hope and expectation was placed on the ability of these structures to influence policy-making from a gender perspective, and to put women's interests on the political agenda. From the point of view of institution-building this was an important development. What the women's movement wanted was the institutionalisation of equality in the norms and procedures of government and to reduce reliance on political will for gender equality (Hassim 2003). The NGM was to provide the channels through which women would exercise policy influence with regard to women's interests, and would ensure women's participation in decision-making.

Now, nearly a decade after the founding of the first structures, optimism has waned and a degree of scepticism colours perceptions about the NGM. The main reasons for this change in opinion are the open conflict between some of the structures, the limited achievements of gender mainstreaming through the gender focal points, and an uneven engagement with women and women's organisations in civil society.

While the NGM was hailed as one of the most integrated and advanced structures in the world, it seems that its problems are related precisely to its comprehensive nature – structural problems tend to arise when many bodies have overlapping mandates. For example, it may be difficult for the NGM to fulfil its function as a watchdog when it is not autonomous from government (the JMC is a government standing committee). As Seidman (2003) points out, policy machineries in advanced industrial societies mainly focus on giving women a voice and representation but in post-colonial societies these structures tend to be oriented more toward mobilising women and seeking to ensure their participation in gender projects, thus putting a double burden on these structures. To further complicate matters the NGM is beset with leadership problems and, in some cases, is seriously under-resourced. It is possible that these problems mask an underlying conflict about what a feminist vision for the NGM should be, or if the vision should be a feminist one at all.

One needs to question therefore what criteria should be used to assess the NGM in South Africa. In her assessment of the CGE, Cherry took 'areas of priority identified by the CGE' (2004: 4) and evaluated how the CGE had realised its mandate in relation to each one. This is a useful yardstick, but would be difficult to use for the purposes of this chapter, as every structure would have to be assessed independently. This chapter aims to consider whether the NGM has fulfilled the expectations of influencing policy and giving organised women's interests access to the decision-making process using an analytical framework developed by Stetson and Mazur (1995). This analysis is followed by a description of the work done to date by the various structures of the NGM and a brief assessment of some of the problem areas.[2] It must be borne in mind that the NGM is only eight years old. Some structures are even younger than that. In a sense, one should expect some teething problems.

Theoretical framework

The analytical model designed by Stetson and Mazur uses two theoretical dimensions to test whether, what they call 'national policy machineries' contribute to gender equality (1995: 14). These dimensions are:
- State capacity: to what extent do women's policy machineries influence policy-making from a gender perspective?
- State–society relations: to what extent do women's policy machineries develop opportunities for society-based actors – feminist and women's advocacy organisations – to access the policy process?

In order to determine whether state capacity and the state–society relations exist, Stetson and Mazur use the following variables:
- The *pattern of politics* surrounding the establishment of women's policy machinery. (Was it created by government, or through party political platforms or through efforts of women's organisations and feminist activists?)

- The extent to which certain *organisational forms* increase the likelihood that policy machineries will further feminist goals. (Is it a single, government bureau, an independent commission or a whole array of bodies?)
- The extent to which the *state has the capacity* to contribute to social change and women's policy machinery can draw on the state for resources.
- The extent to which there is a *coherent women's movement* supporting women's liberation or small divergent women's groups or a combination of the two.

In a comparative study of the national policy machineries of 14 industrialised countries in North America and Europe, Stetson and Mazur (1995) came to the following conclusions:
- First, machineries with a high level of success were all created under initiatives of social democratic governments that placed gender equity on their policy agendas (such as Australia, Denmark, Norway and the Netherlands) and where there was relatively strong pressure from moderate feminist organisations.
- Second, those countries that had a high level of success all had centralised cross-sectoral approaches and promoted gender mainstreaming. Other societies that had either only one structure or dispersed structures with no centralised co-ordinating office had less success with policy influence and limited civil society access was achieved.
- Third, countries with successful machineries brought societal interests into the state and all viewed the state as a major actor for dealing with social inequality. France, for example, is a powerful state but impenetrable to emerging social interests.
- Finally, countries that had successful machineries also had active feminist groups in which women citizens participated, as well as established trade unions and political parties. Radical feminist groups raised gender consciousness, while more moderate feminist groups put pressure on political party elites and politicians to take women's policy machineries seriously.

High access and high influence are therefore related to having a centralised structure concerned with gender equality and also to integrating gender-equity concerns into policy-making while involving women's organisations.

As the authors state in their conclusion:

This study suggests that women's policy machineries will reach high levels of state feminism, on the one hand, when the state is defined as a site of social justice and has the structural capacity to institutionalise new demands for equality, and, on the other, when society sustains widely supported feminist organisations that challenge sex hierarchies through both radical politics from outside and reform politics in unions and parties. (Stetson & Mazur 1995: 290)

In the following section, I apply Stetson and Mazur's four variables to the South African context.

Determining state capacity and state–society relations

Pattern of politics

The establishment of the NGM was championed by civil society organisations in the form of women's groups that came together in the WNC. This alliance experienced a groundswell of support from 1992 to 1994 when the Women's Charter process culminated in the formation of the Charter for Effective Equality.[3]

During the public hearings for the final Constitution, feminist academics contributed to submissions, debating the pros and cons of different types of structures. The support for women's liberation that was vocally and visibly expressed during the period of transition and the formulation of the final Constitution thus formed the backdrop against which the NGM came into existence. This feminist presence opened a space in the state for women to increase their representation in government, also indirectly influencing the quota debate, which ensured that the African National Congress (ANC) accepted a one-third quota for women. The transition to a liberal democracy through which everyone, regardless of race, could claim rights opened the door for a gender-equitable agenda.

This first period during the Charter campaign and the negotiation phase saw women forming alliances across party lines but post-1994, when the ANC came to power, a shift occurred. Loyalties to the ANC and women's participation in the struggle against apartheid on the side of the ANC became an important marker of their capacity to fill positions in the government and the national machinery. In some cases, political credentials replaced specifically gender-related qualifications or expertise when it came to appointments in the NGM.

Organisational form

The organisational form is an integrated set of structures (more integrated than gender machineries in most other countries) that should network between national, provincial and local government and women's organisations in civil society, thus implying vertical (OSW) and horizontal (CGE) accountability (the NGM still needs to be institutionalised at local level).

Figure 6.1 *Structure and components of the national gender machinery*

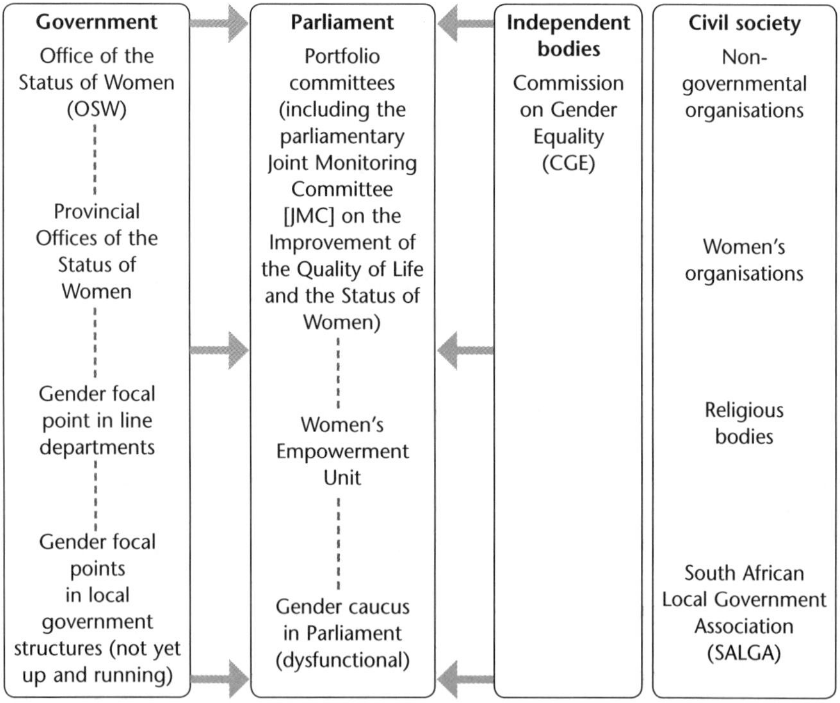

Government	Parliament	Independent bodies	Civil society
Office of the Status of Women (OSW)	Portfolio committees (including the parliamentary Joint Monitoring Committee [JMC] on the Improvement of the Quality of Life and the Status of Women)	Commission on Gender Equality (CGE)	Non-governmental organisations
Provincial Offices of the Status of Women			Women's organisations
Gender focal point in line departments	Women's Empowerment Unit		Religious bodies
Gender focal points in local government structures (not yet up and running)	Gender caucus in Parliament (dysfunctional)		South African Local Government Association (SALGA)

Source: Adapted from OSW (n.d.a)

The apex of the NGM is formed by the OSW which resides in the Office of the State President, giving it the authority and status to be able to co-ordinate and network with other structures in government such as the gender focal points in the state departments and the provincial OSWs.

The CGE is an independent statutory body with the aim of monitoring government, the private sector and civil society. The work done by the main organisations in the NGM is described in more detail later in the chapter.

Capacity of the state

The South African Constitution can be described as one of the most women-friendly constitutions in the world. It embodies the principles of non-sexism and non-racism. It has an equality clause that is interpreted to provide not only formal but also substantive equality. This clause includes 17 grounds on which discrimination may not take place, five of which are related to gender equality (sex, gender, sexual orientation, marital status and pregnancy). The same clause allows for justifiable discrimination through affirmative action. Women are one of the designated groups in the Employment Equity Act of 1999, through which they can claim affirmative action in the workplace.

Since 1994, the state has shown its commitment to gender equality in many different ways, such as the institutionalisation of the NGM as well as through a number of very important laws that have been passed by Parliament to improve the equality of women, such as the Termination of Pregnancy Act of 1997, the Domestic Violence Act of 1998, the Recognition of Customary Marriages Act of 1998, the Maintenance Act of 1998, the Labour Relations Act of 1996 and the Employment Equity Act of 1999.

Social welfare provisions for women have also been improved and equalised across race groups. Women can now access the child support grant, improved old-age pensions and grants for people living with disabilities. Since a large number of women and children live in conditions of extreme poverty, these grants are mostly aimed at improving the living conditions of women. After 1994, policy formulation in development-related issues was also influenced by gender concerns, such as access to land, water, housing, healthcare and public works programmes (Albertyn & Hassim 2003).

While women still battle with conditions that seriously hamper their gender equality, such as very high levels of gender-based violence, HIV/AIDS and customary practices that debilitate their autonomy, the state is seen as being sympathetic to women's equality and is actively involved in initiatives to change the lives of women.

Coherent women's movement

Prior to 1994, the WNC represented an alliance of numerous women's organisations around the single issue of the Charter for Effective Equality. Since then, the mobilisation of women's organisations has changed drastically. Women's organisations now organise sectorally around issues such as violence against women, reproductive health and poverty and the broader alliance of organisations has all but disappeared. Interaction with the state and the national machinery seems uneven. Those who are in close proximity to the OSW head office in Pretoria (such as Gauteng-based organisations) have a greater opportunity to attend the National Gender Forum (NGF) where the NGM interacts with civil society, which will be discussed later in the chapter. On the other hand the Rural Women's Movement has mobilised women in rural areas for submissions on certain Bills.

It is true, however, that there is no broad-based alliance that keeps the NGM accountable to their constituency or maintains pressure on government to deliver on gender equality. For example, it is curious that, in the face of the high mortality rate among women due to HIV/AIDS, no broad-based alliance among women has been formed around this issue.

This 'fragmentation' of women's alliances is common to post-transitional societies where, during the struggle to achieve democracy, women often form alliances as part of community-based organisations against oppressive regimes but when transition is achieved they start to rely on women in government to bring about changes in gender inequality. It seems that the institutionalisation of gender processes defuses the very important gender activism that sustained the struggle against gender oppression in the first place and leads to the marginalisation of women's organisations so that they do not exercise meaningful influence (Waylen 1996).

Given the fact that the state is recognised as being women-friendly and having a commitment to gender equality, combined with an integrated set of state structures, the South African NGM should at least fall into the category of high state capacity, even if on the level of access it is less successful. The tension between exercising policy influence at the same time as mobilising women for a feminist agenda is one of the problems that plagues the NGM. This, combined with structural problems through which power is dispersed unevenly, as well as overly broad and overlapping mandates have contributed to a situation where the machinery is, at the time of writing, perceived to be conflict-ridden and in crisis.

A closer look at the three main structures of the NGM – the OSW, CGE and JMC – is necessary to highlight the successes that have been achieved even though these may now be somewhat overshadowed by internal conflict. The NGF will also be discussed.

The main structures of the national gender machinery

The Commission on Gender Equality

The CGE was established in 1997. It was brought to life through the Commission on Gender Equality Act of 1996, and comprises eight to 12 commissioners, some of whom may be part-time. Presently there are 12 commissioners.

The mandate of the CGE (2002/03) is wide-ranging and includes:
- Monitoring and evaluating the policies and practices of both government and private sector institutions;
- Public education and information;
- Making recommendations to government to promote gender equality, including suggestions for law reform and new legislation (with regard to personal and family law, indigenous law, customary practices and any other law);
- Following up complaints (it has the power to subpoena witnesses), investigating gender matters and complaints, and resolving conflicts by mediation, conciliation and negotiation;
- Monitoring government's compliance with international conventions;
- Submitting reports to government on gender equality.

The CGE started off using a consultative approach through information gathering and evaluation workshops. This indicated a commitment to consultative planning and an understanding of accountability to constituencies of women. An evaluation carried out for the United Nations International Research and Training Institute for the Advancement of Women (Instraw 2000) viewed the CGE as successful in terms of building partnerships with women's organisations and with researchers, as well as engaging the media and raising consciousness around gender issues. While its budget has been small compared to that of the South African Human Rights Commission, donor funding helped with the financial shortfall (Instraw 2000).

One of the key weaknesses singled out in the Instraw evaluation was the issue of horizontal accountability – it seemed that the CGE showed a reluctance to challenge the government when there was backsliding on gender equality. But what the evaluation showed is that the CGE is unique in its monitoring capacity and that no women's organisation alone can fulfil this function.

Yet, while this 2000 report indicated that the CGE was performing well overall, the evaluation was completed before 2000 and by the middle of that year, the CGE was in such disarray it could not co-ordinate activities to commemorate Women's Day that year, and half of the staff and some commissioners had resigned or had been fired under acrimonious circumstances (Seidman 2003). Seidman attributes this immobilisation of the CGE to three factors:

- Its efforts to simultaneously represent feminist voices and to mobilise support for a feminist vision;
- Differences of opinions in the CGE with regard to promoting a feminist vision as opposed to doing gender-development work that risked diluting the feminist vision;
- Adhering to its broad mandate but focusing on rural women (which it had set out as one of its main aims).

Seidman concluded that by not working with feminists who were already organised, the CGE had created a target audience who acted like dependants in need of service delivery.

The CGE subsequently moved beyond this impasse by developing a more strategic focus and a plan of action focused on five priority areas: governance; gender-based violence; gender and poverty; tradition, culture, religion and sexuality; and gender and HIV/AIDS. Annual reports of the CGE for 2002/03 and 2003/04 suggest that the organisation has been active. For example:

- The CGE undertook research in all nine provinces on the local process of drawing up their integrated development plans, thereby monitoring integrated development planning in municipalities.
- In terms of advocacy, it convened workshops on gender and good governance in Limpopo together with the Independent Electoral Commission, the OSW and other stakeholders. A good governance summit was also held in Paarl with the aim of improving service delivery and the lives of underprivileged women.
- Together with the Gender Advocacy Programme and the non-governmental organisation (NGO), Gender Links, it launched the 50/50 campaign for parity in government. It also made a submission to the Electoral Task Team on the advantages and disadvantages for women of different types of electoral systems.
- A gender budget workshop was held with stakeholders on the Gender Budget. It also participated in a mock women's parliament organised by the Mpumalanga Parliamentary Women's Caucus and it held a Young Women's Indaba.
- It made legislative interventions and parliamentary submissions on the Promotion of Equality and Prevention of Unfair Discrimination Act of 2000, and convened the Consultative Conference on the Additional (Women's) Protocol to the African Charter on Human and People's Rights. It also made recommendations to the Second United Nations (UN) World Summit on Ageing, Gender and Older Persons.
- Its advocacy work included a meeting with social partners and stakeholders, including the Sex Worker Education and Advocacy Task Force and the Women's Legal Centre to discuss issues raised by the South African Law Commission's *Issue paper on sexual offences*. As part of its annual campaign to combat violence against women, CGE commissioners and department heads participated in many events during the 16 Days of Activism Against Gender Violence. It also organised workshops in all provinces to promote awareness on the plight of rural women in relation to poverty.
- In performing its oversight functions, it monitored implementation by the private sector of the Employment Equity Act of 1998, as well as the Maintenance Act where it acted as *amicus curiae* in a maintenance case before the Constitutional Court. It is also involved in monitoring implementation of the Domestic Violence Act of 1998. As such, it undertook

a domestic violence survey in Limpopo and, in November 2003, convened a consultative conference on gender-based violence in Bloemfontein and Upington and a summit with major stakeholders in Kimberley.

The CGE has also dealt with a large number of complaints. According to their 2003/04 annual report, the CGE received 2 137 complaints, disaggregated into the following categories: gender-based violence (23%), maintenance (24%), social welfare (7%), customary law (2%), labour-related (8%), divorce-related (4%), media-related (3%), enquiries (9%), employment (6%), and other (14%).

Clearly, in terms of its mandate of public education, consciousness-raising and advocacy, and dealing with complaints, the CGE is succeeding. It has also had success in networking with civil society organisations with an interest in pending legislation and been effective in commissioning opinions from well-regarded human rights lawyers. On some issues it maintained a progressive feminist position, for example, with regard to the Women's Budget Initiative, it held a feminist position on the recognition of unpaid labour and the importance of the role of women in the 'care economy' (Cherry 2004).

Cherry's evaluation, which used the five areas mentioned earlier to look at the effectiveness of the CGE, found that it was relatively successful in all five areas. She points out in regard to the CGE's critical stance on the Communal Land Rights Bill of 2004 and the Traditional Leadership and Governance Act of 2003 that it was effective through obtaining a strong rights-based opinion and forcefully presenting this to the parliamentary portfolio committee but nonetheless failed to prevent the passing of the legislation.

The Office of the Status of Women

The establishment of the OSW was approved by Cabinet memorandum in 1997 as the body that has to implement gender equality in government departments on national and provincial level. The main brief of the OSW on a national level was to develop a national gender policy. This task was completed in 2003. The OSW is situated within the Office of the President and reports to the Minister in the Office of the Presidency. This placement is important because it allows the OSW to draw on the authority of the President.

As the principal structure that co-ordinates the NGM, the OSW's mandate is to maintain a vibrant gender programme. Its functions include:
- Ensuring that each department implements the national gender policy;
- Ensuring that gender issues are routinely considered in departmental strategic planning, and ensuring that departments reflect gender considerations in their business plans and routinely report on them;
- Reviewing all policies, projects and programmes for their gender implications to ensure that departments provide and use gender disaggregated data in their work;
- Establishing mechanisms to link and liaise with civil society;
- Co-ordinating gender training and education in all departments;
- Monitoring and evaluating department projects to assess their gender content. (OSW n.d.a: 28)

Thus, the main task of the OSW is the promotion of gender mainstreaming in government departments through facilitating, monitoring and implementation. It is also responsible for monitoring government's compliance with international accords that the South African government has signed, such as the United Nations Convention on the Elimination of All Forms of Discrimination Against Women.

The OSW was successful in drawing up the national policy framework for women's empowerment and gender equality, even though this took nearly five years to complete. The route that the national OSW followed was to insulate itself from civil society while it consolidated its internal structures and processes. This process made it vulnerable to criticism (Instraw 2000). Another important undertaking of the OSW was the national gender audit (OSW n.d.b) that it undertook of national and provincial government levels during the period 1994 to 1998. The audit looked at the feasibility of the NGM system and the capacity of national and provincial governments to mainstream gender issues. One of the important findings of this audit was that there is a strong political will and a legislative framework in place that will mainstream gender within government but that this is not matched by the administrative will. On the contrary, gender initiatives are sometimes stalled and undermined by the administrative machinery. It also found that there is a general lack of clarity about accountability and reporting lines.

Provincial OSWs have been more active in developing programmes of action and instituting close links with civil society. While this process is uneven in the different provinces, the OSW in the Provincial Administration of the Western Cape is described as an example of a successful provincial OSW.

The provincial OSW in the Provincial Administration of the Western Cape

This OSW has created five programmatic areas:
- Policy development through which it developed a gender strategy baseline document;
- Public education and awareness raising, including involvement in Women's Day events and the campaign of 16 Days of Activism Against Gender Violence;
- Monitoring, evaluating and reporting – departments submit annual reports;
- Capacity building and training – including the development of a unique mainstreaming training package and opening spaces for the NGO sector to help with training, for example the Gender and Education and Training Network. The deputy director ensures that gender focal people are trained;
- Partnership building – one such initiative has been developed with SIDA a donor agency in Canada around gender focal points in which cost-sharing also occurs.[4]

Apart from doing gender mainstreaming inside the provincial government, this OSW also networks with the Cape Town Unicity and with different local governments. A metro-wide gender forum was founded where the OSW and the Unicity came together for workshops. A 'roadshow' was taken to local municipalities in George, Caledon, Beaufort West, Worcester, Moorreesburg, Oudsthoorn, Vredendal, and the Unicity where workshops were held with the aims of:
- Popularising and consulting around the gender equality and women-empowerment implementation strategy for the Western Cape;
- Identifying the needs of women in line with the national theme of '10 years of freedom – What has it meant for women?';
- Raising awareness and determining priorities for the establishment of new disability, youth and gender structures at district level;

- Improving the effectiveness of provincial co-ordination and strengthening existing gender structures. (Directorate Human Rights Programmes, OSW, Western Cape 2004)

The aim is to empower local structures to start their own gender desks. The OSW also co-ordinated a 'train the trainer programme' and developed a gender training course for public-sector managers, as well as assisted in the development of an organisational model for the provincial gender management system.

The Joint Monitoring Committee on the Improvement of the Quality of Life and the Status of Women

This structure was established as an ad hoc committee in August 1996 and later became the Joint Standing Committee on the Improvement of the Quality of Life and the Status of Women (now the Joint Monitoring Committee or JMC) when the need for a permanent committee was recognised (Instraw 2000).

The Committee has to make sure that the UN Convention on the Elimination of All Forms of Discrimination Against Women and the Beijing Platform of Action have been implemented and assess the extent to which departments have prioritised women's needs as well as the differential impact of spending on men and women. It also has to identify gaps in existing and proposed policy and legislation and identify key priorities for women – such as violence and customary law (Instraw 2000).

Since this Committee includes members of different political parties and is situated in Parliament, the question has been raised about the structural anomaly of it having to monitor the legislative process. Nevertheless it has been very successful in getting gender included in legislation and fast-tracking Bills that would have a positive impact on women's lives. With a Committed feminist such as Pregs Govender as the (previous) chair, the committee has been an example of what visionary leadership can do to enhance gender equality.

In a previous study (Gouws 2004) I tracked one piece of legislation to determine the influence of the NGM. My research showed that the input of the JMC was crucial in the making of the Recognition of Customary Marriages Act of 1998, with more limited inputs from other structures. This is an indication that the JMC can play a very important monitoring function in government. The JMC has also hosted a number of key public hearings, such as on the Domestic Violence Bill and the Recognition of Customary Marriages Bill, and also played a central part in the Women's Budget Initiatives.

After the resignation of Govender as the chair of the JMC, and as a Member of Parliament at the end of 2002, the JMC has had a lower profile in government. It was practically dysfunctional in 2004, and seems to have lost momentum. The loss of Govender serves to highlight the importance of having dedicated and skilled feminists within the NGM.

The National Gender Forum

The NGF, which involves civil society in the work of the NGM, was created in 2003, and is co-ordinated by the national OSW with the aim of arranging meetings between the OSW, CGE, JMC and women's organisations once a quarter. When it first started it was highly successful in bringing the different structures together on a platform where information could be shared with civil society and where civil society could give inputs on its needs and interests.

If we look at these structures independently, each one seems to have successfully completed projects related to its mandate. The success rate is uneven but, in a sense, each structure makes a contribution to the struggle for gender equality through monitoring, advocacy, gender consciousness-raising and gender training. However, when we try to assess the relationships between the structures and how they interact with one another, a different picture emerges, one in which structural problems and differential power relations wreak havoc with the national gender project.

Structural problems

Between the structures of the NGM

While it is clear that the OSW, CGE and JMC have had great success with many of their projects that involve monitoring, advocacy and consciousness-raising and have managed to involve civil society, interviews I conducted with members of the NGM, civil society organisations that attended the NGF and consultants to the NGM,[5] show that the boundaries of the mandates of the three major structures in the NGM are not well defined. While overlap may be the logical consequence of the monitoring function of all three of these structures, there is a lack of integrated planning where all three of the structures are present. This overlap also leads to different (and sometimes exaggerated) expectations.

Co-ordinating all these structures is the task of the national OSW. Research has shown that countries in the North with a centralised structure at the top that can effectively exercise authority and engage in cross-sectoral approaches have the highest state capacity, but in the case of South Africa currently, it has led to structural impediments because the top structure (the OSW) is not exercising the necessary authority in the NGM. These problems are compounded by personality clashes and personalised politics within some of the structures.

A lack of co-ordination is also apparent between the provincial OSWs and the national OSW. Initially the national and provincial OSWs held planning meetings where strategy was spelt out and mandates reviewed. These meetings no longer take place. It is argued here that the national OSW is in such an important position that if it does undertake timely strategic planning with the different structures in government and if it has visionary leadership, it could play a crucially supportive role.

The NGF was an admirable attempt by the OSW to get all three structures together and to involve civil society organisations. While these meetings were successful at first, now they are often cancelled, or major stakeholders arrive late or do not turn up. The NGF has been seriously weakened by conflict. In a few instances these forums deteriorated into shouting matches between major stakeholders to the great dismay of civil society organisations, some of which are now reluctant to even attend NGF meetings. A further problem is the lack of continuity in that different people are sent to represent the structures at NGF meetings. This creates frustration among those members who attend on a regular basis.

There is limited co-ordination and communication within the machinery. An example of this lack of communication was the preparation of the final document for the Beijing +10 meeting in New York in March 2005. While it was the responsibility of the OSW to draw up this report, there was no co-ordination with civil society organisations, who also prepared documents. The draft report for government was prepared in such a way that Cabinet rejected it and demanded its revision.

Information is located in different places within the NGM. Getting information from the OSW is important because of its proximity to power and the fact that it has direct links with the UN. It therefore has access to information that is not publicly disseminated. An attempt was made to address the problem of co-ordination within the NGM at the Gender Summit held in August 2001, which brought together the different structures and civil society. But despite the Summit, problems persist.

Within structures: the case of the Commission on Gender Equality

THE SPLIT BETWEEN NATIONAL OFFICE AND PROVINCIAL OFFICES

Because the mandate of the CGE, as defined by the Commission on Gender Equality Act, is so wide and the organisation is small, it is difficult to define the focus of its work. This problem is complicated by the fact that commissioners are national appointees but have to take responsibility for provinces. Where commissioners are allocated to provinces, their interests often shift to the needs and demands of provinces where projects are successfully implemented and stakeholders are better cared for. In contrast, when issues are referred to head office it often takes a long time to get a response (in some cases more than a year). Communication between head office and the provincial offices is often poor, and it is difficult for the CGE to take important decisions if head office and provinces meet in a plenary only once a quarter.

THE SPLIT BETWEEN COMMISSIONERS AND THE SECRETARIAT

There also seems to be a split between the secretariat (administrators) and commissioners (independent) within the CGE. It is unclear where the power resides. This split has resulted in clashes between the Chief Executive Officer and the chair of the CGE – the recent disagreement over which of the two should attend the Beijing +10 meeting in New York is just one example.

Another issue is that when commissioners are appointed it is expected that they will relinquish their party political membership in order to be autonomous. However, it seems that not all CGE members have done this, which tends to compromise the CGE's ability to be critical of government.

STRUCTURAL PLACEMENT OF GENDER FOCAL POINT APPOINTMENTS

While most research and recommendations have made it clear that people who are appointed as officials for the gender focal points should be appointed at high structural levels in the civil service, such as directors (Adams 2001), most have been appointed at very low levels and lack the necessary authority to enforce decisions made. This lack of authority, coupled with a lack of resources and skills, contributes to the less than optimal functioning of the gender focal points. If these focal points are the main strategic points from where gender mainstreaming is to be exercised the problems are self-evident.

The problem of communication

Apart from its lack of internal communication, the NGM also communicates infrequently with the wider public. For example, if civil society is to understand what the CGE is doing, it needs to improve communication with the public about its successes in dealing with complaints from ordinary women and solving their problems. Very often criticism of the CGE arises when complaints are dealt with by the media in a way that the public can neither understand nor accept, as in the case of the South African ambassador to Indonesia who had been involved in more than one sexual harassment case. When the CGE was reluctant to deal with this issue it created the impression that it is not willing to call government to account. While this was only one complaint of many (and one that was *sub judice*), others that were successfully dealt with have not been brought to the public's attention, which leads to the perception that the NGM is ineffective and its staff incompetent.

The problem of accountability

The NGM is involved in two types of accountability – holding government accountable for delivering on gender equality and being accountable to the women in civil society. It is specifically the role of the CGE to hold government accountable but from my interviews it is clear that there is reluctance on the part of the CGE to call government to account. The example where the Minister of Foreign Affairs did not act against the Indonesian ambassador is only one case of this reluctance.

In the absence of a strong women's movement to hold the NGM accountable to a constituency of women, a vacuum has formed in which personalised politics can develop. Unless women's organisations keep the NGM accountable, access to the NGM will be eroded.

The problem of workload

One interviewee indicated that there is a misunderstanding about the creation of gender equality as a *process* that involves more than changing the numbers of women in government, but also changing gender values and norms that are part of the institutional culture. This reinforces the idea that gender mainstreaming does not involve a lot of work. On the contrary, making gender central to all government policies and processes requires the involvement of many people for staff training, policy implementation and follow-up. Most staff members of the NGM are overwhelmed by their workload. A good example of making ends meet against the odds of a heavy workload is the OSW in the Western Cape Province, which consists of only one permanent member of staff and one intern. Despite the lack of support, many projects have been well managed as described earlier in the chapter. In some instances there has been a fast turnover of staff because salaries are not competitive with the private sector.

The problem of strategic leadership

Visionary leadership is crucial for institution-building because future leadership will use practices and policies that have been established. Bad practices are very often hard to eradicate once they are institutionalised. Visionary leadership also understands the difference between practical and strategic gender needs (where the first deals with short-term changes in women's conditions and the latter with long-term, strategic objectives). For strategic needs, a clear feminist agenda is necessary – something that only some members of the NGM are able to articulate. This is one consequence of rewarding loyal party members with positions in the NGM, rather than appointing women with the necessary gender expertise and skills. It needs to be communicated to the Presidency that redeploying skilled women from the NGM (like the removal of Tenjiwe Mtintso, for example), leaves a gap that cannot always be filled with an equally skilled person. It also begs the question of how serious government is about gender equality.

With the change of name from the women's national machinery to the NGM, a corresponding shift in priorities from women to gender has occurred. Many interviewees voiced concern about this, citing a forthcoming 'Men's Summit' organised by the CGE (and involving the project on Moral Regeneration) as shifting the focus from women to men – in a time that women's issues need more articulation than ever, given the high rates of gender violence and HIV/AIDS infections. This is an indication of the difficulty of focusing on a feminist agenda at a time when engaging with tradition and culture is also a priority.

The tendency that has developed in government of dealing harshly with criticism also seems to be present in the NGM, where some staff have become too fearful to criticise, contributing to a spiral of silence that can only be detrimental to the NGM.

While it is not difficult to find solutions for the structural problems in the NGM, strategic leadership is required to transcend personal politics.

Conclusion

This chapter has examined the policy influence that the NGM exercises as an integrated set of structures and the access to policy-making that it accords to organised women's interests. Looking at each structure individually, it can be said that most do exercise some influence through their consciousness-raising activities, inputs on legislation and monitoring of government's actions around gender issues.

However, it is also clear that the NGM is bedevilled by its institutional design and internal conflicts. The authority that should be vested in the OSW as the structure that should steer and co-ordinate the NGM is lacking, partly due to personality politics and partly due to limited capacity. The CGE, while exercising its mandate, is undermined by the dual burden of representing women and mobilising them at the same time, limiting its capacity and resulting in a situation where it seeks to be something, or even everything, for everyone. It has failed to set a clear feminist agenda and therefore one needs to question whether state feminism really exists in the NGM.

Women and women's organisations have themselves forced the CGE into the role of mobilising women as a consequence of the limited mobilisation that has happened since 1994. The reason for this diminishing gender activism in the democratic era is not clear. There does seem to have been far too great a reliance placed on the larger number of women in Parliament and in government. Much work needs to be done to ensure that organisations, other than and in addition to, women's groups take up the challenge of putting gender issues on the political agenda. While the NGM does not yet fall into the category of having high influence and high access, it clearly has the potential to move into that category.

While enabling conditions and environments for gender equality have been put in place in the past decade, certain conditions are needed to shift the South African NGM into the category of successful gender machineries without which enabling environments and conditions mean little. These conditions include the honouring of process, agreements and respect for consultation; a move away from personalised politics; and a move toward strategic leadership. In this regard there is an obligation on women's organisations in civil society to hold the NGM accountable. Viewing the government as a benefactor and only relying on women in government is not enough for healthy democratic gender politics. Probably the most critical need is for the OSW to begin to exercise the authority needed for structural integration, leading to a gender machinery that could be viewed as falling into the categories of high influence and high access.

Afterword

On 31 March 2005 a meeting was held in Cape Town organised by the Western Cape CGE to discuss the problems that exist in the NGM with the aim of making the NGM (in the Western Cape at least) more effective. The meeting involved the CGE of the Western Cape, the OSW in Provincial Administrator of the Western Cape, gender focal point staff and members of civil society. The problems that were spelt out earlier became apparent at this meeting, making it clear that members of the NGM are not unaware of them.

At this meeting, demands were voiced for better structural integration, better and more strategic communication and for a more visible women's movement – something that is difficult to address unless the other provinces are also involved. These demands coincide with the recommendations made in Cherry's (2004) report as well as those of Serote (n.d.b), namely, strategic thinking, putting into place a systematic monitoring process, strengthening partnerships with civil society, identifying priorities and working cross-sectorally.

On the same day, 31 March 2005, a South African Women in Dialogue (SAWID) meeting was held with women from urban areas of the Western Cape (mainly Cape Town). From this meeting it was clear that SAWID is an attempt to mobilise different women's constituencies and to involve younger women in the process. It seems that the new initiative by Ms Zenele Zanele Mbeki, President Mbeki's wife, is an attempt to mobilise women outside of the NGM. According to a brochure they have produced:

> SAWID is conceptualised as 'an initiative…to create a forum where women from all sectors of society can gather to break barriers and to talk and listen to one another. SAWID takes place within the framework of the vision of the African Union and Nepad for the development and regeneration of the African continent'.

The question arises whether this initiative is a vote of no confidence in the NGM. One could also argue that this attempt could alleviate the burden on the NGM to mobilise the women's constituency, something that detracts from its function of representation. The SAWID initiative could fill the gap in gender activism for the time being.

Notes

1   In 1994, 27.7 per cent women were elected, 29.5 per cent in 1999 and 32 per cent in 2004.
2   The author thanks an anonymous reviewer for helpful comments on this chapter.
3   For a more detailed discussion see Hassim 2005: 61–65.
4   Interview with Ms Pat September, Deputy Director of the OSW in the Provincial Administration of the Western Cape.
5   Interviews were conducted with CGE commissioners, consultants to the NGM, members of the OSW in the Provincial Administration of the Western Cape and members of civil society. Most interviewees wanted to remain anonymous for fear of victimisation by other members of the NGM. This is already an indication that a healthy political atmosphere where criticism can be voiced does not exist in the NGM. The chair of the JMC was not available for an interview.

References

Adams UL (2001) Promoting gender equality in the Provincial Administration of the Western Cape: An appraisal based on perceptions of Gender Focal Persons and the Head of the Western Cape Office on the Status of Women for Gender Equality. Unpublished MPhil thesis.

Albertyn C & Hassim S (2003) The boundaries of democracy: Gender, HIV/AIDS and culture. In D Everatt & V Maphai (eds.) *The real State of the Nation*. Johannesburg: Interfund.

CGE (Commission on Gender Equality) (2003) *Annual report 2002/2003*. Johannesburg: CGE.

CGE (2004) *Annual Report 2003/2004*. Johannesburg: CGE.

Cherry J (2004) Overcoming discrimination: Chapter 9 institutions – Commission on Gender Equality. Unpublished paper commissioned by the HSRC.

Gouws A (2004) The politics of state structures: Citizenship and the national machinery for women in South Africa, *Feminist Africa* 3: 24–47.

Hassim S (2003) The gender pact and democratic consolidation: Institutionalizing gender equality in the South African state, *Feminist Studies* 29(3): 505–528.

Hassim S (2005) A virtuous circle: Gender equality and representation in South Africa. In J Daniel, R Southall & J Lutchman (2004) *The State of the Nation: South Africa 2004–2005*. Cape Town: HSRC Press.

Instraw (United Nations International Research and Training Institute for the Advancement of Women) (2000) *Engendering the political agenda: The role of the state, women's organizations and the international community*. Dominican Republic: Santa Domingo.

Office on the Status of Women and Gender Equality, Western Cape Government (Directorate: Human Rights Programmes) (2004) *A decade under review – 10 years of freedom – What has it meant for women?* Cape Town: OSW Western Cape.

OSW (Office of the Status of Women) (n.d.a) *South Africa's national framework for women's empowerment and gender equality*. Pretoria: OSW.

OSW (n.d.b) *South Africa's national gender audit: An analysis, synthesis and presentation of findings and recommendations at the national and provincial level*. Pretoria: OSW.

Seidman GW (2003) Institutional dilemmas: Representation versus mobilisation in the South African Gender Commission, *Feminist Studies* 29(3): 541–564.

Serote P (n.d.a) SADC needs assessment for capacity building for national gender machineries in SADC member states. Unpublished report.

Serote P (n.d.b) Project proposal: Addressing identified needs for building the capacity of national machineries for gender equality in SADC member states. Unpublished report.

Stetson DM & Mazur AG (eds.) (1995) *Comparative state feminism*. London: Sage.

Waylen G (1996) *Gender in Third World politics*. Buckingham: Open University Press.

Part II: Economy

Economy: introduction

John Daniel

The focus in the economy section of last year's *State of the Nation* was a macro one. We surveyed ten years of post-apartheid economics, looked at ownership issues and the attempt by way of black economic empowerment policies (BEE) to deracialise the largely white corporate and industrial-owning class. We also grappled with issues of employment and unemployment, poverty and economic inequality. In this edition, our focus is more micro. We have dispensed for now with the sweeping surveys and broad overview and our focus in this issue is more eclectic.

We open with another look at the BEE issue. In many ways it can be said that the core policy debate around BEE is over. Few now question the need to change the demographic profile of South Africa's owning and management sectors and hardly a day goes by without the financial press trumpeting another empowerment deal. The debate has now moved into the realm of 'broad-based BEE', questioning the fact that only a narrow black elite appears to be benefiting from BEE and asking how larger numbers of individuals and groups can be drawn into the process.

Roger Southall's article is in this vein. Basically, Southall poses the question as to whether BEE is contributing to the democratisation of South African capitalism or, to put it another way, producing what Cyril Ramaphosa (echoing former British Prime Minister Edward Heath) called 'capitalism with a human face'. To this end, he examines the notion of stakeholder capitalism and its potential for transforming the economy in South Africa.

Punted principally in Europe (but with many advocates elsewhere), stakeholder capitalism purports to promote a 'popularisation of share ownership', a harmony of interests between capitalists and workers, a responsiveness of firms to consumers and communities, and corporate social responsibility. However, Southall argues that in today's South Africa there are formidable barriers to the realisation of such goals. These include the fact that domestic capitalism is no longer 'contained and protected by state-imposed barriers', one consequence of which has been that some of South Africa's largest conglomerates (SAB Miller, De Beers, Anglo American, Old Mutual) have unbundled and gone international. In the realm of shareholding there is the fact that more and more stock is held by institutional investors, the managers of which seem increasingly less accountable to either their shareholders or the law. Furthermore, employee share-ownership schemes may have become fashionable as a tool of BEE, yet appear unconvincing as a sustainable mode of democratising ownership of large corporations. Overall, Southall argues that although blacks have made a significant entry into the corporate power elite, and although there is a considerably larger class of black capitalists than is habitually portrayed in analyses of BEE as 'elite empowerment', he remains unconvinced that BEE policies, as presently constructed, will be able to 'propel South African capitalism in a more inclusive, accountable and equalising direction'. At best, Southall suggests, BEE will only 'blur the boundaries of race and class', not break them down.

While Southall focuses his attention on the top echelons of the corporate sector, in her contribution Percy Moleke takes a look at the overall labour market 11 years into democracy. Like Southall, she concludes that while there has been an overall advancement up the economic ladder of black South Africans through such policies as affirmative action and BEE, there are nonetheless areas where little or less progress has been made. One example she cites is that of equity in the workplace. She makes the point that study after study illustrates that white males continue to dominate senior management positions and that Africans remain the largest portion of low-skilled and semi-skilled workers. Moleke does not question that Africans have progressed in the labour market, but she suggests that the pace and extent to which this has occurred needs to be interrogated.

Two factors, Moleke contends, have influenced the slow progress in the deracialisation of South Africa's labour market. One is that most poor black South Africans – and that is most people in this country – continue to receive a poor-quality school education. The significance of that is that, in Moleke's words, 'The education system is a direct feeder of the labour market and does to a large extent determine employability, employment status and earnings.' In short, Moleke argues that unless black South Africans are given access to better education, it is unlikely that a full deracialisation of all sectors of the labour market can be achieved. The second is the fact that equity legislation is not being enforced in a sufficiently concerted manner. Moleke points out that human resource management and development policies and programmes in especially the private sector have a critical role to play in the deracialisation of the labour market and a more vigorous enforcement of equity legislation is required. Without that, progress in this area will lag.

In their chapter, three economists from the School of Development Studies at the University of KwaZulu-Natal, Imraan Valodia, Richard Devey and Caroline Skinner, report on their ground-breaking research on the informal sector. They begin by examining different conceptualisations of the informal sector, a term first coined by Keith Hart in 1973 to describe a range of subsistence activities of the urban poor. Since then the concept has evolved considerably and cannot be captured by one strict definition. What the authors suggest is that in South Africa, as elsewhere, the informal sector is heterogeneous in that it encompasses different types of economic activities (trading, collecting, manufacturing and providing a service), different employment relations (self-employment, paid and unpaid workers and disguised wage workers), and activities with different economic potential (survivalist activities and successful small enterprises).

One of the key arguments in this rich and complex article is the authors' assertion that it is wrong to argue, as the African National Congress now does *ad nauseam*, that the South African economy is a dualistic one and that, moreover, there is a clear dividing line between the first and second economies. In their view there is not because in reality they are integrally linked. There are, they argue, few examples of informal operators who are not linked either through supply or customer networks into the formal economy. Failure to recognise these links has rendered government's support measures to the informal sector 'largely ineffective', Valodia et al. argue.

In their view, what government needs to do is recognise that there is in South Africa one economy within which there are sectors, some of which are working well but others are not. They argue that the 'dualist conception of the economy is misguided not only because it hides some of the "losers" of government's policies but also because it continues to keep elements of the economy invisible.' They go on to conclude that only when government recognises this reality and, moreover, the crucial fact that much of what is regarded by government as the formal economy is actually being rapidly informalised, will it design appropriate support measures for those 'operating at the lower rungs of our economy'.

In their article, sociologists Eddie Webster and Sakhela Buhlungu bring together data from two research projects conducted by their Sociology of Work Unit, based at Witwatersrand University. The first analysed the restructuring of the nature of work and the workplace as a result of what they call the 'triple transition', that is, the transitions from apartheid to a post-colonial order, from authoritarianism to democracy and from a domestically-orientated economy to a globally-integrated one. The second research project was a longitudinal survey of members of the Congress of South African Trade Unions (Cosatu) on their attitudes to democracy. The chapter is organised into four parts. The first identifies the trends in a complex process of workplace restructuring under way in post-apartheid South Africa; the second explores the changing composition of the workforce; while the third examines changing management and labour relations. Finally, the authors examine the future of South Africa's labour movement in the light of these changes. In regard to the South African workforce, Webster and Buhlungu argue that it is being differentiated into three zones – a core of well-paid and secure skilled workers; a non-core zone of semi-skilled and unskilled workers who earn low wages, enjoy few or no benefits and have little security; and a periphery occupied by those in the informal sector and the unemployed. In this restructured workforce, the authors found that union members are concentrated in the core which, however, is a sector diminishing in size while the non-core and those in the periphery are largely unorganised in union terms.

With regard to management and labour relations in the restructured workforce, the authors find that different strategies are being employed to redress the legacies of apartheid and in response to demands for a more democratic workplace. However, they argue that few of these could be judged as successful and they conclude that if one adds in the public service 'a very large number of workplaces, perhaps employing the majority of the country's workers, remain plagued by the kind of racial tension and conflict, including a highly resistant work culture and inefficiencies which characterised the apartheid workplace'.

ECONOMY: INTRODUCTION

With regard to the labour movement, the authors argue that labour – and specifically Cosatu – remains the 'single most powerful civil society organisation in the country'. However, they also make the point that one needs to be aware of the fact that Cosatu represents an ever-diminishing number of workers and that it is making little or no headway in organising workers located in the non-core. Cosatu is, in fact, a federation which represents the more 'skilled, more educated and older' workers. They conclude by asking if we are witnessing the marginalisation of labour or if there could be a revitalisation of the union movement. Their answer is ambiguous, stating that 'labour in general stands between marginalisation and revitalisation'. Which way will it go? They are not sure; time will tell.

In the final article in this section, Michael Kahn and William Blankley look at the state of research and experimental development (R&D) in South Africa. They define R&D as 'the conscious and systematic scientific effort that contributes to the growth of the stock of knowledge that in time may or may not lead to new technical applications'. Overall, the authors conclude, South Africa has in recent years made some good progress in the area of R&D. Investment over the past 30 or so years has created a strong and viable defence and aerospace industry while more recent investments have given rise to such innovative technologies as the pebble-bed modular reactor. Developed by Sasol, the company has become an international leader in the liquid fuels area.

A key factor which the authors identify as a problem and an obstacle to greater levels of R&D innovation is the lack in South Africa today of sufficient high-level person power. They identify a number of factors responsible for this – a brain drain of scientific stock in the 1980s from which the country has not recovered, deficiencies in the education sector, pay constraints and an immigration policy which 'is a barrier to the inward migration of skills'. The result is that South Africa ranks lower than many other countries in the number of researchers per 1 000 employees. For example, South Africa currently has 2.2 researchers per 1 000 employed persons while South Korea (6.8), Australia (7.3) Russia (7.4) and Japan (9.9) all do much better. South Africa also lags behind these countries in terms of expenditure on R&D. Currently, South Africa spends 0.81 per cent of its gross domestic product on R&D while expenditure in the countries named above ranges from 1.28 per cent to 2.64 per cent.

Clearly, therefore, two of the challenges facing South Africa in the area of R&D are to increase its expenditure on scientific research as well as to produce greater numbers of skilled researchers. In regard to the latter, however, the authors identify a second challenge and that is to change the demographics in the R&D research community so as to make that cadre of scientists 'representative of the country's demographics'. None of these challenges, the authors argue, will be easy to attain.

7 Black empowerment and present limits to a more democratic capitalism in South Africa

Roger Southall

In 2002, in the wake of the Enron and other corporate scandals in the US, African National Congress (ANC) Member of Parliament Ben Turok questioned the direction of South African capitalism. Resulting from executive greed, fraudulent accounting, deliberate deception of investors and the misuse of the savings of ordinary American investors, the outrages in the US had demonstrated that an unregulated capitalism, based upon individual greed and which was disregarding of the public realm, was fundamentally flawed. Yet there was an alternative model, for as outlined by Will Hutton (1996), the 'social market capitalism' which evolved in post-Second World War Western Europe, whereby corporations had been constrained by governments and popular pressures to transcend the crude maximisation of shareholders' profits, had evolved into a more democratic system whereby the rights of property were balanced by the pursuit of equality, social solidarity and the public interest. This was clearly a more desirable pattern for South African capitalism, whose development was a product of an apartheid past of brutal racial inequality and the impoverishment of the mass of its citizens, to pursue. In contrast, however, South African capitalism seemed to be 'in the grip of a new drive for greed and unbridled acquisitiveness' (Turok 2002: 6), to which – worryingly – the present policy and practice of black economic empowerment (BEE) appeared to be contributing. Yet, as Turok was to elaborate subsequently, writing in the *Sunday Times* (17.11.04), this need not be inevitable, for while South Africa's new black capitalists cannot be expected to build socialism, they could spearhead a drive towards a more humane capitalism. Even though they may be restrained by resistance to transformation from established white capital and by pressures upon their companies to be globally competitive, they are not without options whereby they can assist the mass of poorer, black South Africans. Eschewing wasteful conspicuous consumption, they may rather choose to promote investment in townships and rural areas, and ensure that their firms establish skills and build black capacity in partnership with government.

Turok's views were echoed by Cyril Ramaphosa, the former trade unionist, ANC secretary-general and now one of the foremost black moguls. Much of the debate about BEE, he maintained, represents:

> a deep yearning for capitalism with a human face. People are saying they expect capitalism which is more responsive to the needs of the people – a human face with compassion not underpinned by greed. It is possible to achieve compassionate ends from a capitalist system. *(Sunday Times* 28.11.04)

The idea of a 'compassionate' capitalism – one contributing to greater equality, social solidarity and the public interest – implies a more democratic capitalism which is more accountable to society as a whole, rather than just to shareholders, and is clearly critical to corporations' legitimacy in post-apartheid South Africa. Equally clearly, the promotion of BEE is central to this enterprise. Yet is the present practice of BEE serving to render South African capitalism more 'democratic'?

Elite or broad-based empowerment?

Turok and Ramaphosa were contributing to a vigorous debate about BEE which, most recently, had been provoked by a number of (completed or mooted) transactions which various outraged critics argued would promote elite enrichment at the cost of broad-based empowerment. Most particularly, criticism had been evoked by two deals constructed around four of the nation's most prominent black businessmen. These were, first, an agreement by Standard Bank whereby it would sell a ten per cent stake in its South African operations to black partners in what would be one of the largest BEE deals concluded so far. Of this ten per cent, 40 per cent would go to black management and staff, and 20 per cent to regional business, community and educational groupings. However, what attracted most attention was that the remaining 40 per cent would go to a consortium led by Saki Macozoma and Cyril Ramaphosa, 'tycoons' already deemed to have been sufficiently 'empowered' *(Sowetan* 15.09.04; *Business Day* 15.09.04). The second deal, following hard upon Standard's announcement, was the proposal by Britain's Barclays Bank to make a R20 billion purchase of 50.1 per cent of shares in Absa which would directly involve the Batho Bonke consortium, led by Tokyo Sexwale, and indirectly, the Ubuntu-Batho consortium, led by Patrice Motsepe (*Business Day* 27.09.04).[1] Although both deals were promoted as providing a model of broad-based empowerment, unions feared that they would reinforce a decade-long trend job shedding throughout the banking sector whilst unduly favouring a few individuals, all of whom enjoyed strong political connections.

Far more significant than the accusations of 'plunder' and 'crony capitalism' which emanated from the opposition Democratic Alliance (DA) (*Business Day* 22.11.04) were the echoing cries emitted by influential commentators both close to and actually within the government. Most notably, ANC Secretary-General Kgalema Motlanthe protested to the Black Management Forum that a small elite of black businessmen were the beneficiaries of one deal after another and proposed that once an individual had been empowered, he or she should no longer be regarded as historically disadvantaged (*Business Day* 01.10.04); and Finance Minister Trevor Manuel and Zwelinzima Vavi, General Secretary of the Congress of Trade Unions of South Africa (Cosatu), both criticised the greed of what Jeremy Cronin, Deputy General Secretary of the South African Communist Party (SACP), labelled the 'BEE-llionaires' (*Business Report* 03.10.04). Although the ANC was later to disparage Archbishop Desmond Tutu for lamenting BEE as simply recycling an elite (*ANC Today* 14–20.1.05), there could be little doubt that it was concerned that such screaming headlines in the popular press as 'Fat cats take loot' (*Sowetan* 13.12.04 – in reference to a deal whereby a handful of ANC luminaries sealed a R1.55 billion deal to purchase assets from Randgold and JCI) were potentially severely damaging to the party's reputation amongst its own constituency.

Although couched in terms of the familiar 'empowerment versus enrichment' debate (Motlanthe, *Business Day* 04.10.04), the issues raised were indicative of deepening frustrations about both the progress and direction of BEE. To be sure, increased government assertiveness with regard to BEE since 2000, notably by pressures upon a wide array of industrial sectors to adopt 'transformation charters' which establish long-term targets aimed at overcoming historical disadvantage, has propelled an increasing number of companies, large and small, into scrambling to find black partners (Southall 2004, 2005a). Hence Ernst & Young, for instance, record that compared with 132 black empowerment deals valued at R23.1 billion in 1999, 126 valued at R28 billion were made in 2000, 101 at R25 billion in 2001, 104 at R12 billion in 2002, and 189 at R42 billion in 2003 (*Business Day* 29.10.04), whilst BusinessMap Director Reg Rumney has promised that the value of transactions struck in 2004 will surpass that of 2003 (*Mail & Guardian* 28.1–3.2.05). However, although these figures are not unimpressive, black control on the Johannesburg Securities Exchange (JSE) amounted to not more than four per cent at the end of 2004, even though the stock market had boomed with a 50 per cent increase in market capitalisation to R2.500 billion (BusinessMap Update 14.01.05). Unless more black-controlled companies apart from MTN (which accounts for around 70 per cent of black-controlled market capitalisation on the stock market) could climb into the JSE's top 40, concluded BusinessMap (2004a), there was little hope of black control becoming significant (*Business Day* 27.10.04).

Such fears fuelled ANC and allied commentators' deep-seated concerns. Motlanthe (*Business Day* 04.10.04) argued that the empowerment elite was largely mired in debt owed to the banks, so the transfer of formal share ownership did little to alter the economic structure. The real problem was not so much that there were four black billionaires out of a population of over 40 million, argued Christine Qunta in *Business Day* (29.10.04), but that so few had been empowered, and by the time debt repayments and fees made over to merchant banks, lawyers and other professionals are accounted for, the major beneficiaries of BEE deals are likely to turn out to be white. Similarly, Essop Pahad, Minister in the Presidency, proclaimed to the fortieth conference of the National African Federated Chambers of Commerce that efforts to build a black business class were blocked by the domination of the South African economy by a handful of conglomerates (*Business Day* 23.11.04), a theme echoed by Mashudu Ramano, Chair of Johnnic Communications, who complained that established business was a 'reluctant player' in transformation (*Business Day* 01.12.04).

That the ANC was indicating its worries about the trajectory of BEE was widely welcomed, yet critics such as DA leader Tony Leon worried that its debate would be the wrong one, concerned principally with placing restrictions upon the emergent 'patriotic bourgeoisie' rather than rethinking BEE more fundamentally. Many of his worries were shared by *Business Day*, which editorialised on 4 October 2004 that the answer to the ANC's worries lay in changing 'the way South African capitalism functions as a whole, and…

(making) it more efficient for the greater good'. More blacks needed to secure a slice of corporate profits, and for that to happen, it would be necessary for South African corporations to become more democratic, notably by including labour in the ownership structures.

> The only way to do that is to make the transfer of equity to labour attractive for the current owners and the only way to do that is to incentivise, through the tax regime, both the ownership of shares by workers and the transfer of shares by owners, [a strategy which should be followed through by the state itself, which as the largest property and equity owner in South Africa should find a way of putting a value on its wealth], then giv[ing] every poor person a share in it that can be traded and mortgaged. (*Business Day* 04.10.04)

The same theme was pursued by Bobby Godsell of AngloGold Ashanti:

> We would like our employees to be meaningful owners and we think it is a very good way of bringing employee interests in line with long-term ownership interests', adding that he saw an opportunity 'to bury Karl Marx's labour theory of value and to develop a twenty-first century model of capitalism, a teamwork model, which eliminates the class conflict of either the shareholders benefiting from the creation of wealth or the workers benefiting, with nothing in between'. (*Engineering News* 25.01.05)

The ANC, DA and influential media and corporate voices, it seems, are all in agreement that South Africa must move towards a more democratic capitalism. Yet it is equally clear that there are immense difficulties in progressing towards such an outcome.

Obstacles to the democratisation of South African capitalism

In the present era, the most widespread model proposed for rendering advanced industrial economies more socially responsible is that of 'stakeholder capitalism', which purportedly represents a third and more humane stage of capitalism. From this perspective, during the first stage of capitalism, that of the industrial revolution, all resources including workers' rights were routinely sacrificed for profit. In the second stage, which extends to the present period and is characterised by the domination of large-scale corporations whose power often exceeds that of the states in which they are based, the interests of workers, customers, communities, the nation and the environment are subordinated to pursuit of 'bottom line' profits, with corporate performance being measured solely in terms of private benefit to the shareholders. The typical response by states to such corporate exploitation is regulation. However, large corporations equally typically manage to find ways to evade regulation, which in any case is often introduced only after an Exxon Valdex oil spill, a Union Carbide disaster in Bhopal, or a Boeing overcharge on defence contracts. In contrast, in the third stage of capitalism, a business exists to earn a fair return for 'stakeholders', that is, all those who commit their resources or labour to the enterprise. Managers in this new stage of capitalism are evaluated by how well they balance the legitimate interests of the several stakeholder groups, whose interests as consumers, workers, local communities, governments or financial investors can be represented upon supervisory boards or councils. Managers, in a word, are rendered accountable (Estes n.d.).

The notion of stakeholder capitalism faces numerous difficulties. Key amongst these is that it does not accurately describe a reality where the world economy is increasingly dominated by a relatively small number of massive corporate conglomerates which appear less rather than more accountable to external interests by virtue of governments' scramble to compete with each other for multinational investment funds. Nor is it clear how the theory of stakeholders tackles the practicality of the pyramid shape of conglomerates, where those who have 'stakes' in subsidiaries (perhaps in impoverished Third World countries) are unlikely to be regarded as stakeholders in the multinational companies (usually based in rich countries) which ultimately control them. Nor again is it clear how ownership rights and privileges are measured against, or even constrained by, those of consumers, workers or communities. Furthermore, in Britain, attempts under Margaret Thatcher to use privatisation of nationalised industries to promote a popular capitalism by selling shares to ordinary people were to become largely discredited as shares were subsequently largely gobbled up by institutional investors, while employee ownership schemes were rarely found to translate into significant worker influence and power. Even so, notwithstanding such difficulties, stakeholder capitalism has become attractive not only to corporate ideologues who are keen to legitimate and stabilise capitalism by making it fairer, but also to social democrats, who see in it a way of taming capital whilst simultaneously harnessing its proven productivity. As elaborated by Hutton (1996), European (notably German) 'social market capitalism' has provided for worker representation upon boards of management and facilitated labour's involvement in corporate decision-making and profit-sharing.

Even if undeveloped, the notion of stakeholder capitalism is becoming increasingly influential in South Africa. This can be ascertained not only by even the briefest of visits to business school websites, but even by reference to key Cosatu documents such as the September Commission (Cosatu 1997), which views the institutionalisation of stakeholder rights as amounting to a 'partial socialisation of capital'. Furthermore, of course, the government has openly committed itself, via such measures as its minerals policy and its recent guidelines for industrial charters to employee share ownership participation, whose thrust is to promote the interests of workers as both co-owners of enterprises and stakeholders alongside other proposals for promoting the black ownership and control of industry and enterprise (DME 1998, DTI 2004). Meanwhile, South African corporations are also becoming subject to demands from a small but increasingly vocal 'corporate social responsibility' lobby (Trialogue 2004).

The notion of stakeholder capitalism undoubtedly has a cosy ring to it, even if it may mean different things to stakeholders as different as Bobby Godsell, who wants to bury Marx, and Cosatu, which continues to cling to collectivist aspirations. Nonetheless, for all that it also provides a convenient framework for the government's pursuit of BEE, it may be that the corporate foundations upon which stakeholder capitalism is supposedly being constructed are already crumbling.

The changing shape of capitalism in South Africa

The structure of capitalism in South Africa remains heavily monopolised, that is, it is dominated by a relatively small group of banks, other financial institutions, mining houses and holding groups which are able to exert massive market influence. This tendency towards the concentration and centralisation of economic power in the hands of a few conglomerates was significantly accelerated by the withdrawals of foreign multinationals from direct investment during the terminal crisis of apartheid, which expanded the asset base of domestic companies, which were restricted in their ability to invest overseas by rigid exchange controls. Hence, as noted previously (Southall 2005a), whereas the top eight South African corporations controlled 61.7 per cent of the total assets of non-state corporations in 1981, the top six controlled 71.3 per cent by 1985. However, since 1994, and especially since 2000, there has been a shift towards the growing influence over the economy of large financial institutions, this accompanied by increasing foreign ownership (the large part of which is also institutional). This trend was facilitated, notably, by the decision by the authorities to relax foreign exchange controls with, for instance, pension funds, life companies and unit trusts being allowed to invest five per cent of their assets overseas, a proportion which was later increased to 20 per cent for pension funds and life companies (*Business Day* 14.01.04). In addition, five major corporations (Billiton, South African Breweries, Anglo American, Old Mutual and Dimension Data) have been allowed to move their primary listings from the JSE to the London Stock Exchange since 1997 (South African Reserve Bank 2002), in preparation for which these companies 'unbundled', sold off and/or delisted various subsidiaries, or bought out minority shareholders.[2] These developments can be illustrated by reference to the changing market capitalisation of the JSE.

Table 7.1 *Share ownership on the JSE by percentage of market capitalisation*

Group and Type	1983	1994	1996	2000	2004
Conglomerate					
Anglo American	52.5	43.3	27.5	23.6	18.7
Rembrandt	2.1	13.0	10.6	11.0	7.9
Sasol	-	1.7	2.1	2.2	4.2
Anglovaal	1.7	3.6	3.0	-	-
SAB Miller (foreign)	-	-	-	2.8	5.1
Subtotal	56.3	61.6	43.2	39.6	35.9
Institutional					
Sanlam	9.4	10.5	11.4	13.2	2.7
Old Mutual	0.6	9.7	10.2	11.0	4.5
Standard/Liberty	1.1	7.2	11.1	5.2	4.7
Absa	-	-	-	-	2.2
Other	18.1	0.9	0.8	6.7	10.3
RMB Firstrand	-	0.5	1.7	2.9	4.9
Investec/Fedsure	-	0.4	1.1	1.9	0.8
Bidvest	-	-	-	1.0	1.2
Subtotal	29.2	29.2	36.3	41.9	31.3

Group and Type	1983	1994	1996	2000	2004
Other					
Foreign groups	5.4	2.2	4.1	3.9	18.5
Black groups*	-	-	6.3	5.7	6.3
Company Directors	9.1	7.0	10.0	8.9	5.8
State	-	-	-	-	2.2
Subtotal	14.5	9.2	20.4	18.5	32.8

Source: McGregor 2004: 69
Note: *Includes all companies that have significant black influence

Anthony Sampson has recorded how after the 'Big Bang' of October 1986, which demolished the closed cartel of British banks and stockholders, European and American bankers gobbled up their British counterparts, the most formidable of whom was Goldman Sachs, a 'tireless advocate of unrestricted free enterprise' (Sampson 2004: 251). Whereas some 80 per cent of shares in Britain were held by private individuals in 1939, by 1998 53 per cent were owned by domestic institutional investors, and another 28 per cent by overseas investors, also mostly institutions (Sampson 2004: 267). The accompanying development has been the rise in influence and power of company directors and managers, whose earnings have grown spectacularly in recent years and whose leading names regularly recur on different boards. Although their actions are supposedly constrained by the presence of non-executive directors who are meant to represent the interests of shareholders, many are chosen by corporate chairs and few have the expertise or inclination to rock the boat (Sampson 2004).

McGregor argues that corporate South Africa is following a similar path (*Financial Mail* 05.11.04). Corporate unbundling and the shift to institutional investment has seen managers become the key decision-makers, often bypassing shareholders' interests. There are now few controlling shareholders, with most large companies having a raft of institutions holding between 10 and 15 per cent of equity. Such institutions cannot be said to 'control' the companies in which they invest, for their task is to judge current and potential performance, and they have an obligation to sell their investment if it does not meet their expectations. Given also a culture of shareholder apathy in South Africa, top managers are increasingly a law unto themselves,[3] their actions only monitored by the financial press and the vicissitudes of the share price, both with a time lag. Such judgements are reinforced by what former Corpcapital director Nic Frangos has opined to be the widespread sentiment within the South African corporate world that corporate criminals will not be brought to book by the authorities. In modern business, he argued, the level of deception is of such complexity and sophistication that it is beyond the ability of the police and specialised agencies such as the Scorpions to decipher it. Such authorities are ill-equipped to understand fraudulent financial engineering, and constrained by the ever present fear that high profile businessmen will act against them. The inevitable result is that whilst corporate magnates may be arrested, few end up behind bars. Eighty-three per cent of fraud cases reported to the police do not make it to court, and only five per cent result in guilty verdicts (*Business Day* 13.09.04).

The saving grace is, in part, that changing ownership patterns and tougher corporate governance regulations have meant a decrease in ownership of multiple directorships. Hence, whereas in 1980, 68 directors served on the boards of seven or more listed companies, that number was down to three by 2004 (*Financial Mail* 21.01.05). This has facilitated an increase in the number of non-executive directors, who now on average make up 67 per cent of company boards. However, these latter remain overwhelmingly composed of white men, with only ten per cent of companies reporting that they have women on their boards, and with 'previously disadvantaged representation' amounting to no more than 23 per cent. Although supposedly assuming greater responsibilities, experience hitherto is far from comforting, with pension fund trustees, for instance, being reported as remaining largely passive whilst simultaneously being blamed by asset managers for tying their hands (*Business Report* 13.05.03).

This unwelcoming corporate culture is undoubtedly an important reason why many black professionals are leaving the corporate world for entrepreneurial, consulting and empowerment opportunities of their own (*Financial Mail* 24.09.04). An outcome is that companies are now having to draw board members from what is described as a shrinking pool of eligible and suitably qualified candidates, resulting in a dramatic increase in non-executive directors' earnings, which reportedly went up by 60 per cent in 2004 (*Business Day* 04.11.04). It is scarcely surprising in this circumstance that black business-people have been accused by one of their own, Nedcor deputy chair Lot Ndlovu, of a 'frightening level of greed' (*Business Day* 26.07.04), although this would seem to reflect a considerably wider (and whiter) phenomenon of high level, managerial rapacity which is supposedly justified by South African companies' need to compete for high level executive skills globally. During 2003/04, South Africa's top executives received pay increases averaging well in excess of 15 per cent, more than double the rate of inflation, widening further the gap between their income and that of skilled and semi-skilled workers. Prominent beneficiaries of corporate largesse were Gold Field's Ian Cockerill, whose package increased by 63 per cent, and AngloGold Ashanti's Bobby Godsell, whose increase of 27.7 per cent appears at odds with his contemporary espousal of stakeholder capitalism. Some packages were downright obscene, topped by that of Steve Ross of Edgars, who earned R42.6 million in 2004, while more and more executives are protected by 'golden parachutes' in the event of their losing their jobs as a result of a takeover. Overall, the differential between executive pay and minimum wages rose from 37 in 1994 to 48 in 2004, and rather than forced disclosure (since 2002) of top executives' pay having contained increases, it has prompted a race to the top (*Financial Mail* 03.09.04; *Business Report* 18.02.05). It was scarcely surprising that Trevor Manuel should condemn salary distortions in South Africa as unsustainable, and should worry that the corporate world was following the example of the US, where the differential between the earnings of executives of large US companies and average workers had recently been reported by *Business Week* as increasing from 42 times in 1980 to 419 times in 1998 (*ThisDay* 17.9.04).

The growing domination of finance capital, combined with managers' increasing control over companies, provides an unlikely background to the development of a more democratic capitalism. Yet the government, for whom BEE represents a key strategy for transforming the advanced sectors of the economy, may dispute this.

Government policy and corporate response

The thrust of government policy concerning BEE is the promotion of black ownership and control of an economy whose commanding heights continue to be dominated by the private sector alongside state-owned enterprises (SOEs) (responsible for around 15 per cent of gross fixed investment). As demonstrated previously, early setbacks to BEE after 1994, notably in the ability of key black companies to withstand the volatility of the market (notably the crash of the stock market in 1998), alongside acute difficulties experienced by the state in utilising privatisation of SOEs to promote BEE, resulted after 2000 in the government resorting to a more assertive and regulatory stance. This was embodied alongside its launch or renovation of various state agencies designed to promote empowerment in its commitment to the promotion of transformation charters, which would establish mid to long-term goals for an increase in ownership, participation and training of the historically disadvantaged for the different sectors of industry (Southall 2004, 2005a). Against the background of the adoption of charters for the petroleum and liquid fuels and the mining industries in 2002, and the financial services industry in 2004, the Department of Trade and Industry (DTI) launched a draft broad-based black economic empowerment code of good practice in December 2004 to assist and guide those 'priority' sectors of industry (agriculture, transport services, automobiles, information and communications technology, engineering and construction) which had yet to complete them, simultaneously announcing a date for their final adoption of June 2005.

The code defines broad-based BEE as 'the economic empowerment of all black people including women, workers, youth, people with disabilities and people living in rural areas, through diverse but integrated socio-economic strategies that include, but are not limited to: (a) increasing the number of black people that manage, own and control enterprises and productive assets; (b) facilitating ownership and management of enterprises and productive assets by communities, workers, co-operatives and other collective enterprises; (c) human resources and skills development; (d) achieving equitable representation in all occupational categories and levels in the workforce; (e) preferential procurement; and (f) investment in enterprises that are owned or managed by black people' (DTI 2004: 11).

The code recommends that companies should seek to achieve clear targets for ownership, management, skills and enterprise development as follows: BEE equity or 'economic interest'[4] levels of 25.1 per cent (such equity to entitle black people to voting rights); black management 40 per cent; employment equity 50 per cent; skills development six per cent; equity procurement 50 per cent; enterprise development (monetary investment in small or medium enterprises with good BEE credentials) eight to ten per cent; and residual elements (such as corporate social investment) three per cent, although deviation from these targets may be tolerated if demonstrably based on a sound economic rationale. Within the broad target of 25 per cent ownership plus one vote by 2014, there is also a set of subordinate and overlapping targets which attempt to ensure that black ownership is relatively broad-based, with specific provision being provided for entitlements for women and designated groups (such as community organisations), as well as for investment trusts, which will qualify as juristic persons representing black economic interests to the extent that voting rights or economic benefits accrue to blacks within them. The date for attainment of these targets, if not specified as earlier, is to be 2014 – in line with the government's overall long-run strategy. Accompanied by detailed weightings for measuring attainment of targets for scorecards, it is further laid down that charters should be the product of 'comprehensive' consultation and 'balanced' negotiation between all major stakeholders. These might include industry bodies, government, trade unions, industry watchdogs and other relevant interests in the participating sector as well as the key enterprises and companies involved. Charters should also provide for establishment of charter councils, equitably composed of stakeholders, whose mandate and powers (whose final approval will be granted by the Cabinet) will provide for the supplying of guidance on sector-specific matters, compiling reports on the progress of BEE within the sector, and sharing information with a national monitoring mechanism, although not having the authority to change targets or weightings. The different charter councils will, in turn, report to the DTI and a Business Black Empowerment Advisory Council (DTI 2004).

The code was welcomed as clarifying the government's objectives and as providing a renewed emphasis upon broad-based empowerment. Industry was also assured by the stress which was laid upon BEE as a process associated with economic growth and not merely with redistribution. However, there were also a number of concerns, the chief of which was that the code was unexpectedly prescriptive in a number of areas, notably regarding ownership, with regard to which the insistence that black equity holdings should entail voting rights was thought likely to inhibit financing structures (including many deals already concluded) which involved share options, preference shares or debt, whilst small business worried that family concerns would be forced to give away equity to non-family members. Mbabane (*Business Day* 10.02.04) similarly objected that the code encourages the 'ridiculous notion' that broad-based empowerment 'should mean that the poor and unemployed should be bused in to buy equity stakes in every enterprise', an 'extreme view' which will require the proposed Advisory Council to distinguish between empowerment and poverty alleviation and job creation. More widely, commentators argued that too much stress had been placed upon ownership at the expense of skills development, enterprise development and employment equity, and that this would make it harder to finance BEE transactions, although some sectors – notably agriculture – were decidedly more negative than others. There were also worries that the code could serve as a deterrent to foreign investment, notably in such areas as information technology, where multinational companies had already been complaining that that sector's draft charter was too demanding *(Financial Mail* 05.11.04, 17.12.04; *Business Day* 20.12.04; *Business Report* 16.01.05). However, the code failed to respond to an earlier demand by Blade Nzimande, who had demanded that all industry charters should be processed through the National Economic Development and Labour Council before they were approved by government (*Business Day* 27.10.04), raising worries in trade union circles that labour's voice as a 'stakeholder' stood in danger of being marginalised.

Towards more broad-based empowerment?

For all that the government regards the draft code as a work in progress, the points system it has devised and the demands it intends to impose upon the corporate sector suggest that it has some potential to change the face of South African capitalism over the medium to longer term. Yet what is likely to be the extent, shape and limits to such a transformation? In this context it is instructive to examine, first, BEE's impact upon the composition of the corporate elite, and second, the extent to which the black corporate elite is underlain by a developing black business class more generally.

BEE and South Africa's power elite

As observed earlier, the broad thrust of much political and media criticism is that BEE is serving to create an unjustifiably enriched black elite. In many ways, this is not surprising, for the wealth amassed by some of the leading black players in a short span of around a decade has been spectacular, and unlike leading white corporate moguls who mostly retain a low profile, they often act out their business lives in the public eye. In a word, such leading figures as Saki Macozoma, Cyril Ramaphosa, Tokyo Sexwale, and Patrice

Motsepe are 'celebrities', not merely businessmen but icons of African success, lauded for their fashionable clothes and lifestyle as much as for the power they wield in a still white dominated corporate world. Take, for instance, Caroline Southey's breathless description of Cyril Ramaphosa, for his entry in the *Financial Mail's* 2003 'power elite'. After the collapse of the Molope Group, which he had founded in 2001, she writes:

> He has since built a substantial corporate presence spanning mining, financial services, the media, advertising and newsprint. He is the largest shareholder in Millenium Consolidated Investments and chairs the boards of Johnnic Holdings, MTN, Sasria, TBWA/Hunt/Lascaris and Rebhold. But Ramaphosa's power lies elsewhere. He has gravitas, charm and exceptional powers of persuasion. He is viewed as a natural leader, a man capable of changing the course of history... Wielding ambition and moral suasion, Ramaphosa has already written himself into SA's history books. But he is associated with power not only because of what he had done but because of the enticing possibility that the main action is to come. (*Financial Mail* 19.12.03)

With credentials like this, Ramaphosa could hardly fail to win an Impumelelo Award as a 'Top Empowerment Business Personality' in 2004 (*ThisDay* 07.05.04). Like Midas, he and his fellow moguls are expected to have the touch of gold. As owner and chairman of Mamelodi Sundowns, Patrice Motsepe is expected to translate his success in the boardroom into triumphs on the soccer field, while the South African Broadcasting Association (SABC) announced that 'charismatic freedom fighter-turned-businessman Tokyo Sexwale' would assume the role of chairman, 'made famous by US property magnate Donald Trump', in a local version of the TV entrepreneurial quiz game *The Apprentice* (*Sunday Times* 13.02.05). Their wealth may be envied, but it is also hugely admired. Yet such adulation, alongside the brickbats, only increases our need to understand the basis of their prominence and power.

According to Mills (1956), the power elite in America is defined by a broad community of interest between those who occupy the 'command positions' in the polity, economy and military. An immediate difference in post-apartheid South Africa is that whereas 'securocrats' undoubtedly occupied key positions of power under the Presidency of PW Botha, democratisation has seen a remarkable reduction of the influence of the military – dramatically illustrated by the notorious 1996 arms deal in which a combination of European government and business interests secured backing from the ANC-led government for the purchase of exorbitantly expensive military equipment which the armed services deemed inappropriate to South Africa's needs (Crawford-Brown 2004). Meanwhile, there is no doubt that with the arrival of an ANC government, there is a major disjunction between the wielding of political and economic power, with the state now controlled by new black incumbents and the corporate world still dominated by whites. Increasingly, however, this situation is changing. On the one hand, SOEs have now fallen largely under black control, while on the other, black executives are assuming top positions in industry.

This changing situation is illuminated by Empowerdex, an empowerment rating organisation, which provides an assessment of black influence that goes beyond direct black ownership to include state and indirect ownership. From this perspective, in June 2002 'empowerment owners' owned R143.4 billion worth (or 9.5 per cent) of the largest JSE-listed companies. Of this, 53 per cent was owned by government agencies and pension funds (such as the Industrial Development Corporation and the Public Investment Commission), 26 per cent by SOE pension funds, eight per cent by municipality pension funds, as well as one per cent and three per cent respectively by historically disadvantaged educational institutions and trade unions. Meanwhile, the proportion of black ownership of the top 20 BEE-owned companies, which included a number of traditional companies, ranged from 58.53 per cent in Real Africa Holdings to 17.42 per cent in Transhex, while overall as many as 68 per cent of the JSE companies could be described as 'black influenced', a term which meant that empowerment wealth could be used to appoint black representation upon boards, and promote employment equity, skills development and social development (Wu & Ngcobo 2002).

Subsequently, Empowerdex (Wu, Ntombela, Ngcobo & Dlamini 2003) concluded that if directorships were equal to influence, then the 260 historically disadvantaged individuals who held 367 directorships in 387 South African-based companies wielded more influence than previously estimated: Ramaphosa headed the list with market influence of R137 billion, and overall, the 25 most influential directors wielded a total market influence of R1 229 billion. Meanwhile, the top ten black chief executives or executive chairs presided over companies with a market capitalisation of R41 634 million.

By its nature, this sort of data is problematic. As noted earlier, the proportion of direct ownership by black businesspeople of companies on the JSE remains extremely low, and less than a quarter of them boast black directors. Nor is the suggestion that indirect black ownership and individual company directorship translates directly into 'market influence' wholly convincing, whilst even direct black ownership has its problems. Although the personal shareholdings of leading black businesspeople (overwhelmingly men) are impressive, these are often held against high levels of debt: for instance, it will reportedly take Cyril Ramaphosa 20 years to pay off the 0.5 per cent of the R200 million worth of shares he has recently purchased under his own name from the Standard Bank (*Financial Mail* 23.07.04). Furthermore, as with all fortunes held in equity, these can fluctuate wildly according to the vagaries of the market: as a result of Gold Field's vigorous resistance to Harmony's US$7.5 billion hostile takeover bid in 2004, Patrice Motsepe was reputed to have lost between R730 million and R1.2 billion as both firms' share prices plummeted (*Financial Mail* 9/10.12.04). Nonetheless, the overall impact of even this fuzzy data is that black executives are undoubtedly beginning to penetrate the highest corridors of corporate power, this illustrated by the fact that South Africa's two largest companies, BHP Billiton and Anglo-American, are now headed by Vincent Maphai and Lazarus Zim respectively.

Similar assessments agree: nine black men were rated by the *Financial Mail* as amongst the 20 most influential people in South African business at the end of 2003 (see Table 7.2). In contrast, no blacks had made it into the top 20 when a comparable list was produced in 1993. Meanwhile, nine out of the ten persons tipped to climb into the top 20 within five years were also black, only one of them a woman.

Apart from omitting to note that it is (and is apparently destined to remain) overwhelmingly male, the *Financial Mail's* comments upon the changing power elite were apt. First, for the first time in South Africa's history, there is a convergence between the political and business elites, although it is probable that this link will become less overt as the black entrepreneurial and business class expands. Second, after proposing that power constitutes the ability to get things done (or stop things being done), the writer observed: 'These people have decisive influence beyond their sphere of business, on the way business is done in South Africa and the way it will be done. They have the ear of policy makers and they can move markets. Their calls are always taken' (*Financial*

Mail 19.12.03). In other words, black owners and managers constitute an increasing proportion of those corporate magnates who deploy the power of money and influence in a way that directly and indirectly determines the fates of millions of South Africans.

Table 7.2 Financial Mail's *top 20 businesspeople in South Africa, 2003*

Black	White
Patrice Motsepe, Chairman, Harmony/ARM. Avmin (2)	Johann Rupert, Chairman, Remgro/Richemont/Venfin (1)
Tokyo Sexwale, Chairman, Mvelaphanda (3)	Tony Trahar, CEO, Anglo American (4)
	Jacob Maree, CEO, Standard Bank (7)
Khaya Ngqula, CEO, Industrial Development Corporation (5)	Laurie Dippenaar, CEO, First Rand (9)
Phuthuma Nhleko, CEO, MTN (6)	Nicky Oppenheimer, Chairman, De Beers (11)
Cyril Ramaphosa, Chairman, MCI/Johnnic/MTN (8)	Maria Ramos, CEO, Transnet (15)
	Bobby Godsell, CEO, AngloGold (16)
Lazarus Zim, Deputy CEO, Anglo American (10)	Brian Joffe, Executive Chairman, Bidvest (17)
	Pieter Cox, Chief Executive, Sasol (18)
Saki Macozoma, CEO, New Africa Investments (12)	Alan Knott-Craig, CEO, Vodacom Group (19)
Sizwe Nxasana, CEO, Telkom (13)	Mark Shuttleworth, Founder, HBD Venture Capital (20)
Reuel Khoza, Chairman, Eskom (14)	

Source: *Financial Mail* 19.12.03

Beyond the elite: the wider extent of black business

It is important to stress that BEE is contributing to the growth of a black business class which extends considerably beyond those few figures constantly cited (and pilloried) as 'the elite'. Most certainly, it remains the case that the BEE heavyweight companies continue to dominate. In 2003, for instance, the DTI reported that 72 per cent of the total deal value involved at least one of six BEE heavyweights (ARM, Mvelaphanda, Shanduka [formerly Millenium Investment Corporation], Safika, Kagiso and Tiso), while R30 billion of the increase (from R43 to R73 billion) in black-controlled market capitalisation on the JSE in the nine months up to the end of September 2004 was largely driven by MTN, Armgold and Mvelaphanda. Against this, Deputy Minister

BLACK EMPOWERMENT AND LIMITS TO A MORE DEMOCRATIC CAPITALISM

Mandisi Mpahlwa is cited as saying that 40 per cent of the transaction value of BEE deals completed in 2004 involved broad-based entities and at least 6.4 per cent involved employees (BusinessMap 2004a; Hassan 2005). Support for Mpahlwa's claim is provided by specification of some of the individual deals completed in 2004 and recorded by BusinessMap (2004b):

Table 7.3 *Selected BEE deals, 2004*

Type	Sector	Stake %	Details
Equity	Defence	25.0	Motswedi Technology Group acquired 25% of IFS Defence SA.
Equity	Telecommunications & IT	30.0	Peter Vundla's New Seasons, which involves black investors, telecommunications professionals and an educational trust, agreed to buy 30% in Alcatel SADC operations.
Equity	Media	42.5	Hosken Consolidated Investments sold its 42.5% stake in 94.7 Highveld Stereo to Primedia and the Mineworkers' Investment Company. Primedia will pay R129m for 30% of the station, MIC R50m for 12.5%.
Acquisition	Cyclical services	25.1	J&J Group will acquire a R4.5m, 25.1% stake in communications software company, Striata.
Equity	Cyclical services	25.0	MIC purchase of 25% stake in Izazi.
Equity	Cyclical services	40.0	Spescom Telecommunications sold 40% stake to Momothekga Trading Company.
Equity	Financial	25.1	Kagiso Investment Trust agreed to buy 25% Holding in Battery Technology.
Equity	Financial	10.0	Makana Investment Corporation paid R4m up front and R37m through borrowing and a preference share scheme in Cadix Holdings.
Equity	Industrial	30.0	Izingwe consortium will buy 30% stake in Aberdare cables over 10 years.
Equity	IT	25.4	Vantage Capital Fund Managers purchased R20m worth of Spescom Telecommunications at a 40% discount.

Type	Sector	Stake %	Details
Acquisition	Consumer goods	49.9	Pamodzi Investment Holdings increased its holding in Foodcorp Ltd to 100% for R2.028 billion. 15% of shares will be allocated to Foodcorp managers, 20% to employees.
Equity	Media & photography	13.1	Naspers granted Johncom rights to acquire 39.1% of M-net/Supersport's shares for R287m.
Acquisition	General retail	65.0	Consortium of Metro Cash and Carry management and African Renaissance agreed to acquire Metro, excluding its Australian subsidiary, for R1 300m.
Acquisition	Mining	100.0	Ilanga Coal Mines (owned by Vela International) bought Spitzkop Colliery from Xstrata Coal for R70m.
Purchase	Food	100.0	Grand Bridge Consortium bought Glenhow Milling and surrounding land from Ilovo Sugar Milling for R335m (10% up front, balance to be paid through sale of coastal land for property development).
Joint Venture	Mining	44.0	Mampa Investment Holdings entered JV with Assore's African Mining and Trust Company to restore Assore's Rustenburg mine.
Equity	Transport	25.1	Orlyfunt Holdings, headed by Mafika Mkhwanazi, acquired stake in Mediterranean Shipping Company.
Equity	Food	54.0	Employees of Philiflora, producing flowers and foliage, acquired stake in company through Khula's Equity Fund programme.
Equity	Beverages	25.1	Phetogo Investments agreed to buy 25.1% of KWV Ltd, which owns 55% of KWV investments, for R200m.
Acquisition	Food	100.0	Investment company Global Makana Strategies purchased home and garden company Agroserve, and established a management share trust.
Equity	Building & construction	25.0	Qakazana will acquire 25% stake in Grinaker-LTA Trident Steel through issue of preference shares valued at R496m, as part of a BEE consortium headed by Tiso Group.

Type	Sector	Stake %	Details
Share buy-back	Computer services	35.0	CEO Nkosinathi Khumalo and his brother bought a 35% stake in Mthombo (M-IT), which they founded, from Dimension Data for R11m.
Equity	Health	25.0	Lengana Investments will purchase 25% in Mx Health, increasing its empowerment shareholding to more than 60%.
Equity	Leisure & entertainment	100.0	Akani Leisure Investments, led by Reuel Khoza, agreed to buy Halcyon Hotels Group for R35m.
Acquisition	Automobiles & parts	100.0	GB Bearings, consortium comprising Federal-Mogul employees, will buy Federal-Mogul. BEE partners will hold a 40% stake.
Acquisition	Mining	51.0	Luvhomba Mining will buy Mooiplats, Holfontein and Zaid mines through structured debt.
Acquisition	Software & computers	63.0	Lithalelanga Connections Holdings purchased Tecor Ltd. 70% was bank financed.
Equity	General retail	39.7	BEE group Ukhamba's subsidiary, Dream World Investments, acquired Imperilog's shareholding in Distribution & Warehousing Network for R147m, payment to be finalised over 5 years.
Partnership	Insurance	60.0	Basebenzi, the investment arm of the Food & Allied Workers' Union, will hold 60% of the share capital of Break-Thru Financial Services. The other 40% will be held by Sanlam.
Joint Venture	Real estate	N/A	Investec and two Indian businessmen will develop the Trade Route shopping mall in Lenasia.
Acquisition	Software & computers	85.2	Zamori 243 Ltd, owned by Bryant black employees, acquired Bryant Technology Ltd for R243 090.
Acquisition	Food	74.0	Eggbert Eggs sold its Boksburg farm to Maye Serobe, a consortium owned 49% by staff, and 25% by the farm's manager, Petrus Fanga.

Type	Sector	Stake %	Details
Buyout	Investment companies	N/A	African Harvest Capital managers bought out Mzi Khumalo, the major shareholder, for more than R200m.
Partnership	Finance	50.0	Leroko, owned by Valli Moosa and Popo Molefe, and private equity fund Metier, formed the R2 billion Lereko-Metier Capital Growth Fund.
Equity	Food	26.8	Agri Sizwe Empowerment Trust (including women's and emergent farmers trusts as beneficiaries) will secure a 25.1% shareholding in Afgri Ltd in 8 years' time, after repaying a loan from the Land Bank.
Acquisition	Clothing & textiles	100.0	A consortium led by SA Clothing & Textiles Workers' Union saved Towles Edgar Jacobs from being liquidated.

Table 7.3 demonstrates that BEE deals, large and small, are being concluded over a wide array of sectors, by a wide array of BEE entities (owned variously by individuals, managers, employees, investment trusts and unions), and through a variety of devices (outright purchase, loan purchase, joint ventures with established firms, buyouts and partnerships). Furthermore, while many deals are funded by borrowing (from established corporates, banks and the state) and represent passive investment, they also suggest strongly that a black business class, even if it remains small, is moving rapidly into hands-on involvement in mining, manufacturing and services. This undoubtedly reflects the post-1994 growth of a black middle class and an increase in the (modest) proportion of blacks who can be described as affluent (Burger, Burger & van der Berg 2004; Southall 2005b). Nonetheless, although it is clear that BEE activity does extend some considerable way beyond the new elite, we should be cautious in rushing to agree with Iheduru that the BEE strategy is serving to establish 'community respect and groundswell legitimacy for capitalism and entrepreneurship among black South Africans' (2004: 19).

For sure, to some extent BEE may be propelling South Africa towards a deracialisation of capital, yet the extent of such a transformation would seem to be of limited benefit to the mass of the black population. Although a number of recent high-profile deals include an element of share purchase by black managers and employees, such share ownership schemes remain very much in the minority, and in any case South African law currently places major tax obstacles in the way of their implementation (BusinessMap 2004c), while Cosatu has recently criticised Old Mutual for using a proposed ten per cent empowerment transfer to employees to weaken their unions' bargaining power and expressed concern that employee ownership plans are rarely linked to effective worker representation upon boards (*Business Day* 18.02.05). Yes, some major deals draw in investments from broad-based trusts and the like, yet they mostly appear to 'tail end' larger players and offer little prospect of active involvement as stakeholders. Meanwhile, whereas the promotion of small enterprises is deemed by many to represent the surest path towards job creation, informed analysis suggests that the government's efforts to promote black enterprises at the ground level, where the need is greatest, constitute the weakest element in its overall strategy for BEE (Rogerson 2004). For the moment, BEE deals overwhelmingly constitute black investment into existing businesses rather than the creation of new ones, and there is little indication that they are altering the economy's path of 'jobless growth'. Alarmingly, the overall black share in South Africa's aggregate household income is said to have *declined* from 54.5 per cent in 1995 to 53.0 per cent in 2000. This, argues Simkins (2004), reflects the deteriorating conditions at the lower end of the labour market. In these circumstances, can BEE be said to be paving the way to a more democratic capitalism?

Conclusion: BEE and the limits to democratic capitalism

A confluence of interests and influences is arguing for capitalism in South Africa to become more democratic. The ANC government is determined that blacks must share in the wealth, ownership and management of the private sector; the new black moguls and white magnates alike are eager to legitimate a 'kinder' capitalism; and even organised labour, although ambivalent, is understandably keen to harness capitalism into providing improved benefits for workers and the wider poor while simultaneously shifting the economy in a more collectivist direction. In this context, widespread perceptions that the government's BEE strategy has done little more than to promote the good fortunes of a small black elite have caused great concern in the highest circles of both state and capital, resulting in the increasing espousal of notions associated with stakeholder capitalism: the popularisation of share ownership (involving notably black employee and broad-based empowerment); the harmony of interest between capitalists and workers; the responsiveness of firms to consumers and communities as well as to shareholders; and 'corporate social responsibility'. Yet this review has indicated that progress towards a more democratic capitalism in South Africa is strewn with obstacles.

Although the white-dominated corporate culture remains uncomfortable territory for many black managers and professionals, the black elite is making visible progress in scaling the walls of corporate power. Importantly, too, far from being isolated in their success, review of the extent of recent deals involving black interests indicates that the elite is merely the advance guard of a considerably larger black capitalist class which, backed by the impetus of the state-driven charter movement (which will link state contracts and procurements to empowerment credentials), is destined to grow in size, skills, weight and depth. Nonetheless, although this represents welcome progress towards a deracialisation of corporate structures, it offers little indication of serious movement towards a capitalism that is more democratic.

The problem for the advocates of stakeholder capitalism is that since 1994, South African capitalism has become more rather than less like the contemporary capitalism of the Western world: no longer contained and protected by state-imposed barriers, domestic conglomerates have increasingly 'unbundled' and internationalised; international and domestic finance capital is increasingly dominant over manufacturing; shareholding is concentrated in the hands of institutional investors, whose fates are determined by managers who are less and less accountable to shareholders and even the law; employee share ownership participation schemes are presently fashionable, yet there seems little guarantee that workers' share ownership will prove sustainable; few women are smashing through the 'glass ceiling' and corporations remain overwhelmingly male territory; and the gap between the financial rewards to top management and their workforces is widening alarmingly in a country where the patterns of inequality are already deeply entrenched. Although the 'broad-based' BEE strategy being pursued by the government will undoubtedly promote the growth of a black bourgeoisie, it appears at present as more likely to blur the boundaries of race and class than to propel South African capitalism in a more inclusive, accountable and equalising direction.

Notes

The author would like to thank the European Union's Conflict and Governance Facility for financial support for the research for this chapter.

1. Sexwale's Batho Bonke consortium owns ten per cent of ordinary shares in Absa, whilst Ubuntu-Batho holds ten per cent of shares in Sanlam, Absa's major shareholder (22 per cent).
2. For instance, Anglo American bought out minorities or delisted: Anglo American Coal, Anglo American Gold Investment Trust, Anglo American Industrial Corporation, Anglo American Investment Trust and Minorco, and disposed of its controlling interests in AECI, Chemical Services, JCI, First National Bank, Southern Life Association, the McCarthy Group, LTA, the Del Monte Group and other substantial holdings, as well as rationalising its crossholdings with De Beers, which was delisted from the JSE.
3. For instance, according to *Noseweek* (December 2004/January 2005) mining magnate Brett Kebble failed to submit tax returns between 1993 and 2000. Eventually, when pressed by the South African Revenue Service (SARS) to submit claims for those years, he admitted to declared income for those years of only R2.2 million, yet his increase in asset value approached R200 million. After further battles with the SARS, he was committed for trial on 8 October 2002, only for SARS to eventually call the prosecution off.
4. 'Economic interest' refers to entitlement which black people or designated black groups may have in an enterprise. However, where there is no economic flow-through to black shareholders or beneficiaries from an enterprise, no points on a scorecard will be allocated.

References

Burger R, Burger R & van der Berg S (2004) *Emergent black affluence and social mobility in post-apartheid South Africa*. Development Policy Research Unit, University of Stellenbosch, Working Paper 04/87.

BusinessMap (2004a) *Black control remains at 3% while JSE market cap increases by 50%*. Quarterly Review of black-controlled companies on the JSE, Ref. No. 004\053\BEE\CR. Johannesburg: BusinessMap Foundation.

BusinessMap (2004b) *Black economic empowerment review*, issues January to November. Johannesburg: BusinessMap Foundation.

BusinessMap (2004c) *Employee ownership for BEE is not as easy as it seems*, Ref. No. 2004\011\BEE\GM. Johannesburg: BusinessMap Foundation.

Cosatu (Congress of South African Trade Unions) (1997) *The report of the September Commission on the future of the unions to the Congress of South African Trade Unions.* Johannesburg: Cosatu.

Crawford-Brown T (2004) The arms deal scandal, *Review of African Political Economy* 100: 329–342.

DME (Department of Minerals and Energy, South Africa) (1998) *White Paper: A minerals and mining policy for South Africa.* Pretoria: DME.

DTI (Department of Trade and Industry, South Africa) (2004) *The codes of practice on broad-based black economic empowerment.* Pretoria: DTI.

Estes R (n.d.) New millenium capitalism: Business for the benefit of all stakeholders. Available at http://www.stakeholderalliance.org/newmillen.html.

Hassan E-K (2005) Black economic empowerment in South Africa, Nedlac (mimeo).

Hutton W (1996) *The state we're in.* London: Vintage.

Iheduru O (2004) Black economic power and nation-building in post-apartheid South Africa, *The Journal of Modern African Studies* 42(1): 1–30.

McGregor R (2004) *McGregor's who owns whom in South Africa 2004*, 24th edition. Johannesburg: Who owns Whom.

Mills CW (1956) *The power elite.* New York: Oxford University Press.

Rogerson C (2004) The impact of the South African government's SMME programmes: A ten year review (1994–2003). Mimeo.

Sampson A (2004) *Who runs this place? The anatomy of Britain in the 21st century.* London: John Murray.

Simkins C (2004) What happened to the distribution of income in South Africa between 1995 and 2001? Available at http://www.sarpn.org.za/documents/d0001234/index.php.

South African Reserve Bank (2002) The impact of offshore listings on the South African economy, *South African Reserve Bank Quarterly Bulletin* September: 60–71.

Southall R (2004) The ANC and black capitalism in South Africa, *Review of African Political Economy* 31 (100): 313–328.

Southall R (2005a) Black empowerment and corporate capital. In J Daniel, R Southall & J Lutchman (eds.) *The State of the Nation: South Africa 2004–05.* Cape Town: HSRC Press.

Southall R (2005b) The black middle class and democracy in South Africa, *Canadian Journal of African Studies* (forthcoming).

Trialogue (2004) *The good corporate citizen: Pursuing sustainable business in South Africa.* Cape Town: Trialogue.

Turok B (2002) Strange silence from the left, *New Agenda* 4: 6–12.

Wu C & Ngcobo L (2002) *Debunking the capital scarcity myth: The hidden empowerment wealth on the JSE Securities Exchange, September 2002.* Johannesburg: Empowerdex.

Wu C, Ntombela N, Ngcobo L & Dlamini A (2003) *Pioneers, powers and pundits: Influential and powerful BEE directors on the JSE, January 2003.* Johannesburg: Empowerdex.

8 The state of labour market deracialisation
Percy Moleke

Introduction

Almost daily concerns are raised in the media about race, racism in the judiciary, in the workplace, in business, in sports, in the media, in fact in almost all segments of society. Are these concerns misplaced or is it a case of 'no smoke without fire'?

Often the reports seem to contradict one another. Affirmative action is often slated as a form of reverse racism and blamed for eroding economic opportunities for whites to the benefit of blacks, yet, in an interview on South African television in 2005, Defence Minister Mosioua Lekota asked when the country is going to stop using race as a measure in employment. On the one hand, reports that the black middle class is increasing in size, and that the number of wealthy black people is rising, are cited as signs of deracialisation and black advancement within South Africa. On the other hand, the pace and extent of deracialisation are questioned. For example, at the Growth and Development Summit in 2003 (GDS 2003) questions were raised about the slow pace with which employment equity is being implemented in the workplace, and again, more recently, Labour Minister Mdladlana raised the same concern and announced that his department is going to be vigilant in following up implementation of equity legislation through a team of inspectors who will physically visit firms to check on progress. The continuing dominance of white males in management positions bears testimony to the Minister's concerns while growing numbers of Africans who are unemployed and continue to live in poverty again raises the question of how much and how fast deracialisation and the economic advancement of Africans is taking place.

This chapter looks at racial skills distribution in the South African labour market and will to some extent respond to the issues raised above. From a labour-market perspective, it is found that deracialisation is happening but the pace is slow and uneven across sectors. An attempt is made to identify some of the reasons for this slow and uneven progress and, while these factors are not weighted in terms of their importance, the need for a focus on education is emphasised. It is also argued that the apparent lack of an integrated and coherent approach to human-resource development renders the various equity laws and regulations powerless and hence ineffective in what they aim to achieve.

Does race matter in South Africa?

There were several assumptions implicit in the transition to democracy in South Africa. It was assumed that all the barriers that forced black South Africans into subordinate status would be quickly eliminated; that increased opportunities would open up for them in business, education, sports and society at large; that repealing apartheid laws (which started long before 1994) and the introduction of new laws on, for example, affirmative action, would gradually increase the participation of black employees in professional and managerial positions. However, South Africa continues to be plagued by huge inequalities, the majority of the population continues to live in poverty, many are unemployed and/or underemployed and race continues to play an important role in explaining the continuing plight of many. This does not refer to racism per se, although undeniably this continues and has a role to play. It is more that the consequences of apartheid continue to play themselves out and unfortunately do so along racial lines. Many black children still do not have access to good quality schooling, healthcare, water or proper housing. This will continue to tarnish their lives as they are denied access to the resources that are critical for positive economic prospects. We cannot be quick to accept that the country is no longer racially divided and that those who are unable to advance have themselves to blame.

On the plus side, black South Africans undoubtedly have political power; the number of black students in higher education has increased dramatically; the number of black business owners is increasing; the number of black managers and professionals has increased within most occupations; and the quality of life for most has improved. However, the gains made so far have not accrued to all black South Africans and progress towards labour-market deracialisation is disturbingly slow. Dismissing the continuing economic disparities between blacks and whites as 'passé, self-serving rhetoric' is an affront to the majority of the disadvantaged in this country. The fact is whites still dominate ownership and management positions in business, social and cultural institutions. Opportunities for whites continue to be abundant – irrespective of income or educational status, it is still far easier for whites to get credit, start a business, find a job, and make more money in their lifetimes than it is for the average black person. This situation affects everyone negatively: the perpetuation of such blatant inequalities means the perpetuation of the social costs associated with them, such as poverty, crime and so on. So yes, race still matters in South Africa.

Inequality in the labour market

The inequalities and racial divisions of South African society are nowhere as evident as in the labour market. Labour-market income accounts for a significant portion of income for the majority of South Africans. Despite legislation and commitment from stakeholders to even out the skills distribution in the labour market, progress is disconcertingly slow. The concerns of Labour Minister Mdladlana cited earlier with regard to the pace of progress towards equity are not misplaced. Based on the Labour Force Surveys, it is evident that Africans constitute over two-thirds of the labour force, while coloureds, Asians and whites constitute 11.8, 3.9 and 18.4 per cent respectively (Stats SA 2002).

Skills composition of workers

A comparison of the distribution of workers with the distribution of racial groups within occupational groups, shows a labour force that continues to be racially divided between skilled white workers and unskilled and/or semi-skilled African workers (see Table 8.1). Table 8.1 also shows the various skills levels in different sectors. Distribution of skill levels within sectors differs according to the skill intensity of the sector. The share of low-skilled and semi-skilled workers is significantly higher than that of skilled workers in almost all sectors. Semi-skilled workers are fairly evenly distributed across all sectors except private households. Skilled workers are concentrated in the technology-intensive sectors, namely, finance; electricity, gas and water supply; transport, storage and communication; and community, social and personal services. The distribution of skills across sectors is important for various reasons. Amongst other things, sectors are a proxy for status in the labour market: for example, a semi-skilled worker in finance has, on average, a better status than a semi-skilled worker in construction in terms of both pay and the nature of their work. Technology-intensive sectors use higher proportions of skilled workers and tend to offer better working conditions.

Table 8.1 also shows the distribution of various race groups in sectors across skill levels. This is important as a proxy for progress in terms of the advancement of Africans. It highlights the relative advancement of Africans into skilled versus semi-skilled categories in various sectors. What is reflected here is the concentration of whites at skilled level in skill-intensive sectors. Highly skilled Africans are mostly in the community service sector, which is mainly government and parastatals in transport, storage and communication and electricity, gas and water supply. It is only in the community service sector and the electricity, gas and water supply sectors that the proportion of Africans in skilled categories exceeds that of whites. The electricity, gas and water supply sector also shows a relatively high proportion of Africans in skilled-level categories, although that of whites is still higher. On the other hand, the proportion of Africans is higher within the semi-skilled and low-skilled categories. The conclusion that can be drawn from this is that the government has made better progress as an employer in terms of advancing Africans into high-level occupations, while the private sector seems to be lagging behind.

The data in Table 8.1 masks the differences within occupational groups due to the grouping of occupational categories into skill level. The skilled group is unpacked in Table 8.2 to show the racial distribution within broad occupational groups: whites are concentrated in high-level positions, top management and senior management, while Africans are concentrated in unskilled and semi-skilled occupations. Within the professional, technical and middle-management levels there is an almost even spread, with the proportion of whites a bit higher. What is also highlighted in Table 8.2 is the change in racial composition within each occupational group: at top and senior-management levels there is positive change shown by an increase in the number of Africans in those levels alongside a decline in the proportions of whites. It is disturbing to compare whites and coloureds in top management between 2002 and 2003: the proportion of whites in top management increased while that of coloureds declined dramatically. It is not clear if this was real or if there were some problems with the data.

Table 8.1 *Distribution of workers within sectors, by percentage, race and skills level*

Sector		2002			
		African	Coloured	Asian	White
Agriculture, hunting, forestry & fishing	Skilled	19.87	4.32		75.82
	Semi-skilled	87.66	2.21	0.26	9.69
	Low skilled	74.91	24.30	0.04	0.74
Mining & quarrying	Skilled	20.85			79.15
	Semi-skilled	71.64	2.46	0.45	25.15
	Low skilled	96.06	1.11		2.83
Manufacturing	Skilled	9.46	8.84	13.13	68.35
	Semi-skilled	52.36	13.34	7.87	26.21
	Low skilled	71.08	17.92	6.91	3.90
Electricity, gas & water supply	Skilled	32.74	18.94	5.95	42.38
	Semi-skilled	60.67	4.23	3.48	31.62
	Low skilled	77.51	13.39	2.44	6.66
Construction	Skilled	19.21	5.18	6.32	69.28
	Semi-skilled	74.26	12.38	2.21	9.98
	Low skilled	83.36	12.55	0.74	3.35
Wholesale & retail trade	Skilled	18.18	4.97	22.61	53.36
	Semi-skilled	60.49	12.32	7.74	18.79
	Low skilled	88.14	6.51	2.37	2.76
Transport, storage & communication	Skilled	46.42	4.74	8.34	39.79
	Semi-skilled	41.27	13.83	8.38	36.39
	Low skilled	78.93	11.09	3.49	6.49
Financial insurance/real estate/business service	Skilled	12.20	5.01	6.81	75.46
	Semi-skilled	39.29	12.94	5.62	41.98
	Low skilled	86.13	8.58	0.59	3.22
Community, social & personal services	Skilled	47.11	5.71	7.40	39.15
	Semi-skilled	61.82	11.29	3.77	22.97
	Low skilled	78.87	17.17	0.96	3.00
Private households	Semi-skilled	89.97	9.36	0.14	0.53
	Low skilled	89.76	9.76		0.13
Other	Skilled	24.42			75.58
	Semi-skilled	32.24	3.05	5.99	58.72
	Low skilled	79.23	20.77		

Sector		2004			
		African	Coloured	Asian	White
Agriculture, hunting, forestry & fishing	Skilled	17.11	12.38		70.52
	Semi-skilled	80.12	6.91	0.29	12.68
	Low skilled	75.38	24.16	0.06	0.41
Mining & quarrying	Skilled	36.06	0.59	1.46	61.88
	Semi-skilled	74.75	1.91	0.03	23.32
	Low skilled	96.99	0.79		1.80
Manufacturing	Skilled	18.76	8.98	11.26	60.32
	Semi-skilled	58.68	15.26	6.30	19.76
	Low skilled	70.05	20.83	5.27	3.86
Electricity, gas & water supply	Skilled	69.31	5.59	5.90	19.20
	Semi-skilled	58.55	18.17	1.38	21.90
	Low skilled	72.94	16.89	6.79	3.38
Construction	Skilled	26.53	20.93	4.04	48.50
	Semi-skilled	76.48	13.83	0.87	8.82
	Low skilled	82.93	12.45	0.16	4.46
Wholesale & retail trade	Skilled	21.57	6.56	15.81	55.74
	Semi skilled	63.87	13.15	5.28	17.57
	Low skilled	88.59	7.22	1.72	2.38
Transport, storage & communication	Skilled	50.87	6.46	4.65	38.01
	Semi-skilled	41.17	14.03	7.06	37.74
	Low skilled	76.98	11.54	3.50	7.98
Financial insurance/real estate/business service	Skilled	20.59	7.13	8.09	64.19
	Semi-skilled	49.11	11.27	6.76	32.81
	Low skilled	79.47	14.76	0.29	5.26
Community, social & personal services	Skilled	50.95	7.31	5.63	35.91
	Semi-skilled	65.71	11.19	3.30	19.81
	Low skilled	84.01	13.19	0.52	2.28
Private households	Semi-skilled	46.18	4.89		48.94
	Low skilled	89.93	9.90	0.04	0.12
Other	Skilled	21.16	5.37	9.81	63.66
	Semi-skilled	35.16	38.72	4.99	21.12
	Low skilled	79.29	20.71		

Source: Stats SA 2002 & 2004
Notes: Low skilled = labourers; Skilled = legislators, senior officials, managers, professionals; Semi-skilled = technical and associate professionals, clerks, service workers, skilled agricultural and fisheries workers, craft and related trades.

At senior management level the decline in the proportion of whites was not balanced out by an increase in any of the other race groups. A dramatic change occurred among the professionals and middle-level management: while all racial groups experienced an increase in this category, the proportion of Africans increased significantly from 33 per cent in 2001 to 40 per cent in 2002. On the other hand, the proportion of whites in this category decreased significantly, from 56 per cent in 2001 to 50 per cent in 2002. (The figures for 2003 were not used in this category because they showed a huge variation that did not allow for a further analysis of the sub-occupational categories.) Unfortunately the data from the equity reports does not enable us to see the occupations in which Africans are advancing most.

Table 8.2 *Distribution of workers in occupational groups, percentage by race, 2001–03*

Occupational categories	African	Coloured	Indian	White
Top management				
2003	10.0	3.4	5.0	81.5
2002	8.0	13.0	4.0	75.0
2001	6.2	2.7	3.8	87.5
Senior management				
2003	10.8	5.3	6.3	77.9
2002	10.0	5.0	5.0	80.0
2001	8.7	4.9	4.9	81.6
Professionals and middle management				
2002	40.0	6.0	4.0	50.0
2001	32.8	5.5	5.8	56.1
Skilled technical and management				
2003	35.8	14.5	7.0	43.1
2002	38.0	13.0	8.0	41.0
2001	34.4	14.6	7.5	43.6
Semi-skilled				
2003	61.9	15.9	5.3	16.9
2002	62.0	15.0	5.0	18.0
2001	58.9	17.7	5.6	17.8

Source: DoL 2001, 2002 & 2003

Nevertheless, the racial division is clear, with whites dominating the first four occupational groups, which represent high-skilled workers, and the reverse true for the semi-skilled group where Africans dominate.

The high proportion of Africans within professional and middle management, and skilled technicians could have positive implications for the future. These categories should provide a base from which Africans can be developed and advanced to senior management levels. It remains to be seen, however, whether employers are able to take advantage of this and translate it into reality over the next few years.

Age distribution of managers

The concentration of whites in management can be attributed to a long history of political and cultural practices in the labour market. Workers do not necessarily occupy management positions overnight – they tend to be 'groomed' and moulded from within the 'system' of the organisation. Hence, in many instances managers are older individuals who have moved up within the system. Alternatively, managers have been 'groomed' elsewhere and have accumulated a wealth of transferable experience. It can be assumed that the high proportion of whites in management is a temporary phenomenon which will dissipate over time as most of these white managers retire. This will then create openings for Africans, who are currently being 'groomed' or accumulating experience, to move up the job ladder to management. According to this theory there should be a concentration of white managers in the older age group (50 years and above). Table 8.3 shows the racial distribution of managers by age groups. This is a selection of all managers who are employed in both the public and the private sectors and excludes those who are self-employed. The figures show that there is a continuation of the disproportionate induction of white workers into management positions relative to other race groups. The distribution of white managers in the given age groups is not significantly different from that of other race groups. More significantly, this distribution does not show signs of ageing white managers who could make way for younger African managers. The current picture clearly indicates that the dominance of whites in management is likely to continue.

Table 8.3 *Racial distribution of managers by age groups, 2004*

Age	African	%	Coloured	%	Asian	%	White	%
15–30	26 893	16.97	11 975	20.97	12 522	23.51	49 578	16.04
31–40	58 521	36.94	23 963	41.95	21 021	39.46	104 087	33.69
41–50	43 322	27.34	11 476	20.09	11 356	21.32	96 298	31.16
51–65	28 269	17.84	9 703	16.99	7 988	15.00	55 659	18.01
> 65	1 431	0.90			384	0.72	3 378	1.09
Total	158 436	100.00	57 117	100.00	53 270	100.00	308 999	100.00

Source: Stats SA 2004

Distribution of workers by gender

The pace of representation with regard to gender shows similar trends to that of race: women continue to be under-represented in skilled occupations.

Table 8.4 *Distribution of workers, percentage by race and gender within skill levels, 2002–04*

	African		Coloured		Asian		White	
2002	Male	Female	Male	Female	Male	Female	Male	Female
Skilled	16.82	11.02	3.77	1.90	7.64	2.92	38.57	16.79
Semi-skilled	36.97	25.83	5.55	4.77	2.46	2.21	10.82	11.05
Low skilled	38.93	43.31	6.79	6.60	1.40	0.53	1.72	0.51
Other	19.24	14.90	6.44	4.82	0.78		37.13	16.70
2003								
Skilled	18.74	12.34	4.43	2.50	5.48	1.79	37.16	17.39
Semi-skilled	37.08	25.41	5.97	5.66	2.63	2.10	10.16	10.80
Low skilled	43.21	39.76	6.92	6.36	1.07	0.41	1.76	0.52
Other	35.77	16.50	3.12	2.07	0.94	0.94	29.01	11.65
2004								
Skilled	19.42	14.09	5.30	2.43	6.69	1.82	32.85	17.10
Semi-skilled	37.88	25.58	6.11	5.90	2.43	1.75	10.14	10.17
Low skilled	44.01	39.02	7.06	6.34	0.94	0.42	1.78	0.38
Other	37.89	14.10	3.19	7.00			29.96	7.86

Sources: Stats SA 2002; 2003; 2004

While women in general were discriminated against during the apartheid era, the racial distribution within gender reflects the advantage that was enjoyed by whites in general. White women tend to be concentrated within the skilled and semi-skilled occupations; in fact, the proportion of white women in skilled occupations is higher than at semi-skilled and low-skilled levels. On the other hand, African women are concentrated within semi-skilled and low-skilled occupations. However, the representation of women also shows signs of positive change, namely, an increase in their proportions between 2002 and 2004, except for Asian women whose proportion declined during this period. Although not shown in Table 8.4, the advancement of women can largely be attributed to their employment in the public sector.

Distribution of workers in the public sector

Although it was shown in the previous section that the government as an employer accounted for most of the progress with regard to racial representation and advancement of Africans in the labour market, all is not well in this sector, as there are signs of racial divisions of labour, albeit not heightened. In the context of equity requirements, it can be safely assumed that the public sector has to live by example. This means that as an employer it can be expected to have a more equitable structure in terms of race and gender, not only in aggregate numbers but also in terms of distribution of workers across occupations. However, there are signs that this is not the case.

As shown in Figure 8.1, although black workers are in the majority in the public sector, they are not evenly distributed across skill levels. Roughly the same proportions of highly-skilled production workers are black and coloured (at about 56 per cent each). Whites and Asians, on the other hand, are represented in higher proportions (74 and 63 per cent respectively). A similar trend is observed with regard to middle (highly-skilled supervision) and senior management. Whereas in numeric terms there are more black senior managers, as a proportion of the total population employed in the public sector they constitute a small proportion at just 0.4 per cent. The seemingly high proportion of skilled workers is due to educators, health workers and security personnel. If excluded, the proportion of skilled workers in the public sector is very small.

Figure 8.1 *Distribution of skill profiles within racial groups as at March 2004*

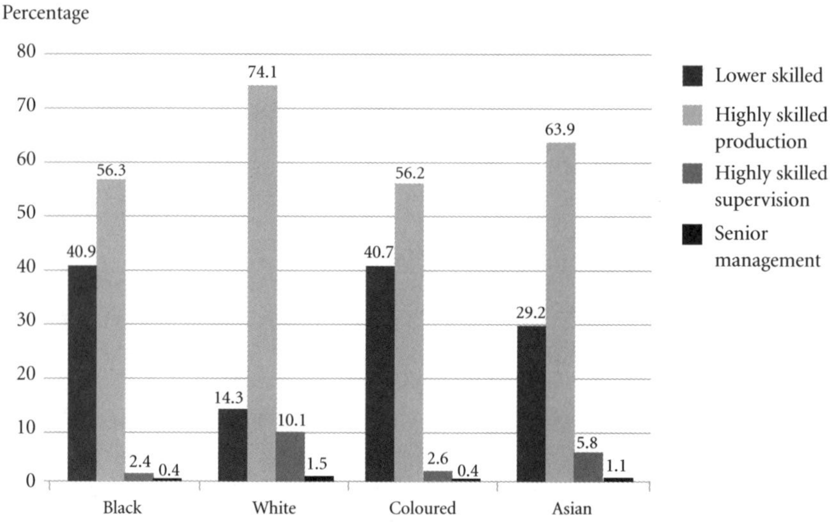

Percentage

Racial group	Lower skilled	Highly skilled production	Highly skilled supervision	Senior management
Black	40.9	56.3	2.4	0.4
White	14.3	74.1	10.1	1.5
Coloured	40.7	56.2	2.6	0.4
Asian	29.2	63.9	5.8	1.1

Source: Calculated from Persal (Department of Public Service and Administration 2004)

The current skills profile of the public sector certainly has to change if the government is to meet its objectives and make its commitments a reality. Skills shortages and gaps are a major constraint blocking achievement of these objectives.

Skills shortages

What accounts for the slow progress towards labour-market deracialisation, particularly in the private sector? Is it a deliberate ploy to perpetuate inequalities and maintain white advantage? Does the current distribution of workers represent a continuation of apartheid's legacy? Or is there a genuine shortage of skilled Africans, making equity targets difficult to meet?

Whether there are skills shortages in the South African economy is an unresolved debate and is not addressed in detail here. But there are indications that there are skills problems, at least in so far as the public sector is concerned.

In his address to the nation, President Mbeki (Mbeki 2005) indicated that the government is looking at ways to source skilled personnel from neighbouring countries. Indeed the government has what they call a scarce-skills policy framework which aims to attract people with relevant skills to the public sector. Failures in service delivery in the public sector are frequently attributed to the lack of skilled personnel to deliver on government commitments. Based on this evidence one can conclude that there are serious skills problems in the public sector.

In the private sector, the picture is not as clear and it is further complicated by the equity target requirements. It is obvious that the private sector is unable to meet equity targets as required by the Employment Equity Act. Notwithstanding the demand-side factors, namely discrimination in hiring, training and promotion, clearly there are problems, particularly with regard to the supply of Africans with relevant skills. This is demonstrated in the education statistics shown in Table 8.5 on p. 214.

In the absence of proper data on vacancies, especially for skilled personnel, or studies to determine this, inferences and perceptions rather than empirical evidence inform conclusions in this regard. Given that the private and the public sector do not operate in two separate markets, the trends observed in the public sector can be inferred to the private sector. Indeed the problems might be considered more acute in the public sector. This is because the public sector is not in a position to compete for skills with the private sector, but also because the private sector tends to be more efficient in its attempts to attract and retain skilled personnel compared to the public sector.

Nevertheless, whether or not there are skills shortages, there are obviously other factors which account for the slow pace of progress. Some are related to the actions of the employers and some fall outside the ambit of the labour market although they directly affect the labour-market outcomes.

Demand-side factors

Discrimination in the labour market, a major source of economic and labour-market inequalities, started to decline prior to the enactment of equity legislation. Indeed it is argued that starting from the 1970s, racial discrimination amongst employers was starting to be replaced by non-racial productive assessments and, in some cases, affirmative action – mostly encouraged by a profit motive. Crankshaw (1997) provides a detailed analysis showing how, at the height of apartheid, despite efforts by the previous government and white trade unions to maintain the racial division of labour, Africans were advancing into previously reserved occupations, albeit only certain occupations. In the 1980s, African trade unions were recognised and workers permitted to join them (Moll 2000). There was also an increase in the number of African students permitted to enter historically white tertiary institutions. Thus post-apartheid reforms and interventions cemented the practices that had already begun.

This does not mean that discrimination was entirely removed after 1994. Repealing apartheid laws could not and did not mean an end to racial discrimination and conflict. Indeed various studies indicate that discrimination continues in the labour market and, it seems, may even have increased over the past decade (Erichsen & Wakeford 2001; Keswell 2002). Rospabé (2000) found evidence of discrimination in hiring in certain occupations and sectors, particularly finance – hence the concentration of whites in that sector. Controlling for all the factors that represent individuals' productivity, it is clear that Africans are still disadvantaged in the labour market with respect to recruitment into certain occupations, promotions and pay.

Another form of discrimination is sometimes overlooked, despite its strength in perpetuating discriminatory practices, namely informal institutional discrimination. Experience from countries such as the US and Canada indicates the links between embedded, informal social relations in organisations and gender and racial discrimination in the workplace. These relations play themselves out in administrative norms and values and institutional practices that perpetuate discrimination (Agocs 2002). Equity legislation to address informal institutional discrimination is lacking in South Africa.

The enacted equity legislation has overtly or discreetly played a role in the declining ability of discrimination to explain the inequalities in some segments of the labour market, but it has not been successful in speeding up deracialisation as such. When one considers that discrimination practices by employers had begun to decline in the 1960s and 1970s, as demonstrated by Crankshaw (1997), it cannot be denied that the progress has been slow. Even within the 11 years of democracy, the progress is disconcerting. However, it is generally accepted that efforts within the labour market alone are not enough to redress labour-market inequalities.

Supply factors

Labour-market inequalities are not only a result of labour-market demand, namely discrimination in hiring, training and promotion. Indeed the supply-side factors under apartheid were designed such that the distribution of various racial groups in occupations and in the accumulation of skills was automatically skewed. With the reported role of discrimination declining as a factor in explaining continued labour-market inequalities, education has now become the major explanatory factor.

Education is inextricably linked to the structure of the labour market. Among its many other functions, it feeds skilled labour into the labour market. Therefore, while there are various factors in the labour market that shape the distribution of labour, education is a major supply factor that affects this distribution and it partly explains the inequalities observed in the labour market. In a similar vein, education and labour-market outcomes are potent tools for eradicating racial inequalities and poverty in South Africa.

From the supply side, it is clear that the legacy of apartheid will take decades to eradicate. The harm done through the education system continues to be felt despite efforts made to transform it. Firstly, a significant majority of African adults in the labour force have no education or have attained low levels of education (see Table 8.5). Overall the proportion of adults with higher levels of education is low at 8.4 per cent. Racial differences show the lowest proportion is among blacks and coloureds – both at about five per cent. These figures, however, mask the tremendous amount of progress made in access to and attainment in education. For example the proportion of Africans with no schooling at all declined from 24.3 to 22.3 per cent in 1996 and those with higher education increased from 3 to 5.2 per cent in 2001. Needless to say these figures are still minuscule and there is need for further improvement in this regard.

Table 8.5 *Highest level of education among those aged 20 and older, percentage by race, 2001*

	No schooling	Some primary	Completed primary	Some secondary	Completed secondary	Higher education
Black	22.3	18.5	6.9	30.4	16.8	5.2
Coloured	8.3	18.4	9.8	40.1	18.5	4.9
Indian	5.3	7.7	4.2	33.0	34.9	14.9
White	1.4	1.2	0.8	25.9	40.9	29.8
Total	17.9	16.0	6.4	30.8	20.4	8.4

Source: Census 2001 cited in SAIRR 2003/04

Despite these gains, a number of dynamics undermine this progress. The denial of quality education to the majority of the population during the apartheid years was exacerbated by policies in the labour market which denied black people access to high-skill occupations, training, promotion and hence accumulation of human capital in the labour market to supplement or complement that received through schooling. Thus the majority of black adults do not possess the education and skills so critical for deployment in the labour market. The consequence of this is that they go through their working lives with low levels of skills.

It seems difficult to reverse some of the trends set in motion during the apartheid era. Participation of black people in education at all levels has increased but there are still concerns with regard to the quality of education received by the majority of Africans. There is little or no integration in predominantly black schools and the outputs of these schools are disappointing in both qualitative and quantitative terms. This is despite the increases in resources and funding for these schools. According to van der Berg and Burger (2003), inefficient management and ineffective use of resources account for most of the poor quality of education in African schools. The quality of education is reflected in the small proportion of those passing the senior certificate with endorsement, the small numbers of students that pass mathematics and science at secondary-school level, and the low throughput rates of Africans at tertiary level, particularly in science, engineering and technology-related fields. The performance of secondary-school students directly affects the tertiary education and labour-market outcomes.

THE STATE OF LABOUR MARKET DERACIALISATION

At tertiary level, there is a concentration of black students in areas of study with poor labour-market outcomes, that is, non-professional fields of study. Table 8.6 shows uneven proportions of racial groups in fields of graduation.

Table 8.6 *Degrees, diplomas, and certificates awarded by public universities, percentage by race and field of study, 2002*

Area of study	African	Coloured	Indian	White
Agriculture and renewable natural resources	46.8	1.4	1.2	50.6
Architecture and environmental design	21.7	4.2	4.6	69.5
Business, commerce and management sciences	25.8	4.8	13.5	55.8
Communication	34.4	2.1	5.9	57.6
Computer science and data processing	28.1	3.7	13.6	54.6
Education	83.7	3.0	2.2	11.1
Engineering and engineering technology	21.4	2.6	11.0	65.0
Healthcare and health sciences	40.4	5.6	12.3	41.6
Home economics	27.9	3.8	3.4	64.9
Industrial arts, trades and technology	5.1	4.1	1.0	89.8
Language, linguistics and literature	46.7	4.6	5.3	43.4
Law	34.9	6.2	9.0	49.9
Libraries and museums	47.4	5.7	4.1	42.8
Life and physical sciences	34.2	4.9	9.8	51.2
Mathematical sciences	38.6	3.5	10.2	47.7
Philosophy, religion and theology	42.5	6.7	5.0	45.7
Physical and health education	13.0	3.1	3.4	80.4
Psychology	32.8	6.8	7.9	52.6
Public administration and social services	69.0	9.0	3.4	18.7
Social sciences and studies	50.8	5.3	7.1	36.9
Visual performing arts	19.5	4.4	2.4	73.7
Total	48.3	4.5	7.7	39.5

Source: Department of Education, cited in SAIRR, 2003/04

Labour-market training

The skewed supply from education partly explains the skewed distribution of racial groups across skill levels. The other explanation relates to the training received in the labour market, which is also a powerful tool to redress the inequalities of the past. The culture of training has apparently picked up with more firms involved in some form of training and skills development of their personnel (Rogerson & Rogerson 2000; HSRC 2003). The Skills Development Act has certainly played a significant role in encouraging this training culture but there is also increasing recognition of the importance of having a skilled workforce. However, the role of labour-market training in redressing the inequalities of the past seems to be limited and constrained by the profit motive among employers. Training tends to be focused on those occupational categories that will most benefit the company. Unfortunately, most of the occupational categories that benefit are dominated by whites, since they dominate in the skilled categories. This can be seen when comparing recipients of training with the proportion of each occupation group by race; it is clear that training as a tool to improve the skills of the previously disadvantaged is not being effected.

Table 8.7 presents the proportion of workers trained as a proportion of the total number of employees by race group in a particular occupational category. The table reflects that a higher proportion of African managers received training. However, within the categories of professionals and technicians and associate professionals, a lower proportion of Africans was trained, while for whites a higher proportion received training.

Some micro-level and qualitative information does, however, give a picture of training-related initiatives. General participation trends show improved access to training for the previously disadvantaged groups, Africans in particular. However, the National Skills Survey revealed that most of the training that Africans had access to was not structured learning (HSRC 2003), which is critical for human capital accumulation and progression in the labour market. Research by Maserumule and Madikane (2004), based on the survey of metal and engineering companies in the East Rand, reported that most of the training was generic or of a basic on-the-job type. Discrimination was also reported in the training of artisans, with whites getting more opportunities and being given higher status through grading and/or being paid more when compared to their African counterparts.

Table 8.7 *Proportion of workers trained in relation to total employees by race group and occupational category*

Occupational categories	African		Coloured	
	% share employees	% share trained	% share employees	% share trained
Legislators, senior officials and managers	17.4	19.2	7.5	8.4
Professionals	37.8	27.6	13.4	6.3
Technicians and associate professionals	31.7	30.8	11.7	11.2
Clerks	35.2	36.4	17.0	15.9
Service and sales workers	57.8	49.3	13.4	15.6

Occupational categories	Indian		White	
	% share employees	% share trained	% share employees	% share trained
Legislators, senior officials and managers	6.3	7.0	68.9	65.4
Professionals	4.9	6.1	43.9	60.0
Technicians and associate professionals	8.0	8.3	48.5	49.6
Clerks	9.1	9.5	38.7	38.2
Service and sales workers	4.8	6.3	24.0	28.7

These studies do indicate that training as a tool for redress is not being used efficiently. This may not be the case generally and some employers may be using training to target Africans in order to upgrade their skills and move them up the ladder within firms. However, current data indicate that training tends to be used for upgrading the skills base of existing employees in their current occupations and workplaces. What is missing from the existing literature on this issue is information about the efforts undertaken by firms to manage change within the workforce. Human-resource management practices have a critical role to play in deracialising the labour force and they speak not only to addressing overt discrimination, but also to informal institutionalised discrimination which occurs between employees.

Conclusion

It is clear that the labour market is far from being deracialised and concerns about the pace of progress in this sphere are valid. While Africans have certainly advanced in the labour market, the fact that Africans constitute a large proportion of workers and are still concentrated in low-skilled and semi-skilled occupations is indeed a cause for concern. The labour market is still racially divided between whites in skilled occupations and management positions, and blacks concentrated in low- and semi-skilled occupations.

It is also clear that the government, as an employer, accounts for most of the progress observed, particularly at management level. Yet even within government there are indications that all is not well, with whites over-represented in skilled occupations and their proportion in senior management relatively higher. Progress in the private sector is slow and uneven.

What must be borne in mind is that the labour market represents only a section of the population – a significant number of Africans, in particular, are unemployed and hence not enjoying those benefits of redress that are, albeit slowly, accruing to those in employment. The increasing opportunities for skilled labour and the decline in demand for unskilled labour have profound implications for new entrants to the labour market.

This speaks directly to the vital role of education as the first port of call for skills accumulation. The poor quality of education accessed by the majority of the population undermines all efforts to undo the injustices of the past. The education system directly feeds the labour market and does, to a large extent, determine employability, employment status and earnings.

Equity legislation, while important in attempting to eliminate discrimination, can only resolve part of the problem as evidenced by the fact that the government sector as an employer has made significant progress in terms of redressing racial distributions while the private sector displays disturbingly slow progress. Current legislation does not address or deal with informal institutionalised discriminatory practices. Perhaps the recent announcement by the Minister of Labour on the monitoring and enforcement of employment equity will encourage progress in this process, particularly in the private sector (DoL 2003). On the other hand it might also be an opportunity for those in the private sector who are committed to transformation to voice some of the problems they are experiencing and that, in turn, may lead to further interventions.

In principle, various policies recognise the importance of integrating efforts to enhance transformation in the labour market. Human-resource development requires a holistic approach with commitment and action from various complementary stakeholders, that is, from *government* (including efforts to improve education and training by the departments of education and labour); from *employers* (in changing their human-resource management practices); and from individual *employees* (in addressing informal discrimination). Initiatives by any of these groupings alone will not be effective without complementary commitments from the others.

References

Agocs C (2002) Canada's employment equity legislation and policy, 1987–2000: The gap between policy and practice, *International Journal of Manpower* 23(3): 256–276.

Crankshaw O (1997) *Race, class and the changing division of labour under apartheid.* London: Routledge.

Department of Public Service and Administration (South Africa) (2004) *Public Service payroll information* (Persal). Pretoria: DPSA.

DoL (Department of Labour, South Africa) (2001) *Report on employment equity registry.* Pretoria: DoL.

DoL (2002) *Report on employment equity registry.* Pretoria: DoL.

DoL (2003) *Report on employment equity registry.* Pretoria: DoL.

Erichsen G & Wakeford J (2001) *Racial wage discrimination in SA before and after the first democratic election.* Development Policy Research Unit (DPRU) Working Paper 01/49. Cape Town: DPRU.

GDS (Growth and Development Summit) (2003) Growth and Development Summit Agreement, June 2003. Available at www.polity.org.za/pdf/GDSAgreement.pdf.

HSRC (Human Sciences Research Council) (2003) *South African national skills survey.* Report for the Department of Labour and the European Union.

Keswell M (2002) Intragenerational mobility: A study of chance and change in post-apartheid south Africa. Paper presented at the DPRU/FES second annual Conference on Labour Markets and Poverty in South Africa, October 2002.

Maserumule B & Madikane M (2004) Is the Skills Act working for workers? *South African Labour Bulletin* 28(3): 30–33.

Mbeki T (2005) Address of the President of South Africa, Thabo Mbeki, to the second joint sitting of the third democratic Parliament. Cape Town, 11.02.05.

Moll P (2000) Discrimination is declining in South Africa but inequality is not, *Studies in Economics and Econometrics* 24(3): 91–108.

Rogerson CM & Rogerson JM (2000) Dealing in scarce skills: employer responses to the brain drain in South Africa, *Africa Insight* 30(2): 31–40.

Rospabé S (2000) Did labour market racial discrimination decline with the end of apartheid? An analysis of the evolution of hiring, occupational and wage discrimination between 1993 and 1999 in South Africa. Paper presented at the International Jubilee Conference of the Economic Society of South Africa, Johannesburg, 13–14.09.01.

SAIRR (South African Institute of Race Relations) (2003/04) *The South African survey 1995–96*. Johannesburg: SAIRR.

Stats SA (Statistics South Africa) (2002) *Labour force survey* (February). Pretoria: Stats SA.

Stats SA (2003) *Labour force survey* (March). Pretoria: Stats SA.

Stats SA (2004) *Labour force survey* (March). Pretoria: Stats SA.

Van der Berg S & Burger R (2003) Education and socio-economic differentials: A study of school performance in the Western Cape, *South African Journal of Economics* 71(3): 496–524.

9 The state of the informal economy

Richard Devey, Caroline Skinner and Imraan Valodia

Introduction

In August 2003, President Mbeki introduced the idea of South Africa being characterised by a 'first economy' and a 'second economy', operating side by side.[1] In November, in an address to the National Council of Provinces, he developed the notion, stating that:

> The second economy (or the marginalised economy) is characterised by underdevelopment, contributes little to GDP, contains a big percentage of our population, incorporates the poorest of our rural and urban poor, is structurally disconnected from both the first and the global economy and is incapable of self-generated growth and development. (Mbeki 2003)

This idea of a 'second economy' is increasingly part of policy rhetoric at all levels of state. For example, the KwaZulu-Natal Minister for Finance and Economic Development, Dr Zweli Mkhize, began his 2005 Budget speech with a description of the economy using the analogy of an apartheid-era train with the first economy occupying the first-class compartments and the second economy being the second- and third-class sections. Having made substantial reference to the notion throughout the speech he argued that interventions in the second economy are 'even more crucial' than projects aimed at stimulating growth in the first economy.

In his 'State of the Nation' speech on 21 May 2004, President Mbeki (2004) argued that the:

> ...core of our response to all these challenges is the struggle against poverty and underdevelopment, which rests on three pillars. These are: encouraging the growth and development of the first economy, increasing its possibility to create jobs; implementing our programme

to address the challenges of the second economy; and, building a social security net to meet the objective of poverty alleviation.

The governing party elaborated on the notion of a dual economy by characterising the second economy as:

> The first and second economies in our country are separated from each other by a structural fault...Accordingly, what we now have is the reality...of a 'mainly informal, marginalised, unskilled economy, populated by the unemployed and those unemployable in the formal sector'. The second economy is caught in a 'poverty trap'. It is therefore unable to generate the internal savings that would enable it to achieve the high rates of investment it needs. Accordingly, on its own, it is unable to attain rates of growth that would ultimately end its condition of underdevelopment. (*ANC Today* 4(47), 26.11–02.12.04)

In his 2005 'State of the Nation' address, Mbeki again refers to the concept of the 'second economy' arguing that:

> We must achieve new and decisive advances towards...eradicating poverty and underdevelopment, within the context of a thriving and growing first economy and the successful transformation of the second economy.

In outlining what government will do about transforming the second economy, the President had this to say:

> To take the interventions in the second economy forward... additional programmes will be introduced or further strengthened by April 2005, as part of the Expanded Public Works Programme.

Although the President does not himself refer to the informal economy, the quote from *ANC Today* above shows that, within the ruling party at least, the informal economy is seen as being located in the second economy. Further, the African National Congress (ANC) sees the second economy, and presumably the informal economy, as being structurally disconnected from the mainstream of the economy.

Arguments about dualism and the relationship between the mainstream of the economy and the periphery have characterised much of South African historiography. This is most prominently captured in the debates of the early 1970s about the relationship between apartheid and capitalism in South Africa with liberals arguing that capitalism would ultimately undermine apartheid as more and more of the African periphery came to be incorporated into the mainstream of the economy (Lipton 1985; O'Dowd 1978), and Marxists arguing that there was in fact a close, but exploitative, relationship between the mainstream and the periphery (Legassick 1974; Wolpe 1972). The re-emergence of a dualist view of the economy is significant not only because it is being articulated by the President and is at odds with the way in which the ANC has traditionally viewed South African society, but also because it seems to inform much of the policy focus of the ANC. Not having had a definitive statement from the President, we can only speculate on why he chooses to use the terms 'first' and 'second' economy, rather than formal and informal economy. As we shall see, these definitions matter. The President's view of the second economy includes the unemployed – implying he is using a conceptualisation of the economy that moves beyond a simple formal–informal dichotomy.

The articulation of the first and second economy conceptualisation of South Africa by the Presidency coincided, we would argue, with a refocusing of economic policy in South Africa (Padayachee & Valodia 2001). This conceptualisation tacitly acknowledges the failure of the trickle-down economic growth policies so central to the post-1996 Growth, Employment and Redistribution (GEAR) era and informs much of government's more recent emphasis on poverty alleviation. However, the dualism suggested by arguments about a 'structural' break between the first and second economy allow government to argue that its economic policies have been successful for the first economy (Naidoo 2004), and as a result of these successes, government is now able to address issues of poverty and unemployment in the second economy. As we demonstrate later, there is in fact a close relationship between the first and second economy (although admittedly we focus only on the informal economy) and government policy for the second economy is either absent, or where it does exist, piecemeal and ineffective.

In the absence of a coherent conceptualisation of – and any systematic data on – the second economy, in this paper we focus on one important element of the second economy – the informal economy. We analyse the nature of the informal economy in South Africa, providing some descriptive statistics and analysis to highlight the nature and extent of the informal economy.[2] Given the present prominence of the 'second economy' concept, we provide some analysis of the efficacy of current government support measures to the informal economy, concluding that these are few and far between, patchy and incoherent, and largely ineffective. We then examine linkages between employment in the formal and the informal economy arguing that, contrary to the views of the President and the ANC, there are in fact fairly close linkages between the formal economy and the informal economy. Finally, by way of conclusion, we use the evidence provided in the paper to comment on the accuracy and relevance of the 'second economy' concept.

The informal economy: conceptual issues and definitions

At this point it is useful to clarify what the informal economy, or the informal sector, comprises. Since Keith Hart first coined the phrase 'informal sector' in the early 1970s to describe the range of subsistence activities of the urban poor, there has been considerable debate about what exactly the term refers to. The most quoted definition is that contained in the International Labour Organisation's (ILO) Kenya Report in which informal activities are defined as 'a way of doing things', characterised by 'ease of entry; reliance on indigenous resources; family ownership of enterprises; small scale of operation; labour intensive and adapted technology; skill acquired outside of the formal school system and unregulated and competitive markets' (1972: 6).

Over the years the definition has evolved, as has the character of the phenomenon it aims to describe. Increasingly, informal activities are the result of formal firms 'informalising'. Further, there are supply relations from the formal to the informal. These trends deem some of the characteristics identified in the ILO definition nonsensical. Lund and Srinivas point out 'we do not think of formal sector procurers of fruit and vegetables from agribusiness who supply to informal traders as "trading in indigenous resources" ' (2000: 9). A machinist doing piecework in the clothing industry is as likely to have acquired her skills in the formal education system as outside of it.

Castells and Portes describe the informal economy as a 'common sense' (1989: 12) notion that cannot be captured by a strict definition. Although the authorities writing on the definition of the informal sector differ markedly as to what criteria they use to define the informal sector and as to the relative weighting of different criteria, a criterion common to all definitions is that these are economic activities which are small-scale and elude certain government requirements or, as Castells and Portes state, are 'unregulated by the institutions of society, in a legal and social environment in which similar activities are regulated' (1989: 12). Examples of such requirements are registration, tax and social security obligations and health and safety rules.

For our purposes, two important points are worth noting. First, the term 'informal sector' disguises a significant degree of heterogeneity. Informal activities encompass different types of economic activity (trading, collecting, providing a service and manufacturing), different employment relations (the self-employed, paid and unpaid workers and disguised wage workers) and activities with different economic potential (survivalist activities and successful small enterprises). A second and related problem is the distinction between the formal and informal sectors as if there was a clear line dividing the two. Closer analysis of this phenomenon demonstrates that they are integrally linked. There are few examples of informal operators who are not linked (either through supply or customer networks) into the formal economy. As Peattie points out, 'if we think about the world in terms of a formal and informal sector we will be glossing over the linkages which are critical for a working policy and which constitute the most difficult elements politically in policy development' (1987: 858).

Using the term informal 'economy' rather than informal 'sector' partially addresses such concerns. The term 'economy' implies a greater range of activities than 'sector'. If both formal and informal activities are seen as part of the economy we are better able to see the linkages between the two. Implied in the notion 'informal' is that there is a formal, a norm, against which these other activities can be compared. As with any norm this will be time and context specific. With respect to the labour market Eapen (2001) points out how some analysts define informality in terms of the absence of characteristics that belong to 'formal' activities like security/regularity of work, better earnings, existence of non-wage and long-term benefits, protective legislation and union protection. She goes on to point out that in a situation in which a number of activities within the formal sector are getting 'informalised' and private, small-scale processing/manufacturing enterprises are growing, 'the borderline becomes blurred' (2001: 2390). Considering this issue from another angle, Bromley asks 'if an enterprise is required to have six official permits, for example, but only has five, should it be considered informal even when the sixth derives from a moribund regulation that most entrepreneurs ignore?' (1995: 146). She goes on to conclude 'formality and informality are really the opposite poles of a continuum with many intermediate and mixed cases' (Bromley 1995: 146).

For statistical purposes, the accepted international standard for defining the informal sector was agreed in a resolution at the fifteenth International Conference for Labour Statistics (ICLS). An important criterion of the ICLS definition is that employment in the informal sector is based on the characteristics of the *enterprise* in which the person is employed instead of the characteristics of the worker employed. The ICLS definition recommends that the informal sector be defined in terms of one or more of the following criteria:

- Non-registration of the enterprise in terms of national legislation such as taxation or other commercial legislation;
- Non-registration of employees of the enterprise in terms of labour legislation;
- Small size of the enterprise in terms of the numbers of people employed.

Statistics South Africa (Stats SA) uses this enterprise-based definition in order to derive estimates of informal employment in South Africa. The ILO (2002) and the seventeenth ICLS have recently proposed an alternative definition which is based on the employment characteristics of the worker. According to this definition – presented at the 2002 International Labour Conference – the informal economy comprises informal employment (without secure contracts, worker benefits or social protection) of two kinds. The first is informal employment in informal enterprises (small unregistered or unincorporated enterprises) including employers, employees, own account operators and unpaid family workers in informal enterprises. The second is informal employment outside informal enterprises (for formal enterprises, for households or with no fixed employer), including domestic workers, casual or day labourers, temporary or part-time workers, industrial outworkers (including home-based workers) and unregistered or undeclared workers.[3]

The difference between these definitions is captured in Table 9.1. The enterprise-based definition, currently used by Stats SA, is made up of cells 3 and 4 with the enterprise being the unit of analysis. In contrast, the new employment-based definition, now recommended by both the ILO and the ICLS, examines the nature of the work being performed and defines the informal economy as being made up of cells 2 and 4. An issue that arises is whether the employment-based definition would be more appropriate to capture the informal economy in South Africa. In related work, we have argued that the employment-based definition would be more appropriate (Devey, Skinner & Valodia 2004).

Table 9.1 *Formal and informal employment – definitional differences*

Production units	Types of jobs	
	Formal employment	Informal employment
Formal enterprises	1	2
Informal enterprises	3	4

Note: Formal employment = 1; enterprise-based definition of the informal sector = 3+4; informal employment (employment-based definition) = 2+4

Trends in the informal economy

Internationally, there is a growth in the numbers of people working in the informal economy, either self-employed in unregistered enterprises or as wage workers in unprotected jobs. A recent collation of international statistics on the informal economy states: 'Informal employment comprises one-half to three-quarters of non-agricultural employment in developing countries' (ILO 2002: 7). Table 9.2 lists the percentages in regions.

Table 9.2 *Informal employment as a proportion of non-agricultural employment*

Region	Percentage
North Africa	48
Sub-Saharan Africa	72
Latin America	51
Asia	65

Source: Adapted from ILO 2002: 7

It is thus clear that in many parts of the world informal employment is the norm. Further, Chen (2001) states that 83 per cent and 93 per cent of new jobs in the 1980s and 1990s were created in the informal economy in Latin America and Africa respectively. This indicates that the trend of informalisation is unlikely to be reversed. Informal employment, however, is not only a phenomenon in developing countries. The ILO (2002) states that three categories of non-standard or atypical work – self-employment, part-time work and temporary work – comprise 30 per cent of overall employment in 15 European countries and 25 per cent of total employment in the United States.

Table 9.3 shows the broad trends in the labour market in South Africa over the period 1997 to 2003, with a sustained growth in unemployment. Figure 9.1, using figures presented in Table 9.3, graphically represents the labour force (those who are working), and shows that employment in the formal economy has demonstrated very limited growth over the period.

Employment in the informal economy,[4] on the other hand, increased from 965 000 in October 1997 to 1.9 million in September 2003, more than doubling over a period of six years.[5] For a number of reasons, this trend must, however, be treated with caution. First, we are using data from the October household survey (OHS) for the period 1997–1999 and the labour force survey (LFS) for the period 2000–2003, two surveys which are not directly comparable. Devey et al. (2004) point to other problems with these estimates of informal employment. They highlight the fact that there are several inconsistencies in the data on informal employment. More importantly, they show that Stats SA has improved its capturing of data on informal employment, which would explain at least part of the increasing trend in informal employment.

Notwithstanding these difficulties it is now widely accepted that informal employment has grown since the political transition and that, as the data show, this growth has declined in recent years (Devey et al. 2004).

THE STATE OF THE INFORMAL ECONOMY

Table 9.3 *Labour market status of workers in South Africa, 1997–2003*

	1997	1998	1999	2000	2001	2002	2003
Formal	6 405 953	6 527 120	6 812 647	6 841 877	6 872 924	7 033 940	7 460 398
Commercial agriculture	495 530	726 249	804 034	666 940	665 941	810 998	831 893
Subsistence agriculture	163 422	202 290	286 856	964 837	358 983	520 259	350 384
Informal	965 669	1 077 017	1 573 986	1 933 675	1 873 136	1 702 415	1 899 114
Domestic	992 341	749 303	798 524	999 438	915 831	875 255	1 022 921
Unspecified	70 986	107 966	92 905	305 797	146 000	85 841	57 534
Unemployed	2 450 738	3 162 662	3 157 605	4 082 248	4 525 309	4 837 493	4 570 566
Not economically active	13 960 772	13 156 940	12 752 967	11 100 135	12 006 413	12 118 060	13 724 114
Total, ages 15–65	25 505 411	25 709 548	26 279 523	26 894 948	27 364 538	27 984 260	29 916 924

Source: Own calculations from Stats SA OHS and LFS (various)

Figure 9.1 *Labour force by type of work in South Africa, 1997–2003*

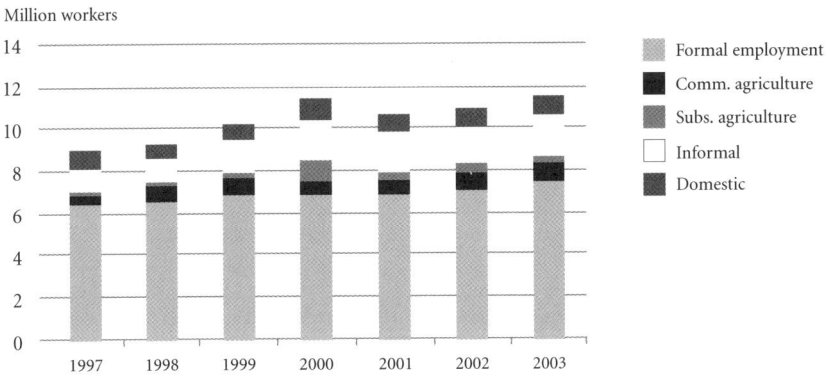

Source: Own calculations from Stats SA OHS and LFS (various)

Drawing on the latest available figures – the March 2004 LFS – Figure 9.2 shows the distribution of workers operating in informal enterprises by industrial sector. Employment in informal enterprises in South Africa is concentrated in trade, with just under half of all informal workers located in this sector. Further, there are significant numbers of people working in construction, manufacturing and services. In comparison to other developing contexts, South Africa's informal economy is disproportionately dominated by trade (see, for example, Charmes' 2000 figures for other African countries).

Figure 9.2 *Workers in informal enterprises by sector, March 2004*

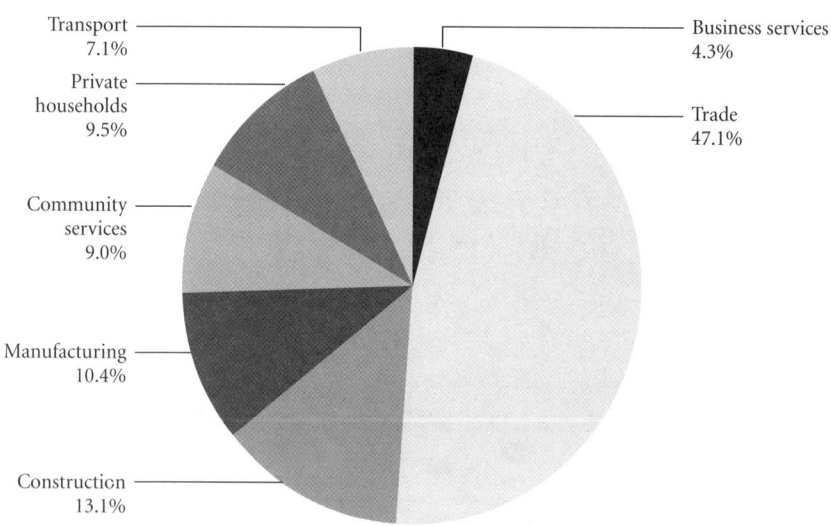

Source: Own calculation from Stats SA, LFS March 2004

Figure 9.3 shows monthly incomes of workers in informal enterprises. According to the survey, 51 per cent of those working in informal enterprises earn R500 or less (with a significant number of people reporting earning nothing) and 92 per cent earn less than R2 501. This suggests a correlation between being poor and working in the informal economy. This relationship is confirmed in previous analyses using LFS data (see, for example, Meth 2002).

Figure 9.3 *Incomes in informal enterprises, March 2004*

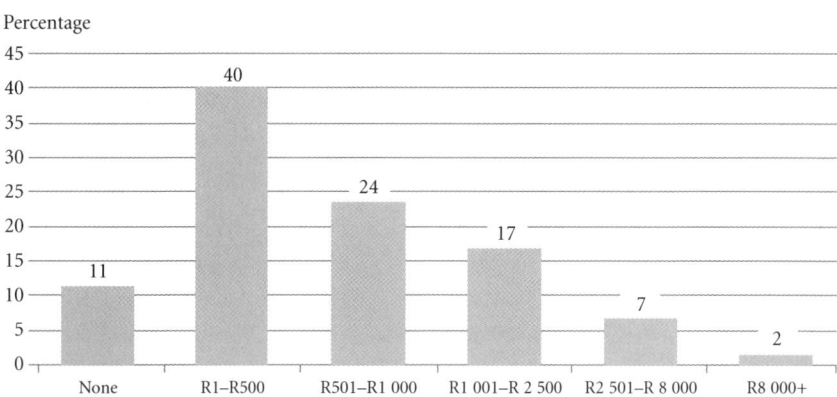

Source: Own calculation from Stats SA LFS March 2004

Table 9.4 contains summary statistics about the sex and race of those working in the formal economy, informal enterprises and domestic work. As is the case internationally,[6] there is a gender dimension to informal work in South Africa. Although more men than women work in the informal economy, the difference is less than is the case for the formal economy. It is also significant that the overwhelming majority of domestic workers are women. Within the informal economy smaller-scale surveys and qualitative research indicate that women tend to be over-represented in the less lucrative activities (see for example Lund's 1998 gendered re-analysis and synthesis of research on street trading). Finally, with respect to race, the majority of those working in informal enterprises are black.

In summary, a large number of South Africans work in the informal economy and this component of employment is increasing. The South African informal economy is disproportionately dominated by the retail and wholesale trade. Further, there is a close correlation between being poor and working in the informal economy. Finally, there is a gender and race dimension to informal work.

Table 9.4 *Formal employment, informal employment and domestic work, percentage by sex and race*

	Formal	Informal	Domestic	Percentage of economically active population
Male	61.9	57.9	3.8	52.3
Female	38.1	42.1	96.2	47.6
Black	60.1	89.3	89.7	79.7
Coloured	14.3	4.8	10.2	8.9
Indian	4.6	1.2	0.0	2.4
White	20.9	4.7	0.0	8.9

Source: Own calculations from LFS March 2004

Government policy on the informal economy

In its policy proposals, the South African government sometimes sees the small business sector as the panacea for South Africa's employment and growth problems. The Department of Trade and Industry (DTI) is charged with the responsibility of developing and implementing policy for the small, medium and micro-enterprise (SMME) sector. The government's 1995 *White paper on small, medium and micro enterprises* was one of the first policy documents of the new government. The White Paper distinguishes four categories of SMMEs: medium enterprises (assets of about R5 million), small enterprises (employ between five and 50), micro enterprises (involving owner, some family members and one or two employees) and survivalist enterprises (activities by people unable to find a job). The White Paper recognises that the survivalist sector has the largest concentration of women and lists as one of its key objectives to 'support the advancement of women in all business sectors'. The document recommends different support strategies for each of the first three categories. Whilst outlining concrete proposals for the small, medium and micro categories, the Paper is mute on support strategies for the survivalist category.

There is evidence that this omission has continued in policy implementation in the post-apartheid period. There are three main DTI small business support programmes – Khula Enterprise Finance Facility, Manufacturing Advice Centres and Ntsika Enterprise Promotion Agency. Khula operates as a

THE STATE OF THE INFORMAL ECONOMY

wholesaler of finance to the retail-banking sector. Khula provides a range of credit guarantee mechanisms that are designed to reduce the risk on SMMEs' loans, thereby encouraging commercial banks to provide finance to those operating in the SMME sector. The responsibility for risk assessment remains with the commercial banks, which each apply their own criteria, most often requiring the minimum of a business plan. This has the effect of excluding most informal economy workers from accessing Khula-backed financial services. The Manufacturing Advice Centres offer sector-specific advisory services to manufacturing SMMEs to enable them to increase their productivity and improve their international competitiveness. Most assessments of the national Manufacturing Advice Centre programme conclude that they have been successful in meeting these objectives (Rogerson 2004).

However, given their focus on manufacturing, and the nature of their objectives and programmes, the activities of the Manufacturing Advice Centres are unlikely to filter down to informal economy workers. Ntsika provides a range of facilities to small business including management and entrepreneurship schemes, technology transfer schemes, market access and business development programmes through a network of local business services centres (LSBCs). By 2003, some 92 LSBCs had been established (Rogerson 2004). The focus of Ntsika's programmes is on assisting SMMEs to improve their market access and to improve their international competitiveness. Much of this focus is implemented by assisting SMMEs to access government contracts and to penetrate export markets. Both of these objectives have little or no relevance to those working in the informal economy. Rogerson's assessment of government's support programmes for SMME's argues that, 'during the period 1994–2003 DTI funding allocations for SMMEs have inevitably favoured and been biased heavily towards support for established small and medium enterprises (often white owned) rather than emerging micro-enterprises and the informal economy' (2004: 9). Rogerson concludes that 'current national support programmes offer little in the way of support for survivalist enterprise, women entrepreneurs and rural SMMEs' (2004: 7).

The scenario of the informal economy falling through policy gaps is echoed with respect to access to training services. There are two potential routes whereby those working in the informal economy can access training – the Sector Education and Training Authorities (SETAs) and the National Skills Fund. As we have outlined in more detail elsewhere (Devey, Skinner &

Valodia 2003) this system does not adequately service those working in the informal economy. The SETAs are funded through the skills levy which is paid by employers who are registered – and thus in the formal economy – and whose annual wage bill is more than R250 000. There is evidence that SETAs tend to prioritise the needs of those contributing to the skills levy. The National Skills Fund relies on training providers responding to incentives. Training providers are often reluctant to service those in the informal economy. The reasons include the lack of profitability because workers cannot cover the costs, the low levels of education of workers, their mobility and thus difficulties of accessing workers, the need to develop non-traditional methods and the fact that many trainers are afraid to enter the areas where people need to be trained (Devey et al. 2003).

The informal economy surveys conducted in Johannesburg and Durban as part of a suite of local economic development surveys included questions on access to support services. In both cases the sample sizes were just over 500 interviews, with respondents operating in a variety of different activities. The fieldwork was conducted in 1999 and 2002 in Johannesburg and Durban respectively. In Johannesburg, of the 12 per cent of enterprise owners who reported trying to obtain a loan from a bank or any other credit institution only 18 firms were awarded the loan (Chandra & Rajaratnam 2001: 36), while in Durban, of the 14.2 per cent who had tried to obtain a bank loan for business purposes only 20 were successful (Skinner 2005: 35). This demonstrates an extremely low level of access to credit. In Johannesburg 81 per cent of all enterprise owners reported that they had never received any business assistance or assistance with training (Chandra & Rajaratnam 2001: 46), while in the Durban survey 88 per cent of respondents had never received help through training or any other assistance programme (Skinner 2005: 41). In both cases, of those who had managed to access assistance it was mostly training. The suppliers of this training were often the private sector or non-governmental organisations. In the Durban survey there were only two cases where an enterprise owner had received assistance from a SETA (Skinner 2005: 41). Skinner concludes that the survey demonstrates how national government support programmes have had little or no impact on those working in the informal economy in Durban.

Budlender, Skinner and Valodia (2004) analyse the budget allocations and programmes of most national government departments to assess the extent and efficacy of support measures for the informal economy. They find that the initiatives at national government level are piecemeal. Their trawling through department budgets, annual reports and other documentation:

> suggests that the approach of most departments is to showcase some or other programme aimed at the poor and marginalised, however small that initiative is in absolute terms. Further, the support often intersects with informal work through specific poverty relief funding. National government lacks a coherent policy on the informal economy and this is reflected in the lack of a coherent programmatic approach to dealing with developments, and supporting economic activity in the informal economy. (Budlender et al. 2004: 86).

An exception to this at the provincial and local government level is the case of the province of KwaZulu-Natal (see the provincial case study of Budlender et al. [2004]), and more particularly in eThekwini (see their local government case study of Durban). Here, the informal economy is recognised as an integrated component of the economy, and support for economic activity in the informal economy is based on a coherent and overarching policy. The result is that budgetary support for the informal economy recognises the particular nature of work in the informal economy and support measures, with a few exceptions, are appropriate for these activities.

Linkages between the formal and informal economy

Drawing on work by Devey and Valodia (2005) we make observations about the informal economy and use this to make some comments about the usefulness and correctness of the argument that is made by the President and more generally in government about the second economy.

One of the arguments the President and the ANC make is that the second economy contributes 'little to gross domestic product (GDP)'. In fact, the informal economy contributes somewhere between seven and 12 per cent of GDP. In its estimates of GDP in South Africa, the South African Reserve Bank uses expenditure surveys of households to estimate the contribution of the informal economy, which it captures via its estimates of private consumption expenditure of households. On this basis, the informal economy contributes some seven per cent of GDP. Using an alternative methodology, Budlender, Buwembo and Shabalala (2001) estimate that the informal economy contributes between eight and 12 per cent of GDP.

A particular problem in policy terms for those working in the informal economy is the idea of the second economy being structurally disconnected from the first. Case study evidence indicates that there are multiple forward and backward linkages between formal and informal activities. For example, Ince's (2003) work on informal clothing manufacturing in a residential area in Durban demonstrated that not only do manufacturers source their inputs in the formal economy, but the garments often end up in formal retail stores. Witt's (2000) work on informal fruit and vegetable distribution demonstrates multiple linkages. It is these linkages that, in policy terms, are often the most interesting areas on which to concentrate.

The panel component of the LFS allows us to explore dynamics in the labour market. The sampling design of the LFS, which is conducted biannually in March (previously February) and September, allows for 80 per cent of the sampling in each wave to remain in the sample. Thus, households remain in the sample over five waves of the LFS. We explore these dynamics beginning in February 2002 for five waves of the LFS ending in March 2004. Matching the individuals in these households over the period, we are able to get some indication of the extent to which workers move between employment and unemployment, and when employed between different segments of the economy, such as formal and informal.[7] In total, we are able to match 5 587 individuals over the period.

Table 9.5 gives a broad overview of how the status of these workers changed over the period. The data show that there is a surprising level of churning within the labour market, with the status of more than half of the workers having changed at least once over the period February 2002 to March 2004. As is to be expected, for those workers whose status remained unchanged, most tended to be employed in the formal sector, or remained economically inactive. Only 1.3 per cent of the 5 587 workers that remained in the panel continued to work in the informal economy over the period under consideration.

Table 9.5 *Labour market status of workers, February 2002 to March 2004*

Type of worker	Frequency	Percentage
Remained in the formal economy	1 175	21.0
Remained economically inactive	1 077	19.3
Remained in commercial agriculture	99	1.8
Remained as a domestic worker	89	1.6
Remained unemployed	74	1.3
Remained as informal worker	71	1.3
Worker status changed	3 002	53.7
Total	5 587	100.0

Source: Own calculations from Stats SA, LFS (various)

In Table 9.6 we remove from the panel all workers who did not engage in informal economy activities over the period, thus only retaining workers who have been engaged in informal economy activities for at least one period. This reduces the number of workers from 5 587 to 1 009. Again, we see a surprising level of churning occurring, with only seven per cent of workers remaining as informal workers over the entire period.

Table 9.6 *Labour market status of informal economy workers, February 2002 to March 2004*

Type of worker	Frequency	Percentage
Informal for 5 periods	71	7.0
Informal for 4 periods	88	8.7
Informal for 3 periods	106	10.5
Informal for 2 periods	202	20.0
Informal for 1 period	542	53.7
Total	1 009	100.0

Source: Own calculations from Stats SA, LFS (various)

Table 9.7 shows the movement of workers that were employed in the informal economy in any one period over the panel. As is to be expected, a large number of workers moved between the informal economy and being unemployed or economically inactive. A significant proportion of workers (18.3%) moved between formal and informal employment.

Table 9.7 *Shifts between informal work and other labour market status*

Type of change	Frequency	Percentage
Informal and unemployed and not economically active	191	18.9
Informal and not economically active	190	18.8
Informal and formal	185	18.3
Informal, formal and unemployed	77	7.6
Informal, formal and not economically active	73	7.2
Remained in informal	71	7.0
Informal and unemployed	60	5.9
Informal, formal, unemployed and not economically active	44	4.4
Other	118	11.7
Total	1 009	100.0

Source: Own calculations from various LFSs

If we reduce the period under consideration to six months, between September 2003 and March 2004 we still find fairly high levels of churning in the labour market. Of individuals recorded as informal workers in September 2003, in March 2004, 44.5 per cent reported working in the informal economy, 17.3 per cent reported working in the formal economy, 11.4 per cent reported being unemployed and 23.7 per cent reported being not economically active. Of individuals recorded as formal workers in September 2003, in March 2004, 3.4 per cent reported working in the informal economy.

These linkages between employment in the formal and informal economy are corroborated by other studies. Devey et al. (2004) show that many workers classified as formal workers have employment characteristics that are consistent with informal work. There is also significant evidence, from micro-level studies, which highlights the growing informalisation of previously formal work. Kenny (2000), in her analysis of the retail sector, not only demonstrates that casual and subcontracted labour constitutes up to 65 per cent of total employment, but highlights how core tasks like shelf packing are increasingly now done by employees of labour brokers, contracted by suppliers. Skinner and Valodia's (2001) analysis of the Confederation of Employers of Southern Africa (Cofesa) – a labour consultancy that assists companies to restructure their workforces, to change employees to contractors and to outsource production to them – reveals Cofesa firms no longer have to adhere to collective agreements on minimum wages or contribute to any of the benefit or training schemes. In the workplace, other than changes in labour conditions, everything else remains the same. Skinner and Valodia demonstrate how, by the end of 2000, Cofesa estimated that this had resulted in the establishment of over 700 000 independent contractors. Cofesa members are involved in many different sectors, notably footwear and clothing manufacturing and also food, farming, transport, construction and engineering. The legislative loophole in the Labour Relations Act that Cofesa was using has recently been changed. It is unclear whether the processes Cofesa set in place have been reversed. Almost all interviewees in Theron and Godfrey's (2000) study of stakeholders from numerous industries – retail, mining, manufacturing (food, clothing, metal and engineering), catering and accommodation, construction and transport – reported an increase in the use of labour brokers and employment agencies.

Using the KwaZulu-Natal Income Dynamics Survey,[8] Lebani and Valodia (2005) explore employment transitions in households between 1993 and 1998. They find evidence of an intra-household link between self-employment activities and formal economy workers. This association suggests that there is a transfer of human and financial capital by the formally employed to self-employment activities since it is the households that have some form of regular income that are mostly involved in self-employment initiatives.

Conclusion

President Mbeki's recent preoccupation with the second economy has undoubtedly raised the profile of an area of employment that has received little policy attention in the last ten years. National government lacks a clear and coherent policy toward the informal economy. National government needs to develop urgently a policy on the informal economy and provide programmatic support. Given the 'space' created by Mbeki, this may be a particularly opportune moment for policy-makers to consider developments in the informal economy more seriously, and to develop a coherent policy to inform programmatic support for informal economy activities.

However, the evidence that we have provided in this paper suggests that the informal economy is not, as suggested by the ANC, structurally disconnected from the formal economy. In fact, the data that we have provided on employment suggest that large numbers of workers may be moving regularly between the formal and informal economy. At the household level, there seems to be an important link between household members' access to employment in the formal economy and informal economy activities. Further, we have argued that much of what is considered to be the 'formal economy' is being informalised.

It is important that government recognises these linkages and develops policy appropriate for the informal economy. Understanding the linkages between formal and informal activities, and the fact that, like the formal sector, the informal economy is made up of a heterogeneous set of economic activities would point to policy which has to be sectorally-based. Internationally there is a trend to apply the commodity chain or value chain approach to growing the informal economy (see for example, McCormick & Schmitz 2001). This entails detailed sector or industry-level analyses outlining the process from product inception to final consumption and identifying the role of those working in the informal economy at each stage. In the process key policy and project-level interventions can be identified to expand the sector and enhance the incomes of those working within it. A good South African example of this is the research and project interventions on the traditional medicine sector in KwaZulu-Natal (see Institute for Natural Resources 2003 for further details). Similar sectoral analyses should be conducted in the segments of the informal economy that both contribute to economic growth and where there are large numbers of people working, such as clothing, craft, fruit and vegetable distribution and waste collection.

The most critical weakness of government policy with respect to the informal economy is one of perception of the informal economy rather than one just of policy design. The 'second economy' arguments of the President and government are based on the premise that the mainstream of the economy is working rather well, and government action is now needed to enhance the linkages between the first and second economy and, where appropriate, to provide relief, such as public works programmes, to those locked in the informal economy. This dualist conception of the economy is misguided not only because it hides some of the 'losers' of government's policies but also because it continues to keep elements of our economy invisible and therefore outside of the mainstream of economic and social debate. Instead, as we have demonstrated, the economy is integrated and government needs to view the informal economy as an integrated and, unfortunately, a growing part of our economy. Rather than design policy for the 'second economy', government needs to ensure that its current policies cater for the realities of our economy and that support measures are appropriately designed to reach those operating at the lower rungs of our economy.

Notes

1. This paper draws on research conducted for a larger research project on the informal economy. The overall research project was funded by the International Development Research Centre and the South Africa-Netherlands Research Programme on Alternatives in Development. The Human Sciences Research Council (HSRC) has commissioned us to write three papers drawing on this research. Some ideas expressed in this paper draw on the papers commissioned by the HSRC.
2. The authors acknowledge permission from Stats SA to access OHS and LFS data. The results presented in this chapter are based on our own data compilations and our own calculations. Our thanks to Debbie Budlender who commented on an earlier draft of this paper, to participants at a workshop where initial drafts of papers in this volume were presented, and to an anonymous reviewer for insightful and helpful comments.
3. Statisticians use the term 'informal sector' to refer to informal enterprises and 'informal economy' to refer to informal employment in both informal and formal enterprises. In the academic and policy arena, given the connotation of the term 'sector', as outlined in this section, we prefer the term 'informal economy' combined with the explanation of whether the *enterprise* or *employment-based* definition is being employed.
4. The other area of employment showing rapid growth (and then rapid decline) is subsistence agriculture. See Aliber (2003) for an analysis of the trend in subsistence agriculture.
5. Stats SA defines someone as working in what they call the 'informal sector' if they work in a firm that is unregistered, in other words, the enterprise definition is being employed.
6. See Sethuraman (1998) for an international gendered analysis of informal sector statistics. Having reviewed substantial country-specific data he suggests that in

the informal sector women's incomes are lower than those of men and that the proportion of women in lower income categories is greater. Sethuraman reports this gender inequality for all countries in Asia, Africa and Latin America from which evidence is drawn.

7   Note that the panel component of the LFS allows us to track *households* not individuals over the five waves of the survey. We have examined the sex and age profiles of workers in these households to confirm that the individuals remain in the panel. We have thus removed from the panel all households where the individuals inside the household may have changed (through, for example, migration).

8   See http://www.sds.ukzn.ac.za for details of the KwaZulu-Natal Income Dynamics Survey (KIDS) data.

References

Aliber M (2003) Small-scale agriculture as revealed by the Labour Force Survey. Unpublished mimeo, Human Sciences Research Council.

Bromley R (1995) Informality, de Soto Style: From concept to policy. In C Rakowski (ed.) *Contrapunto: The informal sector debate in Latin America*. Albany: State University Press of New York.

Budlender D, Buwembo P & Shabalala N (2001) *The informal economy: Statistical data and research findings; Country case study: South Africa*. Document prepared for Women in the Informal Economy: Globalizing and Organizing (WIEGO).

Budlender D, Skinner C & Valodia I (2004) *Budgets and the informal economy: An analysis of the impact of the Budget on informal workers in South Africa*. Durban: School of Development Studies, University of KwaZulu-Natal.

Castells M & Portes A (1989) World underneath: The origins, dynamics, and effects of the informal economy. In A Portes, M Castells & LA Benton (eds.) *The informal economy*. Baltimore: The Johns Hopkins Press.

Chandra V & Rajaratnam B (2001) *Constraints to growth and employment in the informal sector: Evidence from the 1999 informal survey firm*. Washington: World Bank.

Charmes J (2000) Size, trends and productivity of women's work in the informal sector and in old and new forms of informal employment. An outlook of recent empirical evidence. Paper presented at the International Association for Feminist Economics, Istanbul, August.

Chen M (2001) Women in the informal sector: A global picture, the global movement, *SAIS Review* 21(1): 71–82.

Devey R, Skinner C & Valodia I (2003) Human resource development in the informal economy. In HSRC *Human resource development biennial directory*. Cape Town: HSRC Press.

Devey R, Skinner C & Valodia I (2004) *Definitions, data and the informal economy in South Africa: A critical analysis*. Durban: School of Development Studies, University of KwaZulu-Natal.

Devey R & Valodia I (2005) Formal and informal economy linkages. Working paper written for the Economic and Employment Policy Programme, Human Sciences Research Council.

Eapen M (2001) Women in informal sector in Kerala: Need for re-examination, *Economic and Political Weekly* 36(26): 2390–2392.

Hart K (1973) Informal income opportunities and urban employment in Ghana, *Journal of Modern African Studies* 11: 61–89.

ILO (International Labour Organisation) (1972) *Employment, incomes and equality: A strategy for increasing productive employment in Kenya*. Geneva: ILO.

ILO (2002) *Women and men in the informal economy: A statistical picture*. Geneva: ILO.

Ince M (2003) Informal clothing manufacturing in a residential area: The case of Chatsworth. Masters dissertation, School of Development Studies, University of Natal.

Institute for Natural Resources (2003) Strategy and business plan for development of the eThekwini medicinal plants industry. Report prepared for the Durban Unicity Council.

Kenny B (2000) 'We are nursing these jobs': The implications of labour market flexibility on East Rand retail sector workers and their households. Paper presented at the Annual South African Sociological Association, Cape Town, July.

Lebani L & Valodia I (2005) Self-employment in the informal economy and formal employment linkages: An empirical enquiry based on the KwaZulu-Natal Income Dynamics Survey. Unpublished paper, School of Development Studies, University of KwaZulu-Natal.

Legassick M (1974) South Africa: Capital accumulation and violence, *Economy and Society* 3: 253–291.

Lipton M (1985) *Capitalism and apartheid: South Africa, 1910–1986*. Aldershot: Wildwood House.

Lund F (1998) *Women street traders in urban South Africa: A synthesis of selected research findings*. CSDS Research Report No. 15. University of Natal, Durban.

Lund F & Srinivas S (2000) *Learning from experience: A gendered approach to social protection for workers in the informal economy.* Geneva: ILO.

Mbeki T (2003) Speech to the National Council of Provinces, August 2003. Available at http://www.sarpn.org.za/documents/d0000830/index.php.

Mbeki T (2004) Address of the President of South Africa, Thabo Mbeki, to the second joint sitting of the third democratic Parliament. Cape Town, 21.05.04.

Mbeki T (2005) Address of the President of South Africa, Thabo Mbeki, to the second joint sitting of the third democratic Parliament. Cape Town, 11.02.05.

McCormick D & Schmitz H (2001) Manual for value chain research on homeworkers in the garment industry. Available at http://www.ids.ac.uk.

Meth C (2002) What to do until the doctor comes? Relief for the unemployed and for poorly paid workers. A background research paper prepared for the Committee of Inquiry into Comprehensive Social Security in South Africa.

Mkhize Z (2005) Budget address on tabling the Provincial Budget, 03.03.05. Available at http://www.kzntreasury.gov.za/documents/budget_statements/Provincial%20Budget%20Speech%203%20Mar%2005.pdf.

Naidoo K (2004) Operationalising South Africa's move from macro-economic stability to micro-economic reform. Paper presented at the fiftieth Anniversary Conference of the School of Development Studies, University of KwaZulu-Natal, Durban, 20–22.10.04.

O'Dowd M (1978) The stages of economic growth and the future of South Africa. In L Schlemmer & E Webster (eds.) *Change, reform and economic growth in South Africa.* Johannesburg: Ravan Press.

Padayachee V & Valodia I (2001) Changing Gear? The 2001 Budget and economic policy in South Africa, *Transformation* 46: 71–83.

Peattie L (1987) An idea in good currency and how it grew: The informal sector, *World Development* 15(7): 851–860.

Rogerson C (2004) The impact of the South African government's SMME programmes: A ten year review (1994–2003). Mimeo, Department of Geography, University of Witwatersrand, forthcoming in *Development Southern Africa.*

RSA (Republic of South Africa) (1995) *White Paper on national strategy for the development and promotion of small business in South Africa.* Cape Town: Government Printers.

Sethuraman SV (1998) *Gender, informality and poverty: A global review.* Monograph. Geneva: ILO.

Skinner C (2005) *Constraints to growth and employment in the Greater Durban metropolitan area: Evidence from informal economy survey.* School of Development Studies Research Report No. 65. Durban: University of KwaZulu-Natal.

Skinner C & Valodia I (2001) Labour market policy, flexibility, and the future of labour relations: The case of clothing, *Transformation* 50: 56–76.

Stats SA (Statistics South Africa) *Labour force survey, February 2002, September 2002, March 2003, September 2003, March 2004.* Pretoria: Stats SA.

Theron J & Godfrey S (2000) *Protecting workers on the periphery.* Development and Labour Monologues I. Cape Town: Institute of Development and Labour Law, University of Cape Town.

Witt H (2000) *Formal and informal economy linkages in the fruit and vegetable sector.* Study 7.3. Research Report for Durban's Technical Task Team for the informal economy.

Wolpe H (1972) Capitalism and cheap labour-power in South Africa: From segregation to apartheid, *Economy and Society* 1(4): 425–455.

10 Work restructuring and the future of labour in South Africa

Sakhela Buhlungu and Eddie Webster

Introduction

The workplace in South Africa is being restructured under the impact of a complex, diverse and often contradictory range of pressures that could be described as a triple transition – with political, economic and social dimensions.[1] If the apartheid workplace regime was essentially the organisation of exclusion and inclusion on the basis of race, the triple transition has consisted of contested processes of reordering the lines of inclusion and exclusion in post–apartheid South Africa

In the core workplaces of apartheid, the workplace regime consisted of a racially oppressive order derived from South Africa's settler-colonial history. Like other spheres of society, the workplace was a site of racial domination buttressed by racial segregation, and by racist discourses and practices in which the distribution of occupations, skills, incomes and power was racially defined. These structures and practices generated intense racial identity, tension and conflict. While these features were definitive for the apartheid workplace regime, its characteristics did not end there. They extended to hierarchical and authoritarian management styles, extremely adversarial industrial relations, lack of skills – indeed, suppression of skills – and numerous production inefficiencies that sprang from the conflicts, hierarchies, social distances and antagonisms that characterised a workplace with roots in the social relations of settler colonialism and unfree labour (von Holdt 2003).

The transition from authoritarianism to democracy has created a host of new democratic and social rights for workers, trade unions and citizens, and generated at the same time an intense contestation over these rights. The social transition from apartheid to a post-colonial order has impelled profound processes of redistribution of power and access to resources, occupations and skills, together with intense struggles over these.

However, the most significant challenge facing the workplace has been the transition from a domestically-oriented economy to a more globally integrated one. This has led to wide-ranging forms of corporate restructuring effectively integrating companies into more globalised corporate and production structures. For example, BMW (South Africa) is increasingly incorporated into the parent company's global production and marketing operations, AngloGold has moved its head office offshore, and Telkom has been partially privatised to a Malaysian-US consortium (a fate which was avoided by Spoornet only through trade union resistance).

This chapter brings together data derived from two separate research projects undertaken by the Sociology of Work Unit (SWOP) over the past decade. The first project is a set of studies analysing work restructuring under the impact of the triple transition.[2] The second project is a longitudinal survey of Congress of South African Trade Unions (Cosatu) members conducted in 1994, 1998 and 2004 on their attitudes towards democracy.[3] This chapter is divided into four parts. Part 1 identifies the trends in the complex process of workplace restructuring in post-apartheid South Africa. In Part 2 we explore the changing composition of the workforce, drawing on our longitudinal study of Cosatu members. In Part 3 we examine changing management and labour relations and we identify four distinct workplace strategies drawn from the work-restructuring project. Finally, in Part 4 we examine the implications of these changes in the workplace for the future of the labour movement. We conclude by suggesting that the two research projects are intimately connected in that the restructuring is not only profoundly changing the future of labour, it is also having a destructive impact on society which cannot but have a profound impact on the prospects for social reproduction. The reorganisation of the lines of inclusion and exclusion in South African society is producing an enclave of development in a sea of poverty and social stagnation.

Corporate and work restructuring

Domestic corporate restructuring is also proceeding rapidly, often intertwined with processes of internationalisation or increased international pressure in the domestic market. Shoprite, for example, is the product of several mergers and a growing concentration in the retail sector, as well as a growing regionalisation through its expansion into the rest of Africa and internationalisation into India. In a shift that reflects global trends in market and corporate restructuring, several sectors are characterised by the shift of control over products and production from manufacturing companies to large retail chains. Thus, in the wine industry producers find they have to tailor their products and production strategies to the requirements of the powerful retail chains in overseas and domestic markets, placing increasing pressure on consistency, quality, price and volume. In similar fashion, in order to ensure co-ordination, the large supermarkets and retail clothing chains which dominate the South African market are increasingly organising the production of garments while at the same time driving a process of fragmentation, subcontracting and homeworking in response to cheap imports. Similar processes are under way in the footwear sector.

Virtually all private sector enterprises are operating in increasingly competitive, cost-conscious and quality-conscious markets, both international and domestic. Indeed, enterprises can be divided into those that have (relatively) successfully integrated into global markets or production networks and those that are confined to domestic markets. The latter find themselves under assault by cheap, high-quality goods manufactured by multinationals, because they lack the capital base and capacity to break into international markets themselves and compete globally. However, the relationship of state-sector workplaces to the market is more contradictory. Public hospitals are insulated to some extent from the market; however, they draw their skilled staff from a global market and equipment and supplies are sourced from globally competitive suppliers. For example, South African nurses are constantly being attracted to better paid jobs in the North and the Middle East. However, market forces do constrain the options of public hospitals to the extent that private-sector hospitals have secured the revenue from private-sector medical-aid patients, and to the extent that government's conservative fiscal policies limit funding. Similarly, Spoornet is somewhat insulated from the pressure to maximise profits, although market competition from private-sector road hauliers is eroding its customer base. Telkom, in contrast, has been dominated by the profit drive since its partial privatisation. Although there has been competition from cellular and, increasingly, Internet-driven technologies, Telkom has been able to retain its fixed-line market monopoly – indeed, the pursuit of profit has stiffened its resistance to government attempts to liberalise the market.

Overall, these trends tend to reduce the autonomy of South African companies – and of the state – whether with respect to workplace strategies or to national developmental goals such as domestic capital accumulation, job creation or product innovation. Indeed, this reduction in autonomy should be regarded as an important feature of the post-apartheid workplace regime.

Meanwhile, the restructuring of work results in the emergence of three zones in the labour market. Firstly, there is the core, which is occupied by skilled permanent workers who enjoy relatively high wages, benefits, good working conditions and job security. Secondly, there is the non-core zone occupied by semi-skilled and non-skilled workers in precarious jobs who earn low wages, enjoy no benefits, work under poor conditions and have little or no job security. Finally, there is the periphery, which is occupied by those in the informal sector and the unemployed.

South Africa's unemployment rate has steadily increased from 1 912 471 in 1990 (unemployment rate of 15.91 per cent) to 4 789 582 in 2002 (unemployment rate of 30.51 per cent) (UNDP 2003). Significantly, informal employment has increased from 1 742 754 in 1990 to 3 545 284 in 2002 (UNDP 2003). A major contributing factor to the growth of informal employment is the growing number of women who seek employment in the labour market.

Another change worth mentioning at this point is the changing nature and location of the workplace itself. While the typical industrial workplace still exists, the last 30 years have seen the emergence of other kinds of workplaces located in different geographical spaces. Thus, while for some the large factory or mine remains the main place of employment and work, the street, the backyard of one's house or the shade under a big tree have emerged as workplaces in their own right. As we shall see later, this change in the nature and location of the workplace in the context of the economic transition has serious implications for the future of working people, both organised and unorganised.

To sum up, the trends identified in this section suggest that work and workplaces in post-apartheid South Africa are undergoing a complex process

of restructuring, which is producing a work order with the following three features:
- A reduction of autonomy in the context of an increasingly competitive and cost-conscious domestic and international market;
- The differentiation of the world of work into three zones (the core, the non-core and the periphery) through processes of reordering the lines of variable inclusion and exclusion of South African citizens;
- The workplace itself is being redefined in fundamental ways as employment now takes place outside traditional geographical locations.

The state has facilitated many of these processes of corporate and market restructuring through liberalising trade and capital markets, fiscal conservatism and restructuring state enterprises through privatisation. It has also extended labour rights to previously excluded workers and deepened worker rights at enterprise and national level. In particular, it has constitutionalised the right to strike and established institutions and procedures that curb the power of management to act unilaterally. These changes have led to criticisms by employers that the labour market is too rigid and led to calls for greater flexibility. These contradictory interventions have imposed new pressures, constraints and opportunities on workplaces, managers, workers and trade unionists.

Importantly, changes at the level of the workplace also impact on the household and the reproduction of labour. In her research on labour market flexibility in the retail sector, Kenny (2001) found that changing patterns of employment in the workplace impact on households themselves. In the retail sector, cashiers are increasingly being employed on a casual basis, and the employment function of shelf-packers (or merchandisers) is subcontracted out to suppliers. In Kenny's survey questionnaires, a number of questions were asked that related to the quality of life of employees such as access to type of housing, electricity, water and decent sanitation. Whether there was a permanent job in the household was the only consistent predictor as to whether households had access to these services.[4] Those households tended to live in formal housing, whilst households with access to only casual jobs – in some cases more than one casual job – generally lived in informal settlements. Pointing to the longer-term social consequences of this, Kenny summarised her findings as follows:

[F]lexibility not only stratifies workers on the shopfloor...
[H]ouseholds that are supported by a casual wage alone are more
likely to have lower standards of living...[T]hese very households
face diminished future opportunities for their members. Their
members have fewer resources to invest in job search efforts
and networking, and fewer resources to put into means of self-
provisioning that may supplement their poor wages...In the
longer term, far from enabling households to hang on, dependence
on meagre, marginal jobs will erode working-class households'
economic positions and diminish the likelihood of these workers
getting more sustainable jobs. Tenure in 'bad jobs' coupled by a
shrinking 'good job' pool can lead to a disconnection from the
labour market. (2001: 104)

Before examining these pressures we now turn to an exploration of the changing composition of the unionised workforce, taking Cosatu as a case study (Buhlungu 2005).

The changing composition of the workforce

Our data suggest that restructuring is profoundly changing the composition of unionised workers. Increasingly, union members are concentrated in the diminishing core of permanent, full-time employment relations, leaving the non-core and the periphery without an organised voice. Furthermore, those in permanent employment are increasingly better educated and more skilled than their predecessors.

The structure of the black workforce has been changing consistently over the last three decades (Hindson & Crankshaw 1990). A feature of this change has been the decline of the unskilled stratum and the growth of the semi-skilled and skilled strata. This change resulted in the retrenchment of thousands of unskilled workers, thus giving rise to a division between 'the relatively privileged employed workers and the impoverished unemployed workers' (Hindson & Crankshaw 1990: 26). According to Crankshaw (1994), this was achieved through the fragmentation of skilled trades into semi-skilled occupations in which black workers could be employed. The militant unions of the 1980s and early 1990s drew substantial support from the employed and semi-skilled category of workers, many of whom occupied leading positions in the unions.

A survey of Cosatu shop stewards conducted in 1991 (Pityana & Orkin 1992) also showed that although just over half of these shop stewards occupied unskilled and semi-skilled positions, a significant proportion (44%) occupied skilled, supervisory and clerical positions. Similarly, the results of our longitudinal study of Cosatu membership (1994, 1998 and 2004) suggest that this trend has been deepening during the last ten years.

One of the most significant findings of our longitudinal survey is the one concerning the security or insecurity of tenure for Cosatu members. Unfortunately there is no longitudinal comparative data as this question was included for the first time in 2004. Nevertheless, the new data enable us to reach certain conclusions regarding Cosatu. Table 10.1 shows that 92 per cent of Cosatu members are in permanent, full-time jobs. Not only does this project Cosatu members as privileged relative to the growing army of the unemployed and those workers in precarious employment and the informal sector, it also suggests that the federation has failed to make headway in organising beyond the diminishing core workforce in full-time permanent jobs.

Table 10.1 *Security of job tenure of Cosatu members, 2004*

Nature of contract	Respondents
Fixed-term contract (temporary) part-time	10 (2%)
Fixed-term contract (temporary) full-time	30 (5%)
Permanent contract, part-time	11 (2%)
Permanent contract, full-time	604 (92%)

Source: SWOP et al. 2004

The implication of these findings is that in future Cosatu and other unions could find themselves increasingly isolated from the rest of the working class, particularly from the new movements formed to mobilise against the effects of economic liberalisation on the working poor and the unemployed.

Furthermore, the Cosatu survey shows a steady decline of unskilled (and even semi-skilled) workers in the federation occurring at the same time as the steady increase in skilled and supervisory categories of workers. This shows a continuation of the trend noted by Hindson & Crankshaw (1990) in their study of the changing structure of the workforce in the period 1965–1985. But these results also reflect the impact successful public-sector unionisation has had on the composition of Cosatu's membership. In recent years Cosatu's public-sector membership has been estimated to constitute one-third of the total membership (Buhlungu 2001). Table 10.2 gives a breakdown of the federation's membership by occupational position.

Table 10.2 *Occupational category of Cosatu members surveyed, as defined by the company*

Occupational category	1994	1998	2004
Unskilled	190 (30%)	118 (19%)	81 (12%)
Semi-skilled	193 (30%)	223 (35%)	169 (26%)
Skilled	135 (21%)	192 (30%)	275 (42%)
Supervisory	26 (4%)	31 (5%)	61 (9%)
Clerical	64 (10%)	48 (8%)	55 (8%)
Other	32 (5%)	21 (3%)	13 (2%)

Source: SWOP et al. 1994, 1998, 2004

It should be noted that the responses in this table are based on the official designation of workers' positions (as defined by management), and not on the workers' view of how their positions should be graded or designated.

The Cosatu members' survey shows that since 1998 there are proportionately fewer union members under the age of 36. At the same time, the 36–45 age cohort seems to have increased significantly over the last five years. The age profile of Cosatu members as shown in Table 10.3 seems to be a function of recent trends in the labour market. For example, few young workers have been absorbed into formal permanent employment in recent years. Reflecting on a similar finding in the 1994 leg of the study, Ginsburg, Webster, Southall, Wood, Buhlungu, Maree, Cherry, Haines and Klerck (1995) argued that it reflected 'greatly diminished employment opportunities' and that 'people in the formal economy would be less inclined to even temporarily leave their jobs, while those entering the labour market for the first time would be most unlikely to gain formal employment' (1995: 13). What is also striking is the drop in the 26–35 age group, which is the age cohort most likely to be affected by HIV/AIDS.

Table 10.3 *Age profile of Cosatu members, 1994, 1998 and 2004*

Age	1994	1998	2004
18–25	19 (3%)	36 (6%)	37 (6%)
26–35	244 (38%)	233 (37%)	198 (30%)
36–45	219 (34%)	226 (35%)	259 (40%)
46–55	135 (21%)	123 (19%)	130 (20%)
56–65	26 (4%)	21 (3%)	29 (4%)
65 +	–	–	2 (0%)

Source: SWOP et al. 1994, 1998, 2004

The last ten years have seen a remarkable improvement in the educational levels of Cosatu members. Table 10.4 shows that while the proportion of those with educational levels up to, and including, Standard 8 dropped from a high of 65 per cent in 1994 to the present 36 per cent, the proportion of those with Standard 9 and above increased dramatically from 35 per cent in 1995 to 64 per cent in 2004. This finding has far-reaching implications for Cosatu's future. Recent research by Ari Sitas (2004) shows that union activists with higher education stand a much better chance of upward social mobility. While workers with little or no formal education led the mobilisation of the struggle period, the period of democratic consolidation seems to rely on those with higher levels of educational attainment. As Sitas observes, 'The institutional pull of the transition seems not to favour "oral" people in preference of some formal educational competency' (2004: 834).

Table 10.4 *Highest formal educational levels of Cosatu members*

Highest educational level	1994	1998	2004
No formal education	13 (2%)	16 (3%)	3 (1%)
Std 2 or lower	26 (4%)	22 (3%)	14 (2%)
Stds 3 – 5	97 (15%)	66 (10%)	41 (6%)
Stds 6 – 8	283 (44%)	246 (39%)	181 (28%)
Stds 9 – 10	199 (31%)	238 (37%)	247 (38%)
Technical diploma	18 (3%)	31 (5%)	83 (13%)
University degree	0 (0%)	14 (2%)	45 (7%)
Other post-school qualification	7 (1%)	6 (1%)	41 (6%)

Source: SWOP et al. 1994, 1998, 2004

The significant presence of public sector and white workers, particularly in unions such the South African Democratic Teachers' Union, the Democratic Nurses' Organisation of South Africa and the South African Society of Bank Officials, some of which affiliated to Cosatu after the 1994 and 1998 surveys, probably accounts for this dramatic increase in educational levels. But even the traditional Cosatu unions have been gaining members from new sectors of the workforce such as airline pilots, public-sector managers and skilled workers. Significantly, some employers – such as those in auto assembly – have raised educational requirements for new recruits and now insist on a technikon diploma as a minimum requirement.

A consistent finding in the longitudinal study is the one on the gender composition of Cosatu's membership, which continues to confirm Baskin's (1991) estimate of 36 per cent. Table 10.5 presents the gender figures.

Table 10.5 *Gender composition of Cosatu membership, 1994, 1998 and 2004*

Gender	1994	1998	2004
Female	212 (34%)	191 (30%)	225 (34%)
Male	411 (66%)	448 (70%)	430 (66%)

Source: SWOP et al. 1994, 1998, 2004

A subtle but relentless generational change has been taking place in the union movement over the last ten years or so. Understanding this change is key to grasping the changing social composition of union membership during this period. The process of attrition has resulted in the decline of the 1970s' and 1980s' generation of union membership as a proportion of the total. Table 10.6 shows that the majority of Cosatu's current members (55%) joined from 1991 onwards. Of these, 13 per cent joined between 2001 and 2004. Put differently, the table shows that the bulk of Cosatu members (79%) are drawn from a new generation of workers. This suggests that there may have been uneven socialisation of workers into the federation, its policies and organisational traditions. Indeed, it is possible that by the time this majority joined the federation, many of these policies and traditions would have become rituals, which each new member was expected to imitate and repeat in a mechanical, unquestioning way. The loss of large numbers of members and leaders through retrenchments and the brain drain has compounded this problem for the federation.

Table 10.6 *Year in which Cosatu member joined the union*

Year	Percentage of respondents
1970–1980	8
1981–1985	12
1986–1990	24
1991–1995	20
1996–2000	22
2001–2004	13
Do not know	1
Total	100

Source: SWOP 1994, 1998, 2004

How is the restructuring of work and the changing social composition of unionised workers impacting on management–labour relations? This is explored in the following section.

Changing management–labour relations

The South African workplace is facing a challenge constituted by three competing forces. On the one hand, it is facing intensified competition as South Africa is increasingly integrated into the global economy. On the other hand it is compelled to redress the apartheid legacy and respond to the demands for a more democratic workplace and society. In this section we draw on the studies collected in Webster and von Holdt (2005) and identify a pattern of four distinct workplace strategies.

The first of these, 'negotiated reconstruction', refers to a strategy of negotiating the terms of a reconstituted workplace order, and may be driven by management or trade unions or both. 'Wildcat co-operation' describes a managerial strategy for incorporating black workers by negotiating informally with workers and introducing new management practices, but bypassing or marginalising trade unions. 'Authoritarian restoration" is a managerial strategy for reconstituting an authoritarian workplace order which draws on the dominant authoritarian strand of South African workplace history, but which may introduce new features and practices as well. A fourth group of workplaces is characterised by a stalemate brought about by the lack of any specific strategy, or by the failure of an attempted strategy of negotiation or authoritarianism. It should be noted that the success or otherwise of these strategies refers to successful implementation in the workplace – there is no necessary relation between this and the financial success of the company.

While different labour processes, company and trade union capacities, or market conditions may constrain strategic options, the strategic choices made by managers and unions do have a degree of autonomy. Companies may operate in identical markets with virtually identical labour processes, yet have sharply divergent strategies. Nor are these strategies static or fixed. Workplaces may move from one to another over time. Some workplaces or companies may encompass more than one strategy. What emerges from the case studies is that where the union is strong and management is responsive, a successful negotiated reconstruction of the workplace is possible.

Negotiated reconstruction

The strategy of negotiated reconstruction can be initiated by management, as was the case at Sea Harvest and BMW, or it may be induced by intense pressure from trade unions, such as the case of Highveld Steel and Spoornet (Webster & von Holdt. 2005). In the former cases, the result tends to be a relatively stable negotiated relationship between management and unions, with workers articulating more positive attitudes to the company. In the latter cases, however, the resulting negotiated agreement tends to be somewhat unstable because management had been forced to co-operate and was not particularly committed to implementing the agreements.

All four cases of negotiated reconstruction reveal progress towards dealing with the legacy of apartheid, a reduction in racial tension, improved attitudes towards work, a high level of union activity, a focus on production quality, an improved or high level of company performance and, in two cases, the introduction of new work organisation based on teamwork. In the case of BMW we find a lower incidence of increased workload and the introduction of new technology, while in Sea Harvest casualisation and externalisation are widely used.

The poor performance results in Spoornet are partly related to the fact that negotiated reconstruction failed to address the workplace dynamics captured by the nine workplace features – because of the inability or unwillingness of management to respond to union proposals for workplace change on the basis of co-determination. This failure indicates the crucial importance of management's role in addressing the transformation of workplace relations and inefficiencies inherited from the apartheid workplace order.

These correlations suggest that negotiated reconstruction may produce elements of the so-called 'high performance work organisation' (Ashton & Sung 2002: 45), with its emphasis on improved working conditions, the incorporation of workers in decision-making, new forms of work organisation, improved levels of skill and so on. This approach to production performance also appears to be intimately linked to a negotiated and strategic approach to overcoming the legacy of apartheid in the workplace through black economic empowerment, training and employment equity, as well as new forms of supervision and work organisation.

However, the degree of change should not be exaggerated. At BMW, workers display ambivalence towards the company, which matches the contradictions in the company's practice. In addition, workers complain about low wages, increased workload, new shift arrangements and the loss of overtime pay. The persistence of the racial division of labour and of racial tension remains a feature of the workplace despite progress with employment equity (Masondo 2005).

The new technological innovations, Masondo argues, have led to antagonisms among workers based on age. The older generation, it appears, is not comfortable with the introduction of new technology and feels the company prefers young people with skills. Generational differences also relate to union membership. The younger workers seem to be less active in union activities and more interested in career mobility. As one older worker complained, 'These youngsters do not know what solidarity is, and are too selfish and do not want to join the union. They only remember about the union when they have problems' (Masondo 2005: 167).

Wildcat co-operation

Wildcat co-operation is similar to negotiated reconstruction, with the important difference that instead of negotiating change with the trade unions, management seeks to elicit informal consensus and support from workers, bypassing the unions in the process. The implementation of self-directed work teams at AngloGold is an example of wildcat co-operation at workplace level, driven by innovative managers.

At AngloGold there is a formal process of introducing new forms of team training as a basis for new workplace teams, with the aim of producing a new worker for a new twenty-first century workplace, thereby 'sweeping away' the inefficiencies and racial antagonisms inherited from the apartheid era (Phakathi 2005: 173–185). Wildcat co-operation is similar to negotiated reconstruction in its correlation with new forms of work organisation, improved attitudes towards work and the improvement in quality and output of production. The key difference is that there is a relatively low degree of trade union activity (at least in relation to the workplace changes being discussed), as well as a significant increase in workload and output.

However, in the case of AngloGold, wildcat co-operation has not overcome the legacy of the apartheid workplace regime. Instead, Phakathi argues, miners develop an alternative form of teamwork, what he terms '*planisa*'. *Planisa* involves creative, self-organised improvisation and initiative on an individual and collective basis, often circumventing standard work rules. As such it is a double-edged sword. Management not only recognises *planisa*, but also frequently orders workers to *planisa* (Phakathi 2005: 183). However, Phakathi concludes that teamwork is only likely to be successful as a bridge to a new workplace order if the trade unions, and particularly the union which represents the majority of black workers, the National Union of Mineworkers, are drawn into negotiating strategies for skills formation and teamwork training based on the real skills of black mine workers – in other words, if there is a shift to negotiated reconstruction.

Authoritarian restoration

While the studies identified as authoritarian restoration exhibit strong continuities from the apartheid workplace regime in the form of racial authoritarianism, most of them also exhibit proactive managerial strategies for reconstructing authoritarianism under new conditions. Thus managers at Shoprite, footwear and on wine farms have implemented aggressive strategies for casualising and externalising large proportions of their workforces. Shoprite has introduced a strong ideology of marketisation to underpin its racial authoritarianism, while the more far-sighted among the farm managers work to reconstitute racial paternalism in an effort to incorporate their permanent workers.

An examination of workplaces with authoritarian restoration reveals very different patterns from negotiated reconstruction and wildcat co-operation. There is no shift to new forms of work organisation, the workload is high and/or increasing, in half the cases new technology has been introduced with an emphasis on surveillance and production control, and in the majority of cases a concerted strategy of casualisation and/or externalisation is being pursued. The majority of these workplaces are also characterised by racial forms of authoritarianism and the lack of any systematic attempt to address the legacy of apartheid. As a result of all of these factors, workers articulate negative attitudes towards work, but are unable to translate this into a high level of union activity.

The most dramatic example of workplace change is that of the footwear industry. Under the impact of globalisation the industry has been flooded by cheap imports, largely from China, and has only been able to survive through large-scale outsourcing. As Sarah Mosoetsa shows in her study of trade liberalisation in the footwear industry in Pietermaritzburg, the production of shoes dropped from 61.7 million in 1989 to 25 million in 1999 (Mosoetsa 2005). This led to widespread retrenchment and the outsourcing of work to middlemen who have set up sweatshops along Manchester Road, a district set up by the City Council to attract small business. Unable to compete with the imported shoes, people at the sweatshops work in bad conditions for long hours and low wages.

Importantly, Mosoetsa reveals the gendered impact of restructuring and how it poses serious economic and social constraints for many women workers in the sector. As she argues:

> The most common issue raised by the women has been retrenchment. As a result, the workload of the remaining workers has increased and intensified…The hours of work have also increased, but there is no extra pay for overtime work…A high unemployment rate due to factory closures and retrenchments are cited by workers as reasons that compel them to stay in their jobs regardless of their working conditions. Many women workers come from households where they are the only breadwinners, supporting five people on average. (Mosoetsa 2005: 324)

The most important conclusion is that a number of companies are proving successful at reconstituting an authoritarian post-apartheid workplace order in which work organisation and worker attitudes are less important than new forms of control and higher workloads. In several of these case studies authoritarianism is imposed not through direct restoration of racialised authoritarianism, but through a more innovative strategy of reconstituting authority on a new basis – most notably through the large-scale introduction of more precarious forms of employment that disempower and divide workers, new pay systems based on piecework, and new technological forms of control. The result is weaker trade unions and reduced levels of contestation, even quiescence.

Failed strategy, no strategy

In this section we discuss two workplace studies. The first is an example drawn from the domestic appliances industry where management attempts to impose authoritarian restoration but fails in the face of union opposition (Bezuidenhout 2005). Bezuidenhout suggests that the dynamics of race are being reconfigured through the emergence of 'informal colour bars'. Instead of deracialisation, Bezuidenhout describes a situation in which important elements of the apartheid workplace regime persist. In spite of the introduction of the Employment Equity Act of 1998, outlawing unfair discrimination and providing for employment equity for women, people of colour and the disabled, there is a competing logic – a more informal one – that still operates in the workplace. Drawing on Burawoy's (1972) pioneering study of the copper mines in post-independence Zambia, Bezuidenhout identifies the emergence of an 'upward floating colour bar' where black workers are promoted to supervisory level but do not have real authority as whites have simultaneously been promoted above them. Others felt that they were under-qualified for their jobs, and that is why management was able to undermine their positions.

At Chris Hani Baragwanath hospital, management simply fails to implement any strategy for workplace change whatsoever (von Holdt & Maserumule 2005). The profound weakness of the managerial function and the reluctance of government to invest in improving management capacity and systems mean that management is unable to take any initiatives concerning workplace change. If other government institutions in the health sector – or in the public service more broadly – share these problems, then a huge number of workplaces may be subject to the kind of paralysis so evident at this hospital. This paralysis is evident at all levels of the hospital from the chief executive officer to nurses and cleaners. As von Holdt and Maserumule comment, 'Frustration about the declining quality of healthcare delivery at Chris Hani Baragwanath, and their own inability to perform their jobs well, was felt to be profoundly undermining. As one nurse explained, "We used to be proud to work at Bara; even the way you walked to work showed your pride. Now you are just ashamed"' (2005: 454).

Correlations with the nine workplace factors[5] indicate that little has changed in these workplaces. There is no new work organisation or technology, and little attempt has been made to address the apartheid legacy. In the domestic appliances sector there is a strikingly large-scale use of casualised workers, but not at the public hospital. The workload has increased only at the hospital, and there only because budget cuts have led to staff reductions, with a negative impact on attitudes and quality. Work attitudes are uniformly negative, and translate into medium to high levels of union activity. Quality problems are not successfully addressed in any of the cases, and company performance is poor. The domestic appliances companies are facing intense competition from cheap imports, while Chris Hani Baragwanath is characterised by wastage, corruption and poor service delivery.

There are signs that this kind of continuity of the old authoritarian racial order is unsustainable, being eroded on the one hand by processes such as the promotion of black employees into supervisory positions and worker consciousness of the disjuncture between workplace order and broader democracy, and on the other by inefficiency and resistant work culture. The result is a process of decomposition of the workplace regime (von Holdt 2003), which appears in its starkest form at the hospital. More radical solutions may then seem attractive to managers, such as externalising industrial relations into commercial relations with outsourced and informalised forms of production as in the footwear sectors.

The studies also demonstrate the important role played by relatively active trade unionism in preventing management from implementing weakly-resourced initiatives. Trade union presence allows workers to contest workplace order and management strategies or undermine authoritarian restoration as in the domestic appliances industry. Trade unions provide a means for constructing worker solidarity, protecting workers from management control and creating space for workers to maintain or forge a resistant work culture. At the hospital, moreover, membership frustration with workplace conditions has led to trade union pressure on management and government to implement change, which may move this case study into the category of negotiated reconstruction.

There are probably a large number of companies in South Africa – particularly medium and smaller companies – whose workplaces are characterised by failed strategies or little initiative for change. If significant parts of the public service are added to this, we may conclude that a very large number of workplaces, perhaps employing the majority of the country's workers, remain plagued by the kind of racial tension and conflict – including a highly resistant work culture – and the inefficiencies which characterised the apartheid workplace regime.

Implications for the future of labour

The restructuring of the world of work explored in this chapter has implications not only for managers, workers and trade unions, but also for the prospect of broader sustainable social development. Parts of the core workforce have been integrated into post-apartheid society through dynamic trade unionism, workplace participation, the extension of democratic rights, skills development, employment equity programmes, negotiated measures to reduce racial tension, economic incorporation through wages and various benefits, and so on. There has also been a partial integration of other parts of the core workforce, who continue to experience authoritarianism and racial domination. However, this contrasts with the variable socio-economic exclusion of large sectors of the non-core and peripheral workforce.

To the extent that a new authoritarian workplace order is secured through shifting core workers into the non-core zone, or by severing them from employment altogether and casting them onto the periphery, managers may be resolving the crisis of post-apartheid workplace order by displacing confrontation, antagonism and disorder into the family, the household and the community (von Holdt & Webster 2005). This generates a broader social crisis whose symptoms are the breakdown of social solidarity, intra-household and community conflict, substance abuse, domestic violence, and the proliferation of other crimes. The shrinking of the core and the extension of the non-core and periphery have fractured labour solidarity and weakened the trade unions, which are a primary vehicle not only for improving workplace conditions and protecting worker rights, but also for integrating workers into society. What implications do these conclusions discussed in this chapter have for the future of labour?

The labour movement, particularly Cosatu, played a crucial role in the democratic transformation of South Africa (Buhlungu 2005). After the inauguration of the democratically elected government in 1994, Cosatu retained its role as a central player and won many gains for its members, particularly in the form of organising rights and labour-friendly policies. In addition, hundreds of prominent unionists now play leading roles in institutions of the new South Africa and are able to influence the broader processes of change that are unfolding.

Our longitudinal study shows that Cosatu members are happy with the role that the federation continues to play in the democratic transition. They also support the involvement of labour in institutions of the new democracy, including Parliament and municipal councils. It is no exaggeration to say that labour (specifically Cosatu) remains the single most powerful civil society organisation in the country.

However, our examination of the changing workplace and the social characteristics of the membership of Cosatu shows that the federation represents an ever-diminishing section of working people. Furthermore, it is making no headway in organising workers in the growing precarious forms of work – contract workers or outsourced, casual and part-time workers. In addition, the fact that the federation's membership is increasingly becoming more skilled, more educated and older suggests that there are growing layers of workers within and outside the workplace who are without a voice.

Are we about to witness the marginalisation of labour or is a process of union revitalisation likely in South Africa? Our data suggest that what we are witnessing is not simply one or the other of these outcomes. Labour has gained enormous influence over the past decade while at the same time it has been losing organisational power at the workplace level – but it is too soon to suggest that labour has been marginalised during the transition to democracy. Both processes are contested and, as we argue elsewhere, labour in general stands between marginalisation and revitalisation (Webster & Buhlungu 2004).

WORK RESTRUCTURING AND THE FUTURE OF LABOUR

In this chapter we have attempted to bring together data drawn from two separate research projects, the one on the dynamics of workplace change and the other on the changing nature of the labour movement. The conventional approach is to treat the study of the workplace as a domain of human resources and schools of management while labour is relegated to the status of the poorer cousin located in the humanities and social sciences. Our findings suggest that the two projects are intimately connected: in a country with high union density and a tradition of militant mobilisation workplace change succeeds or fails depending on the extent to which the key actors in the world of work understand the changing nature of labour. Equally significantly, we have argued that the broader social crisis facing South Africa cannot be divorced from workplace restructuring. Indeed, until the connection between the spheres of production and reproduction is grasped more systematically, the future not only of labour, but of the nation itself, will remain deeply contested.

Notes

1   In this chapter the term 'labour' is used to describe both the organisation of workers into trade unions and the conditions and rights of working people in general. In other words, our understanding of working people includes those in formal employment as well as those in so-called informal work.

2   These studies have recently been published in a book edited by Webster and von Holdt (2005).

3   This study has recently been published in a book edited by Buhlungu (2005).

4   However, if you are indigent and you are lucky, you can get free services such as an 'RDP House', 6kl of water and R50 worth of electricity per month. The costs are recouped by the municipalities from central government (if they are lucky) under the indigent subsidy scheme.

5   These are identified by von Holdt and Webster (2005) as apartheid legacy and racial conflict; union activity; attitude to work; casualisation and externalisation; new technologies; work organisation; workload; production quality; company performance.

References

Ashton DN & Sung J (2002) *Supporting workplace learning for high performance working.* Geneva: ILO.

Baskin D (1991) *Striking back: A history of Cosatu.* Johannesburg: Ravan.

Bezuidenhout A (2005) Post-colonial workplace regimes in the engineering industry in South Africa. In E Webster & K von Holdt (eds.) *Beyond the apartheid workplace: Studies in transition.* Scottsville: University of KwaZulu-Natal.

Buhlungu S (2001) Democracy and modernisation in the making of the South African trade union movement: The dilemma of leadership, 1973–2000. Unpublished PhD thesis, University of the Witwatersrand, Johannesburg.

Buhlungu S (ed.) (2005) *Fruits of their labour: Cosatu members and the democratic transformation of South Africa.* Cape Town: HSRC Press.

Burawoy M (1972) *The colour of class on the copper mines: From African advancement to Zambianization.* Zambian Papers No. 7. Lusaka: Institute of African Studies, University of Zambia.

Crankshaw O (1994) Race, class and the changing division of labour under apartheid. Unpublished PhD thesis, University of the Witwatersrand, Johannesburg.

Ginsburg D, Webster E, Southall R, Wood G, Buhlungu S, Maree J, Cherry J, Haines R & Klerck G (1995) *Taking democracy seriously: Worker expectations and parliamentary democracy in South Africa.* Durban: Indicator Press.

Hindson D & Crankshaw O (1990) New jobs, new skills, new divisions: The changing structure of South Africa's workforce, *South African Labour Bulletin* 15(1): 23–31.

Kenny B (2001) 'We are nursing these jobs': The impact of labour market flexibility on East Rand retail workers. In N Newman, J Pape & H Jansen (eds.) *Is there an alternative? South African workers confronting globalisation.* Cape Town: ILRIG.

Kenny B & Webster E (1999) Eroding the core: Flexibility and the re-segmentation of the South African labour market, *Critical Sociology* 24(3): 216–243.

Masondo D (2005) Trade liberalisation and work restructuring in post-apartheid South Africa. In E Webster & K von Holdt (eds.) *Beyond the apartheid workplace: Studies in transition.* Scottsville: University of KwaZulu-Natal.

Mosoetsa S (2005) The consequence of South Africa's economic transition: Remnants of the footwear industry. In E Webster & K von Holdt (eds.) *Beyond the apartheid workplace: Studies in transition.* Scottsville: University of KwaZulu-Natal.

Phakathi S (2005) Self-directed teams in a post-apartheid gold mine: Perspectives from the rockface. In E Webster & K von Holdt (eds.) *Beyond the apartheid workplace: Studies in transition*. Scottsville: University of KwaZulu-Natal.

Pityana SM & Orkin M (1992) *Beyond the factory floor: A survey of Cosatu shop stewards*. Johannesburg: Ravan Press.

Sitas A (2004) Thirty years since the Durban strikes: Black working-class leadership and the South African transition, *Current Sociology* 52(5): 830–849.

SWOP (Sociology of Work Unit) (1994, 1998, 2004) Cosatu workers' survey. Unpublished longitudinal survey results.

UNDP (United Nations Development Programme) (2003) *South African human development report 2003: The challenge of sustainable development in South Africa*. Cape Town: Oxford University Press.

Von Holdt K (2003) *Transition from below: Forging trade unionism and workplace change in South Africa*. Pietermaritzburg: University of Natal Press.

Von Holdt K & Maserumule B (2005) After apartheid: Decay or reconstruction in a state hospital. In E Webster & K von Holdt (eds.) *Beyond the apartheid workplace: Studies in transition*. Scottsville: University of KwaZulu-Natal.

Von Holdt K & Webster E (2005) Work restructuring and the crisis of social reproduction: A southern perspective. In E Webster & K von Holdt (eds.) *Beyond the apartheid workplace: Studies in transition*. Scottsville: University of KwaZulu-Natal.

Webster E & Buhlungu S (2004) Between marginalisation and revitalisation: The state of trade unionism in South Africa, *Review of African Political Economy* 100(31): 229–245.

Webster E & von Holdt K (eds.) (2005) *Beyond the apartheid workplace: Studies in transition*. Scottsville: University of KwaZulu-Natal.

# 11 The state of research and experimental development: moving to a higher gear

Michael Kahn and William Blankley

Introduction

Why the 'state of research and experimental development' rather than the 'state of innovation'? After all, it is the broader area of innovation rather than research and experimental development (R&D) that is regarded as key to economic growth (Freeman 1982; Mowery & Rosenberg 1998; Rosenberg 1976).

There are sound reasons to focus on R&D since much technological innovation involves R&D. Moreover, because of our longer history of familiarity with the concept, it is 'easier' to quantify R&D activity than is the case for innovation. In this chapter consideration will first be given to R&D in the broad economy. Next, ways of measuring inputs to and outputs from R&D are examined. This examination provides empirical data on the resources available for R&D. Following this we consider the stocks and flows of R&D personnel. Finally, we make the connection between R&D policy and strategy. These aspects together enable one to construct the snapshot entitled 'The state of R&D'.

Economic considerations

In the process of innovation, R&D is but a component, and not always a necessary component of the web of interactions that give rise to innovation. This is recognised in the current systems approach to innovation. An excellent overview of such thinking is to be found in the United Nations Task Force on Science, Technology and Innovation report (Juma & Yee-Cheong 2005). The previous linear model in which innovation begins with research is deemed to be too simplistic and an inadequate descriptor. It is systems thinking that underpins the national system of innovation (NSI) approach (Freeman 1982) that informs science and technology policy in South Africa. As it happens,

South Africa was one of the first countries to make the NSI approach explicit in R&D and innovation policy through the *White Paper on science and technology* (DACST 1996).

R&D is the conscious and systematic scientific effort that contributes to the growth of the stock of knowledge that in time may or may not lead to new technological applications. In some cases, notably biotechnology, journal disclosure of research findings and patent filing has become almost simultaneous. Where R&D capability is a component of technological innovation, its intensity rises with more complex technology. In addition, R&D capability is necessary for technology transfer and to engage in processes such as reverse engineering. Experimental development on the one hand involves ground-breaking applications, incremental improvements and systematic problem solving, and responses to market pull on the other. The litmus test for the presence of R&D is to ask whether there is a significant element of novelty in the activity.

Innovation on the other hand is the successful dissemination of a new (technological) process or product in the market. The innovation may be new to the organisation, market, country or world. Innovation as a concept thus seems to be easier to understand, but is in fact harder to measure. If innovation is key to economic growth, then R&D capacity is often, but not always, key to sustainable innovation. Without investment in basic research the flow of new thinking may be stultified, and the flow of innovation activity may wither. Indeed, R&D effort has come to be seen as a lead indicator of technological capability.

Then again, it is quite possible for an economy to display high levels of economic growth while investment in R&D is low or barely exists. Examples of this might be Thailand and Hong Kong in the early 1990s (Dodgson 2000) or present-day Botswana and Mozambique. The existence of R&D is not a precondition for economic growth, since steady growth may also come through such diverse sources as operating transnational corporation factories, rents extracted from mineral extraction or plantation crops. Such has not been the case for this country where the challenges of deep mining, low yield ore bodies, weak soils, drought, human and animal disease, and warfare have demanded an R&D response since the advent of industrialisation.

The main organisations that comprise the NSI are the research universities (Cape Town, KwaZulu-Natal, Pretoria, Rhodes, Stellenbosch, Witwatersrand), various government research institutes and museums, the nine science research councils, and firms. These operate in the institutional environment of political, social, moral and legal norms and standards. This NSI has been sufficiently robust to launch the careers of four Nobel laureates – three in physiology or medicine, and one in chemistry – and can deal with the problems of hunger, shelter and health, provided the associated political (and fiscal) will. This was the vision for science held out by then Prime Minister Jan Smuts in the 1940s with the founding of the Council for Scientific and Industrial Research (CSIR).

According to the analysis of Fedderke (NACI 2002), starting in the 1980s, the economy underwent 'innovation-led structural adjustment', whereby productivity gains were provided by technology rather than labour practice. The gradual meltdown of manufacturing resulted in a contraction of employment in this sector as well as a declining share for the sector as a component of gross domestic product (GDP). Fedderke argues that prior investment in creative innovation was expensive and that the country would have been better served by an emphasis on imitative innovation.

In 1995 government opted for its own brand of structural adjustment known as the Growth, Employment and Redistribution strategy (GEAR). A decade later GEAR is hailed as a successful mechanism that has stabilised the currency, reined in inflation, and laid the basis for sustained economic growth. But GEAR came with a price: in order to control the state salary bill public servants were encouraged to opt for a voluntary severance package. As a result some public servants who were disinclined to serve the new government resigned, but a great deal of management skill and institutional memory was also lost. This did open up vacancies for new (black) entrants, but also created skills gaps where black replacements were in short supply, such as in school science and mathematics teaching.

Globalisation

Much is made of country technological performance as measured by the respective country share of world exports in manufactures layered by their technological complexity (Lall 2000). In this typology high technology includes electronics, pharmaceuticals, aerospace, and the information communication technologies (ICTs); medium technology embraces automobiles and steel production; and low technology covers wood products, leather and textile goods, furniture. So Singapore serves as a factory that produces to original equipment manufacture (OEM) specifications and thus has a higher share of medium-level technology exports than South Africa; Malaysia with its massive output of OEM electronics goods has a larger share of high-level technology exports. One must take care in how Lall's typology is applied: wood in and of itself does not make for low technology *vide* Norway's high-technology pulp industry. The South African share of world technology exports is shown in Table 11.1 and appears to relate a dismal tale.

Table 11.1 *South Africa's percentage share of world exports in technology, 1992 and 2002*

Technology level	1992	2002
Low	0.34	0.30
Middle	0.27	0.41
High	0.07	0.07

Source: Kaplan 2004

Table 11.2 presents more detail on the composition of manufactured exports over the periods 1992 and 2002 and confirms that the top ten items are of the medium-technology type. The scale-intensive refinery business is exceptional – not only is this technology among the top five exports, but the balance of trade in this item is strongly on South Africa's side. This is far from the case in the automotive sector.

These data tell the story of export-led growth. That the number two and nine exports are OEM is the result of the Department of Trade and Industry (DTI) Automotive Industries Development Programme and is based on activities that involve considerable R&D by the original manufacturer but low R&D in South Africa.

There is considerable difficulty in defining precisely what is meant by the term 'high-technology export' (Mani 2000) and it requires a finer analysis of the nature and origins of detailed subcategories of exports for accuracy. Nonetheless, a quick analysis of the 1992/2002 manufacturing export data shows that the high-technology share of manufactured exports would appear to have grown from 20 per cent in 1992 to 30 per cent in 2002.

Table 11.2 *Manufactured exports revenue ranked by South African Rands, 1992 and 2002*

	1992		2002		Change in
	Rank	R million	Rank	R million	value (%)
Basic iron and steel	1	10 075	1	25 532	253.4
Motor vehicles	9	1 125	2	18 755	1 666.5
Basic chemicals	3	3 163	3	11 373	359.6
Basic precious & non-ferrous metals	2	5 121	4	11 355	221.8
Other general purpose machinery	17	468	5	10 932	2 334.6
Petroleum/refineries/synthesisers	39	215	6	10 053	4 667.8
Pulp, paper and paperboard	4	2 343	7	6 394	272.9
Jewellery and related articles	5	1 925	8	5 542	287.9
Automotive parts & accessories	6	1 242	9	5 015	403.7
Furniture	24	316	10	4 691	1 484.4

Source: http://www.dti.gov.za

What is perhaps more interesting than the 2002 rankings is the shift in rank across the period since this may give an indication of things to come. Viewed through this lens, the larger data set shows that weapons and ammunition, electronic components, petroleum refineries/synthesisers, engines and turbines, and television and radio receivers have moved up the fastest. Embedded in all of these are high-technology and science-based elements. This thrust rests on the former innovation-led industrialisation that Fedderke has criticised. It is in part a dividend of the apartheid war machine.

South Africa, at this moment in time, is the largest source of foreign direct investment (FDI) into Africa. Its transnational corporations and state-owned corporations have swarmed over the Limpopo, absorbing local banks and breweries, founding mines and chain stores, building communications networks on the ground and in the ether. For the immediate future the northward march of 'Proudly South African' brands seems unstoppable, at least until Chinese business really gets going. This investment has been encouraged by the foreign exchange regime of the South African Reserve Bank. One might ask how sustainable is the northward march, and what will be the role of R&D in maintaining it?

Since 1990 the country has moved from an inward-looking import substitution model toward an outward-looking export-led growth model. While the trade sanctions of the 1980s had most effect on the manufacturing sector rather than commodity exporters (Scerri 1990), all sectors have to grapple with the globalisation of goods, services and personnel.

The problem of measuring R&D

Measurement of R&D activity has a long history. Best practice is provided in the guidelines of the Frascati Manual series (OECD 2002). The resulting science and technology indicators are used for national planning and for international benchmarking as in the *Main science and technology indicators* series (OECD 2003). R&D surveys tend to be conducted biennially and have been conducted in South Africa since the late 1960s. Of recent surveys, that of 1991/92 was conducted by the then Foundation for Research Development (FRD), and the 2001/02 and 2003/04 by the Human Sciences Research Council. These surveys form the basis of what follows.

It is somewhat more difficult to measure and report on innovation activities with accuracy, the guidelines being found in the Organisation for Economic Cooperation and Development's *'Oslo' Manual* (OECD 1993). In South Africa there have been two unofficial innovation surveys (FRD-ISP 1997; Oerlemans, Pretorius, Buys & Rooks 2003), but no large-scale survey so one cannot yet report on the 'state of innovation'.

The R&D surveys record inputs into the conduct of R&D – namely people, equipment and funding. The Frascati Manual defines R&D as 'creative work undertaken on a systematic basis in order to increase the stock of knowledge, including knowledge of humanity, culture and society, and the use of this stock of knowledge to devise new applications' (OECD 2002: 31). This definition works for laboratory R&D or the environment of manufacturing industry. Back in the 1960s when the first Frascati Manual was crafted, measurement of R&D in the service sector was largely ignored. But much has changed since then and the definition is now somewhat frayed. Three cases will suffice to illustrate this.

The first is the area of clinical trials. In this case the Frascati Manual recommends that phases I to III may be included as R&D. Estimates of the size of this 'white coat' economy run between one and two billion rand annually. The pharmaceutical industry, universities and dedicated R&D organisations all contribute to this 'white coat' economy. Indications are that clinical trials account for much of the leap in foreign-funded R&D from six per cent of gross expenditure on R&D (GERD) in 2002 to ten per cent in 2004.

Second is the area of software and information systems development. In the early years of this industry software development was generally excluded as R&D. Now, however, the test of novelty applies. The software does not have to be a fundamental new language or ground-breaking approach to sorting data. If the development is novel and not obvious to the general community of practice, it is included as a legitimate component of R&D. But the closer firms get to being in applications development the more blurred this becomes.

The 2002 revision of the Frascati Manual deals with both the above cases, but it has not yet evolved to deal with the vast diversity of innovative (and possibly research-based) activity in the services sector.

The third is the contradiction found between R&D and innovation surveys. R&D surveys interrogate a small number of targeted institutions – in the case of Italy in 1995 the survey obtained R&D data on 800 firms. The subsequent Italian innovation survey obtained data from 8 000 firms, randomly selected (Sirilli 1998). Now here is the contradiction. The 'lighter' innovation survey often records higher levels of R&D than the 'true' R&D survey does. This is in part because the R&D survey deals with the large firms that conduct most of the R&D, while the innovation survey tends to capture the long tail of small companies. (Innovation surveys also conduct a census of the largest firms.) What this suggests is that many small firms that are innovating believe they are also doing R&D, and many of these small firms are in the service sector. So the challenge is how to measure R&D in small firms and the broader service sector (see Pavitt 1999).

The two conventional R&D output measures are peer-reviewed journal articles and patents recorded in the leading jurisdictions. In the case of the former one must examine journal citation lists compiled by the Institute for Scientific Information (or other such journal citation databases); for the latter, one checks the patent data recorded in the United States, Japan and the European Union – so-called triadic patent data.

R&D performance

Standard practice is to measure GERD across government, higher education institutions and business. In our case we split off the science councils from government and the not-for-profits from business. A full census is conducted for the science councils and higher education institutions, while purposive sampling is effected on not-for-profits, government and business. The reason why a purposive sample is effected is simply that no register of R&D performers exists. With no general R&D tax incentive in place there is no record of who is doing R&D. Currently participation in the survey is voluntary so that coverage is limited. The recorded level of R&D activity must thus be understood to be a floor level, with the ceiling possibly some ten to 15 per cent beyond that. The problem of accuracy is universal: 'The GERD, like any other social or economic statistic, can only be approximately true. Different components are of different accuracy: sector estimates probably vary from ±5 to ±15 per cent in accuracy' (StatCan 2004: 10).

Carrying out the purposive survey is akin to an intelligence-gathering operation. One works through obvious lists such as the Johannesburg Securities Exchange (JSE), support schemes operated by the DTI (for example, the Support Programme for Industrial Innovation) or the Department of Science and Technology National Innovation Fund, as well as lists of technology achievers such as the Technology Top 100. Co-nomination by respondents is also used to build the registry of R&D performers, as are referrals through organisations such as the Biological Research and Information Centres, Blue IQ, Godisa and trade associations. Scanning newpapers and business magazines for announcements about technology development and advertisements for R&D personnel provides additional sources of information.

The conventional indicator of R&D expenditure is obtained by dividing GERD by GDP. It is thus necessary to examine GDP composition and the context in which it is calculated. The composition of GDP is altered from time to time with the consequence that the GERD:GDP series must also be adjusted.

Starting in the mid-1980s, and now with increasing acceleration, the manufacturing component of the economy has shrunk, from 25 per cent of GDP in 1991 to 19 per cent in 2004.[1] In addition, the economy is now open, so that foreigners own some 18.5 per cent of the JSE by value (McGregor 2004).

A number of our leading firms have primary or secondary listings abroad and a number of leading brands have been purchased by foreign concerns. Moreover, the composition of manufactured exports has shown a radical change with the inclusion in the top ten export categories of machinery and refineries, the latter with a high element of R&D. Finally, there is South African FDI with its accompanying outbound technology transfers.

All the above have significant implications for the sourcing of competitive technologies: do these arise through in-house R&D, through inward licensing, contracts performed for offshore clients, through the acquisition of skilled personnel, or reverse engineering?

Figure 11.1 *GERD:GDP, 1983–2003*

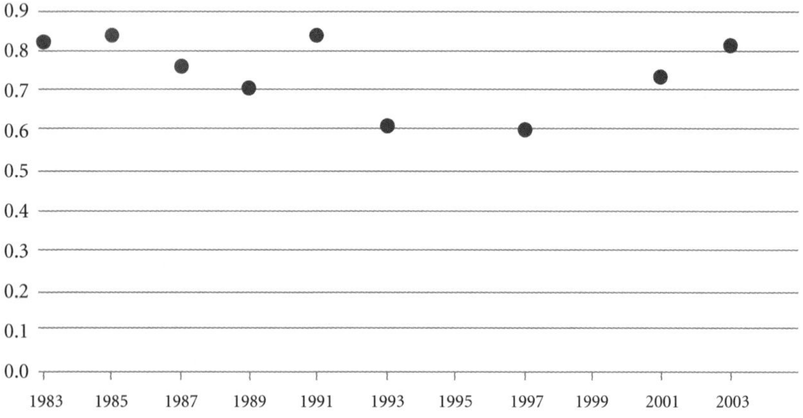

Source: OECD 2005. There were no surveys in 1995 and 1999
Note: Revised GDP records were used.

Figure 11.1 shows that GERD:GDP has a median level of 0.76. GERD is now R10.1 billion; GDP is R1 250 billion – this yields GERD:GDP of 0.806 per cent (DST 2005), still below the one per cent government target, but on a level comparable with Portugal, Poland and Hungary. Sectoral expenditures and relative proportions are shown in Table 11.3.

THE STATE OF RESEARCH AND EXPERIMENTAL DEVELOPMENT

Table 11.3 *R&D expenditure by sector, 2003/04*

Sector	Expenditure R million	Share (%)
Business & not-for-profits (BERD)	5 790	57.4
Government/Science councils	2 210	22.0
Higher education (HERD)	2 081	20.6
Total	10 081	100.0

Source: DST (2005)

R&D expenditure is a proxy of expected benefits, and it is thus important to quantify to what end the funds are committed. The survey uses two main classifications for this purpose – research fields and socio-economic objectives. Expenditure by research fields for the 2001/02 and 2003/04 surveys is depicted in Figure 11.2.

Figure 11.2 *Expenditure on R&D by major research fields, 2003 and 2004*

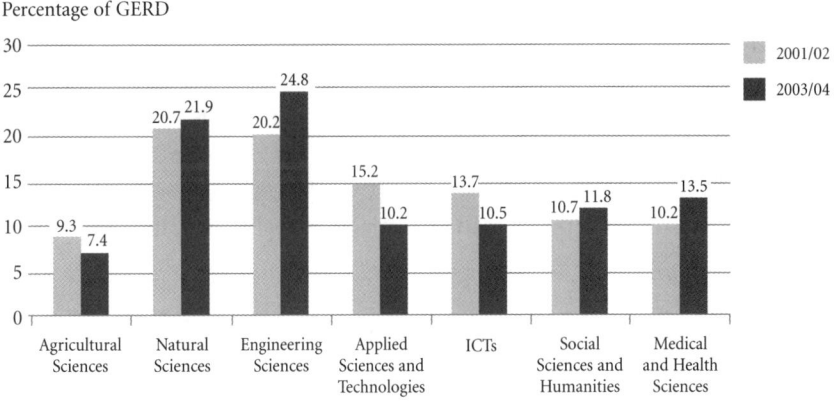

Source: DST 2005

There is concentration in the applied sciences and technology, engineering sciences and ICTs that have grown by ten per cent over the decade. So there is some drift toward the applied sciences and technology that has evoked alarm in social scientists. However, the data show that in the higher education sector some 30 per cent of expenditure is directed toward the social sciences and humanities, a proportion in excess of the level of the 20 per cent recorded in Canada (StatCan 2003). In this sense the social sciences are relatively well funded and the alarm may be misplaced.

There is also concentration of R&D among organisations and regions, a phenomenon that occurs globally. The top four business sector firms account for 40 per cent of BERD; the top six universities for 60 per cent of HERD; the top two science councils for 50 per cent of government direct expenditure. Gauteng province is the site of 60 per cent of R&D effort. Given the openness of the economy it is also instructive to note that ten per cent of BERD is now performed by foreign-controlled firms, with a high concentration in the pharmaceutical industry.

What of R&D outputs, namely publications and patents? Data from the Institute for Scientific Information (ISI) show that the annual number of South African authored publications has remained static at around 3 300 over the last decade; given that world publication volumes have increased our share has necessarily fallen (Pouris 2003). The constancy of our publication output is an unfortunate confirmation that the research capacity of academia has not grown. Worse, Mouton, Boshoff and Bailey (2002) show that the most active publishing cadre consists of 'ageing white males' in the universities. The remaining ten per cent of publications emanates from the science councils, research institutes and museum scientific sections. Industry accounts for less than one per cent of the total.

On the patent front there is a similarly constant level of outputs as shown in Table 11.4.

Table 11.4 *Patents of South African origin granted at the United States Patent and Trademark Office, 1993–2003*

Year	1993	1994	1995	1996	1997	1998	1999	2000	2001	2002	2003
No.	89	99	137	112	112	115	110	111	120	113	112

Source: http://www.uspto.gov

Taking the filings at the United States Patent Office as the prime indicator, the median number of utility patents over the period 1993 to 2003 stands at 112, with the 120 recorded in 2001 being the highest since 1995. One must, however, be circumspect in attributing cause to the patenting behaviour of firms (Granstrand, Patel & Pavitt 1997). The 'low' South African count conceals the contributions of one or two major players, as well as a particular history of managing intellectual property. There is a dearth of research on these issues.

As a whole the evidence on R&D expenditure, journal publications and patenting suggests that the national system of innovation has remained functional, though static, through the transition. It has not collapsed in the way the transitions of Eastern Europe precipitated but has provided the necessary base for the growth in high-technology exports.

What some critics (Kaplan 2004) have overlooked is that while our world share of high-technology exports is steady at 0.07 per cent it mainly consists of our own technologies, not OEM as in the case of Thailand or Malaysia. R&D expenditure in these fields is relatively high. Regarding medium-technology exports, these have grown to 0.41 per cent of the world total, but are essentially OEM. For this activity R&D is minimal. And like many other countries we are unable to retain our share of low-technology exports since our labour productivity (and inadequate technology investment) makes us uncompetitive. This points to two challenges – R&D to compete in low-technology exports and R&D to support the service sector, especially its northward march.

People for R&D

Under globalisation with its open borders, 'free' trade regimes, and knowledge porosity, the knowledge worker has become queen or king. The knowledge worker is increasingly mobile and professionals have greater choice in their domicile as companies and countries fish in the global reservoir of scarce skills. South Africa is but another fisherman constrained by what it can afford to pay. But it competes with fishing technology that is of its own making.

Historically (AS&TS 1988) the country has never produced enough high-level skills to meet its needs. Inward immigration of the highly skilled dried up in the 1980s and has not yet recovered. At present immigration policy is a barrier to the inward migration of skills; policy for human capital is unable to channel sufficient funds to generate new stock from local talent.

Table 11.5 *Researcher full-time equivalents, 1992 and 2004*

Sector	1992	2004
Business	3 395	4 411
Government	2 428	2 342
Higher education	3 631	3 374
Total	9 454	10 127

Source: DST 2005a; 2005b

Table 11.5 shows that across the decade the available number of full-time equivalent (FTE) researchers has remained more or less steady – or is it better to say that the number of FTE researchers has not grown in pace with the economy? The human capital stasis goes some way toward explaining why the NSI appears to be marking time. There are simply not enough researchers in the system to increase the outputs. In fact our levels of researchers – both in absolute and relative terms – and our level of GERD:GDP are very close to where South Korea was in the mid-1980s (Lee 2000). This stasis is particularly troubling since it has been accompanied by a 60 per cent growth in the student population over the decade.[2] Though higher education staff rose by 25 per cent, this lags behind student growth. The consequence is that teaching loads most likely have risen.

The basis of country high-level skill formation lies in the efficiency and effectiveness of its school system to produce school leavers with the wherewithal to proceed to further or higher education. The gateway subject for such progression is mathematics higher grade, whose attainment rests not only upon quality teaching, but also on the communication skills of the learner. Table 11.6 shows the bottleneck in the production of mathematics higher grade passes – the passes have remained around 20 000 for the past 12 years. In 1992 the number stood at 20 500.

Given racial stratification one must ask who these 20 000 learners are. More than half are white; around 30 percent are African, while the remainder is split between coloured and Indian learners. The proportion of African passes has

Table 11.6 *Mathematics higher-grade candidates and passes (thousands), 1997–2003*

Year	1997	1998	1999	2000	2001	2002	2003
Wrote	68.5	60.3	50.1	38.5	34.9	35.5	35.4
Pass	22.8	20.3	19.9	19.3	19.5	20.5	23.4

Source: DoE Examinations Data

grown from 15 per cent in 1992. Under-representation of black students in the cohort led the DoE (2002) to formulate the DiNaledi Schools Project intervention strategy that seeks to correct this imbalance. DiNaledi aims to build capability and capacity in schools located within the disadvantaged communities.

A recent study (CDE 2004) called for the number of mathematics higher grade passes to be doubled within five years. This is perhaps a target too far since it might be argued that the wealthier white and Indian communities are already generating as many passes as they are able to. The increase in pass volumes must come from the most disadvantaged communities and would require quadrupling output from these communities, which is virtually impossible in five years.

The inescapable conclusion is that the education system cannot produce more under present conditions. The nexus is teacher education. To a large extent teacher education has collapsed, with the production of teachers for mathematics and science education lagging behind replacement needs. Without quality teachers quality outcomes are an impossibility.

Conventional R&D surveys cover the basics: disaggregation by gender, group and age is not generally quantified. Given the lack of data on these areas the South African 2001/02 survey included demographic items as well as items on staff mobility. The demographic data is summarised in Figure 11.3, which shows that the average age of researchers in the business and government sectors is some ten years younger than that in higher education.

Figure 11.3 *Demographics of researchers (headcounts) in the NSI, 2001/02*

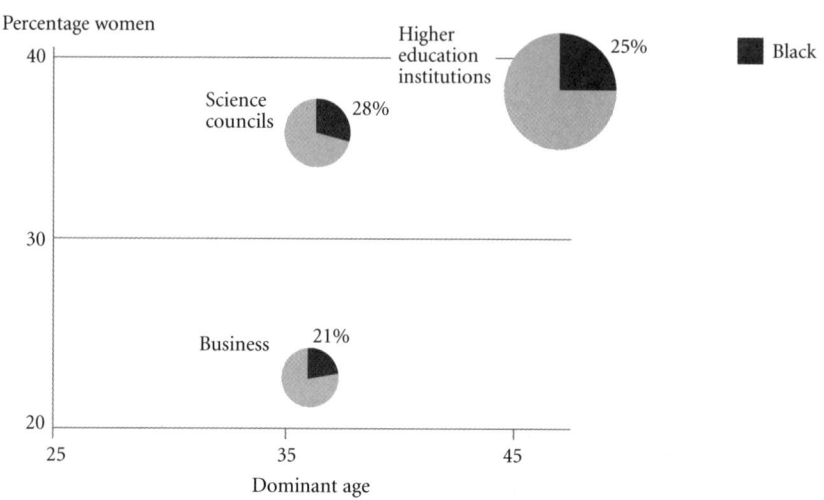

Source: National R&D database 2001/02

The pie areas are proportional to the researcher headcount; the darker slices give the proportion of black researchers; average age is on the x-axis; gender bias is on the y-axis. The data show how a mere eight years after the onset of democracy black staff have come to occupy upwards of 20 per cent of research posts, growing from a very small base. This picture is quite different to that generated in the bibliometric study (Mouton et al 2002). On the gender front South Africa ranks among the countries with the highest proportion of female researchers, though as explained earlier such measurement is the exception not the rule. To recapitulate then, the R&D workforce has remained stable in size and is witnessing a gradual demographic transformation.

The next two issues concern emigration and immigration. The *Flight of the flamingos* (Kahn, Blankley, Pogue, Maharajh & Reddy 2004) compiled a comprehensive picture of the sources, stocks and flows of R&D workers. Regarding emigration, it was indicated that losses had been severe through the previous decade but that it was impossible to provide reliable figures since there was a serious mismatch between emigration statistics and recipient country statistics, with the variance being up to four times higher on the recipient side.

Annual losses appeared to be in the range of 2 500. Conversely, gains to the country were in the order of 500 per year, but similarly distorted by undercounting on the South African side. A significant number of these immigrants hail from north of the Limpopo and are mid- to late-career professionals.

Where there is certainty is in respect of the data on foreign student enrolments in higher education where they comprise in the order of eight per cent of the total, with the countries of the Southern African Development Community (SADC) dispatching the most. In fact, of the SADC states, South Africa is the only one that is able to comply with the norms of the SADC Protocol on Education and Training (SADC 1998) in respect of providing eight per cent of places in higher education for students from SADC member states.

This role of our higher-education institutions as a preferred destination for migrant students represents a return to the days before legalised apartheid. Today migrant students constitute a significant proportion of postgraduates in the sciences, engineering and technology. Their presence naturally raises political and economic questions as to where they will settle down to work.

What is certain is that the South African diaspora has not flocked home in large numbers and it will take a concerted effort from all economic sectors to change this. But there are signs that the large drains have mitigated, and that some reversal is occurring. A number of foreign firms have recently set up shop in South Africa. In one reported case this move was prompted by the large skills base in South Africa. The South African Pharmaceutical Manufacturers Association reports some R400 million of clinical trials funded by multinational pharmaceutical companies.[3]

What must never be lost in the mobility debate is that mobility is necessary for creativity to flourish (and in turn it is only attractive conditions in a country that will encourage inward mobility). So it makes sense for a global player like Sasol not only to fund catalysis research at home, but also to fund a research centre in St Andrews in Scotland to which it sends key staff for intensive periods of R&D after which they return home.

R&D for the people?

What then is to be said in respect of R&D policy and outcomes in the context of the developmental state? Shortly after its establishment as a separate entity the Department of Science and Technology (DST 2002) tabled a strategy for R&D. The strategy followed a long process of audit, foresight studies, organisational review and restructuring of the state-funded science system. It was crafted at the point when an information chasm had arisen through the breaks in the time series of R&D surveys. The preamble of the national R&D strategy avers that:

> Between 1990 and 1994, the strong missions for technology developed by the National Party government (for example, military dominance in the subcontinent, energy self-sufficiency, etc.) were systematically stripped off. The percentage of the South African gross domestic product spent on research and development declined from 1.1 per cent in 1991 to its current level of about 0.7 per cent.[4] (DST 2002: 19)

Was this 'decline' solely due to the end of the *totale aanslag* technology missions? The data show (Blankley & Kahn 2005) that the strong growth in R&D spending since the 1960s had tapered off in the turbulent 1980s as sanctions tightened and business uncertainty grew. There is uncertainty as to how much the curtailment of military and nuclear weapons R&D contributed to this slowdown.

Data provided by Cilliers (1996) allow one to estimate that *budgeted* defence R&D comprised 22 per cent (1989), 25 per cent (1991) and 17 per cent (1993) of GERD. These figures are tentative and further research is needed to be more precise. The record shows that the nuclear weapons programme and large-scale military procurement were scaled down from 1988 onward as the military conflict abated and that the major spending on the weapons programme was incurred many years prior to this. In other words, irrespective of how the budgeted funds over 1989 to 1993 were committed, that is, how beneficiary companies recorded the resulting R&D contracts, there was a steady flow of funds from the state to R&D spending. Arguably, further research is needed to settle the question of 'decline'.

The fall of 27 per cent in GERD:GDP between 1991 and 1994 occurred after the military slowdown and would in any case be the largest such fall in the 30-year time series. It is more likely to have resulted from the changes in measurement methodology that arose as the conduct of the survey migrated across three organisations over this period (CSIR, FRD and a private consultant), rather than sudden changes in R&D investment.

Though the preamble assumptions may have been based on imperfect information there is no argument that new technology missions are needed. The strategy declares these as information and communication technology, advanced manufacturing technology, biotechnology, technologies related to resource-based industries, and technology for poverty reduction. In addition ,attention is given to the endowment of southern earth, oceans and skies that provides for unique scientific study. We now consider the match between the proposed mission areas and R&D activity in these areas (see Table 11.7).

Taken in order of tabulation, one observes that defence (for which read military applications) absorbs 9.3 per cent of effort. This defence expenditure is a legacy of the military-industrial complex that originated in the Second World War and grew during the subsequent cold war and *totale aanslag* (total onslaught) period. It is located in the CSIR, the state-owned Denel group of companies and private sector defence contractors where there is a large spillover into electronics, especially radar and communications technologies. It is substantial, though companies whose products have defence applications do not always report their efforts as such: R&D on military vehicles might be reported as 'transport', not 'defence'.

Regarding the economic development objectives, these may be split into manufacturing and resources on the one hand and services on the other. Of the 60 per cent of expenditure in division 2, the various components that comprise services (24%) represent 'services (that) can be bought and sold, but cannot be dropped on your foot' (Miles 2003: 61). Resources and manufacturing comprise some 36 per cent. Divisions 3, 4 and 5 are all part of the broad services area as well.

Recognising that ICTs are *enabling* technologies that today pervade most industrial and service activity the 5.5 per cent expenditure recorded for ICT appears to be on the low side of actual expenditure. However, this figure represents 'pure' R&D on ICT. Many ICT applications developed in other areas such as environmental sciences, manufacturing, services and mining are likely to be recorded under these sectors of application.

As to manufacturing *per se* this is the single largest slice of the pie. Detecting a match between the 13.8 per cent of R&D expenditure in this sector with the advanced manufacturing technologies mission is difficult and requires a separate dedicated survey.

Table 11.7 *R&D expenditure by socio-economic objective, 2001/02*

Socio-economic objective	Percentage
Division 1: Defence	9.31
Division 2: Economic development	60.26
Economic development unclassified	0.18
Plant production & plant primary products	5.50
Animal production & animal primary products	2.51
Mineral resources (excluding energy)	12.73
Energy resources	0.91
Energy supply	3.66
Manufacturing	13.78
Construction	1.19
Transport	4.08
Information & communication services	5.50
Commercial services	3.76
Economic framework	2.91
Natural resources	3.54
Division 3: Society	12.15
Society unclassified	0.05
Health	6.09
Education and training	2.74
Social development & community services	3.28
Division 4: Environment	5.60
Division 5: Advancement of knowledge	12.69
Advancement of knowledge unclassified	0.14
Natural sciences, technologies & engineering	10.81
Social science & humanities	1.74
Total	100.00

Source: DST (2005a)

THE STATE OF RESEARCH AND EXPERIMENTAL DEVELOPMENT

What of biotechnology? This mission (DST 2001) precedes the publication of the R&D strategy. Department of Science and Technology (DST) funding began to flow to the prescribed biotechnology programme in 2003 (R42 million spent) with steady increases (R116 million in 2004) heading toward an annual R150 million commitment (DST 2005b). Measuring biotechnology effort through the R&D survey is complex since biotechnology activity straddles a number of research fields including bioinformatics, genetics, microbiology, biochemistry, chemical engineering, biotechnology, crop science, agro-processing, mineral extraction and pharmacology, to name but a few. In the 1991/92 survey, where multidisciplinary fields were included, total expenditure on biotechnology R&D equalled R49 million with a further R22.2 million on recombinant DNA R&D and bioengineering at R13.9 million. The 2001/02 and 2003/04 survey databases (see Table 11.8) provide expenditures across business, science councils and higher education in the research fields relevant to biotechnology. And here one finds a clear upward trend that points to evidence of the state injection of funds as referred to earlier. It must be borne in mind that biotechnology is an infant industry in South Africa, with but one biotech company listed on the JSE. The biotechnology strategy is seeking to drive a green field research area with strong growth in the science councils (that are closest to the state). However, much biotechnology R&D in the agricultural, medical and biological sciences is considered as producing genetically modified organisms and potential products face consumer resistance, particularly in Africa and Europe.

Table 11.8 *R&D expenditure by biotechnology-related research field, 2002 and 2004 (R millions)*

	Business		Higher education		Science councils		Total	Total
Year	2002	2004	2002	2004	2002	2004	2002	2004
Biochemistry	3.2	4.7	16.5	12.2	3.0	12.7	22.7	30.0
Genetics & mol. biology	5.4	8.1	13.2	14.8	12.5	25.3	31.1	48.4
Microbiology	9.9	7.1	12.6	26.4	14.4	39.7	38.1	73.4
Genetic engineering	0.0	10.9	6.0	3.7	0.0	13.0	6.0	27.6
Biotechnology	7.7	16.2	17.0	21.7	54.8	42.6	79.5	80.5
	26.2	47.0	65.4	78.7	84.7	133.5	177.5	259.9

Source: R&D Survey database

In the case of R&D related to the resource base, the major mining houses and listed chemicals companies are all active, in-house, in alliance with foreign partners and through local and foreign outsourcing.

In general the reported expenditures and informal interviews do not suggest systematic R&D disinvestment as a consequence of globalisation. The multinational players carry out such R&D as makes sense to them in relation to the commodity cycle, exchange rates, and their own history of technology acquisition, development and protection. In a sense they operate independently of the R&D strategy because of their size and economic trends.

This is to some extent true of manufacturing. Business criteria inform decisions on whether or not to invest in R&D and are difficult to get right. The fate of the local textile market is a case in point. Could investment in R&D have saved the industry; could the industry have afforded R&D at the time? Could the industry have moved up market with sufficient speed in relation to the looming end of tariff protection? If the more advanced European market could not get it right, could one expect smaller players to?

This brings us to the last mission, namely technology for poverty reduction. As already noted, the higher education institutions (and not-for-profits) devote considerable resources to R&D in the humanities and social sciences. Much is known about poverty, its distribution, and the drivers. Also from its earliest days the CSIR had a focus on water supply, low-cost energy and housing, and health. One might therefore argue that technologies and community-based solutions for poverty reduction and eradication exist.

Over 2000–2002 there was a larger than normal seasonal outbreak of cholera in KwaZulu-Natal, with more than 114 000 infections and 260 fatalities.[5] The outbreak is a reality of the second economy and water policy; it should not have occurred since technologies to provide potable water exist. The low death rate is a reality of the first economy. Health (and logistics) technologies to manage the emergency-situation outbreak existed. However, these are not directed at the root causes.

The 'technology for poverty reduction' mission is the most elusive, being so inextricably political.

One might say that the R&D strategy and existing R&D activity areas show synergy. However, there are two fairly obvious silences – defence and aerospace, and nuclear energy. Defence and aerospace is a booming export area; the pebble-bed modular reactor (PBMR) receives passing notice. With R&D expenditures around ten per cent of BERD, Eskom is a major concentration of R&D effort. Where does this effort fit in the broader R&D strategy, and how, if it is important, is it to be supported?

The strategy urges the private sector to commit to R&D and declares the intent of doubling state funding over the period of the medium-term expenditure framework, but exactly which state funding is referred to should be clarified. There is funding under the direct control of government departments and funding that resides in the state-owned enterprises. In the 2004 survey, business (plus the not-for-profit sector) accounts for 57.4 per cent of GERD (DST 2005a). If one strips out the public corporations the share of business falls to around 40 per cent. This share would have been even lower in the past before the sell-off of Iscor, Sasol and Telkom. It may thus be argued that the state is still the major player in funding and performing R&D and has played a major role as an incubator of R&D. What have been termed state-parented organisations (Kahn & Blankley in press) form the backbone of the NSI.

So what is the prognosis? Despite losses through emigration and the disequilibrium of organisational transformations, the NSI has shown stability. This stability has worrying dimensions – the low external efficiency of schooling; frozen demographics in the universities; static journal publication and patent volumes in the United States Patent Office. Most disturbing is that registrations through the less onerous Patent Cooperation Treaty are also not growing from the fairly low average base of around 370 per year between 1999 and 2004 (see Table 11.9).

Table 11.9 *Patents registered under the PCT, 1999–2004*

Year	1999	2000	2001	2002	2003	2004
Number	281	386	419	384	355	399

Source: http://www.wipo.int/pct/en

All the evidence is that the NSI appears to be bumping against a ceiling. Mani praises the construction of South African NSI policy instruments but concludes his study with the observation that 'none of the instruments has effectively addressed, or is poised to address, the severe shortage of skilled manpower, not only for simple manufacturing, but also for research' (2002: 210). Mani then calls for human resources policy with an emphasis on science and mathematics as well as industrial policy, drawing parallels with the miasma facing Malaysia. We would concur with his view, noting the fraught debate that has characterised immigration policy development.

To reiterate: the NSI is functioning at the level that South Korea displayed in the mid-1980s. In particular the universities, with their 3 500 FTE researchers, produce around 3 600 ISI-indexed publications. This is no coincidence – one publication per researcher is a typical output level. If the universities are the heart of future R&D, then capacity must at least double over the next five to ten years. A first step could be the provision of R500 million per annum to recruit and retain an additional 500 FTE researchers and doctoral students in the universities in the key areas that the R&D strategy has advocated. Canada and Singapore have understood the scale of new funding the human capital challenge presents. The volume of undergraduate students now accessing higher education has increased dramatically; now is the time to similarly drive postgraduate research with realistic bursaries and staffing levels.

The value of NSI thinking is that it encourages one to approach policy holistically. In this spirit one might lay out the elements of a skills-focused strategy to 'gain and retain'. 'Gain' implies a well-functioning school system stocked with quality science and mathematics teachers, as well as renewed blood in the researcher cadre through effective redress of the previously disadvantaged and suitable public policies for encouraging returnees. It also requires an open-door immigration policy for the skilled. 'Retain' implies career paths and conditions of service that are attractive to masters and doctoral students and their professors. It means abandoning a fixed retirement age and providing more emphasis on centres of excellence. It requires active and acceptable policies to manage and mitigate the HIV/AIDS pandemic.

In summary, previous investment in defence R&D has now spawned a defence and aerospace industry with a specialisation in electronics that yields R3.7 billion of exports (*Engineering News* 25.03.05). R&D investment over the years has yielded a number of returns such as the PBMR. Similarly, Sasol's previous investment in catalysis R&D has yielded international success. There is the positive trend toward an increasing volume of high-technology exports. In the three cases cited, direct or indirect state control on procurement was pivotal. Together with mining these industries constitute the core of business R&D. The questions for government are how it can both retain the benefits of previous investment and at the same time grow an R&D workforce that is more representative of country demographics. Evidence-based reasoning is needed as to why such R&D and innovation expenditures should be supported through concerted cross-ministry and interdepartmental co-operation. It also needs to be shown how such R&D investment contributes to economic growth and indeed whether present economic growth is in any way attributable to this prior investment. If economic growth can reach the seven per cent that Finance Minister Trevor Manuel is mooting, then tax revenue will grow, and funds for high levels of state-backed R&D will be available. Such R&D may then lay the basis for sustained higher-gear economic performance.

Notes

1   Statistics South Africa (2004) *Fact Sheet 5*. Available at http://www.statssa.gov.za. Accessed 20.11.04.
2   See http://education.pwv.gov.za/ Accessed 18.03.05.
3   See http://www.sapma.co.za/ Accessed 18.03.05.
4   These are historic, not rebased GERD:GDP ratios. The argument is independent of the rebasing.
5   Health Systems Trust. Available at http://www.hst.org.za/healthstats/180. Accessed 18.03.05.

References

AS&TS (Association of Scientific and Technical Societies) (1988) *Human resources for science and technology*. Johannesburg: AS&TS.

Blankley W & Kahn MJ (2005) The history of research and experimental development (R&D) measurement in South Africa and some current perspectives, *South African Journal of Science* (forthcoming).

CDE (Centre for Development and Enterprise) (2004) *From laggard to world class: Reforming science and mathematics in South Africa's schools*. Parktown: CDE.

Cilliers J (1996) Defence research and development in South Africa – The role of the CSIR, *African Security Review* 5(5): 39–52.

DACST (Department of Arts, Culture, Science and Technology, South Africa) (1996) *White Paper on science and technology*. Pretoria: DACST.

Dodgson M (2000) Policies for science, technology and innovation in newly industrialising economies. In L Kim & R Nelson (eds.) *Technology, learning and innovation*. Cambridge: Cambridge University Press.

DoE (Department of Education, South Africa) (2002) *National strategy for science, mathematics and technology education*. Pretoria: DoE.

DST (Department of Science and Technology, South Africa) (2001) *A national biotechnology strategy for South Africa*. Pretoria: DST.

DST (2002) The *national research and development strategy*. Pretoria: DST.

DST (2005a) *Key high level results of the 2003/04 survey* (forthcoming).

DST (2005b) *Corporate strategy 2005/06–2008/10*. Pretoria: DST.

FRD-ISP (1997) *Innovation patterns in South African manufacturing firms*. Pretoria: Foundation for Research Development.

Freeman C (1982) *The economics of industrial innovation*. 2nd Edition. London: Francis Pinter.

Granstrand O, Patel P & Pavitt K (1997) Multi-technology corporations: Why they have 'distributed' rather than 'core' competencies, *California Management Review* 39(4):8–25.

Juma C & Yee-Cheong L (2005) *Innovation: Applying knowledge in development*. Earthscan: London.

Kahn MJ (2004) For whom the school bell tolls: Disparities in performance in senior certificate mathematics and physical science, *Perspectives in Education* 22(1): 149–156.

Kahn MJ & Blankley W (in press) Higher education–industry partnerships: Evidence from the 2001/02 R&D survey, *Industry and Higher Education*.

Kahn MJ, Blankley W, Pogue T, Maharajh R & Reddy V (2004) *Flight of the flamingos: A study of the mobility of R&D workers*. Pretoria: HSRC Press.

Kaplan D (2004) Technology and the growth of manufactured exports: Assessing South Africa's performance and policy. Paper presented at DRUID Summer Conference on Industrial Dynamics, Innovation and Development, Elsinore, Denmark, 14–16.06.04.

Lall S (2000) Technological change and industrialization in the Asian newly industrializing countries: Achievements and challenges. In L Kim & R Nelson (eds.) *Technology, learning and innovation*. Cambridge: Cambridge University Press.

Lee W (2000) The role of science and technology policy in Korea's industrial development. In L Kim & Nelson R (eds.) *Technology, learning and innovation*. Cambridge: Cambridge University Press.

Mani S (2000) *Exports of high technology products from developing countries: Is it real or a statistical artifact?* UNU-Intech Working paper 2000 No. 1, Maastricht.

Mani S (2002) The South African experience since 1994. In S Mani (ed.) *Government, innovation and technology policy.* Cheltenham UK: Edward Elgar Publishing.

McGregor R (2004) *Who owns whom.* 24th edition. Florida Hills: Who Owns Whom (Pty) Ltd.

Miles I (2003) Services innovation: Coming of age in the knowledge economy. In B Dankbaar (ed.) *Innovation management in the knowledge economy.* London: Imperial College Press.

Mouton J, Boshoff N & Bailey T (2002) Promoting South African S&T capacities for the 21st century. Background document for a consultative forum organised by the Academy of Science of South Africa (ASSA), Pretoria, 13–14.09.02.

Mowery D & Rosenberg N (1998) *Paths of innovation: Technological change in 20th Century America.* Cambridge: Cambridge University Press.

NACI (National Advisory Council on Innovation) (2002) *Growth and innovation report.* Pretoria: NACI.

OECD (Organization for Economic Cooperation and Development) (1987) *Structural adjustment and economic performance.* Paris: OECD Publishing.

OECD (1993) *Oslo manual.* Paris: OECD Publishing.

OECD (2002) *Proposed standard practice for surveys on research and experimental development.* Paris: OECD Publishing.

OECD (2003) *Main science and technology indicators,* Volume 2003/2. Paris: OECD Publishing.

OECD (2005) *Main science and technology indicators,* Volume 2005/1. Paris: OECD Publishing.

Oerlemans LAG, Pretorius MW, Buys AJ & Rooks G (2003) *Industrial Innovation in South Africa.* Pretoria: University of Pretoria and Eindhoven: Eindhoven University of Technology.

Pavitt K (1999) *Technology, management and systems of innovation.* Cheltenham: Edward Elgar.

Pouris A (2003) South Africa's research publication record. The last ten years, *SA Journal of Science* 99: 425–428.

Rosenberg N (1976) *Perspectives on technology.* Cambridge: Cambridge University Press.

SADC (Southern African Development Community) (1998) *Protocol on education and training.* Manzini: SADC.

Scerri M (1990) R&D and the international competitiveness of the South African manufacturing sector, *SA Journal of Economics* 58(3): 341–356.

Sirilli G (1998) Old and new paradigms in the measurement of R&D, *Science and Public Policy* 24(5): 305–311.

StatCan (Statistics Canada) (2004) *Estimation of research and development expenditures in the higher education sector, 2002–2003*. Working Paper 88F0006XIE-No. 019. Ottawa: Statistics Canada.

Part III: Society

Society: introduction

Sakhela Buhlungu

The five chapters in this section cover important and topical issues – cities, guns, South Africa's Chinese communities, soccer, mathematics and science education – all of which should give the reader a glimpse of the state of South African society today. At first sight, the diversity of these topics suggests that they are unlikely to have anything in common. However, a closer reading of the individual chapters will reveal a common thread running through this section, namely, that social transformation or transition is a contradictory process. It is not simply about moving from an old order to a new one: it is fact that a new order is built on the ruins of the old.

It is common for today's South Africa to be analysed in terms of 'crises' which are said to have arisen as a result of the transition from apartheid to democracy, and which point to weaknesses or problems in the ways that society is being reconstructed. Indeed, this approach is adopted in one way or another by all the authors of the chapters in this section, with Jacklyn Cock in particular arguing that South Africa's gun culture is an indicator of a severe crisis of social division and fragmentation. Yet a focus on 'crisis' may too often stress the negative, whereas the South African transition is also about aspirations, possibilities and achievements. In other words, what often appears as crisis and social disintegration may also contain great possibilities for social renewal. This, perhaps, is the way to understand the discussion that follows in this section.

Freund's chapter on the cities takes us through the maze of transformation of South Africa's urban environment and how this process is both fraught with problems as well as full of possibilities. On the one hand, there are the 'crises' – the decay of inner cities, the emergence of edge cities and gated communities, crime and the proliferation of private security firms, urban struggles over service provision, the impotence of some local government institutions and functionaries and the marginalisation and exclusion of poor communities. On the other hand, however, Freund raises important questions about innovations in policy that are beginning to bear fruit in terms of governance and urban renewal.

Guns are inextricably linked to such social problems as crime and violence that continue to bedevil the transition process in South Africa. Indeed, Cock argues that gun violence has become 'the most dramatic indicator of the social crisis' in our country. Her discussion reminds us that the problem of guns in general, and illegal weapons in particular, is a bitter legacy of war in the southern African region. Political developments of the early 1990s brought to an end what some have termed the 'Thirty Years War' in the region (Saul 1993). During that period, guns had a special importance to those who maintained authoritarian minority regimes as well as those seeking to replace them through armed struggle. But neither of the two sides were able to control the distribution and use of guns initially intended to serve these two opposing camps, and now they are turned on society itself.

Even so, despite the gloom and doom about the appalling violence and crime which is fuelled by gun ownership, legal and illegal, there is light at the end of the tunnel. An indicator of this is the tremendous public response to the government's recent national gun amnesty whereby those who have chosen to hand in their illegally-owned weapons will not be prosecuted. Much more needs to be achieved before South Africa is rid of the scourge of too many guns and its accompanying robust gun culture, yet there are at least some indications that progress is being made towards a safer, and more caring, society.

The last two editions of *State of the Nation* carried chapters on race and identity issues (Mangcu 2003; Erasmus 2004). Both these analyses took it for granted that South Africa is a country of four racial groups as defined under apartheid. Indeed, this assumption can be found in numerous other accounts and in policy and legislative arrangements of the new 'non-racial' democracy. However, Janet Wilhelm's present survey takes us beyond any neo-apartheid 'four nations' understanding of South Africa by tracing the origins and growth of the Chinese community, and challenges us to adopt an understanding of South African society which can account for diversity without relapsing into racial categories. Her discussion also raises several themes which overlap with the other chapters in the section. Among these are corruption by Immigration and Home Affairs' officials who basically sell citizenship and documents to illegal immigrants, the activities of Chinese gangsters (triads) and the notoriously bad wages and

SOCIETY: INTRODUCTION

working conditions which are said to obtain in many Chinese-owned enterprises in South and southern Africa. Yet Wilhelm also stresses that it is necessary to move beyond the negative stereotypes which have attached themselves to the Chinese community, pointing out that its presence and growth through immigration is also likely to have many positive consequences.

The cliché about sport being the best way to unite people rings as true for South Africa as for many other countries. But it was not always so under apartheid. Indeed, sport often played the dubious role of helping maintain the racial enclaves that have been the determining and divisive feature of this society since the days of colonialism. As a result, certain sports came to be variously associated with the different racial groups: for instance, soccer has for many years been identified as a peculiarly 'African' sport, cricket has been seen as 'white', while rugby has been viewed as played particularly by whites even though there has been a decades-long tradition of it having been enjoyed by Africans in the Eastern Cape. However, the re-admission of the country into the international sporting arena since the advent of democracy has provided the country with endless opportunities to use sport as a source of unity. Witness the way in which Rugby World Cup 1995, African Nations Cup (soccer) 1996 and Cricket World Cup 2003, all held in South Africa, were used for broader political purposes of nation-building. Yet the top international tournament that has been coveted by the country's sports people, politicians and business has always been the Soccer World Cup. After a failed bid to secure the hosting of this major international event in 2006, South Africa was subsequently awarded the right to hold the Soccer World Cup in 2010 and many see this as an event that could propel the country's sports and the economy towards a spectacular take-off into another league. The chapter by Merryman Kunene discusses these issues and locates them in the context of the history of soccer in the country. However, he argues that the sweet victory of winning Soccer World Cup 2010 risks being sullied, not only because of the inequality inherent in the structure of international soccer, but also by issues such as corruption, infighting among administrators and the mediocre record of the national soccer team, Bafana Bafana.

The final chapter in this section focuses on a particular manifestation of the persistence of the apartheid legacy, namely mathematics and science education. Vijay Reddy's study demonstrates the continued existence of the gap in mathematics performance between different types of schools. This uneven performance reflects the old apartheid hierarchy wherein white schools had the best performance, followed by Indian, then coloured and, finally, African schools. It is widely acknowledged that the future of the economy and the overcoming of the racial division of labour within it depend on the elimination of this unevenness in mathematics and science education and performance. On the positive side, Reddy's chapter shows that there is some hope that this could change in the future. She shows that there are now more African schools that are part of the consistently better-performing 'established base' of mathematics performers, and that within them the participation rates of African pupils in mathematics education have increased remarkably well.

Three propositions arise out of a close reading of the chapters in this section. First, in thinking about society we should always bear in mind that change is not merely about crisis and social degeneration; it is also about ordinary citizens trying to realise their hopes and aspirations despite the crises that surround them. Too often accounts of societies in transition focus only on the latter while ignoring other dimensions that drive social change.

Second, there is never any certainty about social transformation and to expect such certainty is to misunderstand the way social change occurs. The chapters here show that from the crises, chaos and muddle that emerges from processes of change, it is possible to discern new opportunities, social patterns and positive developments.

The final point is that the building of the new cannot wait for the removal of the old. Indeed, the two always occur simultaneously. That is what is fascinating about trying to understand society in the new South Africa.

References

Erasmus Z (2004) Race and identity in the nation. In J Daniel, R Southall and J Lutchman (eds.) *State of the Nation, 2004–2005*. Cape Town: HSRC Press.

Mangcu X (2003) The state of race relations in post-apartheid South Africa. In J Daniel, R Southall and J Lutchman (eds.) *State of the Nation, 2004–2005*. Cape Town: HSRC Press.

Saul J (1993) *Recolonization and resistance in southern Africa in the 1990s*. Trenton, NJ.: Africa World Press.

12 The state of South Africa's cities

Bill Freund

If you walk into the spacious and attractive lobby of the Nelspruit Civic Centre, constructed atop a hill in the last decade of apartheid (it was completed in 1987), you will find two pledges from the municipality. First, from the municipal vision statement – 'To be a municipality that provides equal opportunities, sustainable services, economic growth and quality of life for all'. Then, from the mission statement, the visitor reads on, 'to alleviate poverty and promote socio-economic development by providing reliable, sustainable and affordable services to all residents of Mbombela'. These promises of equality and prosperity are prolific in equivalent statements everywhere; every municipality in South Africa has adopted similar mottos. In this chapter, I explore the content of these promises as they look in the second decade of post-apartheid South Africa.

Many contributions to this *State of the Nation* series have been path-breaking, often covering areas which receive little or no attention in the research literature. This is hardly the case with the cities of South Africa. South African urban history, although skewed in some respects, has been strongly developed in the last 30 years. The intensity of the anti-apartheid struggle in the urban context in the 1970s and 1980s drew forth another kind of literature. Urban studies form a major part of the diet for students in geography and planning departments at South African universities and, since 1990, a journal of non-disciplinary South African urban studies, *Urban Forum*, exists. Apart from the reflections of planners and geographers, there is a body of literature inspired by the politics of urban discontent since 1994, for some the Achilles heel of the new political order, reflecting a variety of points of view. Moreover, South Africa's best journalists are far from inattentive to urban issues.

This is not to say that there are not major gaps. Urban economics are not well-developed nor is it very clear how to situate the South African urban situation in the broader African or international one. Most of the best work on South

African cities focuses on the biggest – Cape Town, Durban and especially Johannesburg. The smaller urban communities are very neglected. I have seen my task in this chapter, however, primarily as guiding the reader through a given literature rather than offering a new research agenda. Nonetheless, given my familiarity with Durban, I have tried to supplement that knowledge with interviews with urban officials in Johannesburg and Nelspruit.[1] For the sake of brevity and cohesion, I have decided to divide the discussion into three sections. The first explores the development of post-apartheid urban governance. The second examines some of the determining material forces that push urban change while the third looks at the extremely contentious issue of 'reliable, sustainable and affordable services'.

Urban government in the new South Africa

Before the end of apartheid, South African cities were internationally notorious for their racially divided structuring. Of course, most cities exhibit inequalities that mark histories of colonisation and class formation but the South African case was both extreme and codified by law. Even before 1948 there was a legal racial divide between land owned by black and white. White politics aimed at legitimating the white city as having exclusive rights to urban development within what was determined to be white territory. In practice, this proved unworkable; the real economic development of South Africa drew men and women of all races into the cities in increasing numbers. The Group Areas Act of 1950 was the cornerstone of proclamations that allowed for the racially exclusive development of urban residential areas followed by massive obligatory removals, almost entirely of people of colour. The two racial groups recognised by the South African system, coloureds and Indians, were assigned particular areas to live in. More grudgingly, the state acknowledged the necessity for some Africans to live and work in the city and consequently gave individuals limited rights and created townships for African residence although the emphasis was put as much as possible either on hostel construction or on urban development in the bantustan territories assigned to Africans. Whites possessed the lion's share of urban property, enjoyed dramatically better amenities and facilities and profited from the rates system which taxed industries and commercial property located on what was defined as their turf. They participated in a system of democratic elected local government that derived basically from the United Kingdom in its claims and remits.

Much of the force of insurgency against the apartheid system from the 1970s onward stemmed directly from the contradictory nature of this system and the denial of effective citizenship to what had become the majority of the urban population. In addition, however, the attempts to reform the apartheid system in its final decade of existence through providing somewhat more stability and somewhat more resources to the township population served mainly to aggravate the situation. Large numbers of squatters began to proliferate on the bantustan fringes of the cities, outside what had been small rural centres, in the backyards of township dwellers and elsewhere. The gradual introduction of electrification and other services attached, however, to demands for regular service payments, were intense bones of contention. It proved impossible for the authorities to instal black subaltern bureaucracies that could govern this situation effectively; policemen and councillors were frequently expelled from their homes and met with violence and death. For this reason, the first important step in changing the way cities were governed was the promotion of elite alliances (civic militants, business figures, officials) in the large cities to stabilise a very fragile situation. In Durban, this was Operation Jump Start (Robinson & Boldogh 1994), in Johannesburg the Central Wits Metropolitan Chamber (Tomlinson, Bremner & Mangcu 2003) while in Cape Town, the Metropolitan Negotiating Forum was created in 1992 (Pieterse 2002). These fora considered the future of the fragmented urban areas. In 1993 the Government Transition Act paved the way for the reconstitution of urban space in the country. The Durban Metro, as it was to exist after 1996, for instance, had to be formed from more than 40 separate administrations with widely different levels of capacity and cultures of governance.

A second stage was entered from 1995/96 when unified urban governments based on elections (which still by virtue of the sunset clause agreement of 1994 were not on a one person, one vote basis) were established throughout the country. In the big cities, a two-tier structure was created which allowed an uncertain autonomy to councils embracing subsections of the big metropoles. This was an arrangement which worked quite effectively in Durban, partly due to the success of Operation Jump Start and the apparent early arrival of an 'urban growth coalition' on the scene but problems in Johannesburg, Pretoria and Cape Town proved more serious. In general, cities were now being administered by an uncomfortable combination of bureaucracies from the old regime, sometimes very competent but only within the purview of serving a relatively affluent population along familiar lines, and inexperienced newly-arrived officials and elected representatives who often came from a struggle tradition. These latter figures may have had little sense at first of what was feasible; they were likely used to thinking of the white town as a cornucopia of wealth (Beall, Crankshaw & Parnell 2002).

In Cape Town and Pretoria, Mabin (2004) suggests that the sub-councils achieved problematic autonomy in a context where the African National Congress (ANC) was weak. Johannesburg, the biggest and wealthiest city, was marked by particularly antagonistic politics that reflected the past. It fell quickly into a financial crisis which became obvious and serious by 1997. A major feature of the crisis was the continued non-payment of electricity bills. Bond points out that by this time the national government had shown the way to a solution along lines he calls neoliberal insofar as the pride of place was given to the private sector and the emphasis on internationally modelled governance solutions, often by way of consultancies informed by World Bank and aligned models (Bond 2003; Mabin 2004). Bond has also emphasised to me the reluctance of the Ministry of Finance, which could have eased the situation, to consider any alternative solution. Development had to follow along the fault lines of the private sector's line of investment, never against. The Urban Development Strategy of 1994 already had diverged markedly from the Reconstruction and Development Programme (RDP), which Patrick Bond partially devised on behalf of various NGOs, and on which basis the ANC campaigned in the 1994 elections.

For Johannesburg, the management model that was then put into place is associated with the work of Khetso Gordhan and was elaborated in the eGoli plan of 2001. Gordhan's success in 'turning around' Johannesburg was such as to win the praise of World Bank president James Wolfensohn (Wolfensohn 2001). The key element here was the creation of self-supporting and self-sustaining functional units that operated according to business plans that provided limited, controllable briefs. This system can be called 'corporatisation'.[2] Even where privatisation was not in question, these units were intended to run as though they operated within the private sector. Moreover, 'strategic' partnerships with business were strongly encouraged. This might mean experienced foreign service providers but increasingly in the Mbeki years it has come as well to embrace black economic empowerment (BEE) firms given the state's commitment to the creation of a mainstreamed black business class. Cross-subsidies and decommodified provision of basic needs were not part of this conception. In its own terms, this plan has been quite successful. Johannesburg has been restored to something like fiscal health and gradually a new bureaucratic ethos has been established on a stable basis.

However, this only represents one aspect of what was seen as an administrative crisis of the cities in the later 1990s. One needs also to mention the enormous divergence in capacity and in wealth (given the presence of the rates system) between large, rich municipalities and poor, small ones with the biggest problems often in the smallest towns and the ex-bantustan urban areas where little development of any sort was taking place. In any event, the 1996 arrangements were not considered permanent. From shortly thereafter, the government moved towards reconstructing cities once again. This was heralded in the Urban Development Framework document of 1997.

Reorganisation began to take shape from 1998 with the proclamation of a new *White Paper on local government* (RSA 1998). This was followed by the Municipal Demarcation Act of 1998, which set into place the Municipal Boundaries Commission, the Municipal Structures Act of 1998, which distinguished between the differential status of municipalities based primarily on size, varying the extent of their powers, and the Municipal Systems Act of 1999, which dealt with their capacities and notably with the systematic institution of integrated development plans (IDPs). This menu of legislation, with further supplementation, formed the basis of the present system of municipal administration.

The new set of legislation called for a system of governance in which three layers – national, provincial and local – would co-exist, each with distinct if not always clarified powers which did not overrule one another (subsidiarity). Here too language put an unprecedented emphasis on local government as an agent of development. In this context, the IDP began to be hailed (from the time of the Local Government Transition Amendment Act of 1996 but at first largely nominally or only slowly to be formulated) as the format through which planning in urban areas could be put forward (Pieterse 2003). Each municipality is meant to develop, research and constantly modify a functional and functioning IDP.

One should probably also note some other linkages that have been created. The cities themselves form an association – the South African Local Government Association (SALGA) – under the current chairmanship of Smangaliso

Mkatshwa of Tshwane (Pretoria). SALGA meets annually and serves to create a common discourse among urban bureaucrats and politicians. It is firmly tied into the national administration. At the same time, some of the most forward-looking of the big city administrators formed the South African Cities Network in 2002 which is restricted to the nine major urban centres with the highest level of autonomy; this organisation seems to be falling more directly under central state control. Finally, a financial information network links the financial officers of the big cities.

The Boundaries Commission generally considered greater shopping and commuting areas to form the basis of the new urban boundary network but it faced a particular problem in dealing with South Africa's largest metropolitan area. The largest two South African provinces – the Transvaal and the Cape – were each divided into four and three parts respectively. Gauteng province, carved out of the southern Transvaal, consisted largely of contiguous metropolitan areas. If they were to be joined, they would be very disproportionate to the rest of urban South Africa and the point of having a separate provincial versus local government would be completely unclear. Thus the East Rand cities and townships were made a metropolitan Unicity called Ekurhuleni, which actually abuts Johannesburg. In consequence, both Ekurhuleni and Johannesburg are roughly on the same demographic scale as Ethekwini, the Durban municipality and Cape Town. Khayalami, in-between Pretoria and Johannesburg, was dissolved.

However, the problem is not entirely solved. In Gauteng, the overwhelmingly urban province remains ambitious to involve itself in urban development and the well-known Blue IQ[3] set of initiatives actually emanates from it. Relations are not entirely smooth between provincial and local administrations. In the provinces of KwaZulu-Natal and the Western Cape respectively, the wealth of the two big cities – Durban and Cape Town – creates an uncomfortable balance given that the provinces have little means of raising revenues whilst the cities, through the continuation of the property rates system, have substantial incomes. At the time of writing the Western Cape provincial government is attempting to raise new revenues through new forms of taxation to meet this situation. Instead of the defunct Khayalami and Lekoa, which covered the Vaal Triangle, the Cities Network included the areas emanating from the old centres of Port Elizabeth, East London, Pietermaritzburg and Bloemfontein.

More remarkable though, as the total number of municipalities recognised was reduced substantially (843 to 284), was the melding of urban and rural areas, ex-bantustans and farmlands, into single development-orientated 'urban' areas from 2001. Thus the Mangaung municipality, including Bloemfontein, has in fact a very light population density for the entire area covered, a mere 103 people to the square kilometre, barely one-twentieth of the figure for Johannesburg (that is, 1962 people per km^2) (SACN 2004). Thus the Nelspruit municipality has become the centre of Mbombela, a region that includes parts of what was the KaNgwane homeland, the formerly white town of White River and numerous working farms. In rural areas, land is beginning to be evaluated along urban lines with farms paying rates and chiefly administered land surveyed. In the case of even smaller urban centres, the municipalities are pooled into districts.[4] This is the obvious but quite original response to the problem of poor capacity and concentrations of poverty in the countryside, and administering these new territories will represent a huge challenge.

On the whole this can be seen as a remarkable transformation which represents a major achievement. Outsiders often fail to grasp how thorny and complex a massive restructuring of government agencies can be. There does seem now to be a growing sense of stability and increase of capacity in the system.

Having said this, two obvious problems remain. First, there is the continued remarkable inequality between municipalities. The failure of administration in the poorer and more rural areas has not really been remedied. Some 126 out of 284 municipalities were still described as having 'little or no capacity' by a government audit in late 2004 (*Sunday Independent*). The Mbeki government has in exasperation begun to send administrators directly from ministries to such areas (Project Consolidate) and to make workers in development projects, 'community development workers', directly responsible to the centre (*Weekly Mail & Guardian* 18–24.02.05). Continued financial woes in many municipalities (and not only the small ones: Cape Town is in considerable difficulties at the moment) is to be met with a Municipal Finance Management Act, to regulate and make transparent financial affairs but, at the present moment, the problems continue.

This brings us to the second major dilemma, the creation of local government that is responsible and vibrant, especially where the mass of previously excluded people and the poor can be found. Here we broach the issue of whether the remarkable shifts in governance are actually helping to resolve the urban problems addressed in abstract and philosophical terms in the first paragraph of this chapter. The operating philosophy of so-called governance in the cities follows the lines of what Philip Harrison, using international experience, called 'centralised decentralisation' in a talk at the University of KwaZulu-Natal in February 2005. This presupposes initiatives and energy forthcoming from below but where the centre determines policy initiatives in a co-ordinated manner allowing only limited deviation. There is no question that nationally this approach has so far been very successful in creating simultaneous objectives and practices everywhere as a study of IDPs will reveal.

Whether democratic initiatives from below are allowed significant space in reality is, however, a different question. During the political transition the militant urban civics created the South African National Civics Organisation (Sanco) in 1992. Sanco is a member of the National Economic Development and Labour Council (Nedlac), and is supposed to be a major player in the formation of national policy. In fact, it occupies an uneasy place in-between the government and the ANC on the one hand and complainants protesting against the failures of government urban policy on the other (Heller 2003; Mayekiso 2003; Zuern 2004). The weakness of Sanco is exemplified by a Vaal Triangle activist: 'We are no more a home of boycotters; we encourage people to pay for their services, but we also say to government that they should be sympathetic because people are unemployed' (Zuern 2004). At best, assessments by Zuern and Heller stress that Sanco can serve as an intermediary, a 'pillow' that cushions the punches thrown from either side of the bed. At a national level especially, Sanco is dominated by the ANC and led by top figures in the national government – Elke Zuern terms this more kindly as the enactment of a 'brokerage role'. At local levels, its branches fitfully do represent local interests in poor and needy communities. It is also true that its finances have recently been bathed in scandal. No analyst would give it top marks in successfully bridging the gap between the people and the government.

Elected councillors under democratic conditions should effectively represent their voters but observers tend to concur that this is not often the case. Part of the problem is that the ANC, which now controls all major and almost all minor municipalities, is a huge patronage system that offers great opportunities for upward promotion and operates on a philosophy of 'redeployment' of those found useful and talented. A recent initiative to resolve this problem has lain in the creation of ward committees, currently being introduced in many parts of the country. Cameron (n.d.) reckons that these are also ineffective and that administrative power in the cities, even *vis-à-vis* elected councillors, is growing (as it did under the old regime).

Still less does the vaunted world of participatory public consultation work effectively. The stakeholder democracy idea, whatever its value in wealthy social democracies, falters in the context of a country where some exhibit so much more voice than others. In some cases, the community comes to be represented by special interests who wish to use their position to provide some advantage for themselves. In many more, there is a propensity for 'highly organised and educated middle-classes to hijack participation forums and processes' (Pieterse 2002: 24). In considering the formulations emanating from the state and the Urban Development Framework (UDF) in particular, Pieterse estimates that: 'The UDF displays a romanticised perspective on "communities", an uncritical celebration of partnerships and an over-optimistic approach to what integrated development can achieve' (2003: 128). As Pieterse writes, there is a mystification of the presence through documentation of a plan for integrated development without serious exploration of contradictions or whether any of the desired outcomes will come from this process due to integration alone. Many good intentions are not really supported with funding or personnel and there is little sense of priorities. In the second section of this paper we shall explore where this leads in terms of urban power, and in the third, we shall try to say something about the struggles between urban community activists and the state.

Development trajectories and the cities

To what extent are municipalities fulfilling their development mandates as articulated more and more sharply since the proclamation of the Urban Development Framework in 1997 and the 1998 *White Paper on local government*? This is not an easy question to answer. The presence of well-wrought IDPs and Economic Development Departments in the more progressive cities may indeed provide a helpful facilitative environment for the private sector to invest in but in fact the major shifts of the past decade have depended on other kinds of imperatives that drive that sector. Moreover, the dominance of the national market by big companies and the intensifying dominance of commerce by franchise arrangements make individual initiatives from within a locality unpredictable and difficult. The emphasis the national state lays on (short-term) competitiveness and the immediate need to extend the tax base tend to govern bureaucratic impulses (see Turok 2001 or Pieterse 2002 for judgements along these lines). Indeed, Pieterse suggests that conservative bureaucrats, whose ideas derive from the old regime allied effectively with trade unionists afraid of change that might result in lost jobs, tend to make change that much more difficult.

One might start by looking at population growth. A media cliché is that a 'rural' population, coupled with typically very exaggerated numbers of foreigners, is flooding the city and creating huge challenges for the state. The reality is that urban growth probably is largely governed by the availability of jobs and services and is extremely uneven. According to the *State of the Cities Annual Report for 2004* (SACN 2004), growth has been quite rapid in the Johannesburg and Ekurhuleni municipalities (despite industrial decline and downturn in the latter) and in the City of Tshwane-Pretoria.[5] However, growth is more moderate in Cape Town and particularly in Durban. In the other four associated city municipalities, Buffalo City (East London), Nelson Mandela (Port Elizabeth), Mangaung (Bloemfontein) and Umsundizi (Pietermaritzburg), it has been very slow indeed despite the successes of the automobile industry in the former two. Overall the picture is one that would emphasise increases in migration during the political transition period but afterwards slowing down very considerably. In the nine cities as a whole, the population rate of increase in 1996–2001 was only 2.8 per cent per annum compared to 3.22 per cent over the entire 1946–2001 period despite the absence of passes and other legal impediments to movement compared to the apartheid years. The rate of population growth varied from an annual estimate of more than four per cent in Johannesburg and Ekurhuleni (well over what planners had estimated a decade before) to below one per cent in Buffalo City and Nelson Mandela and just slightly above in Umsundizi, much lower than what was expected (SACN 2004). Of course, the migrants are mainly poor individuals with little capital and limited skills – and, especially initially, their movements are often tentative with much straddling between domiciles – but they probably have a good rational sense of where resources are to be found. Economic growth, where it does occur, is accompanied by demographic growth and new forms of pressure. This can cause serious planning problems such as the environmental threats and traffic concerns that mount in greater Cape Town.[6]

If one considers smaller municipalities, the range is even greater. Rustenberg has racked up the highest growth rates based on the platinum boom (more than six per cent compound economic growth rate from 1996–2001), platinum now rivalling gold as an export earner (*Mail & Guardian* 05–11.11.04). Nelspruit, the core of Mbombela municipality, measured on its own has grown even faster with more than seven per cent growth per annum in business value in recent years, while the overall Mbombela population is growing at approximately the same rate as Johannesburg/Ekurhuleni.[7] This city is a new provincial capital situated on the N4 to Pretoria and profits from massive commercial business on the part of residents of nearby Maputo in Mozambique. It has a strong agricultural base as the closest source of semi-tropical and tropical fruit (mangoes, bananas and so on) to Gauteng and a tourist base given the proximity of the Kruger National Park. The absence of squatter settlements in the vicinity helps account for moderate crime rates in the centre and attracts a middle-class migration in search of an attractive locality in relatively close reach from the metropolises of Gauteng. By contrast, the *State of the Cities Report* notes municipalities that are actually losing population fairly rapidly with Klerksdorp in the North-West province leading the fall most recently. The once thriving gold-mine towns of the northern Free State such as Welkom and Virginia are also bywords for decline (SACN 2004; *Mail & Guardian* 05–11.11.04). In general, shifts in commercial life particularly are tending to cause a concentration of activity and wealth in a smaller number of towns whereby many little centres are losing their *raison d'etre*. Other factors play a role as well – the decline of mines and other extractive activities on the one hand, the pull of tourism and leisure activities on the other. There is little reason to think that the local state has been able to do more than channel or plan new business activities as opposed to promoting any serious counter-hegemonic development that goes against the path of least resistance. A new policy wave to refocus development is the institution of area-based local economic development initiatives; it is unclear yet whether these will make significant headway as here too the competitiveness approach is so dominant.

There is a not entirely fortunate tendency to comprehend all significant contemporary economic and spatial changes in terms of some tsunami-like force called globalisation. At best, this needs far more definition and explanation to be applicable or have any predictive power (Harrison 2003). It is, for instance, the case in South Africa that job creation is happening far more rapidly and directly in finance and commerce than in industry, a pattern observed in the majority of countries today[8] (SACN 2004). However, the preceding discussion and further evidence certainly suggest that the presence of public administration (note the relatively rapid growth of Pretoria and the provincial capitals in general) attracts business and people, not a dictate of neoliberal philosophy.

A few writers have correctly stressed that the urban regime in place today privileges tendencies emanating from the private sector which have been in place in South Africa for a long time. Central here is what is usually termed suburbanisation, which involves the spread of detached single-family housing units, an interiorised and family-orientated mode of consumer expenditure, the provision of good highways allowing for very rapid road transit and the creation of shopping malls and, increasingly, other service/finance/warehousing commercial activities on greenfield sites far from the traditional city centres. Mabin (2005) has argued that this is indeed the central impulse that is in place with regard to changes in urban space. It is one that marginalises those that are unneeded by corporate investor plans. The suburban impulse, linked closely to the provision of mass automobile ownership in the white population from the 1960s (the state playing a key role in the development of the automobile assembly industry in the country from that time) and the critical highway construction that followed, has been potent for a long time. 'Decentralisation started in the early 1960s...Together with the construction of the freeways, pull factors rather than push factors propelled decentralisation' (Tomlinson & Larsen 2003: 44).

Nor is it entirely spontaneous. As Goga (2003) shows, it has in effect been spearheaded and organised by South Africa's heavily concentrated private finance sector so directly involved in property ownership. Many writers have commented on the remarkable shift of business activity in Johannesburg from the old central business district (CBD), which reached its apogee of investment and activity in the generation after 1933 – the golden years of the old South Africa – to suburban Sandton, which is now beginning to equal it in estimated property value.[9] Goga explains how finance essentially organised this shift in Johannesburg. However, similar processes have been in play in virtually every sizeable South African town. The dramatic development of an American-style edge city in Umhlanga to the north of Durban has much to do with the planning initiatives of the landowning sugar giant Tongaat Hulett, itself majority owned by Anglo American.

I have argued elsewhere that, in fact, despite the absence of current terminology, there is also nothing new about urban officials taking crucial steps to invite businesses to settle in their towns and establish close links with them (Freund 2001). For instance, the industrial development of the East Rand depended on the foresight of town fathers making unneeded mining land available for industrial sites at limited or no cost. The British tradition followed in South Africa certainly permitted the municipality to run effective services that would benefit citizens and local capitalism as a whole (gas services, public transport and so on). Under the banner of today's private–public partnerships, it is very possible that the existing major corporate players will be able largely to obtain their own plans for development with the assistance of public sponsorship and moneys. In Durban, it is not only the Umhlanga development that is significant this way but also the creation and extension of the International Conference Centre and the refurbishment of the South Beachfront (uShaka Marine Park) which can be noted (Freund & Lootvoet forthcoming).

Another observation frequently made concerns the importance of security in this spatial shift. Considerable attention has been given to limited access housing tracts, boom gates, security huts, high walls and the widespread employment of private security companies (see for instance, Czeglédy 2003; Bremner 2002). Writers on this theme often have in mind by contrast an idealised version of the interactive, street-lively European city where community consciousness is strong and public space shapes identity. It is questionable whether this ideal much interests South African suburbanites of any colour but the alternative ideal of carefree family existence is potent. Security drives the spatial movement of capital forward.

Although violent crime is largely found in poor urban areas, crimes against property are by contrast prolific in rich ones and fear of violence is far from irrational as measured by crime rates compared to most other countries, even in affluent suburbs. Fulfilling at least some of the desire of the middle class to get out of harm's way has been fundamental to the playing out of these dramatic shifts. Turok has noted that whether in terms of business or residence, the layout of economic activity and class is as dramatically divided in Cape Town today as ever. Businesses move significantly and particular neighbourhoods change character but the broad map of rich and poor in the city does not change; indeed, it arguably is becoming more extreme (Turok 2001).

Counterbalancing movement on the part of the state, the main actor here, has been significant but limited. The ANC has been increasingly perturbed by the apparent abandonment of downtowns, and especially the Johannesburg CBD. In fact this abandonment only represents part of the reality. Since the beginning of the 1980s, the arrival of the shared taxi made town centres easily accessible to black township dwellers and the white upper and middle class began to make itself increasingly scarce. However, the CBDs are intensely used commercially by large working-class throngs. Their streets are densely populated by 'informal' traders and while some residential property has turned into slum, much of it is now inhabited by people with secure jobs who look for an alternative to the single-family township unit.[10] Turning to leisure, you cannot promenade on the Durban Golden Mile beachfront, still very well maintained and secured through city management, without thinking that some aspects of urban life have genuinely opened up to wide swathes of the local population. This is a major central urban amenity which is now very accessible to township dwellers. Thus the picture is not entirely negative.

It is in Johannesburg that the state has placed the most important efforts involved in revitalising the city centre, starting with the creation of the Inner City Office in 1998. Early efforts contained a litany of failures in areas such as co-operative housing for low-income tenants and planned market space for informal traders (Oelofse 2003; Gotz & Simone 2003). Continuing projects include planning middle-income rental and purchased flat accommodation as well as a massive effort to create more security and fight crime (camera placement, community courts, metropolitan police and so forth). However, whether or not the private sector will take the strong hint and move back into the CBD (or use it in new profitable ways) is still largely uncertain. This effort is admired and may be imitated in Durban and Nelspruit while Cape Town's old office blocks are beginning to experience a genuine gentrification.[11]

In an integrated city model, transport is normally a key factor. And yet, despite calls for improved public transport as a means of fighting sprawl and creating compaction, there has been relatively little action in this regard. Thus Durban has actually privatised its public bus company (to the benefit of BEE businessmen) in the questionable hope that a city regulator alone could create the basis for improved public transport (Bellengere et al. n.d.). Cape Town has become more and more spread out and transport clearly is a problem for many poor people but in reality plans have not really developed to change the situation. The suburban trains are rundown and in the massive African township of Khayelitsha, the large majority of African users do not normally pay their fare at all (Behrens & Wilkinson 2003).[11] Taxis have allowed relatively poor people much better access to the city but the impact of growing oil prices here is making this less and less the case. A spectacular part of Gauteng's Blue IQ initiative (see note 3) is the potential train route intended to run from Johannesburg to Pretoria but this train is deliberately being priced at a level to exclude the poor; indeed, its routing is intended to make access from townships difficult (Bénit & Gervais-Lambony 2005). In this sense, it is the opposite of classic plans to unify a city and open up enclaves of the poor through transport initiatives. It was only after protests that some access from Alexandra, the main black township in northern Johannesburg, was envisioned at all.

Currently, there is disquiet at government level about the failure to de-densify and restructure South African cities. Stimulated particularly by the Ministry of Housing, there are plans afoot to move in this direction. However, it is far too soon to begin to evaluate these plans and their outcomes. The situation as it stands in 2005 is that economic development is proceeding in South African cities and some are becoming spatially transformed in consequence quite rapidly. However, the process is mostly driven and largely spearheaded by the dictates of the private sector along long-established lines. Attempts to 'unite a divided city', to steal the title of Beall, Crankshaw and Parnell (2002), have been only very limited in success and defer to the preferences of the market which is largely heading in quite different directions although the beneficiaries today may be better defined in class than in race terms. This balance – or imbalance – certainly is part of current international practice but it is not true that it is an unquestioned imperative everywhere (le Galès 2002). While the post-apartheid government has been very eager to overcome any sense of white exclusivity or dominance, there is little discussion perceivable of how the character of growth today may be hampering redistribution and genuine restructuring of the city in the interest of breaking down historic barriers (Mabin 2004).

There is a final question that can be raised although few have done so (but see Mabin 2004 and Lootvoet & Khan 2001). Can locally-based growth coalitions constructed along the lines of accumulation and growth form significant strategic alliances that may have national political implications? Would this require effective alliances of new and old city-based elites? Here it is too early to tell. At present, the trends are not pointing this way at all. So far the ANC has put measures in place that firmly control any deviant local developments but with time and the possible decline of the centralising post-liberation ethos, this may become a fruitful way of looking at future city development.

Struggles over services: a new age of urban revolt?

In 1990, a truce known as the Soweto Accord was called to the organised urban struggles against the state in that large and famous township. The apparently structured boycott of the late 1980s had focused on five key demands:
- The arrears owed by people who have supported the boycott must be written off;
- The houses must be transferred to the people;
- Services must be upgraded;
- Affordable service charges must be established; and
- A single tax base for Johannesburg and Soweto must be introduced. (Tomlinson et al. 2003: 9)

In this section, I shall consider whether these demands have been met in Soweto or nationally in the ensuing decade and a half and why the last, once very critical, item has proven to be inadequate to establishing a new civil order.

There is little question, in this regard, about the intentions of the ANC. The post-apartheid government has systematically moved to provide black people with the previously rarely available accoutrements of contemporary urban living as defined by the lifestyle of suburbanised whites – secure independent brick homes with supplies of electricity and clean water in communities equipped with schools, health clinics and other such amenities. The state has, in fact, provided more than R1.5 million in subsidies for house purchase in a decade and has, particularly in urban areas, dramatically extended the availability of electricity and clean water. However, with its other hand as it were, it has also insisted on beneficiaries becoming conscientious bill and ratepayers, supporting the 'corporatised' structures of the local state.

The so-called delivery issue is discussed elsewhere in this volume so the following pages try to give only a brief introduction to this crucial issue. The main point I wish to make is that the core ANC policies in this regard are deeply contradictory. ANC economic policy has been hostile to the state creating, or facilitating the creation of, stable permanent jobs below the professional levels. As a result and given the thrust of private investment, South African cities witness massive levels of unemployment and irregular or underemployment. Poor South Africans, and especially women, live in an environment of serious violence, massive health problems and high levels of unpredictability and change. As a result, they are not able to participate in the interactive system the state has in mind except fitfully and tend to become, or wish to become, simple recipients of free services. Mabin has powerfully described these contradictions as follows:

> Many of government's political supporters live in areas whose hopelessness in economic development terms is widely accepted; that public funds created the dilemma under apartheid; and that no amount of fancy consulting work will make it easy for the vast majority in such areas to gain access to decent livelihoods. The consequence is that on one hand government faces a distinct political need to spend money where many of its supporters are; yet on the other, the long-term returns on doing so are likely to be very low indeed. (2004: 12)

It can be said that those black people who can be fitted into professional or at least white-collar jobs are those who have made big gains since 1994. Regular township home-dwellers, especially if there is at least one reliable breadwinner, have gained to a moderate extent on average. Even here, it is noticeable that only a very small upper layer of township dwellers is profiting from the recent dramatic rise in property values; few township houses ever change hands through legal sale while repossessions are a major phenomenon even towards the top end of the value scale[13] (FinMark Trust 2004). Others, of whom there are many millions, have often gained very little (Emdon 2003). The failure of the Seven Buildings scheme in Hillbrow, Johannesburg – where buildings were meant to be 'saved' through co-operative ownership but owners were unable or unwilling to repay bonds or pay for maintenance – was an early public indication of this situation in the city centre milieu (Oelofse 2003). Beall, Crankshaw and Parnell (2003), in observing Soweto suggest, moreover, that there is a fairly marked and noticeable divide between established families with long histories of residence in Johannesburg and backyard tenants and others whose urban roots lie only in the last two or three decades.[14]

The Urban Development Framework proposed urban housing that would be:
- Spatially, racially and socio-economically integrated;
- Economically sustainable;
- Democratically instituted with participatory planning;
- Environmentally sustainable; and
- Adequately financed through the public sector and through public–private partnerships. (Irurah & Boshoff 2003: 257)

However, in operational terms, 'in the field of housing, national policy has called for the delivery of the maximum number of housing subsidies at minimum cost' (Watson 2003: 151). As a result, much of the new housing is located on the edge of established black townships far from city centres, reinforcing old spatial forms of differentiation.[15] This has allowed little space for considering environmental issues or for pursuing the theoretical goal of urban compaction as Watson points out. In fact, the state often saved money by making use of land that already had been allocated for urban development in this way during the late apartheid years.

Let us take an example. Evaton West is such a development adjoining the Golden Highway which joins Johannesburg to the Vaal Triangle cities on its south-west. Created in 1996, this is a built environment characterised by the cheapest possible RDP houses. Electricity is available but most people cannot afford to make regular use of it. Water meters are due to be introduced and are the source of much fear on the part of inhabitants who anticipate serious reductions in their ability to use the water because of costs. There is so far only one primary school and the community development forum with which the state is prepared to deal is not very effective. As Vally and Ciarno point out in the *Sunday Independent* (23.10.05), to the naked eye, there is only a limited amount of improvement compared to the situation before the ANC took power. Similar observations have been made about the gigantic settlement of Orange Farm, south of Soweto (Coalition Against Water Privatisation 2004) and Diepsloot, the largest community of poor, black people between Johannesburg and Pretoria.[16] The latter was described by Mabin (2005) and Beall, Crankshaw and Parnell (2002) as looking much like an apartheid resettlement camp. Nor, as they point out, does the state really know how to deal with the massive population living in 'illegally' constructed backyard shacks in Soweto. It is fair comment to suggest that the dilemma here is not so much what the ANC has done as the limits to what it has done, or seen as possible to do, in terms of its overall sense of budget constraints, its partnership with business and perhaps its vision.

In many areas, there has been a sharp response to these inadequacies charged by some continuity with past protest traditions. Over the past decade, impromptu organisations, often inspired by NGO involvement, have emerged with new leadership and demanded change. Conflict has been most intense over evictions for non-payment, electricity and water cut-offs and the installation of prepaid meters for electricity. However, other issues have also come up at times, including the corrupt or incompetent behaviour of ANC councillors. In the early post-apartheid years, the government instituted Operation *Masakhane* as a means of cajoling township residents to pay their bills which had mounted to dizzying levels. As we have seen, it was electricity non-payment that brought about the Johannesburg fiscal crisis by 1997. Experiments with prepaid meters brought about a massive protest in Tembisa where they were vandalised and destroyed. The next year in Tsakane (also in the present Ekurhuleni) the threat of evictions led to the destruction of considerable municipal property, one claimed death and councillors were forced to flee.

Thereafter all the major cities have witnessed bouts of serious confrontation. In Johannesburg, the institution of eGoli 2001 led to the formation of the Soweto Electricity Crisis Committee with the training of so-called struggle electricians to reinstitute connections and attempts to prevent cut-offs (Bond 2004). Trevor Ngwane, an ANC councillor who took up the struggle, was dismissed for insubordination and became a key figure in the establishment of the Anti-Privatisation Forum. Alexandra, the most important old surviving township from pre-apartheid days in Gauteng, has been the scene of important resistance to these pressures (2001 resistance to apparent forced resettlement plans of some sections) and remains notorious for the extent to which its residents rarely pay bills. Its residents are R750 million in debt.[17] The Coalition Against Water Privatisation was started around events in Phiri, Soweto in 2003 (Coalition Against Water Privatisation 2004). In Cape Town, evictions in Tafelsig occasioned the rise of the Western Cape Anti-Eviction Campaign, while the attempt to evict a large number of very poor families for non-payment of debts from housing erected as part of an apparent liberal experiment by the private sector during the late 1980s in Mandela Park, on the edge of Khayelitsha, led to sustained conflict and growing popular organisation (Desai & Pithouse 2004). In Durban, the threat of evictions touched off the creation of the Concerned Citizens' Forum which transmuted into the Durban Social Forum in 2001 and for a time linked protests in many communities (Desai 1999; Dwyer 2004).

Smaller cities have also not been untouched by this spirit of revolt. In recent weeks (2005), a slew of protests in hitherto obscure northern Free State municipalities (Viljoenskroon, Vrede, Memel, Warden, Hennenman, Ventersburg) have blocked highways and burnt down commercial buildings. Local politics have been part of the picture here and demands for removing particular councillors featured prominently (*Sunday Independent* 26.09– 03.10.04; *Mail & Guardian* 11–17.02.05, 18–24.02.05; see also Krog 2003 in which the distinguished poet talks about the pitifully bad administration of her native Free State town of Kroonstad).

Politics is the reason why numerous eloquent writers have fastened their gaze on these confrontations as the potential embers with which one might create a new kind of liberation or left politics in South Africa, or at least a continuing sense of consciousness that challenges the state (for instance, Desai 1999; Bond 2002; Barchiesi 2004). This is a predictable reaction to the growing bureaucratisation and frequently arrogant self-confidence of the ANC party-state machinery. Such thinking complements (or perhaps rivals) speculation on the future of the Tripartite Alliance between the ANC, the Congress of South African Trade Unions (Cosatu) and the South African Communist Party.

Without entering into the game of political prediction here, it is important to register that thus far urban revolt can legitimately be described as 'popcorn' politics, immensely serious and volatile but unable to transcend the issues of the moment (Dwyer 2004: 28). Trevor Ngwane is an unusual figure in his broader theoretical interests and ambition to create a successful counter-hegemonic politics. In general, protests tend to have had an incandescent but limited life character. It is notable that the finest hours of protest in terms of the scale and presence of mass support have come when large international conferences with lots of alternative NGO attendance and massive media presence have taken place (such as the World Conference Against Racism in Durban in 2001 and the World Summit on Sustainable Development in 2002, which led to a spectacular march from Alexandra township aimed at Sandton). The eGoli 2001 initiative, by threatening privatisation and with it jobs (or at least the conditions under which jobs were made available), in tandem with reforms in many parts of the world, as a result also became a flashpoint and initially met with strong opposition from unionised municipal workers.[18]

Such moments are not frequent, however, and can be avoided by the state if it acts with some dexterity. We have already discussed the failure of the system to bring about (or tolerate?) instruments for effective communication with communities. Systematic organisation brings out very rapidly the possibility of leader opportunism. Numerous writers have commented on the extent to which protests generally depend on community women whose lives consist of coping with basic household and social reproduction issues while formal organisations, especially above the lowest level of organisation, become dominated quickly by men who often have their own personal agendas for advancement.

Government policy with regard to these protests has at times been harsh. Several confrontations have led to individual deaths, for instance, while the beating up of individuals involved in the World Summit on Sustainable Development protests attracted considerable national publicity. Certainly government spokespeople, up to and including President Thabo Mbeki, have not been shy about making threatening and ominous noises about what they are apt to see as treacherous or disloyal activity, above all if there is any suspicion of rival political party involvement. For instance, in the most recent annual address to the National Council of Provinces at Empangeni, the President announced that 'the government will not tolerate violent protests against service delivery' (*Sunday Independent* 11.11.04).

In Johannesburg (but also covering other cities such as Pretoria and Bloemfontein), the notorious Red Ants – employees of a private contracted company – have expelled many thousands of squatters. The famous Bredell land invasion case was resolved by a large-scale eviction, carried out by the central government through the agency of the Red Ants, aka the Wozani Security Company (Bénit & Gervais-Lambony 2005; *Mail & Guardian* 11–17.02.05). Recently an international agency, the Centre on Housing Rights and Evictions in Geneva, Switzerland, has sent a warning to Johannesburg on the human rights violation implications of plans for evictions that go with the enactment of Blue IQ and such plans in the form of a 102-page report (*Sunday Independent* 20.09.05).

This should not, however, make us blind to the large capacity of the ANC (and a government with very substantial resources) to show a softer hand. In rich municipalities such as Johannesburg and Durban, deficits are in fact (despite the neoliberal ideology) carried and sustained with uncertain amounts of assistance from the national government to make up the difference.[19] Not many people in the outlying parts of Mbombela Municipality pay for their water and not many people in Ethekwini Municipality get evicted. The Red Ants' parent company was found guilty of corruption and black empowerment fronting in 2004 and the contract it held with the state has now been severed.

More systematically, the state has turned to policies – these are nationally determined – which guarantee a very limited amount of free water to every household and which provide electricity on the basis of prepaid meters, thus offering the poor a transparent system of self-regulation. There have been many denunciations of these policies as violating the basis of RDP-type promises to poor South Africans but it may be that they, as well as the establishment of regulatory agencies at one remove at least from the state, will take some of the fire out of the urban protest movements more permanently.[20] Thus despite fiery words, President Mbeki went himself to Moqhaka, one of the 'troubled' Free State municipalities, to try and mediate political disputes and sort out the delivery issues early in 2005 (*Business Day* 26.01.05). In 2003, Jeff Radebe, Minister of Public Enterprises and also a Sanco executive member, offered through the offices of Sanco and on the part of Eskom, a huge write-off of the electricity debt of R1.39 billion. Not long before, he brokered a deal on the problem of faulty meters in Soweto, a serious deficiency gradually being tackled, and how users could pay for their supplies in this case (Zuern 2004). An equivalent offer was repeated in Durban at the local level (Dwyer 2004).

Observers have noted the declining participation of poor urban residents in electoral politics (but from very high levels). However, they have tended to admit that alternatives to the trajectory of the ANC as a liberation movement turned government are not really yet visible on the horizon. Such alternatives are not really conceived of as providing a solution; instead, people are apt to turn away from national politics altogether.

Conclusion

From the last section, the main conclusion that one can draw is that urban struggles over rent and housing, over service provision and the politics of local administration have shown considerable continuity in the past decade with those of the late apartheid era and indeed show affinities back to the days of the United Party government in the 1940s when for the first time the black urban population grew dramatically. However, these struggles have not so far shown signs of developing into a consistent and coherent politics. The state has, if awkwardly and grudgingly, usually been able to put out the flames fairly quickly. It continues to commit itself to policies which assume that economic growth and competitiveness together with affirmative action and BEE can, if sufficiently successful and city management is tight, solve the problems of deprivation and poverty that continue to plague urban areas.

The post-apartheid state has gone a long way towards creating a stable local government system dramatically different from its predecessor. It has also helped to foster accumulation in locations where business has shown an interest in development and, as a result, some cities are growing fast. However, this paper suggests that the state tends to ride the horse of private enterprise which often continues, and even magnifies, existing disparities although there is increasingly dynamic economic growth and interesting examples of social and spatial change. This limits the possibilities of creating very different kinds of cities to those that matured under the racial system that prevailed before 1990.

Notes

1 I have summarised my own views on urban history in an article due to appear in the *South African Historical Journal*. For summaries of some of the most perceptive views on urban development in South Africa up to 1994, see the special issue on cities, *Journal of Southern African Studies* 1995, and Smith (ed.) 1992, amongst other collections. For the turbulent world of the townships during the anti-apartheid struggle see van Kessel 1995, Seekings 2000 and Bozzoli 2004. A general introduction to the urban question in post-apartheid South Africa is Harrison, Huchzermeyer and Mayekiso (eds.) 2003. On specific cities see Turok 2001; Beall, Crankshaw and Parnell 2002; Freund and Padayachee 2002 and Tomlinson et al. 2003. A significant source of valuable statistics on the large urban areas can be found in the *State of the Cities Report 2004* (SACN 2004). The new social movements and conflicts over service

delivery are championed in, amongst others, the many works of Patrick Bond such as *Unsustainable South Africa* (2002). The Municipal Services Project reports of Queens University, Canada, and the emerging series of studies of the Centre for the Study of Civil Society, University of KwaZulu-Natal, Durban, must also be consulted. There is also an important developed critical take in the work of what I shall term the 'French school' of South African urban studies: Houssay-Holzschuch 1999, Guillaume 2001, Bouillon 2002, and Bénit and Gervais-Lambony 2005 are amongst the most significant of these studies. I should like here to thank Alan Mabin for his help in several aspects of the researching of this paper, Patrick Bond for comments and to apologise to those writers I haven't been able to mention here.

2   Interview, Roland Hunter, Finance CEO, Johannesburg, 21.09.04.

3   Blue IQ is a R1.7 billion initiative to invest in ten megaprojects (tourism, transport, high-value-added manufacturing). See Tomlinson et al. (2003) and Bénit and Gervais-Lambony (2005).

4   Interview, Roelf Kotze, Nelspruit Deputy Municipal Manager, 08.02.05.

5   However, economic growth in Tshwane is rated at almost the very top end in the country.

6   The most remarkable and unexpected finding across all municipalities but with various serious implications, is the rapid decline in household size throughout. This may be caused by the growing fragility of family life, by the tendency of individuals to retain membership in locationally different households or the impact of disease, notably AIDS, but requires research.

7   Interviews with Roelf Kotze and Susan Oosthuizen/André Schönfeldt, Technical Services, Nelspruit, 08.02.05.

8   Interview, Susan Oosthuizen and André Schönfeldt, Technical Services, Nelspruit, 08.02.05.

9   Interview, Roland Hunter, 21.09.04.

10 It is a general but important point that urban change requires noting the specific characteristics of particular neighbourhoods which can exhibit a dynamism that is not easily predicted by overall stereotypes suggesting no change or little change in the cities has occurred. This point is made explicitly by Jürgens (2003). They have, for instance, researched a grey settlement (integrated) zone from the late 1980s which has developed into a largely black middle-class suburb. The presence of a large squatter settlement adjoining Hout Bay, one of the most beautiful oceanside suburbs of Cape Town, is another type of anomaly.

11 For the ambitious plans of *iTrump* in Durban see the *Independent on Saturday*, 16.09.04. The problem of centre city decay is, however, nowhere so acute as in Johannesburg.

12 The national state is now becoming involved in a special development of land near to the N2 Gateway Project between Cape Town Airport and the centre (*Mail & Guardian* 18–24.02.05). Apart from the airport itself, the environs contain a considerable amount of warehousing and other commercial activity, almost uniquely on the impoverished Cape Flats.

13 The exception here would be in the few elite areas such as Diepkloof Extension and, on a much broader basis, in former Indian and coloured group areas.

14 For a suggestive text which explores some of the cultural consequences of new forms of differentiation, see Ashforth 2000.

15 Although it has been suggested that this is actually beneficial for very low income and migrant individuals (see Todes 2003).

16 For a far more favourable situation as a result of particular circumstances about which I have written elsewhere, Cato Manor Farm in Durban, see Robinson, McCarthy and Forster 2004. This is an unusual case that depended on the work of a very autonomous and dedicated planning unit in the form of the Cato Manor Development Forum, on the prestige of being a Presidential Lead Project and on considerable grants from foreign donors, mainly the European Union.

17 Interview, Roland Hunter, 21.09.04. For Johannesburg protests see Mayekiso 2003.

18 Of course, there is nothing to prevent 'corporatisation' without privatisation from dismissing workers or raising charges to make a profit. I owe this insight particularly to Gill Hart and her research in Newcastle, KwaZulu-Natal.

19 Interview, Roland Hunter, 21.09.04.

20 David McDonald reported plans to create six big regional electricity distributors for whom municipalities will create 'ring-fenced business units' which will act as local redistributors, starting with Cape Town in July 2005 (*Sunday Independent* 31.10.04).

References

Ashforth A (2000) *Madumo; A man bewitched*. Cape Town: David Philip.

Barchiesi F (2004) *Classes, multitudes and the politics of community movements in post-apartheid South Africa*. Centre for Civil Society Research Report No. 20, University of KwaZulu-Natal, Durban.

Beall J, Crankshaw O & Parnell S (2002) *Uniting a divided city: Governance and social exclusion in Johannesburg*. London & Sterling VA: Earthscan.

Beall J, Crankshaw O & Parnell S (2003) Social differentiation and urban governance in greater Soweto: A case study of post-apartheid Meadowlands. In R Tomlinson et al. *Emerging Johannesburg: Perspectives on the post-apartheid city.* New York & London: Routledge.

Beall J, Crankshaw O & Parnell S (n.d.) A matter of timing: Migration and housing access in metropolitan Johannesburg. Unpublished manuscript.

Behrens R & Wilkinson P (2003) Housing and urban passenger transport policy in South African cities: A problematic relationship? In P Harrison et al. (eds.) *Confronting fragmentation: Housing and urban development in a democratising South Africa.* Cape Town: University of Cape Town Press.

Bellengere A et al. (n.d.) Privatiser pour mieux réguler ? le pari de Durban, Afrique du Sud, en matière de transport public. Unpublished manuscript.

Bénit C & Gervais-Lambony P (2005) The poor and the shop window: Globalisation, a local political instrument in the South African city? *Transformation 57* (forthcoming).

Bond P (2000) *Cities of gold, townships of coal: Essays on South Africa's new urban crisis.* Trenton: African World Press.

Bond P (2002) *Unsustainable South Africa.* Pietermaritzburg: University of Natal Press.

Bond P (2003) The degeneration of urban policy after apartheid. In P Harrison et al. (eds.) *Confronting fragmentation: Housing and urban development in a democratising South Africa.* Cape Town: University of Cape Town Press.

Bond P (2004) *South Africa's resurgent urban social movements: The case of Johannesburg 1984, 1994, 2004.* Centre for Civil Society Research Report No. 22, University of KwaZulu-Natal.

Bouillon A (2002) Citizenship and the city: The Durban centre-city in 2000, *Transformation 48*: 1–37.

Bozzoli B (2004) *Theatres of struggle and the end of apartheid.* Johannesburg: Wits University Press.

Bremner L (2002) Closure, simulation and 'making do' in the contemporary Johannesburg landscape. In *Under siege: Four African cities, Kassel Art Festival IX, Documenta 1, Platform 4.* Kassel: Hatje Cantz.

Cameron R (n.d.) Metropolitan restructuring (and more restructuring) in South Africa. Unpublished manuscript.

Coalition Against Water Privatisation (South Africa) (2004) *'Nothing for Mahala': The forced installation of prepaid water meters in Stretford, Extension 4, Orange Farm, Johannesburg, South Africa.* Centre for Civil Society Research Report No. 16, University of KwaZulu-Natal, Durban.

Czeglédy A (2003) Villas of the highveld: A cultural perspective on Johannesburg and its 'Northern suburbs'. In R Tomlinson et al. *Emerging Johannesburg: Perspectives on the post-apartheid city.* New York & London: Routledge.

Desai A (1999) *The poors of Chatsworth.* Durban: Madiba Publishers.

Desai A & Pithouse R (2004) *'But we were thousands': Dispossession, resistance, repossession and repression in Mandela Park.* Centre for Civil Society Research Report No. 9, University of KwaZulu-Natal.

Dwyer P (2004) *The contentious politics of the Concerned Citizens Forum (CCF).* Centre for Civil Society Research Report No. 24, University of KwaZulu-Natal.

Emdon E (2003) The limits of law: Social rights and urban development. In R Tomlinson et al. *Emerging Johannesburg: Perspectives on the post-apartheid city.* New York & London: Routledge.

FinMark Trust (2004) *Township residential property market research report 2004.* Johannesburg: FinMark Trust.

Freund B (2001) City Hall and the direction of development: The changing role of the local state as a factor in the economic planning and development in Durban. In B Freund & V Padayachee (eds.) *The D(urban) vortex: A South African city in transition.* Pietermaritzburg: University of Natal Press.

Freund B (forthcoming) Urban history in South Africa, *South African Historical Journal.*

Freund B & Lootvoet B (forthcoming) 'Où le partenariat public-privé devient l'instrument privilégié du Local Economic Development: l'exemple de Durban, *Revue Tiers-Monde.*

Freund B & Padayachee V (eds.) *The D(urban) vortex: A South African city in transition.* Pietermaritzburg: University of Natal Press.

Goga S (2003) Property investors and decentralization: A case of false competition? In R Tomlinson et al. *Emerging Johannesburg: Perspectives on the post-apartheid city.* New York & London: Routledge.

Gotz G & Simone A (2003) On belonging and becoming in African cities. In R Tomlinson et al. *Emerging Johannesburg: Perspectives on the post-apartheid city.* New York & London: Routledge.

Guillaume P (2001) *Géographies de l'exclusion.* Johannesburg & Paris : IFAS/Karthala.

Harrison P (2003) Fragmentation and globalisation as the new global meta-narrative. In P Harrison, M Huchzermeyer & M Mayekiso *Confronting fragmentation: Housing and urban development in a democratising society.* Cape Town: University of Cape Town Press.

Harrison P, Huchzermeyer M & Mayekiso M (eds.) (2003) *Confronting fragmentation: Housing and urban development in a democratising society*. Cape Town: University of Cape Town Press.

Heller P (2003) Reclaiming democratic spaces: Civics and politics in post-transition Johannesburg. In R Tomlinson et al. *Emerging Johannesburg: Perspectives on the post-apartheid city*. New York & London: Routledge.

Houssay-Holzschuch M (1999) *Le Cap, ville Sud-Africaine: Ville blanche, vies noires*. Paris: L'Harmattan.

Huchzermeyer M (2003) Addressing housing policy through housing policy and finance. In P Harrison et al. (eds.) *Confronting fragmentation: Housing and urban development in a democratising South Africa*. Cape Town: University of Cape Town Press.

Irurah D & Boshoff B (2003) An interpretation of sustainable development and urban sustainability in low-cost housing and settlements in South Africa. In P Harrison et al. (eds.) *Confronting fragmentation: Housing and urban development in a democratising South Africa*. Cape Town: University of Cape Town Press.

Journal of Southern African Studies (1995) Special issue on Urban Studies and Urban Change in Southern Africa, XXI(1).

Jurgens U, Grad M, & Bähr J (2003) New forms of class and racial segregation. In R Tomlinson et al. (eds.) *Emerging Johannesburg: Perspectives on the post-apartheid city*. New York & London: Routledge.

Krog A (2003) *A change of tongue*. Johannesburg: Random House.

le Galès P (2002) Private-sector interests and urban governance. In P le Galès & A Bagnasco (eds.) *Cities in contemporary Europe*. Cambridge: Cambridge University Press.

Lootvoet B & Khan S (2001) La décentralisation sud-africaine et les métropoles : les défis de Durban, *Autre Part*.

Mabin A (2004) Urban policy and power in the cities from late apartheid to the new millennium. Unpublished paper, Queens University seminar.

Mabin A (2005) Suburbanisation, segregation and governance of territorial transformations, *Transformation 57* (forthcoming).

Mayekiso M (2003) South Africa's enduring urban crisis: The local state and the urban social movement with particular reference to Johannesburg. In P Harrison et al. (eds.) *Confronting fragmentation: Housing and urban development in a democratising South Africa*. Cape Town: University of Cape Town Press.

McDonald D & Pape J (2002) *Cost recovery and the crisis of service delivery in South Africa*. London & Pretoria: Zed & HSRC Press.

Oelofse M (2003) Social justice, social integration and the compact city: Letters from the inner city of Johannesburg. In P Harrison et al. (eds.) *Confronting fragmentation: Housing and urban development in a democratising South Africa*. Cape Town: University of Cape Town Press.

Pieterse E (2002) From divided to integrated city? A critical overview of the emerging metropolitan governance system in Cape Town, *Urban Forum* 13(1): 3–37.

Pieterse E (2003) Unraveling the different meanings of integration: The urban development framework of the South African government. In P Harrison et al. (eds.) *Confronting fragmentation: Housing and urban development in a democratising South Africa*. Cape Town: University of Cape Town Press.

Robinson J & Boldogh C (1994) Operation Jump Start: An economic initiative in the Durban functional region. In R Tomlinson (ed.) *Urban development planning*. London & Johannesburg: Zed Press and Wits University Press.

Robinson P, McCarthy J & Forster C (eds.) (2004) *Urban reconstruction in the developing world*. Sandown: Heinemann.

RSA (Republic of South Africa) (1998) *White Paper on local government*. Pretoria: Government Printers.

SACN (South African Cities Network) (2004) *State of the cities report 2004*. Cape Town: SACN.

Seekings J (2000) *The UDF: A history of the United Democratic Front in South Africa 1983–91*. Cape Town, London & Athens, Ohio: David Philip, James Currey and Ohio University Press.

Smith D (ed.) (1992) *The apartheid city and beyond*. London & Johannesburg: Routledge & Wits University Press.

Todes A (2003) Housing, urban development and the compact city debate. In P Harrison et al. (eds.) *Confronting fragmentation: Housing and urban development in a democratising South Africa*. Cape Town: University of Cape Town Press.

Tomlinson R, Bremner L & Mangcu X (2003) The post-apartheid struggle for an integrated Johannesburg. In R Tomlinson et al. *Emerging Johannesburg: Perspectives on the post-apartheid city*. New York & London: Routledge.

Tomlinson R & Larsen P (2003) The race, class and space of shopping. In R Tomlinson et al. *Emerging Johannesburg: Perspectives on the post-apartheid city*. New York & London: Routledge.

Turok I (2001) 'Persistent polarisation post-apartheid?' Progress towards urban integration in Cape Town, *Urban Studies* 38(13): 2349–2377.

van Kessel I (1995) 'Beyond our wildest dreams': The United Democratic Front and the transformation of South Africa. PhD thesis, University of Leiden.

Watson V (2003) Planning for integration: The case of metropolitan Cape Town. In P Harrison et al. (eds.) *Confronting fragmentation: Housing and urban development in a democratising South Africa*. Cape Town: University of Cape Town Press.

Wolfensohn J (2001) The World Bank and global city-players: Reaching the poor. In A Scott (ed.) *Global city-regions. Trends, theory, policy*. New York: Oxford University Press.

Zuern E (2004) *Continuity in contradiction? The prospects for a national civic movement in a democratic state: Sanco and the ANC in post-apartheid South Africa*. Centre for Civil Society Research Report No. 26, University of KwaZulu-Natal, Durban.

13 Guns and the social crisis

Jacklyn Cock

Introduction: a social crisis

Guns are the articulator of a social crisis in contemporary South Africa, one of whose manifestations is the erosion of social relations of caring and responsibility. It was so described by Minister Zola Skweyiya in a half-page advertisement in the *Sunday Times* (16.01.00), in which he warned that 'South Africa is sitting on a time bomb of poverty and social disintegration' and appealed for 'a full understanding of the nature and extent of the social crisis that we face' because it 'has the potential to reverse the democratic gains made since 1994'. Since that time there have been frequent references by labour leaders to the 'crisis' in unemployment levels, and by Archbishop Desmond Tutu and others to the 'time bomb of poverty'.

The indicators of this social disintegration that are usually cited include criminal violence, HIV/AIDS, substance abuse, vehicle accidents, one of the highest rates of rape in the world and other forms of gender-based violence such as femicide. However, the unravelling of relations of caring and responsibility is taking many different forms. It is also manifest in media reports of the nurse whose patient dies while she chats to the driver in the front of the ambulance, the builder who erects sub-standard Reconstruction and Development Programme houses, irregularities in tendering procedures, corruption in the arms industry, the police officer who takes bribes, the currency speculator whose concern for profit obliterates any concern for the well-being of fellow citizens, the public servant falsifying pension claims, the teacher who abuses or neglects his pupils, as well as the owners and drivers of minibus taxis who are indifferent to the safety of their passengers. The perpetrators of gun violence display an extreme form of this indifference. It is in this sense that the current extent of gun violence is the most dramatic indicator of the social crisis in South Africa today.

The extent of gun violence

We are a heavily armed society with over three million (3 737 676) licensed firearms in 2004 (Gould & Lamb 2004: 133). South African civilians have more than six times as many firearms as those held by the state security agencies in the form of the police and army, numbering 567 000. Applications for licences peaked in 1994 with 236 033 new licences issued to individuals in that year. This dropped to 150 928 licences in 1995 (Chetty 2000). The number of licences issued has dropped since then. In 1999, 182 866 licences were issued to individuals, in 2000, 114 893 licences and in 2001, 148 669 licences were issued.[1] Estimates of the number of illegal firearms in the country vary widely but in 2000 the Minister of Safety and Security put the figure at between 500 000 and one million.

In common with other societies experiencing the social turbulence which all too often accompanies political transition, since 1994 recorded violent crimes – such as murder, attempted murder, rape and all forms of robbery and assault – increased dramatically in South Africa. Between 1994 and 1999, violent crime increased by 22 per cent (Schonteich & Louw 2001). In 1994, there were 26 832 homicides and 11 134 of these were committed with a firearm. While the number of homicides since 1994 has decreased, the percentage of people killed with firearms increased from 41 per cent of all murders in 1994 to 49.3 per cent of the total of 10 854 in 2000 (Chetty 2000; Kirsten 2004). The number of robberies involving firearms increased from 51 004 in 1996 to 88 178 in 2000.

The latest South African Police Service (SAPS) statistics show a significant drop in several types of violent crime including murder. Since 1995, when murders peaked at 26 877, the murder rate decreased by 23 per cent to a total of 19 824 in 2003/04. This still means that 54 people are murdered every day in South Africa, but the number involving firearms has not been released. The most recent available firearm homicide figure is for 2000 where they accounted for 31 deaths per day.

Gun violence is the leading cause of non-natural death in South Africa. The fourth annual report of the National Injury Mortality Surveillance System noted that firearms accounted for almost a third – 27.8 per cent – of all non-natural deaths recorded in 2002, a slight increase on the 27.6 per cent recorded in 2001. Road deaths were slightly lower at 25 per cent of all non-natural deaths. The report described 25 494 fatal injuries that were registered at 345 mortuaries in six provinces. The survey found that firearms were the leading cause of fatal injury for all ages from 15 to 65. Of the deaths recorded, 89 per cent were due to homicide, ten per cent suicide and 0.5 per cent were accidental (MRC 2003: 4). An average of two youngsters a day were killed by firearms in 2000, and a total of 375 children under the age of 12 and 324 minors between 12 and 17 years of age were killed by guns that year.[2]

There has been an increase in the number of firearms reported lost or stolen. Between 1994 and 2001, a total of 184 328 firearms were reported lost or stolen – 13 506 were lost by their owners, while 170 822 were stolen from them. In 2001 alone, a total of 23 519 were lost or stolen, an average of 64 guns per day. As these figures are limited to reported thefts or losses, this is clearly an understatement.[3] These stolen or mislaid legal firearms are a major contributor to the stockpile of illegal arms in this country. However, whether legal or illicit, the crucial point is that their status has no relevance to their lethal power.

Many of these illegal weapons are a legacy of war in the southern African region. Thousands of small arms were an important part of the apartheid regime's destabilisation activities. AK47s were included in weapons which were supplied to the National Union for the Total Independence of Angola (Unita) and the Mozambique National Resistance (Renamo), as well as to Inkatha. For example, almost 40 000 AK 47s were purchased by the apartheid state between 1976 and 1986 specifically to be given to Unita (Cameron Commission 1995). This is a large part of the explanation for the current proliferation of arms throughout South Africa.

The role of the post-apartheid state in the proliferation of firearms

The post-apartheid state has contributed – and continues to do so – to this proliferation through its role as a significant arms producer. Private and public companies manufacture a range of arms and ammunition for both military and civilian use and between 1996 and 2001 they exported over R400 million worth of small arms (Gould & Lamb 2004). This trade is regulated by the National Conventional Arms Control Committee (NCACC) which is required to scrutinise export applications in terms of human rights and security criteria. The degree of this regulation is contested as the NCACC has in the past approved the sale of weapons to countries such as Columbia and the Philippines while they were experiencing internal conflict. South Africa has exported small arms to a number of African countries, major recipients being Congo, Uganda and Rwanda. South Africa sold arms worth R43.2 million to six countries fighting on both sides of the war in the Democratic Republic of Congo in 1998 (Batchelor 1999: 17). What this indicates is that the post-apartheid state has moved away from an ethically-driven foreign policy where human rights issues were central, to one which privileges a very narrow conception of national interest.

Furthermore, the security forces of the post-apartheid state possess a significant number of arms. For example, in 2003, the South African National Defence Force (SANDF) held about 350 000 small arms and light weapons – mainly R1, R4 and R5 rifles, machine guns and pistols. Researchers calculated that this amounted to 5.89 firearms per uniformed officer (Gould & Lamb 2004). The SAPS for their part possessed some 262 062 firearms. Of these, 79 253 were handguns issued to officers which could be used in the course of their normal operational duties, and rifles and handguns issued to 903 members of specialised units. As in the case of civilians, loss or theft of weapons is a major police problem. Between 1990 and 1999, an annual average of 1 626 firearms were lost by or stolen from the police (Gould & Lamb 2004).

Since 1994, the post-apartheid state has attempted to address the problem of the proliferation of illegal firearms in a number of ways.

Firstly, it has engaged in the destruction of illegal firearms. For example, in September 2004, 1 000 firearms were destroyed in Cape Town; in October 2004, 12 000 firearms and 67 000 rounds of ammunition were destroyed in Benoni; and in December, another 11 000 firearms were destroyed in Benoni. The SAPS has emphasised that these actions are not only about destroying firearms, but also about preventing violent crimes (GFSA 2004). Secondly, in 2004 the state initiated a well-publicised national gun amnesty calling on people to hand in their weapons. This resulted in some 53 000 firearms being collected in the first three months (*Saturday Star* 22.03.05).

Thirdly, the state has also increased the regulation of the use of firearms in the private security industry. This industry has grown dramatically since 1994 and uses firearms extensively, especially in companies safeguarding assets in transit. According to the Central Firearms Register of the SAPS in September

2003, 1 643 private security companies, out of a total of 3 252, were registered as holding 58 981 firearms. In terms of the Firearms Control Act, private security officers are forbidden from using their own firearms on duty, 'as had previously been commonplace' (Gould & Lamb 2004: 185).

However, the private security industry's regulatory authority has expressed concern that the figures cited may not be a true reflection, and in 2003, in co-operation with the SAPS, launched Operation *Sethunya* to trace illegal firearms and test compliance with firearms legislation. Firearms are also widespread among the 339 companies registered as offering armed response services to private homes and businesses (Gould & Lamb 2004: 188).

Fourthly, there have been a number of other regional and national operations, such as Operation Rachel with Mozambique, geared at reducing the number of illegal guns in circulation. Operation Rachel consisted of a number of phases during which Mozambican and South African police personnel travelled throughout Mozambique identifying and destroying arms caches. 'During the eight operations between 1995 and 2003, over 600 arms caches were discovered and several tons of arms and ammunition were destroyed' (Gould & Lamb 2004: 110). Border control has been tightened up, though the difficulties of monitoring the borders of Mozambique, for example, with its 2 470 km coastline and 14 000 km of inland borders, must be emphasised (Oosthuysen 1996).

Other measures adopted have included actively supporting a United Nations (UN) Programme of Action, playing an active role in framing the continental Bamako Declaration of 2000 which commits African states to a common set of principles with regard to small-arms control and national measures to control firearms, and in framing a regional Southern African Development Community (SADC) Firearm Protocol. This was adopted by the SADC heads of state in August 2001 and was ratified by South Africa in 2003. It seeks to 'combat and eradicate the illicit trade of firearms, ammunition and other related materials… through the mobilisation of a regional commitment to policy and practice' including regional information databases (Stott 2003: 4). Most importantly, the post-apartheid state has passed a new law on firearm control.

Finally, the new Firearms Control Act should make gun ownership more difficult. This replaced the apartheid-era Arms and Ammunition Act of 1969 in July 2004, and put in place a far stricter arms-control regime. Changes included raising the age of legal gun ownership from 16 to 21 years, reducing to one the number of firearms individuals are permitted to own, introducing competency tests for the obtaining of gun licences and a more efficient system of regulation. Individuals seeking firearm licences must now go through a two-step process. The first is to acquire a competency certificate from the police, showing that they are physically fit and know how to use a gun. This requires that the applicants pass national tests on the use of, and law pertaining to, firearms. It also requires local police to do background checks, including interviewing people who know the applicant. Once this competency certificate is issued, the person must then apply for the licence, demonstrating why the weapon is needed. It tightens up control over the carrying and storage of guns and requires that all privately-held firearm licences be regularly renewed. It also imposes stricter penalties for breaking the law. According to the anti-gun lobbying group, Gun Free South Africa (GFSA), the Act was 'the product of many years of lobbying and struggle and can be regarded as a major victory for those individuals and organisations that have battled for greater gun control' (Gun Free South Africa 2004: 8).

GFSA, a small non-governmental organisation (NGO), is a central node in an embryonic demilitarisation network of individuals and organisations in South Africa growing in social cohesion, political reach and geographical spread. But its primary objective of creating a gun-free society involves confronting the legacy of war in the southern African region as a whole.

The legacy of war

The proliferation of firearms is one legacy of the 30 years of war which engulfed southern Africa from about the mid-1960s. In this context, guns are not value-neutral, ahistorical technologies. They are carriers of powerful cultural meanings among different social groups. In contemporary South Africa gun violence is frequently associated with a specific weapon – the AK47 – and a specific social group – ex-combatants.

The AK47 is invested with powerful symbolic force. While the machine gun is a potent global symbol representing the power of the imperial armies, the AK47 is an icon of the anti-colonial insurgent, the symbol of revolutionary resistance throughout the southern African region. Since it first went into production in 1947, some 70 million AK47s have been manufactured. It has been described as the most effective assault weapon in the world and has changed forever the way wars are fought. Especially during the apartheid era, the AK47 became for many black South African youths a mythic icon, a marker of group identity – a kind of code to assert one's political allegiance – which carried great significance for individuals.

Such young people, in diverse conflicts are, in the view of Michael Ignatieff, 'supplying armies with a different kind of soldier – one for whom a weapon is not a thing to be respected or treated with ritual correctness, but instead has an explicit phallic dimension' (1997: 127). In this context, for such soldiers the AK47 is 'a toxic testosterone' (Ignatieff 1997: 127). For all these reasons, the AK47 is appealing to criminals and has also become a powerful symbol of criminal lawlessness. Criminals and terrorists or revolutionaries and freedom fighters – these are the contested political identities that are condensed in the image of the AK47.

But despite the 'common sense' view, the AK47 is not the most commonly used weapon in violent crime in South Africa compared to pistols and revolvers. For instance, in 2000, high-calibre automatic weapons such as AK47s were used in only a small percentage of the murders reported in that year. Of the total of 10 854 firearm murders, the largest category – 6 724 – involved the use of pistols or revolvers.[4] These figures would suggest that the focus on AKs in the contemporary South African media is an ideological hangover from the apartheid era. Furthermore, the AK47 is associated with a particular social category – ex-combatants.

The transition from authoritarian rule in South Africa has created a deep well of social anxiety as the familiar social identities and traditional practices have been disrupted and breached. One consequence of this social anxiety is, as Hall, Critcher, Jefferson, Clarke and Roberts have noted in a different context, the 'emergence of a predisposition to the use of "scapegoats" into which all disturbing experiences are condensed' (Hall et al. 1978: 157). In the South African context, there is one such category – ex-combatants. Much press coverage of gun violence reflects a sense of blame and indignation towards this social group. In the vocabulary of social anxiety, ex-combatants are easy symbols of menace, social dislocation and threat.

As Seegers wrote of South Africa in 1990, the country 'contains large numbers of men with military training and access to arms and ammunition dispersed around the country' (1996: 270). The precise number of ex-combatants is contested. According to a one-time Department of Defence policy analyst, Dr Rocky Williams, in 2003 there could have been as many as 150 000.[5] This number will grow with the planned further downsizing of the SANDF.

Many of these ex-combatants are marked by their experience of war, their training in the means of violence and their lack of marketable skills, as well as their access to weaponry. Throughout the southern African region demobilisation has rarely involved either effective disarmament or effective social integration in the sense of restoring ex-combatants to their communities with demilitarised social identities that involve access to employment and supportive social networks. Instead, many ex-combatants throughout the region have reported a sense of marginalisation and social dislocation (Kingma 2000).

A survey of 180 respondents during the informal demobilisation process which coincided with the 1990 to 1994 period of transition in South Africa found that 72 per cent were unemployed and 67 per cent reported psychological problems (Cock 1993). A sense of marginalisation emerged strongly from a later study which reported that many ex-combatants perceived themselves to have been disregarded and 'wished away' (Gear 2002). The most recent study in 2003 involved 410 questionnaires administered to ex-combatants, defined as members of the Azanian People's Liberation Army (Apla) and Umkhonto we Sizwe (MK) who had received some form of military training under the political leadership of the Pan Africanist Congress (PAC) or the African National Congress (ANC). This survey reported high levels of unemployment (66 per cent of the sample), disrupted education on the part of 60 per cent and a strong sense of social exclusion (Centre for Conflict Resolution 2003).

Numerous press reports have claimed that many of the widespread armed robberies in South Africa have been the work of highly 'professional' bandits with military backgrounds. For example, according to one researcher, 'the increase in crime is partially due to the fact that supposedly demobbed members of MK turned to crime after the struggle ended in 1994' (Anthony Minaar, *Sowetan* 29.09.98). Ex-combatants are thus the target of much contemporary anxiety about gun violence.

The policy solutions generated by this anxiety – the tightening up of gun-control laws and of border security to block illegal immigration and prevent the smuggling of guns by Mozambican ex-combatants – is inadequate. Effective policy solutions have to include an understanding of how guns are invested with powerful social meanings and linked to contested social identities. The present romanticisation of the AK47 and other firearms is partly the historical legacy of colonial conquest and revolutionary struggle in southern Africa.

Much of the literature is flawed by a narrow, technicist approach, which focuses on the supply of guns to the neglect of demand factors. In much of southern Africa there is a robust 'gun culture', which feeds into and reinforces an ideology of militarism. Overall, this culture operates to provide a social sanction to the possession of guns, and much gun violence follows culturally-defined repertoires of behaviour. All of these cultural forms constitute a kind of 'banal militarism'. This is linked to the belief that guns are an effective and necessary form of protection. Now, the gun combines two contradictory images – it is a means of both order and of violence; paradoxically, it is believed to provide protection from violence through the potential threat of violence. However, the psychodynamic power of the gun as protection is largely illusionary; legally-owned weapons contribute to the problem of violent crime.

One of GFSA's first commissioned research reports demonstrated the risks of firearm ownership. One of the most significant findings of a docket analysis on gun use in two police precincts, Bramley and Alexandra, was that victims in possession of a firearm were four times more likely to have their firearms stolen than to use them in self-defence (Altbecker 1997). According to Kirsten, 'this statistic has remained one of the most powerful pieces of information in the gun control debate' (2004: 10). It is powerful because it punctures the current notion of guns as a source of power and protection.

The notion of guns as a means of protection is sometimes linked to masculinity and a man's roles as 'protector' and 'defender'. In most contemporary societies, guns and armies are highly gendered. A distinctive feature of South Africa is that in this context they are also highly racialised and linked to militarised conceptions of citizenship. A militarised form of citizenship characterised the apartheid era in that political citizenship involved compulsory national military service for white males. Blacks were largely denied access to the legal possession of firearms. This prohibition on arms was understood to involve a denial of African manhood as well as citizenship (Hellman 1943).

The outcome of this historical legacy is a militarised citizenship and militarised masculinism, which has devastating social consequences and which will be very difficult to dislodge. Among many black South Africans there is now a widespread understanding that access to all levels of the SANDF, as well as access to legal gun ownership, are markers of liberation and of full citizenship in the post-apartheid state.

It follows that any solution to the proliferation of guns has to deal with these social relations and contested identities that are the legacy of war. A control policy that ignores the historically and socially constructed meanings attached to firearms will not be effective; we need to alter the allegiances and identities which underlie acts of gun violence. Such a policy also has to deal with the class interests and material conditions involved in both the supply of and demand for firearms. While criminal gangs may provide young men with a form of social identity, the gangs themselves are often a response to socio-economic deprivation and exclusion. Naylor has written:

> probably the single most important thing stoking the illegal arms market from the demand side is the prevailing maldistribution of income, wealth and ecological capital. Casting a quick look at the world today, what leaps out is the gross and growing disparities in all three categories. Until these are fairly and frankly addressed, there is little hope of damping the desire of the disadvantaged to seek the tools and rectify those disparities by violent means. (1994: 35)

This points us towards the second component of the explanation of the current proliferation of firearms in South Africa.

Neoliberalism

While Naylor (1994) emphasised the importance of social inequality in the demand for firearms, it is also relevant to understanding the current social crisis. This erosion of relations of concern and responsibility is the outcome of two processes: first, the legacy of 30 years of war and militarisation in the region; and second, the social and economic disruptions brought about by neoliberal policies in South Africa. Together they form a lethal mix.

Neoliberalism is related to the social crisis in three linked ways. First, it is increasing poverty, unemployment and social inequality with South Africa ranking as one of the most extreme cases of income inequality in the world. In January 2005, there were casual workers on chicory farms in the Eastern Cape earning as little as R10 a day. While 57 per cent of our population live in poverty, corporate executive salaries are extremely high. In 2004 the chief executives of Edcon earned R42.7 million, Nedcor R36.7 million, Massmart R36.2 million, MTN R19.7 million, and Telkom R11 million (*The Star* 17.02.05). In some cases such large salaries are paid by corporations which have instituted mass retrenchments. For example, Iscor (now Mittal Steel, the largest steel producer in the world) has retrenched some 20 000 workers since 1994, many of whom are living in extreme poverty. Yet in the 18 months to December 2004, the former chief executive, Louis van Niekerk, was paid a total of R22.57 million in pay and net gains on options (*Star Business Report* 15.04.05). A stable social order cannot afford these extremes.

Second, corporate restructuring is generating what Webster and von Holdt (2005) have termed 'a crisis of social reproduction'. They argue that the sphere of the public is being rolled back and 'instead of extending social rights to all citizens, restructuring in South Africa is transferring the responsibility of social protection to the household and to the poor, threatening the very sustainability of communities and the reproduction of society' (Webster & von Holdt 2005: 35). The privatisation of basic services, such as access to water, has commoditised fundamental human needs and eroded social solidarity. For example, the installation of prepaid water meters in desperately poor communities such as Orange Farm has disrupted social relations and generated new tensions and conflicts (Coalition Against Water Privatisation 2004).

This feature of neoliberalism – the privatisation of state assets and functions – has generated much debate. What has received far less attention is the third factor, namely the privatisation of social relations as people retreat from public engagement in pursuit of individualist goals. Neoliberalism involves the unravelling of the social bonds and solidarities which marked the anti-apartheid struggle. Strong, cohesive group identities have been replaced by an individualism, a competitiveness, an atomisation of collective life.

This process is not unique to South Africa and has been conceptualised by Bauman (2004) as 'the privatisation of the public sphere' – what it means is that individuals have to seek private remedies for socially-produced problems. They cannot trust the state to provide all that is needed in the case of unemployment, illness, security, healthcare or proper education. The implication is that 'the meaning of citizenship has been emptied of much of its past contents' (Bauman 2004: 45). Bauman is writing of a global process but its meaning is particularly serious for our struggle to create a shared, national sense of rights and responsibilities as citizens in an aspirant democracy.

This privatisation of social life has created high levels of anxieties, insecurity and confusion in relation to means and goals. It is the combination of poverty, unemployment and dramatic forms of social inequality, linked to the legacy of 30 years of war, that is at the root of the present social crisis in South Africa. It is dramatically expressed in the current proliferation of guns and gun violence.

Civil society mobilisation against firearms

Established in 1994, GFSA's initial impact was limited. In a gun hand-in campaign in that year, only 270 guns were handed in, mainly white-owned and licensed. But even then, according to ex-co-ordinator Adele Kirsten, the campaign 'raised public awareness about the proliferation of firearms in our society and made it an issue for public debate. It also placed the issue on the political agenda and the ANC national conference in that year adopted a resolution supporting GFSA'.[6]

GFSA is promoting regional solidarity around this issue. In terms of input indicators it is a tiny organisation, with a small budget, no government funding, and only six full-time employees which means that it depends heavily on volunteer energy. It focuses on public awareness and policy advocacy to promote a disarmament culture and, along with the Institute for Security Studies, is strengthening South Africa's role in the UN in the co-ordination of international efforts against the illicit trade in small arms. It is 'particularly committed to work at the grassroots level where we are trying to influence gun-carrying behaviour, with a special focus on young people'.[7]

Since 1994, GFSA may claim to have contributed to changing gun-control policy as in the new Firearms Control Act. The organisation maintains that its successes include the fact that the new South African Constitution excluded the right to own firearms. According to Adele Kirsten, this 'has ensured that gun ownership will remain a privilege rather than an entrenched right'.

GFSA has also gone some way towards shifting the predominant social meanings and stigmatising firearms. This is evident in the increasing numbers of private and public buildings such as schools, churches, NGO offices, government buildings, clinics and taverns, that have declared themselves 'gun-free zones'. This is a space in which firearms are not welcome and is denoted by a no-gun sign (similar to the no-smoking sign). The model is a flexible one and ranges from those gun-free zones that are strictly enforced with elaborate security arrangements, as in some businesses and government buildings, to those that are based on trust and informal social sanctions, as in many townships. One such example is Bophelong, a township near Sebokeng on the East Rand which was the site of much violent conflict in the early 1990s. With an active community organisation, a considerable effort has been made in the township to limit the use of guns. In 2004, GFSA organised a march in Bophelong to mark the 16 Days of Activism Against Gender Violence. A resident, Joseph Dube, explained, 'All too often women become the victims of alcohol abuse and gun misuse. We marched to let the women of Bophelong know that we are taking active steps to make Bophelong a safer place for them' (GFSA 2004: 4). These gun-free zones can be seen as indicators of a desire on the part of many South Africans for a peaceful social order.

These impacts of GFSA can partly be explained by such factors as:
- *Its emphasis on inclusivity* – GFSA places a priority on networking and works with a wide range of organisations from Compassionate Friends (which provides support to bereaved parents) to the PAC. It attempts to maintain a single-issue focus within a flexible framework, co-operating with very different organisations, defining guns as a health issue and a women's issue as a way of mobilising these groupings. It works closely with two other organisations whose activities include engaging with arms issues, the Centre for Conflict Resolution and Ceasefire;
- *Its input into the policy process* – GFSA has made submissions on various policy White Papers; ex-chairperson, Sheena Duncan, chaired an inquiry into the Central Firearms Register, and its co-ordinator, Adele Kirsten, has been active in various policy forums;
- *Its links to the global anti-gun campaign* – GFSA is part of an international network in which increasing numbers of peace, development, public health, gun control, and disarmament interests are represented. This global campaign seeks to build on the successful 1990s anti-landmine

global campaign and 'to capitalise on that momentum. It is already well organised and deeply committed and it brings together everyone from arms control types to humanitarian activists' (Joseph Smaldone, *New York Times* 07.01.98);

- *Its recognition that the proliferation of small arms is a regional problem requiring a regional solution* – These regional connections are part of a shift away from statist and militarist conceptions of security to address issues of human security. Much effort is going into building alliances throughout the region. The regional scope of the campaign is increasing significantly, as evidenced by the geographical spread of attendance at GFSA workshops. A GFSA workshop held in Johannesburg in May 1998 attracted delegates from nine southern African countries. They represented a range of interest groups concerned with human rights, religious groups, advocacy and policy-research groups, thus underlining that a precondition for an effective global campaign is the recognition that small arms are a multidimensional problem;
- *Its extensive use of sound research data* – This is used to support the need for changes in firearm legislation, and to attack some of the myths of power and protection attached to gun ownership;
- *Its reach down into grassroots communities and up into the policy process* – It enables grassroot communities to articulate their concerns with policy-makers in parliamentary hearings and thus engage in policy arenas. 'It became a tool for mobilising people in the public policy process' (Kirsten 2004: 6). This bridging involved 'the redefinition of expertise to include experiential knowledge, whereby "expert opinion" was integrated with the voice of the grassroots' (Kirsten 2004: 7).

In a perceptive analysis of GFSA's strategy, Kirsten (2004) has emphasised the importance of a dual strategy which addressed both supply and demand factors simultaneously. This she claimed was in contrast to many proponents of gun control internationally who focus on questions of supply to the neglect of questions of demand. According to Kirsten:

> By focusing on mobilising at the grassroots GFSA could begin to impact on the demand side by understanding the factors that drive people to want a gun, posing alternatives and explaining ways in which people can live together without guns. This dual strategy was based on the understanding that GFSA needed to mobilise

support for the goal of a gun-free South Africa of constituencies and interest groups, involving people at the local level. (2004: 12)

Conclusion

GFSA is one of a number of 'new' social movements that has recently emerged in response to South Africa's social crisis. Research is still necessary to establish whether these social movements are 'militant particularisms', ephemeral eruptions of the urban poor, the rural landless and other marginalised groups, or components of an emerging counter-movement in the Polanyian sense.

Webster and von Holdt (2005) have emphasised the potential of these movements. They write that 'the significance of social movements located in the community is their potential to re-socialise this crisis – which is experienced as private crisis, distress and conflict in households and communities – by building social solidarity around it, projecting it into the public arena, mobilising support and action and influencing the state and public policy' (2005: 38). A good example of this 're-socialising' potential is Kirsten's description of how the establishment of gun-free zones 'acted as a vehicle to organise communities around the gun issue but more importantly it enabled people to discuss *issues of public safety* in general' (Kirsten 2004: 16, my emphasis). This projection of security into the public arena presents a counter to the privatisation of security whereby people, lacking confidence in the capacity of the state to protect them, resort to private solutions such as private gun ownership, arrangements with private security companies or vigilantism.

In terms of the post-apartheid Constitution, citizens have the right to live in a safe environment. It is the growing gap between the discourse of rights and the reality of unmet needs that is at the base of the current social crisis. While both the supply of and demand for guns are embedded in the legacy of 30 years of war in the southern African region, the distorted social relations – which the extent of gun violence reflect – have a material and ideological base in neoliberal policies. It is in this sense that the solution to gun violence in South Africa will involve deep-seated change.

Notes

1. See http://www.gca.org.za.
2. See http://www.gca.org.za.
3. See http://www.gca.org.za/facts/statistics.htm.
4. See http://www.gca.org.za.
5. Interview with Rocky Williams, Johannesburg, May 2003.
6. Interviews with Adele Kirsten, Johannesburg 2002 and 2005.
7. Interviews with Adele Kirsten, Johannesburg 2002 and 2005.

References

Altbecker A (1997) *Guns and public safety: Gun-crime and self-defence in Alexandra and Bramley*. Johannesburg: GFSA.

Batchelor P (1999) South Africa: An irresponsible arms trader? *Global Dialogue* 4(2): 17–18.

Bauman Z (2004) *Identity: Conversations with Benedetto Vechi*. Cambridge: Polity.

Cameron Commission (1995) *Cameron Commission of Inquiry into alleged arms transactions between Armscor and one Eli Wazan and other related matters*. First Report. Johannesburg.

Centre for Conflict Resolution (2003) Soldiers of misfortune. Unpublished research report.

Chetty R (ed.) (2000) *Firearm use and distribution in South Africa*. Pretoria: National Crime Prevention Centre Firearms Programme.

Coalition Against Water Privatisation (2004) *'Nothing for Mahala'. The forced install-ation of prepaid water meters in Stretford, Extension 4, Orange Farm, Johannesburg*. Centre for Civil Society Research Report No. 16, University of KwaZulu-Natal, Durban.

Cock J (1993) Towards a common society: The integration of soldiers and armies in a future South Africa. Unpublished research report.

Gear S (2002) *'Wishing us away': Challenges facing ex-combatants in the new South Africa*. Violence and Transition Series, Vol. 8. Johannesburg: Centre for the Study of Violence and Reconciliation.

GFSA (Gun Free South Africa) (2004) *Annual report 2001–2002*. Johannesburg: GFSA.

Gould C & Lamb G (eds.) (2004) *Hide and seek. Taking account of small arms in Southern Africa*. Pretoria: Institute for Security Studies (ISS).

Hall S, Critcher C, Jefferson T, Clarke J & Roberts B (1978) *Policing the crisis. Mugging, the state and law and order*. London: Macmillan.

Hellman E (1943) Non-Europeans in the army. In *Race Relations* X(2): 45–53. Johannesburg: Institute of Race Relations.

Ignatieff M (1997) *The warriors honour*. London: Blackwells.

Kingma K (ed.) (2000) *Demobilisation in sub-Saharan Africa. The development and security impacts*. Houdsmills: Macmillan.

Kirsten A (2004) *The role of social movements in gun control: An international comparison between South Africa, Brazil and Australia*. Durban: Centre for Civil Society, University of KwaZulu-Natal.

MRC (Medical Research Council) (2003) *A profile of fatal injuries in South Africa. Fourth annual report of the National Injury Mortality Surveillance System*. Pretoria: MRC.

Naylor R (1994) Covert commerce and underground financing in the modern arms black market. Unpublished paper presented to the American Academy of Arts and Sciences, 24.02.94.

Oosthuysen G (1996) *Small arms proliferation and control in Southern Africa*. Johannesburg: South African Institute for International Affairs.

Schonteich M & Louw A (2001) *Crime in South Africa: A country profile*. ISS Paper No. 49. Pretoria: ISS.

Seegers A (1996) *The military in the making of modern South Africa*. London: Tauris Academic Studies.

Stott N (2003) Implementing the Southern African Firearms Protocol: Identifying challenges and priorities. ISS Paper No. 83. Pretoria: ISS.

Webster E & von Holdt K (eds.) (2005) *Beyond the apartheid workplace*. Pietermaritzburg: University of KwaZulu-Natal Press.

14 The Chinese communities in South Africa

Janet Wilhelm

Introduction

As China claims its place on the world economic stage and its citizens spread across the world, the focus will naturally fall on the Chinese in South Africa. And as it does, it becomes clear that this is by no means a homogenous group. Waves of immigration mean that the Chinese 'community' is such only to the undiscerning eye of those who see only skin colour and racial features. Each group of Chinese in South Africa, old and new, has very different stories to tell and different messages for policy-makers.[1]

The history of the original Chinese migrants to South Africa has been so dissimilar in certain ways from that of other racial groups that it may seem difficult to discern any lessons for cultural identity from their experience. Because of their numerical insignificance they have often been ignored in debates over ethnicity. Little understood, they were subjected to capricious but active discrimination under apartheid, yet do not benefit from legislation designed to redress those injustices. South African in habit and instinct, the descendants of the original small Chinese community nonetheless illustrate that national loyalty and a feeling of belonging are more than a matter of citizenship or a sense of identity.

This has been reinforced by the new waves of opportunistic Chinese immigration from Taiwan and mainland China, where South African citizenship is mainly a matter of mere convenience, and the number of new illegal immigrants is proof of a failure in immigration policy and of widespread corruption in the policing of immigration law.

Waves of migration

That the Chinese South African community has its genesis in the indentured labour brought to work on the mines in the early years of the twentieth century is a common misperception, probably influenced by the origins of the Indian community. Many of these workers died in the mines – the rest were repatriated at the end of their contracts. The original community is descended from independent immigrants – mainly male artisans – who started arriving from the 1870s. These early pioneers came from the southern Chinese province of Kwangtung (now Guangdong) and were from two ethnic groups, the Cantonese and the Hakka.

A feature of Chinese migration to the West is the hundreds of 'Chinatowns' in cities around the globe. By the 1920s, women were following the men and the Chinese were making their presence known in South Africa in what were called '*Malaikam*' in the mining towns of Kimberley and Johannesburg, and in Pretoria, Port Elizabeth, Durban and Cape Town. The Hakka settled in the coastal cities and in Kimberley, and the Cantonese in Johannesburg and Pretoria, establishing themselves mainly as shopkeepers.

Precise population figures are difficult to find. The Chinese, regarded as neither black nor white, were a tiny minority that disappeared in the official records. Figures used are estimates, mainly sourced from records kept by the Chinese community itself. The figures available indicate that in 1946 there were just over 4 000 Chinese in South Africa and 10 000 in 1980.

What these figures do not show is the story of how second- and third-generation Chinese South Africans moved out from behind the shop counters, attended university, and used their qualifications to leave South Africa and migrate to other Western countries. The Chinese faced a variety of restrictions in relation to occupation, residence and movement, which escalated into a full ban on immigration after the National Party came to power in 1948. One reaction to the increasing discrimination under apartheid was a brain drain. By 1967, it was estimated that between 30 and 40 per cent of Chinese graduates had emigrated.[2] This onward emigration continues to this day and there are now Chinese South African communities in the US, Canada, Australia and, more recently, New Zealand.

From the 1970s, even before the demise of apartheid, the Chinese were freed from the restrictions of the Group Areas Act. Most of the original Chinese South Africans melted into the white suburbs, becoming even more invisible as a separate ethnic group. Relics of the apartheid era – shops and restaurants that have been around for decades – remain open in the old Chinatown neighbourhood at the bottom of Commissioner Street in Johannesburg, but the area is rundown, with little sign of life on the street. Kabego Park in Port Elizabeth, the only group area actually proclaimed for Chinese, is now a mixed area.

The face of the Chinese community began to change in the late 1970s after South Africa forged ties with the Republic of China (Taiwan). A second generation of Chinese South Africans was born as, through the 1980s, Taiwanese industrialists set up factories in the homeland areas. These industrialists were joined later by other immigrants from the Republic of China who moved in as entrepreneurs, opening import-export firms, restaurants and small businesses in the metropolitan areas. At the peak, there were between 30 000 and 40 000 Taiwanese living in South Africa. Today there are distinct Taiwanese communities in Newcastle, Bloemfontein and Ladybrand, and there is the bustling New Chinatown in Cyrildene in Johannesburg.

At the time of the first democratic elections in 1994 the Chinese community numbered 20 000. This has since increased to between 100 000 and 200 000, with a third wave of immigrants from Hong Kong and the People's Republic of China swamping the original community. The original Chinese South Africans are now the smallest group – of between 10 000 and 12 000. Most of the Taiwanese have left, and those that remain now number between 12 000 and 14 000. The number of immigrants from Hong Kong is small and they are often described as 'not Chinese, more English'.

The biggest inflow is from the new generation of migrants from mainland China – while exact figures are not known, it is estimated that between 100 000 and 200 000 legal and illegal immigrants have settled in South Africa. They have taken up residence in Cape Town and in a host of small towns around the country, and in Lesotho, but the majority have come to Johannesburg where they have 'colonised' a spread of suburbs in the eastern part of the city, including Bruma Lake, Kempton Park and now Edenvale.[3]

It is staggering to think that so many migrants could enter a country almost unseen. While their arrival has changed the dynamics of the Chinese communities in South Africa, in terms of the Chinese diaspora, this inflow into South Africa is almost negligible as 36 million Chinese now live outside China.

Stumbling blocks to belonging

The story of the original Chinese South Africans is one of a group trying to find a place for itself in an environment that was at best ambivalent, at worst hostile, towards them. For most of the last century, they straddled the colour line but were not socially accepted by either blacks or whites. At the same time they were gradually losing their language and their religion as Christianity spread along with the provision of education by the churches. As their connections to China withered, they became more westernised and joined the middle class. Ironically, apartheid kept alive a sense of being Chinese as discriminatory legislation brought them together as a group, giving rise to a plethora of social and cultural organisations.

After the arrival of the Taiwanese, discriminatory blocks were removed – except for the franchise. At the time of the first democratic elections in 1994, the Chinese were the only group that had not been given franchise in one or other apartheid political structure. The easing of restrictions was, however, a concession to the Taiwanese and not a right, a grievance that still rankles today.

There are now two distinct generations within the original Chinese community: the older generation who grew up with and remember the humiliations of apartheid, and the younger generation who grew up with economic and social mobility. The latter were allowed to live where they liked, to attend any school and to open businesses wherever they wanted. Most have tertiary degrees and work in professions and business. Chinese essentially became a racial description rather than a cultural one – this generation socialised with whites and were accepted as, and identified themselves as, South African.

The re-racialisation of South Africa through affirmative action legislation has, however, put Chinese ethnicity back on the agenda. The exclusion from affirmative action laws on employment equity and black economic empowerment is a controversial topic in the community. Once again they, like many Indians and coloureds, feel pushed aside by the present government, saying that under apartheid they were excluded as non-whites and now they are being excluded because they are non-black. The case of Phil Ah Hing is a good example. Her application for a shop at the Emfuleni casino in Port Elizabeth was refused on the grounds that at least 30 per cent of the businesses needed to be black-owned. Her response was bitter: 'We didn't count before and we don't count now.'

While some of the old organisations are becoming redundant and fading as the older generation passes on, affirmative action legislation has given the Chinese Association of South Africa a role in democratic South Africa. In 2003, the Association made a presentation and submission to Parliament regarding their legal status during apartheid and protesting against their exclusion from the definition of those who should benefit from employment equity, but as yet there has been no response from the labour committee of Parliament.

This exclusion has led to confusion in practice, with some companies including Chinese as previously disadvantaged and others excluding them. It is noteworthy, in terms of how the Chinese community feels about their place in democratic South Africa, what the Association said in its submission to Parliament: 'The amendment to the Employment Equity Act would allow us as South Africans to believe that we are part of one nation.'[4]

While this statement underlies the feeling of not belonging, the original Chinese community nevertheless has a strong sense of themselves as South African – even after they have emigrated. Many still have family connections in South Africa, and in cities like Toronto and Vancouver there are cultural groups for Chinese South Africans that arrange social functions.

On its website, the Canadian Chinese Association South Africa describes itself as an organisation aimed to foster social contact among Chinese from southern Africa now living in Canada. The Transvaal Chinese Association (which has been around since 1903 and is changing its name to the Chinese Association Gauteng) facilitates links between those who have emigrated and those still in South Africa on its website. According to Park (2005), what underpins the desire to maintain links is the fact that as they encounter other Chinese they feel less Chinese and more South African.[5]

The new immigrants from the People's Republic of China have brought these issues of identity to the fore, with a marked schism between the two groups, and growing resentment from the original Chinese South Africans of what they say is behaviour that is damaging the image of Chinese people. When the Taiwanese arrived, the local community went out of its way to make them welcome, even though the original community spoke Cantonese and the Taiwanese speak Mandarin. There are fault lines between the two communities. Tensions initially arose when the Taiwanese began to make their presence felt in local Chinese politics and tried to assume leadership of several regional associations. Another source of tension is the reputation of Taiwanese factory owners as bad employers, which members of the original community consider reflects badly on them as Chinese.

Links between these two communities essentially remain more about business than social activities, but there is no sense of a class difference. However, the attitude of the original community towards the mainland Chinese is vastly different and at times quite hostile. In this instance, there is a class difference. A common refrain heard is that the newcomers are low-class, dirty, uneducated and embarrassing, evidenced in comments such as, 'they don't use curtains but newspaper to cover their windows,' and 'they use the swimming pool as a fish pond'. The Taiwanese share some of these concerns. However, they also share a language with the mainland Chinese and make a distinction between those who are here illegally and law-abiding legal immigrants. Exacerbating these concerns is the negative media coverage about these new immigrants, which has focused mainly on the criminal activities of the Chinese triads, and more recently on job losses that are being blamed on cheap Chinese imports.

A valid concern expressed by members of the original community is that they will be identified with the newcomers as they say that other South Africans do not distinguish between those who have been here for generations and the new immigrants. These worries are not unfounded – there have been stories of local Chinese being stopped by the police and asked for their passports and being accused of being here illegally. There is a genuine fear that they will be treated as foreigners in their own country.

Underlying this inability to make distinctions is the fact that the South African Chinese experience is a closed book to most other South Africans. The community still remains almost invisible. The first non-academic book about the community – not fiction but a memoir – is Darryl Accone's (2004) *All under heaven: The story of a Chinese family in South Africa*, in which he uses his family's experience as a mirror to explore the social history of the original community. It is an illuminating account of how apartheid laws damaged the lives of ordinary people. When asked in an interview why so little had been written about the Chinese, Accone pointed out that historically the Chinese had not really entered public life because it was exceptionally difficult to do so, for various reasons. However, he also acknowledged that some of the difficulties the Chinese had in fitting in were probably due to the dearth of books and plays by Chinese South Africans about their experience. By contrast, members of other immigrant groups have produced plays about their search for identity. For example, Irene Stephanou explored what it meant to be young and of Greek origin, growing up behind the counter at the corner shop, in her play *Meze, Mira and Make-up*, and Rajesh Gopie's *Out Of Bounds* delves into the Indian experience in South Africa. These works have opened those worlds to a larger audience.

Ten years after democracy the voice of the original community remains low-key. Significantly, the campaign to be included in affirmative action legislation was channelled through an extra-parliamentary body dating from the apartheid era. This contrasts with the Taiwanese, who have entered public life and see Parliament as a forum to represent the Chinese community. Since 2004 there have been four Taiwanese-born Chinese Members of Parliament: Sherry Cheng (Democratic Alliance); Eugenia Chang (Inkatha Freedom Party); Chris Wang (Independent Democrats); and Charlie Huang (African National Congress), who has also held the position of deputy mayor in Newcastle.

Influx from the East

The first wave of new Chinese immigration was swept along by the odd friendship forged in the late 1970s between the two international pariah states of the Republic of China (Taiwan) and South Africa as the two countries tried to give each other a sense of legitimacy. Having spent decades blocking Chinese immigration, the Nationalist government did an abrupt about-turn and actively encouraged immigration as a way to bolster its homeland border industries policy.

State visits, cultural exchanges, treaty ratifications, medal swapping and city twinning accompanied the drift of Taiwanese into the country in the 1980s and 1990s. As part of the package the government made a number of concessions, such as allowing permanent residence to these new immigrants.

But the real drawcard was the generous incentives offered to set up shop in Bophuthatswana, KwaNdebele, Venda, Lebowa, Gazankulu, Transkei, Ciskei Qwa Qwa and KwaZulu, which included relocation costs, subsidising wages for seven years and rent for ten. These homeland factories mainly produced clothing and items such as kitchenware, and their owners ranged from small businessmen who relocated their factories to these areas, to subsidiaries of companies in Taiwan. Ladysmith and Newcastle became sites of secondary investment when white local government officials in small, mainly Afrikaans-speaking towns bypassed the national government in an attempt to attract Taiwanese into their fiscal nets.

Many of the Taiwanese immigrants came with capital. Others made an instant fortune – 'buckets of gold' – from round-tripping[6] the financial rand. There are stories of industrialists who neglected their businesses for this more lucrative source of income. Factory management and technical staff brought out on contract also cashed in. Some used the money as capital to set themselves up in business.[7]

From the start the Taiwanese factories were bedevilled by labour problems. The juxtaposition of radically different cultures and work ethics caused clashes. While people wanted work, the local black population resented the sweatshop conditions that the Chinese seemed to accept as the norm. On the Chinese side they were baffled by high staff turnover, low productivity and theft. Another major problem was communication, with myriad difficulties caused by a Mandarin speaker and a Sotho or Zulu speaker having to grope towards understanding in broken English. Communication remains a problem today, particularly for the immigrants from mainland China.

One result of this situation is uneasy race relations, with Chinese employers being viewed as exploiters by black workers – despite new labour legislation, post-1994 stories of poor Chinese labour practices in areas like Newcastle persist. However, international pressures accompanying increased access to the US market – the US Africa Growth and Opportunity Act (AGOA) allows complying sub-Saharan countries to export to the US duty-free – are forcing changes. Non-governmental organisations in the US have put pressure on large retail buyers and brands like the Gap and Levi Strauss to adopt progressive policies that avoid sourcing goods from outlets that have abusive labour practices. The improvement in working conditions in Lesotho is said to be marked.

Over the past few years several clothing factories have moved to Swaziland and Lesotho to take advantage of AGOA. As less developed countries, these countries offer greater incentives – and labour is cheaper and less organised. Others have returned to Taiwan or relocated to southeast Asia or the mainland, where the Taiwanese are now being treated as VIPs and even granted tax incentives to take their capitalist skills to the country. Labour is also cheaper in Asia. The Chopstick Products Company is an example of this – established with incentives on the edge of the Langeni Forest in Transkei in the late 1980s, it was the world's largest disposable chopstick factory, producing two million chopsticks a day, mainly for export to Japan. It has now relocated to southeast Asia.

There are various reasons given by the Taiwanese for their dwindling numbers, including the crime rate, the fact that it is difficult to make money here because labour is unskilled and the appreciating rand, which is hammering exports. The textile industry in general is taking a knock as low-cost clothing from China floods onto the international market, and this is also pushing Taiwanese factories in the region out of business.

Despite this disinvestment, in the industrial and manufacturing sectors there are still about 250 Taiwanese factories in South Africa, with the biggest concentration in Newcastle and Ladysmith. There are about the same number of companies operating in the commercial and service sectors – ranging from banking to travel and ocean freight, import-export and real estate – mostly in Johannesburg.[8] One of the most successful is David Kan's Mustek Electronics, established in 1987 and now the largest maker and distributor of computers in South Africa, including those under the Mercer brand.

Another major reason for the withering of links with Taiwan is the government's decision to cut ties with the Republic of China and recognise the People's Republic of China in 1998. In contrast to the situation in the 1980s when red tape was cut to facilitate immigration, now Taiwanese companies have difficulty getting work permits to bring in skilled staff. There are no longer even direct flights between the two countries.

From the start, the Taiwanese became socially integrated into white South Africa – only in conservative Bloemfontein did the Chinese have difficulty renting houses during the apartheid era. Children were allowed into white schools, although many attended private schools. Many of those that have

THE CHINESE COMMUNITIES IN SOUTH AFRICA

stayed talk of South Africa as their second country. A significant number of their children have been born here, with English becoming their first language, although Mandarin is still taught in weekend schools.

However, ties with Taiwan remain strong. There are three Mandarin newspapers printed locally, which cover community news, international news, news from Taiwan, mainland China and Hong Kong, entertainment and sports. Newspapers from Taiwan and mainland China are readily on sale and satellite television offers channels from both countries.

There is an increasing engagement with local issues by the Taiwanese, such as the Tzu Chi Foundation, a charity which distributes food parcels in black communities. The Taiwanese have also introduced dragon boat racing, a spectacle of boats decked out with the head and tail of a dragon moving on the water to rhythmic drumming. Since the first regatta on Bruma Lake in 1999, the Gauteng Dragon Boat Association was formed and it is now a league of clubs across the racial spectrum – white, black and Chinese. There are a number of cultural clubs and business associations, although it seems that many of these are more about form than substance and are part of the business-card culture of the Chinese – an essential networking tool, which is not complete without association membership credentials.

The Taiwanese also brought Buddhism to Africa. While this generation of migrants is more religious than the first and the third – from mainland China, where religion under Communist rule withered – the Taiwanese say that their children brought up in South Africa are starting to lose their religion. A physical manifestation of Taiwanese religious life is the Buddhist Temple in Bronkhorstspruit in Gauteng – and the sight of it rising out of the veld at the side of the N4 between Pretoria and Witbank is incongruous. It could easily be mistaken for a Chinese theme-park casino. It contains a guesthouse and meditation retreat centre (popular with stressed-out Johannesburgers) and a seminary. The main temple is due to be opened to the public in October 2005, and is an awesome celebration of Chinese art with three giant Buddhas and intricate craftsmanship. Among artists brought in from abroad to work on the temple were a team from Beijing. Built on 15 hectares of land donated to the Taiwanese Fo Guang Shan Buddhist Order by the Bronkhorstspruit Council in 1992, the multimillion-rand temple is funded by devotees in South Africa and Taiwan and is the first Buddhist seminary in Africa. It is intended as a base for the dissemination of Buddhism throughout the African continent. While the monks are from Taiwan, the novices are mostly from Africa and the present intake includes students from Congo, Madagascar, Malawi, Tanzania and Swaziland. There are also two South African novices, a white male and a white female. The three-year training course is intensive and includes learning Mandarin for two hours a day. The order based at the temple minister to the remaining Taiwanese community, and also maintain cultural centres with shrines in Bloemfontein, Ladybrand, Newcastle, Cape Town, Pretoria and Johannesburg. The monks would like to reintroduce the Buddhist way of life to the new immigrants from mainland China, but have not had much success yet. However, Master Hui Fang, the temple's abbot, pointed out that thousands of mainland Chinese visited the temple in February this year, not to worship but to attend the festival to celebrate the Chinese New Year. This was in contrast to 2004, when only a handful of mainland Chinese attended.

Moving from the mainland

If China is becoming the factory of the world, then China City, behind Ellis Park in Johannesburg, is one of its depots. This sprawling maze of traders, selling clothes, shoes, glasses, toys, leatherwear, electronic goods and food is open seven days a week, shunting thousands of boxes of goods, mainly imported from China. The customers are mainly black and Indian, hawkers in the local informal sector, small-town traders and shopkeepers who come in from all over the country, as well as from countries such as Botswana, Zimbabwe, Angola and even Nigeria and Ghana. As one shopper from Port Elizabeth, who was stocking up for his township shop, put it: 'Everyone wants cheap clothes. You can buy here and still make a profit.' In addition to China City, several Chinese shopping complexes have been built in Johannesburg – Asia City, Hong Kong City, Crowne Square, Gold Reef Emporia and the African Trade Centre – each an economic web of China meets Africa, oiling the second economy and supplying small retail outlets.

The earliest record of the new immigrants from mainland China dates back to 1991 when 42 were arrested in Boksburg and appeared wearing headbands with Chinese script that translated as 'hunger strike'. They were all deported. The next time the presence of these new immigrants sprung into the public's awareness was several years later when there were clashes on the streets of Johannesburg between Chinese and black hawkers. The latter objected to the Chinese muscling in on their turf. In contrast to the Taiwanese – manufacturers who came with capital to open businesses, bringing with them skilled staff to work in their factories – most of the Chinese from the mainland arrived without money and with few skills other than the ability to work hard.

Since the finalising of diplomatic relations with the People's Republic of China at the beginning of 1998, Chinese companies have begun investing in South Africa, although foreign direct investment remains low. There are now essentially three strata of mainland Chinese in South Africa: diplomats; entrepreneurs setting up businesses and also investing in property and acting as export agents for commodities such as fruit; workers and traders. And the days of hawking on the street are over as China City and the other complexes have provided them with an economic base. Some of those who have been around for a while have prospered – the route to wealth was hawking, then branching out to supplying hawkers, then becoming a wholesale supplier, and then an importer.

It would be a mistake to view the mainland Chinese in South Africa as a cohesive group. They come from different provinces, speak different dialects, and sometimes even have difficulties understanding each other. There are already signs of a division between those who have been here for a while and those who have arrived more recently – 'from farm' is how an 'old hand' of eight years described a newcomer. The reason most of the migrants have come to South Africa is economic. Their stories echo those of the first Chinese immigrants early in the last century who arrived with little apart from a desire to improve their lot and give their children a better chance in life. Take the case of Lin who has been here for ten years, has a shop in China City and rents a house in Sandton. She echoes the refrain of migrants around the world when she talks of her aspirations for her daughter, who attends a private boarding school in the Free State: 'I don't like her same like me. A doctor is fine.'

Another way in which these migrants resemble the early settlers is that often a family member – male or female – comes on their own. Sometimes they bring the family out later, but many essentially remain migrant workers who remit money back to their families. A few years ago the first stopping-off point for these migrants was blocks of flats near Joubert Park called Shanghai One and Shanghai Two. However, Edenvale has become the latest centre, with 'guesthouses' for individuals. The problem of language (not speaking English) is avoided by living in an almost enclosed economy – working for other Chinese and buying from Chinese shops.

It is estimated that many of these migrants are in South Africa illegally. People enter in various ways. Some arrive as visitors and stay, forfeiting their deposits lodged at the South African Embassy in Beijing. Others are enticed to come with false promises of work, and some are then forced into prostitution. Yet others are victims of scams – after paying a large fee they are abandoned, often at the airport or in a hotel. Smuggling rings are trafficking illegal immigrants into South Africa using men known as 'snakeheads'. Some stay while others are in transit to other destinations. They stay in South Africa for a couple of months, get false papers and then move to South America and finally, the Chinese dream destination, the US.[9]

According to the South African Police Service Aliens Investigation Unit, one of the illegal migrant entry routes is air travel to South Africa via Johannesburg to Mbabane or Maputo or Maseru, where migrants buy false identity documents and passports and use these to enter South Africa by road. Chinese nationals have also been heavily implicated in the false marriage scam. And there are now firms of lawyers specialising in helping Chinese nationals get legal papers, such as upgrading from a visitors visa to a business visa or the self-employed category.

The extent of the Chinese presence can be illustrated by the number of small towns in South Africa and Lesotho which have a Chinese shop. Peter Sapire is an attorney who has acted on behalf of a number of Chinese businesses which have had problems with goods impounded by customs. He describes the business community as: 'Hundreds of small companies importing and retailing or wholesaling goods. The structure is hierarchical with everyone deferring to a big boss. It is an extremely closed community. It's even difficult to serve a summons and to trace people. People in the building say they are not there or that they don't know where the person is. People vanish. They assume another name, start another company.'

Harassment for bribes is reportedly common. According to Sapire: 'They pay up and agree to anything – anything from the price of a coke to a few hundred rand.' Stories of bribes are repeated over and over. Stall owners at China City say the police wait to be paid off in the streets outside the centre on Sundays when Chinese shop owners from smaller towns come in for supplies. It seems clear that bribery is widely used to avoid arrest and deportation. In early 2005, the Parliamentary Portfolio Committee undertook a fact-finding mission and found only African detainees being held at Lindela repatriation centre prior to deportation. The Committee has asked the Home Affairs Ministry to provide answers as to why there are no Asians or whites in Lindela, and for clarity on the deportation figures. To date it has not had a reply.

Crime and corruption

The Chinese community in general bears the brunt of the common public perception that illegal immigrants are responsible for crime. While it is certainly the case that many Chinese migrants break the law to enter the country, in the broader picture of crime, they are often the victims. This applies particularly to Chinese women who are victims of human trafficking in the illicit sex trade. The International Organisation for Migration in Pretoria assists, on average, seven Chinese women each month who have been to South Africa to return home.

Most of the women were lured to South Africa from China on the pretext that they would be working in a luxury hotel or in Chinese restaurants, shops and businesses, where the fact that they do not speak English will not matter. Recruiters are said to target poor women, often from southern China, who sign a contract to repay their travel expenses from their future earnings. They are given documents and tickets before they leave for South Africa, but on arrival are told they will have to earn their keep through sex work. Chinese triad societies direct this lucrative industry, often using the threat of harming the girls' families if they do not co-operate and 'repay their debt'.

Another method used to entrap women is to tell them they are coming to South Africa to study English. They arrive legally with study permits. In Cape Town, syndicates use schools for teaching English to foreigners. Girls are taught basic telephone technique, like how to say, 'Hello my name is Lulu.' After a month they are told there is no more money for food or studies and they are forced to earn their keep in the sex trade.[10]

The International Organisation for Migration also has evidence of South African women being trafficked to the East Asia city of Macau, which became a special administrative region of China in 1991, and is known as the Las Vegas of China for its casinos, nightclubs and brothels, called 'saunas'. Young South African women are lured there with false job offers before being forced into prostitution. A police source believes that South Africans were first trafficked to Macau in 2000.

This human trafficking is the work of organised crime in the form of Chinese triad societies, which made their way into South Africa in the 1970s when they became involved in the trade of shark fin in Cape Town. By the 1980s they had moved into other cities and expanded their activities to include trading in abalone (and products from other protected species such as rhino horn), drug trafficking, diamond smuggling, human smuggling, illegal gambling, extortion, prostitution, vehicle theft and illegal imports. The police know of seven triads working in the country, some from Hong Kong and Taiwan. There are clubs and restaurants around South Africa owned by triads for the exclusive use of the Chinese community at which both South African and Chinese women work.

The Chinese community are also concerned about what they call 'gangsters'– free agents not attached to the triads – who are moving in. In recent years there have been a number of contract killings of Chinese businessmen. According to Simon Shi of the Chinese Community and Police Co-operation Centre in Johannesburg, there were 19 murders of Chinese people in and around Johannesburg last year. The most recent such case was a gruesome murder of a couple and their two children who were then dumped near the highway. It is rumoured that the murders were linked to a property deal and that hitmen were brought in from China to do the killings (*Sunday Times Metro* 28.11.04).

The other side of the coin is the fact that Chinese crime would not exist without local collusion. Corruption plays an important role in facilitating the activities of the triads. Home Affairs officials issue false papers to facilitate illegal immigration, and officials from the Department of Customs and Excise are involved in clearing counterfeit goods, often with forged documents.

Citizenship, identity and the Chinese community

In *Blood washes blood*, a search by Italian-American Frank Viviano (2001) to understand his ancestry, he wrote: 'The past is not another country it is the country within...Identity, in the end, rests in the tension between conflicting plots, a lasting tension between the dramas we inherit, consciously or not, and the drama we choose to write for ourselves.' Among the dramas the original Chinese South Africans inherited was the legend of a great China, a land of traditions and dignity. The reality of the new Chinese immigrants has deflated this idea of China and has unsettled the way the original Chinese see themselves, increasingly making them acknowledge their South African identity. However, that sense of 'being South African' does not necessarily translate into a sense of belonging. Many members of the younger generation in the Chinese community have emigrated. However, when they leave it is with this sense of themselves as South Africans, as evidenced in the existence of Chinese South African communities in cities such as Vancouver and Toronto.

Citizenship does not always equate with loyalty to a country. The Republic of China allows dual citizenship. Most Taiwanese who came to South Africa were granted permanent residence and later took out South African citizenship. As many as 60 per cent of the Taiwanese who emigrated to South Africa have now re-emigrated or returned home. This would suggest that their South African citizenship was more about expedience than commitment, a practical way to avoid bureaucratic hassles. The question is, what will happen with the generation of Taiwanese who were born in South Africa or arrived when they were young? The first generation of Taiwanese was self-employed. The second generation, who are approaching adulthood, is English-speaking, well-educated and skilled. Like many young white South Africans, their perception is that jobs will go to black applicants before them. Affirmative action is highlighted as one reason why young Taiwanese want to emigrate after completing their tertiary education. Many of these younger Taiwanese get a Taiwanese passport, but they do not return to Taiwan, often moving instead to Australia and New Zealand.

In contrast, the People's Republic of China does not allow dual citizenship and large numbers of this group are unlikely to relinquish their Chinese citizenship for South African citizenship. Many have drifted here on an economic tide and will leave if business opportunities dry up. In general, members of this group do not see a future for their children in South Africa. However, history shows that this wave of immigration is likely to create a new Chinese South African group.

Conclusion

In his 2005 'State of the Nation' speech President Thabo Mbeki noted inspiringly: 'We can and shall build a South Africa that truly belongs to all who live in it, united in our diversity.' The experience of the older Chinese groups in South Africa suggests that this will be far more difficult than the rhetoric suggests. As a group the Chinese continue to be treated differently, unsure whether they are defined as 'previously disadvantaged' and fearful of discrimination in job opportunities. In some ways their experience of democratic South Africa mirrors that of white South Africans, with the inevitable change to majority rule and the growth of African nationalism instilling feelings of marginalisation, whether these are based on fact or perception.

The presence of a large number of new Chinese immigrants shows the power of economic forces in an era where globalisation has generated an unprecedented movement of the world's people. It also underlines the failure of immigration law in practice, undermined as it is by widespread corruption.

Notes

1   In the course of researching this paper, I conducted interviews with the following people: Vance Chang: Director of Information Division, Taipei Liaison Office in the RSA; Sherry Chen: MP Democratic Alliance, Executive Member of RSA-ROC Economic Relations, owner of Top International Traders and clothing factories; Master Fang, Abbot of the Fo Guang Shan Buddhist Temple; Gino Feng: Editor, *China Express*; Alice Hu: Alice Hu Properties; Sandy Kalyan: MP Democratic Alliance and DA Home Affairs spokesperson; Eugene Kanson: Chinese Association of South Africa; Peter Sapire: Attorney; Robin Xu: Director China JiLin Provincial/Commercial Liaison Association in South Africa and director of the African Trade Centre, Johannesburg.

2   A detailed discussion of the population shifts in the original community is provided by Yap and Leong Man (1996).

3   Gastrow in 2001 said there were 100 000 Chinese citizens/residents and quoted police sources as saying there were between 100 000 and 200 000. Since then this figure of 100 000 illegal immigrants has been mentioned in a number of newspaper articles and has become a consensus – though not necessarily correct – figure alongside the figure of 80 000 legal immigrants, the figure given by the embassy of the People's Republic of China in Pretoria. The embassy accept that their figures are not

accurate and do acknowledge that there are illegal immigrants. However, they do not think it as high as 100 000. In my interviews with people from the mainland community some also said the figure was too high and that it did not take into account migratory flows as many people have gone back to China or moved on. Also, they say that the situation has changed and that people get papers once they are here, and that this is becoming easier. The evidence is that although this is being done legally in some cases, people are also obtaining papers illegally and I go into this in more detail later. In the end no one really knows how many mainland Chinese are here.

4   The perceived Chinese exclusion from the employment equity legislation was one of the most controversial issues Park (2005) found in her research.

5   One of the findings from interviews by Park with Chinese South Africans who had emigrated.

6   Round-tripping was a way of profiting from the difference between the two types of currency created under the apartheid regime to protect the economy from abnormal outflows through capital flight. Foreign investment and disinvestment in South African assets was effected through the 'financial rand', which traded at a discount to the 'commercial rand'. The commercial rand was used for all other transactions, such as buying overseas goods, or paying dividends. The idea was to insulate the normal currency, the commercial rand, from volatility, especially a fall in value against other currencies. The dual currency system also created an opportunity, which some sharp-eyed businessmen took advantage of. Bringing in money as an investment through the financial rand and taking it out shortly afterwards through the commercial rand route meant an immediate profit – and risk of prosecution.

7   Interview with *China Express* editor Gino Feng.

8   *Taiwanese investment in South Africa, Swaziland and Lesotho: A case study* by Representative Du Ling, Taipei Liaison Office in the Republic of South Africa.

9   Interview with IOM official based in Cape Town tracking human smuggling rings in Lesotho.

10 Interview with IOM official based in Cape Town tracking human smuggling rings in Lesotho.

References

Accone D (2004) *All under heaven: The story of a Chinese family in South Africa*. Cape Town: David Philip.

Gastrow P (2001) *Triad societies and Chinese organised crime in South Africa*. Occasional Paper No. 48, Institute for Security Studies.

Hart G (2002) *Reworking apartheid legacies: Global competition, gender and social wages in South Africa, 1980–2000*. Social Policy and Development Programme Paper No. 13. United Nations Research Institute for Social Development.

Martens J, Pieczkowski M & van Vuuren-Smyth B (2003) *Seduction, sale & slavery: Trafficking in women & children for sexual exploitation in Southern Africa*. Third Edition International Organization for Migration (IOM) Regional Office for Southern Africa. Pretoria: IOM.

Mbeki, T (2005) Address of the President of South Africa, Thabo Mbeki, at the second joint sitting of the third democratic Parliament. Cape Town, 11.02.05

Park YJ (2005) Citizenship and identity dilemmas for Chinese South Africans in post-apartheid South Africa. PhD thesis, Sociology Department, University of the Witwatersrand.

Pickles J & Woods J (1989) Taiwanese Investment in South Africa. *African Affairs* 88: 507–528.

Viviano F (2001) *Blood washes blood*. New York: Pocket Books.

Yap M & Leong Man D (1996) *Colour, confusion and concessions: The history of the Chinese in South Africa*. Hong Kong: Hong Kong University Press.

15 Winning the Cup but losing the plot? The troubled state of South African soccer

Merryman Kunene

South Africa's winning of the right to host soccer's World Cup in 2010 was received by the nation with triumph. First and foremost, it signified global recognition of the enormous steps which a racially divided country had taken in putting its house in order since 1994, and seemed set to promote further nation-building and social cohesion. Secondly, for the majority of South Africans, it offered glittering prospects of developmental gains, with the estimates suggesting that the event could generate about R20 billion, yield some 160 000 jobs, provide a huge boost to tourism and lead to hugely improved infrastructure in and between South Africa's cities. Third, the award was seen as offering huge opportunities for South African soccer and the reputation of African soccer generally. Hence, for Danny Jordaan, the Chief Executive Officer (CEO) of the local organising committee, 'The World Cup must be both African but above all be world-class. This way, we will be making the point to the international community that there is no contradiction in being African and world-class' (*City Press* 26.03.05). Finally, and most importantly, in the eyes of millions of supporters, hosting the World Cup is seen as an opportunity to promote the international ranking and status of the national soccer team, Bafana Bafana, and in so doing, promote the long-term development of the game domestically. Yet for all the opportunities it represents, planning for the World Cup represents far greater challenges than it has to any host country so far, for this mega-event – as large in investment and audience terms as the Olympics – is being undertaken by a country whose domestic game is poorly run, poorly financed, and too often poorly played in an era when globalisation is in any case underdeveloping the game in Third World countries. If the opportunities of hosting the World Cup in 2010 are to be maximised, then much must change locally.

A diary of disarray: the chequered development of South African soccer

After South Africa's re-admission to world soccer in 1992, the team won the African Cup of Nations in 1996 at the first attempt. For some, this was even a greater triumph than South Africa's winning the Rugby World Cup in 1995, for although that moment had been famously celebrated by Nelson Mandela donning a Springbok rugby jersey and delighted many who otherwise had no interest in the game, the team which triumphed was entirely white, the sport had an unenviable reputation as a redoubt of racism, and whilst having significant black pockets of support around the country, was undoubtedly a minority sport in national terms. In contrast, although the Nations Cup was only a continental competition, and although the triumphant Bafana Bafana team was captained by Neil Tovey, a popular white centreback, the team was nonetheless largely black and representative of a sport which was enjoyed and fêted by the majority of the population and which, after numerous struggles, appeared to have overcome the legacy of apartheid. Yet Bafana Bafana's success (like that of the rugby team, it has to be said) was fleeting, and although the national team managed to reach the World Cup finals in 1998 and 2002, its performance was otherwise disappointing, its regression marked by its failure in successive African Nations Cups to make any significant mark. Team managers came and went, racial tensions tore at the fabric of the team, and some European-based players at times simply decided to opt out of playing for their country. Yet the chaos in the Bafana Bafana camp simply mirrored soccer's troubled historical development and present state.

The game arrived in South Africa as a by-product of Britain's commercial and imperial expansion, brought and played by mainly white working-class Britons,[1] but thereafter became hugely popular among the black population, encouraged by the schools and missions, and in the Transvaal, by the mines and the close-knit conditions of the African townships (Couzens 1983; Alegi 2004). The first league became a reality in 1892 with the formation of the Natal Football Association, a body which subsequently presaged the foundation of the (whites only) South African Football Association (Safa) in 1892. The latter hosted the first-ever visits by a team from Britain with the arrival in 1897 of the then mighty Corinthians (and then again in 1903 and 1906), this followed by tours by squads despatched by the English Football

Association in 1910, 1920, 1929, 1939 and 1956, whilst Scotland contributed tours by Aberdeen in 1927 and 1937 and Motherwell in 1931 and 1934. Yet it was only after the Second World War that the tempo changed markedly, with Clyde, Wolverhampton Wanderers, Leicester City, Newcastle United, Preston North End Tottenham Hotspur, Dundee and Arsenal and other clubs all arriving to play matches against South African (segregated) opposition, games which led to many white South African players being lured to play for British teams, whilst in return, many British players were to sign for South African teams in their declining professional years (Raath 2002).[2] Overall, the British influence was to leave a marked impact upon the local game, not least in the style of play and its lingering affections (Alegi n.d.).[3]

However, the promise that such visits held for South African soccer was to be denied by the plunge of the domestic game into nearly 30 years of isolation, following the final imposition by the Federation of International Football Associations (Fifa) in 1964 of a ban on South African teams touring abroad or receiving overseas teams (SAIRR 1964).

Fifa's ban was the culmination of a struggle for legitimacy within South African soccer in the apartheid years. The most broad-based of the domestic soccer groupings was the South African Soccer Federation. Established in 1951, it brought together African, Indian and coloured bodies and from the outset made representations to Fifa that it, rather than the white-run Safa, should be recognised internationally. These failed as in 1952 Fifa admitted Safa as South Africa's sole member of the international body. Under continuing domestic and international pressure, in 1956 Safa deleted a colour-bar clause from its constitution and changed its name to the Football Association of South Africa (Fasa). But in reality nothing changed. Fasa insisted that it had to operate within the laws of the country which, since passage of such legislation as the Group Areas and Population Registration Acts of 1950, had rendered racial segregation compulsory.

Despite the cosmetic nature of the changes within Safa/Fasa, in 1958 Fifa re-affirmed its recognition of Fasa as the governing body of soccer in South Africa and Fasa continued to preside over the development of soccer along separate (yet distinctly unequal) lines, even acquiring some so-called Bantu, Indian and coloured affiliates in line with the government's doctrine that sport should be organised along 'multinational' lines. What made Fifa's action surprising was the fact that soon after Fasa had in 1957 become a founder member of the Confederation of African Football (CAF), it was suspended for attempting to enter an all-white, and when that was turned down, an all-black team into the inaugural African Cup of Nations tournament. Failed attempts to enter non-white teams into a subsequent Nations Cup and World Cup preliminaries followed. The events in South Africa post-1960 saw Fifa subjected to ever-mounting pressure to exclude Fasa from the international body. The result was that, despite continuing Western support for Fasa within Fifa – on the grounds that the former body was supposedly rendering increased support for the development of non-white soccer – it was eventually suspended in 1964 (Couzens 1983; SAIRR 1955–56; 1964).

South African soccer subsequently continued to develop along separate lines. On the one hand, Fasa continuously sought to urge its case with Fifa, and presided over a series of 'multinational' competitions and a tour by a professional British Stars XI in 1973.[4] Yet they were unable to combat the energetic campaigns by groups like the South African Non-Racial Olympic Committee (Sanroc) to have South Africa banned from international sport completely. By this time, it was clear that the future of South African soccer lay in the hands of black groups whose club affiliates enjoyed enormous popularity. Many of these clubs had a close (but unofficial) relationship with the African National Congress (ANC). This was no surprise given that for decades leading ANC figures had also been prominent in organising football amongst Africans. These included Chief Albert Luthuli, who became ANC President in the 1950s, and who had been the first secretary of the South African African Football Association (SAAFA) on its launch in 1932 and subsequently helped establish the Natal Inter-Race Soccer Board in 1946 (Couzens 1983: 209; SAFA 2001). By the early 1970s, Soweto alone reportedly had as many as 1 000 amateur and 15 professional teams which, despite grossly inadequate facilities, were able to draw large crowds (SAIRR 1972).

In order to both plead its case before Fifa and to shore up the financial basis of its affiliates, Fasa had begun to contest government policy by arguing for 'multiracial' support whereby teams from different racial groups would be enabled to play against each other. In 1977, this culminated in a proposal for a Super League which would draw 16 of the country's top professional sides into a mixed league. However, in the wake of the Soweto protests, this failed and the plan collapsed when the nine top black teams which had been drawn into negotiations opted to stay with the black National Professional Soccer League (NPSL). Later in 1977, five leading white clubs, including Highlands Park and Wits University, decamped from their white soccer grouping (the National Football League [NFL]) to join the NPSL. By December 1977, 19 teams (including eight from the NFL) had been accepted into a newly constructed NPSL which operated under the auspices of George Thabe's predominantly African South African National Football Association (SAIRR 1972, 1973, 1977; Safa 2001). In 1979, Kaizer Chiefs took the politically momentous step of signing the first white player to join a historically black club, a veteran midfielder 'Lucky' Stylianou who, according to North, 'instantly…became one of the best-known whites in black South Africa, with a name recognition on a par with the prime minister and other leading political figures' (1985: 146).

In the early 1980s, the NPSL went from strength to strength. One reflection of this came in the form of increasing sponsorship, notably from South African Breweries. In 1983, it was estimated that some four million fans went through turnstiles of the NPSL, netting the league and its clubs some R8 million in revenue. In September 1984, after moving their home from Orlando Stadium in Soweto to the Ellis Park stadium in Johannesburg, the prominent NPSL team Kaizer Chiefs drew a crowd of 100 000 fans to their clash with rivals Orlando Pirates, a record for any soccer match in South African history (SAIRR 1984).

Yet the increasing flow of money into the game induced bitter rivalries, and in 1985, Thabe – increasingly under attack for his tolerance of 'multiracialism' – was unable to prevent the formation of a breakaway National Soccer League (NSL) which was headed by Abdul Bhamjee who enjoyed the support of the real kingmaker in the form of Kaizer Motaung, owner of Kaizer Chiefs. The divide was violent, with some clubs like Orlando Pirates and Moroka Swallows being split right down the middle. Players and officials were caught in deadly fights, and some said that Swallows had their captain (Aaron Roadblock Makhathini) murdered for allegedly refusing to join the NSL faction. Indeed, early in 1985, fans at the FNB stadium in Johannesburg watched in dismay as Pirates took to the field with two different teams, and China Hlongwane, the captain of one of them, was stabbed several times in full view of supporters and viewers watching the drama on TV (Safa 2001). Yet backed by the key emerging soccer bosses, notably Motaung and Irvin Khoza of Orlando Pirates, it was the NSL which prevailed and vanquished the NPSL.

The end to division was at long last in sight with the approach of democracy and a non-racial society. With the support of the ANC, which the NSL and a new non-racial South African Soccer Association had travelled to meet in Lusaka, in early 1989 (SAIRR 1988–89), all the different groupings within the game at last agreed to merge under one umbrella of a unified and non-racial South African Football Association, which was launched in 1991. Under the chairmanship of Mluleki George, with Solomon Sticks Morewa as the general secretary, it was under this body that South Africa was re-admitted into the international arena (in 1992, even before the country's formal progression to democracy). Nonetheless, despite this welcome attainment of unity, the future development of South African soccer in the post-apartheid period was to remain hugely problematic.

The political economy of soccer in South Africa

As already suggested, although the history of South African soccer was severely distorted by the internal and international implications of apartheid, by the early 1990s it had achieved unity and, increasingly fuelled by lucrative commercial sponsorships, was rapidly developing into a multimillion rand sport. Yet in so doing, it was also transforming itself into an 'industry', and whilst retaining many of the imprints of its troubled past, it was simultaneously acquiring the characteristics, both bad and good, of soccer internationally.

Soccer is by far the world's most valuable spectator sport, and it translates into very big business indeed. The combination of a highly competitive team sport, in which it is undesirable for one team to be unbeatable if popular interest is to be sustained, and free-market business, which seeks to maximise power and profitability at the expense of any opposition, inevitably leads to contradictions and conflicts which the controlling bodies seek to regulate. These trends have been most exemplified in England, where the impact of an explosion of live television coverage of games has driven an apparently unstoppable trend towards the greater commercialisation and corporatisation of football, at least at the topmost levels.

The sudden availability of huge amounts of money from televised coverage, most of it devoted to broadcasting the games of the leading teams, was to result in the establishment in 1992/93 of the Premier League, an independent breakaway by the old First Division from the long established Football League, which was left to administer the lower and poorer divisions. Operating under the broad-based authority of the English Football Association, the Premier League – which from the beginning was dominated by a handful of leading clubs – was founded upon huge sponsorships, which were to increase in time with the rapid expansion of satellite television as matches were beamed to numerous countries around the world, including South Africa.[5] Increasingly, the leading clubs acquired international followings, established overseas marketing corporations, and some listed as public companies on the London Stock Exchange. Financial success accompanied success on the field, and following the logic of the free market, the Premier League itself increasingly became an unequal battlefield where the half dozen or so leading clubs claimed most of the trophies, most of the better players, and most of the money, enviously tailed by the majority of teams whose great fear was the dramatic loss of gate revenues and loss of sponsorships which would follow upon relegation back to the old Football League. At the same time, as the Premier League became global, so it became less British, and whereas only a decade before the overwhelming majority of players had been drawn from England, Scotland, the Irelands and Wales, now it became the venue for increasing numbers of foreign players, many of whom (so long as they were recognised internationals) were drawn from countries of the Third World.[6] As similar developments took place in the other major leagues of Europe as well, global soccer increasingly fell under the sway of Europe, where the major clubs were not only enabled to pay huge salaries to talented players, but also impelled to do so if they were to retain their 'stars', whose bargaining power was to be greatly amplified by changes in Fifa regulations which were required to comply with European Union legislation regarding employee freedom of movement (although only after a Belgian player, Jean-Mark Bosman, had tested the matter in court). Hence, whilst star-struck crowds in England, Italy, Spain and Germany flock to stadia that are constantly being enlarged, countries in Latin America, Asia and especially Africa (accounting for less than five per cent of the global soccer economy) increasingly struggle with the quality of play and the competitiveness of their domestic leagues, which are increasingly becoming training grounds for Europe.

In keeping with its early history, South African soccer was to be significantly influenced by the English example, not least because the English Premier League was soon to become broadcast regularly upon the commercial station,

M-Net (which, with the satellite revolution, was soon to be beaming the English game over much of Africa too). Most notably, however, it sought to emulate the English example with the transformation of the NSL into the Premier Soccer League (PSL) in 1996/97. Yet rather than inaugurating an era of uncomplicated prosperity and growth, the PSL has tended to replicate the worst aspects of the English Premier League whilst only dubiously reaping its benefits and also having to cope directly with the competition of Europe for both its players and its audiences.

Although securing increased sponsorships, the 'Castle' PSL was always going to be disadvantaged, not only by its heritage of clubs with inadequate grounds, poor playing pitches and dismal training facilities, but also by the limited availability of television revenue. For M-Net (later DSTV), initially the English and later other continental leagues were a major drawcard for viewers able to afford a pricey monthly subscription, its appeal being increased by the rapid appearance of 'sportsbars' where substantial crowds regularly gathered to watch live games. In contrast, although the PSL was non-racial, it was played principally by African and coloured players and appealed mainly to African audiences, the mass of whom had no direct access to television, and if they did, were unable to afford subscriptions to DSTV. Consequently, it fell to the South African Broadcasting Corporation, the public broadcasting channel, to cover the PSL, and the resulting financial benefits which accrued to the clubs were correspondingly modest. One result was that in a bid to boost revenues, the launch of the PSL was to be accompanied by the running of a host of cup competitions, none of which was able to secure a stature of the analogous English FA Cup, and all of which contributed to an almost continuous season, with no extended break in playing to revitalise interest, and an arguably deleterious impact upon the quality of play and excitement.

Nonetheless, whereas the early years of the English Premier League were to be dominated by just two teams (Manchester United winning eight out of the first 12 championships and Arsenal three), the PSL was won by six clubs between 1997 and 2004, with only Mamelodi Sundowns and Kaiser Chiefs securing repeat triumphs. Even so, the league – and the too numerous cup competitions – remain dominated by a handful of teams. These are drawn principally from Gauteng, by far the richest province, which reaps the largest crowds and most lucrative sponsorships, leaving teams from the other metropoles – and particularly from the more rural areas of the country – in their wake.

An accompaniment of this development is that the administration of the game has become dominated by a handful of moguls. In the early days of African soccer, club ownership and control rested with particular communities. For instance, Pirates was initially owned by residents of Orlando, a location in Soweto, where office holders were elected every year by the club's members and supporters. Yet in an impoverished community with limited resources and few opportunities, this soon gave way to squabbling and the capture of control, in this case by Irvin Khoza, who emerged as general secretary of the club and who was able to provide it with a greater sense of direction, and later became its owner. Yet he was but one of a number of African entrepreneurs who, in one of the few fields of economic enterprise left open to them under the restrictions of apartheid, used football as an avenue to accumulation and wealth. Other individuals who emerged to similarly dominate their clubs were Jabu Phakathi of Amazulu, Melika Madlala of Golden Arrows, David Chabeli of Moroka Swallows, and not least Jomo Sono, who purchased Highlands Park, a historically-white club based in Johannesburg's northern suburbs in 1983, and renamed it Jomo Cosmos. Yet none was to become so prominent as Kaizer Motaung, who, drawing inspiration from the clubs he had played for in the US (particularly Atlanta Chiefs), used his own capital to found his own club in Soweto. As the club was under his control from the beginning, it was run on a considerably more professional basis than its rivals, and was able to avoid the infighting which so characterised their management. Kaiser Chiefs rapidly amassed the largest support base in the country, and Motaung's national influence was to rise accordingly.

Motaung was to work closely with Sticks Morewa, and was also part of the delegation which visited the ANC in Lusaka in 1988. With Morewa subsequently emerging as President of Safa, and Motaung wielding major influence within the NSL, they played a major role in the transformation of the latter into the PSL. However, their domination of the game was not to last for long, for together with Brian Mahon, who ran a sponsorship marketing company, they were to be pronounced 'an undesirable connection' by the Pickard Commission, a body which had been established to enquire into allegations of mismanagement and corruption in top-flight soccer (Safa 2001). Many believed that this was just the tip of the iceberg, for one of the unfortunate facets of the game was that numerous rumours circulated that soccer administration replicated many of the features of township gangland culture – a belief which a recent scandal concerning allegations of club bosses bribing referees has done nothing to suppress.⁷

After capturing control of Pirates, Khoza had rescued the club from the brink of collapse in the early 1990s, not least by negotiating lucrative sponsorship deals and by beginning a brand merchandising campaign modelled on those of English premier clubs such as Manchester United (*Sowetan* 03.05.05). In the wake of the Pickard Commission, he seized the opportunity to use his popularity with other club owners whom the Motaung/Morewa regime had marginalised to wrestle control of both the PSL and Safa, earning himself in so doing the sobriquet the 'Iron Duke'. Although a controversial figure – in 2002 he was investigated for non-payment of tax and eventually had to settle a claim of R7.2 million – Khoza has utilised his position to draw in sponsors and to extend commercial backing for the game. In January 2004, for example, his Orlando Pirates and arch rivals Kaizer Chiefs teamed up with the Zionist Christian Church to sell Vodacom's mobile-phone cards at matches and religious services.

One outcome of the trend towards commercialisation has been the increased attraction of the game to wealthy individuals and interests from outside football. By far the most high profile of these is African Rainbow Minerals magnate, Patrice Motsepe, who now bankrolls Mamelodi Sundowns, whilst another important instance was provided by the decision of M-Net – initially felt by many to be doing nothing for local football – to take over second division Pretoria City in 1994 and convert them into the more professionally-run SuperSport United (a move which it has followed with the expansion of satellite television by broadcasting more local and African soccer content). Although there has as yet been no development equivalent to the takeover of Chelsea by the Russian oil multi-billionaire Roman Abramovitch (resulting in the effective purchase of the English Premier League title in 2005) and the more recent corporate raid on Manchester United by the American sports tycoon Malcom Glazer, the growing commercialisation of the South African game is nonetheless encouraging its effective domination by a handful of self-made African millionaire PSL club owners.

Yet while the owners may prosper, the players are unable to secure the rewards they feel are due to them. The better South African players look to migrate to better paid leagues all over Europe and Asia, depriving the local game of local talent, their place taken by players from other African countries whose own leagues cannot match the relative wealth of the PSL. Meanwhile, the patterns of sponsorship, ownership and governance reinforce rather than address the disparities. On the one hand, as in England, relegation from the PSL to the Mvela Golden League is a financial disaster. In 2005, PSL clubs received R320 000 a month from league sponsorship, whilst standing to earn millions more from the South African Airways-sponsored Supa 8, and the Absa and Coca-Cola Cups, which are reserved for the 16 top-flight clubs. In contrast, Mvela sides received just R30 000 per month (*Business Day* 24.05.05), forcing relegated clubs to offload their better players. Meanwhile, whilst teams from Gauteng mostly thrive, teams from other provinces battle to survive: poorer provinces like Mpumalanga and Northern Cape have no representation in the premier league, while teams from KwaZulu-Natal, the Eastern Cape and Free State regularly struggle to avoid relegation. Nor is such inequality adequately addressed by the game's wider development strategy.

Development and grassroots structures: divergent approaches

Safa has overall responsibility for the game's administration and for the running of its wider facets: amateur and women's soccer and player development. According to its official manifesto, it is committed to promoting and facilitating the development of football through a sustainable and integrated approach to all aspects of the game. For the national association, player development programmes are carried and sponsored through every level of junior football, providing regional and national competitions, coaching, talent identification, a soccer school of excellence and national squads with their own training camps and international competition schedules.

The association has acquired such sponsors as Transnet, Chappies and Simba to finance the programme of leagues and organised tournaments designed to guide youngsters through a structured development process. However, for all the fanfare which has accompanied Safa's national development strategy, only a handful of players have emerged through it to the ranks of top professionals. To be sure, when the programme was started in 1994, a number of youngsters like Lucky Maselesele (who now plays for Black Leopards) and Steven Pienaar (who now plays for Ajax Amsterdam) demonstrated what a school of excellence with proper management and talent scouting could produce. Yet, in more recent times there have been few equivalent outputs, and it would seem that if the programme is not being undermined by, then it is certainly not being co-ordinated with, the development efforts run by the larger and more powerful clubs of the PSL – some of them in collaboration with overseas teams – nor indeed with other significant initiatives. It almost goes without saying that the majority of all such efforts are devoted to the male game, and that the development of women's soccer is largely ignored, and that the women's national team, Banyana Banyana, receives little attention from Safa, the media and sponsors.

One of the more successful contemporary club development programmes is run by Orlando Pirates, which, with the assistance of the Johannesburg-based Boston City College, former national team coach and Peruvian international Augusto, is turning out promising youngsters in significant numbers. According to Pirates, its approach is informed by the club's desire to fulfil the ideals of the National Skills Development Strategy, and is designed to not only produce top quality players on the field but also to empower them socially and academically off the field. The system has served the club well, for many of its products have gone on to play for the national under-17, under-20 and under-23 teams, while some like Benedict Vilakazi and Mbulelo Mabizela have become regulars in the Bafana Bafana squad.[8]

The other larger PSL clubs have run similar programmes, with Kaizer Chiefs and Ajax Cape Town, for instance, having worked together with the then Rand Afrikaans University to run soccer schools for youngsters. Yet although all the professional clubs seek to develop and scout their own talent, the present structures work to reinforce inequality within the game, a development which Safa's efforts do little to counteract. Two factors in particular add to this trend.

First, urban clubs like Pirates, Chiefs, Wits University FC, and Ajax (of Cape Town) capture most of the available soccer talent for the simple reason that they offer career prospects and facilities which few smaller, provincial and lower division sides can match. Importantly too, as was expressed by aspirant players to the author in a review of youth programmes in 2000, not only is the coaching provided by lesser teams perceived as poor, but the pitches upon which they play are poor and conducive to career-threatening injuries.

The second factor is the partnerships that certain clubs in the PSL have developed with European clubs like Manchester United (with Wits University), Ajax Amsterdam with Ajax Cape Town and Feyenoord Rotterdam (with SuperSport United). The understanding is that links between local clubs and their more professional overseas counterparts allow clubs to attract the best talent available and expose them to the best training methods at an early stage. The further implication, of course, is that the European teams will cherry-pick the best talents and acquire them at transfer fees which, whilst providing significant funds for the South African club, will be modest in global terms, perhaps enabling a huge profit if the more successful players are then sold on to other clubs. Hence, Ajax Amsterdam claim that their development programme costs about $800 000 a year, whereas their products – which in the past have included South Africa's Benni McCarthy and Aaron Mokoena – were sold on for millions.

A further important initiative in youth development in South Africa lies with the United Schools Sports Association of South Africa (Ussasa) which runs what has been described as the world's second biggest school tournament (*Soccer News* November 2000). Sponsored by KFC, MTN and Coca Cola, it is an inter-schools competition, two of whose winners (Madibane High, Soweto [1997] and Kgorathuto High, Free State [2000]) have gone on to represent South Africa in schools world cups. It was at Ussasa competions that future stars like Doctor Khumalo, Steve Lekolea, Thabo Mooki, Braina Baloyi, Sibusiso Zuma, Benedict Vilakazi and Matthew Booth, who have all represented the national team, were first spotted and signed up by professional clubs while playing in schools sport competitions. Surprisingly, this programme seems to have few or no links at all with either Safa or the PSL. Instead, Safa is running a national talent-scouting exercise, the *Wonke Wonke* project, as part of its Vision 2010, which is headed by its national youth team coaches, but with little or no organic connection to Ussasa.

In sum, the overall development for South African soccer is poorly co-ordinated, and lacks the organisation and drive suitable for a country not only hosting but aspiring to win the 2010 World Cup. The local game's weaknesses are also illustrated by South African soccer's less than happy relations with the rest of Africa.

South Africa's relations with Africa – still estranged?

When South Africa was re-admitted into the international fold after years of isolation, Africa opened its arms and heart. Safa received a standing ovation at the CAF congress in Dakar in 1992, and Mustapha Fahmy, the secretary general of that organisation, declared that soccer in the wider continent would make substantial gains from the technology and commercial infrastructure which South Africa had to offer. Yet over the decade that followed, the initial good relations soured, with the result that many African countries denied South Africa their support in its bid to host the 2010 tournament. The reasons for this estrangement lay in politics as well as in the 'business' of football. It is a relationship from which neither party emerges with clean hands.

A key moment occurred in 1995 when then President Mandela openly and correctly criticised the Abacha military regime in Nigeria for the execution of human rights activist Ken Saro Wiwa and some of his colleagues. However, rather than receiving widespread continental support, Mandela's action was widely perceived by many of his African peers as 'unAfrican' and inappropriate. Disgracefully, Abacha gained much quiet support when he responded to Mandela's condemnation by withdrawing the Nigerian football team from the then forthcoming African Cup of Nations tournament, which was due to be played in South Africa in 1996 as a gesture of welcome to the country as it came back in from the cold. Although Abacha's action cost Nigeria three years in isolation from the biannual tournament as a punishment by CAF, it nonetheless served notice that, for all its weight, South Africa had much to learn about how to conduct diplomatic relations in Africa. It also served to cheapen South Africa's winning of the Cup as the Nigerian team was widely regarded as the continent's best.

Despite this unsavoury beginning to South Africa's soccer (and other African) diplomacy, it was widely hoped that South Africa would use its financial muscle to play a crucial role in uplifting football on the continent. To some extent this has occurred. For instance, key South African companies operative in Africa – notably MTN in Uganda, Cameroon and Swaziland, Vodacom in the Democratic Republic of Congo (DRC) and South African Breweries in southern Africa, and for a time in East Africa – have sponsored local leagues (*Swazi News* 30.04.05). MTN has also recently contributed major funding to CAF and to some of its development programmes. Nonetheless, with such largesse also comes some resentment, and some African critics argue that South Africa's financial muscle has added little to African football. For instance, every year Vodacom spends huge amounts to bring teams from the DRC and Ghana to South Africa for a two-week tournament with Orlando Pirates and Kaizer Chiefs (which, as already noted, are also sponsored by the company) and from which it is alleged that the South African teams are by far the biggest beneficiaries. Similarly, Vodacom sponsors the under-20 tournament of the Congress of Southern African Football Associations, yet whereas most participating countries would prefer the competition to rotate, South Africa has hosted it for the last five years.

Much African criticism was directed at South Africa during the country's preparations for the 1998 World Cup when it rarely considered African teams for friendly preparatory matches, preferring European and South American teams. For South Africa the reason was quite straightforward. Most teams it would be meeting in the World Cup were from Europe or South America, and thus it made better sense to prepare against such teams rather than against ones from Africa. Nonetheless, it seemed to many African countries that South Africa regarded the continent with disdain, and it reinforced the belief in some quarters that, even after the end of apartheid, South Africa still considered itself more a European enclave than a part of Africa. Such adverse feelings have only been compounded by the reluctance of major teams like Kaizer Chiefs and Moroka Swallows to play in African club competitions, citing lack of incentives and funds, with the recent decision by Kaizer Chiefs to pull out of a match in the African Champions League – for which it has received a three-year ban from the competition – being only the most recent example. It is likely that its decision not to appeal that ban will be interpreted by CAF and others in Africa as a snub to the continent. To many observers, South Africa's once enforced isolation in Africa is now voluntary.

Such tensions have worked their way into the more formal international relations of soccer on the continent. For instance, in the intra-African contest to host the 2010 World Cup the final choice boiled down to Morocco and South Africa. Even though the former had withdrawn from the African Union (AU) over the latter's recognition of Western Sahara and is in colonial occupation of an area that the AU and the United Nations regard as sovereign territory, it gained the majority of African votes.

In short, while in South African eyes its hosting of the World Cup in 2010 represents a triumph and major developmental opportunity for the continent, it will have to work hard to ensure that the event serves to narrow rather than widen its at times testy relations with Africa.

The 2010 World Cup: a double-edged sword?

As noted earlier, the award of the World Cup to South Africa was met with widespread celebration and it was seen by most commentators as heralding an economic bonanza. It is also, however, an opportunity stalked by hazards.

Although owned by Fifa, the World Cup is hosted every four years by a member country, and is much valued not only for the economic benefits it promises but also for the international prestige and attention it confers. Historically dominated by, and shared between, Europe and South America (continents which have consistently provided its winners), in recent times it has become more genuinely global, not only with the rise of football prowess in Asia and Africa, but with the arrival of satellite television which beams the competition to virtually all countries in the world. It was only a matter of time, therefore, before the transcontinental duopoly was broken, and the decision taken that the right to stage the competition should be distributed more equally, with the first World Cup to be held outside Europe or South America being shared between Japan and South Korea in 2002.

Yet what economic gains flow to the host country, and more particularly, what benefits can South Africa expect to reap from hosting the event in 2010? In his presentation to Fifa prior to South Africa winning the bid, President Mbeki hailed the World Cup as 'one of the biggest festivals of our age', and as providing 'a global stage on which nations and peoples of the world come together to reaffirm our humanity', yet noted that South Africans would be looking to use the event to boost the country's long-term development prospects. According to Tito Mboweni, Governor of the Reserve Bank, hosting the Cup is expected to promote a significant influx of foreign capital into investment, whilst simultaneously providing positive spillovers in terms of the development of tourism, transport and communications throughout the entire southern African region. Similarly, project assessors Grant Thornton Kessel Feinstein expect that, apart from a massive inflow of capital, 'worldcupanomics' will create something like 160 000 jobs. Meanwhile, it is estimated that South

Africa will need to invest about $511million (about R3.5 billion) in order to reach a state of readiness for the Cup, the largest part of such expenditure going on infrastructural developments like the upgrading of stadia, building five new ones, telecommunications and information technology solutions, safety and security, and the improvement of transport. Although much of this investment will be guaranteed by central government and local municipalities (which are keenly competing for part of the action), it will necessarily have to be made in close collaboration with private capital, both local and international (*Finance Week* 17.05.04).

Whether or not South Africa attains its development objectives depends on several factors. Managing the relationship between Fifa and the host country is key, not least because the sponsorship and marketing rights belong to the world federation, which sees its mandate as fulfilling its obligations to all its members. Hence, while the World Cup in the US in 1994 was hailed as a major commercial success – not least in the way that stadium attendance averaged 70 000 per game – organisers were taken aback by the manner in which the financial spin-offs from sponsorships accrued to Fifa, leaving the hosts to scramble for pickings in order to balance their books. The even more successful competition in France in 1998 similarly attracted huge crowds, not least because of the excitement generated around a peculiarly attractive host national team who swept all before them and emerged as champions. But will a tournament held in South Africa be able to fill the stadiums, especially if Bafana Bafana fail to progress much beyond the early group rounds? Then there is the added potential complication that the tickets will be too expensive for the majority of ordinary South Africans (in 1998 an average ticket price was R600, or R826 in contemporary terms), and for all the promises being made that ticket prices will be lowered to allow locals to fill the stadiums of especially the less attractive games, there is a serious prospect of some matches being played in front of near-empty stands.[9]

There are other concerns. The Cup is earmarked to spur the development of infrastructure around the country. According to *Finance Week* (17.05.04), 'The 1995 Rugby World Cup resulted in improved road networks in Cape Town, while the 2002 World Summit in Johannesburg got authorities to address Sandton's long overdue road improvements.' Much is similarly made of the boost that World Cup 2010 will give to projects that will have lasting value. Hence, it has added momentum to the controversial commitment by Gauteng

Premier, Mbazima Shilowa, to building the so-called 'Gautrain', a proposed rapid rail link between Johannesburg, the International Airport and Pretoria, which it is claimed will create some 57 000 jobs during its construction phase and more than 2 000 permanent job once the train becomes operational.[10] However, major concerns remain as to how functional this high-tech transport link will be in the long term, with many critics arguing that it will do little to take commuter traffic off the roads because of inadequate provision in the plans for feeder roads and parking. Similarly, besides suggestions that South Africa's construction plans are already lagging behind the proposed timetable, South Korea has cautioned that the plans to build new stadia should be re-examined, as its own experience is that a number of the new arenas it built for World Cup 2002 became white elephants and had to be demolished. Yet the principal worry must be that, whilst infrastructure expenditure should serve to improve transport linkages between towns, the overwhelming benefits of preparation will flow to the principal urban centres where the majority of games will be played, thereby reinforcing regional inequalities. Nor is it unlikely that the vast proportion of the estimated R12.6 billion direct expenditure (R4.6 billion of which will come from ticket sales) upon the Cup will land in the pockets of Fifa and huge corporations (international as much as domestic) rather than accruing to the benefit of poorer South Africans.

Finally, there is the matter of organisation, governance and co-ordination. Danny Jordaan, CEO of the local organising committee, has identified the three main challenges facing his association between now and 2010 as developing a 'world-class' national association, a 'world-class' national team, and a 'world-class African World Cup'(*City Press* 26.03.05). However, present structural issues within Safa inspire little confidence.

Jordaan became CEO of Safa after Morewa was forced to leave the organisation following the findings of the Pickard Commission. Together with Molefi Oliphant (who replaced Morewa as President) and Irvin Khoza, whose presence in Safa was courtesy of his chairmanship of the PSL, Jordaan was central to what Fifa's Sepp Blatter later termed South African soccer's 'three musketeers'. Although there were reportedly tensions between the three in the aftermath of the failed bid in 2006, they subsequently regrouped with the encouragement of Blatter, who was pushing to bring the next Cup to Africa (and to shore up his position at Fifa by extending his support from the Third World in the face of European member associations' concerns about his unorthodox dealings). Yet although Jordaan was subsequently to spearhead the successful 2010 bid, tensions had re-emerged over concerns around alleged financial maladministration (or worse).

At Safa's annual general meeting (AGM) in 2002, it had revealed a R2.5 million debt. After failing to hold an AGM in 2003 (as it was constitutionally required to do), the organisation subsequently recorded a surplus of R13 million in 2004, yet had recorded a loss of R25.5 million the previous year, during which it had been involved in a major dispute with the South African Revenue Service and had failed to make regular, scheduled payments to its regions. Furthermore, although the Pickard Commission had recommended that its members should not be remunerated because membership of Safa's executive was honorary, the 2002 statements indicated that R3 887 598 had been paid out to them over the course of that year. Meanwhile, Safa was also said to be being kept afloat financially by loans of R4 million from Khoza and R4.6 million from the PSL, which doubtless helps explain why club owners had been insistent that the former retain his place on the organisation's executive.[11]

It was against this background that, following the award of the 2010 Cup, it was reported that Khoza was seeking to oust Jordaan from his position and that Blatter had contacted President Mbeki directly to register his concern. In the event, whatever disagreements there were were smoothed over and Jordaan was subsequently confirmed as CEO at Safa's AGM in 2004. However, this was only after Blatter had indicated a decision by Fifa that it was going to become more firmly involved in preparations for 2010.[12]

Amidst the bickering, Safa made the controversial decision of appointing a relatively unknown Englishman, Stuart Baxter (previously coach of England's under-18s and under-19s), to manage the national team. One of his immediate successes was to attract back into Bafana Bafana a number of overseas players, such as Benni McCarthy of Porto and Quinton Fortune of Manchester United, who had withdrawn from the national squad following differences with his predecessor, Ephraim 'Shakes' Mashaba. Furthermore, after an uncertain start, he took the team to its present position at the head of its group (which sensibly doubles up as the qualifying group for both the 2006 African Cup of Nations and World Cup competitions), yet in concentrating upon obtaining results, he has presided over a team whose style of play is said by critics to be unattractive and un-South African. It was probably no coincidence, therefore, that in early 2005, Baxter was the victim of a concerted attack by the Sowetan newspaper. In a campaign which bordered upon xenophobia, he was accused of having been manipulated in his team selections by a particular agent for some overseas-based players whom he preferred to play at the cost of South African-based talent. The effect of this is that local agents lost revenue from the fees they earned from the selection of their clients to the national team. Baxter survived the campaign, but only at further cost to the confidence which surrounds the management of both the national team and the national game by Safa.[13]

Clearly, for South Africa to achieve Jordaan's ambition of a 'world-class African World Cup' which will prove of lasting rather than fleeting benefit to the country, there is much to be done if the host association and the host team are to make a decent showing.

Conclusion

South African soccer has come a long way since the days of apartheid when so much energy was directed into struggles around legitimacy and unity. Yet it is now faced with the challenge of developing in an era when the global political economy of the game is presenting major challenges to African and Third World soccer generally.

Soccer, once the game of the working class, has increasingly become the property of multinational business, or at least, those aspects have which present opportunities for the making of money. Increasingly, the game revolves around television, and it is the revenue it generates, both directly and indirectly, that lies behind the increasing domination of the European Champions League and European national leagues of a handful of elite clubs – based principally in England, Germany, Spain and Italy. As money increasingly finds its way into their hands, their superiority is confirmed, and ironically, the competitiveness and long-term viability of their own national competitions is undermined, whilst less fortunate clubs below them become engaged in an increasingly difficult struggle for survival.

It is this model – one which exacerbates inequalities between and within the world's soccer nations – that the South African game is virtually compelled to follow, and to attempt to 'live up to'. In a country with the most advanced communications network on the continent, it has to compete with televised (and heavily marketed) European soccer for audiences, sponsorships and, increasingly, players – even if ironically it may be said that at present the underdevelopment of the game in South Africa is reflected by the relatively small number of players 'plying their trade' (an antiquated phrase much loved by football commentators) in the major leagues in Europe.[14] Yet there can be little doubt that the difficulties posed by these challenges are much compounded by the historical legacy of disarray within the South African game and the divisions within and between its leading organisations. It is in this context that the staging of the World Cup offers both threats and opportunities – the danger that preparations for what is one of the world's greatest spectacles become a source of power and wealth for a few, against the prospect that if well managed the competition could provide a source of pride and development for many.

Notes

1   The first documented football match in South Africa was played in Cape Town and Port Elizabeth between white civil servants and soldiers (Safa 2001).

2   White players who were lured to Britain included Stuart Leary, Syd O'Lynn and Eddie Firmani (later an Italian international), who all played for Charlton Athletic, and Bill Perry, who scored the winning goal for Blackpool in the famous 'Matthews' Cup Final of 1953. Perry later became an England international. Stephen 'Kalamazoo' Mokone became the first South African black player to play in Britain after signing for Cardiff City in 1956, while Leeds United winger Albert 'Hurry Hurry' Johannessen became not only the first black South African but the first black person to play in an English Cup Final in the Leeds-Liverpool clash of 1965.

3   A typical instance of the British influence is provided by the Mthatha-based Bush Bucks, whose team slogan is 'You'll never walk alone' because the club was founded (in 1957) by African supporters of Liverpool FC (http://www.bushbucks.co.za/history.php). In similar vein, the legendary Kaizer Chiefs goalkeeper of the 1970s, Joseph Sethlodi, was nicknamed 'Banks' after the Engish goalkeeper of the day, Gordon Banks (North 1985).

4   But Fasa retained friends within Fifa, which wobbled badly in the early 1970s. It temporarily lifted Fasa's suspension in 1973 after it had agreed to allow foreign teams to go to South Africa to play in the multiracial South African Games, only to withdraw that permission when it found that Fasa was planning separate teams for

different ethnic groups. Fifa sent a delegation to South Africa in 1974 to investigate conditions, the outcome being Fasa's expulsion in 1976 (Safa 2001).

5   The first English game televised in South Africa was the Manchester United v Liverpool Cup Final in 1975. Two of the editors of this book, both strong supporters of the anti-apartheid movement and who were then teaching at the then University of Botswana, Lesotho and Swaziland, had fervently hoped before that game that the attempts by anti-apartheid activists in Britain to stop the game being broadcast to South Africa would fail!

6   Under EU regulations only established international players from non-EU countries can obtain work permits, although many players (notably from Latin America) duck the regulations by claiming a European nationality through legal 'grandfather' clauses.

7   Especially as police investigations concern only referees in the PSL's Mvela Golden League (its second division), and not the Premier League itself.

8   See http://www.orlandopiratesfc.com.

9   See http://sport.iafrica.com/soccer/2010/324799/htm.

10 See http://www.sa-venues.com/2010.htm.

11 See http://sport.iafrica.com/soccer/2010/324806.htm.

12 See http://sport.iafrica.com/soccer/2010/86775.htm and 348399.htm.

13 Prior to a crucial away game with Cape Verde in May 2005, Baxter's preparations were hampered by Safa's failure to provide a goalkeeper coach. Baxter also battled because Jim Lawler, who does all Baxter's video analysis, refused to fly to South Africa from England because in his year of working for Safa he had yet to receive a contract (*The Star* 30.05.05).

14 For instance, there were only four South African players playing in the English Premier League in 2004/05 – Shaun Bartlett and Mark Fish of Charlton Athletic, Quinton Fortune of Manchester United, and Aaron Mokoena of Blackburn Rovers – although of course the much loved and outstanding Lucas Radebe, who retired at the end of that season, had previously played with distinction for Leeds United in that competition until they were relegated in 2003/04.

References

Alegi P (n.d.) Katanga vs Johannesburg: A history of the first sub-Saharan African football championship, 1949–50. Available at http://www.unisa.ac.za/default.asp.

Alegi P (2004) *Laduma! Soccer, politics and society in South Africa*. Pietermaritzburg: University of KwaZulu-Natal Press.

Couzens T (1983) An introduction to the history of football in South Africa. In B Bozzoli (ed.) *Town and countryside in the Transvaal*. Braamfontein: Ravan Press.

North J (1985) *Freedom rising: Life under apartheid*. New York: MacMillan.

Raath P (2002) *Soccer through the years 1862–2002. The first official history of South African soccer*. Cape Town: Juta.

Safa (South African Football Association) (2001) South African Football Association (Safa) profile. Available at http://safootball.co.za/safa.htm.

SAIRR (South African Institute of Race Relations) (various years) *A survey of race relations in South Africa*. Braamfontein: SAIRR.

16 The state of mathematics and science education: schools are not equal

Vijay Reddy

Introduction

Mathematics and science are key areas of knowledge and competence for the development of an individual and the social and economic development of South Africa in a globalising world. Since 1994 the new democratic government has emphasised the centrality of mathematics and science as part of the human development strategy for South Africa (Mbeki 2001, 2005). Performance in this area is one of the indicators of the health of our educational system, makes an important contribution to our economy and has been a contributor to inequalities of access and income.

Most South African citizens meet mathematics and science knowledge for the first and last time in the schooling system. Competency in these gateway subjects at a school level opens up opportunities for empowerment through an understanding of common technologies on which all depend and provides better access to tertiary education and higher skilled jobs and livelihoods. By most performance indicators, South Africa is performing poorly in mathematics and science. This chapter is not about rehashing the poor performance statistics, but rather provides a more nuanced analysis of performance indicators, reflects on experience of attempts to improve mathematics and science education and offers suggestions to improve access, participation and outcomes at the school level.

The first part of the chapter reviews how the situation in mathematics and science has evolved since 1994, and comments on the policies and programmes introduced to address the new needs. The second part of the chapter offers an analysis of the current state of the mathematics and science sector through an analysis of the performance of learners. This draws on two empirical studies: Trends in International Mathematics and Science Study (TIMSS) (Mullis, Martin, Gonzalez & Chrostowski 2004), which compared

South African performance with other countries; and a Human Sciences Research Council (HSRC)-conducted study of a six-year trend analysis of matriculation mathematics performance at school level.

The state of mathematics and science will be illustrated primarily using statistics from mathematics. About half the learners who take mathematics take physical science and performance between the two is highly correlated. Many of the observations based on the mathematics data resonate with those in science but space prevents a full analysis of both.

The mathematics and science story

The pre-1994 situation

In 1953, Dr HF Verwoerd, then Minister of Education in the National Party, argued in Parliament that there was no use in 'teaching the Bantu mathematics when he cannot use it in practice. The idea is absurd' (RSA 1953 vol. 83, column 3585). The result was an education policy that ensured racially-differentiated access to mathematics and science within the framework of Bantu education, a policy designed to under-educate black South Africans.

The state of mathematics and science education just before the first democratic elections in 1994 is outlined in Kahn's (1993) sector study of science and mathematics education and the Foundation for Research Development's *Science and Technology Indicators* (FRD 1993). Table 16.1 indicates participation and performance patterns in mathematics for the different racial groups in 1990.

Table 16.1 *Participation and performance in mathematics in 1990, percentage by racial groups*

	Participation rate in matriculation mathematics	Pass rate in mathematics	Participation in higher-grade mathematics
White	64	97	60
Indian	70	76	74
Coloured	45	74	38
African*	24	15	65

Source: FRD 1993
Note: *Education for Africans was fragmented and offered in the homeland and self-governing states as well as 'South Africa'. The statistics for the African group are from the Department of Education and Training schools.

This analysis points starkly to the not unexpected differences in participation and performance of learners from the different ex-racial departments with results for the African group being the poorest by a wide margin. A further indicator of the differences in performances is provided by examining which schools are dominant suppliers of science and engineering students to universities. Auret (in FRD 1993) determined that nine per cent of white and 29 per cent of African students came from the ten most prominent schools in their respective racial departments of education, illustrating a very high degree of polarisation in access and performance, especially in African schools. Only 0.4 per cent of African schools provided one-fifth of the students to science and engineering faculties.

The situation since 1994

Since 1994, all sectors (government, business, academia and parents) have recognised the importance of science and mathematics for the development of the country. It has also been recognised that the African population was most disadvantaged and needed a programme of redress to ensure better participation and performance in mathematics and science. Commitment to this has been outlined in various government gazettes and policy documents (DoE 1996; DoE & DoL 2002; DST 2002). These policies affirm that capacity interventions are needed at the school level in order to build mathematics, science and technology. This is the only way to meet the demand from higher education and workplaces and to rebalance participation in more equitable ways.

In 2001, the Department of Education (DoE 2001) unveiled a national strategy to improve participation and performance in mathematics and science education. The flagship programme in the strategy was the identification of 102 schools in the *Dinaledi* project. This strategy selected schools in each province that showed the potential to perform well (and therefore could increase higher-grade mathematics participation and performance). The schools received additional facilities, equipment and support for effective mathematics and science teaching and learning. While the *Dinaledi* vision of investing in schools with potential to succeed appears sound there have been problems in the selection of schools according to the predetermined criteria and the implementation of the interventions in the schools has been uneven. The *Dinaledi* intervention has yet to be independently evaluated, or to demonstrate the kinds of gains in participation and performance that were anticipated. Prior to the *Dinaledi* initiative the government had embarked on the Students and Youth in Science, Technology and Mathematics (SYSTEM) programme to increase the number of mathematics and science graduates from the schooling system. There have been other interventions by government, private sector and non-governmental organisations (NGOs), which have attempted to improve education. Many of these were abandoned after a few years and there have been limited evaluation accounts and thus limited lessons learnt from interventions.

In the last decade there has been large-scale and radical curriculum reform in South Africa. In the old curriculum all learners took general science and mathematics up to the end of Grade 9. In Grade 10 learners could choose to enrol for mathematics, physical science or biology. In 1997, Curriculum 2005 (C2005) with an outcomes-based education philosophy was launched. Through Grades 1 to 9, it made the natural science, mathematics and technology learning areas compulsory for all learners. However, much criticism was directed at C2005. In regard to these learning areas, it was criticised for the under-specification of content and lack of structured resource materials for teachers since they departed from the traditional content-based approach. In the short term, this may have negatively affected learners' knowledge in these learning areas as teachers tried to understand the outcomes-based approach and teach it with unfamiliar learning materials.

The revised version of C2005 introduced in 2002 provided greater structure for teachers to organise their classroom activities. The outcomes-based education curriculum for the further education and training (FET) phase (Grades 10–12) will be introduced in 2006. This FET curriculum is oriented to high knowledge and high skill – this is necessary as South Africa has committed itself to a science and technology pathway for development. All learners in this phase must study mathematics, either in the form of mathematical literacy or mathematics. This essential addition poses challenges of how learners will cope with a Grade 10 mathematical literacy curriculum, given their poor performance in mathematics at the Grade 8 level (as evidenced by the results of TIMSS 2003).

Teachers with expert knowledge in mathematics and science are essential for a quality delivery of the curriculum, especially in the FET phase. The concepts in science are often counter-intuitive and formal instruction is essential to shift the learner to scientific understandings of concepts. South Africa is grappling with teacher shortages, which are acute in mathematics and science (Arnott & Kubeka 1997; Ministerial Committee on Teacher Education 2004). National and provincial departments of education have introduced bursary schemes to attract undergraduate students to become mathematics and science teachers. Because of the under-supply of suitably qualified mathematics and science graduates from the schooling system and the range of options offered to undergraduates these bursaries have not been taken up. The new cohorts of students in undergraduate teacher education courses are mostly female, white and training to teach in the general education and training phase. It is unlikely that many of these graduates will teach in township and rural schools where there is the greatest need for qualified teachers. More innovative strategies are needed to attract knowledgeable people to teach mathematics and science in different environments or to use different strategies to communicate the educational experiences.

Although most mathematics and science teachers have accredited teaching qualifications, less than half have at least one year of specialised training in either mathematics or science (Arnott & Kubeka 1997). For teachers to access the requisite knowledge to teach mathematics and science, the national and provincial departments of education, with tertiary institutions, have set up professional development qualifications for science and mathematics teachers (for example, the National Professional Diploma in Education and Advanced Certificate in Education). The programmes are offered as a mixture of contact and distance learning and as yet there has not been an evaluation of the improvement of disciplinary knowledge of teachers or the impact of these qualifications on classroom practice.

In addition to the challenge of addressing the present shortages of mathematics teachers, the educational system will also have to face the challenge of finding teachers to teach the new mathematics literacy courses. This has created additional demand since all learners will take either mathematics or mathematical literacy at FET level. Many tertiary institutions are offering upgrading qualifications for teachers of mathematical literacy, but given that it is a high-knowledge and high-skill subject, the challenge will be of providing the appropriate knowledge to non-mathematics teachers.

In 1990, the Grade 12 mathematics enrolment was made up of 54 per cent males and 46 per cent females. There were an almost equal number of African males and females and for the other race groups the proportion was 57 per cent male and 43 per cent female. Of those who passed mathematics, 55 per cent were male and 45 per cent female (FRD 1993). Analysis of participation and performance by gender in 2003 indicates that the participation and performance patterns are almost equitable for both groups. However, further analysis of performance by gender, race and class (using the proxy indicator of attendance in ex-racially classified schools) indicates that there is a difference by race and class. There is a significant gender difference in performance in African schools, with the girls having lower performance scores but not a significant gender difference in the other former racially classified schools (Kahn 2004; Perry & Flesich 2005; Reddy 2005).

Performance in mathematics and science

While we have many policies and programmes to improve the state of mathematics and science education, the ultimate indicator of success is the performance of learners. The analysis in this part of the chapter is framed by two starting points. First, the South African population is diverse and any meaningful analysis must involve a disaggregation of the performance scores into relevant groupings. Second, schools are the institutions where learners are exposed to knowledge and skills in mathematics and science and thus we need to provide a school-level analysis. This analysis is a response to the question raised by President Mbeki (forthcoming) when he asked: 'How many young black people are matriculating with exemptions in mathematics and the sciences?' The answer illustrates the continuing racial inequalities in the country.

South Africa has participated in a number of large-scale systemic studies (conducted by international and national agencies) to assess the performance of the country in science and mathematics. The Department of Education's systemic evaluation at the Grade 3 level revealed that the national average score for numeracy was 30 per cent (DoE 2002a). In the Unesco co-ordinated Monitoring Learner Achievement studies for Grade 4 learners, the average numeracy score for South Africa was 30 per cent compared to Mauritius with a score of 59 per cent, Senegal 40 per cent and Malawi 43 per cent (Chinapah, H'ddigui, Kanjee, Falayajo, Fomba, Hamissou, Rafalimanana & Byamugisha 2000). In the TIMSS 2003, which tested mathematics and science proficiency at the Grade 8 level, South Africa came last of the 50 countries participating (Mullis et al. 2004). The Grade 12 mathematics performance is unsatisfactory and, in particular, there is the concern about the small number of learners passing with higher-grade mathematics. In 2002 there were 19 765 mathematics higher-grade passes. Of this there were 4 637 African learners who passed higher-grade mathematics (Perry & Fleisch 2005).

South African society is characterised by high levels of poverty and vast inequalities, a legacy of the policy of apartheid. An indicator of the poverty level is that in 2000, in South Africa, 13 million people (30 per cent of the population) were living on less than $2 a day (World Bank 2002). The Gini coefficient, which measures the distribution of the national income, was 0.6 in 2000, showing that, with Brazil, South Africa has one of the most unequal income distributions in the world (Stats SA 2002). The consequence of South Africa's racial politics and poverty is that Africans are the poorest group and in African schools there are vast backlogs to the provision of basic infrastructure, learning materials and qualified teachers – all of which affect science and mathematics participation and achievement.

In the last ten years the government has attempted to improve the infrastructure and resources in schools previously designated for Africans but this is 'unfolding at a much slower pace than envisaged' (Mbeki 2005). One-quarter of schools (mostly African) do not have access to running water and about 45 per cent of schools do not have access to electricity (DoE 2001). About half the schools sampled for the TIMSS 1999 and 2003 study do not have a biology, general science or physical science laboratory (Reddy 2005). Any analysis of performance must consider the racial and poverty dynamics in South Africa.

South Africa and TIMSS 2003

In November 2002, the HSRC assessed a national sample of 9 000 Grade 8 learners (15 year olds), as part of TIMSS 2003. The results show that the Asian countries (Singapore, Republic of Korea, Hong Kong and Chinese Taipei/Taiwan) were the top performers in mathematics and science (Mullis et al. 2004). Six African countries participated – Egypt, Tunisia, Morocco, Botswana, Ghana and South Africa. South Africa had the lowest score in science and mathematics. This poor performance echoed the performance of 1999 when South Africa had the lowest score of 38 countries.

THE STATE OF MATHEMATICS AND SCIENCE EDUCATION

The South African mathematics mean score of 264 (SE 5.5)[1] and the science mean score of 244 (SE 6.7) are well below the international mathematics mean of 467 (SE 0.5) and international science mean of 474 (SE 0.5) (Reddy forthcoming). An important characteristic of the results is that South Africa had the widest distribution of scores in mathematics and science of all the countries that participated. This wide range means that there were very low as well as a few very high scores. South Africa is not a homogenous society and the single aggregated score is misleading to understand the mathematics and science performance in the country. Disaggregation of the mean scores of learners by the previous racial departments is essential to understand current patterns. Figure 16.1 illustrates the differences in performance of learners attending the different types of schools.[2]

Figure 16.1 *TIMSS 2003 mean mathematics scores of schools categorised by ex-racial departments*

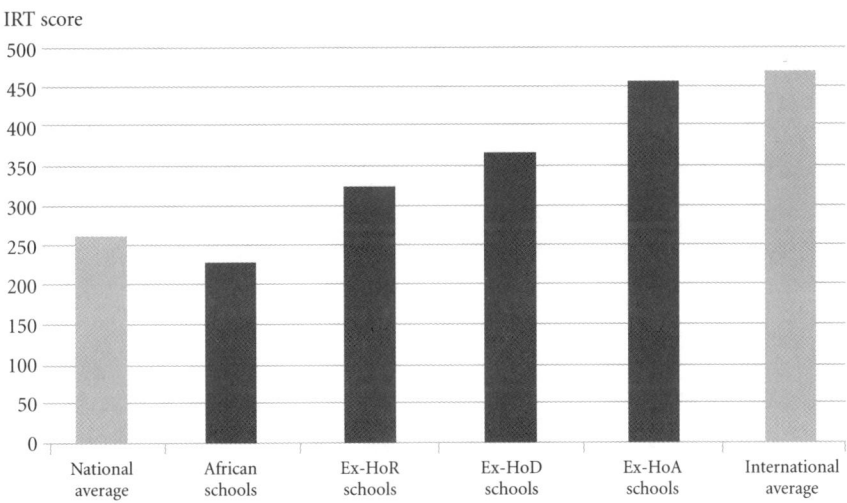

Source: Own calculations from TIMSS 2003 South African data
Note: DET – Department of Education and Training; HoA – House of Assembly; HoR – House of Representatives; HoD – House of Delegates

Learners in the African schools have the lowest average scores, and learners in the former House of Assembly schools have the highest score. Learners attending the former House of Assembly schools have a mean score close to the international mean score.

Since 1994 there has been an increasing racial integration of students in the ex-House of Representative (former coloured), ex-House of Delegates (former Indian) and ex-House of Assembly (former white) schools.[3] The degree of integration in each school varies. The teaching and management of the schools is still essentially by the race group for which the schools were originally designated. In the past, access to the different types of schools had been determined by race; now access is determined by the ability to pay the school fees, stay in an area where one was previously excluded from, and travel to schools which are outside the township. Learners attending the different types of schools have different educational experiences and very different performances in mathematics and science.

The delivery of and support for education is a provincial responsibility. Each of the provinces has a different resource base, different human resource capability and different gross domestic product (GDP) per capita. Figure 16.2 illustrates the mean mathematics score for each of the provinces. The GDP per capita for each of the provinces is also superimposed against the performance graphs.

Figure 16.2 *TIMSS 2003 mean mathematics scores by provinces*

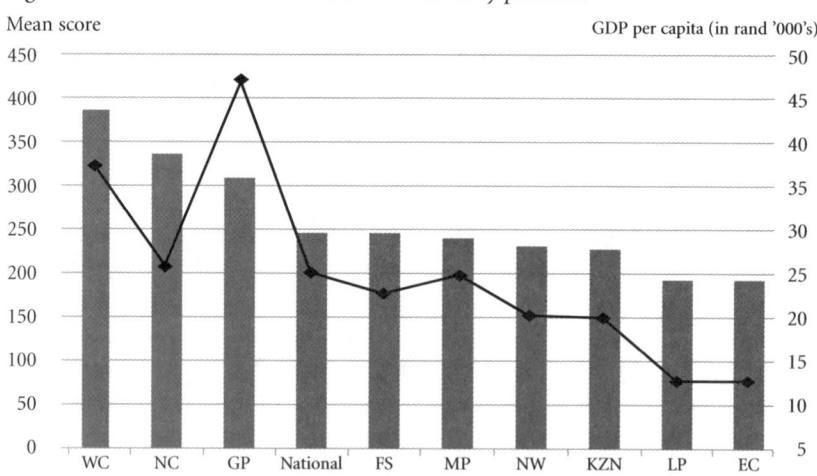

Source: Own calculations from TIMSS 2003 South African data and Stats SA (2002, 2003)
Note: WC – Western Cape; NC – Northern Cape; GP – Gauteng; FS – Free State; MP – Mpumalanga; NW – North West; KZN – KwaZulu-Natal; LP – Limpopo; EC – Eastern Cape

The top performing provinces (Western Cape, Northern Cape and Gauteng) have almost twice the scores as the lowest performing provinces (KwaZulu-Natal, Limpopo and Eastern Cape). In addition, the provincial mean scores, with the exception of Gauteng, closely mirror the trends in GDP per capita for each of the provinces.

These disaggregated scores reflect the continuing inequalities in education in South African society. The mean scores in mathematics and science by ex-racial department and by province differ by more than two to one from the best to the worst, reflecting differences in provision and socio-economic conditions. The inequalities persist and there is still a gap between what happens in former white schools and African schools.

Trend analysis of school-level mathematics performance

Educational inputs take place largely in schools and we need to examine how those institutions are performing.[4] Schools almost certainly have a much greater importance for performance in poorer communities than in middle-class communities because they are the institutions that can substitute for lack of cultural capital and home support to facilitate educational experiences for students. The question is whether schools provide this opportunity for the majority of learners, especially in mathematics and science which are subjects not accessible without quality formal instruction. School achievement is likely to be the major, if not the only, vector for disadvantaged children to acquire competence, skill and access to employment of a different quality to that of their parents. Low school achievement is part of the definition of poverty as well as the means to reduce it.

We will now examine how performance in mathematics has changed in the last six years and how this may relate to school quality indicators. We will examine this question for one of the provinces, Gauteng. In this case study we will describe the schools and then look at the trends (for the period 1998–2003) in participation, performance and school-level quality (using a proxy of matriculation performance) and then identify schools that consistently produce high quality mathematics and science results. We are in the process of analysing the data for all the other provinces and Gauteng is presented initially to illustrate the trends in mathematics and science. The performance at the exit-level examination gives us a proxy indication of performance at the other levels of the system.

Gauteng is the smallest province by area, with a population of 8.8 million, of which 97 per cent is urbanised and has the highest population density (365/km^2). There is a high population diversity and this is reflected in the percentage of schools from the former racial departments. Of the schools who take the matriculation examination offered by the Department of Education, 42 per cent are African, 26 per cent are former white, 24 per cent are independent,[5] four per cent are former coloured and three per cent are former Indian. The other provinces do not have the same level of diversity.

The public schools in Gauteng have different histories. Table 16.2 describes the profile of public schools in Gauteng according to the former racially-based Departments of Education (giving an indication of the availability of resources in these schools) and poverty quintile rating (reflecting socio-economic status of the community in which the school is located), with 1 being the poorest quintile and 5 the most affluent. The resources available to teach learners, the socio-economic background as well as the culture of teaching and learning are all likely to influence learning outcomes. The schools belonging to the former African departments are mostly in the lower quintile rating and schools belonging to the former white departments are in the higher (more affluent) quintile rating.

Table 16.2 *Public schools in Gauteng offering mathematics in 2003, categorised by ex-racial Departments of Education and poverty rankings*

Ex-department	Poverty quintile					Total
	1	2	3	4	5	
Ex-DET	59	67	94	41	2	263
Ex-HoA	0	0	0	53	115	168
Ex-HoR	0	7	12	7	0	26
Ex-HoD	0	0	3	13	6	22
Total	59	74	109	114	123	479

Source: Own calculations using data provided by the School Register of Needs and the School Funding Norms of the provinces
Note: DET – Department of Education and Training; HoA – House of Assembly; HoR – House of Representatives; HoD – House of Delegates

Since the 1990s there has been a deracialisation of learner enrolments at schools. Sujee (2004) tracked the trends of learner enrolments, by race, into the schools of the different ex-racial departments in Gauteng. He found that there has been a 25 per cent shift of African learners from the African schools to the other former departments and independent schools for the period 1996 to 2002. In 2002 the distribution of African learners at the different school types was that 72 per cent were in African schools, three per cent in former Indian, three per cent in former coloured, 13 per cent in former white and six per cent in independent schools. While there has been a decrease in the percentage of African learners in African schools, the actual number of learners has increased.

In 2002, the pattern of racial integration in the different types of school was as follows: the former coloured schools had 44 per cent African learners and 56 per cent coloured learners; in the former Indian schools there were 63 per cent African learners and 31 per cent Indian learners; in former white schools there were five per cent coloured, three per cent Indian, 34 per cent African and 57 per cent white learners. The trends in the participation and performance in mathematics in the different school types must be read against the backdrop of the migration of students across the school types.

PROVINCIAL PARTICIPATION AND PERFORMANCE PATTERNS

Table 16.3 paints a picture, over the six-year period, of the *participation patterns* of matriculation mathematics candidates. Almost 99 per cent of the schools offering matriculation subjects offer mathematics as a subject. The number of matriculation candidates dropped from 1998 to 2003. The contributory factors to this could be the imposition of age restrictions on overage learners in the school system; increased attention to matriculation pass rates and schools 'holding back' Grade 10 and 11 learners who were less likely to pass Grade 12; and learners moving to FET colleges. The drop in matriculation numbers is concentrated in African schools. The numbers in the other former racial school departments have increased slightly. This might have resulted from the shift of better-performing African learners to the 'non-DET' schools. The mathematics participation rates remain around 60 per cent in Gauteng. In African schools there is a decrease in numbers but an increase in participation rates and in the former HoA schools there is an increase in numbers but a decrease in the mathematics participation rate.

It is important to examine whether learners take the subject at higher or standard grade since this is what provides access to science and technology careers. The

Table 16.3 *Trend of mathematics participation in public schools in Gauteng*

	1998	2001	2003
Learners in public schools			
Total matriculants	69 189	59 627	63 514
Mathematics entrants (% of matriculants)	39 291 (57%)	37 453 (63%)	38 253 (60%)
Learners in ex-DET schools			
Total matriculants	41 058	29 295	32 316
Mathematics entrants (% of matriculants)	19 887 (48%)	17 202 (59%)	18 372 (57%)
Learners in ex-HoA schools			
Total matriculants	22 866	24 733	25 413
Mathematics entrants (% of matriculants)	16 117 (70%)	17 124 (69%)	16 924 (67%)
Learners in ex-HoR schools			
Total matriculants	2 850	3 149	3 172
Mathematics entrants (% of matriculants)	1 647 (58%)	1 536 (49%)	1 525 (48%)
Learners in ex-HoD schools			
Total matriculants	2 415	2 450	2 613
Total mathematics entrants	1 640 (68%)	1 591 (65%)	1 432 (55%)

Source: Own calculations using data provided by the DoE

importance of increasing the number of higher-grade mathematics graduates is also mentioned as a priority in the provincial 'State of the Nation' speeches of Gauteng and the Western Cape (Rasool 2005; Shilowa 2005). Table 16.4 indicates the higher-grade mathematics participation for the different types of schools.

Table 16.4 *Higher-grade mathematics participation in Gauteng (no. and % of entrants)*

	1998	2001	2003
Mathematics HG entrants in public schools	8 028 (20%)	7 492 (20%)	8 059 (21%)
Mathematics HG entrants in ex-DET schools	1 802 (9%)	1 006 (6%)	1 480 (8%)
Mathematics HG entrants in ex-HoR schools	88 (5%)	76 (5%)	45 (3%)
Mathematics HG entrants in ex-HoA schools	5 589 (35%)	6 009 (35%)	6 109 (36%)
Mathematics HG entrants in ex-HoD schools	549 (33%)	401 (25%)	425 (30%)

Source: Own calculations using data provided by the DoE

THE STATE OF MATHEMATICS AND SCIENCE EDUCATION

Higher-grade students are overwhelmingly in the former white schools. The overall numbers have not changed much between 1998 and 2003. An alarming phenomenon is the number of schools that offer mathematics only as a standard-grade subject and Table 16.5 illustrates the trend.

Table 16.5 *Trends of schools in Gauteng offering only standard-grade mathematics (no. and %)*

	1998		2001		2003	
Public schools	55	(12%)	107	(22%)	81	(17%)
Ex-DET schools	43	(17%)	90	(34%)	65	(25%)
Ex-HoR schools	9	(36%)	14	(54%)	14	(54%)
Ex-HoA schools	2	(1%)	1	(1%)	1	(1%)
Ex-HoD schools	1	(5%)	2	(9%)	1	(5%)

Source: Own calculations using data provided by the DoE

About one-fifth of Gauteng learners write mathematics at the higher grade and about one-fifth of the schools only offer standard-grade mathematics at their schools. These provincial statistics mask the different patterns in the different school types. In former Indian and white schools this enrolment trend has been constant over the six years with about one-third of learners writing higher-grade mathematics.

In African schools fewer than ten per cent of the learners write mathematics on the higher grade and a quarter of the schools offer mathematics only at the standard grade. This proportion is lower in the former coloured schools where about five per cent of the learners write mathematics on the higher grade and half the schools only offer mathematics on the standard grade. There was a decrease in the number of learners and schools offering higher-grade mathematics from 1998 to 2001, but this trend changed slightly from 2001 to 2003.

In addition to participation we need to track the trends in matriculation mathematics performance, at a provincial level, for the period 1998–2003. To track performance change over time we used the indicator of the number of learners who gained either an A, B, C or D in higher-grade mathematics in each year (see Table 16.6).

Table 16.6 *Trends of higher-grade mathematics performance in Gauteng schools, by ex-racial department*

Ex-racial department	A	B	C	D	Total
Ex-DET (1998)	5	9	11	50	75
Ex-DET (2001)	16	25	53	83	177
Ex-DET (2003)	49	54	107	161	371
Ex-HoA (1998)	476	526	840	1 072	2 914
Ex-HoA (2001)	746	648	1 045	1 312	3 751
Ex-HoA (2003)	1 041	757	1 038	1 218	4 054
Ex-HoD (1998)	10	11	30	59	110
Ex-HoD (2001)	35	31	57	73	196
Ex-HoD (2003)	22	29	45	74	170
Ex-HoR (1998)	0	0	1	5	6
Ex-HoR (2001)	0	1	1	6	8
Ex-HoR (2003)	0	0	3	3	6

Source: Own calculations using data provided by the Examinations Section of the DoE

Assuming the equivalence of quality of the higher-grade mathematics examination papers, it seems that for the period 1998–2003 the quality has improved. There is an overall improvement in the number of students acquiring higher-grade mathematics passes in all schools except ex-HoR schools. There were 3 105 A, B, C and D higher-grade mathematics passes in Gauteng public schools in 1998 and this number increased to 4 601 in 2003 – an increase of 48 per cent. In 1998, the African schools contributed 2.4 per cent of these passes and in 2003 the contribution increased to eight per cent.

SCHOOL-LEVEL QUALITY IN MATHEMATICS AND SCIENCE

The preceding discussion analyses participation and performance patterns at the provincial level. Learning occurs in schools and we need to understand how quality changes at a school level. We created an index of quality, using the proxy of performance in matriculation mathematics for each school. The index was based on the number of students who are eligible to enter a tertiary institution and the quality of the performance (the methodology is described fully in Reddy & van der Berg with Berkowitz & Lebani 2005). Figures 16.3 and 16.4 illustrate the pattern of school quality categorised by their former racial departments.[6]

Figure 16.3 *Mathematics school quality in Gauteng public schools in 2003, by ex-racial department and independent schools*

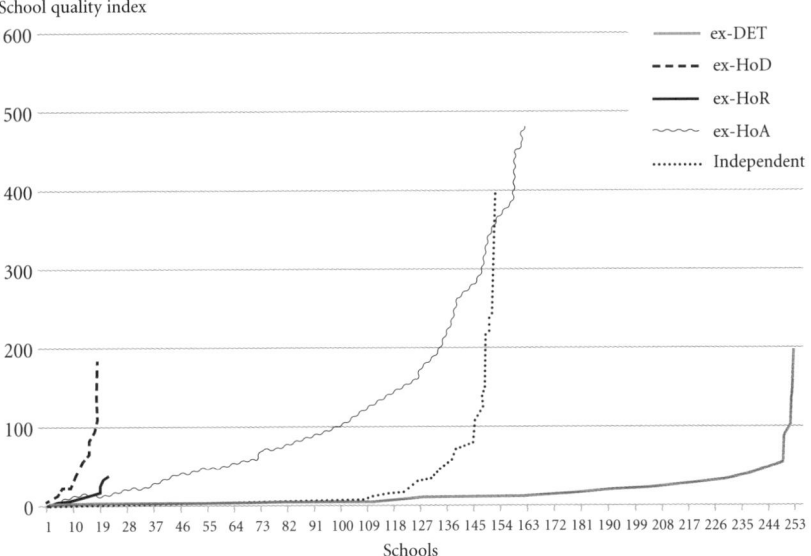

Source: Own calculations using data provided by the DoE

Schools from the different ex-departments show a different profile for school quality, with the schools from the former white department being distributed fairly evenly across a wide range. African and former coloured schools have uniformly low quality with only a few schools scoring highly. The independent schools show two distinct profiles: schools that perform well and schools that have poor quality mathematics passes. Many parents would have made the choice, at a higher fee structure, to send their children to independent schools because they believe that it would provide better opportunities.

Figure 16.3 provides an indication of school quality for a single year. We need to track how this quality has changed over time. Figure 16.4 presents the changes for the two biggest sets of schools by ex-racial departments – African and former white schools. One would also have to interpret the change of school quality in African schools against the backdrop of the migration of probably the better performing and better resourced learners to schools of the other former racial departments.

Figure 16.4 *Change in school quality in Gauteng over time (1999, 2003), for ex-DET and ex-HoA schools*

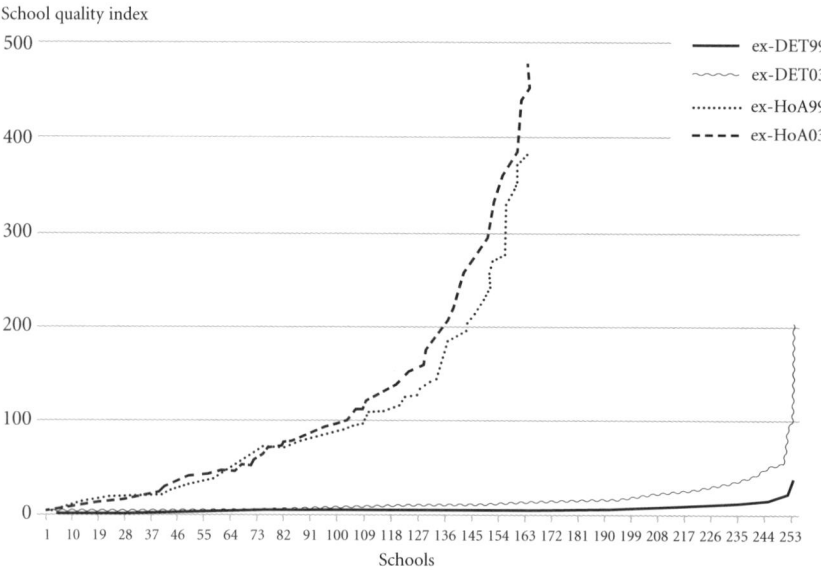

Source: Own calculations using data provided by the DoE

Assuming the equivalence of the passes over the time period, it would seem that the system and schools in each of the former racial departments has shown an improvement. However, it is clear that the gap between different school types has not closed at all, indicating that differences are entrenched and have not shifted following recent policy interventions.

While analysis of quality for the group of schools (Figure 16.4) indicates the quality is improving, we need to track how individual schools perform over time. The correlation co-efficient for quality of individual schools in different time periods shows a different pattern for African and former white schools.

Table 16.7 *Trend in correlation of school quality in Gauteng for ex-DET and ex-HoA schools*

Year of correlation of performance	1998–2003	1999–2003	2000–2003	2001–2003	2002–2003
Ex-DET schools	0.15	0.18	0.20	0.37	0.51
Ex-HoA schools	0.78	0.80	0.82	0.89	0.90

Source: Own calculations using data provided by the DoE

Table 16.7 shows that the correlation co-efficients for African schools are low, which means that the school performance varies from one year to the next. The high value for the ex-HoA schools demonstrates performance endures. The performance correlation co-efficient has been improving in recent years, especially in the African schools – but for some schools this may be due to correlation of low performances. Predictability of performance or an enduring quality of good performance is an important indicator of school quality and the challenge is how to support schools to ensure that the quality endures over time.

From the analysis of the correlation co-efficients of performance we know that there are some schools that consistently produce good results and others that do not. It is important to categorise the schools as either consistently better-performing schools, which we have called established schools, and schools which show potential for good performance, called emergent schools[7] (see Reddy et al. 2005 for definitions). Using the six-year trend data we have established a pattern for Gauteng schools (see Table 16.8).

Table 16.8 *Established and emergent schools in Gauteng*

Ex-department	Total number of schools	Established base	Emergent base
Ex-DET	258	4	49
Ex-HoA	168	119	34

Source: Own calculations using data provided by the DoE

As expected there are very few African schools in the established base. However, the promising aspect is that about one-fifth of the African schools show reasonable performance and the potential for improvement. The challenge is to support these schools to move from the emergent to the established base. Having an increased number of African schools with an enduring quality of performance will afford a greater number of African learners a chance for a quality education – and 75 per cent of African learners in Gauteng are in African schools – and better life chances.

How far have we come?

Given the historical legacies of apartheid and ten years of democracy with a commitment to the improvement of mathematics and science, how are we doing? In this concluding section we measure our progress and the nature of the progress since 1994, and suggest ways to improve the school mathematics and science system.

Since 1994, there has been strong acknowledgement of the importance of mathematics and science for the social, human and economic development of the country. This recognition is from all sectors including the President, the Ministries of Education, Labour, and Science and Technology, business and private sector, NGOs and academia. There have been investments and intervention programmes from these different sectors.

Comparing the state of mathematics and science between 1990 and 2003, there have been improvements. One of the goals of the mathematics and science strategy of the new government was to ensure that participation rates in these subjects increased, especially for black learners. Comparison of the mathematics participation rates for 1990 (using the national data) and 2003 (using the Gauteng dataset) indicates that participation rates have remained the same for the former white and coloured schools, have dropped in the former Indian schools and have increased considerably (from 24 per cent to 57 per cent) in the African schools. African schools started off from a very low base in 1990 and since then there has been an increase in the number of African learners enrolling for the matriculation examination and matriculation mathematics.

While the increased participation rate is commendable, during this same period (1990 to 2003) there has been a drastic reduction in higher-grade participation rates. In African schools the higher-grade participation rate dropped from 65 to eight per cent, in former white schools from 60 to 36 per cent, in former Indian schools from 74 to 30 per cent and in former coloured schools from 38 to three per cent. The challenge for the educational system is to ensure a higher number of quality mathematics passes since access to key science and technology careers is dependent on performance in these subjects.

Performance in the key areas of mathematics and science is poor by international, regional and national assessment standards. In addition, performance across the educational system varies widely and disaggregation of performance scores of learners in schools belonging to the ex-racial groups illustrates this. The former racial departments of schools are located in communities with different socio-economic conditions. The areas where most Africans live and where most African schools are located still rank the lowest on the scale of socio-economic conditions. The lowest performance is in the African schools and this forms the majority of South African schools.

Mathematics and science are subjects that require formal instruction for learners to access the knowledge. Schools are the institutions mandated to provide formal instruction. In conditions of poverty, schools take on greater importance as they are the only resource that most learners are able to access. Furthermore, school achievement may provide disadvantaged children with access to opportunities and employment of a different quality to that of their parents. However, the analysis demonstrates that the former white and Indian schools are the better performers. There is a small improvement in African schools – participation rates have increased and performance is slowly increasing – and this is commendable given the migration of learners. However, the gap in the performance of the different types of schools is not changing. Educational inequalities are continuing in South African society.

Presently, access for individuals to better learning opportunities is determined by access to economic resources. Individuals who have the financial resources (or social class) to access schools from other ex-racial departments have a better chance for improved learning opportunities, improved performance and hence improved life prospects. Schools are not serving the majority of learners in the country equitably. The learners who live in poorer areas, and who are particularly dependent on the school, are not getting sufficient input from these institutions to improve their life chances.

So where do we go in the next ten years?

First, our policy frameworks (for example, curriculum) are in place for a quality science and mathematics education. However, like other sectors of the society, implementation of policy has not proceeded according to the initial intention. Importantly, human resources needed for the implementation of those policies are scarce. In the next ten years there is the parallel challenge of developing human resources to manage the educational system and ensure there is quality support for the implementation of the policies, especially at school level. The policy frameworks must include detailed and realistic implementation plans and human resource needs.

Second, in the past decade there have been many interventions from government, the private sector and NGOs to improve mathematics and science education. These interventions provide creative programme plans but often lack a detailed implementation plan to effect the innovation. The intervention is abandoned after a few years because it does not demonstrate the expected results. The reason for the lack of progress may be that the project had not been implemented with the necessary support or there had not been enough time to embed it into the educational system. Further, we do not have adequate evaluation studies about the interventions to use as a learning tool to guide future efforts. It is important that when an intervention is introduced into the system we have a clear implementation plan, provide adequate resources to support the intervention, set realistic timetables regarding when we expect to see the impact of the intervention, and that we study the intervention and implementation process in order to derive lessons for ways to improve the process. We should not move from one intervention to the next and become 'serial innovators'.

Third, given the problems of teacher shortages and teacher quality, it is important to consider providing high quality structured learning materials (for example, textbooks) to learners. Structured learning materials, especially in poorer learning environments, can provide a fail-safe mechanism for learners to acquire knowledge. Given that the nature of mathematics and science knowledge is cumulative, the structured learning materials can provide a way to acquire this knowledge even if there is no teacher. These materials can also allow communication between the school and the community so that other individuals can assist in the learning process.

Fourth, given that African female learners in African schools experience the highest gender disadvantage in mathematics and science, particular strategies need to be directed to this group of learners. Participation rates are equitable, so that strategies must focus on ways to improve performance for these learners. Since overall performance in mathematics and science is low, an overall improvement of the system will benefit both males and females.

Fifth, the performance analysis presented in this chapter is for the secondary level, but the performance in mathematics/numeracy and science is poor at all levels of the educational system. The interventions for improvement must be aimed at the entire system and not only at the secondary level. It is important to build mathematics and science concepts from the early stages.

Sixth, and most importantly, we must invest in African schools which show the potential to succeed, to improve mathematics and science education in the country. There are schools that have achieved some successes and the strategy must be to invest in them so that they consistently produce quality results. This will involve a whole school development and then a specific focus on mathematics and science. At the moment African schools have to contend with the disadvantages of apartheid as well as the migration of probably the more resourced and better performing learners to schools from the other former departments. Individuals will continue to migrate to different schools, but the systemic level intervention must be to strengthen the institution of the school. There will be a tension about whether the intervention must be implemented in all schools or a selection of schools; however, it is not possible to strengthen all schools at the same time. It is more strategic to start with the emergent schools and ensure that they produce consistently good results and then expand the intervention to all schools.

This strategy of investment in schools mirrors the present Dinaledi strategy. However, in continuing with this strategy there must be a careful selection of schools (and use of more objective tools like the emergent schools analysis); a greater investment in project implementation which would involve provincial personnel supporting professional activities on a sustained basis to schools to ensure their improvement; ongoing careful monitoring and evaluation which would inform the implementation plans and setting realistic timeframes to allow the programme to be implemented, the innovation to be embedded in the system and impact measured.

Therefore, in returning to the question raised by President Mbeki about the number of black students matriculating with exemptions in mathematics and science, we can answer that the numbers are very small. But we can also answer that African students who have the economic resources to access private and former white schools have better chances of performing well. To improve the quality of mathematics and science for all, it is important to invest in strengthening the school to provide a quality education. Therefore we suggest that the future monitoring tool for the President to measure progress in science and mathematics education, includes the number of African learners graduating from African schools with exemptions in mathematics and science.

Notes

1. This is an IRT score and one could consider that the maximum score is 800. SE denotes standard error.
2. In the national sample there were 189 African, nine former Indian, 32 former coloured and 24 former white schools.
3. In the analysis we have to refer to schools by their ex-racial classification. They are ex-House of Representatives (HoR, former coloured), ex-House of Delegates (HoD, former Indian) and ex-House of Assembly (HoA, former white) schools. The ex-Department of Education and Training (DET) schools are almost 99.7 per cent African and will be referred to as African schools.
4. The research reported in this section has been developing in the HSRC and has had inputs from Servaas van der Berg (Stellenbosch University) and Keith Lewin (Sussex University). The interns Likani Lebani and Robert Berkowitz have provided invaluable support in setting up the datasets.
5. The number of independent schools in Gauteng is higher than the national average.
6. In reading the graph the x-axis indicates the number of schools in that racial group. The y-axis indicates the school quality index. The lower the line is along the x-axis, the poorer the school quality.
7. We looked at the six-year period of performance and categorised established schools as those schools that produced at least ten students who were eligible for tertiary-level admission in at least five of the six years (1998–2003), and emergent performing schools as those that had at least six tertiary-level eligible students in three of the six years and one of those good performances being in the last two years (2002 or 2003).

References

Arnott A & Kubeka Z (1997) *Mathematics and science teachers: Demand, utilisation, supply and training in South Africa.* Pretoria: Edusource.

Chinapah V, H'ddigui EM, Kanjee A, Falayajo W, Fomba CO, Hamissou O, Rafalimanana A & Byamugisha A (2000) *With Africa for Africa: Towards quality education for all.* Report for the Joint International Unesco-Unicef Monitoring Learning Achievement Project. Pretoria: HSRC Press.

Chisholm L, Volmink J, Ndhlovu T, Potenza E, Mohamed H, Muller J, Lubisi C, Vinjevold P, Ngozi L, Malan B & Mphahlele M (2000) *A South African curriculum for the twenty-first century: Report of the review committee on Curriculum 2005.* Presented to the Minister of Education, Professor Kader Asmal, Pretoria.

DoE (Department of Education, South Africa) (1996) National Education Policy Act, No. 27 of 1996. Pretoria: DoE.

DoE (2001) *National strategy for mathematics, science and technology education in general and further education and training.* Pretoria: DoE.

DoE (2002a) *National report on systemic evaluation: Mainstream education.* Pretoria: DoE.

DoE (2002b) *Revised national curriculum statement for Grades R to 9 (schools) policy.* Pretoria: DoE.

DoE & DoL (Department of Labour, South Africa) (2002) *Human resource development strategy for South Africa: A nation at work for a better life for all.* Pretoria: DoE & DoL.

DST (Department of Science and Technology, South Africa) (2002) *South Africa's national research and development strategy.* Pretoria: DST.

FRD (Foundation for Research Development) (1993) *SA science and technology indicators.* Pretoria: FRD.

Kahn M (1993) *Building the base: Report on a sector study of science and mathematics education.* Pretoria: Commission of the European Communities.

Kahn M (2004) For whom the school bell tolls: Disparities in performance in senior certificate mathematics and physical science, *Perspectives in Education* 22(1): 149–156.

Mbeki T (2001) Address of the President of South Africa, Thabo Mbeki, at the joint sitting of the second democratic Parliament. Cape Town, 09.02.01.

Mbeki T (2001) Address of the President of South Africa, Thabo Mbeki, at the second joint sitting of the third democratic Parliament. Cape Town, 11.02.05.

Mbeki T (forthcoming) Response of the President to the debate of the State of the Nation address, Cape Town, 17.02.05.

Ministerial Committee on Teacher Education (2004) *National report on teacher education.* Presented to the Minister of Education, Ms Naledi Pandor, Pretoria.

Mullis IVS, Martin MO, Gonzalez EJ & Chrostowski SJ (2004) *TIMSS 2003 international mathematics report.* Chestnut Hills, Mass: TIMSS & PIRLS International Study Center, Boston College.

Perry H & Fleisch B (2005) Gender and educational achievement in South Africa. In V Reddy (ed.) (forthcoming) *Marking matric: Proceedings of a colloquium.* Cape Town: HSRC Press.

Rasool E (2005) State of the Province address to the Western Cape legislature, Cape Town, 18.02.05.

Reddy V (2005) Cross-national achievement studies: Learning from South Africa's participation in the Trends in International Mathematics and Science Study (TIMSS), *Compare* 35(1): 63–77.

Reddy V (forthcoming) *The South African national report for TIMSS 2003.* Cape Town: HSRC Press.

Reddy V & van der Berg S with B Berkowitz & L Lebani (2005) A trend analysis of matric mathematics performance. In V Reddy (ed.) (forthcoming) *Marking matric: Proceedings of a colloquium.* Cape Town: HSRC Press.

RSA (Republic of South Africa, Parliament) (1953) Debates of the House of Assembly (Hansard). First session – Eleventh Parliament. 3rd July–2nd October 1953.

Shilowa M (2005) State of the Province address to the Gauteng legislature, Johannesburg, 18.02.05.

Stats SA (Statistics South Africa) (2002) *Earning and spending in South Africa. Selected findings from the income and expenditure surveys of October 1995 and October 2000.* Pretoria: Stats SA.

Stats SA (2002) *Mid-year estimates 2002.* Pretoria: Stats SA.

Stats SA (2003) *Gross domestic product: Annual estimates 1993–2002, Annual estimates per region 1995–2002.* Pretoria: Stats SA.

Sujee M (2004) Deracialisation of Gauteng schools – A quantitative analysis. In M Nkomo, C McKinney & L Chisholm (eds.) *Reflections on school integration: Colloquium proceedings.* Cape Town: HSRC Press.

World Bank (2002) An overview of poverty and inequality in South Africa. In I Woolard *An overview of poverty and inequality in South Africa.* Working paper prepared for DFID, South Africa.

Part IV: South Africa in the world

South Africa in the world: introduction

Roger Southall

In this final section, Jesmond Blumenfeld reviews South Africa's foreign trade strategy, Sanusha Naidu asks whether South Africa's strengthening relations with China offer more opportunity than threat, and John Daniel and Jessica Lutchman focus upon South Africa's drive for energy sufficiency and the contribution of the African market to the attainment of that goal.

Blumenfeld argues that although the post-1994 government has successfully restored fiscal and monetary stability, implementation of requisite policy reforms of the trade regime, notably liberalisation and deregulation of the financial (including foreign exchange) markets, has been much less certain. Indeed, the results have been 'unspectacular': whilst South Africa's trade with other countries has grown, South Africa's share of world manufactured exports has declined from 0.5 per cent in 1980 to 0.3 per cent in 1999.

Blumenfeld locates the origins of South Africa's trade regime in the 'Pact Government's' bid back in the 1920s to address the so-called 'poor white' problem without raising the cost to the mining sector. The resulting import-substitution policy was directed at benefiting whites rather than promoting industrial development per se, with increased political support for protection being generated by the expansion of local industry during the Second World War. It was not until the 1970s that the urgency of increasing manufacturing exports began to receive serious attention. Even so, the extent of liberalisation that was achieved thereafter was limited. As a result, the key features of the trade regime inherited by the new government in 1994 were the relatively high level of protection it afforded, its strong bias against exports and its administrative complexity.

The new African National Congress (ANC) government faced two major challenges: should it focus its trade policy efforts upon its African hinterland, or upon its established trading partners (Western Europe, the US and Japan)? Second, how should South Africa relate to the General Agreement on Tariffs and Trade (GATT), and its successor body, the World Trade Organization (WTO)?

Initially, the new government signalled its belief in multilateralism via an unexpectedly strong commitment to trade liberalisation. In practice, however, the results have been modest, and the tariff regime remains relatively complex and cumbersome. This is explained in significant part by the fact that South Africa has three distinct tariff schedules – those relating to the WTO, the European Union (EU) and the Southern African Development Community (SADC).

Blumenfeld argues that while South Africa's initial orientation to the WTO favoured liberalisation, its attitude was largely self-interested. Subsequently, however, this shifted to an ambition to play a more substantial role in multilateral trade negotiations on behalf of all developing countries, even though the interests of South Africa and other developing countries do not always coincide. Consequently, as multilateral negotiations have become more complex, South Africa has become increasingly concerned with regional and bilateral relations.

The potential for strengthening South Africa's economic relations with Africa was self-evident, yet complicated by unease amongst neighbouring countries about domination by the regional giant. Pretoria sought to assuage fears by joining the SADC (which initially did not require much market integration) rather than the more demanding and more dynamic Common Market for Eastern and Southern Africa. Subsequently, however, the SADC has moved towards economic integration, with a protocol which sees South Africa liberalising faster than other members, although its implementation remains slow. In contrast, a substantial renegotiation of the Southern African Customs Union (SACU) was far more urgently pursued. Although proving unexpectedly complicated, this resulted in a new agreement, which came into effect in 2004. This is much fairer to Botswana, Lesotho, Namibia and Swaziland, and has accordingly reduced tension between South Africa and its immediate neighbours.

Nonetheless, Blumenfeld warns of the knock-on effects for the rest of southern Africa of South Africa's negotiation of bilateral agreements with different partners. By far the most significant of these is the EU – South Africa Trade, Development and Co-operation Agreement, which came into effect in 2000.

This provides for an asymmetrical phasing out of duties across a range of manufacturing sectors in South Africa's favour which allows improved access to the EU market. Nonetheless, Blumenfeld judges that the benefits that South Africa – and other regional countries – will derive from this are unlikely to be significant until the EU's common agricultural policy is substantially liberalised. Similar ambiguities attend negotiations which have been conducted with the US, Mercosur, the European Free Trade Association, and other countries, notably China. His overall conclusion is that the three major thrusts of South African trade policy – substantial unilateral liberalisation of the domestic trade regime, improved market access to the EU, and consolidation of trade relations with neighbouring states in SACU and SADC – are not always compatible, and have little systematic connection to a coherent industrial strategy.

In her chapter, Sanusha Naidu addresses South Africa's relations with the People's Republic of China (PRC), a country whose global economic and political weight is growing dramatically. While South Africa seems to be scrambling to strike up trading relations and friendship with Beijing, it by no means follows that its interests with China are as well-matched as glowing rhetoric implies.

South Africa's formal links with China began in the 1920s, when Pretoria entered relations with the nationalist regime of Chiang Kai Chek. Ties with the mainland initially survived the latter's ousting from power and the isolation of his regime in Taiwan in 1949, but were terminated in the 1960s as a consequence of the PRC's increasingly vigorous anti-imperialism. Instead, in 1976 Pretoria established diplomatic relations with Taiwan, a regime which, like itself, lived in a half-world of political isolation. Subsequently, ties between South Africa and Taiwan grew apace, albeit mostly in the latter's favour, with Taiwanese investment assuming an increasing presence in light industries like clothing and textiles. However, even during this period, South Africa and China maintained trade links, albeit clandestinely.

Such continuing ties contradicted China's commitment to the liberation struggle. This had been instrumentalised through fraternal relations between the ANC and the Chinese Communist Party, but fell victim to the ideological struggle between Moscow and Beijing, with the ANC opting to retain its much stronger alignment with the Soviet Union. However, differences were narrowed in the wake of the rapprochement between Moscow and Beijing in the early 1980s, by the Kremlin's shift of focus away from southern Africa, and by China's declaration that all liberation movements in the region would be treated alike. Yet in the wake of the massacres of Tiananmen Square and China's own resistance to democratisation, these closer relations were to pose a major dilemma for the ANC once it moved into office, for its initial foreign policy was centred around the espousal of human rights, an orientation which implied a maintenance of diplomatic relations with Taiwan.

South Africa was faced with the dilemma of whether to maintain the status quo, and hope that time resolved the difficulties; attempt dual recognition, which was contrary to Beijing's One China policy; or downgrade relations with Taiwan in favour of the PRC. Abandonment of a democratic Taiwan would send out the wrong message internationally concerning South Africa's foreign policy, while also resulting in loss of benefits emanating from Taipei's 'chequebook diplomacy'. However, Pretoria could not in the long term afford to ignore the imminent rise of China as a global giant. Hence it was that pragmatism prevailed, and the Mandela government established diplomatic relations with the PRC from January 1998.

Naidu discusses how subsequently, links between South Africa and China have grown apace, with President Mbeki inaugurating a Bi-National Commission in December 2001 and numerous official visits either way having occurred before and after that. The volume of bilateral trade has increased considerably, rising by an annual 36 per cent from R5.3 billion in value in 1998 to R23.3 billion in 2003. Yet the balance and nature of trade is very much in China's favour, with South Africa being cast primarily in the role of an exporter of raw material and an importer of agricultural, capital, and manufacturing goods. The investment relationship is similarly skewed, with Chinese foreign direct investment in South Africa far exceeding the reverse (although this imbalance may be corrected by a growing list of South African companies, amongst them leading conglomerates and financial houses, which are looking to invest in China), whilst importantly, South Africa is becoming a major destination for Chinese tourists. Meanwhile, mutual trade appears set to expand markedly as a result of a pending SACU-China Free Trade Agreement. Nonetheless, that there may be costs to this is denoted by the deleterious impact upon the South African clothing and textile industries resulting from the recent influx of cheap imports from China, whilst other challenges are posed to other sectors of industry from competition from Chinese investors.

Naidu concludes that while there are important synergies between China and South Africa, there are key issues which need analysis. The PRC is making a major thrust into Africa, from which it now imports 25 per cent of its oil requirements. However, many of its aid, trade and investment links are with oppressive African regimes, and these ties may well serve to undermine South Africa's commitment to propelling its continental peers towards greater accountability and better governance. Furthermore, South Africa will face Chinese investment competition within its own 'backyard', especially as African countries may use the Chinese presence to weaken Pretoria's own continental leverage. In short, whilst the relationship will continue to grow, there are problems ahead, and Naidu warns that South Africa must remember that Chinese policy is guided by realpolitik rather than solidarity.

In their paper, John Daniel and Jessica Lutchman pick up from previous reviews of South Africa's economic expansion into Africa in the first two volumes of *State of the Nation* to focus upon its urgent search for energy (oil, gas and hydropower) resources. South African capacity to generate its own electricity production will peak in 2007, so increasingly Africa is assuming centre stage as a new source of energy supply. However, in looking to the continent, South Africa is facing increasing competition.

South Africa's investment dash into Africa slowed in 2004, resulting in a near-stagnant level of exports to the continent. Against this, the value of imports from Africa grew, the increase being made up almost entirely of crude oil. Furthermore, while the expansion of most sectors of South African industry into Africa stalled, there were major initiatives in two resource-related areas: mining and the one which is the focus of this paper, energy. In this area, however, its search for energy on the continent is being matched by non-African investors – China in particular, the US, France, India and Brazil. A number of factors have combined to generate their interest. African oil offers an alternative supply source to the troubled Middle East; most African oil exporters (led by Algeria, Libya, Nigeria, Angola and Egypt) have chosen not to join the OPEC oil cartel; most of Africa's oil is high grade; and Africa's known oil reserves seem set to grow in an era of growing global consumption and depleting supplies. Furthermore, many new African oilfields are located in countries which are weak, dependent and easily manipulable.

These factors are producing a sudden scramble for Africa's oil, led by the US and China, vast countries with an unquenchable thirst. Though obviously on a lesser scale, South Africa's own drive is motivated by the same factors, yet also by a concern to win a larger part of the 'secondary' aspects of the oil sector, the bulk of which presently goes to non-African business.

This provides the cue for Daniel and Lutchman to provide a detailed analysis of South Africa's energy sector and its expanding relations with Africa. They describe how policy and action involves a slew of legislation and a complex set of public–private companies. At the level of the state, strategy is driven by the Department of Minerals and Energy, which via the Central Energy Fund has established four subsidiaries, PetroSA, the Petroleum Agency of South Africa, Oil Pollution Control South Africa, and iGas, all of which have separate functions, but which together form a complex designed to acquire, explore, manufacture, market and distribute any energy form.

They describe South African energy strategy as having three major components – electricity, natural gas and oil – for all of which the African marketplace is central. With regard to electricity, the need for South Africa to diversify away from coal-generated electricity (90 per cent of South Africa's production) and to go beyond production from nuclear reactors (seven per cent), is encouraging greater investment in hydroelectric power. Much of this is drawn from the Cahora Bassa scheme in Mozambique, yet by far the most ambitious scheme is the upgrading of the Grand Inga project, the world's largest hydropower project, centred in the troubled eastern Democratic Republic of Congo (DRC). Set to be developed by a joint venture of the national utility companies of Botswana, Angola, Namibia, the DRC and South Africa (Eskom), Grand Inga is the vital element in South Africa's long-term objective of ensuring its self-sufficiency in electricity. It is little wonder, Daniel and Lutchman comment, that South Africa is expending so much time and effort to secure peace and stability in the DRC.

Meanwhile, South Africa, via joint investments, will soon be purchasing more gas from Namibia, although the largest gas venture is the 865-kilometre gas pipeline being constructed to supply natural gas from central Mozambique to Sasol's plant in Secunda, east of Johannesburg. By 2010, gas could account for ten per cent of South Africa's energy consumption, part of it supplied by Sasol's growing involvements in gas-to-liquid plants located in Qatar and Nigeria's delta region.

Finally, drawing 75 per cent of its oil from the Middle East and 23 per cent from Africa, South Africa is moving to reduce its import dependency through a process of buying into the African oil market, using a mix of economic muscle, technical edge and tactical diplomacy. PetroSA is currently involved in joint-venture agreements in Algeria, Angola, Gabon, Nigeria and Sudan, working with a variety of different partners. Bilateral agreements with Angola have facilitated PetroSA's involvement in an Angolan offshore concession, although in Angola, the South African presence is receiving strong competition from China. Similarly, Sasol is involved directly (with four foreign partners) in crude oil production in Gabon and has secured exploration rights in Equatorial Guinea, this backed by a commitment to co-operation in defence and security. Meanwhile, South African efforts to gain a share of secondary aspects of oil production are being led by the Cape Oil and Gas Supply Initiative in a bid to position Cape Town as a regional supply and fabrication hub for the Atlantic Coast and central African oil sectors.

These three absorbing chapters offer different challenges to the developmental state. Blumenfeld views the South African trade regime as contradictory, and as lacking connections to a coherent industrial policy. Naidu views South Africa's closer relations with China as deliberate, yet largely reactive. Daniel and Lutchman, in contrast, suggest that the post-apartheid government is responding to South Africa's foreseen energy needs with a comprehensive, state-led strategy. Yet all three papers appear to concur that if South Africa were to move to an integrated and single-minded external economic policy, as implied by the shift to a developmental state, then troubling trade-offs may be required of Pretoria's commitments to democracy, human rights and development in the wider continent more generally.

17 South Africa's evolving foreign trade strategy: coherence or confusion?

Jesmond Blumenfeld

Introduction

South Africa's growing political isolation during the decades of apartheid was accompanied by intensified economic isolation, especially from the mid-1970s onwards. Externally, boycotts and sanctions distorted and inhibited trade relations, investment and other financial flows, and technology and knowledge transfers. Internally, inward-looking, interventionist and 'defensive' economic policies and controls were reinforced, when economic logic increasingly favoured more outward-looking policies and less state regulation of markets and prices. Although some significant attempts at liberalisation were made, they were outweighed by moves in the opposite direction. Increased protection of domestic industries, exchange controls, interest-rate manipulations, a moratorium on foreign debt repayments, and suppression of market information about many aspects of international economic relations were at the heart of the policy responses to the sanctions and disinvestment campaigns.

Economic stagnation ensued, putting paid to hopes – at least for the foreseeable future – that South Africa would emulate the recently industrialised 'tiger' economies of south-east Asia by becoming a major exporter of manufactured goods with sustainably high rates of output and employment growth. In global terms, South Africa's share of total world trade had collapsed from a peak of 1.43 per cent on average from 1965–69 to 0.72 per cent from 1985–89 and 0.60 per cent from 1990–94 (Absa/SA Financial Sector Forum 2004).

The distortions engendered (or reinforced) by isolation – and the policy responses to it – included:
- Increasing international uncompetitiveness of South African-produced goods;
- Increasing concentration of productive assets in the hands of local capital, especially a small number of 'conglomerates';

427

- Extension of the anti-export and pro-capital-intensity biases inherent in existing policies;
- Exacerbation of the long-standing structural 'balance of payments constraint' on economic growth;
- Double-digit annual inflation rates; and
- Increased flight of capital and skills.

From the onset of the political transition process in 1990, the external isolation diminished, and following democratic elections in 1994, all remaining sanctions were lifted. However, removal of the formal external barriers to participation in the global economy did not in itself restore full participation. Moreover, many of the domestic structural obstacles to foreign trade and investment remained. Consequently, there was a need to devise policies to facilitate trade and investment flows, and to effect the structural changes required to engage successfully with the forces of globalisation. More generally, among the many trade-related challenges facing the new government was the strategic need to formulate a new 'trade diplomacy' for South Africa: a key issue was how would the new democracy view its role and identity within the global trading system?

At the macroeconomic policy level, there was an urgent need to restore fiscal and monetary stability, and to create a policy environment broadly conducive to fixed investment, economic growth and trade. Considerable progress has been made since 1994 in these directions. Indeed, macroeconomic stability has been the cornerstone of economic policy. Fiscal policy is now firmly set within a clear medium-term expenditure framework, and monetary policy has focused on seeking to tame inflation, at least within a modest range. As a result, South Africa is now perceived globally as a significant 'emerging market' with rising stability and improving credit ratings. Barring unforeseen circumstances, or an out-of-character departure from the current broad policy objectives, these achievements should be sustainable.

At the microeconomic level, the requisite policy reforms and structural changes included:
- Reform of the foreign trade regime;
- Liberalisation and deregulation of financial markets (including the foreign exchange markets); and
- Reduction of market power and other barriers to entry in domestic markets for goods and services.

These changes have been accompanied by a host of other reforms impacting on financial and labour markets, competition policy, industrial structures and regulation of public utilities, foreign investment, and export promotion – not to mention education, health, social and other public services. Each of these reforms in turn, together with exogenous external factors such as global economic growth and international commodity prices, will have played some role in determining South Africa's post-transition foreign trade performance.

Evaluation of the separate effects of each (or any) of these reforms – many of which remain works-in-progress – on foreign trade, or any of South Africa's other global reintegration objectives, is far beyond the scope of this chapter.[1] However, available data suggest that their collective impact on overall trade performance has been positive, but – at best – unspectacular:

- Growth in non-gold export volumes accelerated in the mid-1990s, but fell away sharply thereafter, even contracting in 2002 and 2003, leading to an average annual growth rate of 6.1 per cent from 1994–2003.
- During the same period, merchandise exports increased from 63 per cent to 71 per cent of total export earnings and from 14.5 per cent to over 19 per cent of GDP.
- However, South Africa's share of total world trade continued to decline, falling to 0.53 per cent between 1995 and 1999 and 0.44 per cent between 2000 and 2003 (Absa/SA Financial Sector Forum 2004; South African Reserve Bank 2004).

In short, while trade has grown since the transition, it has grown much more slowly than world trade in general.

The story is only marginally better for manufactured exports. Although total manufacturing output growth in the 1990s showed almost no change from the one per cent annual average of the 1980s, manufactured exports grew by 5.4 per cent per annum from 1990–95 and 11.6 per cent per annum from 1995–2000. As a result, the share of manufacturing in total non-gold exports (including service exports) rose from 39.5 per cent to 56.2 per cent over the decade (McCarthy 2003: 180). Despite this, South Africa's share of world manufactured exports declined from 0.5 per cent in 1980 to 0.3 per cent in 1999. Moreover, the growth did not appear likely to be sustainable: globally, in 1998, the 20 most 'market-dynamic' product groups grew at an average rate of 12.9 per cent, and accounted for 22.6 per cent of total world exports (28.7 per cent of developing country exports). In South Africa, these products contributed a mere three per cent of total exports (Kaplan 2004: 623–5).

Against this background, this chapter explores the broad policy framework within which South Africa's post-transition foreign trade has operated. It explains the nature and origins of the inherited trade regime, examines the changes in trade policy that have taken place in the past 15 years, and evaluates progress towards articulation of a coherent role for South Africa within the global trading system.[2]

Towards a new trade diplomacy

The new African National Congress (ANC)-led Government of National Unity (GNU) faced daunting challenges in two foreign trade-related policy areas: the nature of the trade policy regime and the wider issues of trade strategy.

The trade regime

The policy stances of the apartheid-era governments towards trade issues were unabashedly protectionist. Initially, however, it was social policy – rather than trade – considerations that provided the impetus for the development of local manufacturing industries from 1925 onwards. South Africa's gold-mining-based development path was already impoverishing people of all races, whilst simultaneously enriching the minority. However, the primary political concern of the post-1924 'Pact' government was the growing 'poor white problem'. While economists of the day almost universally favoured free trade, most policy-makers were concerned to avoid any actions that would raise the cost of inputs to the gold-mining industry. 'Import substitution' as such was therefore not an issue for the government, which viewed industrial development mainly as an instrument of its so-called 'civilised labour policy', directed at solving the poor white problem (Horwitz 1967).[3]

However, there was also widespread recognition that South Africa's traditional export profile, and particularly its heavy reliance on gold production, was as much a weakness as a strength. The gold reserves would not last forever, and the (fixed) price of gold was beyond the control of the producers. It was imperative, therefore, for the country to develop 'secondary industries' to counter the eventual and inevitable decline of the gold industry. However, as the Customs Tariff Commission emphasised in the mid-1930s, if such industries were not 'economic' they would prove ruinous of the country's interests (Horwitz 1967: 250). The Commission's concerns about the detrimental effects of protection may have been somewhat overstated, but the underlying logic of the longer-term need to generate non-gold exports was irrefutable.

The Second World War brought a *de facto* state of generalised protection. The physical impossibility of importing many goods rendered their local production essential and the manufacturing sector expanded dramatically. The creation of these new economic interests rendered post-war continuation of this industrial thrust politically inevitable. However, the balance of economic opinion about the benefits of protection had also shifted in relation to the industrial aspirations of commodity-exporting countries. The economic arguments in favour of import-substituting industrialisation thus became more prominent, although the socio-political objective of increased self-sufficiency, particularly in 'strategic' industries, was also a major driving force in the specific circumstances of South Africa.

In the meantime, other mineral finds led to an expansion of non-gold mineral exports. In addition, the new manufacturing industries were finding success in exporting, if only to neighbouring African countries. Consequently, the need for non-gold exports was being partially met in the post-war years. Neither individually nor collectively, however, did these developments constitute a solution to the underlying problem. Other minerals suffered from much the same disadvantages as gold, particularly in the exogeneity of their prices and demand. Although manufacturing exports were competitive in parts of Africa, despite the costs of protection, they were far less competitive in markets further afield. Moreover, following the uncoupling of the rand from sterling in the 1960s, these two problems became interconnected: during commodity price booms, the rand appreciated and manufacturing exports contracted.

Even more fundamentally, South Africa's limited domestic market dictated that local production of most capital and many intermediate goods employed in domestic production across all sectors of the economy was uneconomic. The import-intensity of production was therefore high. Consequently, attempts to raise the (patently inadequate) growth rate of output were not generally sustainable, because the increase in import demand would outstrip the growth in exports, and the resulting deficit on the current account of the balance of payments would necessitate the curtailment of economic growth. Only in circumstances where capital inflows were sufficient to fund the current account deficit – as in the 'miracle' years of the mid-1960s – could higher rates of growth be sustained for more than two to three years. Despite this – or perhaps even because of it – the protective system grew ever more extensive and complex.

It was not until the early 1970s that exports received significant policy attention (Holden 1990). This coincided with the growing recognition within the economics discipline of the limitations of inward-looking industrialisation strategies that failed to promote the growth of manufactured exports. Over the ensuing two decades, there followed intermittent periods of trade policy liberalisation, punctuated by a succession of official reports. A variety of direct export incentives was introduced and the overall level of protection reduced, mainly through reductions in the use of quantitative restrictions (QRs) on imports (Bell 1997). However, the positive effects of these liberalisation efforts were prematurely attenuated. The 'culprits' were commodity (especially gold) price booms, which resulted in currency appreciations and politically-related crises (including sanctions, civil unrest, and a foreign debt moratorium), which led to the imposition of import surcharges and other directly and indirectly protective measures.

According to at least one commentator, 'by the beginning of the 1990s, South Africa had made substantial progress towards trade liberalisation' (Bell 1997: 71).[4] Others have regarded the impact of the changes as more modest. For example, Cassim (2003) believes there was little effective reform of the tariff system, with changes limited to export incentives – pre-1990s liberalisation 'had minimal political costs, as it continued to protect complacent firms while marginally changing the price incentive structure for firms keen to export' (Cassim 2003: 78).

Whatever the net extent of these earlier liberalisation efforts, the key features of the trade regime inherited by the GNU were (McCarthy 2003; Cassim 2003, 2004; Cassim & van Seventer 2004; Cassim & Zarenda 2004):
- The relatively high overall level of protection it afforded;
- The exceptionally high rates of protection against many individual product lines;

- Its strong anti-export bias;
- Its highly discretionary nature (the result of the selective basis of protection);
- The unfair burden imposed on consumers through high tariffs; and
- Its administrative complexity.

Anti-export bias will always be present when tariffs on imports lead to higher prices for domestically-produced goods, thereby making the latter less competitive in international markets. However, the high import-intensity of much South African production renders the anti-export bias particularly unfortunate, since this increases the burden on exports to generate the foreign exchange needed to sustain production levels of many goods.

The high level of protection was evident not simply in the many high nominal tariff rates but also in the fact that the effective rates of protection in many cases exceeded the nominal rates, sometimes significantly so.[5]

The complexity was the result of the multiplicity of protective instruments employed: tariffs (formula, specific and *ad valorem*), QRs, import surcharges and export subsidies – often used in combinations. The tariff structure was also extremely cumbersome, with a very wide dispersion of tariff bands and categories. In 1990, there were some 12 500 tariff lines and 200 tariff rates (bands), the latter ranging from nought per cent to almost 1 400 per cent, with an (unweighted) average of 27.5 per cent (Cassim & van Seventer 2004: Table 1). On the export promotion side, 1990 had seen the introduction of the General Export Incentive Scheme (GEIS) which, by 1994, had already been widely acknowledged as ineffective, very expensive and contrary to international rules.

Strategic challenges

Historically, after the Second World War, South Africa's trade relations were strongest with western Europe, the US and Japan. Typically, South Africa exported minerals, agricultural products and other commodities and raw materials to these markets, and imported capital equipment, intermediate goods and consumer goods from them. Typically, too, South Africa ran a substantial balance of trade deficit with these countries. Europe (especially Britain) and the USA were also the main sources of foreign direct investment (FDI) inflows, while Britain and southern Africa were the main destinations for FDI outflows (Blumenfeld 1982).

Southern Africa was also important, albeit on a much smaller scale, in that it absorbed the great majority of South Africa's manufactured exports, but had little to offer in return. Consequently, this regional trade not only contributed significantly to the viability of South Africa's manufacturing industries, but also generated a surplus that did much to offset the deficit with the rest of the world. The fact that the nature and extent of export trade with, and fixed investment in, Africa had been curtailed (and/or disguised) during the sanctions period did not alter their potential strategic importance after 1994. Indeed, there was every expectation that both would resume and expand quickly and on a significant scale: according to the popular cliché of the mid-1990s, South Africa was destined to be the continent's 'engine of growth'.

While all these 'traditional' markets were bound to remain important, two strategic issues needed addressing:
- First, in the new globalising and post-sanctions environment, it was not clear whether South Africa should focus its trade policy efforts mainly on its African hinterland, or on its global trading partners – or, indeed, how much it should seek to diversify its trading relations by concentrating on new markets, for example among the 'Indian Ocean Rim' countries (including India and Australia), or in Latin America or the post-socialist countries of Eastern Europe.
- The second question concerned South Africa's stance towards global trade issues. Apartheid South Africa had been a founding member of the General Agreement on Tariffs and Trade (GATT) since 1947. Most developing countries had – at best – reservations about the underlying liberal principles of GATT and its successor body, the World Trade Organization (WTO). How should post-apartheid South Africa, both as an 'emerging middle power' and a 'regional big power' (Schoeman 2003), relate to the GATT/WTO and the associated 'North-South' cleavages in trade policies?

The answers to these essentially strategic questions held potentially profound consequences for future trade relations and policies. In any circumstances, the formulation of quick and coherent responses would have been unlikely. In the specific circumstances of South Africa, it was impossible. As Carim puts it, 'In framing a trade policy…the government had to respond to South Africa's developmental imperatives in the context of rapid changes in the global economy…trade policy reform is a political process that needs to be managed carefully' (2004: 2–3).

Moreover, notwithstanding the government's expressed desire to engage positively with the global economy, its main preoccupation was with the broader policy issues of growth and employment and the associated challenges of 'redistribution'. In 1996, the Growth, Employment and Redistribution strategy (GEAR) (DoF 1996) became the centrepiece of economic policy. The only substantive references in the programme to trade policy issues were to the effect that 'the central thrust of trade and industrial policy [must] be the pursuit of employment creating international competitiveness' and that a 'competitive platform [was required] for a powerful expansion by the tradable goods sector'. An appendix to the GEAR document noted that the recent (1996) depreciation of the rand presented 'a significant window of opportunity...[to] take advantage of the implied shift in the prices of tradables and non-tradables, and to lay the basis for an export-led revival' (DoF 1996: Appendix 2).

These preoccupations presumably explain why it was not until 2000 that the Department of Trade and Industry (DTI) was able to produce a 'Global Economic Strategy', which sought to integrate the 'three distinct terrains of strategy formulation: multilateral, regional and bilateral' within a common framework (DTI 2001: 2). In the interim, the practical demands of trade diplomacy forced the government to ride all three of these horses simultaneously, if not necessarily always harmoniously.[6]

Multilateral trade policy and the trade regime

The GNU evinced an unexpectedly strong commitment to the GATT/WTO. Indeed, the first step taken towards rebuilding the country's global trade relations was an offer of a substantial, but phased, reform of South Africa's tariff schedule. The offer, made to the GATT Uruguay round of multilateral trade negotiations, was remarkable for the apparent depth of the proposed reforms (discussed later); that it was made in advance of the conclusion of the political negotiations over South Africa's future was all the more remarkable. The terms, negotiated in the National Economic Forum in 1993 and approved by the Transitional Executive Council, had the support of the ANC, the unions, the business community and the outgoing National Party government.

The politics underlying this surprising consensus on an issue of such importance (and potential conflict) are not clear. At face value, the agreed submission appeared to reflect a recognition on the part of all stakeholders of the urgent need, in the interests of improved competitiveness, to liberalise the country's trade regime and to bring it more firmly within the GATT/WTO norms. However, Bell (1997) has plausibly suggested that the unanimity masked wide differences among the various parties in motivations and assumptions about both the signals and the expected impact of the offer.

Whatever the initial motivations of the respective interest groups, the government was keen to maximise the political benefits. The widespread support was presented as confirmation of a belief in the principles of multilateralism and in the value of the WTO, both as a framework for managing global trade and as a useful mechanism for offering reassurance to potential investors about the new government's future economic policy intentions (Cassim & Zarenda 2004). The virtues of the WTO's role as an external 'agency of restraint' have been underlined by Carim's assertion of the government's belief that 'the WTO...[has] strengthened [the] rules-based trading system, ...enhanced security and predictability in market access, [and] reduced the scope for unilateral trade measures...[E]conomic interactions, including the resolution of disputes, are governed by rules and not solely by economic power' (2004: 3).

The government was also keen to represent the decision as pro-competitive. Thus, the GEAR document claimed that the 'far reaching programme of liberalisation...launched in 1995 [was] aimed at increasing competitiveness' (DoF 1996: Appendix 10). More recently, Carim has argued that the offer was a 'strategically courageous policy [decision...to promote structural reform... by opening up the economy to international competition' (2004: 3).

Tariff reforms

The GATT offer, which took effect from January 1995, included:
- A phased reduction in (simple) average tariff levels from 11.7 per cent in 1995 to 5.5 per cent over five years;[7]
- Replacement of all remaining QRs and formula duties on imports by *ad valorem* duties;
- Reduction in the number of tariff bands to six ceiling rates (0, 5, 10, 15, 20 and 30 per cent), and significant reduction in the number of tariff lines;

- Introduction of a 'cascading' tariff structure for primary products and capital goods (0–10 per cent), components (10–15 per cent) and consumer goods (15–30 per cent).

The proposed reforms also reflected a shift towards productivity-enhancing (and WTO-compatible) – rather than price-distorting (and WTO-incompatible) – measures in support of exports (Cassim & Zarenda 2004). Thus GEIS was to be phased out by 1997, and replaced by supply-side incentives, such as grants for research and development, technological innovation and skills development. (Cassim & van Seventer 2004).

At first glance, the phase-down has resulted in significant reform of the tariff regime. By 1999, the number of tariff lines had fallen by 38 per cent to around 7 700, and the number of lines on which positive (non-zero) tariffs were levied was less than 2 500. The unweighted average rate had declined to 7.1 per cent (although, when zero rates are excluded, the average was still relatively high at 16.5 per cent). However, of the reforms that were implemented, most had already taken place by 1996, and further progress since then has been slow at best (McCarthy 2003; Cassim et al 2002). Moreover, on closer inspection, the extent of reform becomes questionable:

- The number of unique *ad valorem* tariff rates is still far from the six-band, 30 per cent maximum target – there were still around 40 rates in 2001, with many more combining both specific and *ad valorem* rates;
- As tariff levels have fallen, increasing – and seemingly disproportionate – use has been made of non-tariff barriers, including anti-dumping actions;
- Phasing out of export subsidies has meant that, despite lower tariffs, the anti-export bias has been little diminished;
- Effective rates of protection have been little changed.

A further complication is that, following separate late-1990s negotiations, South Africa now has three distinct tariff schedules: the WTO (or 'most-favoured-nation') schedule; and EU and Southern African Development Community (SADC) schedules. The latter arose from additional tariff-reduction commitments made during bilateral free trade area negotiations with the two groups of countries.

In short, despite the mid-1990s liberalisation thrust, and despite the key objective of creating transparency and predictability in the structure of protection and the underlying policies, the tariff regime has remained relatively complex and cumbersome (Draper 2003). Although the average tariff rate is modest by international standards, the numerous remaining 'peak' rates imply continuing high levels of protection for a significant number of product lines.

Global player?

Initially, post-apartheid South Africa's attitude to the WTO was largely self-interested: the primary concern was to use the multilateral rules system to promote pro-competitive domestic reforms. By the late-1990s, however, this concern had been replaced by an evident ambition to play a more substantial role in multilateral trade negotiations themselves. Believing that 'WTO agreements exhibit a range of imbalances and inequities that are prejudicial to the trade and development interests of developing countries' (Carim 2004: 3), Pretoria sought to offer leadership and support to other developing countries on the global stage. During the recent WTO Doha round negotiations, the main vehicles for this role were membership of the Cairns Group of agricultural exporting countries and of the Group of 20 (G20) trade bloc, led by China, India and Brazil. Through its pre-eminent role in promoting the New Partnership for Africa's Development (Nepad), South Africa has also acted as spokesman for the economic interests of African countries at meetings of the G8 (the world's leading economic powers).

Although Pretoria has appeared to take this advocacy role seriously, it has not proved entirely unproblematic, since the interests of South Africa and those of the poorer developing countries (especially in Africa) do not always coincide. Moreover, the lack of progress (to date) in the Doha negotiations has undermined hopes for early progress in achieving major benefits (Draper 2003). With the immediate relevance of multilateral negotiations declining, South Africa – in common with other countries – has opted to concentrate more on regional and bilateral negotiations, predicated on reciprocal moves towards freer trade. Indeed, Cassim and Zarenda argue that this focus on bilateral and regional trade agreements, rather than on WTO commitments, as the main vehicle for phasing out protectionist policies, has been a 'recurrent feature' of the post-transition trade-policy landscape (2004: 14).

Regionalism and the pull of Africa

Africa's potential importance as a destination for South African goods (and services) and for new outward investment by South African firms in mining, manufacturing, financial and business services and construction was self-evident. But relationships with Africa, both political and economic, were sensitive. During the apartheid era, Pretoria had projected not only its economic but also its military power into southern Africa in damaging and destructive ways. In 1980, its regional neighbours had formed the Southern African Development Co-ordination Conference (SADCC) with the two key objectives of reducing their economic 'dependence' on South Africa and of promoting development through 'collective self-reliance'.

There were many who believed that the new democracy owed a major political debt to Africa – especially its southern African neighbours – for moral and material support during the liberation struggle. However, even in an age of increasingly fashionable regionalism, it did not necessarily follow that regional trade relations should be the top priority for Pretoria's trade diplomacy. On purely mercantilist reasoning, it was unlikely, if not improbable, that – even in the aggregate – Africa, with its low income levels and high instability levels, would emerge as a major trading partner for many years to come. Moreover, many Africans remained naturally wary of domination by the regional giant. In 1993, as South Africa's political liberation approached, SADCC had abandoned its avowed aims and reconstituted itself as the Southern Africa Development Community (SADC), with aspirations for a regional free trade area (FTA) agreement, including South Africa. However, Pretoria's putative role within the new organisation was viewed by some with apprehension. It was not even certain that South Africa would join the SADC; an alternative (or additional) option was to join the rival – and much larger – Common Market for Eastern and Southern Africa (Comesa), to which most (though not all) SADC members also belonged.

Nor were SADC and Comesa the only regional bodies for which South Africa's economic power was problematical. South Africa, together with four of its neighbours – Botswana, Lesotho, Namibia and Swaziland (BLNS) – constituted the long-standing Southern African Customs Union (SACU), and the four smaller partners were seeking a review of the highly unequal balance of power within this institution.

In the event, South Africa took two steps at an early stage:
- It opted to join SADC; and
- It entered into negotiations with the BLNS countries for a revision of the SACU agreement.

SADC

At least in the short-term, joining SADC was a relatively cost-free option. SADC's programme of enhanced 'economic co-operation' did not (at that stage) involve much market integration – it had only the most minimal institutional infrastructure – and there were no demands for reciprocity. Had South Africa opted instead to join Comesa, this would have involved a 'heavier political burden…than it was prepared to accept' (Cassim & Zarenda 2004: 6). This was partly because of the greater diversity – in levels of development and political stability – of Comesa's membership, and partly because Comesa had a more explicit demand-led and rules-based integration agenda.

SADC has since undergone a major restructuring, including adoption of a common development and integration agenda, a more centralised approach to policy-making, and a free-trade protocol which has now been ratified by most member states. However, the secretariat in Gaborone, Botswana, remains small, with limited powers, and there are still no formal institutions, other than ministerial and standing committees. The trade protocol sets a target of 2012 for zero tariffs on all intra-SADC trade, with South Africa liberalising further and faster in the earlier stages, giving the weaker economies more time to adjust. Despite attempts to bring this timetable forward, implementation remains slow. This judgement, made in 1999, is probably still largely valid.

> SADC is largely a political organisation in which regional co-operation and integration are perceived as functions of the political relations between member states [that is, at the intergovernmental level] rather than an economic and technical arrangement that is required of any community-in-the-making (Evans, Holmes & Mandaza 1999: 23)

Moreover, little formal attention has been given by SADC to the compatibility between the SACU arrangements and SADC's proposed FTA, let alone the potential points of friction between SADC and Comesa.

SACU

By contrast, the SACU renegotiations were more a matter of necessity than choice for South Africa. Moreover, they threatened to impose significant sacrifices on South Africa. BLNS were not only seeking major changes in the balance of policy- and decision-making power – hitherto concentrated in South Africa's hands – but also a real redistribution of the resources in the common revenue pool. The negotiations proved unexpectedly difficult, taking eight years to conclude. They were complicated by several factors:

- The revenues received by BLNS were proportionately important, ranging between one-fifth (for Botswana) and one-half (Lesotho) of total government revenues in 1992. However, under an earlier (1976) revision of the revenue-sharing formula, South Africa had seen its share of the common revenue pool decline sharply. While the smaller countries were concerned to protect their shares, South Africa – which faced major demands for higher social spending – considered the existing formula increasingly unaffordable.
- BLNS were concerned that the absolute size of the revenue pool might decline as a result of the tariff reforms unilaterally agreed by South Africa in its GATT offer, and by the switch in several countries (including South Africa) from sales taxes to VAT.
- BLNS felt threatened by the concurrent negotiations between South Africa and the EU for an FTA agreement (see below). They were excluded from direct participation in these negotiations, even though – by virtue of their membership of SACU – they would be directly affected by the outcomes. Unless compensated for by increased import volumes, further lowering of South African tariffs could have potentially serious consequences for the smaller countries: apart from the budgetary impact, their industrial ambitions could be adversely affected by competition from EU producers.

The new agreement only came into effect in 2004. SACU's institutional structures have been fully democratised, with ultimate authority resting with a Council of Ministers, a rotating chair, and a requirement for unanimity in decision-making. The setting of tariffs, customs duties and rebates, and the regulation of trade policies, unfair competitive practices, countervailing measures and anti-dumping policies have been devolved to a 'commission of experts' from the member countries. A permanent secretariat is located in the Namibian capital, Windhoek, and an ad hoc tribunal, reporting to the Council, will adjudicate in any disputes between member states. A new revenue distribution formula has been agreed. It includes a 'development component', strongly skewed in favour of the poorer countries.

The new agreement is manifestly fairer than its predecessor and, in the short term, should protect BLNS revenues. However, the size of the revenue pool may diminish further as general levels of protection decline. It also remains to be seen how effectively the new political and institutional arrangements will work, particularly in dealing with the inevitable tensions between South Africa and the smaller countries. Initial impressions appear reasonably positive, in that SACU has been brought more directly into recent negotiations and discussions over the prospective bilateral trade agreement with the USA (among others). However, the possibility that South Africa's *de jure* dominance will be replaced by *de facto* dominance cannot be ruled out.

Bilateral relations

Since the Second World War, the UK, Germany, the USA and Japan had consistently been South Africa's largest bilateral single-nation trading partners. However, with the advent of the single market in Europe, attention had naturally focused increasingly on the EU. In 1990, the EU accounted for around 40 per cent of South Africa's total merchandise trade, and it was also the major source of FDI inflows. Looking ahead, the EU was likely to retain this predominant position. Moreover, despite earlier differences between the ANC and the UK and German governments over the issue of economic sanctions, there was strong political support for the new democracy within the EU. Against this background, it was unsurprising that economic relations with the EU were high on the new government's agenda.

EU-South Africa free trade agreement

All South Africa's neighbours were party to the Lomé Convention, signed in 1975, between the EU and the African-Caribbean-Pacific group of developing countries. Lomé accorded them non-reciprocal preferential market access to the EU for most of their exports (among other benefits). Early indications from Brussels suggested that a favourable non-reciprocal trade agreement, with preferential access for South African exports, would also be on offer to South Africa. Indeed, an Interim Co-operation Agreement, incorporating duty-free access to the EU market for some 2 000 industrial and semi-industrial products, was signed within months of the 1994 election, and improved access for almost 60 per cent of agricultural exports followed a year later.

Despite this seemingly positive start, relations were soured at an early stage by the EU's rejection of South Africa's formally expressed wish to join the trade (but not the aid) provisions of the Lomé agreement. The EU did not regard South Africa as a developing country. This opposition to the 'Lomé-minus' option was regarded within South Africa as a betrayal of the supportive promises made by EU political leaders at the time of the 1994 elections.

The European Commission (EC) subsequently proposed a twin-track approach involving 'qualified' or 'political' membership of Lomé, coupled with a bilateral trade agreement leading asymmetrically towards free trade. The asymmetry would give South Africa more time to reduce its general trade barriers; there would also be the opportunity to negotiate special arrangements for 'sensitive' products. The central message from the EU was that improved access to its markets would not be forthcoming without reciprocity. This course was eventually, albeit reluctantly, accepted by Pretoria. However, the negotiations proved to be tortuous and protracted.

REGIONAL IMPLICATIONS

Not the least of the difficulties was the potential effect on BLNS, who feared profound consequences. Although the EC undertook to be sensitive to regional issues, in practice South Africa's neighbours felt excluded from the process. As a result, the SACU renegotiations were paralysed for extended periods of time. There were also concerns within SADC about competition from EU, as well as South African, producers. However, escalating diplomatic tensions within SADC – most notably between South Africa and Zimbabwe – effectively diminished Pretoria's inclination to push harder to protect its neighbours' interests.

MARKET-ACCESS ISSUES

A far more significant obstacle was the EC's determination to exclude many South African agricultural products from the terms of any trade agreement.

For South Africa, significantly improved access to EU agricultural markets constituted the main potential source of direct gains from a trade pact. However, the EC's negotiating mandate sought to exclude some 40 per cent of South Africa's agricultural exports – four per cent of its total exports – to the EU. There were stronger-than-anticipated EU demands for wider and more rapid reciprocal market access in several of South Africa's most sensitive industrial sectors, including chemicals, textiles, dairy products and automobiles. The EU also appeared to be seeking to introduce linkages or additional conditions designed to extract further concessions, particularly in respect of fisheries and fortified wines.

AGREEMENT TERMS

The eventual agreement – known as the EU-South Africa Trade, Development and Co-operation Agreement (TDCA) – came into effect in 2000. It provided for the asymmetrical phasing out of duties on 90 per cent of the then annual total of $20 billion worth of bilateral trade. Liberalisation covered 95 per cent of South African exports, worth $9.7 billion, and 86 per cent of EU exports, worth $10.3 billion. EU tariffs are being abolished over ten years, with the main reductions coming in years three to six. South African tariffs are being phased out over 12 years. Of South African farm products, 63 per cent were granted unrestricted access to EU markets, with a further 12 per cent entering under duty-free quotas. EU imports of several products originally on the 'excluded' list were partially liberalised. The annual duty-free quota for South African wines was increased by three per cent, but South Africa agreed to phase out its use of the terms 'sherry' and 'port' over 12 years. South Africa also agreed to the conclusion of separate substantive negotiations on fishing rights.

BENEFITS

The value of two-way trade flows did increase in the wake of the TDCA: exports to the EU rose from R54.0 billion in 1999 to R100.1 billion in 2002, before falling back to R85.1 billion in 2003; and imports from the EU rose from R63.4 billion to R117.0 billion between 1999 and 2002 and back to R111.9 billion in 2003. However, exports to the EU remained within the range of 31–33 per cent of total exports, while imports from the EU still accounted for between 41 per cent and 43 per cent of total imports (Absa/SA Financial Sector Forum 2004: 15). This suggests that, until the common agricultural policy is substantially liberalised, South Africa is unlikely to derive significant direct benefits from the agreement. In the meantime, the main hope must be that the agreement will bring indirect (or 'dynamic') gains, with increased confidence in Pretoria's commitment to more market-oriented policies leading to more fixed investment, both domestic and foreign, thereby boosting growth and exports. This hope, together with the negative confidence effects that would have come from abandoning the project, kept South Africa in the negotiations, despite at times serious disillusionment with the process.

Beyond the EU

Following the successful, if complex and difficult, negotiations with the EU, Pretoria – now increasingly constrained to act in concert with its SACU partners – embarked on a seemingly aggressive strategy to conclude a series of new bilateral FTAs with other potential partners. These included the Mercosur group of countries in Latin America, the four-nation European Free Trade Association (EFTA) and, most significantly, the USA. More recently, exploratory talks have been initiated with several other 'Southern' countries. To date, however, these negotiations have borne little fruit.

USA

This proposed FTA agreement would replace (and strengthen) the unilateral provisions of the existing 2000 US Africa Growth and Opportunity Act (AGOA), due to expire in 2008. If successful, the negotiations would lead to the first FTA involving the US and sub-Saharan Africa. Negotiations began in June 2003, but lost momentum in late-2004 as major differences emerged over several issues.

Total bilateral trade between the US and SACU is estimated at around $7 billion annually. SACU absorbs $2.5–3.0 billion of US goods per year, making it the largest market for the US in sub-Saharan Africa. In addition, total US FDI in SACU countries was $2.8 billion in 2000. For its part, the SACU region contributes more than one-third of all non-fuel imports into the US from all AGOA-eligible sub-Saharan countries.

The negotiations fit into the broader US strategy of opening key developing country markets by promoting competitive trade liberalisation through bilateral and regional accords (Draper & Soko 2004). SACU members have been among the leading beneficiaries of AGOA, which currently accords them preferential access to US markets for some 1 800 products. The poorer SACU members have preferential access for a further 4 650 products under the US Generalised System of Preferences. Consequently, an estimated 95 per cent of SACU products exported to the US already enter free of duty. However, there are no reciprocal arrangements for US exporters, and some US producers claim to have been disadvantaged by the EU-South Africa TDCA. US firms also find the southern African market difficult to penetrate, because of the concentration of domestic ownership and control, and perceived non-tariff protectionist barriers, including restrictive licensing and other regulatory or procedural requirements.

For SACU, the FTA agreement would represent a strategic insurance against potential US protectionism. Even if AGOA is renewed, it has three deficiencies that render an FTA agreement desirable for SACU members:

- Although beneficiary countries will have an option to negotiate reciprocal trade access when it expires, AGOA remains a unilateral US initiative that can be withdrawn arbitrarily. This possibility underlines the merits of seeking to 'lock in' the benefits of preferential access at an early stage.
- Some of SACU's key agricultural exports, particularly sugar and tobacco, are excluded from benefits under AGOA.
- AGOA's rules-of-origin – designed to benefit the least developed nations – do not favour South Africa's clothing producers.

A dauntingly wide range of contentious issues – including many so-called 'second generation' (or 'Singapore') issues – has yet to be resolved in the negotiations. They include market access for industrial and agricultural goods, trade in services, intellectual property rights, investment, government procurement, trade remedies, dispute settlement, and labour and environmental standards. Whether a satisfactory deal encompassing all, or even most, of these issues can be reached remains an open question.

MERCOSUR

Mercosur is a free-trade bloc comprising Brazil, Uruguay, Paraguay and Argentina. In economic terms, Mercosur is much larger than SACU: Brazil's GDP alone is four times that of SACU. Trade integration arrangements within Mercosur are well advanced. However, trade flows between Mercosur and SACU are minimal – Mercosur absorbs only around one per cent of SACU's total exports – although they have recently grown rapidly from this very small base (*Business Day* 29.12.04). Despite extended negotiations over several years, an FTA agreement remained an unlikely outcome, since few of the critical conditions and interdependencies, whether economic or political, were present (White 2002, 2003; Roberts 2004). The two sides finally acknowledged this reality and, in late 2004, they concluded a more limited agreement in the form of a fixed tariff preference (FTP) arrangement. The FTP agreement embraces some 2 000 specified products in a selected range of sectors, for which exporters from both sides will now face lower tariffs. Efforts to expand the agreement towards an FTA will continue.

EFTA

Negotiations for an FTA agreement with the four non-EU EFTA members – Switzerland, Lichtenstein, Norway and Iceland – began in mid-2003. The objective was to bring economic relations with EFTA in line with the EU-South Africa TDCA. As with the US negotiations, however, second-generation issues, including intellectual property rights, investment and government procurement, created obstacles, in part because SACU members had yet to adopt convergent policies and positions among themselves. A scaled-down version of the original proposals, limited mainly to improved market access arrangements, now appears the most likely outcome.

Other agreements

FTA negotiations between SACU and India, China, Nigeria, Kenya and Egypt have also been mooted. In recent years, India, and especially China, have evinced growing interest in Africa, including South Africa, as a source for raw materials and a market for consumer goods. Although substantive talks have yet to begin, a framework for SACU's approach to negotiations with India was agreed in late 2004. As in the case of Mercosur, progress is more likely to be made via sectoral-specific FTP agreements than full-blown FTA arrangements. India, Brazil and South Africa have also begun promoting the tripartite 'IBSA' forum for boosting their mutual trade links, although the current intention is to proceed formally via bilateral, rather than trilateral, agreements. On China, Pretoria has taken the preliminary, but significant, step of according Beijing 'market economy' status but a SACU negotiating mandate remains some way off.

Coherence or confusion?

As noted earlier, an ad hoc multi-track approach to post-apartheid trade relations was unavoidable pending formulation of an overarching strategic trade agenda. Seen in retrospect, Pretoria's initial post-transition trade diplomacy incorporated three main objectives:
- Substantial unilateral liberalisation of the domestic trade policy regime, through the WTO, in the interests of increased competitiveness;
- Improved market access for South Africa's exports to the EU; and
- Consolidation of trade relations with neighbouring states in SACU and SADC.

However, these aims proved to be not always compatible either with each other or with other core policies. For example, the negotiations with the EU and with SACU presented significant obstacles for each other; and there was considerable political concern that the employment consequences of reduced protection were inconsistent with the GEAR objective of employment growth. By the end of the 1990s, unilateral liberalisation had been largely abandoned in favour of bilateral negotiations for improved trade preferences. In addition, Pretoria's view of the WTO as a useful agency for promoting domestic competitiveness had given way to that of a forum for exercising an advocacy role on behalf of poorer countries. Subsequently, the reciprocal market access objective moved centre stage, with actual and prospective bilateral negotiations not only with traditional 'Northern' trading partners, but increasingly also with other 'Southern' countries.

The trade policy–industrial policy nexus

Although the focus of this chapter has been on trade policy, the analysis would be incomplete without some reference to industrial policy, the two being intimately interlinked, especially with regard to the promotion of manufactured exports. There have been two policy aspects to the latter objective:

- Reducing the anti-export bias created by pre-transition policies by lowering the levels of protection; and
- Encouraging export-oriented (and employment-generating) industrial growth through 'supply-side' measures, such as tax incentives and productivity-enhancing support programmes.

Both prongs of the export promotion strategy appear to have been weak. The disappointing post-1994 performance of manufacturing (and manufactured exports) confirms the doubts (noted earlier) about the real extent of the tariff reforms; and independent survey evidence indicates that take-up of the support measures and their effectiveness have both generally been modest. Two sectors – automobiles, and clothing and textiles – have benefited from sector-specific support programmes with wider take-up, but both sectors have retained relatively high protection levels, and only the auto industry has expanded successfully (McCarthy 2003; Kaplan 2004).

More broadly, industrial strategy has undergone several changes of approach since 1994 as the DTI's increasingly hard-pressed policy-makers have sought 'to develop focused sectoral strategies and policies…a complex undertaking, with mixed results' (Draper 2003: 21). As Draper goes on to say:

> Effective trade negotiations…should be an extension of coherent, focused industrial strategy. In turn, sectoral strategies must be based on the sectors' integration into the global economy… [O]pening up access to key markets abroad, and increasing the competitiveness of domestic markets, should be key premises of industrial strategy. (2003: 22)

'Global Economic Strategy'

In addition to the weaknesses of the required 'feedback loop' between industrial and trade policies, analysis of the *Global Economic Strategy* (GES), published by the DTI in 2001, and the main features of the post-2000 trade policy agenda, reveal a continuing lack of clarity about some of the key post-transition trade policy issues facing South Africa.

Perhaps the single most important issue is where South Africa's priorities should lie. The GES accords greatest priority to relations with African countries, which occupy a significant proportion of the document. The strategy:

needs to respond to the economic marginalisation suffered by our neighbours...on the African continent...[It] must provide economic content for the vision of an 'African Renaissance'. More broadly, it should seek to promote a developmental agenda, in which South Africa will find allies across the developing world. (DTI 2001: 1)

The methodology adopted in the strategy formulation process was to rank countries in 'descending order of importance or intensity of engagement [as] strategic partners, strategic countries, and priority countries' (DTI 2001: 5). However, 'the African Renaissance concept determines that *all* African countries be regarded as strategic' (DTI 2001: 5, emphasis added), and the 'continental agenda' requires an assessment of whether SADC should be expanded to include other key bilateral partners or other regional groupings. Furthermore, a 'central consideration...is that each of the instruments or areas of engagement (with Africa) requires strong government-to-government interactions at the bilateral level' (DTI 2001: 10).

The GES confirms the downplaying of the multilateral 'terrain', at least from the domestic perspective. Within an increasing emphasis on regional and bilateral relations, it distinguishes mainly between North and South. Deepening of economic relations with key Northern countries, especially the EU and the US, is regarded as 'imperative to lock in supplies of capital, technology and finance' (DTI 2001: 12). However, Japan – the world's second largest economy, which alone accounts for almost eight per cent of South Africa's exports and over seven per cent of its imports, as well as being the sixth largest post-apartheid foreign investor – is seen as a 'strategic country', rather than a 'strategic partner', on the grounds that 'we do not share perspectives on most issues' (DTI 2001: 13). For its part, however, Japan 'clearly views South Africa as its strategic partner in Africa' (Skidmore 2004: 9).

In relations with the South, the GES takes SADC and Africa as the starting point, but with Brazil and India both designated as strategic partners. Yet trade with India remained static (proportionately) at around one per cent of both total exports and total imports from 1998–2003; and while imports from Brazil rose sharply in the same period to two per cent of the total, the export share remained well below one per cent (Absa/SA Financial Sector Forum 2004). By contrast, China – which is rapidly emerging as a significant trading partner (6.4 per cent of imports and 2.5 per cent of exports in 2003) – is seen only potentially as a strategic partner. Numerous other countries are also identified as having 'strategic' or 'priority' characteristics, and the GES acknowledges that many other countries 'which are important in their own right' for foreign trade relations are not mentioned at all.

The status of the GES is open to some doubt. It is not much referred to by officials or by independent commentators, some of whom question whether it truly reflects the DTI's strategic thinking. However, it is currently the only available formal policy statement covering the broad spectrum of South Africa's international economic relations. Taken at face value, it raises some questions about the direction and control of Pretoria's trade diplomacy. In particular:

- The strategy lacks a convincing 'big picture'. It prioritises (many) countries rather than issues and objectives, other than the broad priority of reversing Africa's marginalisation.
- The document stresses that the DTI's trade policies need to be consistent with those of other government departments. While accepting that a country's global economic strategy can never be concerned solely with trade relations, and that it 'should inform – and be informed by – the wider considerations of…foreign policy' (DTI 2001: 2), the content of the GES raises questions about the location within government of the driving forces behind South Africa's trade strategy.
- The prioritisation of Africa appears to stem from a moral and political, rather than a calculated economic, stance. As expected, exports to Africa expanded rapidly after 1994, rising from less than nine per cent of the total in the early 1990s to a peak of almost 15 per cent in 1997 (McCarthy 2003). Since then, however, the proportion has stabilised around the 13.5 to 14 per cent level (Absa/SA Financial Sector Forum 2004). Further growth spurts are possible under various scenarios, but the most likely scenario is that 15 per cent will remain the ceiling for the foreseeable future. Imports from Africa have retained their two to three per cent share of total imports throughout the last 15 years (Jones 2003; Absa/SA Financial Sector Forum 2004), although this may change if South Africa's ambitions to source much more of its oil and energy supplies from Africa are realised.[8]
- The GES offers no serious analytical basis for its emphasis on South–South trade links, beyond asserting that they offer 'vast export opportunities'

and, by virtue of 'the complementarities that emerge from comparable levels of industrial development...[they] offer unique opportunities... [for] investment, joint ventures and technology transfers' (DTI 2001: 11). However, despite some recent analytical support for South–South trade links (Australian Government 2004), the advantages remain uncertain. Such initiatives have been criticised for being 'politically driven' and 'lack[ing] real economic and commercial incentives' (White 2003: 2), and there is a danger that they will not move beyond the signing of agreements between government officials to involve the people who actually undertake trade, namely private enterprises (Joubert 2005). All free or preferential trade agreements offer scope for 'dynamic' gains, especially through new FDI flows, but these are, by their nature, unquantifiable and uncertain, and they are heavily reliant upon successful implementation by all the signatories of a whole package of essential and complementary regulatory, policy and market reforms (Hartzenberg 2005). Several studies (White 2002, 2003; Roberts 2004) have emphasised the limited scope for gains from the long-running SACU–Mercosur negotiations; and similar reservations have been expressed about the forthcoming SACU–India negotiations (Alves 2004).

The high level of generalities in the GES, and the absence of well-motivated arguments, do not inspire confidence in the thrust of the strategy. Perhaps as a consequence of this, the practice of trade diplomacy – which appeared to have clear (if not always consistent) objectives in the early years – also appears to lack strategic direction. There has seemingly been an increased focus on negotiations per se, and it is not clear how much this approach has been based on policy analysis and strategic thinking. The danger is that South Africa will devote increasing resources to the negotiation of trade agreements that will boost the profile of South–South linkages, but may have limited relevance in addressing the major challenges facing the country's trade diplomacy.

Conclusion

In several respects, trade policy in South Africa has come a long way in difficult circumstances:
- The protective structure has been substantially (if still incompletely) liberalised;

- A major FTA agreement has been forged with the country's most important – and now substantially enlarged – trading partner, the EU;
- The SACU treaty has been substantially renegotiated, with South Africa committed to more generous and more equitable forms of economic co-operation;
- South Africa has joined SADC, a move significant not only for political and security issues in the region, but also – potentially – for economic integration; and
- Trade relations are in the process of being forged and deepened with other traditional and non-traditional partners in the Americas, America, Europe, Asia and Africa.

In addition, mainly through the negotiations with the EU, which provided a major learning experience, South Africa's policy-makers were afforded good insight into both the technicalities and the realpolitik of trade negotiations.[9]

Despite these achievements and the accumulation of this wealth of experience, however, the formulation and implementation of trade policy still retain a distinctly ad hoc appearance. Post-apartheid trade performance has proved lacklustre, yet there remains a lack of clarity both about the priorities for, and the determinants of, a more successful trade strategy. The progressive implementation of existing and future regional and bilateral trade agreements will continue to lower protective trade barriers. However, the initial conviction that liberalisation was a necessary condition for successful engagement with the global economy has seemingly faded, and there is no evidence of a coherent alternative strategy. Nor has an effective 'feedback loop' yet been created between industrial and trade strategies. Much general progress has been made in reforming economic policies and structures; where foreign trade is concerned, however, the anti-export bias of policy, the structural lack of competitiveness of South African manufactures, and the balance of payments constraint on growth remain unresolved.

Notes

1   See Cassim (2004) for a discussion of the relationships between those policies aimed at improving productivity and efficiency, and those with redistributive objectives.

2   The author is grateful to the School of Economics and Business Sciences at the University of the Witwatersrand and to the South African Institute of International Affairs for the provision of research facilities in connection with this project.

3   Horwitz's analysis contrasts with that of more recent authors, who tend to attribute the origins of protectionist policy primarily to the desire to reduce the reliance on gold and agricultural exports. (See, for example, Cassim & Zarenda 2004: 6, and the references cited therein.)

4   It should be noted that the term 'trade liberalisation' is open to different interpretations. A strict definition would regard liberalisation as applying only to measures resulting in the 'lowering or removal of the trade barriers that may exist in the encouragement of either export production or the protection of import-competing industries' (McCarthy 2003: 163). By contrast export subsidies, whether direct or indirect, may assist exporters but do not 'liberalise' the import regime.

5   The extent of protection that is afforded to production of a good (for example, clothing) does not depend only on the tariff applied to imports of the good itself. It also depends on the (weighted rate of) tariffs applied to inputs used in the production process (for example, textiles). In broad terms, if the tariff rate on the output (clothing) is higher than that on the inputs (textiles), the effective rate of protection will be higher than the nominal rate (and vice versa). Since, in general, consumer goods face higher import tariff rates in South Africa than intermediate goods (including raw materials) or capital equipment, the effective rate of protection exceeds the nominal rate in a wide range of sectors. In some sectors, most notably textiles, leather goods, footwear, clothing, motor vehicles, motor parts and food processing, the effective rates are high by comparative international standards. (See Cassim & van Seventer 2004: 49–56.)

6   The nature and development of this framework has been discussed in varying detail by several authors (Carim 2004; Draper 2003; Cassim et al. 2002; Cassim 2003; Cassim & van Seventer 2004; Cassim & Zarenda 2004; Bell 1997).

7   The reduction in the average rate from 27.5 per cent in 1990 to 11.7 per cent in 1995 is indicative of the strength of the (unilateral?) liberalising thrust of the outgoing administration.

8   See the chapter by Daniel and Lutchman in this volume.

9   For a detailed review of the negotiations process from South Africa's perspective, see Bilal and Laporte 2004.

References

Absa/SA Financial Sector Forum (2004) *South Africa's foreign trade* (2004 edition). Rivonia: SA Financial Sector Forum.

Alves P (2004) *Understanding Indian trade policy: Implications for the Indo-SACU agreement*. SAIIA Trade Policy Report No. 5. Johannesburg: South African Institute of International Affairs (SAIIA).

Australian Government (2004) *South–South trade: Winning from liberalisation*. Canberra: Economic Analytical Unit, Department of Foreign Affairs and Trade.

Bell T (1997) Trade policy. In J Michie & V Padayachee (eds.) *The political economy of South Africa's transition: Policy perspectives in the late 1990s*. London: Dryden Press/Harcourt Brace.

Bilal S & Laporte G (2004) *How did David prepare to talk to Goliath? South Africa's experience of trade negotiations with the EU*. ECDPM Discussion Paper No. 53. Maastricht: ECDPM.

Blumenfeld J (1982) Economic relations and political leverage. In J Barber, J Blumenfeld & CR Hill *The West and South Africa*. Chatham House Papers No. 14. London: The Royal Institute of International Affairs/Routledge & Kegan Paul.

Carim X (2004) SA's trade policy: Ten years on, *TIPS Trade & Industry Monitor* 31 (Sept): 2–5.

Cassim R (2003) The pace, nature and impact of trade policy in South Africa in the 1990s, *South African Journal of Economic History* 18 (Sept): 76–95.

Cassim R (2004) Reflections on South Africa's first wave of economic reforms. Unpublished paper, School of Economics and Business Sciences, University of Witwatersrand, Johannesburg.

Cassim R, Onyango D & van Seventer D (2002) *The state of trade policy in South Africa*. Johannesburg: Trade and Industrial Policy Strategies (TIPS).

Cassim R & van Seventer D (2004) South African merchandise trade reform since democracy: An overview. Unpublished paper, School of Economics and Business Sciences, University of Witwatersrand, Johannesburg, and TIPS, Pretoria.

Cassim R & Zarenda H (2004) South Africa's trade policy paradigm: Evolution or involution. In E Sidiropoulos (ed.) *Apartheid past, renaissance future: South Africa's foreign policy 1994–2004*. Johannesburg: SAIIA.

DoF (Department of Finance, South Africa) (1996) *Growth, employment and redistribution: A macroeconomic strategy*. Pretoria: Department of Finance.

Draper P (2003) *To liberalise or not to liberalise? A review of the South African government's trade policy*. SAIIA Trade Policy Report No. 1. Johannesburg: SAIIA.

Draper P & Soko M (2004), *US trade strategy after Cancun: Prospects and implications for the SACU-US FTA*. SAIIA Trade Policy Report No. 4. Johannesburg: SAIIA.

DTI (Department of Trade and Industry, South Africa) (2001) *South Africa's global economic strategy*. Pretoria: DTI.

Evans D, Holmes P & Mandaza I (1999) *SADC: The cost of non-integration*. Harare: SAPES Books.

Hartzenberg T (2005) South–South trade liberalisation: Competing amongst ourselves. *Tralac Documents* 8 February 2005. Available at: http://www.tralac.org/scripts/content.php?id=3393.

Holden M (1990) The choice of trade strategy: Past reflections and future prospects. In N Nattrass & E Ardington (eds.) *The political economy of South Africa*. Cape Town: Oxford University Press.

Horwitz R (1967) *The political economy of South Africa*. London: Weidenfeld & Nicolson.

Jones S (2003) External trade in the 1990s, *South African Journal of Economic History* 18 (Sept): 332–365.

Joubert N (2005) South–South cooperation: Real action or political daydreams? *Tralac Newsletter* 22 February. Available at: http://www.tralac.org/scripts/content.php?id=3455.

Kaplan D (2004) Manufacturing in South Africa over the last decade: A review of industrial performance and policy, *Development Southern Africa* 21(4): 623–644.

McCarthy C (2003) Manufacturing during the 1990s: Facing up to trade liberalisation, *South African Journal of Economic History* 18 (Sept): 159–187.

Roberts S (2004) *Reflections on approaching an FTA negotiation with Mercosur: A review of key issues*. SAIIA Trade Policy Report No. 6. Johannesburg: SAIIA.

Schoeman M (2003) South Africa as an emerging middle power: 1994–2003. In J Daniel, A Habib & R Southall (eds.) *State of the Nation: South Africa 2003–2004*. Cape Town: HSRC Press.

Skidmore N (2004) *Japan and South Africa: Deepening economic relations*. SAIIA Report No. 42. Johannesburg: SAIIA.

South African Reserve Bank *Quarterly Bulletin* (various issues)

White W (2002) *South Africa-Mercosur: Long process, little progress*. SAIIA Report No. 23. Johannesburg: SAIIA.

White W (2003) *Driving South Africa-Mercosur: Trans-Atlantic co-operation in the automotive industry*. SAIIA Report No. 34. Johannesburg: SAIIA.

18 South Africa's relations with the People's Republic of China: mutual opportunities or hidden threats?

Sanusha Naidu

> China is a sleeping giant. Let her lie and sleep, for when she awakens she will astonish the world.
> *Napoleon Bonaparte, 1803*
>
> Looking into the future, Sino–SA friendly co-operation has broad prospects for development. Our two countries are highly complementary in terms of economy and trade. We share identical or similar views on many major international issues. I believe that with the deepening of mutual understanding between our two countries, bilateral co-operation in all fields are sure to bear more fruits. China-South Africa relations is bound to have a brighter future.
> *HE Liu Guijin, Chinese Ambassador to South Africa, 29.04.04*
>
> China is both a tantalizing opportunity and a terrifying threat to South Africa.
> *Moeletsi Mbeki, allAfrica.com, 24.10.04*

Since the demise of the cold war, the geopolitical importance of the People's Republic of China[1] (PRC) has increased dramatically. The international community sees the PRC as an increasingly important player in the global economy as well as a significant force on the diplomatic stage (Grant 1995).[2] Indeed, for those small developing nations without substantial political muscle, having the PRC as a potential ally in international fora like the Security Council or World Trade Organization (WTO) can be a boon, while for others like South Africa, Brazil and India, alignment with Beijing is considered a priority, particularly in terms of mainstreaming development in the South and challenging the unilateral character of the post-cold war order. Yet such relations should not be overemphasised. Even though the PRC has tantalised the world with its vast reservoir of economic opportunities, distinguishing whether its interests dovetail with those of its diplomatic partners remains less clear. This is because the Chinese leadership's commitments to South–South solidarity are obscured behind a veil of enigmatic rhetoric which masks Beijing's commercial and political interests. Nevertheless, the global community remains attracted to the PRC despite their many reservations, not least those regarding lack of progress towards democracy.

That post-apartheid South Africa chose to follow the mainstream international consensus was undoubtedly one of the critical tests in Pretoria's foreign policy. Debating the Two China Policy was not easy for the newly-elected government given the high premium it placed on human rights in its foreign policy formulation in at least its early years. But even if the Mandela Presidency was to stand by its universal approach to foreign policy, it could ill afford to ignore Beijing, which was fast becoming an alternate centre of power in an otherwise unilateral post-cold war world order. Moreover, both governments demonstrated resounding synergies in their global outlook around South–South co-operation, multilateralism, and the promotion of a fairer international economic order. From a cursory perspective, this appeared to make them likely allies in the context of a highly unequal world.

The forging of formal relations between Pretoria and Beijing was heralded as the dawning of a new chapter in Sino–South Africa relations. Such rhetoric has been echoed repeatedly by the authorities from each side at various meetings of the Bi-National Commission (BNC) as well as by the business community and mainstream commentators and media in the respective countries. But is this rhetoric as positive as we are led to believe? Undoubtedly, as Peter Draper wrote in the *Taipei Times* (28.12.04), 'engaging with China politically and recalibrating our economic policies towards her are absolute necessities', but complacency in this regard could lead to complications that are already beginning to test this relationship.

Firstly, opening up to Chinese investment could unleash a rush of cheap Chinese products onto the South African market. Not only might this endanger and crowd out local industries, but China's mass of cheap labour could jeopardise South African plans for poverty reduction and job creation, particularly in the clothing and textile sector. Secondly, the lure of the potential of China's huge market may imperil South Africa's own foreign direct investment (FDI) competitiveness. Thirdly, Beijing's outward economic strategy, which is geared towards meeting China's growing domestic demand for commodities, tends to confine South Africa's role in this relationship to that of a primary exporter of raw materials. Fourthly, China's considerable investment and economic interests in Africa pose significant challenges to Pretoria's African Renaissance project and President Mbeki's efforts to establish a code of good governance across the continent. Fifthly, South Africa's candidacy for a permanent seat in the reformed United Nation Security Council – and how this plays itself out at a global level – will certainly have implications for South–South co-operation, especially over competing interests in the South and the common task of development between Pretoria and Beijing. Lastly, trade practice and competition can strain relations if either country lodges a dispute at the WTO over what either may construe as the other's protectionist trade policy. In this regard, pressure from the domestic clothing and textile industry on the South African government to stave off 'unfair' competition from China could prove to be a thorn in the relations. Seemingly, then, underneath the rhetoric of Sino–South African relations there are clashes of interest which dictate that a more cautious approach is necessary.

This chapter therefore seeks to assess the balance of the mutual opportunities and the inherent threats which are embedded in South Africa's evolving relations with China. It does this by analysing the following set of questions. Is it a relationship borne out of political expediency? Or is it one that is crafted out of economic pragmatism? Where do the lines of complementarity lie and what are the divisions? Do Pretoria and Beijing speak with one voice when it comes to the South, especially regarding African issues? Or is it a case of differing agendas? Answers to these questions as well as the above concerns will be discussed in the latter part of the chapter. But first a brief historical overview will be provided, followed by the political and economic dimensions of the relationship.

Historical relations

South Africa's diplomatic relations with China date back to the 1920s when the nationalists took power in the mainland under the auspices of Chiang

Kai Chek.³ These continued even after the nationalists were ousted from power in 1949 by the communist movement of Mao se Tung and established a parallel government on the island of Taiwan that became known as the Republic of China. Despite the communist regime's anti-imperialist and anti-colonialist stance, the apartheid government maintained relations with Beijing rather than Taipei. However, by the late 1950s Pretoria was becoming increasingly nervous about PRC's solidarity with the colonially oppressed in the developing world, particularly in Africa. The PRC's participation at the Asia–Africa Conference or Bandung Conference in 1955 did little to allay Pretoria's fears. Furthermore, the Chinese Communist Party's (CCP) support for non-alignment and the promotion of anti-colonialism and racial equality reinforced Pretoria's fears that the PRC government could lend support to the liberation struggle and undermine its economic and security interests inside South Africa as well as within the region (Singh 1997). Even though the PRC's purpose at the conference was to offset what it saw as the Soviet Union's growing hegemony in the anti-colonial struggles in the Third World, Pretoria feared that the CCP's position could pave the way for communism to take root in Africa through violent means that could threaten the security of the apartheid state. Consequently, official ties between the two sides ended in July 1960.

Subsequently, Pretoria established diplomatic relations with Taiwan in 1976.⁴ This relationship was politically expedient given that both governments were increasingly isolated within the international community and saw themselves at risk from communist aggression (Geldenhuys 1990). Political, economic, cultural and military ties expanded between the two sides in the 1980s with bilateral trade and investment increasing substantially, albeit significantly in Taiwan's favour. Investors from the island took advantage of the apartheid government's industrial decentralisation policy, particularly in the homelands. Light industries like clothing and textile factories became the trademark of Taiwanese investment in areas like Ladysmith and Newcastle in northern KwaZulu-Natal and parts of the Eastern Cape. Moreover, the surge of Taiwanese investments in the so-called 'regional growth points' was influenced by the considerable tax breaks that were part of an incentive package which offered a good return on investments (Mills 1995). Meanwhile, the Taiwanese also played a critical role in enhancing the apartheid state's capacity in low-intensity warfare, particularly that of psychological operations.

This strengthened relations with the South African Defence Force, which sent officials to the island for training.

Evidence provided by Larkin (1971) and Hutchison (1975) indicates that, despite the cessation of official relations, Pretoria and mainland China maintained a clandestine economic relationship. Allegations were rife that sanction-busting trade persisted surreptitiously until the demise of apartheid.[5] By engaging in such illicit trade with South Africa, the PRC contradicted its own public condemnation of the apartheid regime.[6]

The CCP's posturing towards liberation organisations in Africa, including the African National Congress (ANC) and the Pan Africanist Congress (PAC), was guided by two issues: the ideological polemic[7] between Beijing and Moscow and Taiwan's position in the United Nations (UN). With Taiwan being a permanent member of the UN, winning support from the African bloc was crucial in replacing Taipei in the Security Council, which Beijing managed to achieve in 1971.

At the outset, relations between the ANC and the CCP were cordial, with the ANC sending cadres to the PRC for various kinds of assistance ranging from education to military training. However, as the ANC positioned itself within a pro-Moscow camp of liberation organisations, relations between the two came under increasing strain. This was compounded by the ANC's alignment with the pro-Soviet South African Communist Party (SACP). These developments inevitably caused relations to sour for almost two decades, with Moscow becoming the ANC's main source of financial and technical assistance. In contrast, the CCP and the PAC developed closer relations because of Beijing's traditional support for pan-Africanism.

Sino–PAC relations were somewhat uneven and prescribed by expediency rather than ideology. On the one hand, the PAC saw China's growing friendship as one way of compensating for its lack of international patrons. On the other, 'China's attitude towards the PAC was intimately linked to its wider foreign policy on the continent and the continued anti-Soviet position in Beijing' (Taylor 2000: 96). However, PRC aid to the PAC never came close to what the ANC was receiving from Moscow, and Lodge was to conclude that Beijing's support for the movement was 'meager and unreliable' (1983: 304). This was due to the internal feuding, organisational weakness and leadership crises within the PAC and the CCP's military and financial incapacity to support any broader external campaign.

Détente in Sino–ANC/SACP relations was partly due to the rapprochement between Moscow and Beijing following Brezhnev's conciliatory speech on the PRC in September 1982. The changing policy environment in Moscow shifted the Kremlin's focus away from southern Africa. Unable any longer to bear the costs of supporting liberation movements in the region, the Gorbachev government encouraged the ANC to participate in additional coalitions and engage with those powers willing to involve themselves in their liberation struggle. Hence Sino–ANC ties improved, notably after 1983 when the CCP authorities redefined their policy towards liberation organisations by declaring that all such movements would be treated alike without discrimination (Taylor 2000). Naturally, this policy marginalised the PAC, as Beijing was inevitably drawn to the ANC, whose friendship offered it much greater kudos in the Third World. Consequently, within a short space of time, the Chinese leadership and media became ardent promoters of the ANC as the movement with the legitimacy to govern a democratic South Africa. Beijing, like Moscow, also began to encourage moves to a negotiated settlement as a political solution to South Africa's stalemate. This was a radical departure from its earlier stance where violence was the only way of defeating counter-revolutionary forces. That China was pushing for a political settlement and democratisation in South Africa was ironical given its brutal suppression of democracy protests in Tiananmen Square, which scarred its international image and also threatened its future linkages with the post-apartheid state.

Beijing's anti-apartheid rhetoric endorsed the ANC's call upon the international community to maintain sanctions against Pretoria. But this did not deter Beijing from pursuing surreptitious relations with the apartheid government.[8] By courting both sides, Beijing indicated that it wanted to cement relations with all those forces which were going to play a significant role in a post-apartheid era, especially in the context of the Taiwan issue and the CCP's outward global strategy. This kind of thinking reflected what Taylor describes as being 'based on a cool rationalization of the situation and…grounded in *realpolitik*' (2000: 105). This continues to characterise Beijing's current modus operandi in the global arena.

With the world edging closer to a unipolar configuration, the ANC needed to ensure that its vision regarding global issues found synergies with like-minded allies with whom it could advance a global agenda that reflected 'harmony without uniformity'. Establishing formal relations with the PRC was deemed just that since Beijing espoused similar principles, although the economic factor was not lost on the ANC leadership. However, the latter became the subject of much debate during the transition phase and after the 1994 democratic elections, not least because the Two Chinas issue was the first fraught test in South Africa's post-apartheid international relations but also because it exposed the ambiguities and contradictions of Pretoria's foreign policy ideals and principles.

The Two Chinas dilemma

Since April 1994 South Africa's foreign policy-making has frustrated commentators who have complained about its incoherence and contradictory nature. What perturbs them most is Pretoria's vacillation between 'realist' and 'moral' internationalism (Le Pere, Lambrechts & van Nieuwkerk 1999: 1). It was within this context of hesitancy that the Two Chinas dilemma tested Pretoria's ambitious (albeit ambiguous) international relations.

That the newly democratic South Africa would extend relations with Beijing was never in doubt, though what interested Pretoria's new leadership and the foreign policy fraternity was how this relationship would be expressed in diplomatic terms. On the one hand, there were the extensive trade and investment linkages with Taiwan to consider, while on the other, mainland China's increasing political and economic ascendance in the global setting could not be ignored. As part of this debate, Greg Mills (1995: 85) outlined three possible scenarios. The first scenario called for the maintenance of the status quo. This option meant that Pretoria could 'wait and see' whether the issue of recognition could rectify itself through the developments in the PRC and Taiwan before making its own choice while at the same time continuing economic relations with Taiwan and procuring gains by being courted by both sides.

The second scenario – *attempt at dual recognition* – meant that Pretoria could avail itself of its universal approach to international relations and seek to establish diplomatic ties with the PRC while retaining official linkages with Taiwan. This stance would have aligned Pretoria to the UN charter on the principle of universality and with international law on statehood, for which Taiwan fulfils most of the requirements. This position would also have dovetailed with the UN's 'model of parallel representation of divided countries' such as the two Koreas and the former East and West Germany. But, while option one would have meant exclusive recognition of Taiwan, option two was irreconcilable with Beijing's One China policy (Suttner 1995).

The third scenario – *downgrade relations with Taiwan in favour of the PRC* – flowed from international consensus. This was primarily based on China's rapidly growing economic influence and the opportunities this opened up for South Africa's business community.

But the Two Chinas dilemma forced the Mandela Presidency to realise that arriving at a decision was fraught with internal contradictions. Firstly, forging ties with Beijing would send out a confused message about its own values in terms of its democratic and human rights norms, especially after the Tiananmen Square crisis. Secondly, if the leadership sought to switch ties to Beijing, it had to reconcile itself to the loss of the financial inducements it received from Taipei as part of the latter's chequebook diplomacy which was designed precisely to encourage Pretoria to retain the status quo.[9] In the early 1990s, Taipei announced increased investments in South Africa through a series of loans and contracts to Eskom, MacSteel, and the Development Bank of Southern Africa while making commitments (on paper at least) to undertake projects valued at over R1 billion linked to the Reconstruction and Development Programme (RDP).[10] Such inducements compelled the Mandela leadership to evaluate the implications which disinvestment by Taiwan would have for the South African economy and other cultural and educational exchanges if diplomatic ties were switched to the mainland. However, what concerned the Mandela Presidency most was whether the comparatively small amount of PRC investment in the country would increase to match that of the Taiwanese, especially in terms of financing the RDP.

The Hong Kong factor was another consideration. With Hong Kong destined to return to Chinese rule in 1997, Pretoria had to consider the implications this would have for its economic linkages with the island, which was South Africa's fifth largest trading partner at the time. Since there were no formal ties between the PRC and Pretoria, South Africa's economic interests and political status on the island were not protected by basic law. This meant that the status of its mission, the air service agreements as well as duties on goods entering the market would be at the discretion of the PRC and determined by whether Pretoria afforded Beijing diplomatic recognition. Against this, the dynamism of Hong Kong being included into China's economy and the rising living standards on the mainland would open up new opportunities for South African goods which could well surpass those offered by maintenance of relations with Taiwan.

Even before coming to power, there were signs that the ANC was wavering. During a visit to Taipei in 1993 Mandela appeased the Taiwanese government's anxieties by noting 'a democratic South Africa will not abandon its long-term friend who assisted the ANC during its worst time' (*Sowetan* 02.08.93). Yet, in the following year, after the elections, indications from the newly-elected ANC government were that it was willing to enter into diplomatic relations with China, although it would not consider severing ties with Taiwan. Meanwhile, senior members of the ANC, like Deputy President Thabo Mbeki, who were more clear-sighted about South Africa's engagement with PRC, stated as early as 1993 that normal diplomatic relations would be pursued with Beijing (*Weekly Mail* 03.12.93). In part, the uncertainty surrounding the Two Chinas issue reflected the determination of the Mandela government to assert its sovereignty while simultaneously attempting to promote South Africa's rapid reintegration into the world community. Yet in the ultimate analysis, Pretoria could not ignore the rise of China in the global system and the attendant benefits that establishing formal ties with Beijing would bring, especially with regard to the new regime's aspirations in the reformed Security Council and in the context of South–South co-operation. That South Africa dragged its feet in making its choice may well have reflected the new government's recollection of Beijing's initial inability to commit wholly to the ANC's anti-apartheid struggle, as well as clandestine trading with the apartheid regime (Taylor 2000). In the end, however, pragmatism prevailed, and scenario three obtained when South Africa established diplomatic relations with the PRC on 1 January 1998.

The logic of formalising relations with the PRC was the anticipation that it would have the following spin-offs:
- Allow access to a burgeoning consumer market;
- Establish a strategic partnership for promoting the interests of the emerging markets of the developing world;
- Facilitate sharing of the common task of development and the advocacy of a multipolar rather than a unipolar world system; and

- Promote a common agenda for the reform of the global political and economic system.

The unfolding of formal relations

After reaching agreement on relevant issues, the two countries signed a Joint Communiqué on the Establishment of Diplomatic Relations in December 1997 whereby the South African government affirmed that it would adhere to the One-China position. On 1 January 1998, the two countries formally established diplomatic relations and thereby opened a new chapter in their relations.[11]

Since then, bilateral co-operation has burgeoned, and there has been a flurry of high-level visits. Since 1998, on the South African side, Deputy President Mbeki (April 1998), Speaker Ginwala of the National Assembly (October 1998), President Mandela (May 1999), President Mbeki (December 2001), Ms Pandor, Chairperson of the National Council of Provinces (October 2002) and others have paid visits to China. On the Chinese side, Vice President Hu Jintao (February 1999), Chairman Li Peng of the Standing Committee of the National People's Congress (November 1999), President Jiang Zemin (April 2000), Chairman Li Ruihuan of the National Committee of the People's Political Consultative Conference (April 2001), Premier Zhu Rongji (September 2002), Vice Premier Li Lanqing (January 2003) and others have paid visits to South Africa.

On his state visit in April 2000, Chinese President Jiang Zemin joined President Mbeki in signing the Pretoria Declaration, marking the formal establishment of 'partnership' between the two countries. In the document, the two sides announced the founding of the high-level BNC in order to further enhance the partnership and promote co-operation in political, economic and other fields. In turn, President Thabo Mbeki officially inaugurated the BNC during his return state visit to China in December 2001, and together, the two heads of state presided over the first plenary session of the BNC. Separate talks on co-operation in relevant areas were held between leading members and their counterparts from ministries and departments of foreign affairs, economic co-operation and trade, public security, justice, science-technology, energy and tourism. Subsequently, four sectoral committees on foreign affairs, economy and trade, science-technology and national defence have been established, while various other counterpart government departments have also set up channels of communication at different levels and stayed in regular working contact.

In June 2004, the second South Africa–People's Republic of China BNC issued a communiqué which indicated that the two countries had reached broad consensus on and reaffirmed commitments to the following:
- Promoting peace, stability and development in Africa through the Addis Ababa Action Plan and the Forum on China–Africa Co-operation;
- Mutual support for the New Partnership for Africa's Development (Nepad);
- The launch of the Southern African Customs Union (SACU)–China free trade agreement negotiations;
- South Africa's recognition of China's market economy status;
- The inauguration of the sectoral committee on education for further co-operation and the confirmation and establishment of the Centre for Chinese Studies at the University of Stellenbosch;
- The need to advocate multilateralism and equality in addressing and resolving international issues like the reformation of the trading regime, the war on terrorism, and so forth;
- Confirmation of their position as important partners in the pursuit of a new international political and economic order based on peace, stability, justice and equality;
- Strengthening their co-operative South–South relationship; and
- Commitment to the One China policy.

This second meeting of the BNC concluded with:
- Agreement on education co-operation;
- An exchange of letters in regard to grant aid for human resources projects in South Africa;
- Agreement on administration of quality supervision, inspection and quarantine;
- Understanding on a sanitary and phytosanitary consultation mechanism; and
- Signing of the Protocol of Phytosanitary Requirements in June 2004 for the export of citrus fruits from South Africa to China.

However, while the BNC has cemented ties politically between Beijing and Pretoria, it is uncertain whether these relations extend much beyond the realm of technical co-operation.

Economic relations

It was in the early 1990s that the two countries commenced open commercial exchange. The volume of bilateral trade in 1991 was US$14 million and in 1997 over US$1.5 billion. Since the establishment of diplomatic ties, bilateral trade has grown rapidly. It stood at US$2.58 billion in 2002, of which China's imports amounted to US$1.269 billion and exports US$1.311 billion. Between 1998 and 2003 trade between the two countries rose by an annual 36 per cent from R5.3 billion in 1998 to R23.3 billion in 2003. By the end of the first half of 2004, the volume of China–South Africa trade had grown substantially to US$2.75 billion, a 64 per cent increase over the same period. Furthermore, it was estimated that the total trade volume for 2004 may well surpass US$5 billion. China is now South Africa's fifth largest trading partner while South Africa is currently China's biggest trade partner in Africa, accounting for about 20 per cent of the total volume of its trade with the entire continent. Moreover, South Africa has granted China market economy status, which is a much sought-after status for Beijing, even if this is a politically motivated decision rather than commercially driven. This is because under the WTO accord China must be granted market economy status by 2015 and with Europe and the US still classifying the PRC as a 'non-market' economy, it has begun to lobby developing country economies to meet the requirement. Market economy status is important for Beijing because it is a precursor for free trade negotiations.

However, as Figures 18.1 and 18.2 illustrate, trade between Pretoria and Beijing is heavily weighted in China's favour. According to Davies (2004), South Africa's trade deficit with China stood at R9.85 billion in 2004, which was a substantial increase of 88 per cent since 2001.

As Figure 18.3 shows it is mainly manufactured products from China that dominate this trade relationship, followed by high-technology goods. Other products that South Africa imports from Beijing include agricultural goods, capital equipment, TVs, electronic goods and 'white goods' and garments/textiles.

Figure 18.1 *South Africa's bilateral trade statistics with China*

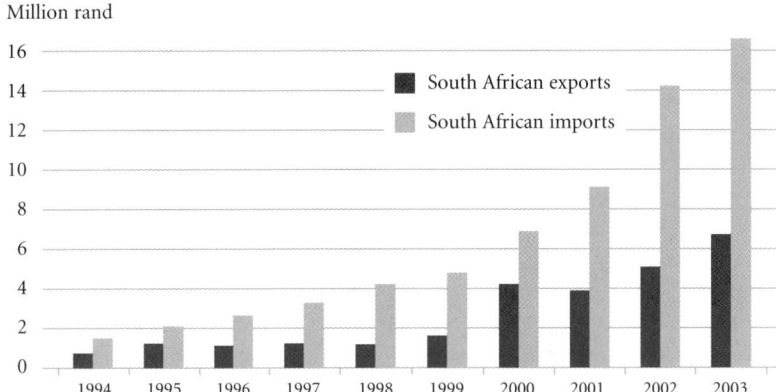

Source: Davies (2004)

Figure 18.2 *China–South Africa bilateral trade*

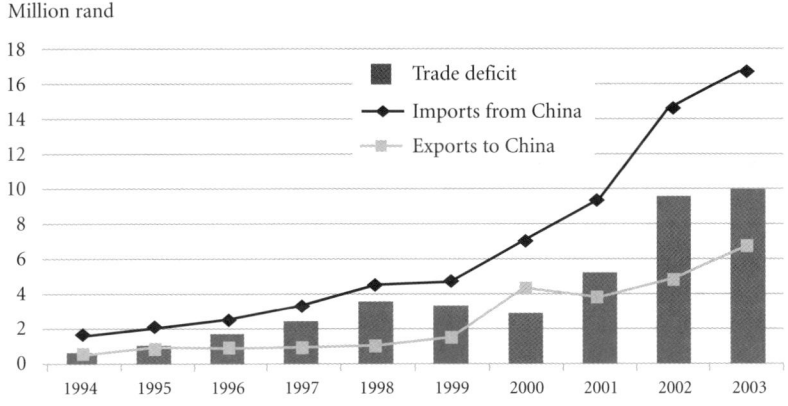

Source: Davies (2004)

Figure 18.3 *Commodity imports from China to South Africa*

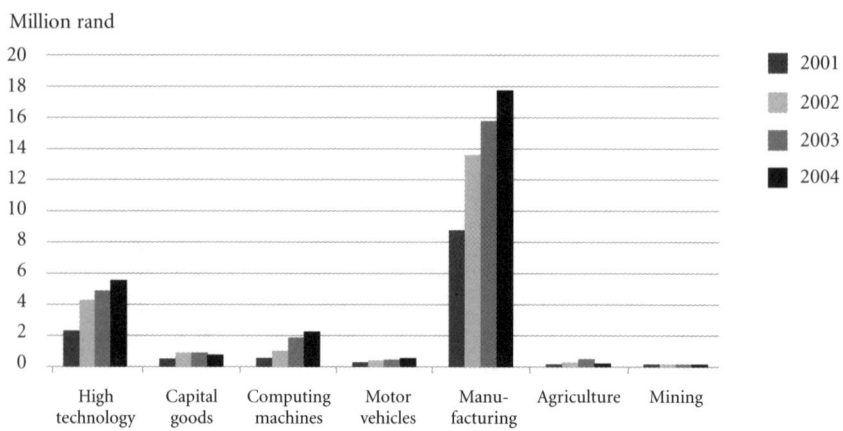

Source: DTI economic database[12]

On the other hand, South Africa's main exports to the mainland are iron ore, manganese, chrome ore, tobacco, wool, granite, gold, copper, aluminium and auto components, thereby making South Africa a net supplier of raw materials to the Chinese market while imports from China are manufactured goods for sale on the domestic market.

Two-way investment has also been on the increase. By the end of 2002, Chinese enterprises had invested US$160 million in 98 projects in the fields of agriculture, textiles, electronics, mining as well as banking, transportation, and communications in South Africa, while South African enterprises had invested in 206 projects in China. There are currently around 20 South African-based businesses with offices in China, and some 187 Chinese companies in South Africa with a stake of around US$100 million in investment. By March 2004, 111 Chinese investors had registered with China's commerce ministry to invest in South Africa, representing a total investment of US$210 million. As of 2004 Chinese FDI to South Africa had amounted (cumulatively) to about R500 million, while South African FDI to China amounted to about R4 billion.[13] In addition, Beijing is also expanding its interest in the South African market to include technologies in mining, electricity supply and power stations, water management, solar energy, pollution control and military and nuclear research. Clearly, with a population of over one billion people, the Chinese government needs to boost alternative sources of energy supply, whilst it also has major concerns about water. Moreover, a Memorandum of Understanding has been signed between South Africa's pebble-bed modular reactor (PBMR) company and China's Chinergy to co-operate in the development of the PBMR. China's interest in the PBMR is based on expanding its electricity capacity, although the nuclear component of the PBMR has caused concern that China could have other designs in mind.[14]

The list of South African companies investing in China is impressive and includes a basket of resource, mining and financial conglomerates that anchor the South African economy. These include Anglo-American, Anglo Gold, Anglo Platinum, Anglo Coal, Kumba Resources, Old Mutual, Standard Bank, De Beers, Sasol, Absa, MIH (M-Tel), Sappi, SABMiller plus smaller specialist entities such as Landpac and consultancies like Beijing Axis. Over the last two years, there has been a 65 per cent growth in trade in mining equipment and transport from South Africa to China. In addition, Sasol has signed a memorandum of understanding – with the Combined Chinese Working Team, on the one hand, and Shenhua Coal Liquefaction Corporation and Ningxia Coal Group Company on the other – to develop two plants in the coal-rich western part of China, namely Ningxia Autonomous region and Shaanxi province to convert coal into liquid fuels by 2011.[15] The projects are expected to cost about US$3 billion each and, if economically viable, they will have a combined annual production of 60 million tons of oil.[16]

Furthermore, the Gauteng Economic Development Agency (Geda) has established a virtual mining initiative with China whereby if a Chinese company needs mining equipment or any other mining needs, a request can be made to Geda, which will, in turn, facilitate contact with appropriate Gauteng-based suppliers. A recent deal concluded under this initiative saw China's largest manufacturer of gas-detection devices, which supplies 80 per cent of mines in China, enter into a venture with a Gauteng-based gas detection manufacturer for products. Geda has also led a South African business delegation to China where new partnerships and business deals were on the cards (*Engineering News* 21–27.01.05). Emerging Markets Focus is another South African-based consulting group which offers similar products as well as briefings on Sino–South African political and economic relations.

The fact that these two organisations have made China a pivotal focus of their operations signifies the importance for South Africa to be doing business with China. Clearly, if South African companies are going to have a global presence, it would seem that the Chinese market would be the first step in this direction since it is considered one of the core economies of the global economic architecture.

With China being the fourth largest gold producer and consumer, there is a natural synergy between it and the world's largest producer of gold. This is particularly so because of a growing demand for gold products from China's rapidly growing middle class. However, the concern is that South Africa remains a primary exporter of gold and needs to transform this advantage into value-added manufactured products destined for the Chinese market. Meanwhile, South Africa became the first sub-Saharan African country to be granted approved destination status by the Chinese government in 2002. The South African authorities see this as an important benefit in boosting its tourism and service industry. More than 33 000 tourists from the mainland visited South Africa in 2003 and they are becoming one of the fastest growing groups of visitors to the country.

The rate of air cargo has also increased dramatically between the two nations. With South African Airways' introduction of the Airbus on the Hong Kong route, the volume of cargo inbound from the Far East escalated by 86 per cent in the last year. On the other hand, exports flown by South African Airways cargo to the Far East grew by 35 per cent and tended to include mostly mining equipment, telecommunication materials and large consignments of Chinese favourites: abalone and lobster (*Engineering News* 21–27.01.05).

In the telecommunication sector, MIH, a subsidiary of media giant Naspers, invested up to $45 million to become the biggest single foreign media investor in the listing of Chinese newspaper group Beijing Media Corporation in December last year (*Business Day* 14.12.04). Naspers took a 9.9 per cent stake in Beijing Media, which gives the group a foothold in China's potentially huge print and television markets. The group also has an interest in Tencent Holdings Ltd., a telecommunication company that is a leading provider of Internet and mobile services in China, while it holds an 87 per cent interest in Sportscn.com, which is one of the principal suppliers of sports news and results via its mobile phone and fixed-line platforms.[17]

There are also local companies like Leitch Chance, a property specialist agency, which has launched a service to find and manage offshore property investments for South African clients with surplus capital from the domestic property boom. Its first project is Talent Studios, being built in China's fast-growing city, Shanghai. The project, which is being developed by Shanghai Fudan Science Park, will be used for accommodation for workers at the Science Park and MBA students from Fudan University. With property prices soaring in Shanghai, a 99 square metre two-bedroomed flat will cost the equivalent of R1 121 900, which is comparable to prices for an off-plan flat in Sandton. Leitch Chance notes that investors are guaranteed an income of R5 799 per month (*Financial Mail* 18.02.05).

In contrast, China's footprint in the South African market consists mainly of business interests in the 'mom-and-pop' trading operations. Trade between the two countries is likely to increase with the pending SACU–China Free Trade Agreement (FTA), which is expected to act as a stimulus to all sectors of the South African economy in terms of exports and employment, and boost South–South trade. Yet the agreement has aroused mixed feelings. Some are confident that, if managed correctly, the FTA will open up opportunities for South Africa's (and SACU's) export of agricultural products. Davies (2004) highlights that with a middle-class population of over 100 million people, demand for fruit, vegetable, meat and dairy products is increasing rapidly. Writing in *Business Day* in October 2004, Peter Draper supported this view, highlighting that China's agricultural imports will rise as more and more economically active people leave the rural areas for the cities. This is underpinned by China recently granting South Africa formal access to its citrus market. Other product markets that South Africa is well poised to take advantage of include beef, fruit juices and wine, especially since tariffs for these products have been reduced dramatically over recent years. The FTA could also have positive spin-offs for both sides in the services sector, with banking being the one area which could benefit significantly. To date this sector has been protected by China, but once expected reform takes place, this should create new opportunities for South Africa's financial giants (Dietrich 2005). Finally, southern Africa stands to gain from its abundant mineral deposits as China's manufacturing sector booms.

Unfortunately an FTA with China will have a negative impact on the clothing and textile sector across the region. The garment industry has already suffered as a result of the influx of cheap Chinese imports into the market, due to China's cheap labour and undervalued currency. In South Africa, Chinese imports account for 74 per cent of all apparel imports into the country. Local companies are also concerned that the expiry on 1 January 2005 of the Multi-Fibre Agreement, which limited Chinese and Asian textiles exports to Europe and the US, will add to the competition currently facing clothing manufacturers at home and in the region. Local manufacturers say that rising imports from China could threaten at least 30 000 jobs. The Congress of South African Trade Unions has joined local industry in appealing to the government to impose certain measures to limit the flood of Chinese apparel imports. According to the WTO, rules countries can adopt certain measures such as curbs on exports in cases where the entire market could be disrupted. However, Pretoria seems to be moving cautiously in this regard. Some believe that it does not want to start employing WTO mechanisms before it finalises a trade agreement with Beijing, while others contend that it is politics guiding the trade relationship. Even so, the more Pretoria delays on this matter, the more dire the implications will be for the clothing and textile industry.

Other concerns surrounding the FTA relate to unfair trading practice in the steel industry, issues of reciprocity and symmetrical versus asymmetrical reduction in trade tariffs. China has opposed South Africa's proposal for asymmetrical reduction in trade tariffs because it does not believe that the South African economy needs to be protected from Chinese competition because Pretoria is a signatory to the WTO rules on open trade. There are also political concerns that Swaziland's diplomatic ties with Taiwan could delay the negotiations around FTA, as is the case with Lesotho, which provides incentives to Taiwan based on the African Growth and Opportunity Act (AGOA) (Reddy 2004).

Apart from the FTA concerns around increased competition from Chinese companies, a recent contract awarded to a Chinese consortium, CITIC-ARCE, by steelmaker Ispat Iscor has raised eyebrows in the industry and the media (*Business Day* 28.02.05). The controversy surrounding the contract relates to the fact that several hundred Chinese workers are to be brought in to work on the construction of a coke oven battery and gas plant at the steelmaker's Newcastle plant. Ispat Iscor defended its decision, arguing that local expertise did not exist, despite the fact that two of South Africa's construction giants, Murray and Roberts and Aveng Grinaker Ltd., were among the bidders for the contract. Industry experts are worried that this move could set a precedent in the domestic market for preference for Chinese companies, which can provide cheap labour. Sasol has also indicated recently that it would have to import about 2 000 qualified artisans, mainly from Asia, due to shortages in the domestic economy (*Business Day* 28.02.05). Meanwhile, the automotive industry is another area wherein China poses a challenge, for many of the major global automotive component manufacturers have already established operations in China, and may drain investment away from South Africa (*Engineering News* 05–07.11.04).

Despite such concerns, the two countries have signed a series of government agreements on the protection of investments, trade, economic and technical co-operation, avoidance of double taxation, civil air transport, maritime transport and so forth. With the Sectoral Committee on Economy and Trade under the BNC serving as a contact channel, the relevant government departments have stayed in close consultations on matters concerning China–South Africa co-operation in WTO, protection of intellectual property rights and Nepad, as well as specific issues relating to the bilateral economic co-operation and trade.

On balance South Africa's economic relations with the mainland raise concerns about Pretoria's industrial strategy. With few core industries gaining from the economic opportunities present in the Chinese market, consideration must be given to those industries where South African competition is threatened. As economic relations progress, negotiators of the FTA – particularly from SACU – need to assess whether the opportunity exists for the region to export value-added goods to the Chinese markets or whether it will be condemned to remaining a source of primary exports. Moreover, South Africa also needs to understand how its economic relations with China will impact on its presence in the immediate region and the wider continent. In addition, a more pertinent issue that must be evaluated is whether China's economic boom is sustainable. Finally, South Africa must remain conscious of its FTA with Europe and the trade deficit that exists between itself and Brussels. In other words, can the Mbeki government afford to have another negative trade balance if it is to deliver on its people contract in 2014? Meanwhile, although both governments have become allies in various trade groupings (G20), challenging the dominance of the established economies in the WTO trade negotiations, China's own economic fluidity and market barriers, especially in the banking sector and price controls, raise concerns around China's trade liberalisation and how South Africa will deal with this.

These considerations notwithstanding, economic relations between South Africa and the mainland are set to continue and intensify – but Pretoria needs to proceed cautiously if it wants the relationship to be pragmatic.

Conclusion

At the beginning of this chapter, two questions were posed concerning the nature of the relationship between Pretoria and Beijing: how should it be conceptualised; and are there common synergies in their relationship that make them common allies in the South and within the global community? The answer to the latter question is yes and no while the simple response to the former is expediency. In exploring both questions, however, several issues come to the fore which warrant further analysis.

Firstly, Africa has become a new frontier for both Pretoria and Beijing politically and economically. With Chinese exports and imports looming large in African markets, this poses some critical political and economic concerns for the Mbeki administration. China's rampant industrial growth is playing a huge role in the scramble for the exploitation of Africa's resources. China is currently the world's second largest consumer of oil and this is fuelling its drive into the continent. There is a significant presence of Chinese companies strewn across the continent which have interests in, amongst others, Sudan, Angola, Nigeria, Equitorial Guinea, Gabon, Libya, Niger, Central African Republic and the Congo. These companies are involved in a variety of activities ranging from building pipelines to oil and gas exploration. West African oil is particularly appealing to the Chinese companies because of its high quality – light, waxy and low in sulphur – which is similar to the grade used in the domestic oil market. Another bonus is that, apart from Nigeria, West African producers do not belong to the OPEC cartel and therefore are not obliged to follow the group's production and export caps. All of which makes the region attractive to Beijing. China now depends on Africa for about 25 per cent of its oil imports (Giry 2004).

It is not only in the oil sector that China's African footprint can be found. Chinese companies are also involved in developing Africa's infrastructure: rail and roads in Ethiopia, Sudan and Rwanda; a new hospital in Sudan; a farm and bridge across the Nile; as well as tendering for a stake in Nigeria's state-owned Nigerian Telecommunications Ltd., for which South African-based MTN and Telkom are also making a bid (*Financial Mail* 11.02.05). Chinese telecoms firm, Huawei, is said to have won contracts worth $400 million to service mobile-phone networks in Kenya. Moreover, China Railway First Group Company Ltd. is one of the nine companies that have pre-qualified for the 25-year tender concession to manage freight traffic on the Mombasa–Kampala railway and it is envisaged that work on the Benguela Railway will resume. In addition, Chinese contractors were said to be ready in November 2004 to begin work on a $600 million hydroelectric plant in Kafue Gorge in southern Zambia, while Chinese agricultural firms tender for land in Zambia. At the same time Chinese textile firms are said to be exploiting Africa's AGOA status (*Daily Champion* 28.04.05).

The attractiveness of China's investment is that it appears to come with no strings attached. For African governments this departure from the tied aid that is normally associated with the West is seen as respect for sovereignty with mutual value and regard for diversity that may be construed as an alternative to the 'Washington Consensus' (Thompson 2004). Yet China's brand of co-operation obscures Africa's – and in particular South Africa's – efforts to bring good governance and human rights to the continent. It also complicates issues surrounding the transparency and accountability of governments in Africa and puts at risk the work of institutions like the African Peer Review Mechanism, especially if Beijing is seen to be supporting questionable regimes. A recent $2 billion credit facility extended to Angola is testimony to this point (IRIN 2005), while Sudan is another example of how China used its veto power in the UN Security Council to foil efforts to impose sanctions on the country (Stakelbeck 2005).

Furthermore, if South Africa were to take a more interventionist approach to Zimbabwe, it would have to contend with the presence of China and the developing relationship between Beijing and President Mugabe. With Zimbabwe almost isolated in the West, Mugabe's 'look East' policy has paid dividends with Beijing extending a hand of friendship. The Chinese have provided Harare with military hardware and software (*Vancouver Sun* 28.10.04), supported the Zimbabwe African National Union-Patriotic Front's electoral campaign in the 2005 parliamentary elections and sealed a $600 million deal with the Zimbabwe Electricity Supply Authority to expand two power generation plants (*Sunday Times* 07.11.04). Consequently, if any remedial action is going to be taken against Harare, consideration must be given to the assertion by Emmerson Mnangagwa, former Speaker of the Zimbabwe Parliament, that: 'With all-weather friends like the People's Republic of China…Zimbabwe will never walk alone' (*YaleGlobal* 03.01.05).

While China increases its political influence across the continent, some see its presence on the global stage as an emerging pole that can counter Western 'culture and values that have come to dominate the rules of the world' (*Guardian* 11.09.04). But this can also be problematic for Mbeki's twin projects of the African Renaissance and Nepad. This is because some of his detractors on the continent may view China as a counterweight to what they perceived as Pretoria's increasing presence and growing hegemony across the continent. This could also fuel sentiment about using China as a countervailing force against South Africa's growing economic hegemony. In Kenya, where South African investors have had a rough ride, the winds from the East are beginning to blow strong with President Kibaki calling for the Chinese to increase their investments in the country (*The Standard* 29.01.05).

Secondly, with cheap Chinese products entering African markets, South African corporates face competition within their own backyard, especially the immediate region. This could raise unease in the relationship between Pretoria and Beijing, particularly if the South African business community pressurises the government to lobby African governments on their behalf.

Thirdly, consideration must be given to how China perceives its role in the UN Security Council and within the South. It is clear that Beijing sees its position in the Security Council as being the voice representing the developing world and the South. If so, what implications will this have for Pretoria's role if it does, indeed, secure a seat in the reformed Security Council structure? Moreover, with China's increasing ties with Nigeria and Egypt, which country will Beijing back for the African candidacy?

Lastly, even though some African nations perceive China's friendship as without political strings, the evidence indicates that the Chinese determine the rules of the trade game, especially when it comes to labour-intensive contracts in which they ensure that Chinese labour is used. This could put at risk Mbeki's vision of building a downstream mineral beneficiation sector not only in South Africa, but across the continent. Moreover, China's friendship also comes with the disadvantage that most of the returns on its investments offer little direct benefit to the local African economy, as in the case of Sudan's oil sector, where half of the $2 billion that Khartoum earns each year in oil exports goes to China (*YaleGlobal* 03.01.05).

Nonetheless, it remains the case that China represents both opportunity and threat to South Africa. If defined from the realist perspective of international relations, China's behaviour is anything but anomalous. Realist theorists conceptualise the behaviour of states in the international system as based on national interest and survival of the fittest within a hostile environment. In light of these assumptions, China conducts its current international relations according to its self-interest, and pursues its foreign policy with aggression and on its own terms. Yet liberal theorists would counter that China's foreign policy behaviour undermines the foundations of the international system, namely co-operation, democracy, transparency, and human rights.

The argument here is that, in the case of Sino–South African relations, the realist interpretation of China's behaviour holds true. The Chinese government has aligned its national interest to its economic sustainability and political ambitions. Meanwhile, whereas the post-apartheid government would similarly argue that its formalising diplomatic ties with the PRC was dictated by South Africa's national interest, seven years later the benefits flowing from these considerations are still debatable. Economic relations remain in China's favour while Pretoria is uncertain how China will react on issues relating to security in the UN. Moreover, China is becoming an important economic and political force in Africa which may unsettle Pretoria's Africa policy. And even within the dynamic of the South, China remains the dominant pole with much more influence than South Africa. Considering these assessments, the nature of Sino–South African relations extends beyond just expediency – if anything the relationship masks more of the hidden threats than the mutual opportunities.

As this relationship grows, the inequality already evident in it will also increase. What this means is that the post-apartheid government must be more cautious in how it engenders its future relations with China. While it makes infinite sense for South African corporates to penetrate the Chinese market if they want to have a global presence, it is even more imperative and logical that the South African government understands that relations with

China are fundamentally about the 'business of business is business' within the confines of realpolitik.

Notes

1. The terms PRC, China and mainland China are used interchangeably throughout this paper to refer to the People's Republic of China.
2. This is also driven by the inclusion of Greater China or China Inc., which comprises of the economies of the PRC, Taiwan and Hong Kong. China Inc. is certainly the most significant economic development in the last two decades of the twentieth century and will become an important factor fuelling the global economy in the future (Mills 2004). Driven by exports, China Inc. has a combined economy of approximately US$1.5 trillion, impressive growth rates averaging 9.7 per cent over the last two decades to 2000 and ranging from 7.5 per cent in 2001, eight per cent in 2002 and 9.1 per cent in 2003, and is considered to be the fourth largest economy in the world.
3. See Taylor (2000) for a concise overview of historical relations.
4. In 1966 the South African regime opened a Consulate General in Taipei.
5. Goods allegedly purchased from Pretoria included uranium, copper, diamonds, lead and zinc, where the latter products were processed through middlemen in Hong Kong, while China supposedly supplied Pretoria with oil and grain.
6. In 1973 China, which became a member in 1971, was one of four members of the UN Security Council to vote against Pretoria's credentials to address the General Assembly. When its actions failed to stop South Africa from addressing the body, China walked out in protest. The following year China supported the vote to exclude South Africa's representatives.
7. The rivalry between Moscow and Beijing was borne out of the ideological enmity between the two centres over the interpretation and application of communism. As the rivalry intensified, so too did the competition where each tried to influence and support opposing liberation movements involved in independence struggles by providing aid (including military capabilities). The split saw blocs develop amongst these movements either aligned to Moscow or Beijing. Wherever there were signs that an organisation indicated a willingness to deal with Moscow, Beijing encouraged a rival organisation by switching aid to them. But this rivalry and competition for influence weighed more heavily on China and radically affected Beijing's Africa policy where the latter was seen to be aiding ineffective organisations because

of their hostility to Moscow, for example the PAC and SWANU. Thus by the mid-1960s Sino–Soviet relations had frozen.

8   Taylor (2000) notes that in May 1991, Pretoria denied a secret visit by a PRC delegation to discuss trade links. According to the *Star* newspaper, the visit reflected China's 'determination not to let ideological scruples get in the way of commercial benefits' (31.05.91). In addition, Taylor highlights that there were reports from Hong Kong, which indicated that China was importing iron ore from South Africa but claiming that it was from Australia.

9   It was reported that the ANC received R33 million from Taiwan for its electoral campaign in 1994 but Taipei denied this and instead argued that the money was earmarked for assisting returning ANC guerillas (Mills 1995). The *Star* newspaper of 25 February 1995 reported that following the democratic elections in 1994, the Taiwanese authorities embarked on a massive sponsorship drive of all expense-paid trips for South Africa's new parliamentarians (248 members including key Cabinet Ministers like Joe Modise and Jeff Radebe as well as controversial personalities like Winnie Mandela and Peter Mokaba) and members of the media and academics to visit Taipei hoping to lobby support for the maintenance of relations.

10 Mills (1995) notes that the announced Taiwanese investment comprised of the following: the Taiwan Railway Administration awarded a contract of R420 million to Union Wagon and Carriage of South Africa, a joint computer venture with ACER, that the Taiwan Feed Industry Association would purchase 300 000 tonnes of maize before April 1995 worth R122.5 million while the Taiwan Power Company would also increase the purchase of coal by 0.5 million tonnes and R140 million would be donated to vocational training under the RDP. The loans to Eskom, MacSteel and the Development Bank of Southern Africa were valued at R105 million, R70 million and US$15.5 million respectively (Mills 1995).

11 See http://www.dfa.gov.za/docs/2004/chin0621.htm.

12 See http://www.thedti.gov.za/econdb/raportt/rapstruc.html.

13 See http://www.dfa.gov.za/docs/2004/chin0621.htm.

14 See http://www.engineeringnews.co.za/eng/sector/energy/?show=64356.

15 See http://www.miningweekly.co.za/eng/features/sasol/?show=58298.

16 See http://www1.cei.gov.cn/ce/doc/cenf/200407012185.htm.

17 See http://www.naspers.co.za/English/inter.asp.

References

Beijing Domestic Service (Beijing), 11.01.78.

Beijing Review, 22.09.86.

Beijing Review, 21.12.87.

Botha PJ (2004) China Inc: An assessment of the implications for Africa: New diplomatic initiatives. In G Mills & N Skidmore (eds.) *Towards China Inc? Assessing the implications for Africa.* Johannesburg: South African Institute of International Affairs (SAIIA).

Davies MJ (2004) Evaluating free trade between South Africa and China: Who are the winners, who are the losers? Unpublished presentation at the Sandton Convention Centre.

Dietrich J (2005) In fear of Asian competition, *Development and Co-operation*. Available at http://www.inwent.org/E+Z/content/archive-eng/01-2005/tribune_art4.html.

Geldenhuys D (1990) *Isolated states: A comparative analysis.* Johannesburg: Jonathan Ball.

Giry S (2004) China's Africa strategy, *New Republic Online*, 11.15.04.

Grant RL (1995) An international opinion on the recognition issue. In *South Africa and the Two Chinas dilemma.* Johannesburg: SAIIA and Foundation for Global Dialogue.

Hutchison A (1975) *China's African revolution.* London: Hutchinson.

IRIN (Integrated Regional Information Network) (2005) Angola: Oil-backed loan will finance recovery projects. In *UN Office for the Co-ordination of Humanitarian Affairs (OCHA),* 21.02.05.

Larkin BD (1971) *China and Africa 1949–1970: The foreign policy of the People's Republic of China.* Berkeley: University of California.

Le Pere G, Lambrechts K & van Nieuwkerk A (1999) The burden of the future: South Africa's foreign policy challenges in the new millennium, *Global Dialogue* 4(3) 3–8.

Lodge T (1983) *Black politics in South Africa since 1945.* London: Longman.

Mills G (1995) The case for exclusive recognition. In *South Africa and the Two Chinas dilemma.* Johannesburg: SAIIA and Foundation for Global Dialogue.

Mills G (2004) Spots on the butterfly's wings? Developing a South African diplomatic strategy towards Asia. In G Mills & N Skidmore (eds.) *Towards China Inc? Assessing the implications for Africa.* Johannesburg: SAIIA.

Reddy L (2004) A China-SACU FTA: What's in it for South Africa? *South African Foreign Policy Monitor*, August/September. Johannesburg: SAIIA.

Singh S (1997) Sino–South African relations: Coming full circle, *African Security Review* 6(2). Available at http://www.iss.co.za/pubs/ASR/6N02/Singh.html.

Snow P (1988) *The star raft: China's encounter with Africa*. London: Weidenfeld and Nicholson.

Stakelbeck FW Jr. (2005) China's growing influence in Africa, *The American Thinker* 06.05.05. Available at http://www.americanthinker.com/articles.php?article_id=4474.

Suttner R (1995) Dilemmas of South African foreign policy: The question of China. In *South Africa and the Two Chinas dilemma*. Johannesburg: South SAIIA and Foundation for Global Dialogue.

Taylor I (2000) The ambiguous commitment: The People's Republic of China and the anti-apartheid struggle in South Africa, *Journal of Contemporary African Studies* 18(1) 91–106.

Thompson D (2004) Economic growth and soft power: China's Africa strategy, *China Brief: Journal of Analysis and Information* 4(24). Washington: The Jamestown Foundation.

19 South Africa in Africa: scrambling for energy

John Daniel and Jessica Lutchman

> Our forecasts indicate a steady increase in demand for electricity... If we do not take corrective measures now, South Africa will run out of excess peaking capacity by 2007 and excess base load by 2010.
> *Thulani Gcabashe, Chief Executive of Eskom*
>
> Investment in Africa's offshore oilfields is really going crazy.
> *Dr Philip Lloyd, Energy Resource Centre, UCT*
>
> The third scramble for Africa continues apace...
> *Duncan Clarke, Chair of Global Pacific and Partners*
>
> The fact that the 18th World Petroleum Congress is taking place in South Africa in September is indicative not only of Africa's prominence in the global oil industry but also of South Africa's increasingly important role within it.
> *Business in Africa 09.02.05*

Introduction: the changing African economic environment

In the first two *State of the Nation* volumes, analyses were presented of post-apartheid South Africa's rapid corporate expansion into the African economy and its emergence in less than a decade as the continent's economic powerhouse (Daniel, Naidoo & Naidu 2003; Daniel, Lutchman & Naidu 2004). In the year since our second article appeared, the fundamentals of the South African–African economic relationship have remained intact. South Africa remains a colossus in the African economy. According to the International Monetary Fund (IMF), South Africa's gross domestic product (GDP) in 2003 accounted 'for nearly one-third of Africa's on a purchasing power parity basis and to 38 per cent of African nominal GDP at market exchange rates'(Arora

& Vamvakidis, 2005: 4). In regard to the GDP of the Southern African Development Community (SADC) region, South Africa's share was in the region of 80 per cent. Despite an increased interest in the African economy on the part of some non-African investors, South Africa remained the largest source of new foreign direct investment (FDI) on the continent, while the trade balance continued to favour South Africa.

In this article, we focus on a particular aspect of South Africa's interaction with the African market, namely, its resort to the continent's oil, gas and hydropower resources as a means to meeting its growing energy demands.[1] Current estimates are that South Africa's capacity to generate electricity from its current sources will peak in 2007. With a limited capacity to generate new power from domestic sources, Africa is assuming centre stage in South Africa's unfolding energy strategy. In this context, however, South Africa is finding that there are other energy-hungry powers scrambling for Africa's power resources. This competition is just one of a number of emerging changes to the continent's political economy.

In regard specifically to South Africa's interaction with the African market, one of the features of the last 12 months has been a levelling-off of the pan-sectoral nature of South Africa's involvement in that market. Overall, the near decade-long dash into the African market slowed in 2004, while some sectors, like aviation, banking and road construction, actually showed a decline. In aviation, South African Airways' goal of establishing a West African hub in Nigeria was set back when its acquisition of a 30 per cent stake in the new Nigerian national carrier, Eagle Airlines, was abruptly cancelled by the Nigerian government in favour of the British airline, Virgin Atlantic.

In the banking arena, none of South Africa's private-sector banks or financial services institutions made any new acquisitions in 2004, while Nedbank sold off its poorly-performing Zimbabwean operation altogether. This stall in the expansion of South African banking operations in Africa will likely, however, be temporary. In early 2005, Absa moved into Angola while its pending link-up with Barclays plc – in terms of which Barclays will acquire a 60 per cent shareholding in Absa – will significantly boost its African presence and profile. According to Absa's Chief Executive Officer (CEO), Steve Booysens, the deal could make Absa 'a pan-African powerhouse. Our dream of becoming the "Lion of Africa" is in our reach'[2] – a grandiose statement which will be seized upon by those analysts who see imperialist and/or hegemonic intentions in everything South Africa and its corporates do in Africa

Road construction groups like Aveng continued to scale back on their African involvements in 2004 with Aveng's chief executive admitting that the company was not 'making money out of a significant portion of our African activities' (*Financial Mail* 06.05.05).

Even the expansionist high-flyer of recent years, Shoprite Checkers, slowed to a near standstill, opening only one new store in Africa in 2004 (Lagos). While turnover in its African stores outside of South Africa increased by 26 per cent in the period July–December 2004, its profits from these same stores dropped by a massive 71 per cent. The fact that the company in this same period opened its first outlet outside of Africa (a hyperstore in Mumbai in India) suggests that its appetite for new African outlets may have peaked.

This slowdown contributed to a second significant development in 2004, namely, the near stagnant nature of South Africa's export sales into the continent. In rand value terms, South Africa's exports were just over R37 million more in 2004 than 2003, a negligible statistical increase of 0.11 per cent.

In two cases where conditions for trade were more favourable than for many years, there was an actual decline in trade volumes. One was Libya. Despite the lifting of UN sanctions, the existence of a binational commission between South Africa and Libya and the signing of seven agreements on co-operation – including a trade agreement – exports in 2004 declined by more than half to only 44 per cent of their 2002 value. Likewise, in the case of post-civil war Angola, South Africa's exports declined in 2004 by nearly R1 billion (from R3.39 billion to R 2.5 billion).

In part, this decline and the overall poor African export performance was attributable to the strengthening in the value of the rand over the course of the last year, a factor which disadvantaged the export sector while facilitating imports. However, this is not a sufficient explanation as it applied to the export sector overall which, nonetheless, globally grew by 9.5 per cent.

It was only in fact in regard to Africa that export performance was sluggish in 2004. In the case of each of South Africa's other trading regions, export volumes grew. Thus, even though in regard to export-market share by region Africa retained the third place it achieved in 2003, its overall share declined for the first time in the post-1994 era. In 2004, the figure was 14.7 per cent compared to 16.48 per cent in 2003. The Americas remained in fourth place with 12.2 per cent of total share. Exports to Europe, Asia and the Pacific all increased, albeit by marginal percentage points in the region of one per cent. By rand value, however, they increased significantly – by 12 per cent for both Europe and Asia and 25 per cent for the Pacific.

While South Africa's export drive into Africa flagged, its imports from Africa grew in 2004. Nonetheless, as noted earlier, the imbalance in the South African–African trade relationship noted last year persisted. It did, however, continue its downward dip from 5:1 in South Africa's favour in 2001 to 4:1 in 2003 and 3:1 in 2004. While statistically a drop of just over one per cent in a one-year period could be said to be significant, in trade terms it was less so because this increase was made up almost entirely of crude oil. It added no real value to any other sector of the African economy.

Despite this increase, Africa remained in global terms in fourth place as an import source by region (4.2 per cent) of South Africa's imports. However, the point to note is that were oil to be excluded, it would lag behind the Pacific and in last place. It is hard to imagine but the fact is that were it not for oil, South Africa would import more from Australia, which accounts for 90 per cent of the Pacific region's exports to South Africa, than from the whole of the African continent.

That said, Europe and Asia remain by some distance the primary sources of South Africa's imports with between them 80 per cent of the total. What is worth noting here is the sharp escalation in 2004 of Asian imports, up by 29 per cent. What this probably reflects is the growing Chinese, Korean and Indian penetrations of the local commodities market. Table 19.1 and Figures 19.1, 19.2 and 19.3 illustrate the points made above.

STATE OF THE NATION 2005-2006

Table 19.1 *South African exports, imports and trade balance by region, 2004 (R millions)*

Region	Exports			Imports			Trade balance	
	2003	2004	Change (%)	2003	2004	Change (%)	2003	2004
Africa	39 000	39 037	0.0	8 217	13 000	58	-30 783	-26 037
Americas	34 161	36 571	7.0	36 436	40 158	10	2 275	3 587
Asia	65 176	73 200	12.0	89 131	114 806	29	23 955	41 606
Europe	92 019	102 969	12.0	116 597	129 398	11	24 578	26 429
Pacific	6 331	7 921	25.0	6 765	8 118	20	434	197
Total	236 687	259 698	9.5	257 146	305 480	18	-20 459	-45 782

Source: Preliminary statement of trade statistics for RSA for January–December 2003 to January–December 2004 released by SARS (2004); and Department of Trade and Industry economic database[3]

Figure 19.1 *South African exports by region, 2003 and 2004*

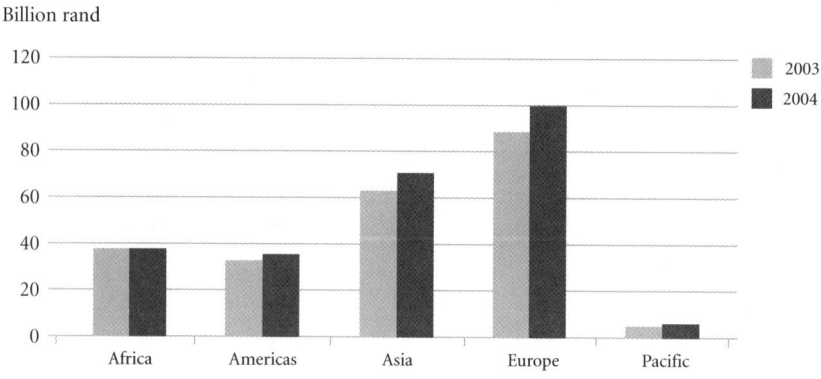

Source: HSRC, Corporate mapping database

Figure 19.2 *South African imports by region, 2003 and 2004*

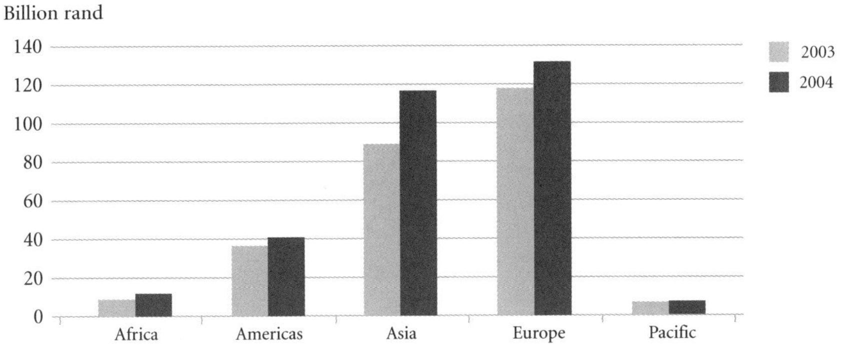

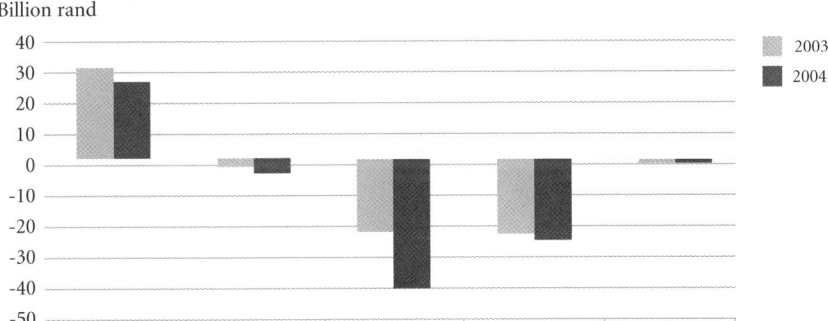

Source: HSRC, Corporate mapping database

Figure 19.3 *South Africa's trade balance by region, 2003 and 2004*

Source: HSRC, Corporate mapping database

Having noted the general slowdown in the South African penetration of the African market, and in some cases a retreat from it, in 2004 there was an intensification of interests and activities on the continent in two niche areas. Both were resource-related – mining, on the one hand, and energy, broadly defined, on the other. In fact, as Figure 19.4 indicates, these two were the largest stand-alone sectors operative in Africa over the four-year period 2000–03, as opposed to the collective infrastructural sector which is actually a composite of six related but distinct sectors.[4] They will presumably have further extended their prominence as a result of their expanded operations in 2004.

Figure 19.4 *South African business activity in Africa by sector, 2000–03*

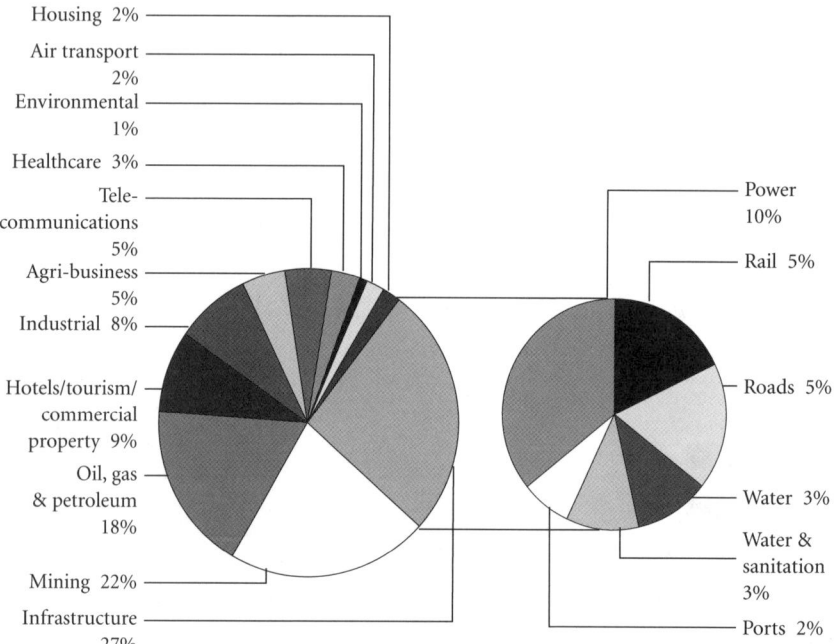

Source: South African Foundation (2004)

In the mining sector, South Africa's two largest African players are Anglogold Ashanti and Randgold Resources. Of the two, only Randgold was in expansionist mode in 2004. With operations in Mali, Angola, Burkina Faso and Ghana, it launched exploratory probes in both Angola (diamonds) and Burkina Faso (two for diamonds) and a joint venture with a Ghanaian company probing for gold in the Ashanti region. However, in Mali it consolidated by selling its interests in the Syama gold mine while upping its investments in the Loulo and Morila gold mines.

An interesting new South African entrant into the African mining sector in recent years has been Mvelaphanda Holdings. Established by Tokyo Sexwale in 1998, it is now one of South Africa's more prominent black-managed and black-owned investment groups. Commencing seven years ago with a capital base of R1 000, the company now has gross assets exceeding R2.5 billion. Much of this has been materialised through the resource and energy sectors and by way of a number of strategic investments in private equity, property development and financial services. Analysing these, it seems clear that Sexwale is seeking to position Mvelaphanda Holdings as a pan-African minerals and mining company. Thus, for example, by acquiring equity in the Absa banking group, in Goldfields and in the insurer African Life, the company has acquired a presence in Namibia, Tanzania, Zimbabwe, Burkina Faso, Ghana, Botswana and Zambia.

However, it is through its subsidiaries, Mvelaphanda Resources and Mvelaphanda Energy, that the company is staking out a claim as a mining entity. Mvelaphanda Resources gained its first foothold in the rest of Africa when Tokyo Sexwale obtained two diamond-mining licences in Angola (Luarica and Fucuama). These concessions were then passed through to its diamond-mining subsidiary, Trans Hex. At present, Trans Hex is operating one diamond mine in Angola, is developing another and has launched two exploration projects. It was also recently awarded a contract to mine diamonds in Namibia. In January 2004, Mvelaphanda Resources also managed to secure mining concession rights in the Democratic Republic of Congo (DRC). These were in regard to parts of the Kilomoto gold region and the Ruashi copper cobalt project.

The other subsidiary, Mvelaphanda Energy, has recently moved into the African oil and gas sectors. This it has done by acquiring a majority stake in Ophir Energy, a London-based company. Through Ophir, Mvelaphanda is seeking, or has gained, oil concessions in Libya, Gabon, Guinea, Nigeria and Somaliland. In the latter case, it has been dealing with the Kenyan-based provisional Somali government, which, despite the fact that it is unable to set up base in its own country, felt able to grant offshore oil concessions. The company has recently begun drilling operations off the Somali coast. While this may sound impressive, in the world of oil Ophir and Mvelaphanda are minnows.

This brings us to the second of the significant changes to the African economic environment, namely, the renewed and intensified interest in the continent on the part of major non-African investors, including some oil giants.

The end of the cold war ushered in an era of intensified African peripheralisation from the mainstream international economy, as well as one of politico-strategic insignificance. This was exemplified both by Africa's declining share of global trade, which dropped below two per cent in the 1990s, and by a steady disinvestment from the African market by most foreign investors, notably the British, Americans, Japanese and Portuguese. China also ceased its prominent role as a donor as it turned inwards as part of its embrace of the capitalist mode. The one exception to this trend of African disengagement was France, which continued to be involved deeply in the economies of its former African possessions but which did little to open up new areas of African trade. The dismal nature of both the African economic performance in the 1990s and of its future prospects (as one African diplomat put it, 'people are tired of Africa. So many countries, so many wars') was aptly summed up by an American business executive who commented to the political economist, Thomas Callaghy, 'Who cares about Africa. It is not important to us; leave it to the IMF and the World Bank' (Callaghy in Harbeson & Rothchild 1991: 41– 42).

This Western withdrawal from Africa coincided with South Africa's post-1990s 'discovery' of the African market documented in previous *State of the Nation* volumes. What this meant was that for the best part of the decade 1994–2004 not only was South Africa the 'new kid on the block' in the African marketplace, it was also frequently 'the only show in town'. Under the impact of global and globalising forces, the door to the African economy was flung wide open in the 1990s but often it was only the South Africans that entered. However, in the last year or two this has changed and South Africa is increasingly finding itself having to share its place at the table with two big players in the form of the US and the China, and two important regional actors in the form of India and Brazil. What these countries all have in common – amongst themselves and with South Africa – is their growing focus on Africa's energy and mineral resources, amongst which the first prize is oil.

Africa's oil: the global context

The oil industry is comprised of three main components – upstream activities in the form of exploration and production, midstream in the form of pipelines and so-called tanker farms and downstream functions in the form of refining and retailing. As of 2003, it was estimated that Africa held about nine per cent (or 105 billion barrels) of known world oil reserves. It was in that year exporting 5.9 million barrels per day, equivalent to 14.8 per cent of the world's total and putting it third behind the Middle East (36.7%) and Eastern Europe (16.1%). Five countries (Algeria, Libya, Nigeria, Angola and Egypt) dominate the African oil sector. Together they are responsible for 85 per cent of upstream production while also holding 91 per cent of Africa's proven reserves. There are, however, nine other African crude oil producers. This does not include South Africa which is an oil producer but of synthetic or bituminous (oil from coal) fuel and not crude. In terms of downstream activities, South Africa is the continent's third-largest refiner of oil (after Egypt and Algeria), generating 15.6 per cent of the continent's distilling capacity. Most of this is domestically consumed, though a small proportion is exported.

A number of factors have combined to generate the current interest on the part of the major oil importers in the African oil market. The first is that African oil offers an alternative to the Middle East, which particularly in the light of its post-9/11 security review and its perceived need to reduce its dependence on Middle Eastern sources, is a considerable factor for the US. Hence the growing emphasis of the US on oil-producing African states, moving beyond Nigeria and Angola where it has had oil interests for some years, to develop oil ties with Equatorial Guinea, Gabon, Chad, the Republic of Congo (Congo-Brazzaville) and Libya.[5]

A second incentive is the fact that most African oil exporters have chosen not to join the Organisation of the Petroleum Exporting Countries (OPEC), which means that they would likely increase their output in the event of OPEC imposing production quotas. Third, most of Africa's oil output is high grade ('high-quality sweet crude', as it is known in the trade) and thus easy to pump and refine as it has a low sulphur capacity.

Finally, recent discoveries have suggested that Africa's oil reserves, which as noted above stand at just over 100 million barrels, could grow by as much as a quarter in the decade ahead. Much of this is held by states which are not amongst the big five, are not members of OPEC and which are either dirt poor (like Equatorial Guinea, Chad and the Republic of Congo) or whose economies have been wrecked by war and armed conflict (such as Sudan and Cote d'Ivoire). They are thus highly dependent and weak states susceptible to manipulation and big-power pressure. What gives these African reserves added significance is the fact that currently the world is consuming oil at a rate faster than it is discovering new sources. It is furthermore estimated that global consumption of oil will increase by some 70 per cent in the next 25 years – from the current six billion barrels per year to about 27 billion.

All of this has combined to produce the current 'scramble' for Africa's oil. For the US this is, as suggested earlier, a product of both security considerations and its virtually unquenchable thirst for oil. Currently importing about seven per cent of global production, this figure is rising by some two per cent per annum. Africa's reserves thus form an important component of its forward planning. The same applies to the Chinese for whom the combination of its extraordinary growth rate since it embraced the market economy, its vast population, booming vehicle sales, rapid rural electrification and the policy decision enunciated in the Chinese Five-Year Energy Plan (2000) to double the country's strategic oil stockpile to between 10 and 12 million tons has generated an unprecedented thirst for oil, as well as energy and mineral resources. Within two to five years, it is estimated that China will surpass Japan as the world's second largest oil importer.

Though obviously on a far lesser scale than China, many of these same factors are driving South Africa's thrust to gain a foothold in the African oil market. However, as this paper will argue, this is driven more than just by the need to acquire new sources of crude oil. What South Africa is also seeking is a greater share of what are referred to as the 'secondary' or 'local contact points' of the energy industry, the bulk of which business currently goes to non-African-based companies. This is the supply side of the industry ranging from large-scale machinery (drilling equipment, for example) to the clothing, food and other needs of offshore oil workers. South Africa's economic planners have identified this sector of the business as one in which it, as Africa's economic powerhouse, can reap the benefits of what economists refer to as 'sideways benefication'.

South Africa and energy

The South African energy sector comprises four fuel components – oil, petroleum, natural gas, and electricity (nuclear and non-nuclear-generated). Overall, South Africa's energy strategy has a dual focus. One is the goal of long-term self-sufficiency while the other is the short-term one of not exhausting its supply of energy in the next two to three years. If it does, the power failures which plagued downtown Johannesburg and its wealthy northern and western suburbs in the summer of 2004/05 will become a national phenomenon. The strategy is pursued in a host of ways involving a slew of legislation and a complex set of public–private sector arrangements.

At the level of the state, the strategy is driven by the Department of Minerals and Energy (DME). Central to the operational delivery of the strategy is the Central Energy Fund (CEF), which is a sub-component of the DME and which came into being with the enactment of the 1997 Central Energy Fund Act. The CEF reports directly to the Minerals and Energy Minister. Its first task was to develop a *White Paper on energy policy,* which Cabinet approved in 1998. Its implementation since then has been effected through no less than 12 pieces of legislation. These have dealt with the production and regulation of the whole gamut of fuels – nuclear energy, natural gas, petroleum products and electricity. More recently, a second White Paper dealing with the issue of renewable energy was approved. Its proposals were included in the 2004 National Energy Act, which also made provision for the setting up of both a National Energy Advisory Committee and a National Energy Data Base and Information System.

Since 1998, the CEF has spawned the confusingly-termed Central Energy Fund (Pty) (Ltd). While part of the state, it operates as a private company in terms of the Companies Act. Its role is in many ways not that dissimilar to those of the science councils, which although answerable to the state through a designated minister, operate with a very high degree of autonomy. Its mandate is a broad one, namely, the acquisition, exploration, generation, manufacture, marketing and distribution of any energy form, as well as research relating to the energy sector. In pursuit thereof, it has set up four subsidiary companies.[6] These are:

- PetroSA which engages in the exploration and production of crude oil and the harnessing of natural gas. It is the product of a merger and restructuring of two state-run apartheid-era companies, Mossgas and Soekor, which undertook offshore oil explorations as the then government sought ways around UN sanctions on the supply of oil to South Africa.
- The Petroleum Agency of South Africa whose role it is to promote the exploration and exploitation of crude oil and natural gas.

- Oil Pollution Control South Africa (OPCSA) which manages oil pollution prevention and control.
- iGas which is responsible for the development of the hydrocarbon gas industry.

Figure 19.5 reflects the full range of the CEF's concerns.

Figure 19.5 *Organogram of the Central Energy Fund*

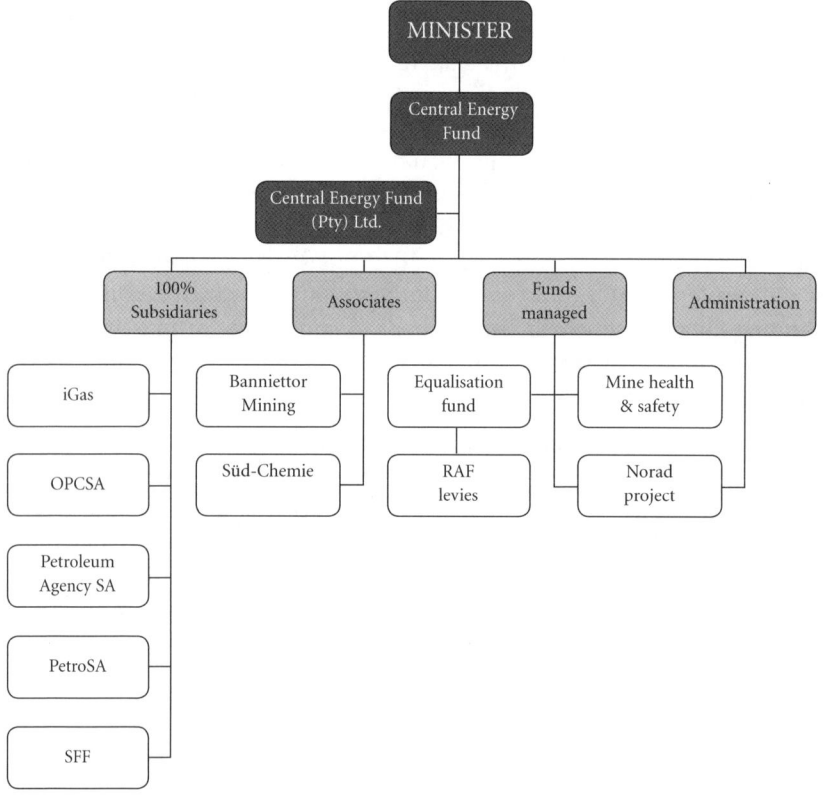

Source: http://www.cef.org.
Notes: RAF = Road Accident Fund
SEF = Strategic Fuel Fund

Impressive though this might all look on paper, the CEF has in its short lifespan not been free from scandal. Like the energy industry virtually everywhere, South Africa's energy sector has proven to be no exception to the industry's general reputation for sleaze. Of the four CEOs to have held office in the CEF, only the current incumbent – in office since early 2003 – has not been forced to resign under a cloud.[7] In April 2005, the *Mail & Guardian* (19–26.05.05) reported that PetroSA had knowingly allowed itself to be used as a front or conduit for the siphoning of R11 million of oil-generated revenue to the ANC for its 2004 election campaign. The announcement by the chair of the Parliamentary Portfolio Committee on Minerals and Energy that his committee would not be investigating the allegation suggests that the energy sector need have little concern for the supposed oversight role of the national legislature.

South Africa's energy strategy by component

South Africa's energy strategy has three components to it – electricity, natural gas and oil – and the African marketplace is central in regard to each of these.

Electricity

South Africa generates two-thirds of Africa's electricity. Just over 90 per cent of this is sourced from coal, seven per cent is nuclear-generated while only two per cent is in the form of hydroelectric power. As a consequence of its substantial coal reserves, South Africa is the second cheapest electricity producer in the world. South Africa's state-owned utility, Eskom, manages the country's demand for power and produces some 90–95 per cent of the electricity generated in South Africa. Independent power producers, imports and municipal generators account for the other four to five per cent.

Eskom, which is Africa's largest energy utility and the world's fourth largest, has since its inception been a vertically-integrated monopoly. It owns and operates 24 of the country's 53 central-station power plants. The rest are owned by municipalities (22) while private interests run the other seven. In late 2004, the government invited the private sector to bid for the construction of one 1000 MWe oil-fired power station or two with a capacity of 500 MWe each. Ultimately, the government intends for the private sector to generate 30 per cent of South Africa's future energy needs. In the meantime, it has also begun work on recommissioning three Gauteng-based power stations closed down in the late 1980s and early 1990s when the country had an excess of capacity.

Of Eskom's 24 power plants, 15 are coal-fuelled, two are gas-turbine plants, six are water-driven hydroelectric plants while one is a nuclear power plant. This is located at Koeberg in the Western Cape and is the only commercially viable nuclear power plant in Africa. The licensed capacity of Eskom in 2000 stood at 39 870 MWe (92 per cent of total licensed capacity in South Africa) and its net capacity was 35 584 MWe. Of its net capacity, 88 per cent is derived from coal, six per cent from water, five per cent from nuclear energy and one per cent is from liquid fuels.

The DME's forward planning in regard to electricity reflects a concern that, based on the current three per cent per annum increase in the rate of domestic consumption, South Africa could run down its surplus power capacity (currently 36 000 MWe from all electricity producers) in this decade. A second factor is that coal-fired power is a significant polluter and, consequently, a growing environmental hazard in the industrial heartlands of the country. The DME's strategy, therefore, to ensure future energy security is to diversify its power sources from coal to nuclear and hydroelectric power and to develop a liquid fuels (processed natural gas) industry.

In terms of enhancing nuclear energy, the DME and Eskom are involved in the development of a pebble-bed modular nuclear reactor (PBMR) at Koeberg. A new type of high temperature helium gas-cooled nuclear reactor, a PBMR would be a faster, cheaper and more efficient form of nuclear energy than the current technology used at Koeberg. A private partner is currently being sought for the US$1.2 billion cash injection needed for the project.

The virtues of the PBMR notwithstanding, hydroelectric power is regarded as a more viable option for South Africa at present and it is in this context that South Africa's developing trade and other ties to Africa loom large. Being on the whole a dry or arid country, South Africa has a limited domestic hydroelectric capacity. Currently it generates only 2 267 MWe per annum of hydroelectric power. Its largest hydroelectric power plant is the Drakensberg Pumped-Storage Facility which generates 1 000 MWe per annum. However,

South Africa's neighbour, Mozambique, possesses substantial hydroelectric capacity, some of which it sells to South Africa. This is sourced from the Cahora Bassa hydroelectric power-generation scheme on the Zambezi River.[8] South Africa's relations with its neighbours in terms of power are facilitated through Eskom Enterprises, the international arm of Eskom, and it is to the wider African region that Eskom Enterprises is looking – not only to secure South Africa's electric power needs but also as a source of revenue. Currently, Eskom Enterprises' largest external project is its participation in the Southern African Power Pool, a scheme which encompasses a common power grid among SADC-member countries. The company, however, is active in the energy field in at least 17 countries across the length and breadth of the African continent.

Its largest and most ambitious scheme is the Grand Inga project. This is actually the world's largest hydropower project and will be implemented in three phases over a time span of some 20 years. The project is centred in the troubled eastern region of the DRC. Parts one and two of the project involve an extension and upgrading of an existing hydroelectric facility built in the DRC some two to three decades back. Under-investment and poor maintenance has led to a steady degradation of the infrastructure.

Phase three of the project – 'Grand Inga' – is the responsibility of the Western Power Corridor joint venture company, or Westcor, made up of the national utilities of five Southern African Power Pool member utilities – Botswana, Angola, Namibia, the DRC and South Africa. Westcor's initial task is to connect Inga to southern Africa and to feed electricity into the grids of its members. About 3 000 MWe per annum of power is scheduled to be transferred from Inga 3, of which 2 000 MWe per annum will be destined for South Africa. Once Westcor has completed this western corridor, it will move to 'lighting up Africa' by linking the western corridor to planned or existing southern, eastern and northern power pools. Once completed in the 2020s, Grand Inga is expected to generate 40 000 MWe of electricity, sufficient to meet the needs of the entire continent as well as generate revenue for its members by exporting its surplus power to Europe.

Grand Inga is the vital element in South Africa's long-term objective of ensuring its self-sufficiency in electricity. It is little wonder then that the South African government has committed so much in the way of time and effort, as well as military peacekeepers, to the task of bringing political stability to the DRC and to ending the endemic conflict in particularly the eastern region (Ituri) of the country. This is where its peacekeepers are located, part of a UN force. A peaceful and stable DRC forms an important element in South Africa's economic future.

Natural gas and the liquid fuels industry

The acquisition of natural gas for processing into liquid fuels is another important component of South Africa's energy strategy. To the fore in this regard is Sasol. In recent years it has moved beyond its oil-from-coal pioneer technology to the point where it is now regarded as the world's leading natural gas processing company. To this end, it has in recent years negotiated a number of mega-deals in order to secure an abundant supply of natural gas.

South Africa has no significant natural gas reserves of its own but Namibia and Mozambique do. In the case of the former, South Africa will soon be purchasing natural gas from the Tullow Oil's (an Irish company) offshore Kudu field. The gas produced from these will be developed and commercially operated by NamPower (Namibia's national power utility) for resale into the Namibian and South African markets. Also, new reserves of gas discovered offshore but in an area that straddles the South African–Namibian border could turn out to be beneficial for South Africa. Known as the Ibhubezi Prospect, the majority shareholding is held by two US companies – Forest Oil and Anschutz – with PetroSA having a 30 per cent share and Mvelephanda Holdings ten per cent.

Sasol is at the centre, however, of South Africa's largest natural gas venture. In 2002, Sasol, in partnership with the South African and Mozambican governments, launched a joint venture for the construction of an 865 km gas pipeline for the supply of natural gas from the Pande and Temane onshore fields in central Mozambique to Sasol's plant in Secunda, east of Johannesburg. Here it is processed into synthetic liquid fuel. The pipeline came on stream in February 2004 and the goal is to pump about 120 million gigajoules a year. This will increase natural gas's contribution to South Africa's primary energy supply from 1.5 per cent to about four per cent. If, as seems likely, some of the independent operators in the energy sector take up government's invitation to build gas-fired power stations, gas could by the end of the decade account for ten per cent of South Africa's energy consumption.

Sasol has also moved into, and beyond, Africa to develop gas-to-liquids plants. Late in 2005 Sasol's first offshore gas-to-liquids plant located in Qatar will be commissioned. It will also be involved in the operations of a gas-to-liquids plant being constructed in Nigeria's Delta province. While not involved in the ownership of the plant, Sasol will supply its production technology for a licensing fee. It is also looking at opportunities to be involved in the construction of similar plants in Australia and Iran.

As part of its strategy to acquire natural gas, government has also developed a gas infrastructure plan. It is in four phases, the first of which has been completed. That involved the construction of the Mozambique–Secunda pipeline and the upgrading of the now ageing pipeline between Secunda and Durban. Phase 2 will involve either the construction of a pipeline from the Kudu fields in Namibia to the Western Cape, or an offshore pipeline from Ibhubezi to Saldanha and then on to Cape Town, Mossel Bay and Port Elizabeth. Phases 3 and 4 will involve, respectively, pipelines from the West Coast to Gauteng via Sishen in the Northern Cape and one from Port Elizabeth to Durban via East London.

Oil

South Africa is dependent for approximately 98 per cent of its oil needs on imports. Of this, 75 per cent is imported from the Middle East and 23 per cent from Africa. This latter figure reflects a considerable increase in recent years. In 2001, for example, African imports stood at only nine per cent. Its main African supplier is Nigeria with the others being Angola, Cameroon and Gabon. In the last five years, however, South Africa – or more precisely South African companies operating with state support – has moved to reduce its import dependency through a process of buying into the African oil market as either a sole proprietor or in a partnership arrangement. In pursuit of this goal, South Africa has employed a combination of economic muscle, technical edge and tactical diplomacy.

Leading the attempt to secure this greater stake in African crude oil production have been Sasol and the CEF-owned PetroSA. The latter is currently involved in joint-venture arrangements in Algeria, Angola, Gabon, Nigeria and Sudan. A state-owned company which, however, receives no funding from the state, PetroSA sources its funds from its own resources or by borrowing from the private sector. While obviously respondent to the state's demands, seeking business opportunities internationally is seen in the oil trade as key to PetroSA's long-term viability as it will exhaust its gas supplies from its fields off Mossel Bay in the course of this decade.

Operationally, its approach internationally is to work with a strategic partner either as a co-equal partner or a minority shareholder. Thus, for example, in Algeria, PetroSA has an 18.75 per cent stake in block 402d operated by US company Burlington, and jointly they are involved in an oil-exploration concession off the Algerian coast. In Nigeria, PetroSA acquired a 40 per cent interest as a technical partner in an oil-producing bloc in the Niger Delta, with the Nigerian independent Moni Pulo retaining 60 per cent of the field. In January 2005, at the conclusion of President Mbeki's state visit to Sudan, PetroSA signed an agreement with the Sudanese state oil company, Sudapet, for oil concession rights in oil block 14. This is one of the very few of Sudan's new concessions not to have been awarded to one of the three major foreign players in the Sudanese oil sector, China, Malaysia and India. It was almost certainly an expression of gratitude to the South African government for its role in brokering the comprehensive peace agreement between the government of Sudan and the southern Sudanese group, the Sudanese People's Liberation Movement. Signed in the same week as the oil agreement, the comprehensive peace treaty brought to an end Africa's longest-running civil war.

In February 2005, a state visit to Angola led by then Deputy President Zuma concluded with the signing of four bilateral agreements. One of these was to facilitate the granting of permits and licensing agreements necessary for investment. A second on electricity was geared at facilitating Eskom's growing role in Angola in the refurbishment and development of the country's national electricity grid. Other agreements related to defence co-operation and social development programmes. The first of the agreements could also lead to greater involvement in the oil sector to complement PetroSA's single Angolan offshore concession. As in the case of Sudan, an obstacle in the way of South Africa's desire to secure a larger stake in Angola's oil industry is the growing Chinese involvement in the economy of Angola. This has come about largely as a result of the Chinese government extending a $2 billion line of credit to the Angolan government and its offer to rebuild at its expense (and by using some 200 000 imported Chinese labourers)[9] the Benguela railway which runs from the Angolan coast to the DRC and which has been inoperative since the South African apartheid government destroyed large parts of it during its campaign of military aggression in the 1980s.

Elsewhere on the continent, PetroSA is negotiating oil rights with the governments of Equatorial Guinea, the Central African Republic, Libya and Egypt.

In crude oil production, Sasol is involved only in Gabon where, in tandem with four other operators (from the US, Canada, the Philippines and Japan), it has a production licence in the Etame Marine field offshore of southern Gabon. Its shareholding in this venture is 30 per cent. It also has an exclusive technical evaluation agreement with the Gabonese government for exploration in the new so-called Phenix block while it is also negotiating with the government for rights in a promising new field it discovered in shallow water at Ebouri in the southern region of the country.

In Equatorial Guinea, Sasol has oil exploration rights. These stem from the signing in February 2004 of a trade and investment promotion accord between the South African and Equatorial Guinean governments. According to a statement issued by the Department of Foreign Affairs at the time, the two governments also committed themselves to co-operation in the 'security and defence spheres'. It was only a few weeks later that the South African government informed the Zimbabwean and Equatorial Guinean governments of plans for a military coup involving South African and other mercenaries. There can be little doubt that this 'shopping' of the mostly South African coup makers facilitated South Africa acquiring a stake in Equatorial Guinea's state-run energy industry. Since then, Sasol has acquired ten per cent and 20 per cent stakes respectively in oil and gas fields located in the Rio Muni Basin while it has also been given the option to acquire up to 50 per cent equity in two other blocks in the Basin.

Sasol's only other involvement in the African oil market is as a supplier of refined fuels. In 2004, the company, through its black empowerment partner in Namibia, Namibia Liquid Fuels, was awarded a three-year contract worth R800 million per annum to supply fuel to the National Petroleum Corporation of Namibia. It also has a lucrative, multi-year deal to supply fuel to the Swaziland Independent Oil Company. Figure 19.6 depicts the involvement of South African corporates in Africa's oil and natural gas markets.

Figure 19.6 *South Africa's involvement in the African oil and natural gas markets, by company*

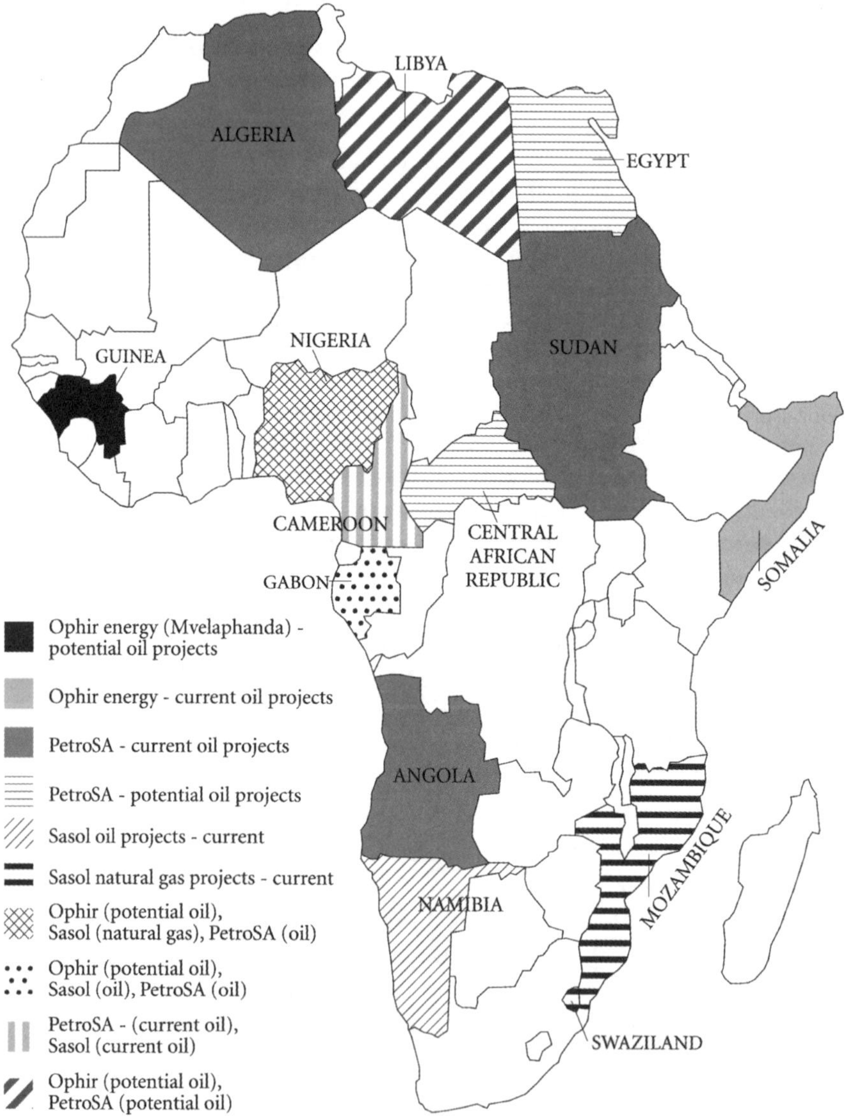
LIBYA
ALGERIA
EGYPT
NIGERIA
GUINEA
SUDAN
CAMEROON
CENTRAL AFRICAN REPUBLIC
GABON
SOMALIA
ANGOLA
MOZAMBIQUE
NAMIBIA
SWAZILAND
Ophir energy (Mvelaphanda) - potential oil projects
Ophir energy - current oil projects
PetroSA - current oil projects
PetroSA - potential oil projects
Sasol oil projects - current
Sasol natural gas projects - current
Ophir (potential oil), Sasol (natural gas), PetroSA (oil)
Ophir (potential oil), Sasol (oil), PetroSA (oil)
PetroSA - (current oil), Sasol (current oil)
Ophir (potential oil), PetroSA (potential oil)

Source: HSRC, Corporate mapping database

COGSI: in pursuit of secondary points

Earlier mention was made of the government's ambition to acquire a larger share of the supply side of the African energy industry, a sector currently dominated by non-African corporates. Realisation of this goal is being driven by the Cape Oil and Gas Supply Initiative (COGSI), a venture funded jointly by the Western Cape government and the City of Cape Town Metro Council, and to which the two groups have committed R2.5 million and R0.35 million respectively.

The city's goal is to become the regional supply and fabrication hub for the Atlantic coast and central African oil sectors – that is, Angola, the two Congos, Gabon, Sao Tome and Equatorial Guinea. Currently it is estimated that some US$10 billion is spent annually on the secondary or supply side of this particular energy market. COGSI is seeking to capture a share of that lucrative market for the Cape Town–Saldanha region.

To that end, Saldanha's oil-rig construction facility – used originally to build oil platforms for Mossgas – is being refurbished. With the number of operational rigs off the West African coast increasing by 11 per cent per annum, this would seem a sensible business decision from which a good return can be anticipated.

A new dry-dock facility for oil supertankers is also being built at Saldanha. When operational, this will be the only dry dock for oil supertankers between Dubai and the Mediterranean.

COGSI has also compiled a database of about 1 500 South African companies currently providing or capable of providing products and services to the offshore oil and gas industries. These firms have in turn been divided into three groups: those able to supply products and services; those with a capacity for the fabrication of all or parts of offshore oil rigs; and those that can undertake oil-rig repairs.

The existence of this register is now being marketed throughout the target region as part of a lobbying exercise to persuade African oil-producing governments to recognise 'African content' as a preferred source of procurement. The initiative is bearing some fruit. In March 2005, a Cape-based engineering firm was awarded a contract to service three oil-drilling vessels, an oil rig and its supply ships.

Conclusion

In the course of only two decades, South Africa has moved from an energy-surplus situation to one approaching deficit. This is part testimony to South Africa's accelerated rate of post-apartheid economic growth but is also a product of the increased supply-side demands created by a public housing strategy based on the construction of individual housing units (each of which requires an electricity link-up) rather than communal housing blocs which are easier and cheaper to supply with power. Midway through these two decades, South Africa underwent a regime change which brought to power a government which was both short on state policy-planning expertise and experience as well as burdened by a number of burdensome apartheid-era state projects and institutions. Some of these, like Sasol and Mossgas, were in the energy field and had operated for decades in a cocoon-world business environment, ring-fenced by the apartheid state from the cut and thrust of the market. In short, they could lose money hand over fist (and did) secure in the knowledge that the state would pick up the tab. In this context, four points merit comment by way of conclusion and summary.

One is the impressive and proactive manner in which the post-apartheid state has dealt with the energy sector. In regard to Mossgas and Sasol and Eskom's external arm, Eskom Enterprises, it has applied market principles and for the most part, their turnarounds have been successful in commercial terms.

The second is the speed and adeptness with which the 'new' ANC government has responded to the country's changing energy needs and the comprehensive nature of its strategy. While it cannot guarantee that there will be no disruptions as the country adapts to being a net importer of energy, the country will not be 'caught short' and will not have to resort to emergency, ad hoc and often costly damage-control measures.

The third is the largely state-driven nature of the new energy scenario. While allowance has been made for the participation of the private sector in the new energy scenario – and there will be some – the ANC has acted out of a recognition that there is little scope for profit in supplying a new consumer market comprised largely of the poor and economically marginalised. What it has developed is an energy strategy consistent with the interventionist, proactive development-state model outlined in the introduction to this volume.

Finally, it is clear that access to Africa's range of energy resources will be a key to the success of South Africa's developing energy strategy. It is similarly clear that this sector is already contested terrain and that other energy-deficit states are eyeing the African market. In its scramble to acquire a share of this market, the ANC government appears to have abandoned any regard to those ethical and human rights principles which it once proclaimed would form the basis of its foreign policy. Its approach in regard to energy is one in which the national interest is being interpreted purely on material grounds. To this extent it has a cold-war feel to it with the imperatives of democracy and good governance subordinated to expedient and material factors.

The ANC has in the last decade moved a long way from its condemnation of the execution in Nigeria in 1995 of the anti-oil campaigner, Ken Saro Wira, to the point where it is now prepared to deal in oil and energy matters with one of Africa's most corrupt and unaccountable regimes, Angola, and in the cases of Sudan and Equatorial Guinea, with two of the most abusive regimes on Earth, let alone in Africa. When it comes to South Africa's economic relations, it now seems that anything goes – or perhaps rather that if it has oil any government will do. In this regard, it seems that the South African government is not unlike the Bush administration.

Notes

1. The authors are indebted to Reg Rumney of *BusinessMap* and Claire Pickard-Cambridge of the *Petroleum Argus* for their invaluable comments on earlier versions of this article.
2. *Sundaytimes*.co.za 09.05.05.
3. See http://www.dti:gov.sa/econdb/.
4. With the exception of a few private road construction companies, all the South African companies active in this sector in Africa are parastatals. The largest are Eskom in the power sector and Transnet (incorporating Spoornet, Petronet, Portnet and Transtel) in the road, rail and port sectors with Umgeni Water monopolising the water and sanitation sector.
5. Growing links to Libya offer an insight into the extent to which pragmatism in the form of the oil needs of the US economy has trumped ideological factors on the part of even the most ideologically-driven US administration in 50 years. Similarly, the fact that the Libyan government in recent months awarded almost all of its new oil

and gas concessions to two US companies (Occidental and Chevron), and none to European concerns, shows how it too has de-ideologised its foreign relations and the priority it now accords to being 'on-sides' with the US.

6   The CEF is also responsible for the administration of a number of funds set up to facilitate the energy strategy. These include the Strategic Fuels Fund (SFF) which is responsible for the strategic inventory of crude oil, and the Equalisation Fund which finances any premiums required to obtain crude oil.

7   First to go was Don Mkhwanazi who was alleged to have awarded a R3 million contract to a Liberian politician without going through tendering procedures or consulting the CEF Board. His successor, Keith Kunene, resigned after it emerged that a joint South African–Dutch company, High Beam Trading International, had bribed South African state oil officials with $60 000 in exchange for a contract which gave the company control over South Africa's strategic oil stock. The contract had been signed without the knowledge of the DME and sealed without an open tender. It was cancelled. This was followed a year later by Renosi Mokate's suspension and then resignation after an audit of the SFF revealed losses of R40.8 million.

8   Ironically, while South Africa purchases hydroelectric power from Mozambique, it sells back to it coal-generated electricity at a fixed and low price in terms of an agreement negotiated between the apartheid government and the Portuguese colonial authorities in 1970. This agreement fixing the price of the sale was for 60 years and runs until 2030. Not surprisingly, the company which operates Cahora Bassa is in debt to the tune of $2.5 billion. South Africa also sells electricity to each of the member states of the Southern African Customs Union (SACU). This is largely a legacy of the close integration into the South African economy of the member states of the SACU, an arrangement which dates back to 1909, and the fact that Namibia was administered as part of South Africa from 1949 to 1990. In recent years, as the economy of Zimbabwe has spiralled downwards, South Africa has become a supplier of electricity to that country. In fact, it would be no exaggeration to suggest that if South Africa ceased to supply electricity to Zimbabwe, the lights in that country would go out.

9   A feature of Chinese aid largely overlooked, especially by those scholars critical of Western and South African involvement in Africa, is that where it involves large-scale construction or large-scale investment in infrastructure, the Chinese use huge amounts of their own cheap and poorly-skilled labour, and not the abundant numbers of equally unskilled and cheap local labour. Thus, for example, there are at least 200 000 Chinese labourers in the Sudan. These are deployed to protect China's oil facilities in that country. If one considers the fact that the majority

of these Chinese workers are men who will also have had at least three years of military training, then it is not entirely fanciful to see them as a 'reserve army' in a military sense. In a refreshing break from the tendency of the left to ignore these uncomfortable facts, Mandla Maseka, chief economist at Eskom Treasury, recently described China's ventures in Africa as 'colonialisation' and 'exploitative' (*Business Report* 11.03.05).

References

Arora V & Vamvakidis A (2005) *The implications of South African economic growth for the rest of Africa*. IMF Working Paper (WP/05/58). Washington DC: IMF.

Callaghy T (1991) Africa and the world economy: Caught between a rock and a hard place. In J Harbeson & D Rothchild (eds.) *Africa in world politics*. Boulder: Westview Press.

CSIR (Council for Scientific and Industrial Research) in conjunction with Shell (2003) *CSIR energy scenarios for Africa*. Pretoria & London: CSIR/Shell.

Daniel J, Lutchman J & Naidu S (2004) South Africa and Nigeria: Two unequal centres in a periphery. In J Daniel, R Southall & J Lutchman (eds.) *The State of the Nation: South Africa 2004–2005*. Cape Town: HSRC Press.

Daniel J, Naidoo V & Naidu S (2003) 'The South Africans have arrived': Post-apartheid corporate expansion into Africa. In J Daniel, A Habib & R Southall (eds.) *The State of the Nation: South Africa 2003–2004*. Cape Town: HSRC Press.

Daniel J, Southall R & Lutchman J (2004) Introduction: President Mbeki's second term: opening the golden door? In J Daniel, R Southall & J Lutchman (eds.) *The State of the Nation: South Africa 2004–2005*. Cape Town: HSRC Press.

De Pontet P (2004) *Sub-Saharan Africa-energy: Strategic implications of growing competition for African Oil*. Intellibridge: Global Energy Solutions.

SARS (South African Revenue Services) (2004) Preliminary statement of trade statistics for RSA for the period January–December 2003 to January–December 2004. Pretoria: SARS.

South African Foundation (2004) *South Africa's business presence in Africa*. Occasional Paper No. 3. Johannesburg: South African Foundation.

Contributors

William Blankley
Chief Research Manager,
Knowledge Management Research Programme
HSRC

Jesmond Blumenfeld
Associate Senior Lecturer,
School of Economics and Finance
Brunel University
London

Sakhela Buhlungu
Lecturer and Deputy Director,
Sociology of Work Unit
Department of Sociology
University of Witwatersrand

Jacklyn Cock
Professor,
Department of Sociology
University of Witwatersrand

John Daniel
Chair of the Editorial Board,
HSRC Press

Richard Devey
Research Fellow,
School of Development Studies
University of KwaZulu-Natal

Judith February
Political Analyst,
Political Information and Monitoring Service
Institute for Democracy in South Africa

Bill Freund
Retired Professor,
Department of Economic History/ Development Studies Programme
University of KwaZulu-Natal

Amanda Gouws
Professor,
Department of Political Science
University of Stellenbosch

Karthy Govender
Professor,
School of Law
University of KwaZulu-Natal

David Hemson
Research Director,
Integrated Regional and Rural Development Programme
HSRC

Michael Kahn
Executive Director,
Knowledge Management Research Programme
HSRC

CONTRIBUTORS

Merryman Kunene
Honours Student in Development Studies,
School of Social Sciences
University of Witwatersrand

Jessica Lutchman
Researcher,
Democracy and Governance Programme
HSRC

Wiseman Magasela
PhD Student,
St. Antony's College
Oxford University

Percy Moleke
Senior Research Specialist,
Employment and Economic Policy Research Programme
HSRC

Sanusha Naidu
Research Specialist,
Integrated Regional and Rural Development Programme
HSRC

Michael O' Donovan
Research Consultant,
Hlakanaphila Analytics

Vijay Reddy
Research Director,
Assessment Technology and Education Evaluation Research Programme
HSRC

Caroline Skinner
Research Fellow,
School of Development Studies
University of KwaZulu-Natal

Roger Southall
Distinguished Research Fellow,
HSRC

Imraan Valodia
Senior Research Fellow,
School of Development Studies
University of KwaZulu-Natal

Cherryl Walker
Chief Research Specialist,
Integrated Regional and Rural Development Programme
HSRC

Eddie Webster
Professor and Director,
Sociology of Work Unit
Department of Sociology
University of Witwatersrand

Janet Wilhelm
Independent Journalist, formerly with the *Mail & Guardian* and *ThisDay*

Index

A
Absa, 177, 199, 485, 491
acts
    African Growth and Opportunity Act (2000), 357, 445, 474
    Arms and Ammunition Act (1969), 337
    Central Energy Fund Act (1997), 495
    Commission on Gender Equality Act (1996), 151, 160
    Companies Act (1973), 495
    Domestic Violence Act (1998), 149, 153
    Employment Equity Act (1998), 153, 213, 263
    Employment Equity Act (1999), 149, 354
    Firearms Control Act (2000), 337, 344
    Government Transition Act (1993), 305
    Group Areas Act (1950), 74, 79, 84, 85, 90, 304, 352, 371
    Intestate Succession Act (1987), 100
    Labour Relations Act (1995), 149, 241
    Local Government Transition Amendment Act (1996), 307
    Maintenance Act (1998), 149, 153
    Municipal Demarcation Act (1998), 307
    Municipal Structures Act (1998), 307
    Municipal Systems Act (1999), 307
    National Conventional Arms Control Act (2002), 8, 129
    National Energy Act (2004), 495
    Native Land Act (1913), 70, 89
    Native Land and Trust Act (1936), 89
    Population Registration Act (1950), 371
    Promotion of Administrative Justice Act (2000), 112
    Promotion of Equality and Prevention of Unfair Discrimination Act (2000), 103, 153
    Protection of Constitutional Democracy against Terrorism Act (2004), 131
    Recognition of Customary Marriages Act (1998), 149, 157
    Regulations of Gatherings Act (1993), 111
    Restitution of Land Rights Act (1994), 67, 69
    Skills Development Act (1998), 218
    South African Schools Act (1996), 102
    Termination of Pregnancy Act (1997), 149
    Traditional Leadership and Governance Act (2003), 154
affirmative action, 106, 170, 202–203, 214, 325, 353–354, 356
African Cup of Nations, 370, 372, 382–383
African Growth and Opportunity Act (2000), 474
African National Congress (ANC), xiii, xvii–xviii, xix–xxv, xxvii–xxviii, xxxiii, xxxviii–xxxix, xl, 5, 11–13, 15, 21, 25–27, 34, 37, 51–52, 58, 67–71, 79, 87, 109, 118, 124–125, 129, 131, 134–135, 137, 147, 171, 175–179, 190, 197, 213, 224–226, 237, 242, 306, 310, 316–322, 324, 340, 344, 356, 372, 374, 377, 419, 421–422, 430, 435, 442, 461–463, 465, 481, 497, 506–507
African Nations Cup 1996, 301
African Union (AU), xiii, 165
Ajax Cape Town, 380–381
Anglo American, 170, 182, 191, 199, 314, 471
AngloGold, xix, 179, 185, 249, 261, 490
anti-retroviral treatment (ART), xiii, 34
Anti-Terrorism Bill, 137
apartheid, xvii, xxvi, xxxiii, xxxvi, xxxviii, 5, 50, 56, 58, 67, 83–84, 88, 95–96, 103, 127, 129–130, 134, 172, 175, 181, 203, 211, 214–216, 225, 248, 259–262, 264–265, 273, 285, 299–305, 312, 319–320, 325, 335, 338, 341, 350–354, 356, 359, 370–371, 374, 383, 388,

398, 410, 413, 427, 430, 439, 460–462, 465, 503, 506, 508
Arms and Ammunition Act (1969), 337
arms deal, 8, 124, 129, 133–135, 190
authoritarianism, xl, 172, 248, 259, 261–263
Azanian People's Liberation Army (Apla), 340

B
Bafana Bafana, 301, 370, 380, 385, 387
bantu education, 393
bantustans, 88, 304–305
Banyana Banyana, 380
Barclays Bank, 176
Basic Income Grant Coalition, 61
Batho Bonke consortium, 177, 199
BHP Billiton, xix, 182, 191
Bill of Rights, 6, 52, 58–61, 93, 97–101, 103–104, 111–112, 118–119
Bi-National Commission (BNC), xiii
black economic empowerment (BEE), xiii, xix, xxiii–xxiv, xxvi, xxxiii, xxxvi, 169–170, 175–176, 178, 181, 185–188, 192, 196–198, 259, 306, 316, 324–325, 353
    deals, 177, 196
    strategy, 197–198
    firms, 306
Black Management Forum, 177
Botswana, Lesotho, Namibia and Swaziland (BLNS), xiii, 440–443
brain drain, 173, 257, 351
business and not-for-profits R&D (BERD), xiii

C
Cape Oil and Gas Supply Initiative (COGSI), xiii, 425, 505
capitalism, xxvi–xxviii, xxxii, xxxv–xxxvi, 169–170, 175–181, 185, 188, 197–198, 225, 315
    compassionate, 176
    democratic, 176, 179, 185, 197–198
    global, xxxv
    stakeholder, 179–181, 185, 198
Central Energy Fund (CEF), xiii, 424, 495, 497, 508
Central Energy Fund Act (1997), 495
Charter for Effective Equality, 143, 147, 150
child support grant (CSG), xiii, 4, 13, 30–31, 149
Chinese Association of South Africa, 354
Chinese Communist Party (CCP), xiii, xxviii
Chinese community, 299, 301, 350–353, 356, 363–365
Chinese triads, 300, 355, 363–364
Chinese, sex trade, 363–364
coal-generated electricity, 424
Coalition Against Water Privatisation, 321
cold war, 457, 492
colonialism, xxviii, 248, 301, 304
commercialisation, 378
Commission for the Promotion and Protection of the Rights of Cultural, Religious and Linguistic Communities, 127
Commission on Gender Equality (CGE), xiii, 9, 127, 145, 148–149, 151, 153–154, 158, 160–161, 163, 165
Commission on Gender Equality Act (1996), 151, 160
Commission on Restitution of Land Rights, 67
Committee of Inquiry into a Comprehensive System of Social Security for South Africa, 55
Common Market for Eastern and Southern Africa (Comesa), xiii, 439–440
Communal Land Rights Bill, 154
communication, 136, 205, 384
communism, xxx, 460, 480
community courts, 13, 36
community water programme, 17
Companies Act (1973), 495

Comprehensive Plan on HIV and AIDS, 13, 34
Confederation of African Football (CAF), xiii, 372, 382–383
Confederation of Employers of Southern Africa (Cofesa), xiii, 241
Congress of South African Trade Unions (Cosatu), xiii, xviii, xxiii, xxvii, 132, 136–137, 172–173, 177, 181, 197, 249, 253–254, 256–258, 265, 322, 474
Congress of Southern African Football Associations, 383
Constitution, xxxiv, 5–7, 9, 46, 49, 52, 55, 58–62, 69, 93, 96–97, 99–111, 114–116, 118–119, 121, 126–127, 129–130, 133, 135, 139, 147,149, 344, 347
Constitutional Court, 3, 6–7, 59, 99–101, 107, 109, 114–116, 119,153
constitutional democracy, 94, 97, 102, 108, 110–111, 117, 119–120, 127, 129, 133
Convention on Torture and Other Cruel, Inhuman or Degrading Treatment or Punishment, 94
Convention on the Elimination of All Forms of Racial Discrimination, 94
Convention on the Elimination of Discrimination against Women, 94
Convention on the Rights of the Child, 94
Convention Relating to the Status of Refugees, 94
Council for Scientific and Industrial Research (CSIR), xiii, 272, 286–287, 289
crime, 204, 299–300, 315–316, 334, 336, 338, 340–341, 358, 363–364
customary law, 154, 157

D
De Beers, 170, 471
democracy, xvii, xxiii, xxix–xxx, xxxviii, xxxix–xl, xlii, 6–7, 15, 52, 59, 94, 97, 102, 105, 107–111, 117, 119, 120, 123, 127, 129, 133, 140, 143, 150, 170, 172, 203, 214, 248–249, 284, 299–301, 311, 344, 356, 374, 410, 425, 428, 439, 442, 458, 479, 507
constitutional, 94, 97, 102, 108, 110–111, 117, 119–120, 127, 129, 133
direct, 107
liberal, xl
multiparty, 97, 109
participatory, 107, 111, 140
representative, 107–108
stakeholder, 311
democracy/development trade-off, xxx, xxxvii
Democratic Alliance (DA), xiii, xxiv, xx–viii, xl, 108, 124–125, 138, 177–179, 356
Democratic Nurses' Organisation of South Africa, 257
Democratic Party, 108, 137
Department of Education (DoE), xiii, 32, 283, 394, 397, 402
Department of Housing, 57
Department of Land Affairs (DLA), xiii, 71, 73, 89
Department of Minerals and Energy (DME), xiii, 498
Department of Science and Technology (DST), 286, 289
Department of Science and Technology National Innovation Fund, 277
Department of Science Support Programme for Industrial Innovation, 277
Department of Social Development (DoSD), xiii
Department of Trade and Industry (DTI), xiii, 186–187, 192, 234–235, 273, 277, 435, 449, 451
Department of Water Affairs and Forestry (DWAF), xiii, 17, 27, 57
deracialisation, 202–203, 212, 214, 263
developmental state, xvii–xviii, xx–xxv,

xxvii–xxxii, xxxii–xxxiii, xxxv, xxxvii–xxxix, xl–xliii, 3
Dinaledi, 283, 394–395, 413
disability grant, 30
discrimination, 94, 100, 103–106, 213–215,
219–221, 350–351, 366, 462
dispossession, 84, 87
District Six, 81–82
Domestic Violence Act (1998), 149, 153
Domestic Violence Bill, 158

E

East Asian Growth and Development Plan,
xxi
economic empowerment, xxiv, 186
economy, xviii, xix, xxi, xxiv–xxv, xxvi–
xxviii, xxxiii–xxxiv, xxxix, xl–xlii, 39,
49–50, 52, 79, 81, 169, 171–172, 178,
180, 182, 185, 189, 197, 212, 223–230,
232–233, 235–243, 249, 258, 270–
272, 276–277, 280, 282, 289, 302, 360,
362, 392, 428, 431, 435–436, 448–449,
450, 453, 457, 464–466, 468, 471,
473–475, 479–480, 484–485, 487,
492, 494, 502, 508
African, 484–485, 487, 492
formal, xl, 171–172, 226–230, 233, 236,
238, 240–242
global, xviii, 223, 258, 428, 435, 449, 453,
457, 480
informal, 224–226, 232–233, 235–243
market, 448, 468, 494
political, xxvii–xxviii, xli, 81, 485
education, xviii, 4, 12–13, 22, 27, 32, 47, 94,
98, 102, 112, 122, 136, 151, 156, 170,
173, 203, 213, 215–216, 220–221,
226, 256, 277, 279, 283, 285, 289, 292,
299, 301–302, 340, 344, 353, 392–
397, 400–401, 412–414, 429, 461, 467
Bantu, 393
mathematics and science, 393–394, 397,
412–414

outcomes-based, 395
science and mathematics, 299, 301, 302
system, 102, 170, 215, 220, 226, 283
election(s), 9, 15, 127, 305, 352, 393, 428,
465
Electoral Commission, 108, 127
Electoral Task Team, 153
electricity, xix, xxvi, 4, 13, 16, 20, 22–23,
27, 29–30, 38, 105, 205, 252, 318,
320–321, 324, 327, 398, 423–424,
471, 484–485, 494–495, 497–499,
502, 506, 508
electrification, 29, 305
Elimination of All Forms of Discrimination
Against Women, 155, 157
emigration, 284, 351
Employee share-ownership schemes, 170
Employment Equity Act (1998), 149, 153,
213, 263, 354
employment, xviii, xix, xxxvi, xlii–xliii, 25,
50, 154, 169–171, 186, 188, 190, 202,
211, 220, 226, 229–230, 232–234,
237, 240–243, 251–254, 259, 263,
265, 267, 272, 315, 353, 427, 435,
448, 473
equity, 186, 188, 190, 202, 259, 263, 353,
367
formal sector, xix, 229, 240
informal, 228–230, 240, 251
relations, 171, 237, 253
empowerment, 186–188, 190, 197–198
energy, xlii, 4, 289, 291, 419, 423–425, 470–
471, 485, 491, 494–495, 497–500,
505–508
consumption, 500
demands, 485
industry, 494, 497, 505
low cost, 289
needs, 425, 498, 506
nuclear, 291, 495
resources, 507
renewable, 495

sector, 424, 491, 494–495, 497, 506
self-sufficiency, xlii
strategy, 500, 507–508
solar, 470
equality, 6, 9, 60, 100, 103, 106–107, 111, 143–147, 149–152, 154–158, 161–162, 164, 175, 303, 460, 467
gender, xxxvi, 9, 143, 144, 145, 146, 149, 150, 151, 152, 154–158, 161–162, 164
racial, 143, 460
equity, 146, 170–171, 179, 186, 191, 202–204, 208, 211, 213–214, 220
legislation, 171, 202, 214, 220
Eskom, xx, xxxvii, 30, 289, 324, 464, 494–499, 507, 509
European Commission (EC), xiii, 443–445
European Free Trade Association (EFTA), xiii, 445
European Integration Programme, xxi
European Union (EU), xiv, 136, 420, 437, 442–444, 448, 453
EU-South Africa Trade, Development and Co-operation Agreement (TDCA), 444
evictions, 321–323
Expanded Public Works Programme, 224

F
Federation of International Football Associations (Fifa), xiv, 371–372, 375, 384–387, 389–390
femicide, 333
firearms, 334–336, 337–338, 341, 342, 344–346
illegal, 334, 336–337
legal, 335–336, 338, 342
legislation, 346
Firearms Control Act (2000), 337, 344
fixed tariff preference (FTP), xiv, 447
Football Association of South Africa (Fasa), xiv, 371–372, 389
foreign direct investment (FDI), xiv, 274, 452, 459, 470, 485, 433
foreign exchange, 182, 433
foreign investment, xxix, xxxix, 188, 367, 429
foreign policy, 422, 458, 461, 463, 507
foreign trade, 419, 428–430
formal economy, xl, 171–172, 226–230, 233, 236, 238, 240–242
formal sector, xix, 224, 227
Forum of South African Directors-General, xx
Foundation for Research Development (FRD), xiv, 286
free trade area (FTA), xiv, 437, 439, 440–441, 445–447, 453
Freedom Charter, 11–12, 58
full-time equivalent (FTE), xiv
further education and training (FET), xiv

G
gas, 315, 476, 485, 490–491, 494–498, 500–501, 503–505, 508
Gauteng Economic Development Agency (Geda), xiv, 471
Gender Advocacy Programme, 153
Gender and Education and Training Network, 156
gender, xxi, xxxv–xxxvi, 8–9, 143–146, 148–158, 161–165, 211, 257, 283, 397, 413
-based violence, 150, 152, 154, 333
equality, xxxvi, 9, 143–146, 149–152, 154–158, 161–162, 164
General Agreement on Tariffs and Trade (GATT), xiv, 419, 434–436, 441
General Export Incentive Scheme (GEIS), xiv, 433, 437
Global Economic Strategy (GES), xiv, 450–452
global warming, 34
globalisation, xxxii, 281, 289, 313, 366, 369, 428
Government of National Unity (GNU), xiv, 435

Government Transition Act (1993), 305
gross expenditure on R&D (GERD), xiv, 277–278
Group Areas Act (1950), 74, 79, 84–85, 90, 304, 352, 371
Growth, Employment and Redistribution (GEAR), xiv, xvii, 12, 50, 225, 272, 435–436, 448
gun, 299–300, 333–341, 344–347
   amnesty, 300, 336
   control, 340, 344–346
   culture, 299–300, 341
   hand-in campaign, 344
   -free zones, 345, 347
Gun Free South Africa (GFSA), xiv, 338, 341, 344–347

H

health, 4, 13, 27, 32–34, 37, 47, 60–61, 318–319, 429
healthcare, 57, 61, 112–113, 115–116, 119, 121–122, 149, 203, 264, 344, 490
higher education R&D (HERD), xiv
HIV/AIDS, 18, 34, 105, 117, 138, 150, 163, 292, 326, 333
homelands, 23, 352, 357, 460
household subsistence level (HSL), xiv, 51
housing, xviii, 4, 12, 14–15, 19, 22–25, 37–39, 47, 57, 81, 98, 112, 114, 119, 121–122, 149, 203, 252, 289, 316, 320–321, 325, 490, 506
Human Rights Committee, 94
human rights, 3, 7, 46, 59–60, 93, 95–97, 118, 120, 129–130, 154, 323, 335–336, 346, 422, 425, 458, 464, 477, 479, 507
Human Rights Watch, 118
Human Sciences Research Council (HSRC), xiv
hydroelectric power, 424, 497–498

I

immigration, 22, 173, 281, 284, 292, 301, 340, 350–351, 356, 364, 366
   Chinese, 350, 356
   illegal, 340, 364
   law, 350, 366
   policy, 173, 292, 350
Independent Democrats, 356
Independent Electoral Commission, 102, 153
industrialisation, xxii, xxv, 271, 431–432
inequality, xviii, xxiii, xxv, xxx, xxxvi, 52, 118, 140, 146, 150, 175, 301, 342–344
informal economy, 224–226, 232–233, 236–243
informal employment, 228–230, 240, 251
informal sector, xli, 171–172, 226–228, 243, 251, 254, 360
informal settlements, 23, 25, 252
informal traders, 226, 316
information communication technology (ICT), xiv
Inkatha Freedom Party (IFP), xiv, 109, 134, 137, 335–356
Institute for Scientific Information (ISI), 276, 280
Institute for Security Studies (ISS), xiv
Institutions Supporting Democracy (ISD), xiv, 138
integrated development plan (IDP), xiv, 307, 310–311
International Labour Organisation (ILO), xiv, 220, 226, 230
International Monetary Fund (IMF), xiv, xx, 484, 492
Intestate Succession Act (1987), 100
investment (s), xxi, xxiii, xxix, xxxii, 173, 175, 181, 185–186, 188, 197, 224, 271, 306, 314, 360, 384, 413, 423–424, 427–429, 433–434, 439, 445, 447, 452, 458, 460, 463–464, 470, 473, 475, 477–479, 491, 502–503, 508

J

Jacobins, xxii, xxiv, xxvii–xxxiv, xxxvii, xlii

Johannesburg Securities Exchange (JSE), xv, 178, 182, 191–192, 277, 289
Joint Monitoring Committee (JMC), 144, 148, 151, 157–158, 165
Joint Rules Committee (JRC), xiv, 138–139
Jomo Cosmos, 377

K
Kaizer Chiefs, 373, 376–378, 380, 383
Khomani San, 68, 80, 88
Kruger National Park, 68, 313

L
labour, xv, xxi, xxiii–xxiv, xxix, xxxi–xxxii, xl, 20, 50, 55, 88, 154, 170–173, 179–180, 197, 202–204, 209, 211–212, 214–221, 223, 227–228, 230–231, 238–241, 248–249, 251–253, 259–260, 265, 267, 302, 351, 357, 429–430, 446, 458, 474–475, 478, 508
  brokers, 240–241
  labour force survey (LFS), xv, 20, 204, 230
  legislation, 228, 357
  movement, 172–173, 249, 265, 267
Labour Relations Act (1995), 149, 241
land, 3, 5–6, 9, 19, 37, 57, 67–75, 77, 79–86, 88–89, 119, 149
  claims, 67–68, 72, 79, 83, 85
  dispossession, 69–70, 82–84
  redistribution, 67
  reform and redress, 5–6, 67, 69–70, 80–81, 85
  restitution, 3, 5–6, 37, 57, 67–75, 77, 79–86, 88–89
  restoration, 6, 80–81, 88
Land Claims Commission, 69, 89
liberalisation, 419, 427, 444, 448, 453
Local Government Transition Amendment Act (1996), 307
Luthuli, Albert, 372

M
Maintenance Act (1998), 149, 153
malaria, 13, 33–34
malnutrition, 19–20
Mamelodi Sundowns, 376, 378
Mandela, Nelson, 143, 370, 382, 422, 458, 464–466
Manuel, Trevor, 18, 70 185, 293
mathematics and science education, 299, 301–302, 393–394, 397, 412–414
Mbeki, Thabo, xvii–xviii, xix–xx, xxii, xx–viii, 3, 11, 29, 31, 35–36, 38, 46, 67–68, 70, 81, 85, 123, 138, 165, 213, 223, 241, 306, 309, 323–324, 366, 384, 387, 397, 414, 422, 465–466, 475–476, 478
migration, 17, 312–313, 350, 403, 413
militarism, 341–342
minimum living level (MLL), xv, 51, 55
Moroka Swallows, 373, 377, 383
Motsepe, Patrice, 177, 188–189, 191–192
Mozambique National Resistance (Renamo), 335
MTN, 178, 192
Mugabe, Robert, xl, 477
multilateralism, 420, 436
Municipal Demarcation Act (1998), 307
Municipal Finance Management Bill, 309
Municipal Structures Act (1998), 307
Municipal Systems Act (1999), 307
Mvelaphanda Holdings, 192, 491, 500

N
Naspers, 472
National African Federated Chamber of Commerce (Nafcoc), xv, 178
National Assembly (NA), xv, 126–128, 131, 135, 137–138
National Conventional Arms Control Act (2002), 8, 129, 131
National Conventional Arms Control Bill, xv, 130–131, 353

National Conventional Arms Control
  Committee (NCACC), xv, 130–131
National Council of Provinces (NCOP), xv,
  127–128, 132
National Economic Development and
  Labour Council (Nedlac), xv, 188, 310
National Energy Act (2004), 495
National Football League (NFL), xv, 373
National Gender Forum (NGF), xv, 150–
  151, 158–159
national gender machinery (NGM), xv,
  3, 9, 137, 143–145, 149–151, 155,
  157–165, 174
National Party, 96, 135, 286, 351, 393, 435
National Professional Soccer League
  (NPSL), xv, 373
National Skills Development Strategy
  (NSDS), xv, xix, 380
National Soccer League (NSL), xv, 373–374,
  377
national system of innovation (NSI), xv,
  270–272, 282, 291–292
National Union for the Total Independence
  of Angola (Unita), 335
Native Land Act (1913), 70, 89
Native Land and Trust Act (1936), 89
neoliberalism, 14, 342–343
nevirapine, 7, 115–117
New National Party (NNP), xv, xxxviii,
  108, 137
New Partnership for Africa's Development
  (Nepad), xv, 467, 475, 478
nuclear energy, 291, 495
nuclear weapons programme, 286
nutrition, 20, 39, 61

O

October Household Survey (OHS), xv, 20,
  23, 53, 230
Office of the Status of Women (OSW), xv,
  9, 143, 148–151, 153–160, 162–165
oil, 317, 423–425, 471, 476, 479–480, 484–
  485, 487, 490–497, 501–505, 507–508
  concessions, 491, 502
  market, 425, 493–494, 501, 503
  pollution, 496
  production, 425, 501, 503
Oil Pollution Control South Africa
  (OPCSA), 424, 496
Oilgate, 8, 125
Old Mutual, 170, 182
Organisation of the Petroleum Exporting
  Countries (OPEC), xv, 423–424, 476,
  493
Orlando Pirates, 373, 378, 380, 383
outcomes-based education (OBE), 395

P

Pan Africanist Congress (PAC), xv, 340,
  345, 461, 481
pan-Africanism, 461
passes, 312
paternalism, racial, 262–263
pebble-bed modular nuclear reactor
  (PBMR), xv, 173, 291, 471, 498
pension(s), 4, 149, 182, 190, 333
  claims, 333
  funds, 182, 190
Petroleum Agency of South Africa, 424, 495
petroleum, 490, 494–495
PetroSA, 125, 135, 424–425, 495, 497,
  500–504
Pickard Commission, 377–378, 386–387
Pollution, 470, 496
Population Registration Act (1950), 371
poverty, xv, xviii, xx–xxi, xl, 3–5, 14, 18,
  38–39, 46–58, 60–62, 80, 114–115,
  149–150, 169, 188, 202–204, 215,
  223–225, 237, 249, 289, 303, 325, 333,
  342–344, 398, 401–402, 411, 458
  alleviation, xxi, 14, 114–115, 188,
  224–225
Premier Soccer League (PSL), xv, 374–381,
  386–387, 390

Pretoria Declaration, 466
primogeniture, 100
private sector, xx, xxii, xxiv–xxvi, 171, 185, 209, 213, 220, 236, 250, 306, 311, 314, 316–317, 395, 497–498, 501, 506
private security companies, 315, 337, 347
privatisation, xxii–xxiii, xxxvii, 250–251, 306, 322, 343–344, 347
Programme for Land and Agrarian Settlement (PLAAS), xv, 73
Promotion of Administrative Justice Act (2000), 112
Promotion of Equality and Prevention of Unfair Discrimination Act (2000), 103, 153
Protection of Constitutional Democracy against Terrorism Act (2004), 131
Protection of Constitutional Democracy against Terrorism Bill, 7
Protection of Constitutional Democracy against Terrorist and Other Related Activities Bill, 132
public sector, xxviii, 211–213, 257, 320
public works programme, 37, 57, 149
public-sector unionisation, 254

R
racial authoritarianism, 261–263
racial discrimination, 48
racial paternalism, 262–263
racial segregation, 248
racial skills distribution, 202
racism, 95, 202–203, 370
Ramaphosa, Cyril, 176, 188–189, 191–192
Randgold, 177, 490
Recognition of Customary Marriages Act (1998), 149, 157
Recognition of Customary Marriages Bill, 158
Reconstruction and Development Programme (RDP), xv, 11–12, 19, 21–23, 25, 37, 39, 52, 306, 320, 324, 333, 464
Regulations of Gatherings Act (1993), 111
Restitution of Land Rights Act (1994), 67, 69, 90
retrenchment, 253, 262, 343
rights, 52, 58–62, 93-95, 98, 112–118, 122
  civil and political rights, 58, 93–94, 98, 122
  economic and social, 61
  socio-economic, 52, 55, 59, 60–62, 94–95, 98, 112–118, 122

S
sanctions, 13, 16–17, 19-20, 22–23, 27–28, 32–33, 37, 39, 114–115, 252, 286, 427–428, 432, 434, 462, 486, 495
sanitation, 4, 21, 28, 57
Sasol, 173, 285, 291, 424–425, 471, 475, 500–501, 503–504, 506
Scorpions, 184
Sector Education and Training Authority (SETA), xvi, 235–236
Select Committee on Public Accounts (Scopa), xvi, 8, 124–125, 129, 133–135
sex trade, 363-364
Sex Worker Education, 153
Sexwale, Tokyo, 177, 188–189, 192, 491
Shoprite, 250, 261, 486
Sino-South Africa relations, 458–459, 471, 479
Skills Development Act (1998), 218
slavery, 94, 98
slums, 12, 24–25, 27
small, medium and micro-enterprise (SMME), xvi, 234–235
soccer, 299, 301, 369–375, 377–382, 386, 388–389
Soccer World Cup in 2010, 301
social grants, xviii, 31, 39
social security, 4, 13, 22, 30–31, 55, 57, 60–61, 94, 98, 112, 119, 121–122,

190, 224, 227
child-support grant, 4, 13, 30–31, 149
disability grant, 30
pensions, 4, 190
social services, 61, 116, 149
social welfare, 149, 154
socialism, xvii, xxiii, xxvi, xxviii, 175
solar energy, 470
South African Football Association (Safa), xvi, 370–372, 374, 377–382, 386–388
South African Airways (SAA), xvi, xix
South African Breweries, 170, 182
South African Broadcasting Corporation (SABC), 189
South African Communist Party (SACP), xvi, xviii, xxiii, xxvii–xxviii, 177, 322, 461
South African Defence Force, 461
South African Democratic Teachers' Union (Sadtu), 257
South African Human Rights Commission (SAHRC), xvi, 6, 61, 68, 107, 112, 115, 117–118, 121, 127, 152
South African Local Government Association (SALGA), xvi, 148, 307–308
South African National Civics Organisation (Sanco), xvi, 310, 324
South African National Defence Force (SANDF), xvi, 133, 336, 340, 342
South African Non-Racial Olympic Committee (Sanroc), 372
South African Police Service (SAPS), xvi, 13, 35, 38, 334, 336–337
South African Reserve Bank (SARB), 274
South African Revenue Service (SARS), xvi, 199
South African Schools Act (1996), 102
South African Soccer Association, 374
South African Soccer Federation, 371
South African Women in Dialogue (SAWID), xvi, 165
Southern African Customs Union (SACU), xvi, 420–422, 439–443, 448, 452–453, 467, 473, 475, 508
Southern African Development Community (SADC), xvi, 285, 337, 420–421, 437, 439–440, 443, 448, 450, 453, 485, 499
Soweto Accord, 318
Spoornet, 249–250, 259
Standard Bank, 176, 191
State of the Nation address, xviii, 3, 5, 11, 15–16, 21–22, 24, 27, 36–37, 67, 70, 81, 85, 123, 224
State of the Nation speech, xxxvii, 366, 404
state-owned enterprises (SOE), xvi, xix, xxi, xxxvii, xli, 185, 291
Statistics South Africa (Stats SA), xvi, 18, 20, 23, 53, 228, 230, 243
Strategic Defence Procurement Package ('arms deal'), 8, 129
Students and Youth in Science, Technology and Mathematics (SYSTEM), xvi, 395
SuperSport United, 378, 380
Surplus People Project (SPP), xvi 83–84

T
tariffs, xxx, 432–433, 435–437, 441, 444, 447, 449, 454
technical state capacity, xix, xxxv, xxxvii, 20, 39, 472, 490
Telkom, xix, 249–251, 291
Termination of Pregnancy Act (1997), 149
terrorism, 132, 467
Thatcher, Margaret, xl, 180
Tiananmen Square, 422, 462, 464
tourism, 313, 326, 369, 384, 466, 472, 490
trade, 262, 275, 419–423, 427–430, 432–448, 451–454, 459–461, 463, 466–469, 471, 473–476, 478, 485–489, 492–493, 498–499, 502–503
bilateral, 444, 445, 460, 468–469
China-South Africa, 468–469
free, 430, 443, 467–468

liberalisation, 262, 420, 432, 445, 454, 476
policies, 419, 421, 434–435, 441, 448–449, 451–452, 459
relations, 427–428, 433, 435, 439, 448, 451
SACU-China Free Trade Agreement, 473, 475
sanctions, 275
trade union(s), xli, 94, 132, 146, 187, 214, 248–249, 258–261, 264–267
Traditional Leadership and Governance Act (2003), 154
Transnet, xix, 507
transport, xix, 136, 205, 316–317, 326, 384–386
Travelgate scandal, 124, 126, 140
Treatment Action Campaign (TAC), xvi, 7, 115, 117, 136
Tripartite Alliance, xviii, xxviii, xxxvii, 322
Tutu, Archbishop Desmond, 177, 333

U
Ubuntu-Batho consortium, 177, 199
Umkhonto we Sizwe (MK), xv, 340
unemployment, xviii, xxi, xxx, xli, 12, 18, 47, 50, 60, 169, 225, 230, 251, 262, 319, 333, 340, 342, 344
United Democratic Movement (UDM), 109
United Nations (UN), xvi
United Nations Development Programme (UNDP), xvi, 18, 38, 54
United Nations International Research and Training Institute for the Advancement of Women (Instraw), 152
United Schools Sports Association of South Africa (Ussasa), xvi, 381
Universal Declaration of Human Rights (UDHR), xvi, 93, 95
Urban Development Framework (UDF), 307, 311, 320
US African Growth and Opportunity Act (AGOA) (2000), xiii, 357, 445

V
ventilated improved privy (VIP), xvi, 27–29
vigilantism, 347
violence, 157, 300, 305, 315, 319, 333, 340–341, 462

W
Washington Consensus, xx, xxi, 477
water, xviii, xix, 4, 12–17, 19, 21–23, 25–27, 32–33, 38–39, 57, 60–61, 98, 105, 112, 114–115, 119, 121–122, 149, 203, 205, 252, 289, 318, 320–321, 324, 343, 398, 470–471, 498
  clean running, 12–13, 25
  portable, 22, 114–115
  cut-offs, 321
  delivery, 26–27
  policy, 289
Western Cape Anti-Eviction Campaign, 321
Wildcat co-operation, 258, 260–262
Woman's Charter, 143, 147
Women's National Coalition (WNC), xvi, 143, 147, 150
Wonke Wonke project, 381
World Bank, xx, 5, 52–54, 306, 492
World Cup 2002, 386
World Cup 2010, 369, 384–385, 389
World Health Organization (WHO), xvi, 115–116
World Summit on Sustainable Development, 74
World Trade Organization (WTO), xvi, 420, 434, 437–438, 448, 457, 459, 468, 474–475

X
xenophobia, 388

Z
Zuma, Jacob, 8, 134